12 Jan 87

America's First Battles

Modern War Studies

Raymond A. Callahan
Jacob W. Kipp
Jay Luvaas
Theodore A. Wilson
Series Editors

America's First Battles

1776–1965

EDITED BY

Charles E. Heller

LIEUTENANT COLONEL, UNITED STATES ARMY RESERVE

&

William A. Stofft

BRIGADIER GENERAL, UNITED STATES ARMY

Maps by Laura Kriegstrom Poracsky

UNIVERSITY PRESS OF KANSAS

To the United States Army,
its soldiers: past, present,
and future.

Published by the University Press of Kansas (Lawrence, Kansas 66045), which was organized by
the Kansas Board of Regents and is operated and funded by Emporia State University, Fort Hays
State University, Kansas State University, Pittsburg State University, the University of Kansas,
and Wichita State University

Library of Congress Cataloging-in-Publication Data
America's first battles, 1776–1965.
  Includes index.
  1. United States—History, Military. 2 Battles—
United States—History. I. Heller, Charles E.
II. Stofft, William A.
E181.A46   1986   973   86-7825
ISBN 0-7006-0276-3
ISBN 0-7006-0277-1 (pbk.)

Printed in the United States of America
10 9 8 7 6 5 4 3 2 1

Contents

List of Maps

Preface

The world in the late twentieth century clearly has become a more dangerous habitation than ever before for all human beings. The age-old pattern of conflict among and between peoples has become intertwined with newly created capabilities for global destruction. In this environment of challenge and conflict, the United States bears broad responsibilities for maintaining a precarious peace and protecting its own and its allies' vital interests. The United States Army—today as throughout the nation's history truly a manifestation of a democratic republic—has thus been given challenging missions and heavy burdens by the makers of national policy. With little prior warning, the Army must be capable of fighting in a variety of geographic locales against any one aggressor or a coalition of potential aggressors in joint and combined formations. The Army's officer corps not only must prepare for the war that could begin today but must also anticipate the nature and evolution of likely future conflicts. One means currently employed to assist in preparing and planning for war is study and analysis of military history. As was true for military thinkers of earlier times, now, when discussions arise with regard to problems facing the Army and the nation, a question that continually surfaces is: "How have we prepared for war and gone to war in the past?" The idea for the present work took shape as an effort to answer that question from today's perspective.

Underlying what has become *America's First Battles* is the assumption that it makes a great deal of difference how the U.S. Army prepares in peacetime, mobilizes for war, fights its first battle, and subsequently adapts to the exigencies of conflict. This assumption was tested by inviting eleven historians, each a nationally known specialist in a particular period of military history, to write essays on the first battle or campaign in each of nine wars in which the U.S. Army has fought. The editors, who were at the Combat Studies Institute (CSI, the history department of the U.S. Army Command and General Staff College [CGSC], Fort Leavenworth, Kansas), transformed general concepts into a scholarly examination of the way the U.S. Army has prepared for, fought, and learned from first battles. On the completion of the first drafts a working seminar was held at CGSC, at which the authors and

ix

editors refined the direction of the essays. The aim was to provide concise accounts of how the peacetime American military establishment is transformed when plunged into hostile circumstances. The essays analyze the ability of a prewar army, once in battle, to adjust to conflict. The final essay assesses similarities and differences among the case studies and traces the "rhythms" of the historical experience in order to comprehend how America has gone to war.

The editors devised a list of topics to be treated in each essay and set to work. Included were such issues as strategic and political background, the circumstances in which the U.S. Army found itself when the war began, strengths and weaknesses of the opponent, organizational and tactical procedures, weaponry, creation of a plan of operations, combat performance and leadership in the battle itself, and lessons learned (or not learned) from the experience of this first battle. The assignment posed numerous interesting problems for the editors. In several instances, the issue of which engagement should be selected as the "first" battle of a war had to be thrashed out. After much research and discussion, ten "first battles" were selected from America's major wars. Because of the breadth of World War II, two battles were selected from this conflict, reflecting the very real differences in how war was waged in the Atlantic and Pacific areas. In two instances—the Mexican War and the Spanish-American War—the editors and authors decided that a study of the battles would not be complete without examining either an engagement immediately following the battle (as with Palo Alto and Resaca de la Palma) or a simultaneous battle (as with San Juan and El Caney).

The first engagements in the Mexican War, the Civil War, World War I, World War II (Atlantic area), Korea, and Vietnam were universally agreed on as appropriate choices. The initial engagements of the American Revolution, the War of 1812, the Spanish-American War, and World War II (Pacific area) were not so clear-cut. Here, the battles selected were those that best matched the Army's current doctrinal interests without sacrificing the first-battle concept. For example, purists might argue that Bunker Hill was the first test of arms for Americans in the Revolutionary War. However, Long Island was the first battle fought by the newly formed Continental Army regulars commanded by George Washington. Similarly, Detroit is a logical first engagement in the War of 1812, but that was essentially a long march followed by a quick surrender and did not lend itself to any real consideration of military organization, training, and tactical doctrine. Queenston, on the other hand, took place a short time later but possessed many of the ingredients that made it appropriate for close scrutiny. Cantigny is a World War I set-piece battle. U.S. forces had been engaged earlier, but Cantigny was the first test for the Army of 1918 in an offensive setting. Buna, the first large-scale combat experience of the mobilized Army in the Pacific, followed by some eight months the disaster in the Philippines. However, it was fought with a mobilized citizen force—a National Guard division—and it was an offensive battle in the spirit of the United States Army's traditional doctrine. Conversely, the battle of Kasserine Pass was placed before Buna in order of presentation, even though this bloody baptism of American troops in North Africa began nearly six weeks after their comrades had engaged the Japanese in New Guinea; the reasoning here was that Kasserine better reflected the strategic assumptions and other intellectual baggage, training, and doctrine that the U.S. Army carried into World War II.

In certain instances, the absence of information about various dimensions of a battle hindered authors' efforts to deal fully with all topics in the common outline. Nonetheless, we believe that, as John Shy's overview, "First Battles in Retrospect," asserts, there exist significant patterns as well as startling differences in the stories of these ten initial engagements in America's nine wars. We also believe that the separate essays, each comprising a coherent narrative of an individual battle, will be found to be fascinating and to evoke America's tumultuous military history. Overall, the emphasis on the operational and tactical levels of war, as well as information about prewar circumstances, justify for the collection a claim of uniqueness in military history studies.

In the midst of preliminary efforts to bring into being the idea of a methodical examination of America's first battles, the Combat Studies Institute undertook to expand its teaching and research roles within the Staff College and to reach out Army-wide. Today's officer corps leads the army of a highly industrialized, technologically oriented nation. CSI has accepted the assignment of helping convince this technically competent and dedicated group of officers—today's and tomorrow's leaders—that systematic and progressive study of military history is of value to the professional soldier. Army leaders—active duty officers and reservists alike—have a compelling need to know the history of war.

That need has never been more compelling than it is today. As the United States Army settles into an extended interwar routine, arguably for the first time since 1939, it does so in an era of unprecedented change in both the pace and scope of warfare. For the military leader confronting the potential of war in a prewar environment, constant effort is required to reduce the gap between training and battle. The luxuries of time and distance the United States Army once enjoyed no longer can serve as brakes on requirements for rapid deployment of forces and their possible use in widely spread theaters of operation across the spectrum of conflict. The Army may no longer proceed to battle on its own timetable. Because armies generally fight along the lines of how they were prepared, it is worth examining how the U.S. Army has developed its organizations, equipment, war planning, training, and rules for war—its battle doctrine—and then how it has applied these plans and principles in initial combat in the wars it has fought.

To envision and describe accurately the features and dimensions of the landscape of future battle is a nearly impossible task. The record of Americans' ability to predict the nature of the next war (not to mention its causes, location, time, adversary or adversaries, and allies) has been uniformly dismal. Of course, such flawed records are typical worldwide. But the myopia of the past in no way lessens the need to prepare. Quite the contrary. Preparations of the most certain sort possible are required for a most uncertain future. To be effective, such preparations entail making the laboratory of war as realistic as possible. To date, no more realistic laboratory for the study of war has been discovered than past wars.

A thorough knowledge of war demonstrably and dramatically increases the competence—and thus the self-confidence—of the military leader. He must come to know, for example, that risk is inherent in war and that there is a clear difference between risk and gamble. American military leaders may not gamble with the lives entrusted to their care. To that end, they must grasp the important difference between spending combat power profitably and wasting it through bravado or paralytic hesitation. They must understand and seek to reduce what Clausewitz referred to as the ''fog and friction'' of battles. They must appreciate the limits of that experience as well as its benefits. It is in these subtle and sophisticated fundamentals of the art and science of war that systematic and progressive study of military history can most benefit today's army officers. Because there is no time to study, pause, and reflect on the contemporary battlefield, these activities must be completed in advance. The intellectual preparation of the military leader has never been more important. The basic themes and principles of war have not changed since 1776, but war has become more complex—and far more deadly. It is through creative leadership that one simplifies the complexities of war and thus renders the combat environment more manageable. For today's officer corps, creative leadership requires the traits that the British general, tactician, and historian J. F. C. Fuller recommended: wisdom, courage, and fitness. War fighting necessitates a mastery of the profession of arms in our times, a mastery that can be gained by analyzing and reflecting on the art and science of war. It is in this spirit that *America's First Battles* was written.

General Donn A. Starry, Training and Doctrine Command (TRADOC) commander at the time this project was launched; General William R. Richardson, then-commander of the Combined Arms Center (CAC); and Major General Robert Forman, then-deputy commandant, CGSC, gave full support to the concept and plan that were developed. As the project progressed, CSI received valuable encouragement from Brigadier General James L. Collins, Jr., U.S. Army Chief of Military History at the Center of Military History (CMH) in Washington, D.C., who has since retired. All four of these Army general officers helped see the project to completion, convinced that sustained study of military history is crucial for today's professional leaders. A debt is also owed to our colleagues in the Combat Studies Institute for their unfailing support and thoughtful critiques. Finally, our profound gratitude goes to Professor Ted Wilson of the University of Kansas, who served as the John F. Morrison Professor of Military History at the Command and General Staff College in 1983–84. He has been a vital part of Carl Becker's "intellectual West" and of this project.

Whatever the book's shortcomings, they are ours alone.

Charles E. Heller
William A. Stofft

1

America's First Battle: Long Island, 27 August 1776

IRA D. GRUBER

America's first battle—that is, the first general engagement involving an army of the United States—took place on Long Island, New York, on 27 August 1776. That battle, fought by citizens of the new nation to sustain their claim of independence from Great Britain, was by no means America's first experience with war. For nearly two centuries before they rebelled, English colonists had fought to maintain and extend their control over the Atlantic coast of North America from Florida to Nova Scotia and Quebec. At first, they struggled mainly with American Indians, employing small, mobile bands of militia in a succession of skirmishes and short, inconclusive campaigns. By the eighteenth century, they were engaged in increasingly bitter fighting against French and Spanish colonists on their frontiers—fighting that drew Indians and regular European forces to each side and that led after 1740 to full-scale war and the Anglo-American conquest of Canada in 1760. Thereafter, during the last years of royal government, the colonists continued to battle Indians while preparing to use force—and using it—to protect their liberties against an increasingly assertive king and Parliament.[1]

For all their experience with warfare, Americans remained innocent of battle—of general engagements—until August 1776. If during the colonial period they had seen or taken part in intense fighting, they had never yet experienced fighting of the scale and duration of a general action, of anything comparable to the Battle of Long Island. Encounters between colonists and Indians were comparatively small, sharp, and brief; it was far easier to break the power of Indians by destroying their crops, supplies, and villages than by bringing them to action. Imperial conflicts of the eighteenth century required much larger forces and extended service. But the colonists served mainly as auxiliaries to British troops, and most campaigns ended with sieges or with engagements in which regulars did much of the fighting. New Englanders, sustained by a British fleet, captured Louisbourg by siege in 1745; so too did

1

regulars and provincials take Louisbourg in 1758 and Ticonderoga in 1759; and in the climactic battle of the French and Indian War, colonists skirmished along the flanks of a British army that swept the Plains of Abraham and captured Quebec. Even during the opening year of the Revolutionary War, Americans fought only detachments of regulars at Lexington and Concord, Bunker Hill, Quebec, and Charleston. Casualties were high, but forces were small and fighting was brief.[2]

It would seem then that Americans entered their first battle at a decided disadvantage. Not only had they never fought a general action, but they had very limited experience with managing the kind of forces needed for such an action. They had relied traditionally on militia to fight Indians or neighboring colonists; they had rarely cooperated in intercolonial expeditions that were not given coherence and direction by the British Army; and their success against the British had been in small engagements and under unusually favorable circumstances. Was it possible that they could form, lead, and supply an army of Continental, state, and local forces capable of standing successfully against a professional army of more than 20,000 men? What, in fact, were the relative merits of the opposing forces that gathered on Long Island in August 1776—of their leaders, their ideas about war, and the organization, training, discipline, morale, health, and equipment of their rank and file? Last, how well did each side use the forces at its disposal on Long Island and how did the Battle of Long Island—the first battle of the Revolutionary War—affect the remainder of that war?

Although senior American officers at Long Island were less experienced than their British counterparts, their comparative inexperience was neither as great nor as decisive as it might at first glance seem to have been. To say merely that the twenty-one American generals at New York in 1776 were, on average, forty-three years old with slightly over two years' military service and that the fifteen British generals were forty-eight with thirty years' service is to create a misleading impression—an impression of decisive disparity. At a time when there was no systematic education or training for officers, when only one of the British generals had attended a military academy, experience was particularly valuable in preparing an officer for command. The senior British officers at New York were certainly men of experience—and, presumably, the right kind of experience. With one possible exception, all had proved themselves in combat; eleven of fifteen had commanded a brigade or regiment in action; and eleven had served in America before the campaign of 1776. Yet on average, these fifteen generals had seen combat during only four of their thirty years' service.[3] The American generals, by contrast, had served almost exclusively during wartime and in North America. Fourteen of twenty-one had been in combat before coming to New York in 1776, and seven had commanded brigades or regiments in the opening engagements of the revolution.[4] In short, American generals were not professional soldiers, and they were not as familiar with combat or command as were the British; but neither were they by the summer of 1776 without valuable, practical experience in war.

Apart from experience, what about the personal qualities of the opposing generals? Although there may have been more talent—more natural aptitude for command—among the American generals than among the British at New York in August 1776, the British were able to put their most talented men in command on Long Island while the Americans were not. British success and American failure in this instance resulted from a fortuitous interplay of officer selection, tactical circumstance, and illness. King George III, who sought the best available men to command his forces in America, was ultimately to be disappointed in his choice of Maj. Gen. William Howe as commander in chief and Henry Clinton as second-in-command. Yet Howe and Clinton—together with their principal deputies, Hugh, Lord Percy, and Charles, Earl Cornwallis—were clearly among the best general officers in the British Army and better than any other British general at New York in 1776.[5] Howe had established himself not merely as an excellent regimental and brigade commander during the Seven Years' War in North America, Europe, and the West Indies but also as an authority on the light-infantry tactics that were expected to be most useful in the American war. Clinton, Percy, and Cornwallis had won similar reputations: each had distinguished himself as a regimental commander in Germany at the close of the Seven Years' War, and each was recognized as an accomplished student of war. These four general officers did have reservations about Britain's coercive policies, about relying primarily on force to end the rebellion. Yet each had a keen sense of obligation to serve his king and country and to sustain royal government in America.[6] Because Howe proposed to use his whole force to attack the rebels on Long Island, it followed that he, Clinton, Percy, and Cornwallis—the most senior as well as the most accomplished of the British generals at New York—would exercise tactical command in the first general action of the war.

The Americans were not to be so fortunate. In choosing George Washington as commander in chief and appointing other leading patriots to serve as major generals and brigadier generals, the Continental Congress had sought to find able, experienced soldiers and to satisfy political interests in the states. Congress could not always do both, and Washington was left to discover talent among his generals by the costly process of trial and error. At New York in 1776, he had the additional problems of having to divide his forces and attention among Manhattan, Long Island, and New Jersey and of replacing his ablest general, Nathanael Greene, who had been forced by illness to give up the command on Long Island just a week before the battle. As a result, Washington was unable to supervise closely all preparations to receive the British, was not present when the Battle of Long Island began, and was forced to rely on Israel Putnam and John Sullivan to command in place of Greene.[7] Washington, who had served as commander of Virginia militia during the French and Indian War and as commander in chief of the Continental Army since its creation, was sometimes too aggressive, but he was also an extraordinarily effective leader of revolutionary soldiers. He had found in Nathanael Greene an ideal lieutenant, a man who had prepared for command by reading extensively in military history and theory and by training Rhode Island militia and who, since joining the Army at Boston, had proved as successful in disciplining troops as in combining military theory and practice. But Washington could not put the same confidence in Putnam or Sullivan. Putnam had considerable experience in leading men against the French and Indians, and he was a charismatic—even legendary—personality who had taken a prominent part in the fighting at Bunker Hill. But he was not the man for an independent command. Nor was John Sullivan, an impetuous lawyer and politician from New Hampshire, whose ambition and enthusiasm for the revolution exceeded his capacity for command.[8] Of course, Putnam's and Sullivan's weaknesses were not fully apparent when Greene became ill, but circumstances did deprive American forces on Long Island of their best generals before the British attacked.

However much experience and circumstances favored the British, neither side had an advantage in military theory. Indeed, the opposing generals at Long Island shared a single military tradition. With few exceptions, Americans had experienced war only while serving with or against the British, and their military heroes had been, until the Revolutionary War, British generals or generals the British admired. When the colonists prepared their militia for war, they relied almost exclusively on British manuals—provided, that is, they could not find a British soldier to conduct their training. In the twenty years before the Battle of Long Island, American presses issued sixteen British manuals in thirty-two editions; and Edward Harvey's *The Manual Exercise as Ordered by His Majesty in 1774,* which appeared in Boston, Newbury Port, New Haven, Providence, Baltimore, Williamsburg, and Philadelphia between 1774 and 1776, went through more printings than all non-British military texts published in the colonies in the two decades before 1776.[9] When American officers wanted to go beyond the mechanics of marching and firing, when they wanted to learn how to manage an army or a war, they turned to the very books and authorities then most popular among British officers. Henry Knox, the Boston bookseller who was Washington's chief of artillery at New York, complained that "good books on military subjects were almost impossible to obtain in America."[10] Yet he, Greene, and Washington not only owned such standard works as Caesar's *Commentaries* and Saxe's *Reveries* but also cited them when discussing tactics or strategy.[11]

Although American and British officers shared a single military tradition, that tradition was itself ambiguous in both theory and practice. To judge by the books they read and wrote, by the commanders they admired, and by wars they waged, British and American officers were unable to decide between the limited war of posts that was then in vogue on the Continent and the unlimited war of conquest that had been practiced occasionally in the ancient world. The most popular contemporary authorities, the Marquis de Feuquieres and Maurice de Saxe, advocated limited war. Rather than risk their expensive and highly trained professional soldiers in a general action, they sought military advantage through skillful maneuvers and limited engagements. Feuquieres would invade enemy territory to demoralize the population and weaken the opposing army by disrupting its lines of supply. Saxe would exhaust the enemy with frequent small-scale attacks. But Feuquieres and Saxe were not as popular in Anglo-American military circles as Julius Caesar, whose *Commentaries* was a textbook for aggressive, mobile warfare culminating in a decisive engagement. When outnumbered, Caesar might avoid battle or resort to siegecraft; more often, he had both troops and authority enough to risk a general action—to overthrow his enemies by destroying their armies and exploiting victory with ruthlessness or even generosity. Here, then, were two distinctly different styles of war: a limited war of maneuver, skirmishing, and siegecraft, and an unlimited war of general engagements, destruction of the enemy's army, and conquest. The two styles were not necessarily incompatible, but British authors, ignoring the styles' fundamental differences, promoted ambiguity in British military theory. The Earl of Orrey and Samuel Bever, the most popular of mid-eighteenth-century British writers, advocated limited war; but they also celebrated Caesar as the greatest of all generals, a man who knew how to "engage, defeat, and destroy an enemy."[12]

Nor was this theoretical ambiguity resolved during the French and Indian War. At the beginning of the war, British colonists in America and imperial authorities in England had very different intentions: the colonists wanted to end French influence on their frontiers by conquering Canada; the British government sought to maintain its frontiers against French encroachments by a limited use of force. The government came to share the colonists' preference for conquest, but it continued to recommend—and for the most part its commanders pursued—the strategies of a limited war. Loudoun, Abercromby, and Amherst, successively commanders in chief, all sought conquest without a climactic battle. Each sent separate columns converging on Canada by way of the St. Lawrence River, Lake Champlain, and Lake Ontario. These columns were to capture French outposts by siege and bring at last overwhelming pressure on Quebec and Montreal, the principal towns of Canada. Although Loudoun lacked the energy and Abercromby the patience to carry out this strategy, Amherst had the right combination of persistence and prudence to see it to fruition and become one of the most celebrated commanders of the war. Ironically, Amherst's success depended in part on James Wolfe's capture of Quebec—on Wolfe's having risked and won a decisive battle.[13] So it was that the French and Indian War left a confusing legacy: the British government had conquered with a conventional war of posts, and the greatest heroes of the war, Amherst and Wolfe, seemed as different as Saxe and Caesar.

Most senior officers at New York, being veterans of the French and Indian War, were heirs to this confusing legacy. But what of those British officers like Clinton, Percy, and Cornwallis who had studied the art of war on the Continent, served in Germany during the Seven Years' War, and admired Prince Ferdinand of Brunswick as the consummate commander in chief? Their theoretical training was not substantially different from that of officers who had served primarily in America: they read the same books, attended the same peacetime encampments, and associated with the same kinds of men. But in Germany they experienced only limited war. Their commander in chief, Prince Ferdinand, was charged with defending Hanover, Brunswick, and other German principalities against decidedly superior French forces. To parry armies advancing through both Westphalia and Hesse, he relied on combinations of maneuvers, sieges, and sharp attacks on enemy detachments. At least twice—at Minden in 1759 and Vellinghausen in 1761—Ferdinand fought general actions. But he never had the forces to exploit his victories or to try to end the war by destroying opposing armies. His was an aggressive, successful war of posts to preserve German territory. It was strategically more consistent than the war being waged in North America by Amherst and Wolfe.[14] Even so, British officers of the German school would not be free from the ambiguities of the Anglo-American military tradition. They too dreamed of Caesar and Saxe, and they knew that Ferdinand had been forced—by politics as well as by persistent shortages of men and supplies—to keep within the bounds of limited war.[15]

However ambiguous their strategic heritage, British and American officers at New York in 1776 had a relatively clear understanding of tactics. They agreed not only that most fighting in America would be done by infantry but also that infantry would fight, according to circumstances, in prescribed formations. Europeans, who thought of infantry, cavalry, and artillery acting together in battle and of formal siegecraft, debated the proper proportion of cavalry to infantry in an army or the relative merits of columns and lines for an infantry attack.[16] Anglo-Americans understood that in New England and the middle states, they would rely on infantry and earthworks with only modest support from artillery and that cavalry would be little more than mounted infantry employed in scouting and skirmishing. They also understood that columns and lines had specific tactical applications. They would use columns screened by skirmishers in loose lines to advance toward battle. If they found the enemy was not entrenched, they would deploy into lines of two or three ranks so as to make the most of massed musket fire. But if attacking earthworks, they would divide their men into thin, narrow columns and rely primarily on bayonets.[17] Thus, James Wolfe had used a line of infantry, two ranks deep, and musketry to shatter the French Army on the Plains of Abraham; and thus William Howe, finding a variety of American defenses at Bunker Hill, had employed both lines and columns to win a costly victory.[18] Although earthworks and artillery remained important in their tactics, Anglo-Americans were—by the time of the revolution—losing their enthusiasm for sieges.

Just as British and American officers shared a single strategic and tactical heritage, so too did they work within similar military organizations. The British Army was, of course, under more centralized direction than the American: it was a national professional force under a parliamentary monarchy; the American Army was a combination of local, regional, and national forces under the loose control of a confederation of states. But more important than this difference were the similarities between the two armies. Both were clearly subordinate to their governments. Congress and the state governments, like the king in Parliament, created the Army, commissioned and promoted officers, defined terms of service for the rank and file, established military justice, and approved plans of campaign. Both armies were controlled by a commander in chief in consultation with division and brigade commanders and with the assistance of a secretary, an adjutant general, and four or five aides-de-camp. Both armies were structured around infantry regiments. The American regiment was intended to be slightly larger than the British—608 as against 477 men—and there were six American regiments and only four British to a brigade. But when the armies assembled at New York and allowances were made for Americans who were ill and British who were withdrawn to form elite units of light troops and grenadiers, infantry regiments on both sides usually contained between 300 and 350 men.[19] Finally, the administration and supply of both armies were managed by line officers (sometimes civilians) serving as quartermaster, commissary, paymaster, and muster master generals who worked with various governmental agencies, the commanders in chief, regimental quartermasters, and private contractors.

It might seem that the organization of the British Army, being more centralized and better established than that of the American Army, would have given the British advantages in the Revolutionary War. In fact, it did not: both armies suffered periodically from the absence of strong executive authority and clearly defined bureaucratic responsibility in their governments. Executive authority in the British government was divided between the crown and Parliament—between King George III and his ministers. The king selected officers for high command and issued formal instructions; ministers corresponded regularly with the commander in chief and other senior officers discussing plans of campaign. Because senior officers always had powerful friends in society and government—Howe, Clinton, Percy, and Cornwallis all were members of Parliament—command in the British Army was regularly weakened by senior officers who took considerable latitude with their orders or who thwarted their superiors by appealing—or threatening to appeal— unofficially to the government. Thus, commanders in chief like Howe and Clinton deviated from the government's orders and were in turn frustrated by subordinates like Percy and Cornwallis who corresponded unofficially with the government.[20] Equally serious, there was no clearly defined bureaucratic responsibility for managing the logistics of the American war. The War Office, the Treasury, the Navy Board, and the Board of Ordnance shared the burden of supporting the Army. Because no one coordinated their efforts or inquired into their weaknesses, these bureaus competed with each other and remained inefficient, if not corrupt, throughout the war. The Army, which relied on Britain for most of its food as well as its cash, clothing, camp equipment, arms, and ammunition, was frequently immobilized for want of supplies or overland transportation. Nor could it depend on impressment to offset shortages: foraging parties were always vulnerable to attack and often plundered friends and foes alike.[21]

The American Army suffered from the same ills—the absence of strong executive authority and of well-defined bureaucratic jurisdictions. Having rebelled against a central government, abuses of executive power, and a standing army, Americans were unwilling to give too much power to Congress and reluctant to create through Congress and their state governments either powerful executive agencies or standing armies. But controlling and support- ing an army made up of Continental and state units without a strong central government or executive authority was nearly impossible. Officers who did not get the commands or recognition they sought turned to Congress or state governments for redress. Their appeals were at best troublesome; at worst, destructive of military authority.[22] Congress did appoint men to assist Washington in gathering supplies for and administering the Army, men to serve in such posts as quartermaster and commissary general. Congress also created a Board of War and Ordnance charged with "overseeing all military stores, superintending the raising, equipping, and dispatching the land forces, and supervising the army generally."[23] But Congress did not separate the jurisdictions of those charged with gathering supplies or, until 1781, give the Board of War power to match its responsibilities; and Washington refused to assume powers that Congress would not grant its agents. No wonder then that representatives of various supply departments—both Continental and state— frequently competed for scarce military supplies or that their competition did more to drive up prices and promote corruption than to alleviate shortages. Because Washington did not wish to tarnish the revolution by resorting to impressment, the American Army was, for much of the war, "poorly housed, miserably clothed, ill-equipped and underfed"—and smaller than Congress had intended.[24] Some of the Army's troubles were the unavoidable consequences of primitive systems of manufacturing and finance; more were the result of weak executives and conflicting jurisdictions.

Notwithstanding organizational flaws, the armies that gathered at New York in 1776 were adequately equipped and supplied—certainly better than they had been in 1775 or would be during most of the ensuing campaigns. It is true that Americans did not have uniforms or standardized small arms in 1776—that most on Long Island wore work clothes or hunting shirts and carried any musket, rifle, or fowling piece that could be found. Yet, with an adequate supply of cannon, powder, food, and camp equipment, they had the means to meet the British. In the sixteen months since fighting had begun at Lexington, Americans had made heroic efforts to equip their army. Finding domestic manufactures wholly inadequate, they had come to rely primarily on what they could capture from the British or buy from the French and the Dutch. New Englanders took 72 serviceable cannon from Fort Ticonderoga; privateers captured a succession of transports bringing munitions to Howe at Boston and New York; and American merchantmen exchanged grain for powder at the Dutch West Indies island of St. Eustatius. By August 1776, such efforts had enabled Washington to assemble 121 cannon and 19 mortars at New York and to have, for the first time since becoming commander in chief, a surplus of powder. His forces were also by then well fed and adequately sheltered. The British were, all considered, even better off than the Americans. Although they had been forced to endure short rations during the previous winter, they now had provisions for nearly five months and hopes of securing fresh food and forage from the Loyalists of New York and New Jersey. And if their uniforms were too heavy for Long Island in August, they did have complete uniforms and camp equipment, standardized muskets (.75 caliber with reasonable accuracy at 80 yards and a capacity to kill at the point-blank range of 250 yards), fourteen-inch socket bayonets, a regular complement of artillery, and the close support of 30 warships and nearly 400 transports.[25] Temporarily at least, equipment, supplies, and transportation were not major problems for either army.

But what of the men who would use this equipment—the rank and file and junior officers of the opposing armies? Who were these men? What were their origins, their places of birth, their family backgrounds, and their early training? How had they been recruited? And were they required to meet minimal standards of age, health, strength, and intelligence? What kinds of lives did they lead in the army? What were their aspirations and their prospects? How, moreover, were they trained to fight, and how effective was that training in achieving technical competence as well as discipline and sound morale? Were British common soldiers no more than beggars and criminals shaped into regiments by numbing discipline? Were the Americans, conversely, all sturdy, independent craftsmen and farmers who had taken up arms in self-defense, in a desperate effort to resist a tyrannical imperial government? Was this a contest between unthinking professionals and inspired citizen soldiers? If so, would the citizen soldiers have a chance of success in formal engagements decided by intricate maneuvers, disciplined fire, and unified bayonet attacks? In short, who were the soldiers of the American war and with which side did the advantage lie?

British common soldiers of the Revolutionary War era were not typically beggars or criminals; they were, on the contrary, men of respectable origins who volunteered for the army, accepted privation, and became—as much through motivation as discipline—effective fighting men. Twice during the American war, the British government did sweep men from poorhouses and jails into the army. But because opinion was against impressment, the government usually relied on volunteers. Most of the rank and file were solid, productive members of society who, thrust out of work by industrialization or temporary shifts in the economy, entered the army to get bounties and permanent employment. The typical soldier was a former weaver, shoemaker, or carpenter; he was unmarried, about thirty years old, with ten years' service; and he was no more sickly than any other British subject. His days were filled with manual labor, marching, enforcing the law, and, occasionally, preparing for war. He learned, during periods of training, how to keep cadence, deploy from column into line, ploy from line to column, load and fire his musket on command, and ply his bayonet. If he sometimes deserted or mutinied, he was far more often an obedient soldier and a formidable enemy. His collective strength lay in long, common service: years of living in the same regiment (possibly with other members of his family or with men from his native town or county), years of being isolated from society at large, of wearing a scarlet coat and regimental facings, of honoring his regimental colors, of enduring battle, and of acknowledging duty to king and country. Such shared experiences made ordinary, solid Englishmen into disciplined, determined soldiers. Those who served at Long Island would prove capable of maintaining their morale and effectiveness through a long, discouraging, and difficult war.[26]

That the rank and file performed so well may be attributed in part at least to the competence and spirit of British junior officers. Those junior officers were, paradoxical as it may seem, products of a system of selection and promotion that put more emphasis on money, influence, and longevity than on talent or theoretical studies. To be sure, there were in this system some who were ignorant of their profession and irresponsible in their duty—some who survived because there were no periodic reviews of performance and because influence could offset incompetence in particular cases. There were also many young officers who knew little of military theory: only those entering the artillery or engineers or attending an academy on the Continent were likely to study the art of war. Yet, despite its faults and inequities, this system did produce many competent, highly motivated junior officers. Because even lieutenants and captains could find security, exclusive company, and respect in the army, there were always more candidates than vacancies for commissions; and the candidates were far more often able men from the ranks or sons of accomplished members of the middle class (army officers, doctors, lawyers, provincial officials, clergymen, or merchants) than scions of noble families. It did take, above all, money and social standing—or a patron with both—to get permission to buy a first commission; but it also took a basic education in literature, language, and mathematics as well as a reasonably sound body and character. Thus, newly commissioned officers were frequently young men of talent and ambition. Although only those with considerable wealth and influence could hope to rise to the highest ranks, the remainder could look forward to satisfying careers as lieutenants, captains, and majors—often within a single regiment and sometimes in company with many near relatives. Such junior officers gave the army experienced, competent, and dependable leadership and strengthened the corporate spirit of individual regiments. Moreover, when the American war began, the purchase system allowed those officers with qualms about fighting British subjects to sell their commissions and leave the army—thereby enhancing the loyalty of the officer corps throughout the Revolutionary War.[27]

The American Army was, of course, far less homogeneous than the British. Each royal regiment had its distinctive characteristics; yet each drew officers and men from throughout the British Isles, and each was controlled by one goverment and one set of regulations and customs. By contrast, the American forces on Long Island in August 1776 included regiments from eight states under thirteen separate governmental jurisdictions and the operational control of George Washington, commander in chief of Continental forces.[28] Because each government established slightly different terms of service for its troops, used different criteria in selecting officers, and provided different training and regulations and because each unit reflected the peculiar characteristics of the community from which it was drawn, the American Army was a true conglomeration. Washington already knew what battle would prove: that the quality of his army was as varied as its origins—that discipline, morale, and effectiveness were strikingly different from regiment to regiment.

Although Washington thought the militia the least dependable of the troops under his command, the militia was more representative of American society, more popular with ordinary citizens, and more consistent with republican ideals than state or Continental forces. State laws required that every adult white male be in the militia, furnish his own weapons and clothes, train periodically, and be available for service in time of trouble. Because the militia, in turn, furnished officers and men for long-term service in state and Continental forces, it might seem that all forces came in time to mirror white male society, that the militia was no more representative than state or

Continental units. Not so. The militia drew upon the full range of the adult white male population; the state and Continental forces, upon its extremes— the more prominent for officers and the poorest and most obscure for rank and file. Those citizens who had the means and standing to choose where they would serve and who were not so zealous or ambitious as to want commissions in state or Continental forces usually preferred the militia. They preferred to be with friends and neighbors, to elect their own officers, to enjoy relaxed discipline, and to serve for comparatively short periods near home. Moreover, the militia continued to seem ideally suited to carrying on a revolutionary war. Representing all classes, led by trusted local men, and organized loosely for temporary service, the militia offered a means of overthrowing the royal government without jeopardizing republican institutions, without replacing one standing army with another. Washington might mistrust the militia because of its lax discipline and its members' refusal to serve for more than brief, appointed periods. But many Americans wanted to rely primarily on the militia, supported by a minimum of state and Continental troops, to defeat the British. Would not the militia, inspired by a love of liberty and a sense of divine providence, be able to overcome regular British forces? Would not courage and simple tactical skills offset discipline and the most intricate maneuvers?[29]

Washington did not think so. He believed that only a regular army—only an army with discipline and coherence enough to fight effectively in open country—could defeat the British. Although he was unable to create such an army before the Battle of Long Island, he did succeed in making some Continental and state troops more like regulars than militiamen. To be sure, until January 1777, all Americans were serving for relatively short periods. When enlistments expired at the end of 1775, Washington recommended that Continentals should thenceforth serve for the duration of the war. Congress, thinking those terms would discourage all save the most impoverished men and being unwilling to rely on such men in a standing army, authorized enlistments for just one year.[30] Even so, only the most desperate signed on for 1776. Those in the Massachusetts Continental Line were "poor farmers and artisans, young and almost totally indifferent to the cause of independence, who were enticed into service by the promise of land, steady wages, and easy discipline."[31] Much the same was true of the Virginia Continental Line and Maryland state troops. In Virginia, the officers were the best people; the rank and file were the sons of poor farmers and laborers, crudely educated boys of twenty who, knowing little of politics, enlisted for the rewards of bounties and land. Maryland recruits, also young and poor, enlisted "not because of a sense of duty or patriotism, but because Maryland society offered them few opportunities for employment."[32] With such young men, similar in social origins and motivation to the British common soldier, Washington sought to build a regular army. He emphasized respect for rank, discipline, cleanliness, and order as well as tactical skills and loyalty to regiments and the revolution. By August 1776, he had had modest success with some regiments—enough to form the nucleus of what would be a regular army.

Notwithstanding his success, Washington's Army was, in August 1776, decidedly inferior to the British forces assembling at New York. The Americans did have the moral advantage of fighting in defense of their homes, families, and institutions; they were buoyed by a general enthusiasm for a revolution that was then at its zenith; they knew as yet comparatively little of the defeats and suffering that could and would come with war; and they had in Washington a commander in chief who knew how to make the most of popular feeling. But apart from their enthusiasm and innocence, there was little that favored the Americans. It was not just that the British generals were more talented and more experienced in combat than the Americans commanding on Long Island or that the British had better weapons and more abundant supplies. It was primarily that the British Army was far better prepared than the American to endure the shattering experience of battle, of a general action fought at close quarters with muskets, bayonets, and cannon. British regiments were stronger and more resilient than even the best of the American. They were filled with soldiers who were, on average, five to ten years older and who had served together nine to ten years longer than the rank and file of the Continental or state line; and there were in some regiments, like the *Royal Welsh Fusiliers* and the *37th Foot,* men who had fought at Minden, Quebec, and Vellinghausen, men whose presence alone could steady their younger comrades. In short, British regiments had had time to build the deep sense of community and the automatic response to command that were essential in eighteenth-century combat—that sustained a regiment under fire and that, in turn, made its fire truly destructive.

That these two armies met for the first time in a general action sixteen months after the war began was primarily the result of the difficulties both sides had in mobilizing their forces. The Americans, who had the advantage of being closer than the British to their sources of men and most supplies, had considerable trouble transforming militiamen into a Continental army. From Lexington and Concord to the Battle of Long Island, Americans were ready to defend themselves against the British—whether at Boston, Charleston, or New York. But only rarely did Washington have enough disciplined troops with an adequate supply of arms and ammunition to consider a general action. His troubles were those inherent in a weak central government, an inefficient military organization, a primitive economy, and an undisciplined populace. The British, for their part, had the advantages of a standing army of 45,000 and a comparatively well-developed economy. But they had to maintain garrisons from North America and the West Indies to the British Isles, the Mediterranean, and India; and before regulars could be assembled for a general action at Boston or New York, the British government had to raise substantial additional men and solve formidable problems of supply and transportation. The government lost little time after Bunker Hill in deciding to increase its forces in America. But King George III refused to create new regiments, and recruiting for the old went slowly. Thus, his ministers had to find mercenaries for the war in America, and not until the late spring of 1776 were large reinforcements on their way across the Atlantic. In the interim, the main British Army remained too small—little more than 6,000 men—to risk a general engagement.[33]

While the British mobilized their forces, they decided on the strategy that would take them to New York and to the Battle of Long Island—a strategy based both on their assumptions about the rebellion and on their ambiguous understanding of how war should be waged. They had learned very quickly at Lexington and Concord and at Bunker Hill that they would not be able to restore royal government with a mere show of force. But believing that New England was the center of discontent, that a majority of Americans remained loyal to the crown, and that force could be used successfully against the rebels, the British decided on a comprehensive plan to end the war in 1776—a plan that owed as much to Saxe as to Caesar. The main British Army would leave Boston, go to New York, and, with reinforcements from England and the support of loyal colonists, begin strangling the rebellion in New England. A detachment advancing north along the Hudson River would join another moving south from Canada across Lake Champlain to cut overland communications between the Middle Colonies and New England and to launch attacks on western Massachusetts and Connecticut. Other detachments of ships and men would take Rhode Island and range north as far as Maine, raiding colonial ports and attacking all American shipping. These measures, designed to isolate the most disloyal provinces and subject them to relentless military pressure, would have pleased the most cautious strategist. But the British also proposed to seek, engage, and destroy the Continental Army—to risk, as General Howe put it, "a decisive Action, than which nothing is more to be desired or sought for by us as the most effectual Means to terminate this expensive War."[34]

British strategy for 1776 had another dimension. A minority within the government as well as a number of prominent generals and admirals, including General Howe and his brother Admiral Richard Lord Howe, the commanders in chief of British forces in America, favored a negotiated settlement of Anglo-American differences. None wished to make concessions on the fundamental question of sovereignty. All believed that ultimate authority within the empire had to reside with the king in Parliament. Yet all thought that concessions might be made on specific issues such as taxation and that concessions leading to an amiable settlement would be preferable to the most complete military victory. Although these moderates did not succeed in controlling British policy, which since the Battle of Bunker Hill had become ever more bellicose, they did persuade a majority in the ministry and in Parliament to authorize sending a peace commission to America. The majority agreed to the commission mainly to satisfy critics of the war and to hasten the colonies' surrender. It had no intention of allowing the commission to undertake negotiations until the colonies had formally surrendered—to do more initially than offer pardon to those who pledged allegiance to the crown. But the majority did agree to permit the Howe brothers to serve as peace commissioners as well as commanders in chief; and the Howes, among the most enthusiatic proponents of a negotiated settlement, would be sorely tempted to allow their hopes for peace to interfere with conduct of the war.[35]

American strategy for 1776 was far less complicated. Washington shared the ambiguous heritage that left British generals groping between wars of posts and of decisive battle. Yet circumstances allowed him little choice for 1776. Even before the British sailed from Boston, he assumed they would go to New York to occupy the Hudson River valley and isolate New England from the remainder of the colonies. He also assumed that the British fleet and army, acting together around Manhattan, would be superior to any forces he could assemble there. But he felt obliged to defend New York not only to satisfy Congress and keep up American morale but also to protect vital lines of communication along and across the Hudson—lines stretching north through Albany to American forces in Canada and lines binding "the northern and southern Colonies, upon which depends the Safety of America."[36] Once he had decided to defend New York against superior forces, he found himself committed to a war of posts. At least, to hold the city and block the Hudson without benefit of warships, he had to depend on a web of fortified posts stretching from Long Island and Governor's Island, which together commanded New York City and the East River, to Manhattan and adjacent parts of New Jersey, which guarded the city itself and the mouth of the Hudson.[37] Defending places and routes of strategic consequence and relying on fortifications—even sacrificing garrisons—to obstruct and delay the enemy were the conventional ends and means of a war of posts. But in one important respect, Washington was violating convention. By placing his forces astride the Hudson and East Rivers without having control of these rivers, he jeopardized his entire army.

Although well aware of the weaknesses in Washington's position, General Howe was not prepared to exploit them to the full. He reached New York in June 1776 determined not merely to isolate and exhaust the rebellion in New England but also to engage and destroy the Continental Army. In early July, he was "still of opinion that peace will not be restored in America until the Rebel Army is defeated."[38] Although he did not then have the men or the equipment to attack the rebels, he knew that by sending warships into the Hudson and East Rivers and by landing troops north of the Harlem River, he

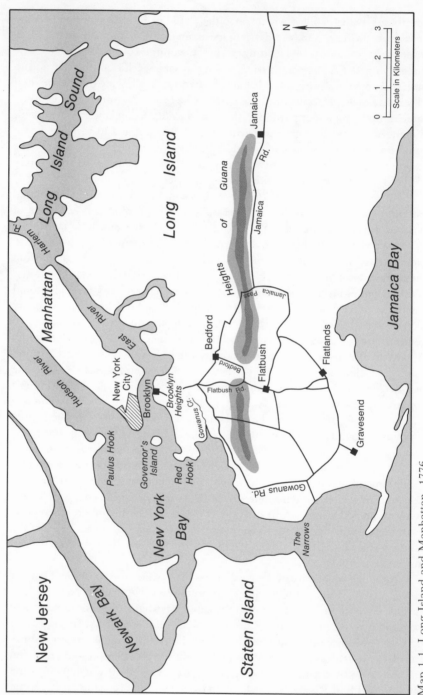

Map 1.1. Long Island and Manhattan, 1776

could trap nearly the whole of Washington's Army. But while he awaited reinforcements and while his brother tried repeatedly—and unsuccessfully—to open negotiations with the rebels, Howe began to think that driving Washington from New York was preferable to trapping him there. By 12 August, when at last he had all the men and equipment he needed to open the campaign, he had decided to land on Long Island, disperse the rebel detachment, and, by mounting cannon on Brooklyn Heights, which commanded lower Manhattan, force Washington to abandon New York City. He would subsequently occupy the remainder of Manhattan and send detachments to capture Rhode Island and join troops from Canada along the upper reaches of the Hudson River.[39] Here was a plan designed to recover New York and bring pressure on New England with only minimal risks to the British Army, a plan that gave Washington every opportunity to avoid being forced to accept a general action.

What caused Howe to modify his plans? Why did he decide against trying to end the rebellion by destroying the Continental Army—by trapping it at New York or by engaging and defeating it in a single climactic battle? It is impossible to be sure, but it seems likely that he gradually changed his plans in response to a combination of tactical and political considerations. He may well have decided that American positions at New York were too extensive to be besieged successfully and too strong to be attacked directly. His experience at Quebec in 1759 argued against investing an extensive position and, at Bunker Hill in 1775, against assaulting rebel entrenchments. He also may have decided that engaging and destroying the Continental Army would work against his hopes for Anglo-American reconciliation. He knew that some force would have to be used to make the colonists more tractable. But he hoped that a skillful suite of maneuvers, forcing the Americans to give up New York and creating the impression of British invincibility, would be as effective as—and less hazardous than—a decisive battle in promoting negotiations. Certainly maneuver and siegecraft were orthodox parts of British military thinking. When Howe rejected Clinton's proposal for a landing on Manhattan and chose instead to approach New York City through Long Island, he was pursuing an entirely conventional war of posts; and when he justified his prudent strategy by saying he had to preserve his army as "the stock upon which the national force in America must in future be grafted," he was making both political and military sense.[40]

While Howe gathered forces and changed plans, Washington struggled to strengthen the defenses of New York—to raise additional men, complete his extensive fortifications, and decide how best to deploy his forces. He did receive substantial reinforcements of state troops and militia after the British reached Staten Island, enough to increase his army from about 10,000 men in mid-July to 20,000 fit for service by late August. But even with these

additional men he was not able to complete or to garrison all the fortifications
he had undertaken, and he had no prospect of contesting every mile of
shoreline about New York. To defend the city and the Hudson River—to
pursue his strategy—he had to concentrate his men in a few posts and rely on
fortifications to sustain them against an enemy that would be superior
wherever he chose to strike. By mid-August, Washington expected the British
to attack first on Manhattan. Knowing he could not prevent a landing, he
decided to place most of his forces in and around New York City, which lay at
the southernmost tip of Manhattan and at the center of his defensive line
across the mouths of the Hudson and East Rivers. Although he risked having
most of his forces—perhaps 11,000 men and 64 of his 121 cannon—trapped in
the city, he had to take that gamble to keep the city and defend the Hudson.
The remainder of his forces were deployed so as to complement the defenses of
the city and the river (in fortified posts at Brooklyn on Long Island,
Governor's Island in the East River, and Paulus Hook in New Jersey) and to
secure overland communications between Manhattan and upstate New York
(at Kingsbridge on the Harlem River, a dozen miles north of New York
City).[41]

The largest and most important of the detachments outside the city was
across the East River at Brooklyn. It was there because Brooklyn commanded
the river and the city—was indispensable to the defense of both—and because
holding Brooklyn required elaborate and extensive fortifications. On the
landward side, Brooklyn Neck was covered by three forts and two redoubts
linked together by more than a mile of entrenchments stretching from
Wallabout Bay on the north to Gowanus Creek on the south—entrenchments
that commanded clear fields of fire and that were everywhere strengthened by
a ditch, a fraise, and an abatis. Behind this line were additional entrenchments, three forts, and a redoubt to defend the bay and river fronts of
Brooklyn from Gowanus Creek and Red Hook on the south to Wallabout Bay
on the north—a distance of nearly four miles. Two of the interior forts,
Defiance at Red Bank and Stirling opposite New York City, also were sited to
cover the mouth of the East River. Although the works at Brooklyn remained
unfinished in August 1776 and may have been too extensive for the 28 cannon
and 3,500 men assigned to them, they were still "of very respectable
strength."[42] And they were, until 20 August, under the command of
Nathanael Greene, the best of Washington's generals, who had been driving
his men for nearly four months to complete the works and to achieve the high
levels of discipline, physical fitness, and training that would be needed to
defend them.[43]

But the British were not planning to assault these works. As early as 12
August, Howe had decided to try to end the rebellion without risking a
general action—to employ a series of flanking maneuvers to drive the rebels
from New York and encourage a negotiated settlement. He would begin by

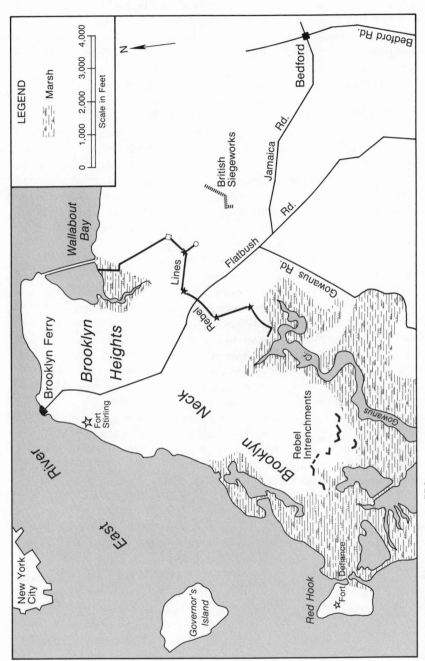

Map 1.2. Brooklyn, August 1776

clearing the rebels from Brooklyn Heights so that he could mount artillery there, make New York City untenable, and recover the city without a costly battle. It is not entirely clear how he intended to take the works at Brooklyn, but to judge from his actions, it seems that he planned to rely on siegecraft or intimidation—that his tactics on Long Island were to be consistent with his strategy of avoiding battle. It also seems that he assumed—perhaps as a result of intelligence from Loyalists—that nearly all American forces on Long Island were concentrated within their lines. At least, he chose to land six miles south of Brooklyn at Gravesend, presumably to avoid disembarking under fire; and once ashore, he pushed forward as rapidly as possible—and by a circuitous route—toward the American lines, presumably to reach them before the rebels could march out and contest the densely wooded ridge that separated Gravesend and Brooklyn.[44] If he could get to Brooklyn without opposition, he could then begin a regular siege that, with minimal risks, would force the rebels to surrender or withdraw. In either case, he would have Brooklyn and, with it, command of New York City.

If these were Howe's plans, all did not go according to plan. The reinforcements that arrived on 12 August did give him the men and equipment he needed to open the campaign: between 23,000 and 24,000 troops, fit for duty, supported by nearly 400 transports and 30 men of war. On 22 August, he and Lord Howe did succeed in landing 15,000 men on Long Island without opposition and without loss. And, within several hours of their landing, his advanced guard of 4,000 men under Lord Cornwallis did reach Flatbush unopposed. But when Cornwallis tried to advance from Flatbush to Brooklyn, when he tried to pass through the densely wooded ridge that separated the two villages—the Heights of Guana—he found his way barred by rebels. At that, Cornwallis retired to Flatbush to await reinforcements and further instructions. Howe was now faced with a difficult tactical problem: how to advance on Brooklyn without having to fight his way across a formidable natural fortification, the wooded ridge forty to eighty feet high, that lay across all roads leading north to Brooklyn. Finding that the rebels intended to defend the three roads nearest to New York Bay, Howe encamped, sent to Staten Island for another 5,000 men, and began searching for a relatively safe approach to Brooklyn.[45]

It is unclear whether Washington or Sullivan, who commanded on Long Island 20–24 August, first decided to oppose the British along the Heights of Guana; but it is clear that Washington heartily approved of the decision and that Sullivan consistently sought to carry it out. When the British landed at Gravesend on 22 August, Sullivan sent detachments to watch them, destroy crops and cattle in their way, and resist any attempt to cross the heights. Washington, who was then on Manhattan and who feared that the landings might be a diversion, sent only 1,800 men to reinforce Sullivan; but he ordered that some of the reinforcements be used to block the passes through the heights and the remainder, to strengthen the Garrison at Brooklyn. Twice during the next four days, Washington went to Long Island to confer with his generals, encourage his men, and reconnoiter the British Army in its camp near Flatbush. After his first visit, he appointed Putnam to command over Sullivan, perhaps because he thought Sullivan ignorant of the terrain or because he disapproved of some of Sullivan's actions. But on each visit, Washington saw and accepted the dispositions Sullivan had made to defend the Heights of Guana, and after each visit he sent additional troops to strengthen those dispositions. By 26 August, about 7,000 American troops were on Long Island: 4,000 within the lines at Brooklyn and 3,000 on the Heights of Guana. Most of those on the heights were concentrated at the three passes nearest to New York Bay—800 each on Gowanus, Flatbush, and Bedford Roads—and 500 were vaguely assigned to watch the Jamaica Road, which led to a fourth pass nearly five miles east of Brooklyn. These four detachments, together with small parties ranging among them, were responsible for watching and defending more than six miles of wooded ridge against an army of 20,000 men.[46]

In deciding to defend the heights—to engage the British before they reached his lines at Brooklyn—Washington chose an understandable, if hazardous, course. To await the British at Brooklyn was virtually to concede the loss of that post and New York City; at least with a superior fleet and army and with a full siege train, the British could be sure eventually of taking Brooklyn. It did, therefore, seem reasonable to use the Heights of Guana as a giant outwork, as a place where inexperienced and outnumbered troops might delay or possibly defeat the British. The heights were too steep and too thickly covered with trees and brush to invite frontal assault, and they were too extensive to be taken by siege. Yet they were also too extensive to be safely held by relatively small forces without cavalry, forces like those under Sullivan's command on 26 August. It was simply not possible for 3,000 infantrymen to defend a ridge that stretched northeast from New York Bay for more than ten miles; even to try to cover the six miles and four passes from the bay to the Jamaica Road was a hazardous undertaking. Should the British succeed in breaking through or turning the American position, the whole of the position would be in danger of being cut off from the lines at Brooklyn, which lay from 1½ to 3 miles behind the principal detachments. In short, the success of the defense and the safety of the defenders on the Heights of Guana depended on accurate and timely intelligence. On the night of 26 August, they depended on five young officers sent to watch the Jamaica Pass.[47]

While Washington committed ever more men to the Heights of Guana, Howe searched desperately for a way to pass those heights without serious losses. By 26 August, after five days of probing and reconnoitering American positions, he knew he could not afford the casualties that would be required to force the Gowanus, Flatbush, or Bedford Passes. He also knew that apart from those passes, the heights were impenetrable within six miles of New York Bay—that the terrain was too difficult and too closely patrolled to admit an attack between the principal roads. He even doubted he could successfully turn the exposed eastern flank of the American position. But, after receiving a reinforcement of 5,000 Hessians and after considering alternatives, he agreed to try a flanking maneuver. General Clinton, who had personally reconnoitered the heights, believed that the Jamaica Pass was unguarded and that it could be used to envelop the Americans on the heights—to break their resistance and to open all roads to Brooklyn. Clinton's plan required the close coordination of more than 20,000 men and several warships. While a detachment of 5,000 British troops made a diversionary attack on the Gowanus Pass and another regiment drove off American patrols east of the Bedford Pass, 10,000 men would make a long night's march to the Jamaica Pass. At dawn, while ships and men created diversions from the East River to the Gowanus and Flatbush Passes, the main British force of 10,000 would push through the Jamaica Pass and envelop Americans on the heights, forcing them to withdraw or face a concerted British attack and destruction. Howe doubted that such an elaborate plan could succeed—that 10,000 men could get through the Jamaica Pass undetected and unopposed—but he accepted the plan, presumably because it seemed less certain to end in disaster than any other that had been proposed.[48]

The plan was far more successful than Howe expected not only because each British unit performed well but also because chance and inexperience worked against the Americans. Shortly after dark on 26 August, Howe, Clinton, and the main British force assembled near Flatlands, about two miles southeast of Flatbush and well clear of American outposts and patrols. By 2100, Clinton and the van were marching for the Jamaica Pass covered by skirmishers ranging along the Heights of Guana and by a diversionary attack on the Gowanus Pass. As he approached Howard's House, which was only "a few hundred yards" from Jamaica Pass, Clinton sent out a patrol to see whether the house and pass were, as he hoped, unguarded. The patrol promptly met and captured the only American soldiers within miles of the pass, the five young, inexperienced officers who had been sent to watch the exposed eastern flank of American positions on the heights.[49] It was, of course, naive of Sullivan, who commanded on the heights, and perhaps of Washington, who had visited Sullivan on 26 August and reviewed his preparations, to rely on five young and inexperienced men to secure the flank of an army. It was also naive of Sullivan, who had anticipated an attack each day since the British landed, to let 10,000 men steal a march on him. But the British had masked their intentions and actions skillfully; they were fortunate to capture all the men watching the Jamaica Pass, and they exploited their good fortune promptly and efficiently. As soon as Clinton learned that the pass was unguarded, he sent troops to secure it, and at first light, he crossed the heights on his way toward Bedford and Brooklyn.[50] He had turned the American flank.

Thereafter, Howe's execution deviated little from his design. While he and Clinton were clearing Jamaica Pass, other British forces were creating diversions in New York Bay and on the Heights of Guana: seven British warships rode a flood tide toward the American works at Brooklyn; General James Grant with 5,000 men broke through the Gowanus Pass; and General Philip von Heister moved forward with 4,000 Hessians to threaten Flatbush Pass. The Americans, unaware that their flank was being turned and alarmed by their failure to hold the Gowanus Pass during the night, now concentrated on stopping Grant and von Heister—leaving the Jamaica Road open for Howe and Clinton to complete their envelopment of the heights. Indeed, for three hours—even longer along New York Bay—Americans believed that they were holding firm against the British. Alexander Lord Stirling of New Jersey took command of fresh troops, went to the Gowanus Road, and formed a line of battle that checked Grant; Sullivan, reinforced by 500 men who had withdrawn from the Jamaica Road, had no trouble stopping von Heister at Flatbush Pass. But neither Stirling nor Sullivan realized that he was meeting only a diversionary attack, that the forces opposed to him would be content to skirmish until the main British force was in his rear. So successful were the British that each American detachment was in turn surprised to find itself attacked by converging forces. There was little that Sullivan or Stirling could do except try to save as many of his men as possible. About 1000, Sullivan began a general retreat from Flatbush Pass, a retreat that sent his men scrambling along the heights looking for ways to Brooklyn. Stirling held out an hour longer, using Smallwood's Maryland regiment to cover a withdrawal over Gowanus Creek. Both Sullivan and Stirling, together with 897 men, were captured, and by 1400, all fighting had ended. Although some British officers and men now wished to exploit their success by attacking the lines at Brooklyn, Howe did not. He was unwilling to deviate from his plan—to risk heavy losses taking by storm what he would soon have by siege.[51]

The first battle of the Revolutionary War was a British victory, but it was less decisive than it seemed or might have been. Howe certainly had achieved all that he had intended tactically and without heavy losses. His men had driven the rebels from a formidable position; they had killed, wounded, or captured more than 1,000 of the enemy while losing only 370 of their own; they had destroyed nearly every unit that stood against them; and they had trapped what remained of American forces on Long Island in their works at Brooklyn, had trapped them where they might soon have been reduced by a regular siege.[52] Yet for all their success in surprising, surrounding, and destroying American forces, the British had not made the most of their opportunities on 27 August. When the Battle of Long Island began, they had had nearly every advantage. They had turned the American flank, surprising the defenders, depriving them of prepared positions, making it impossible for Washington to reinforce his units on the Heights of Guana without jeopardizing his works at Brooklyn, and threatening to cut off all who remained on the heights. The British had, moreover, overwhelming superiority in size and quality of forces. It was not just that they outnumbered the rebels on Long Island by more than two to one or that they had a five-to-one advantage in men engaged but also that they were better led, equipped, and disciplined than their heterogeneous opponents. Considering, then, their multiple advantages, it should be asked why the British did not kill, wound, or capture more than 1,000 of the 3,500 men defending the Heights of Guana, why they did not complete their victory by taking the works at Brooklyn, and why they allowed the remnants of a defeated army to withdraw unscathed from Long Island.

To answer these questions, it is essential to look more closely at the battle. Although the British succeeded at the onset in depriving the rebels of formidable defensive positions on the Heights of Guana, they fought the Battle of Long Island on ground that favored the surprised and scattered defenders. The gentle northern slope of the heights was, as one British officer said, "entirely after [the rebels'] own heart covered with woods and hedges"; the cultivated fields were small; and the roads narrow and high crowned.[53] Such countryside provided cover for the rebels—places where they might make a stand or find refuge once their units were broken.[54] More important, such countryside inhibited the movement and use of British forces, making them much less effective in killing and capturing rebels than they might otherwise have been. In turning the American flank, Howe had to move his army in a long, slow procession, "the Country not admitting two Columns of March"; in advancing their artillery, the Hessians had first to level the roads; and in attacking through woods, British and Hessians alike had to resort to columns of "two men abreast and rather far apart."[55] Occasionally the British were able to employ whole regiments and disciplined fire across open ground: Lord Percy leading a battalion of guards near Bedford had "just Time to give [the rebels] one Fire," and the British grenadiers contributed a heavy, distant fire to the collapse of the American right wing.[56] But clearings were too small for "drawing up two armies regularly opposed to each other" or for using cavalry in customary ways.[57] Clinton recalled his dragoons at the beginning of the battle because he was unwilling to use them against rebels who were retiring into a wood, unwilling to let them attack "under such disadvantages." Nor was British cavalry able to pursue effectively when the rebels gave way: "The Light Horse could not act for a swamp that was in front."[58] So it was that the nature of the ground worked against the British— keeping them from moving more rapidly to envelop the rebels, from making the most of their superior discipline in formal lines of battle, and from taking more prisoners.

These were not the only ways in which the ground worked against the British. The mere extent and strength of the American position on the Heights of Guana exacted their toll. To turn the American flank, Howe had to take the main body of his army on an eight-mile night march, a march that was, according to Captain Sir James Murray of the *57th Regiment,* "as disagreeable a one as I remember to have passed in the course of my campaigning. . . . We dragged on at the most tedious pace from sunset till 3 o'clock in the morning, halting every minute just long enough to drop asleep and to be disturbed again in order to proceed twenty yards in the same manner. The night was colder too than I remember to have felt it, so that by day break my stock of patience began to run very low."[59] No wonder that once Howe had gotten safely through Jamaica Pass, he stopped to give his men time for food and rest. But in stopping, he delayed the envelopment of the rebel forces on the Heights of Guana; and when he did resume his march toward Brooklyn and Gowanus Creek, his men were forced to overcome fatigue as well as an enemy that might contest every hedge and copse.[60] Although 20,000 British troops at last converged on 3,500 rebels and although the British behaved with great "Spirit and Intrepidity," they managed to kill, wound, or capture only a third of the rebels. The two-thirds who got away did so by taking advantage of terrain—a large and difficult battlefield and Gowanus Creek that covered their flight to Brooklyn.[61] Even so, had the British begun the battle more rested, they might have achieved more decisive results—might have surrounded the rebels sooner and pursued them with greater resolution.

Just as terrain and fatigue worked against more decisive results, so too did Howe's intentions. Unwilling to risk heavy casualties and eager to promote a reconciliation, Howe sought to end the rebellion without a decisive battle. He would use flanking maneuvers and siegecraft to drive the rebels from Long Island, establish the superiority of British arms, and make conciliation more appealing. Thus, he was all too willing to rest after his night's march on 27 August—all too willing to delay his envelopment of the rebels—and he subsequently refused to pursue them into their lines at Brooklyn: "It was apparent the Lines must have been ours at a very cheap Rate by regular Approaches. I could not risk the loss that might have been sustained in the Assault. . . ."[62] Nor did he make any serious effort to keep the rebels from evacuating Long Island after their defeat, from saving that portion of their army remaining at Brooklyn. Although Howe's subordinates were, in general, sympathetic with his intentions, they also lamented the opportunities he had lost. Maj. Gen. Archibald Robertson, who was commanding a brigade on the twenty-seventh, thought "the whole of this days Manoeuvre was well plann'd and Executed, only more of the Rebels might have been cut off had we pushed on . . . sooner towards General Grant." Capt. Frederick Mackenzie of the *23d Regiment* agreed: "Many are of opinion that [Howe] should have followed up the advantage he gained on the 27th of

August and either on that day or the following attacked the Rebels in their lines at Brooklyn, yet it must be allowed that it was extremely proper in him to consider what fatal consequences might have attended a check which the Army might have received in the first action of the campaign."[63]

Terrain, fatigue, and Howe's intentions clearly worked against a more decisive British victory on 27 August. Yet to appreciate the full significance of these factors, it is essential to see how together they affected tactics—how they kept the British from exploiting the numerous small victories they had won on Long Island. Unable to use infantry, cavalry, and artillery in a conventional line of battle, the British relied primarily on their infantry acting in companies or regiments and employing General Howe's tactics: "It was the General's order that the Troops should receive the Rebels first fire and then rush on them before they had recovered their arms, with their bayonets, which threw them into the utmost disorder and confusion they being unacquainted with such a maneuver."[64] These tactics did cost the British some casualties—more, the Hessians believed, than necessary to defeat the rebels. But most British officers considered their casualties light and their tactics highly successful: "We soon saw them come through the woods to attack us. We routed them the first onset, and pursued them so close through the thickest woods that they never could rally"; and: "The Light Infantry who were first engaged dashed in as fast as foot could carry. The scoundrels were driven into the wood and out of the wood, where they had supposed that we should never venture to engage them."[65] However successful these small-unit tactics were in shattering resistance, they did not lead to a complete victory. Small-unit bayonet attacks tended to disrupt and tire the attackers, especially those who had marched all night to turn the rebel flank. Thus, the British infantry were far more successful in routing than in pursuing the rebels: they advanced rapidly enough to keep the rebels from re-forming, but they were too tired or perhaps too wary of the rebels to overtake more than a third of them in terrain that was ideally suited to rear-guard actions. "From what I saw myself," said Lord Howe's secretary, "nothing could exceed [the British and Hessian soldiers'] Spirit and Intrepidity in attacking the Enemy. In one thing only they failed— they could not run so fast as their Foes, many of whom indeed were ready to run over each other."[66] Had the British been faster in pursuing and cutting off the rebels or had they been permitted to follow them into their lines at Brooklyn, they might well have taken all of the American forces on Long Island. "Not a man," Clinton thought, "would have escaped."[67]

There was at least one other reason why the British were slow to cut off or overtake the rebels: they were reluctant to engage their own men. Howe's plan for the battle required British and Hessian units to converge on each other as well as on the rebels defending the Heights of Guana. Because visibility often was restricted by woods, hedges, fences, and folds in the ground and because some rebels wore uniforms that resembled those of the

British light infantry and the Hessians, there was a real danger of confusing friend and foe. At least twice, the British took casualties because they failed to recognize the rebels or because they ran afoul of their own men. "Two companies suffered an unfortunate mistake which might have created a good deal of confusion. They took a large body of the rebels dressed in blue for the Hessians and received a fire from them at a very small distance before they discovered their mistake. The two captains Neilson and Logan were killed upon the spot." A number of men were wounded, and at least one officer and twenty marines were taken prisoner.[68] On another occasion, an officer was, as he said, "ordered to draw up my Highland Grenadiers on the right of the Grenadiers by doing which one of the squares blocked me and my men were gauled very much, 17 were killed and wounded. . . ."[69] When such accidents were possible—when British and Hessian units were converging in a close country against sporadic resistance—there was reason to be doubly wary. Plunging after the rebels might well bring death by friendly or hostile fire.

Although the rebels were nowhere able to withstand a determined British attack, they did provide resistance enough to delay the British and help secure the retreat of two-thirds of their men. On the left and in the center of their position—on the Jamaica Road and at the Bedford and Flatbush Passes—the Americans offered little organized opposition. Two regiments did set out from the Bedford Pass to secure the Jamaica Road early on the morning of 27 August. But finding that the British had already turned their flank—were already proceeding along the Jamaica Road in overwhelming strength—they decided to give up any idea of attacking the British and to try to slip around them and into the lines at Brooklyn. When discovered and attacked, both American regiments disintegrated, offering at best sporadic resistance. Lt. Col. Daniel Brodhead stated, "Did all in my power to rally the musquetry and Riflemen, but to no purpose, so that when we came to engage the Enemy, I had not fifty men. . . ." Such small parties temporarily checked the British and may have helped some rebels escape to Brooklyn. Yet all fighting soon came to an end on the American left; more than half of the two regiments that went to defend the Jamaica Road were killed or captured.[70] In the center, the Americans were even less effective in stopping the British and Hessians. Major General Sullivan began the day by sending units from Bedford and Flatbush Passes to help secure the American flanks and by taking another party to reconnoiter east along the Heights of Guana. While he found that the British were in his rear and that he was trapped, the rest of his men spiked their guns, abandoned the Bedford and Flatbush Passes, and sought a way to Brooklyn.[71]

Only on their right were the Americans able to provide sustained, organized opposition. Although that opposition was the result as much of British restraint as of American discipline, it did allow hundreds of rebels time to escape to Brooklyn. General Grant, who was ordered to create a diversion on the American right while Howe turned their left, was slow to press the rebels defending the Gowanus Road. Throughout the morning of 27 August, he was content to skirmish and exchange desultory cannon fire. The forces opposing him under Lord Stirling were some of the best in Continental service—regiments like William Smallwood's of Maryland and John Haslet's of Delaware. These regiments were not to be broken by a mere show of force, and they stood firm against Grant—gaining confidence in themselves and allowing stragglers from the left and center of the American line to pass behind them to Brooklyn. When about 1200, Howe came down on the flank and rear of Stirling's men and Grant attacked their front, the Americans continued to fight even though Stirling was unable to coordinate their efforts. His main body, including Haslet's regiment, faced about, broke through the British, and "effected a most Noble Retreat up to the middle thro a Marsh of Mud and brought off with them 23 prisoners. . . ."[72] His left flank was not so fortunate. Failing to receive orders to retire, the left was soon cut off and broken into small units, many of which fought stubbornly until forced to surrender.[73] Stirling himself, with a substantial portion of Smallwood's regiment, stayed behind to cover the retreat and was captured.[74] The American right had at last collapsed under the combined weight of Howe's, Grant's, and von Heister's men. But it had fought well enough to save hundreds of men and to help prevent the British from completing their victory.

Although Americans knew they had been defeated in the Battle of Long Island, they temporarily minimized that defeat and reinforced their troops at Brooklyn. They conceded that the loss of the Heights of Guana was a serious blow—that the heights had been their "principal barrier" against the British and were more defensible than the lines at Brooklyn.[75] They also recognized that a number of their men were missing, possibly prisoners, and that some units had been "cut to pieces."[76] Yet they congratulated themselves on having stood well under fire. General Samuel Holden Parsons thought "the trial of that day far from being any discouragement . . . in general our soldiers behaved with firmness."[77] He described American losses in dead and wounded (apart from prisoners) as "inconsiderable," and Col. Gold S. Silliman described the battle as little more than a skirmish: "We have had no General Engagement yet. . . . We are in constant Expectation of a General Battle. . . ." Even those like Sullivan and Stirling who had been taken prisoner were, according to the British, "rather impudent than otherwise in talking of yesterday's engagement."[78] Washington was at first more pessimistic than most. Having watched from Brooklyn while his men were overwhelmed, he was proud of the discipline some had shown but was ready to abandon Long Island; in fact, he might have done so late on 27 August had his troops not been so disordered. The next day, when the British began digging trenches for a formal siege, and on the twenty-ninth, he brought reinforcements to Brooklyn.[79] It is not clear whether he was buoyed temporarily by the rising spirits of his officers or whether he sought merely to restore confidence among his men so that they could withdraw safely. But he committed more of his meager resources to Long Island, risking the destruction of an even larger portion of his army.

Even as reinforcements went to Long Island, Washington and his generals were deciding to give up Brooklyn Heights and, with it, command of New York City. They did so in part because they thought their men were in poor condition to withstand a siege or an assault and in part because they thought it unwise to bring the rest of their army to Brooklyn. It had rained very hard for two days following the battle, and by 29 August, Washington's men were wet, cold, and dispirited—their arms and ammunition spoiled. Was it likely that fewer than 10,000 men, discouraged by the loss of their outworks and their weapons, would be able to hold extensive works against more than twice their number? Washington and his generals did not think so. Would it then be wise to bring over additional reinforcements, to commit the whole of the Army to the defense of Brooklyn? Certainly not—at least, not when the British seemed capable of using their superior fleet to close the East River, trapping the Americans at Brooklyn where they might soon be forced to surrender by a regular siege. To avoid either prospect, Washington and his general officers decided to abandon Long Island during the night of 29 August. By the next morning all but three stragglers and several cannon were safely across the East River on Manhattan.[80]

Why were the Americans able to escape from Brooklyn, to save such a large part of their army? Much credit belongs to Washington. To avoid panic and mask his intentions, he told his rank and file that they were to be relieved. He then withdrew the least reliable units, leaving the remnants of Small-wood's and Haslet's regiments to hold the lines until the last possible moment; and he stayed on Long Island until all of his men were safely embarked. He was also favored by the weather. During the night, the wind came fair for the boats pushing back and forth across the East River, and early in the morning, a thick fog covered the final embarkation.[81] But as important as Washington's skill and fortune, the British had done nothing to prevent the escape. No one really expected the rebels to give up their "stupendous works" without a fight. Assuming that such works "might easily have been defended for a consider-able time" and that time was a valuable counter in a war of posts, British officers were astonished to discover that the Americans had fled.[82] General Howe, anxious as ever to avoid losses and foster a reconciliation, had taken no precautions against a withdrawal: "Had our Troops followed them close up, they must have thrown down their arms and surrendered; or had our Ships attacked the Batteries, which we have been in constant Expectation of being ordered to do, not a Man could have escaped from Long Island."[83] In fact, to judge by the mood at headquarters, the Howes were "most agreeably surprised to find the Rebels had entirely abandoned Long Island.'' This victory was "as complete as could be wished and with much less loss than could possibly have been expected.''[84] It would take the Howes some months to realize that the appearance of British superiority would not bring the Americans to accept a negotiated peace. Once Washington was safe on Manhattan, Congress refused to negotiate except as representatives of independent states.[85]

In retrospect, it does seem that Washington and his inexperienced, outnumbered men had been exceptionally lucky on Long Island. In their innocence of battle, their enthusiasm for the revolution, and their determination to hold New York City, they had courted disaster on Long Island. They had undertaken to defend Brooklyn against forces that clearly had the power to trap them there. They had established themselves on the Heights of Guana which, while naturally strong against a frontal attack, were too extensive for their numbers and quality—vulnerable both to a flanking maneuver and to separate, simultaneous attacks. And once they had decided to defend the heights, they had failed to take reasonable precautions against surprise. Considering, then, the fundamental weaknesses in their strategy and tactics and the uneven quality of their forces, they were indeed fortunate to have engaged the British and escaped to Manhattan without losing more than one-seventh of the men committed to the defense of Brooklyn. It is true that they had provided formidable works to protect themselves, that some of their units had fought well on 27 August, and that they had planned and carried out a most skillful withdrawal. Yet that they escaped complete destruction on Long Island was more a matter of chance and General Howe's intentions than of their own prudence or skill. The battle took place on terrain that no one chose but that clearly favored the Americans. The British could not find enough open space to coordinate infantry, cavalry, and artillery in large-scale attacks or to take advantage of their superior discipline and firepower. Instead, they had to rely primarily on infantry and limited bayonet attacks. Such tactics, carried out by men who were tired from a long approach march and wary of encountering their own men among the trees and hedges, succeeded in breaking resistance but not in capturing large numbers of fleeing rebels. But even those tactics might have yielded more decisive results had General Howe not been preoccupied with sparing lives and making peace—had he been determined to trap and destroy the Americans on Long Island.

Because the Battle of Long Island was followed by a succession of British victories, it is difficult to establish clear relationships between events on Long Island and the subsequent conduct of the war. It does seem that the battle had little effect on what the British did subsequently. Having defeated the rebels convincingly, if not decisively, and assuming that the war would soon be won, the British were not inclined to criticize their performance or to consider changes in the administration or application of their forces. General Howe, who was more pessimistic than most of his subordinates—who anticipated that the war would last until 1777—asked for reinforcements, especially light troops and cavalry to cover the flanks of his army. But there had been enough men on Long Island; their equipment and supplies were certainly adequate; they had been well supported by the navy; and they had fought with discipline and determination. If some officers complained that Howe had lost opportunities to exploit his victory, most celebrated his prudent, conventional tactics—his success in taking Brooklyn without suffering heavy casualties. The British government, which was eager for victories that would break the rebellion as quickly as possible, was so pleased with news of the battle that it created Howe a Knight of the Bath. Indeed, it would be nearly six months before Howe or the ministry questioned his basic strategy of combining a war of posts with conciliatory efforts and more than a year and a half before the ministry made a fundamental change in the conduct of the war, before it abandoned a war of posts and sought victory either in a decisive battle or in a gradual reconquest of the colonies with the help of Loyalists.[86]

Although Americans were equally slow to modify their strategy, they did make a greater effort than the British to learn from the Battle of Long Island. Their defeat was in part the result of their strategy—their determination to defend New York City against a superior fleet and army. But if Washington came to see that preserving his army was more important than holding New York or any other place, that the essence of a war of posts lay in avoiding a decisive defeat, Congress persisted in urging a more aggressive strategy. For at least two years after the Battle of Long Island, Congress goaded Washington to seek a decisive engagement, to wage a "short and violent war."[87] However unrealistic such a strategy was, Congress did recognize that Washington had not had enough well-trained men to defend Long Island against the British and that he would need a larger and better army to win the war. Thus, soon after he withdrew from Brooklyn, Congress voted to raise eighty-eight battalions to serve for the duration of the war and to stengthen discipline throughout the Army. Congress remained uneasy with the prospect of creating a professional army; it continued to compete with the states for recruits, driving up bounties and forcing some communities to resort to conscription or even to hiring soldiers; and it did not provide uniform training for recruits—standardized instruction in tactics—until the winter of 1777–78.[88] Even so, as a result of the Battle of Long Island, Congress set aside its opposition to long-term enlistments—suppressing its fears of a standing army—and began creating the kind of force Washington would need to fight and defeat a major power.

The Battle of Long Island, the first battle of the War for American Independence, is important primarily for what did not happen during and after the action. The British, having every advantage that numbers, discipline, and experience could confer, succeeded in shattering American troops defending the Heights of Guana, but they killed or captured only a third of them. After the battle, it seemed certain that the British would be able to capture the troops remaining at Brooklyn—nearly half the Continental Army—without the risk of a general action. They failed, however, to take ordinary precautions, and the Americans were able to withdraw safely across the East River. Although Howe still hoped that the clarity of his victory on Long Island would make conciliation more appealing, it did not: Congress remained intransigently committed to independence. Congress also remained committed to the unrealistic strategy that had jeopardized its forces at New York, but it did not insist that Washington continue to fight the war with short-term enlistees. After Long Island, it began to create the kind of professional army that could sustain the revolution. It is, of course, impossible to know whether a decisive British victory on Long Island would have destroyed the Continental Army and, with it, the revolution. It is certain that the survival and improvement of the Army contributed a great deal to the winning of independence.

2

The Battle of Queenston Heights, 13 October 1812

THEODORE J. CRACKEL

As the American nation moved toward war through the spring of 1812, the prospects seemed encouraging. Forts and gunboats to defend the coasts were in place, stocks of cannon and muskets were laid up in national arsenals, a small but promising regular force existed and in reserve was a huge militia organization. The conquest of Canada was the logical objective—regardless of what motivated the war—and the task looked easy. On paper, the fighting strength of the United States was near colossal. The regular Army had almost 36,000 troops, and Congress had recently added a volunteer force of 50,000 and a militia contingent of 100,000 drawn from over 700,000 listed on the rolls. Additionally, the Army now was supplied with officers from its own military academy.

But not everything was as it seemed. Some forts had been decaying for years; others had never been completed. No port had a fully integrated defensive system; few, in fact, had ever had any carefully drawn plans. Like many of the forts, the weapons that filled the arsenals were often relics of earlier times. Cartridges were apt to be older than the soldiers who were to use them. Another problem was recruitment of soldiers to use the weapons and man the forts. Voting battalions into existence was one thing, enlisting them another. Of the 36,000 authorized in the regular force, fewer than one-third had been enlisted by July 1812, when war was declared. What is more, the units that were raised were virtually untrained, and most remained so. They were wholly unprepared for the war on which they embarked.

The disasters of the first year of the War of 1812 were followed by disasters of the second. The lessons of that first year were imperfectly learned. New generals—even better generals—could not overcome the dead weight of an undrilled, undisciplined force. Even in the third year of the war, the singular efforts of just one officer, who trained one brigade, created the only real successes the Army enjoyed: two tactical victories in the midst of a

33

strategic defeat. A political settlement that owed nothing to the efforts of the Army ended this disgraceful affair. One positive result was that before the "Peace of Christmas Eve," the need for an accepted system of infantry employment, along with training and discipline, finally was recognized.

Twenty-five U.S. Army infantry regiments were on the books in July 1812. The 1st and 2d had been created in the reorganization and consolidation of the Army under President Thomas Jefferson in 1802. In 1807, the British attack on the American naval ship *Chesapeake* caused Jefferson again to enlarge the force, adding five regiments, the 3d through 7th,[1] though filling the rosters proved difficult. There was no further augmentation of the Army until the eve of the war. In January 1812, however, Congress authorized ten additional regiments of regulars but in so doing mandated an organization that was at variance with established units. The regiments created in 1802 and 1808 differed only slightly—ten companies of 76 and 78 men respectively—but the 8th through 17th regiments authorized in 1812 were composed of eighteen companies of 110 men, arranged into two battalions. Some of these bulky eighteen-company regiments recruited actively, but most never raised their second battalions.

In the midst of regimental recruiting, Congress acted to rationalize the force structure. In June 1812, the Army was reorganized into twenty-five infantry regiments of ten 102-man companies. On paper at least, the infantry regiments were made uniform.[2] All twenty-five regiments organized and recruited actively, but during the first two years of the war, they attracted less than half the total number authorized. A bounty of sixteen dollars was offered to stimulate enlistments; a bonus of three months' pay and 160 acres of land was added for those who completed their service faithfully. The enlistment, however, was for five years, a length that proved to be a powerful disincentive.

Supplying its far-flung forces was another difficulty the Army faced. When Jefferson and Henry Dearborn, his secretary of war, reorganized the Army in 1802, they eliminated the position of quartermaster general and divided those responsibilities between the secretary of war and three civilian military agents. The secretary of war became the focal point of requisitions, while supplies were dispersed through the new military agents and assistants appointed as needed from among officers of the line. For the most part under this arrangement, supplies were purchased centrally and shipped to agents for issue, though agents were allowed to purchase supplies locally if they could be had more cheaply that way. That seldom proved to be the case; besides, purchases totaling more than fifty dollars had to be cleared with the secretary of war. Most ordinary military supplies, including food, clothing, and medical supplies, were obtained by the contract system, with contracts usually awarded to the lowest bidder by the secretary or an agent. This highly centralized system obviously involved the secretary in a huge amount of detail work. Under the watchful eye of Dearborn, the system functioned reasonably well and, in peacetime, promoted economy. However, with the Army scattered in small, isolated posts that—except for New Orleans and St. Louis—seldom housed more than a single company, there was little opportunity to learn the lessons of supply essential for large campaigning forces to be supported. In one sense, a peacetime economy was achieved at the expense of wartime effectiveness; but in a larger sense, that may have been unavoidable. The size and disposition of the Army in peacetime made unnecessary—even undesirable—the creation of staff departments that would provide effective logistical support in time of war.[3]

American tactical doctrine borrowed heavily and directly from both the French and British and cannot be understood without reference to them. For the British Army, Frederick the Great's organization and methods had had a profound influence since his infantry regulations were first translated and published in English in 1754.[4] In 1785, at the last maneuvers of the Prussian Army under Frederick's eye, one British observer, Col. David Dundas, was so impressed that he returned home and reduced what he had seen to a volume, *Principles of Military Movement* (1788). Four years later this work, substantially reorganized and revised, was issued under the authority of the adjutant-general at the British War Office as *Rules and Regulations for the Formation, Field Exercise, and Movement of His Majesty's Forces.*

Dundas' drill, inspired as it was by the Prussian system, incorporated little that had been learned about the employment of light infantry in the two recent wars in America. To many of the officers who had served there, his system seemed excessively rigid and formal.[5] Dundas, however, argued that there had been too much emphasis on light infantry and that it should be considered as nothing more than a simple accessory to the standard infantry formation. "[Light forces] have become the principal feature of our army," he complained. "The showy exercise, the airy dress, the independent modes which they have adopted, have caught the minds of young officers and made them imagine that these ought to be general and exclusive."[6] In *Rules and Regulations,* Dundas specified the formation of the company in three compact ranks, usually arranged in long linear formations. His eighteen maneuvers were designed to attain this linear formation from the march column (or re-form the column), to move the formation on the battlefield, and to shift it into the famous square to confront cavalry.

The weakness of the work lay in its intentionally cursory treatment of light infantry. The value of this formation was just then becoming widely accepted, and the role of light-infantry skirmishers was being refined in most other modern armies. Nevertheless, the work served the British well for Dundas did lay out a sound scheme of training and a system of tactical formations that could be modified as circumstances deemed necessary. Over time, three ranks gave way to the two-deep line that brought more firepower to the front, and light-infantry skirmishers found more and more systematic employment. Otherwise, his system remained essentially in force up to the time of the Crimean War.

While the British debated whether light infantry or line infantry would dominate, a quite different controversy raged among the French. There, "firepower" competed for primacy with "shock action." Those who favored shock action advocated a formation in depth—*ordre profond*—which, in the attack, would concentrate the force of the blow on a small area. In this formation, the companies (or pairs of companies, called divisions) formed two or three men deep would be arrayed in column one behind another. To this school, deployment into lines for fire purposes was secondary to the weight achieved in column. Indeed, some urged dispensing with the line altogether. The supposed ease with which green troops could be trained to maneuver in column (as opposed to linear formations) also enhanced its appeal.

Those who believed that musket fire was the primary source of infantry power naturally advocated a thin order—*ordre mince*—which would bring into action the maximum number of weapons. Here, all the companies would be arrayed on line. When units formed two men deep (rather than the traditional three), the number of weapons on line was increased substantially; thus, this formation gained favor among many who preferred the *ordre mince*. Both schools favored extensive employment of light troops as skirmishers in front and on the flanks, and in both schools their employment had become a matter of systematic study. The freer, more dispersed movements of light troops promised quick mastery. Experience in the early years of the French Revolution seemed to confirm this belief.

This debate, particularly after the Seven Years' War, was often heated, but gradually the more extreme positions were abandoned. Ultimately a compromise was attained that became the basis for the tactics of the wars of the revolution and of Napoleon and that influenced the small community of doctrinal thinkers in the United States. The Ordinance of 1791, though drawn up by partisans of the *ordre profond,* represented the compromise that had come to prevail. Both concepts were prescribed in this new infantry regulation suggesting to some, including Napoleon, the *ordre mixte*—a combination of the two orders with some elements in column and some on line in the advance.

In the early years of the nineteenth century, a doctrinal debate sprang up in the United States. In contrast to the debate in Europe, however, this was less a technical debate over shock action or firepower, or light or line infantry, and more an issue of politics in and out of the Army. For years, the Americans had followed the Prussian-like drill laid down by Baron von Steuben during the American Revolution—modified only so much as necessary to accommodate the organizational differences of the militias of the various states.[7] Even the prospect of war with France in 1798–99 prompted no alterations, though

Americans were not oblivious to changes that had taken place in the French Army and the success that had followed them.[8] Only after the Republicans came to power in 1801 did any serious debate ensue.[9] Doctrinaire Republicans struggled to come to grips with a threefold dilemma: the growing need for a trained force; the poor quality of the militia (and the inability to reform it); and, at the same time, the perceived danger of a standing army sufficient to meet the threat Europe posed. The leading character in this debate—and the central figure in subsequent debates of the period concerning American military doctrine and discipline—was William Duane, the editor of Philadelphia's staunchly Republican *Aurora*. For Duane, a militia officer who ultimately accepted a regular commission under Jefferson, the solution to the political dilemma lay in a correct military doctrine, a doctrine suited to the American political temper.

The catalyst for Duane's work seems to have been Maximillian Godefroy's *Military Reflections, on Four Modes of Defense, for the United States,* which appeared in August 1807.[10] Godefroy examined America's defense posture and found it wanting. He rejected two of the staples: the militia and the system of discipline created by Steuben during the revolution. Only forces trained according to modern French discipline, he argued, could meet the new European armies on equal terms. Duane debated Godefroy in two extended articles in the *Aurora*.[11] He conceded much of Godefroy's argument. The militia, he admitted, was ineffective. "Courage and good intentions," he agreed, "do not alone make soldiers." Moreover, with recent changes in warfare, Steuben's military tactics of the revolution would no longer do.[12] He would not concede, however, that the militia should be replaced. Instead, he proposed a new militia organization and new training in the French tactics Godefroy had suggested. The nation needed only to adopt correct organization and discipline for the militia. He proposed a militia of cavalry, artillery, and infantry but emphasized the light elements of these, particularly the flying artillery, light infantry, and riflemen.

To those who suggested that only regulars could acquire the necessary skills to adequately defend the nation, Duane answered that tactics were "more a matter of common sense" than military men would usually admit. The militia could be prepared to meet and defeat the enemy; no great "scientific acquirements" were necessary. "Skill in military affairs may be reduced . . . to a few principles." He laid out three objects of study: the nature of men, military discipline, and weapons. "Modern tactics," he asserted, "[are] the result of that experience, which men of intelligence have derived from the study of history, and the study of mankind."[13]

Duane expanded on these ideas in his two-volume *American Military Library* to which he appended a translation of the French drill.[14] He had hoped that the United States Army would adopt his work, and there was reason for optimism. The Jefferson administration had been supportive. Duane was given a commission as lieutenant colonel in 1808 and was assigned as an assistant inspector general, a position that allowed him to complete and issue the two-volume *Library* and then *A Military Dictionary*.[15] Even so, the *Library* did not finally appear until after Jefferson and Dearborn had left office, and William Eustis, President James Madison's first secretary of war, had considerably less interest in such undertakings than had his predecessor.[16]

By 1810, the nation still had no prescribed discipline other than the long-outdated Steuben manual. In any case, the regulars who were spread out by company and detachment had little opportunity for the kind of drill that would have counted in combat. As for the militia, which Americans touted as the first line of defense, few units were more than vaguely acquainted with even Steuben's simple work. William Henry Harrison observed that if, outside of towns with volunteer associations, there is "a single brigade from St. Mary's to the Hudson, and from the Atlantic to the Mississippi, so well disciplined as to perform the commonest evolution . . . it has escaped my observation and inquiry." Muster days, he insisted, were wasted. "In nineteen out of twenty instances little else is done that relates to military duty." What was needed, he said, was an established discipline and extensive training. "Some weeks at least must be devoted to the purpose, and the men must be taught in camps of discipline. . . ." In a few years, "our militia would become formidable to any European army which should land on our shores. . . ."[17] Without such an effort, however, America effectively had no militia. The "untutored rifleman," long touted as "the most formidable of all warriors," would find himself unequal to European soldiers trained in the new military art. "No alternative is left to the [Americans] but to perfect themselves in the same arts and discipline."[18]

In 1810 and 1811, a "school of discipline" was established for the regular forces under the command of General Wade Hampton at Cantonment Washington in Mississippi Territory. For a time, drill was given regularly. The French system was prescribed, but where those manuals were not available, Steuben was substituted. This, however, was just one portion of the Army—and, at that, not the portion that was to carry the brunt of the burden in the upcoming war. The western force was generally maintained in some semblance of preparedness and had the advantage of being more concentrated. The forces on the northern frontier were, at best, ill prepared for the war that was to come. The militia was not prepared at all.[19]

The presence of factions within the Army itself was nearly as debilitating as the lack of a uniform discipline or system of tactics. In actuality, these factions had existed for some time. The centerpiece was Brig. Gen. James Wilkinson; officers split into either pro-Wilkinson or anti-Wilkinson camps. These factions had roots in events that had occurred years before—certainly as far back as his efforts in 1792 to undermine Anthony Wayne's authority when the latter was appointed his superior.[20] In the Jeffersonian era, the anti-

Wilkinson faction had been led for a time by Col. Thomas Butler, who commanded the 2d Infantry regiment. When he died in late 1805, he was replaced by his second-in-command, Thomas H. Cushing, a Wilkinson man. The administration, which had ample reason to be circumspect where the general was concerned, made every effort to install an anti-Wilkinson man as Cushing's deputy—someone who would serve as a rallying point for the now leaderless "antis." Twice they attempted to circumvent the traditional process of promotion by seniority, and twice Congress refused to consent to the appointments proposed. These efforts, which continued for two years, were ultimately abandoned—but only because another solution was in sight. With the enlargement of the Army in 1808, the appointment of Brigadier General Hampton solved the problem. As Winfield Scott recalled, the officer corps had become divided between partisans of Wilkinson and Hampton.[21]

That rift widened as the years passed. By 1811, "intrigue" and "bitterness of party" had "been generated so long, and grown to so great a height, in the army and out of it," Hampton wrote Eustis in a plea for backing, that "nothing but the highest confidence of support of government can sustain the officer to whom the command of the army is confided."[22] Eustis was incredulous. "It was not to have been expected that a party spirit could have so far diffused itself throughout the Army as to render an expression of the confidence of the executive necessary. . . ." Nonetheless, the required assurances were forthcoming.[23] This general enmity between officers of the two factions manifested itself in every aspect of the Army's performance and became linked with the doctrinal debates that were to continue throughout the war.

In 1811, as the prospects for war again heightened, Duane and others returned to efforts to supply the nation with a military discipline. Alexander Smyth, who also had been appointed to the service originally in 1808, adapted the French regulations of 1791 for use by the American Army. He published them in 1812 with the official sanction of Eustis, who ordered their adoption by the infantry of the Army. Duane, who had for some months been working on a set of new manuals, immediately attacked Smyth's work and the haphazard organization of the Army.[24] In a pamphlet addressed to Congress and signed simply "A Private Citizen," Duane asserted that only Congress (not the executive branch) could establish a system of discipline for the nation's armed forces. Smyth's work had no such seal of congressional approval. Duane pointed out the difficulty in adapting these or any regulations to the diverse organizations that had accumulated not only among the militia of the various states but within the federal Army itself. Duane went to some lengths to point out how each new law, from 1802 to the spring of 1812, had created a new and sometimes vastly different structure. After a detailed critique of Smyth's manual, Duane concluded that it was "no more than a

very injurious mutilation of the French infantry system,'' in which ''essential
parts'' had been totally cut out.[25]

A response to Duane's critique appeared a few days later in the *National
Intelligencer* and was probably written by Smyth himself, though it was signed
only ''An Officer of the Army.'' As for congressional sanction, the author
insisted that the manner in which an army shall maneuver was not a proper
question for a legislature to answer, though Congress could prescribe such
rules for the militia. The author then rejected Duane's criticisms one by one.
He concluded by citing Duane's suggestion that Smyth should have consulted
''experience'' before publishing his work. The critique writer replied that
there was no such applicable experience and that in terms of what might be
called doctrinal thought, ''I find that truly the Army has been STULTIFIED.''[26]
There could be no argument with the author's conclusion on that count. The
Army was infertile ground in which to plant any such ideas. Few officers made
any move to adopt his new work—or any other.

Duane's pamphlet did prod Congress into action on one front. In June
1812, the Army was reorganized into uniform regiments of ten companies
each. As Duane wrote Jefferson, ''The extraordinary effect it produced on
men's mind I cannot describe, but it has produced action correcting almost
everything pointed out as to the organization. . . .'' Moreover, he noted,
Smyth's *Regulations* had been withdrawn and were ''now undergoing another
metamorphosis.''[27] In the meantime, Duane had completed his own *Hand
Book for Infantry*. He submitted it to Congress with a cover letter describing the
work as a ''military discipline founded on rational method.'' It would, he
argued, ''explain in a familiar and practical manner . . . the modern
improvements in the discipline and movement of armies.''[28]

The House Committee on Military Affairs responded with a resolution
authorizing the president to prescribe the discipline for both the Army and the
militia, but the full House did not act.[29] Congress was now fully occupied with
the war it had just declared. The Army was left to prepare for the conflict with
no accepted discipline and no common tactical system.

As war with Great Britain approached in spring 1812, Congress,
desperate to fill the ranks it had created, authorized the enlistment of up to
5,000 men and reduced the term of enlistment from five years to one. Even
this drastic reduction in length of service did not have the desired effect. By the
time Congress declared war the Army had filled only about one-third of its
ranks. Moreover, the units that had been recruited were so poorly prepared
that little could have been expected of them. New company officers were
almost uniformly ignorant of their duties and noncommissioned officers were
little more than recruits themselves. A camp for instruction and training had
been established near Philadelphia in July 1812, but recruiting had proceeded
so slowly that the camp was abandoned in the autumn when the demand for
troops in the north required that all recruited units be sent directly to the

front.[30] Without training, these units were "little better than an undisciplined rabble," and with unschooled officers, there was little prospect for immediate improvement. "It may be a question," remarked one officer, "whether they are not of more dis-service than of use."[31] "If taken into action in their present state," complained another, "[they] will prove more dangerous to themselves than to their enemy."[32]

The Jefferson administration had in 1802 taken steps to revive the Army's neglected supply and administrative departments. The net effect was to disestablish the quartermaster system and bring supply under the direct control of Dearborn, the secretary of war. In March 1812, an administration-sponsored bill was passed that reestablished the quartermaster's department under a quartermaster general with a staff of deputies and assistants. The new scheme did make some improvements; the old had been designed to serve small, far-flung garrisons. But even the most efficient system would have been strained. The system with which the United States entered the war made no pretense of being perfect. With the rapid expansion of American forces, the supply system nearly ground to a halt. Some regiments were provided with arms so old and poorly maintained that as many as one in five was unfit for service. Cartridges were so old that some officers insisted that they may have been made up nearly twenty years earlier for Wayne's campaign. Even such ordinary items as shoes and stockings were in short supply, and as fall turned into winter, many of the men still had no woolen clothing and no coats. Tentage was always in short supply. Medicine, hospital stores, and surgical instruments went unissued while the War Department debated about what size medicine chest to supply. As the forces gathered, few if any signs augured an auspicious beginning.[33]

British forces in Canada in early 1812 consisted of elements of six regiments and some garrison detachments from the *Royal Veterans Battalion*. Two of the regiments had been raised in Canada: the *104th Regiment* (originally the *New Brunswick Fensible Infantry*) and the unnumbered *Royal Newfoundland Regiment*—which is said to have suffered more than one-fourth of all British casualties in this war. In addition, there was the *Irish 100th Regiment* and battalions from the *8th*, the *41st*, and the *49th Regiments*. Two additional infantry battalions arrived late in 1812 (one each from the *1st* and *89th Regiments*), but the latter closed so late in October that it had to winter in Halifax. The infantry in Canada was supported by eight companies of the *Royal Regiment of Artillery*. Except for concentrations at Quebec and Montreal, most of the British troops were assigned, like their American counterparts, by company or detachment to the numerous posts that dotted the shores of the lakes dividing the two nations. For the most part, these units had been in the provinces for some time. Scattered as they were, they suffered some of the same deficiencies in training as did the American units; but they did have the advantage of a coherent and reasonably modern system of discipline.

In 1812, the forces in Canada were an afterthought in a larger struggle. The British Army had its hands full as Wellington campaigned in the Iberian peninsula. The crown did, however, in 1813, dispatch several additional battalions to Canada. Then, after Napoleon's defeat the next year, the British poured troops into Canada as fast as shipping could be arranged. Elements of at least twenty-one regiments arrived in late spring and early summer 1814.[34] The Canadian militia consisted of supposedly trained units and unorganized or sedentary militia. In practice, their manner of performance varied as much as did that of their American counterparts. Any advantage that accrued to them came from the role they generally played: defending the homeland. They were seldom used in any numbers on offensive forays.

The British system of supply was not markedly different from that of the Americans. In fact, the Americans had borrowed their system from the British during the revolution. The British, too, had made some modifications. The hitherto-civilian commissary recently had been uniformed and given an assimilated rank; but as with the changes in the American system, this solved few problems. If the British system functioned more smoothly than its American counterpart, it probably reflected British control of the lakes and shipping thereon during the early years of the war. Ironically, the long haul from England to Canada proved less of a problem than the cross-country movement the Americans were required to make. British command of the seas and its extensive merchant fleet had the effect of shrinking distance.

The American campaign of 1812 was directed as much by chance and circumstances as by strategy. Canada, like America, was largely undeveloped. The scattered settlements that did exist were for the most part still located near the rivers and lakes that divided the two nations. The best strategy might have been to concentrate on taking Montreal or even Kingston and to cut communications with the posts to the west, which then would have fallen of their own accord. Madison had favored such an approach, but practical difficulties prevented the necessary concentration of effort on a single objective. Congress had increased the authorized strength of the Regular Army to nearly 36,000, but fewer than 12,000 had actually enlisted when war was declared, a number that included 5,000 very recent recruits. Moreover, the veteran troops were scattered throughout the country, with the greatest concentration near strategically important New Orleans. To take Montreal quickly, it was essential to employ New England militia, supposedly the best prepared in the country. But when, on 15 April, the president called for troops, Massachusetts Gov. Caleb Strong replied that he, rather than the president, had the power to decide when constitutional exigencies actually existed. Because he expected no invasion, he refused the requisition except for three companies of militia sent to the Canadian border. Connecticut took a similar view and furnished nothing. The prowar sentiment of the nation actually lay in the West, particularly in Ohio and Kentucky, but the governors of New York, Pennsylvania, and the other states generally complied with levies placed on them.

Without New England troops, Dearborn proposed a move against Montreal only after preliminary offensives from Detroit, Niagara, and Sackett's Harbor. The hope was that these secondary efforts, which could use available local militia, would siphon off British forces that could otherwise have been moved to defend Montreal.

General William Hull, governor of Michigan Territory, was appointed to conduct operations from Detroit. Hull took command of his army in Dayton, Ohio, where that governor had called out three regiments of volunteers. They were joined en route to Detroit by a regiment of regulars. The force reached Detroit on 5 July. Hull crossed into Canada a week later but vacillated, unable to work up the courage to attack. Meanwhile, the Canadians, under Sir Isaac Brock, moved to threaten Hull's tenuous line of communication along the shores of Lake Erie. Hull withdrew to Detroit. Under siege by a mixed force of British regulars, Canadian militia, and Indians totaling perhaps 1,300, Hull surrendered his entire force of 2,500 to Brock. The American regulars were sent as prisoners to Lower Canada, but the militia were contemptuously released to return home on parole.

While this disaster was being played out at Detroit, a considerable American force was gathering on the Niagara frontier. Daniel D. Tompkins, the Republican governor of New York, appointed Federalist Stephen Van Rensselaer commander in chief of the New York militia. The appointment gave a nonpartisan aspect to the war effort and tied down a troublesome political opponent. Van Rensselaer had no military experience and requested that Col. Solomon Van Rensselaer, a relative and a man of much wider military experience, be appointed his aide. By October, over 6,000 troops stood at the various posts along the Niagara frontier. Though formidable in sheer numbers, the Americans were plagued by inadequate supplies, improper food, wretched discipline and training, and much illness.[35]

It was generally understood that when Stephen Van Rensselaer had enough troops, he would move. Moreover, the only way to retain this largely militia force was to commit it to action. After the daring capture of two small British ships upstream across from Buffalo, his troops insisted on action. "This was expressed to me through various channels," wrote Van Rensselaer, "in the shape of an alternative, that they must have orders to act or at all hazards they would go home."[36] His plan called for simultaneous attacks on Fort George and nearby Queenston with its commanding heights. If successful, the move would sever British communications between Lakes Erie and Ontario and deny the British a strong rallying point on the Niagara frontier. Besides, wrote Van Rensselaer, "we shall save our own land—wipe away part of the score of our past disgrace, get excellent barracks and winter quarters, and at least be prepared for an early campaign another year."[37] General Smyth, who was then at Buffalo with 1,650 regulars, was to move his force overland to Lake Ontario and then by boat to a point from which Fort George could be attacked from the rear. Smyth, who cared little for this plan and less for the notion of serving under a militia officer, refused to cooperate. Van Rensselaer, whose troops were growing more restless by the day, decided to move without Smyth.

A first attempt to cross the Niagara in the dark and rainy early morning hours of 11 October failed when the officer who was to lead the force across the river crossed in a boat that contained nearly all the troops' oars and sailed past the intended landing site. When he put ashore far up river, he abandoned his detachment and fled. Whether he acted through ignorance or through treachery is even now unknown. Before the command could recover from this setback, the opportunity to cross under the cover of darkness had been lost.[38]

This initial failure had done little to release the pressure for action, and unable to resist the clamor of his men, General Van Rensselaer ordered that a second attempt be made the night of 12 October. Col. Solomon Van Rensselaer, in overall command of the assaulting party, was to cross with a force of about 300 militia; Lt. Col. John Chrystie was to cross simultaneously with his regulars—a force of about the same size. They were to be followed by a party of about 550 regulars, some pieces of flying artillery, and then the balance of the militia on order as the situation permitted.[39]

That night, the lead detachments marched up from their bivouacs to the river. At the point chosen for crossing, the river was about 250 yards wide and, though the current was strong, a skillful boatman could execute the crossing in about fifteen minutes. The landing site on the far shore was near a point where the bluffs that dominated Queenston joined the low plain on which the town was situated. To the right of the landing site lay the town. To the left, jutting up some 275 feet, were bluffs so steep that the British believed them impassable. Though plans had called for about thirty boats, each of which would carry about twenty men, only twelve or thirteen boats were actually available. The lack of boats was troublesome, but after some discussion, Van Rensselaer ordered men into the available craft. They pushed off about 0400. They would soon lose what concealment darkness gave. At best, the exercise was problematical, but matters worsened when Canadian sentries discovered the crossing attempt and gave the alarm. The two companies of the *49th English Regiment* and some detachments of Canadian militia that were stationed at the town—about 300 men in all—fell out and engaged the landing party. At the same time, artillery on the Canadian shore opened up on the boats and men on the river. The assault was so disorganized by this resistance that by the first light of day, only about 200 men had crossed—essentially the first wave.

Meanwhile, the firing was heard at Fort George, six miles downstream, where the river empties into Lake Ontario and where General Brock was making his headquarters. Concerned that the attack on Queenston might be a feint, Brock instructed Maj. Gen. Roger Sheaffe to open fire on Fort Niagara opposite them and to ready for an attack. He then set off for Queenston. A brief inspection of affairs at Queenston convinced him that the main attack was against that point, and he sent orders to Sheaffe to march from Fort George with every available man.

Meanwhile, the Americans who had crossed tried to organize their assault. Colonel Van Rensselaer had been seriously wounded upon landing and was ineffective, but Capt. John Wool assumed command and found a narrow, unguarded path up to the heights above Queenston. He immediately led a party of some sixty men to a spot behind and above a key gun position firing against the American crossing. Unaware that the enemy had gained the heights, Brock, who had just arrived, stationed himself at the battery. He was giving directions for correcting its fire when Captain Wool and his troops descended on him. Hastily retreating to the village, Brock placed himself at the head of a company of the *49th* and charged up the hill to retake the gun. A bullet fired at close quarters hit him in the chest, and he died almost instantly.

With this initial success, General Van Rensselaer had begun to make plans to consolidate his position on the Canadian shore. Capt. Joseph G. Totten, of the engineers, was ordered across to lay out a fortified encampment, and plans were made to move Lt. Col. Winfield Scott and his artillery across to strengthen the force.

At the embarkation point, troops continued to cross, but no one had been placed in charge of activities, and conditions deteriorated rapidly. American batteries had succeeded in silencing most of the British artillery, but one remaining heavy gun pounded away with some effect at the boats and troops attempting to cross. As if an ill omen, much of the small flotilla in use that morning had been lost or damaged. Only three remained serviceable by midmorning. In the confusion and lacking any direction, detachments attempting to cross the river had hurried into the first boats they could find, crossed, and abandoned them on the far shore, perhaps to go adrift or else to be brought back by the wounded or deserters.

Some of the units that were to have followed the first elements were held up for hours while they waited for ammunition to be issued. When they finally arrived at the crossing long after daylight, they found so few boats that less than a company could be transported at any one time. "This," reported one commander, "prevented the security soldiers would feel in their own protection when in a considerable body, and also delayed the others by obliging them to stand on the bank after their arrival, and seeing the wounded in the return boats added very little to their inducement to go over."[40] Suddenly, the sounds of musketry and the war cries of Indians were heard from the

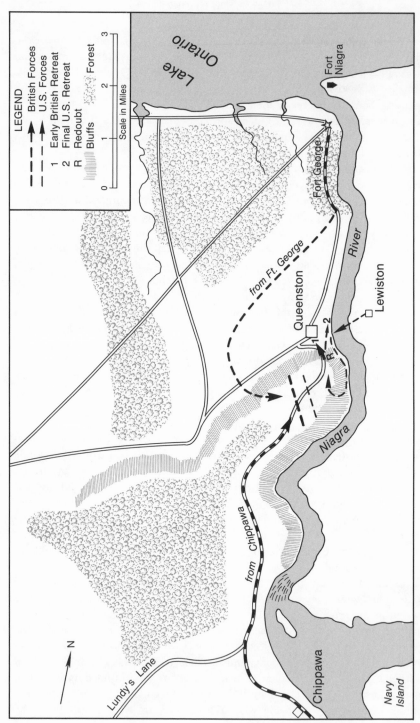

Map 2.1. Queenston Heights, October 1812

LEGEND

British Forces
U.S. Forces
1 Early British Retreat
2 Final U.S. Retreat
R Redoubt
Bluffs
Forest

Scale in Miles
0 1 2 3

N

Lake Ontario

Fort Niagra

Fort George

River

Niagra

Lewiston

Queenston

from Ft. George

from Chippawa

Lundy's Lane

Chippawa

Navy Island

Canadian shore as a British force from Chippewa arrived and attacked the Americans on the heights. The attack itself was beaten back handily, but its psychological effect on the troops waiting to cross was less easily dealt with. "The commencement of [this] battle, and a considerable number of dead and mangled bodies which were brought to our shore in the return boats, caused a depression of mind on this side which could not be effaced," wrote one young gentleman to his father. "Though our troops were again completely victorious . . . none could be got to cross, and many were constantly deserting. . . ."[41] Chrystie noted a similar occurrence. "A company of men very handsomely equipped, which was just on the point of entering the boats when this firing was heard . . . thereupon halted and absolutely refused to cross, regarding neither the orders nor threat nor remonstrances of the General."[42] Chrystie, whose own crossing had been thwarted, took matters into his own hands, organized the crossing site as best he could, and began to push units across. Even that, however, was to little avail.[43] The battle had begun just before daybreak, but delay had followed on delay. By 1400, no more than 700 to 800 Americans had made the crossing.

On Queenston Heights, Lieutenant Colonel Scott had replaced Captain Wool in command of the troops and had established a defensive position in the vicinity of the captured battery. He had led a spirited defense against the Chippewa force and had kept them effectively at bay, though they constantly sniped at the right flank of the position. Without more troops (and almost none were now crossing), there was no way to take the offensive against even the small British and Canadian force that still held key positions in the town below. The Americans clearly understood that if their position on the bluff were to be saved, it would have to be reinforced before the garrison from Fort George arrived.

Shortly after the refusal by some American troops to cross, Sheaffe's red-coated regulars from Fort George emerged from the forest on the river road to the north of town. This sight further dampened the spirit of the undisciplined forces on the American shore. "The sight of another reinforcement of red coats, who had marched directly within our view, decided their fears. The panic became universal. . . ." General Van Rensselaer again urged the unengaged troops across the river, but as he later reported, "to my utter astonishment I found that at the very moment when complete victory was in our hands, the ardor of the unengaged troops had entirely subsided. I rode in all directions; urged the men by every consideration to pass over, but in vain."[44]

Sheaffe conducted the counterattack with skill. His main body of troops made a wide detour inland to avoid the American artillery fire that still pounded Queenston from across the river. They then would attack the American position from along the broad ridge on which the battery was situated. With the small garrison from Chippewa, the British force included

300 to 400 regulars, a slightly larger group of militia, and some 200 to 300
Indians. It was supported by a detachment of four artillery pieces. The British
were quite deliberate in their moves; they marched and countermarched
across the front and left of the American position, awaiting a favorable
opportunity.

The Americans on Queenston Heights could do little but await the
British assault and parley among themselves, trying to decide what to do in
light of Van Rensselaer's failure to reinforce them. On their side, only about
500 men remained effective, supported by but one piece of artillery with no
more than a dozen rounds to serve it. A number of the wounded had been
evacuated, but at least 200 men had deserted the heights and now huddled
wherever they could find cover along the shore. As many more had already
been captured, largely as a result of abortive landings. At length, the
Americans decided to alter their position in such a way as to avail themselves
of a route of retreat along the road that led down the hill to the village and the
river. Unfortunately, that maneuver was begun by shifting a detachment of
militia. Sheaffe saw the move, seized the opportunity, and ordered his forces
forward. Without the discipline instilled by long drill, the now-exposed
American militia broke and ran. Their action precipitated a general flight. All
semblance of order dissolved, and a rout ensued.

In all, over 900 Americans were captured, at least a third of them
regulars. As many as 300 had been either killed or wounded. The British once
again showed their contempt for the American militia by simply freeing them
under parole. For the British, casualties had been remarkably light. But the
price was higher than it might have seemed at first glance. They had lost
General Brock, who had engineered the British successes to date. An officer of
his caliber could not be easily replaced.

After the defeat at Queenston, Van Rensselaer resigned and Alexander
Smyth, who had refused to cooperate in the effort, assumed overall command
along the Niagara frontier. Smyth, however, could never quite bring himself
to action. His troops, disgusted at being marched down to the river time and
again only to have their commander lose his nerve, gradually melted away.
Finally, at the end of November, the volunteers were sent home, and the
regulars were ordered into winter quarters. Smyth's request for leave was
granted, and his name soon was quietly dropped from the rolls. Except for a
few insignificant raids across the frozen St. Lawrence River, the inglorious
campaign of 1812 was over.

In the aftermath of the campaign, the Army and the nation assessed the
battle's implications. At the tactical level, several lessons were clear, but all
seemed to stem from inadequate planning. "The first and principal [cause of
the failure at Queenston was] that the plan was not sufficiently matured before
the operation commenced," wrote a militia commander whose regiment,

which was to have followed the first elements across, was delayed four hours waiting for ammunition. With ammunition finally issued, they encountered another problem.

> When we were prepared for crossing, instead of a sufficient number of boats to convey a large body at a time there were only three. . . . After the first body, the crossing was continued in a scattering, irregular manner, without plan or preconcert or cooperation, many going to the river and returning for want of means to get over.
> This misfortune could have been remedied by providing a sufficient number of boats and appoint proper officers to take command of the same and regulate the crossing of the men.[45]

Clearly, it was foolhardy to have attempted the crossing without a sufficient number of boats and boatmen. "You should, if possible, be prepared for crossing with three thousand men *at once*," Dearborn later warned Smyth, adding that site selection was crucial. "You will pardon me for being this particular," Dearborn wrote. "The most important consideration will be that of ascertaining and agreeing on the best and surest points of crossing; [and] much will depend on a judicious selection of the principal landing places."[46]

At a higher level, the criticisms took a different tone. "Detroit, Queenston, and Buffalo are all the fruit of the shocking disregard of common sense in the choice of unfit, incapable, and profligate men," William Duane wrote to Thomas Jefferson. "What could we expect but reverses, when one general was appointed full of years only to prevent his being a rival candidate to a member of Congress from the same district."[47] Jefferson replied in a similar vein that "three armies [had been] lost by the treachery, cowardice, or incapacity of those to whom they were entrusted. I see that our men are good and only want generals."[48]

Few were inclined to argue with Jefferson's analysis of the leadership— Hull, Van Rensselaer, and Smyth were in one manner or another replaced— but there was some quarrel with his assessment of the men. The Army clearly needed more than just good generals. It is badly in want of men who were thoroughly disciplined by training and drill. Events had demonstrated that point, but the need for officers was easier to perceive and easier to act on. In 1813, the theater received a new set of generals but no system of discipline and no emphasis on training that the defeat at Queenston should have brought in its wake. Those alert to the need were unable to sway Army leadership. The nation plodded along from failure to failure until events demonstrated dramatically the value of an instilled tactical system. Three years of campaigning were lost before the Army acted.

The disastrous campaign of 1812 did, however, prompt some to act. Duane again went to Congress with his *Hand Book* on infantry discipline.[49] Smyth, whose manual still had official sanction, had been professionally

discredited by his conduct on the Niagara and had no champion. Congress
was in the mood to do something, and much needed to be done. The militia
had demonstrated its inability to supply the substantial, trained force
theoretically promised, and few now held any real expectation of improvement. Even Duane, who earlier had insisted that only proper discipline was
needed to make the militia effective, was beginning to lose confidence.
Regular forces were the apparent solution, but they were needed quickly, and
the newly created regular units left much to be desired. What was needed, and
what Duane believed he offered, was a system of discipline that could be
instilled very quickly, a system that could produce trained forces in a
minimum of time. Units could be trained more quickly and effectively with his
discipline, he insisted, than with any other available.[50]

To achieve that purpose, Duane had modified the French scheme of 1791
in three areas: the drill (the movement of soldiers on the battlefield); the
manual of arms (the handling and firing of weapons); and the method of
instruction. Gone from the drill manual were those features he believed
applied only to parades or to guard mount. "A good method in instruction in
military discipline should exclude everything that is unnatural or not applicable to actual military service in action," he insisted. The result of his tailoring,
however, had a rather shocking effect on the old-line professionals. The
appearance of soldiers at drill under Duane's system was a rather radical
departure from any accepted system. He had dropped the emphasis on
precision of lines or intervals between soldiers—aspects that give the drill its
martial character—and executed all movements and facings from "mark
time"—marching in place. Though the changes were calculated to attain
efficiency, old soldiers thought the new drill "unmilitary" and resisted its
introduction.[51]

Similarly, Duane relegated some portions of the manual of arms—"the
performance of certain unmeaning and frivolous motions with the firelock in
the hand"—to a decidedly secondary position. The manual exercise, he
maintained, should consist of two parts: a "manual of discipline" and a
"manual of parade." The former consisted of the minimal motions required
to use the weapon in action; the latter were unessential and should be
excluded when imminent danger necessitated the rapid training of a large
force. "The only effectual parts of the manual are those which go into action,
they are the priming, loading and firing, the fixing and charging of bayonets,
and the manner of carrying the firelock." All else were "motions of
convenience" and could be "rejected without disadvantage."[52]

These changes simplified the training task. Instruction no longer needed
to begin by rehearsing one or two recruits at a time. Duane's discipline was
designed to be taught to larger groups. Recruits were to be trained in parties
of not fewer than twenty. Fifty, he insisted, would be better than ten or
fifteen.[53] His aim was to create a scheme that would produce competent

soldiers out of raw recruits or undrilled militia in as brief a period as possible.
He was confident that his discipline had accomplished that. "Militia, which
had never been before at a drill, have been exercised by the whole company in
the very first drill, and in a fortnight made more competent to maneuver, and
marched better, than companies which have been in regular service three
years," Duane bragged.[54]

Movements on the battlefield were also subject to simplification. In the
attack, Duane favored the column for much the same reason the French had
adopted it in their revolutionary army: it was "less liable to error" and
rendered the movements of the army "simple and easy." "The column
contains *the great secret of modern tactics,* it is the most certain lever in the hands of
a skillful officer."[55] The alternative, an extended line, was both more difficult
to handle and less well adapted to the rough terrain that characterized most of
the areas where the American Army was expected to be employed. Duane
objected to the fixed maneuvers or evolutions Dundas had popularized and
opted for a more flexible system.

> So soon as the evolutions are begun [in training] they should constantly vary,
> that is, the evolutions should never succeed each other in the same order any
> two times; the drill should one day move from the right, another from the
> left, and so on . . . ; by this means the soldier will never know what
> movement is to follow any other . . . : the contrary practice is too prevalent,
> and the practice of what is called the *nineteen manoeuvres,* is held as the
> consummation of military perfection; when in fact, a well disciplined soldier
> may never have seen a single one of these manoeuvres, and yet perform them
> or any other at the first word of command.[56]

Upon the advice of the new secretary of war, John Armstrong, the House
voted in early 1813 to adopt Duane's system. The Senate, however, chose
simply to authorize the president to establish a discipline system for the time
being and to subsequently recommend to Congress a permanent system; the
House went along.[57] With Armstrong's support, the selection of Duane's
Hand Book for Infantry was a foregone conclusion.[58]

Formally adopting a system of discipline, as the Army had done with
Duane's *Hand Book* in 1813 (or Smyth's the year before), and implementing its
instruction throughout the Army proved to be entirely different matters.
Duane's discipline, though based on the French system, was so remarkably
different in style from anything the Army had previously seen that it was
strongly resisted in the field. Duane's critics focused their attacks on the very
aspect that was supposed to have made the Army more efficient: simplification
by omitting unnecessary aspects of the system. Almost all criticized his failure
to stress posture and alignment—features that give formations their military
appearance. To Duane, the critics had missed the point. The real object of a
system was to provide large numbers of men trained for combat: "If by one

method 50 or one hundred men may be brought to the required habit with nearly the same labor and in nearly the same time as one may by another method, the advantage must be . . . obvious."[59]

The advantages of Duane's system, however, escaped the notice of most of his contemporaries, though a growing number began complaining about the lack of some form of established discipline. Opposition was so great to his new system—which had been adopted for Army-wide use in March 1813— that early in 1814, a number of senior officers were asked if Duane's handbook should be altered or replaced. They overwhelmingly favored replacing it.

Duane attributed their opposition to the "prejudice or the jealousy which has always been the attendant of improvements in the arts, and in none more than in the military art."[60] But even he found it difficult to ignore the near-total rejection the work had received. "At a period when a method adapted to teach hundreds in a shorter time than by any other means before devised was so much wanted, the *Hand Book* found only a few regiments in the United States Army who obeyed the regulation." To a larger degree, he blamed "the spirit of political party, and even of parties in the Army." Duane had long been a Wilkinson supporter but could hardly admit it openly. "Not to be the partisan of one general," he insisted, "was to incur the imputation of being the friend of another; thus all the friends of one violently condemned, while the friends of the other were totally indifferent to the subject."[61] He increasingly took the rejection as a personal affront, and the attacks on him somewhat justified that view. By some he was viewed as little more than an opportunistic bookseller; his work, one officer opined, was "almost universally despised" by knowledgeable military men.[62] John Quincy Adams accused Duane of "fleecing the public by palming upon the Army, at extravagant prices, a worthless compilation upon military discipline that he had published."[63]

In January 1813, Congress enlarged the Army to forty-five regular infantry regiments. The campaign plans again called for a series of actions: the recapture of Detroit; an attack on Canada across Lake Ontario; and the opening of operations in the Southern Theater. The latter, conducted by Andrew Jackson, ultimately led the next year to the best remembered victory of the war—the Battle of New Orleans.

Madison had picked William H. Harrison, governor of Indian Territory and hero of Tippecanoe, for the Detroit operation. Despite the difficulties inherent in a winter campaign, the loss of Detroit had so affected the nation that Harrison was ordered north later in 1812 with some 6,500 men. In January 1813, the forward elements of this force were soundly defeated along the Raison River some twenty-six miles south of Detroit. Harrison then withdrew and spent the spring and summer of 1813 waiting for the Navy to gain control of Lake Erie. This victory finally came in September, but that left little time for campaigning. Harrison nonetheless pushed on. The British, now outnumbered on land and exposed from the lake, retreated. Harrison followed them and finally brought them to battle some eighty-five miles up the Thames River in Upper Canada. Instead of attacking with infantry in the traditional way, Harrison ordered a mounted attack. The British, unprepared for this tactic, crumbled under the onslaught. This victory ended major activity in this theater for the balance of the war and left the Americans in control of Detroit, Lake Erie, and a portion of Upper Canada.

To the east, the Ontario campaign had been entrusted to General Dearborn, former secretary of war under Jefferson. The American strategy was sound, but Dearborn was a poor choice to implement it. He was to capture Kingston, the only effective naval station on the Canadian side of Lake Ontario, thereby winning control of the lake for the Americans. Dearborn, however, became concerned that the British had reinforced Kingston and opted for a less direct route that called first for the defeat of the British garrison at York. There, the chance explosion of a British powder magazine killed Zebulon Pike, commander of the American forces ashore, and a number of others and so disorganized the attack that the initial advantage they had gained was not pursued.

While Dearborn attacked York, American units from Niagara forced the British out of Fort George and Queenston. An immediate pursuit might have sealed the victory, but Dearborn delayed several days. The smaller British force, now reorganized, thoroughly routed the Americans sent after them in a fierce night attack. A second similar reverse brought an end to any further action on the Niagara frontier that year. Dearborn's decision to first secure the west end of the lake had uncovered the strategically important Sackett's Harbor. Only the brilliant action of Jacob Brown saved this key American post when the British attacked the weakened force that remained there.

That fall, after the indecisive campaign on Lake Ontario, a two-pronged attack on Montreal was ordered. One army of 4,000 men under Wade Hampton was ordered to attack the city from an encampment at Plattsburg on Lake Champlain, and another of about 6,000 under the command of James Wilkinson was to attack down the St. Lawrence from Sackett's Harbor. The operation was one of the worst fiascos of the war. The two commanders refused to cooperate. Hampton retreated after his first contact. Wilkinson followed him into winter quarters at Plattsburg after an action in which about one-third of his force was severely mauled. The personal animosity between these two men—leaders of the Army's main factions—played no small role in this debacle.

Early in 1814, three volunteer regiments were brought into the regular establishment and designated the 46th, 47th, and 48th regiments.[64] The authorized strength of the Army now exceeded 62,000 men. Recruiting efforts were again intensified, and the bounty was once more increased. Though total

strength never approached the authorization, it did increase dramatically—
from some 19,000 in the previous year to just over 38,000 by September.

In March 1814, Wilkinson made a foray from Plattsburg with about
4,000 men but was turned back only eight miles into Canada by a British and
Canadian force numbering barely 200. It was an even more miserable failure
than that of the preceding fall. After this setback, Wilkinson was replaced by
Jacob Brown, now a major general.[65] A lull settled on the northern frontier
while Brown prepared his forces to fight. Among his officers was Winfield
Scott, who had distinguished himself at Queenston and had recently been
promoted to brigadier general and placed in command of one of Brown's
brigades.

Scott had no time to be drawn into the debate over discipline. He simply
rejected Duane and began immediately to train his troops in the French
system. "I have a handsome little army of about 1,700," he wrote. "The men
are healthy, sober, cheerful, and docile. The field officers highly respectable,
and many of the platoon officers are decent and emulous of improvement. If,
of such materials, I do not make the best army now in service, by the 1st of
June, I will agree to be dismissed from the service."[66] Ignoring the order to
use Duane's *Hand Book,* he drilled his men up to ten hours a day for three
months in the French system he preferred. When the units finally graduated to
large-scale drills, the precision was so great that even the troops took delight in
it. "[They] began to perceive," wrote Scott, "why they had been made to fag
so long at the drill of the soldier, the company, and the battalion. Confidence,
the dawn of victory, inspired the whole line."[67]

Scott so thoroughly drilled and trained his forces at Buffalo that later in
the summer they provided the United States Army with its proudest moments
of the war. In July, at Chippewa and again at Lundy's Lane, his troops
displayed such discipline and skill that they drew praise from even the British
commander. Scott and his disciplined troops were unique, however, and when
he was severely wounded and his brigade withdrawn, the campaign again
faltered.

With Napoleon's defeat in 1814, the British were able to reinforce
Canada and begin a series of adventures along the Atlantic seaboard and in
the South. The most famous of these raids was the foray into Chesapeake Bay,
which resulted in the sacking and burning of Washington. At about the same
time, the enlarged British forces that had been gathering in Canada began to
move south toward Lake Champlain. At Plattsburg, New York, a British force
of 11,000 regulars faced an American force of only about 4,500, many of them
militia. Alexander Macomb, another of the new brigadier generals, was in
command of American forces. Only his skillful cooperation with a superior
American naval force on the lake saved the day. The subsequent British
withdrawal ended the greatest threat thus far to American territory. The
prospects for the next year, however, with further British reinforcement likely,

spurred efforts to improve the effectiveness of the Army. In the last months of 1814, nearly 27,000 men were enlisted, and once again the issues of training and discipline came to the fore.

Despite all that had transpired, the nation's prospects for a campaign in 1815 were in many ways brighter than they might have seemed. It was true that the British, now freed from the Continental war, could introduce a number of battle-hardened regiments, but three years of war had brought about significant changes in the American forces. By 1815, the most incompetent of the senior commanders had been shunted aside in favor of younger men who were both more proficient and more energetic. Moreover, the factionalism that had plagued the service had largely been eliminated with Wilkinson's demise.

Jacob Brown, for one, looked forward to the next campaign, but he recognized the importance of an immediate solution to the discipline issue. "If you establish a system of tactics . . . and place a copy of the work in the hands of every commissioned officer," he wrote, and if it was made "obligatory upon him to produce the work at every inspection under a penalty of no less than the loss of his commission," it would be worth 5,000 men. It was an essential and hopeful step. It could, he said, "be the means of saving us from the total destruction."[68]

Improved prospects notwithstanding, the situation of the nation as 1815 approached was simply too dangerous to allow the conflict over discipline to continue through another campaign. Twice a discipline had been prescribed, and twice the Army had refused to follow it. Duane had recently completed a new rendering of the French system but was pessimistic about its being greeted with favor.[69] Nonetheless, realization was dawning that something had to be done.

In November, Congress again inserted itself into the debate. Scott had demonstrated admirably what could be done with disciplined, drilled troops, yet the Army persisted in disorder. John C. Calhoun rose and demanded to know why no one system of discipline was used throughout the Army. "So great was this variance," he reported, "that no large body of our Army, Brown's command perhaps excepted, could be properly exercised together." Was the Army being trained by any one system of discipline? If not, why not? the House wanted to know. The Army confirmed that no uniform system was then being practiced but proposed that a board be formed immediately to recommend such a system.[70] Duane suspected that his own system was to be abandoned. "I can anticipate what will be the course pursued, and almost who will be the members of this Board," he wrote, "and I can even anticipate that the thing is already arranged by one of those whose enmity to me has been most active. . . ."[71] His hunch was correct.

Jacob Brown summed up the attitude of many officers on the issue of discipline. Any system but Duane's was better than none, he wrote. "I beg to be delivered from any patched up system conceived by book-makers, who for the sake of gain, labor to make a mystery of what is purely mechanical.''[72] In December, the House agreed with the War Department proposal and directed that a board be convened to establish a system of discipline for the Army. Furthermore, the House specified that the new system be drawn directly from that of the French. The House, which had once promoted Duane, had turned around. Lobbying by the Hampton faction had paid off.

Winfield Scott was chosen to head the board, which began to meet in January 1815. Duane made one last effort to salvage something for his efforts and wrote directly to Scott, but to no avail.[73] Scott's manual, copied from the French system of 1791, became the basis of American drill, but it came too late to influence events in this war. The Peace of Ghent was signed on 24 December 1814 and was ratified in Washington in February 1815—even before the new system was fully fashioned. Scott's drill, however, was adopted and was to be the basis for American discipline for years.

In retrospect, it was unlikely that any such "unmilitary" system as Duane had proposed would have gained wide acceptance, particularly by the Regular Army establishment. Nonetheless, the scheme did face up to a political reality that few others would address. For years to come, soldiers would lament the shortsightedness of politicians who insisted on maintaining the smallest-possible regular establishment and who relied in war on a largely citizen army. The Battle of Queenston Heights had shown how impractical such policies were. Duane's system of discipline was one of the few efforts to deal with the political realities that derive from our republican nature. Few military figures before or since have understood those imperatives so thoroughly.

3

The Battles on the Rio Grande:
Palo Alto and Resaca de la Palma,
8–9 May 1846

K. JACK BAUER

The Mexican War arose from a clash of American and Mexican national interests. While psychological and philosophical pressures aplenty assailed both nations, it was the presence of the three Mexican states of Texas, New Mexico, and Alta California in the path of the inexorable westward drive of American settlement that brought the two countries to war. President James K. Polk wanted California and considered a Rio Grande boundary a desirable by-product of any negotiations. To secure a Pacific terminus for the American march toward the setting sun, Polk devised an ingenious scheme. He proposed to use as a lever the more than $5 million in outstanding American claims against Mexico. Because the Republic of Mexico was broke and could not pay her debts, Polk proposed to assume them in return for Mexico's recognition of the Rio Grande border plus at least northern California. It was an offer that the American president believed no rational and bankrupt nation could refuse.[1]

As viewed from Washington, the problem was how to convince a reluctant Mexican government and populace that the offer was a reasonable solution to their problems. Mexico had severed diplomatic relations in the spring of 1845 following the U.S. annexation of Texas. Following annexation, the administration sent Brev. Brig. Gen. Zachary Taylor there with a small force of regulars, to which he gave the unfortunate name of the Army of Occupation.[2] Taylor's force arrived at Corpus Christi, Texas, in late July 1845. During the succeeding months, it built up to approximately 4,300 men, slightly over half of those in service.[3] Although Taylor initially instituted a strenuous training program, the effort slackened as the evil weather of the fall and winter attacked the troops in their poorly protected encampment. Despite a growing sick list and the presence of increasing numbers of grog shops,

57

prostitutes, and gambling dens, the Army maintained its underlying discipline.[4]

Meanwhile, the administration's diplomatic efforts to settle the dispute foundered. When it became clear that Polk's negotiator, John Slidell, would not be received in Mexico City, the administration decided to demonstrate its seriousness by increasing the pressure on Mexico. Naval squadrons on both coasts received orders to concentrate off Mexican ports; Secretary of War William L. Marcy simultaneously directed Taylor to move from his station at Corpus Christi to the banks of the Rio Grande.[5] This moved American troops into territory to which Texas had scant claim and where it had no actual presence. To the Mexicans, who did not even recognize the alienation of the land between the Sabine River and Corpus Christi, this represented a flagrant invasion of their territory.[6] While Taylor prepared his force to march, diplomatic efforts died. In late December, the moderate government of José Joaquín de Herrera was deposed by the opportunistic and implacably anti-American General Mariano Paredes y Arrillaga. Paredes refused to recognize or negotiate with Slidell, who departed on the last day of March 1846.[7]

While Slidell made his way back to Washington, the Polk administration relied on the shift of Taylor's army to the Rio Grande as the lever to force Mexico into serious negotiations. It failed. Instead of talking, the Mexicans launched a drive to remove the Americans from the disputed area, which brought about the Battles of Palo Alto and Resaca de la Palma described in this chapter. Neither the defeats north of the Rio Grande nor a series of American thrusts into northern Mexico and California changed the Mexican stance. As a result American leaders, in the fall of 1846, abandoned their strategy of graduated pressure in favor of an amphibious assault into the heartland of central Mexico. That campaign, brilliantly conducted by Maj. Gen. Winfield Scott, ultimately forced Mexican politicians to negotiate and gained for the United States the great swath of territory that stretched from Texas to the Pacific and from Oregon to Baja California.

During the spring of 1846 the pressure upon which the Polk administration relied to achieve its diplomatic objectives was the Army of Occupation in Texas. "A better little army than this never took the field," one enthusiastic young West Point graduate wrote in April 1846.[8] Because the force contained only regulars, more than one-third of the entire Army, it was the most professional and best-trained body with which the United States ever had fought the initial battles of a war. The battles it fought reflected the competence of the officers and men of the American Army of 1846, a force that would redeem the clouded reputation the service had earned during the War of 1812.

Despite its professionalism, the United States Army in 1846 had its flaws. The appointment of Taylor, colonel of the 6th Infantry, to command the force in Texas illustrated a major problem: the Army lacked an expandable, experienced senior officer corps. It had only three general officers of the line. The senior officer, Maj. Gen. Winfield Scott, served as general in chief of the Army. The post's title promised more than it delivered because the incumbent's authority was ill defined and he lacked a supporting staff. What power he wielded resulted from personal influence with the secretary of war and the president. With Secretary Marcy and President Polk, Scott's influence was limited. The two line brigadier generals were Edmund P. Gaines, a superannuated hero of the War of 1812, who commanded the Western Division from New Orleans, and the martinet John E. Wool, who headed the Eastern Division from Troy, New York. Neither could be spared for the Texas assignment.

Taylor was one of the United States Army's fourteen line colonels, six of whom held brevet commissions as brigadier generals. All commanded regiments, and four of the six were on detached duty as the head of a territorial department, as were four of the colonels who had yet to earn their brevets. The cumulative effect of the detachments, which were matched by special assignments for junior officers, was to strip the Army in the field of a large portion of its officer corps. For instance, only three regiments assigned to Taylor's force were accompanied by their colonels. One resigned his commission before the start of hostilities, and a second was sent home for drunkenness.

Taylor's blue-clad force contained the elements of four infantry and one dragoon regiments plus a regiment-sized battalion of "red-legged infantry"— artillerymen serving as infantry. The infantry and dragoon units arrived in Texas fresh from service on the Indian frontier, while the artillerymen came from coastal defenses. All were well drilled and were commanded by experienced officers. The infantry regiments were organized in accordance with the Act of 23 August 1842 into ten forty-two-man companies. Each regiment contained one company formed as a grenadier unit, although the use of hand grenades had effectively vanished from the American Army. A second company was trained and equipped as light infantry. It was frequently combined with the light companies of other regiments to form a special battalion.

In 1846, the standard arm for the American infantry was supposed to be the Model 1841 percussion musket, which fired a .58 caliber ball and was fitted with a 33-inch bayonet. In practice, many, if not most, of the troops with Taylor retained their older .69 caliber flintlock muskets, either Model 1822 or 1840, fitted with 16- and 18-inch bayonets, respectively. Foot soldiers carried "buck-and-ball" cartridges for their muskets; the cartridges contained a ball and three buckshot in addition to a charge of powder. Smoothbore muskets were seldom effective beyond 100 yards, although the troops were trained in marksmanship.

The foot soldiers had been trained since 1825 in accordance with Winfield Scott's *Infantry Tactics,* considered by most to be a thoughtful revision of William Duane's *Hand Book for Infantry.* Following the *Infantry Drill Regulations of 1815,* Scott formed his units in two lines, increased cadence from seventy-five to ninety steps per minute, and stressed target practice. The men were trained in three phases: the School of the Soldier, the Company, and the Battalion. American infantry were well trained in individual and company drills, but the normal practice of stationing troops in small, two- to five-company detachments offered little opportunity for battalion drill. Taylor instituted a battalion training program at Corpus Christi in autumn 1845, but its effectiveness was questionable.

The horse regiments were dragoons rather than true cavalry. In keeping with American practice, the mounted men were armed and trained to fight on foot in preference to horseback. They carried breechloading Hall rifled carbines, pistols, and heavy sabers, but not lances. Nor were the American horses as heavy as those European armies used for their cavalry shock units. The American dragoons, whose regiments consisted of ten companies of fifty-four men each, had been formed and were normally used for frontier police duties which placed a premium on movement and required them to be, in effect, fast-deployment infantry. As prescribed in the 1822 *Tactics,* they were normally employed in two ranks, although the only charge executed during the Rio Grande fighting employed a column of fours because of local conditions. The mounted men, historically a neglected arm in the American service, were too few in number to play a major role in the Rio Grande actions or other battles of the day.

The artillery regiments were trained to serve both as gunners for the coastal defense batteries and as temporary infantry in support of the local militia when containing an enemy landing party. Their versatility allowed the artillery companies to function as the Army's strategic reserve. When reinforcements for the troops were needed in the field, as in Texas, one or more artillery companies could be dispatched with the confidence that they would serve creditably as infantry. One company in each of the four artillery regiments was armed as a light or field battery of four guns, usually a pair of six-pounder guns and two twelve-pounder howitzers.[9] The six-pounder hurled a 6.1-pound projectile about 1,500 yards, while the howitzer lofted an 8.9-pound shell some 1,070 yards. Both were cast of bronze. In 1840, the Army adopted Lt. Robert Anderson's translation of the French manual of *Instructions for Field Artillery, Horse and Foot.* As modified in 1845, it contained drills for the piece, the driver, and the battery.

The American Army in 1846 contained no special troops. Engineering work was accomplished by fatigue parties drawn from line units and supervised by engineer officers. The latter were normally among the most promising graduates of West Point Military Academy, which in the 1840s was still the nation's largest single source of trained engineers. In May 1846, Congress authorized the formation of the Company of Sappers, Miners, and Pontoniers, but it would not see action until spring 1847. Logistic support of the Army in the field was the responsibility of the quartermaster, commissary, forage, and ordnance departments. Each relied on hired civilians to man its wagons and depots under the control of officers belonging to the departments. Similarly, the medical department consisted of medical officers but no enlisted men. Nurses and others who helped staff the hospitals were either civilians or soldiers detailed by their superiors to that duty.[10] While graduates of the military academy dominated the junior ranks, no West Pointer present in the actions along the Rio Grande held a permanent rank higher than captain; only five individuals did, in fact, in the entire Army. The senior West Pointer with the force was Brev. Lt. Col. Thomas Childs, the commander of the artillery battalion. Nevertheless, it would be the young company officers who would carry the brunt of the leadership in the initial battles and the campaign that followed. In part, this resulted from the physical nature of the battlefields, which tended to break up the combat into small-unit actions, and in part, from the paucity of Regular Army field officers available for service in Mexico.

The company commanders serving with Taylor were experienced and mature. Many, if not most, had served as post commanders on the frontier and were accustomed to making independent decisions. As a result, they were inclined to make quick judgments on the battlefield rather than refer problems up the chain of command. Because in most instances they knew or could deduce Taylor's plan of battle, this generally brought favorable results. Equally valuable was the standardization of tactics introduced by Scott's *Infantry Tactics*. American small-unit commanders could generally be relied on to follow tactics that were understood by their fellow officers. This guaranteed that abnormal gyrations likely to upset neighboring units seldom occurred.

The experience of the Regular Army, growing out of its frontier service, had its limitations. Seldom did units larger than small battalions serve at one post, a circumstance that ensured that few field officers had experience in handling large numbers of men on a battlefield.[11] Luckily, the battles north of the Rio Grande did not require the maneuvering of units larger than regiments nor any drill more complicated than the formation of a regimental square.

On paper, the opponent was formidable. The Mexican Army in 1846 numbered about 35,000 men, nearly five times the number of American regulars. The Mexican regular regiments—twelve infantry, three light infantry *(ligero)*, and ten cavalry—were supported by twenty-five reserve, or *activo*, infantry units and five *activo* cavalry regiments. There also existed about 3,000 port defense *(guardacosta)* militia and about fifty companies of *presidiales*, irregular light cavalry that normally patrolled the Indian frontier. The

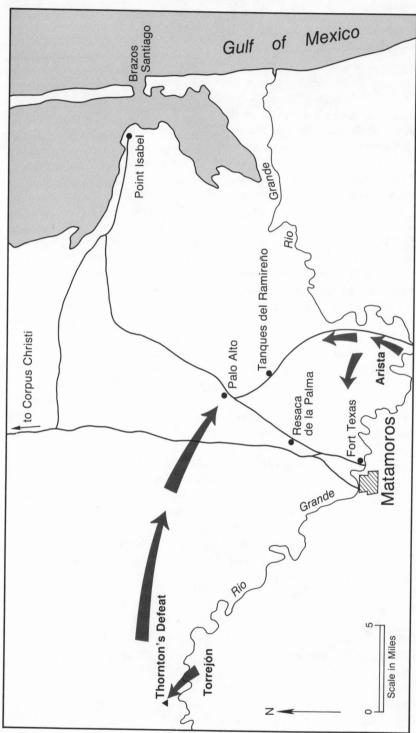

Map 3.1. Southern Texas

Mexican soldier was commonly an Indian conscript who was a courageous, long-suffering, but often ineffectual soldier who frequently lacked training. Mexican marksmanship was miserable because the infantrymen fired from the hip and usually overloaded the powder in their muskets. Most of the muskets were discarded British flintlock Tower models that had seen extensive service. The cavalry generally carried lances as their main weapon, although some units, notably the *presidiales,* were armed with swords and a short blunderbuss called an *escopeta.* Nearly all horsemen rode small, wiry Mexican ponies which had great endurance but limited shock power.

The Mexican Army's artillery was weak. It was formed into fourteen batteries of varying strength; most of the guns were defective and the officers assigned often incompetent. Moreover, Mexican guns still utilized the ponderous stock-trail mounts, and individual batteries lacked organized transports, making it difficult to shift them once they were situated on the battlefield. Unlike the U.S. Army, the Mexican force contained organized engineer units, but they were commonly used as a line infantry unit in battle. Mexican engineer officers, like their American counterparts, were generally well trained and skillful.[12] Overall, the Mexican army on the battlefield was a determined, disciplined force resplendent in its predominantly blue uniforms. It suffered from weak leadership at both the junior and senior levels and from a tendency to panic when pressed beyond its expectations or when the men could be led to believe that their leaders had deserted the cause.

In March 1846, Taylor sent his force south toward the Rio Grande along a trail that led from Corpus Christi to the Mexican town of Matamoros. The heavy artillery, supplies, and the sick traveled by water under naval escort to Point Isabel on the coast just north of the mouth of the Rio Grande. That Mexican settlement would become Taylor's supply base. The troops marching overland traversed a desolate, semiarid land populated by jack rabbits, centipedes, and tarantulas, as well as occasional herds of mustangs, which dashed about among the tangles of chaparral and stunted trees. As the leading elements of the U.S. Army approached the Arroyo Colorado, they encountered Mexican troops who threatened resistance about twenty miles north of the river. Taylor brought up his trailing brigades and prepared to make an assault crossing of this shallow, ox-bow stream. His light troops and dragoons dashed across on the morning of 20 March while the artillerymen stood by their loaded guns. The Mexican patrol offered no resistance and scampered back to the river.[13] American dragoons occupied Point Isabel on 24 March while the main body of infantry continued on to the river. They set up camp across the river from Matamoros four days later. The engineers promptly laid out an earthwork, Fort Texas, which signified the American presence on the waterway.[14] From there Taylor rebuffed demands by General de brigada Francisco Mejía, the commander at Matamoros, that he return to Corpus

Christi. Such an action, Taylor pointed out, was beyond his orders.[15] The two forces glowered at each other across the Rio Grande for another five weeks, but neither side was prepared to initiate an attack. Taylor's orders were not to precipitate any hostilities; the Mexican, who consistently insisted that by the very fact of marching into the area south of the Nueces River the Americans had declared war, refrained from acting until reinforced.[16]

During the period of peaceful confrontation, the Mexicans made strenuous efforts to induce American Catholic enlisted men to desert. Mexican leaders expected to lure as many as 1,500 men across the Rio Grande and at one time believed that the U.S. Army's entire 7th Infantry, a largely Irish and German unit, would desert en masse.[17] The actual number of deserters crossing into Mexico is difficult to determine but apparently was well under 100 men.

The first blood flowed on 10 April. Col. Trueman Cross, the highly regarded quartermaster of the Army of Occupation, was murdered by Mexican highwaymen while riding outside the American camp. On the eighteenth, Lt. Theodoric H. Porter and one of his men were ambushed and killed while searching for Cross. None of the three was killed by Mexican troops, but most Americans at Fort Texas believed that the bandits responsible had been incited by Mexican authorities.[18] General de división Pedro de Ampudia, who replaced Mejía as commander at Matamoros on 12 April, formally demanded that the Americans withdraw to the Nueces. Taylor refused, again arguing that he had been ordered to the Rio Grande by his government, but he reiterated the peaceful nature of his orders. Two days later, he instituted a blockade of the Rio Grande to prevent supplies from reaching the Mexican army gathering at Matamoros.[19]

Ampudia planned to start his offensive on 15 April following the arrival of his awaited reinforcements. He cancelled the operation on learning that General de división Mariano Arista, commander of the Army of the North, was en route. Arista reached Matamoros on 24 April. He immediately sent the Americans their fourth notice that hostilities had commenced.[20] Taylor, who had been using the time since his arrival to stock Fort Texas with food and ammunition, sent his supply train back to the safety of Point Isabel.[21]

Arista launched an attack on 24 April. His plan called for General de brigada Anastasio Torrejón, with about 1,600 sappers, cavalry, and light infantry, to cross the river at La Palangana, west of Matamoros. From there, they would strike east to sever the American supply line to Point Isabel and cover the crossing by the main body. About 1500 on the twenty-fourth, Taylor received a false report of Mexicans crossing the river below him. Eight hours later, he learned of Torrejón's passage and sent Capt. Seth Thornton with a squadron of dragoons to investigate.[22]

The following morning, Thornton carelessly led his command into an ambush at the Rancho de Carricitos, about twenty-eight miles from the American camp. In the effort to break out, eleven Americans died and twenty-six, including Thornton, were captured. News of the debacle reached Taylor at daybreak on the twenty-sixth when Thornton's guide, who had not been at the ambush, rode into camp. He was followed later in the morning by a dragoon whose wounds could not be treated by Torrejón's surgeon on the march. The two men quickly made clear the magnitude of the defeat.[23] Taylor reported to Washington that "hostilities may now be considered as commenced" and called upon the governors of Louisiana and Texas for volunteers. Any units organized and dispatched would be in addition to four companies of the 1st Infantry and 300 recruits then en route in response to earlier requests.[24]

After his clash with Thornton, Torrejón led his troops toward their objective. On the twenty-eighth, a Mexican patrol surprised an encampment of Texas volunteers about seven miles from Fort Texas, killing five men. The unexpected proof of the proximity of Mexican cavalry caused a near panic at Point Isabel until Maj. John Munroe hastily improvised a 500-man force of artillerymen, Texans, and sailors from ships in the harbor to defend the base. Torrejón, however, had no designs on the port, nor did he attempt to block the road to Fort Texas. Instead, he hastened to rejoin Arista as soon as the Mexican main body crossed the Rio Grande.[25] Capt. Samuel H. Walker, the legendary Texas Ranger whose men had been so ignominiously surprised, carried Munroe's appeal for assistance to Taylor during the evening of 29 April. The general realized the importance of securing both installations. He put every man "not detained by other indispensable duty" to work completing the fort's walls so that it could withstand a siege. Once that had been accomplished, the army could march to the aid of Munroe.[26] Taylor's efforts came none too soon. Ampudia led the first brigade of Mexican infantry across the river at Longoreño, downstream from Matamoros, on the last day of the month. Arista followed the next day with a second brigade. General Mejía remained behind with 1,400 men to protect Matamoros.[27]

Taylor learned of the crossing about 1300 on 1 May. By then it was too late to attempt to attack the Mexican bridgehead. The American commander assumed that Arista's objective was the supply depot at Point Isabel. It was a logical deduction because the Mexican force had to be supplied by sea, normally from New Orleans, and American vessels had shut the mouth of the Rio Grande. Taylor lost no time in starting for Point Isabel. Led by Capt. George A. McCall's battalion of light infantry, the army cleared Fort Texas by 1530. The Mexicans watching from across the river rejoiced, for they assumed the departure signaled an American retreat. They were misled. Maj. Jacob Brown remained at the still-uncompleted American work with about 500 men of the 7th Infantry, Capt. Allen Loud's battery of four eighteen-pounders, and Lt. Braxton Bragg's field battery. The American main body bivouacked shortly before midnight about eighteen miles from the river. They reached the coast at about noon the next day, whereupon Taylor ordered them to work to strengthen the Point Isabel defenses.[28]

Once he completed ferrying his men across the Rio Grande on 2 May, Arista divided his command. Ampudia led the *4th Infantry,* the *Puebla Battalion,* some sappers, and about 200 light cavalry toward Fort Texas. They began an attack on the fort at 0500 on the third of May in conjunction with the batteries at Matamoros.[29] The defenders responded with both heavy and light guns and scored a hit on one Mexican twelve-pounder, silencing the incoming fire until the surviving guns shifted to safer locations. The Mexican gunners kept up their fire until midnight but did little damage. The Americans ceased replying at 2200 in order to conserve ammunition. By then, it was evident that Bragg's guns were too light to be effective against the Mexican batteries and the eighteen-pounders too few to suppress them. Loud attempted to fire hot shot against Matamoros; this action was not successful because his men could not adequately heat the shot. Taylor could hear the bombardment at Point Isabel. His initial reaction was to lead the field force back to Fort Texas, but he soon abandoned the idea. Instead, he sent Walker and a few of his men to work their way through the Mexican lines to deliver instructions to remain inside the post and defend it—if necessary, to the last man. Walker was to return with a report on the situation of Brown's command. The Texans were escorted part of the way by a squadron of dragoons under Capt. Charles A. May, who had orders to await their return. Walker reached the fort early the next morning, conferred with Brown, and returned that night only to discover that May had left. Without a dragoon escort, Walker had to turn back but was able to make the trip safely on the fifth. He reported that the fort had suffered little damage and could hold out until relieved.[30]

Meanwhile, the siege of the American fort continued. On 4 May, Mexican light cavalry cut the road to the coast while the artillery exchange continued. At daylight on the fifth, Mexican guns resumed firing and soon afterwards General Ampudia moved his 1,000 men and four guns into position to invest the fort. During bombardment on the sixth, Major Brown received a mortal wound; command passed to Capt. Edgar S. Hawkins. When Arista formally summoned the fort to surrender that afternoon, Hawkins responded with understated bravado: "My interpreter is not skilled in your language but if I understand you correctly . . . I must respectfully decline to surrender."[31] Hawkins was in a strong position. As long as his supplies lasted, he was in no immediate danger from either the generally ineffectual Mexican artillery or from Ampudia's inactive infantry. Indeed, Arista's division of forces to lay siege to the post would have invited disaster had he faced a more imaginative or energetic opponent than Zachary Taylor. Arista's strategy was flawed in an even more basic sense. His proper objective was neither the post on the Rio Grande nor Taylor's field force but the depot at Point Isabel. Had it been destroyed, Taylor would have had no choice but to fall back to Corpus Christi because he could not live off the land.

Taylor delayed his return to Fort Texas until sufficient reinforcements reached Point Isabel to ensure its safety. They arrived on 6 May along with the news that the 1st Infantry companies and the initial group of Louisiana volunteers were close behind. The following morning he alerted the troops to be prepared to march at 1500. "The Commanding General has every confidence," he told the men, "in his officers and men. If his orders and instructions are carried out, he has no doubt of the result, let the enemy meet him in what numbers he may. He wishes to enjoin upon the battalions of infantry that their main dependence must be in the bayonet."[32] The reports of Walker and May incorrectly placed the main Mexican force astride the Matamoros Road about twenty miles from Point Isabel. Actually, Arista had concentrated his command, except for the troops besieging Fort Texas, at the Tanques del Ramireño, about three miles south of the road, because of the availability of good water.

Taylor burdened his column with 200 wagons loaded with supplies, despite the hindrance to rapid movement and the possible embarrassment they might prove in an engagement. He further limited his mobility by adding to the force a pair of eighteen-pounders, each drawn by six yoke of oxen. Neither was necessary. Fort Texas faced no immediate shortage of food or ammunition, and the eighteen-pounders contributed little to the army's battlefield strength. Once he had reopened the supply corridor to Fort Texas, an operation more easily conducted by troops unfettered by slow-moving wagons and heavy artillery, and driven Arista's forces south of the Rio Grande, sufficient time would have remained to resupply the river post. Because of the late start and the slow pace, the American force bivouacked after marching only seven miles.[33] When Arista learned that the Americans had left Point Isabel, he moved to intercept them. The main body of his force marched along a track that intersected the Point Isabel–Matamoros road at Palo Alto. Ampudia's comand abandoned its siege and hastened to rejoin the main body. Both armies reached the vicinity of Palo Alto about 1200 on 8 May. The Americans had marched about eleven miles. The Mexicans, having come less than half that distance, were already in place. The Mexican cannon greeted Taylor's men with a few rounds that caused no damage.

The plain of Palo Alto took its name from a band of tall timber that began there and, interspersed with chaparral and patches of open ground, stretched southwards toward the river. The plain, about a mile and a half wide and somewhat longer, was flat except where pocked by shallow, marshy depressions filled with runoff water and a boundary ridge extending northeastward from the Tanques del Ramireño road. Stiff, shoulder-high, sharp, pointed

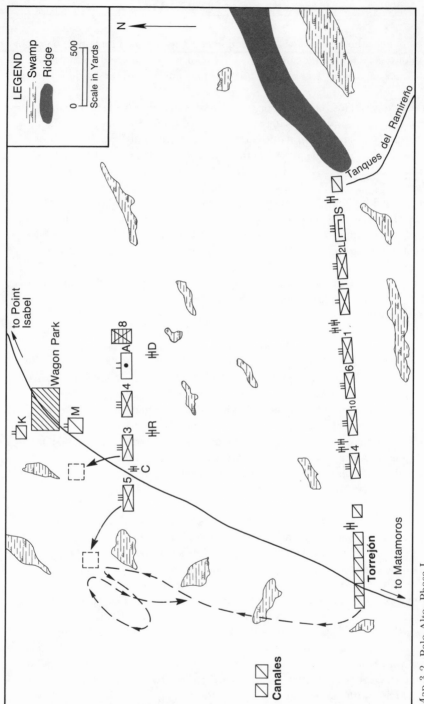

LEGEND

Swamp

Ridge

0   500

Scale in Yards

N

to Point
Isabel

Wagon Park

K

M

A 8

D

4

R

3

C

5

to Matamoros

Torrejón

Canales

Tanques del Ramireño

S

L 2

T

1

6

10

4

Map 3.2. Palo Alto, Phase I

grass called *zacahistle* by the Mexicans inhibited movement by foot soldiers. Chaparral fringed the west side of the battleground where several small marshy depressions marked its limits.

Taylor halted his column about two miles from the Mexican line to allow the wagon train to close. Then the Americans, still in a column, moved forward again until they were about three-quarters of a mile from the enemy. Taylor halted his men once again, this time to allow canteens to be filled from a nearby water hole "with a view to rest and refresh the men," in his words.[34] He also used the time to move the wagon train into a defensive position nearby under the watchful eyes of a squadron of dragoons under Capt. Croghan Ker. While the American units shifted positions to form a column of divisions and individual soldiers stared at the Mexican bayonets and lances glistening in the sunlight and the pennons and flags rippling in the breeze, Lt. Jacob E. Blake reconnoitered the field. He noted the artillery positions and verified that no unpleasant surprises lay hidden in the tall grass. About 1400, Taylor ordered his 2,228 men forward again. His plan was to concentrate his strength on his right, adjacent to the road, and open a passage with a bayonet charge. The strategy proved impractical once the battle began because of the danger of an attack on his flank or rear by the Mexican horsemen. Taylor, whose experience with both cavalry and artillery was nearly nonexistent, had underestimated their impact in an open-field battle.

Ampudia's men arrived as the Americans formed. They took position on the left of Arista's infantry except for General de brigada Antonio Canales' irregular cavalry, which moved into the chaparral west of the battlefield. Whether Canales hoped to be in a position to cut off the American retreat or wished to avoid a clash with them is uncertain, but the move effectively removed his men from the battle. Arista formed his army into a thin, mile-long line running roughly east and west. Torrejón's thousand lancers formed the left flank. His westernmost unit, some companies of *presidiales* (mounted rangers), were astride the road and the rest of the corps *(8th* and *7th Cavalry,* two light field pieces, and the *Light Cavalry Regiment)* extended about 800 yards east of it. Then came the main body of infantry interspersed with artillery. From west to east stood the *4th, 10th, 6th,* and *1st Infantry,* a company of sappers, a battery of five four-pounders, the *Tampico Battalion, 2d Light Infantry,* more sappers, and a single four-pounder. General de brigada Luis Noriega held the east end of the Mexican line with 150 light cavalrymen. All told, Arista commanded about 3,270 men of mixed quality. Some units, notably the *4th Infantry* and *2d Light Infantry,* were well equipped and led by professionals; others were little more than half-trained collections of Indian conscripts. Arista's formation was well conceived as a trap for any force launching an infantry attack down the road or across the plain. In either case, Mexican cavalry could envelop any attackers. The formation's weakness was the length of the Mexican line, which absorbed all the available men, leaving

Arista no reserves to contain a breakthrough or shape a counterattack. Moreover, because Mexican artillery was difficult to shift on the battlefield, he could not substantially rearrange his formation once it had been set.

As soon as the Mexican batteries opened fire, Taylor deployed his troops and ordered the American guns to return the compliment. In keeping with his plan of a thrust down the road, Taylor placed Brig. Gen. David E. Twiggs' right wing astride it. The 5th Infantry (Lt. Col. James S. McIntosh) took the extreme right followed by Brev. Maj. Samuel Ringgold's field battery. Then came the 3d Infantry (Capt. Lewis N. Morris) and the pair of oxen-drawn eighteen-pounders under Lt. William H. Churchill. The 4th Infantry (Brev. Maj. George W. Allen) was Twiggs' easternmost unit. He held in reserve Ker's and May's dragoon squadrons. Brev. Lt. Col. William G. Belknap's left wing deployed from the west to east: the regimental-sized Artillery Battalion (Lieutenant Colonel Childs), Capt. James Duncan's battery, and the 8th Infantry (Capt. William A. Montgomery). The latter was slightly refused as a precaution against any attempt by Mexican cavalry to turn the flank.

At 1500, the American line was within a half-mile of the Mexicans. Twiggs threw forward Ringgold's battery with May's squadron in support to within about 700 yards of the Mexican position. Belknap also advanced Duncan's guns about the same distance ahead of his line. The accurate fire of the two field batteries and of Churchill's eighteen-pounders induced Arista to abandon an intended infantry attack. Instead, he ordered Torrejón to turn the American right. Because it involved a difficult passage through the chaparral, the cavalryman accepted the assignment with reluctance. He was correct. His horses became bogged down in one of the swales that appeared unexpectedly among the tangled growth. That gave the Americans time to form defenses. When the impending attack was reported to Taylor, he laconically replied, "Keep a bright lookout for them," and returned to his contemplations. Twiggs, whose responsibility that portion of the battlefield was, reacted more assertively. He sent his right flank regiment, the 5th Infantry, about a quarter-mile to its right and rear. There it formed a square. Torrejón attacked in column with his poorest troops, the *presidiales,* in the van. The horsemen were twice driven off by volleys from the ranks of infantry delivered at a range of about fifty yards. Torrejón then attempted to slide past the 5th Infantry toward the wagon park, only to be dissuaded by the sight of the 3d Infantry also forming a square and the arrival of Lt. Randolph Ridgely's section of guns from Ringgold's battery.

Arista planned a second attack involving the infantry and cavalry on his right. It never started because of the withering fire of Duncan's guns. Mexican artillery, on the other hand, inflicted little damage despite its constant fire. The Mexican brass cannonballs seldom reached their targets on the fly, apparently because of faulty powder. They ricocheted along the ground, giving American troops a chance to dodge them. In several American units, notably the Artillery Battalion and the 8th Infantry, officers had their men throw themselves on the ground to avoid the bouncing balls. About 1600, a wad from one of Duncan's guns set the grass on fire. It burned with clouds of intense, acrid smoke that blew toward the Mexican lines. The smoke so obscured their targets that the American guns ceased firing for nearly an hour. While the artillerymen enjoyed the respite and replenished their ammunition, both armies changed their positions. Taylor took advantage of the absence of Torrejón's horsemen to send Twiggs' wing forward about a thousand yards. Its effect was a thirty-five-degree counterclockwise revolution of the American line. At the same time, Arista shifted his force about the same amount, so that the relative position of the two forces remained nearly unchanged.

When the artillery resumed thundering about 1700, Taylor ordered May's squadron, supported by the 4th Infantry, to turn the Mexican left. Because May shied from pressing his attack against superior numbers of Mexican cavalry, the maneuver accomplished nothing. The 4th Infantry, meanwhile, had received "a most galling fire" from the Mexican batteries while supporting Ringgold.[35] It drove Major Allen's men back, but the Artillery Battalion moved up. It held its ground between the heavy battery and the 5th Infantry along the road under intense Mexican fire for an hour and a half. By then, the Mexicans had exhausted their ammunition.[36] Torrejón's cavalry again approached the American line but fell back under the combined weight of canister fired by the eighteen-pounders and the musketry of the Artillery Battalion's square. Because of the damage being wrought by Ringgold's and Churchill's guns, the Mexican artillery concentrated on them. So effective was the counterbattery fire that it drove back even Ringgold's gallant unit, and one round mortally wounded its commander.

The Mexican units on the right flank began to waver under the effective shelling of Duncan's cannoneers. When the Mexican troops demanded to be ordered either to attack or allowed to withdraw outside of artillery range, Arista ordered an attack. Duncan, whose targets had been obscured by the smoke of battle, at that moment was harnessing up his battery to go to the assistance of Ringgold. He spotted the Mexican move and realized that, left unchecked, enemy horsemen could reach the supply train. Duncan quickly shifted his guns to shield the wagons. He placed one section ahead of the Mexican column and the second in a position to fire canister into its flank. The artillerymen were soon joined by Ker's squadron and the 8th Infantry, but it was the fire from Duncan's battery that forced the Mexicans to break off their attack. When the Mexicans fell back, Duncan took advantage of the smoke to move his guns unobserved to within 300 yards of the Mexican right flank. From there, he opened an unexpected enfilading fire that rolled back the Mexican line. Noriega's cavalry increased the panic among the infantry by riding through them. Arista and some of his officers halted the flight, but to prevent a rout from developing, he had to order a second attack. It was

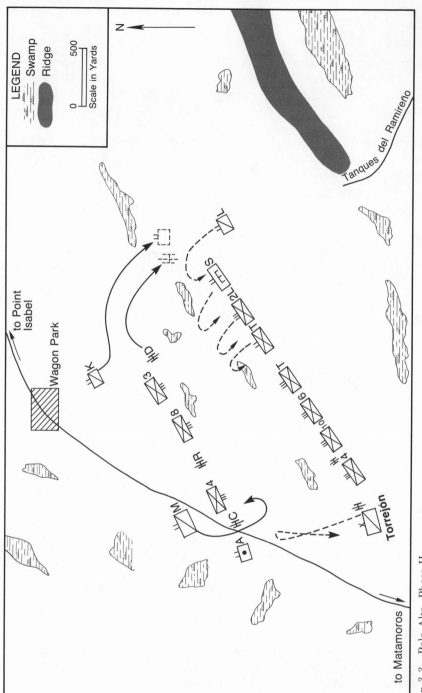

LEGEND

Swamp

Ridge

0   500

Scale in Yards

N

to Point Isabel

Wagon Park

to Matamoros

Tanques del Ramireño

Torrejón

Map 3.3. Palo Alto, Phase II

supported by Col. Cayetano Montero's *Light Cavalry Regiment.* The Mexican troops were too disheartened to push home the attack and were easily turned aside by the Americans.

It was now 1900. Because Arista's artillery had expended its available ammunition, he ordered his army to withdraw onto the chaparral-covered high ground behind its right wing. There they bivouacked. Taylor made no effort to pursue, apparently fearful for the safety of the wagon train in the encroaching darkness. The Americans bivouacked on the battlefield, unsure whether morning would bring a renewed conflict or a Mexican flight.

Technically, Taylor's men had won the battle, for they held the field. But the Americans had not destroyed the Mexican force, nor had they driven it south of the Rio Grande. Credit for the victory clearly rested with the artillery. Duncan's, Ringgold's, and Churchill's cannoneers had inflicted the bulk of Mexican losses. American infantry proved steady in the face of Mexican shelling, but only the 5th Infantry and the Artillery Battalion had directly faced the enemy. Nor had the battle been waged as Taylor had anticipated. He was content to allow his army to fight on the defensive all afternoon, eschewing the bayonet on which he had proposed to rely. Taylor's apparent flexibility probably reflected his inexperience as much as anything. Palo Alto was his first large engagement and the first time he had seen in action the horse or "flying" batteries developed by Ringgold and Duncan. Their performance could not have failed to impress him. In addition, the battle was the only time Taylor had seen cavalry perform in battle. Their flexibility and speed of movement clearly worried a general whose force was hobbled by a large and vulnerable wagon train. The threat of any assault force to the train and to the flank is the probable explanation for the decision not to attack. Casualties during the battle reflected the deadliness of the artillery. Mexican casualties were 102 killed, 129 wounded, and 26 missing, about 7 percent of their force. The American army reported 9 killed, 44 wounded, and 2 missing, or 2½ percent of those engaged.[37]

During the night of 8 May, Arista recalled the remaining troops besieging Fort Texas.[38] He decided against renewing the action at Palo Alto. Instead, he ordered his army to retire behind the Resaca de Guerrero or, as the Americans called it, Resaca de la Palma, a strong defensive position about five miles from Palo Alto. The troops at Point Isabel spent a worried day. They could hear the thunder of artillery but had no news of its outcome. Luckily, Commodore David Conner with four ships of the Navy's Home Squadron hove into sight off the port during the late morning. Conner had concluded from information reaching him at Vera Cruz that Arista had been given orders to attack. He hastened north in hopes that his presence might prevent hostilities. Conner responded to Munroe's request for assistance by landing 500 sailors and marines during the morning of the ninth. Although the

Mexican raid Munroe feared never materialized, the naval party stayed
ashore until 13 May.[39]

When the morning mists lifted from the Palo Alto battleground about
0700 on 9 May, American eyes could see the Mexican rear guard riding south.
Taylor promptly held a council of his senior officers when Twiggs reported
that most wished to halt and await reinforcements. The preponderant opinion
of the council was to go on the defensive, but Taylor, supported by McIntosh,
Morris, and Duncan, overruled it and ordered an advance.[40]

Resaca de la Palma was to mark the end of the first phase of the Mexican War.
On the morning of 9 May, Taylor dispatched a dragoon patrol to verify that
the Mexicans had departed. Captain McCall, with 220 light troops, followed
with instructions to keep contact with the retiring column. The rest of the
Americans broke out picks and shovels to construct a breastwork strengthened
by emplacements for the eighteen-pounders and a pair of twelve-pounders to
protect the wagon park. Unlike the preceding day, Taylor did not want to be
encumbered by the vulnerable train. Construction of this works took most of
the morning.

The Resaca de la Palma to which Arista's army withdrew was a bow-
shaped, shallow, brush-covered ravine that had once been a channel of the Rio
Grande. The Point Isabel–Matamoros road crossed at about the center; east
and west of the crossing, narrow ponds served as obstacles to channel any
attack. Arista placed most of his men behind the Resaca, whose south bank
formed a natural parapet. A three- or four-gun battery swept any approach
along the road, while other guns occupied commanding positions to its west.
Arista placed the *6th* and *10th Infantry,* the sappers, and the *1st Infantry* on the
right of the road. The *2d Light Infantry* and part of the *4th Infantry* deployed in
the chaparral north of the crossing near the road to ambush any Americans
who got that far. The remainder of the *4th Infantry,* the *Tampico Battalion,* and a
small detachment of sappers held the south bank west of the road. Arista had
his headquarters tent pitched in an clearing about 500 yards behind the front
to the left of the road. Torrejón and his cavalry served as a reserve as well as a
blocking force should the Americans attempt a wide encirclement of the
position. Canales with the light cavalry and a pair of light field guns watched a
vital crossroad that led to the Mexican rear. The Mexicans felt confident
about their position. "If I had with me . . . $100,000 in silver," General de
brigada Rómulo Díaz de la Vega later mused, "I would have bet the whole of
it that no 10,000 men on earth could drive us from our position."[41]

The position was not as formidable as it appeared at first glance. Arista's
force was too small to defend it properly as he lacked the necessary infantry
reserve to contain any penetration of the defenses. The siting of the guns and
the presence of Mexican units on the north bank of the Resaca combined to
limit severely the arcs of fire available to the artillery. Moreover, the chaparral

broke up the Mexican units and eliminated the psychologically important feeling of unit integrity. A substantial number of the men had not eaten in twenty-four hours. In many instances, too, they had lost confidence in their leaders, notably Arista, because of what they perceived as his culpable hesitation of the previous day. The result was dampened morale in the Army of the North.

The Americans advanced with high spirits, buoyed by the successes at Palo Alto and a growing confidence that they could best any group of Mexicans they chanced to engage. Taylor left the Artillery Battalion to guard the wagon park and set the rest of this army in motion about 1400. Meanwhile, McCall's skirmishers felt their way cautiously forward. Shortly after 1400, they sighted the Mexican guns guarding the passage of the Resaca. Instantly, the guns spoke and a half-dozen Americans were struck. The others retired. McCall's report of the contact reached Taylor about an hour later. He pushed on to the front where about 1600 he encountered McCall. Taylor ordered the light troops to start the engagement and attempt to work around the Mexican flanks. "I will push the regiments in to support you as they come up," the general promised.[42] Taylor instructed Duncan's battery, now commanded by Lieutenant Ridgely, to move up along the road after a patrol under Lt. Stephen D. Dobbins drew fire to locate the Mexican guns. As the artillerymen pushed their guns forward, McCall's men deployed on both sides of the road. Unfortunately, their obstructed view of the Mexican position precluded rendering the usual support that the artillery expected. Even so, Ridgely's gunners continued to work their pieces down the road and even beat off an attack by Mexican lancers. By showering the Mexican positions north of the Resaca with grapeshot, they drove the defenders back across the ravine.

As different American units reached the battlefield, they moved into the chaparral, the 8th and 5th Infantry to the east and the 3d and 4th Infantry to the west of the road. The fight now became one of small groups. An officer or noncommissioned officer would lead a small number of men, isolated from the rest of the line by the dense chaparral in their private war against nature and comparably detached groups of defenders. It was the type of action at which the Americans, trained in the hard school of the Indian frontier, excelled. Yet the struggle was not easy. Some Mexican units, notably the *4th Infantry* and *2d Light Infantry,* fought tenaciously. The Americans to the west of the road faced fewer foes and had the good fortune to strike a path that carried them west of the ponds and around the Mexican flank. The defenders there were too few to halt even the uncoordinated assaults of the small American groups. Capt. Robert C. Buchanan and ten men of the 4th Infantry seized a gun emplacement and beat off an attack by 150 enemy soldiers. Another group under Capt. Philip N. Barbour suddenly broke out of the chaparral into the clearing containing Arista's headquarters. That unnerved the defenders, and

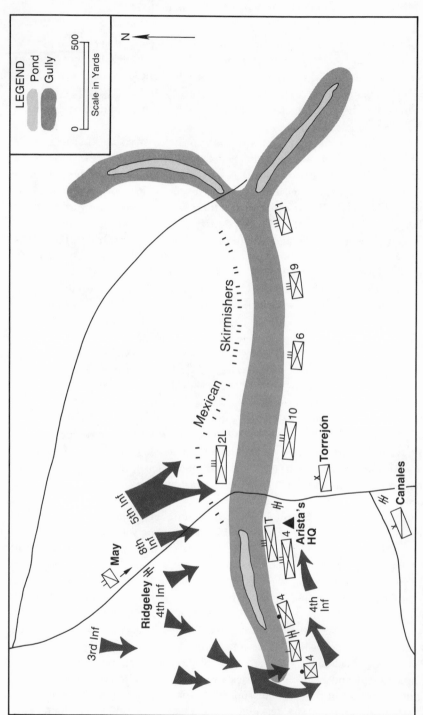

Map 3.4. Resaca de la Palma

it also insured that Arista's correspondence and silver service fell into American hands.

Meanwhile, Taylor's attention remained fixed on the fight along the road. Having lost tactical control over most of his units because of the chaparral, he was unaware of the impending collapse of the Mexican defense. Therefore, when he received a request from Ridgely for assistance in eliminating the battery confronting him, he ordered May to charge the guns. When May hesitated, Taylor in frustration called out, "Charge, Captain *nolens volens!*"[43] May remained uncertain of the location of his objective when he reached Ridgely. The artilleryman responded: "Hold on, Charlie, 'till I draw their fire and you will see where they are."[44] The American guns barked and drew a reply from the Mexican battery. Before the Mexicans could reload, May's dragoons galloped down the road in a column of fours. The charge drove the gunners from their pieces, but the Americans could not stop their horses until a quarter-mile beyond the Mexican lines. They re-formed and returned through a hail of Mexican musketry that inflicted heavy casualties. In repassing the battery they took several prisoners, including General la Vega.[45] They re-formed and repeated the exercise, taking even heavier losses.

Each time the dragoons passed the guns, the Mexicans returned and resumed firing. Only infantry, as Taylor should have realized, could take and hold the position. Finally, he turned to Colonel Belknap and said: "Take those guns, and by God keep them!"[46] The 5th and 8th Infantry rushed through the decreasing crash of musketry to seize the battery. At some points, Mexican resistance was ferocious. Belknap was wounded, and Colonel McIntosh found himself in combat with five Mexicans. He received three bayonet wounds before his subordinates could come to his assistance. Taylor intended to have Ker's dragoon squadron and the Artillery Battalion add their weight to the attack, but their orders miscarried. They arrived only in time to pursue the fleeing Mexicans.

The attack of the 5th and 8th Infantry was aided by the collapse of the Mexican line as a result of the successes on the American right, especially Barbour's sudden appearance in the headquarters clearing. Arista, ever a brave soldier, took personal command of the cavalry and attempted to salvage the situation with a charge down the road, but it accomplished little beyond easing the escape of some of the infantry. By then, the Mexican front had broken and the troops were in full flight. The fleeing Mexicans scattered. Individuals, groups, and occasional units streamed toward the various crossings of the Rio Grande. Many brushed past Fort Texas, but the garrison made no effort to speed or impede their passage. The panic-stricken soldiers overwhelmed the guards at the main ferry crossing, seized the lumbering craft, and commandeered anything else that would float. Others, fearful of being left behind, tried to swim, only to fall victim to the swift currents. Arista and most of the cavalry crossed at various lower fords without much difficulty. The army commander himself reached Matamoros at 2200. Arista reported 154 men killed, 205 wounded, and 156 missing, about 13 percent of his force of 3,758. The Americans reported that they buried about 200 Mexicans, captured eight artillery pieces, and took the colors of the *Tampico Battalion*. American casualties were also heavy: 49 dead and 83 wounded, approximately 9 percent of those actually engaged.[47]

Although he still had Ker's squadron, Duncan's battery, and the Artillery Battalion in reserve, Taylor's pursuit of the broken Mexican Army was lackluster. The Artillery Battalion marched all the way to the river bank but reported taking only thirteen prisoners.[48] Taylor missed an opportunity to eliminate the Mexican Army of the North, but that was in keeping with his character. At no time during his entire military career did he exhibit the instinct for the kill that makes the truly great field commander.

Although Taylor can be faulted in detail for his conduct of the campaign and for his battlefield tactics, his army fought with valor and intelligence. At Palo Alto, the Americans used their superiority in artillery to overcome inferior numbers; but even more significant was Ringgold's and Duncan's innovative use of the weapon. They employed the mobility of the horse batteries to shift them about the battlefield to locations where they were most effective. It was an unusual freedom that they would seldom again experience, but it demonstrates the tactical benefits to be gained from imaginative deployment of weapons. At Palo Alto, the advantage of well-trained troops also showed. The American infantry withstood both cavalry charges and artillery fire without flinching, unlike the less well-trained though no less brave Mexicans.

At Resaca de la Palma, the small-unit experience of the American troops carried the day. That battle relied on the good sense, combat skills, and leadership of junior officers and noncommissioned officers (NCOs) to lead their men through the barrier formed by the chaparral and to push home the attack. The Army proved on 9 May 1846, if there had been any question, that it was a professional force capable of overcoming unexpected difficulties and of exploiting unforeseen opportunities. During the battle, the junior officers demonstrated that well-trained leaders, given only very general direction, could fashion the tactics necessary for victory even if their commander lacked talent and finesse.

Taylor's force could not follow up the victories north of the Rio Grande with an attack into Mexico. It lacked bridging equipment and boats or the raw materials from which to construct them, largely because of Taylor's failure to foresee his needs. As a result, American troops did not cross the stream until 18 May. Even then, it was an administrative crossing because Mexican forces had abandoned their positions around Matamoros the preceding day. Three

days later, on 21 May, the first two of the emergency, ninety-day regiments
Taylor had called following the attack on Thornton finally arrived. Their
service time was too short to permit their participation in the Monterrey
campaign in September, and they were too green to contribute much except
problems to the occupation force.[49]

Congress formally recognized the state of war between the United States
and Mexico on 13 May following consummate political maneuvering by the
administration. Included in the war act was provision for 50,000 volunteers.
Secretary of War Marcy and President Polk anticipated a short war and
limited enlistments to one year. The bulk of the volunteer units was recruited
in the southern and western states where suppport for the war was strongest.
The legislation provided for ten company regiments commanded by a colonel,
lieutenant colonel, and major. Their companies contained three officers, eight
NCOs, two musicians, and 84 to 100 privates. Because the units were
organized under the state militia laws, they normally elected their officers.[50]
None of the new regiments received extensive training before being sent to the
war zone. They arrived ignorant of military drill, customs, discipline, and
camp sanitation; only a few units were ready for combat before September
when two volunteer divisions participated in the attack on Monterrey.

On 18 June, Congress authorized the addition of one major and two
brigadier generals to the Regular Army for the duration of hostilities. The law
also allowed the president to appoint generals to command the volunteers.[51]
The clear distinction between wartime and regular officers was an innovation
in American practice that protected the service from the messy, morale-
shattering selection process that had followed the War of 1812. It was a
solution to the rapid increase of officers that has been followed in differing
guises in all mobilizations since 1846. Polk selected Taylor to receive the
major generalcy and the two dragoon colonels (Stephen W. Kearny of the 1st
Dragoons and David E. Twiggs of the 2d) for the one-star rank. He added two
volunteer major generals and six brigadiers. The latter were a mixed group.
Some had substantial militia or regular service, while others were deficient in
both experience and command sense.

The administration initially decided to replace Taylor with Scott as
commander in Mexico, but when General in Chief Scott delayed his departure
for the front, the assignment was canceled.[52] Taylor continued in command of
the forces in northeastern Mexico with the task of seizing the commercial and
communications center of Monterrey. Simultaneously, three other thrusts into
northern Mexico added impetus to Polk's continuing policy of graduated
pressure on the Mexican government in hopes of bringing it to the diplomatic
table without further fighting. These included the dispatch of a column under
General Wool from San Antonio, Texas, to Chihuahua; the occupation of
Santa Fe, New Mexico, by Kearny's Army of the West; and the seizure of
California by the Navy.[53] The failure of this strategy, which also included the

restoration to power in Mexico of exiled strongman Antonio Lopez de Santa Anna, forced the Polk administration to strengthen the forces in the field and launch a second drive into eastern Mexico—Winfield Scott's skillful Mexico City campaign.

The 1846 campaign's failure to "conquer a peace" had profound political repercussions. Most American troops who had headed for Mexico had expected an easy victory and were convinced from accounts of the early battles, the patriotism of the moment, and their own ethnocentrism that Mexican soldiers were incapable of standing against American men at arms. That was no more true than the notion that soldiering involved only dressing in a new blue uniform and sleeping in a tent. As a result, disillusionment rapidly set in, public support of the war atrophied, and the political benefits of the war declined. This meant that recruiting for the second group of volunteer units, which began in the late fall of 1846, would be slow and difficult.

The Army learned little from the Rio Grande battles but that it could fight well. The very success of the engagements seemed to most officers to confirm the validity of prewar doctrine and training. Beyond greater reliance on field artillery and its forward deployment, which became so painfully a part of the initial clashes of the Civil War, few changes were evident in either Taylor or Scott's later battles. Palo Alto has been properly described as a battle won by the artillery, but its role there was eclipsed by its more dramatic part in salvaging victory at Buena Vista in 1847. It also can be argued, but less convincingly, that the failure of Mexican cavalry to affect the outcome of any of the battles of the war proved to military thinkers that the American inclination to ignore the arm was a sensible view for North Americans. The shortcomings of the supply system, which became so evident later in the war, did not affect the Rio Grande battles. They were fought by a force small enough to be served adequately by the Army's peacetime logistical machinery.

The totally regular composition of Taylor's Army of Occupation is unique among the forces that fought America's first battles. In no other initial clash was the American force composed entirely of trained regulars. All others were fought by a combination of regulars and green men or by green troops alone. Whether because of the makeup of Taylor's force or because of a poor opinion of his tactics, contemporaries studied neither Palo Alto nor Resaca de la Palma. Even though the success of the mobile field batteries at Palo Alto was noted by many writers, no discussions of the lessons learned have come to light. Neither can there be found any consideration of the probably decisive role of small units at Resaca de la Palma. It is also clear from their memoirs that the leaders of Civil War armies did not view their Mexican War experience as particularly enlightening. Yet for most of the officers involved, the clashes along the Rio Grande served as their initial exposure to the realities of a major conflict. Whether acknowledged or not, Mexican battlefields were the practice grounds for the men who would become the field leaders of the two great armies that were to clash a decade and a half later.

4

First Bull Run, 19 July 1861

W. GLENN ROBERTSON

The complex web of constitutional, economic, political, and moral issues that for years had been generating tension among the states of the Union had become by 1860 too weighty for the American political system to resolve peacefully. The South had built an entire economic and social structure on a system of slavery, and many Southerners looked on any attempt to alter or eliminate the institution as an attack on the very foundation of their civilization. In sharp contrast, many Northerners fervently believed slavery to be an abomination that must be eradicated posthaste from all parts of the nation. For other Americans who cared little about slavery, the issue was simply a question of which held supreme power: the central government or the individual states. By autumn 1860, the opposing positions had become clearly delineated. When Abraham Lincoln, the antislavery candidate, was elected president, South Carolina led six other Southern states out of the Union. The seven subsequently formed a central government, the Confederate States of America. Now it was no longer a question of politics. If the Union were to be preserved, the federal government would have to apply military force. That meant the direct involvement of the United States Army, which had long attempted to remain aloof from the crisis.

On 31 December 1860, the strength of the U.S. Army stood at 16,367 officers and men, present and absent. Of the 1,108 officers, only 745 were present, while no more than 13,918 noncommissioned officers and enlisted men were at their duty stations. The Army was organized into nineteen regiments—ten of infantry, four of artillery, two of dragoons, two of cavalry, and one of mounted riflemen. No regiment was concentrated at any one location; instead, individual companies were distributed among large numbers of small posts scattered about the nation. Most of these posts were located in the western half of the country, reflecting the Army's primary mission of frontier protection. Of 198 company-sized units, 183 were stationed west of the Mississippi River or en route there. The remaining 15 companies either

81

watched the border with Canada, manned fixed fortifications on the Atlantic and Gulf Coasts, or guarded twenty-three arsenals. Indicative of the Army's emphasis on western deployment, there was one soldier available for every 129 square miles west of the Mississippi River and for every 1,300 square miles in the eastern half of the nation.[1]

General in chief of the U.S. Army in 1861 was Brev. Lt. Gen. Winfield Scott, hero of the war with Mexico. Born in Virginia in 1786, Scott had entered the Army in 1808 during the presidency of Thomas Jefferson. Rising to prominence in the War of 1812 because of his exploits on the Niagara frontier, Scott had become general in chief in 1841. His brilliant campaign from Vera Cruz to Mexico City in 1847 had further enhanced his position as the foremost American soldier of the age. An unsuccessful candidate for the presidency in 1852, Scott had clashed frequently with his civilian superiors during the 1850s and had moved the Army's headquarters to New York City. By the time the Civil War broke out, he had returned to Washington, but advanced age and poor health precluded his leading the Army in the field. Nearly seventy-five years old and unable to ride horseback, Scott nevertheless retained his mental faculties. He could provide the Army with strategic concepts, but younger commanders would have to implement them.[2]

Below Scott in the Army hierarchy were the chiefs of the eleven semi-independent bureaus and departments that composed the Army staff. The average age of these men at the time of the Fort Sumter crisis in 1861 was sixty-four, and six were over seventy. Similarly, the three general officers of the line in addition to Scott—Brev. Maj. Gens. John E. Wool and David E. Twiggs and Brig. Gen. William S. Harney—were all past their prime. Wool and Twiggs were in their seventies, while Harney, the youngster in the group, was sixty. None of the four generals of the line was a West Point graduate, and only Scott had experience in maneuvering more than 5,000 troops in a body. These men remained on active duty primarily because there was no provision for retirement on grounds of age or disability. Thus, when war came, the upper echelons of the Army's command structure would prove unequal to the demands placed on them.[3]

At lower levels of command, the problem was lack of knowledge. The deployment of the Army in minuscule detachments of company and platoon strength, while necessary for frontier police duty, seriously hindered officers from preparing for large-scale field operations. Unless a major Indian campaign were in the offing, the component companies of a regiment never gathered in one location. Even battalion-sized operations were rare. Because field exercises or maneuvers were unknown, officers had little or no opportunity to gain practical experience in maneuvering large tactical formations. Thus, tactical training for officers above the rank of captain was almost totally theoretical and lacked doctrinal foundation. Similarly, neither a theory of staff work nor practical staff training existed. As Confederate general Richard S.

Ewell so aptly remarked, prewar regular officers knew everything about commanding companies of fifty men and nothing about anything larger. In sum, the doctrine, training, and deployment of the U.S. Army on the eve of the Civil War was essentially that of a frontier constabulary, supplemented by a handful of coastal artillerists. Although occasionally overextended, such an army had served the nation well through 1860. The crisis of 1861, however, required a far different sort of force.[4]

In theory, the nation's militia stood ready to reinforce the Regular Army. Hallowed by traditions dating back to the days of Lexington and Concord, the militia had unfortunately been allowed to degenerate into relative impotence. Organized under the authority of the Militia Acts of 1792 and 1795, with subsequent modifications, more than 3 million officers and men were on the rolls as of January 1861. Of that number, 350,729 were credited to the seven states that had already left the Union. All such computations were meaningless, however, because many of the state rolls were badly out of date. Delaware's latest count dated from 1827, Indiana's from 1832. Other states were more current in their record keeping, but even so, the fact that a man's name was on the rolls did not indicate anything about his state of training or readiness. In fact, unless he belonged to one of the few organized companies that drilled regularly, a militiaman of 1861 probably had received no useful training whatsoever. Both the North and the South claimed a few militia companies that were militarily excellent, but they represented an exceedingly small proportion of the great unprepared mass.[5]

The inauguration of hostilities at Fort Sumter on 12 April 1861 found the military forces of the United States ill prepared to take action against the Confederacy. The units deployed on the frontier could not immediately withdraw from their distant stations without leaving the western settlements to the mercy of their Indian neighbors. In Texas, General Twiggs had surrendered 2,430 officers and enlisted men of the Regular Army when that state seceded from the Union. This force, approximately 16 percent of the Army, had been permitted to withdraw to friendly territory, but little more than half had done so by 12 April. The remainder therefore became prisoners of war and were unavailable for service until exchanged. This loss of experienced troops at the beginning of the conflict was a serious blow to Federal hopes.[6]

Unable to redeploy the Regular Army immediately, Lincoln initially chose to rely on the militia. The Acts of 1792 and 1795 empowered the president to activate militia units for three months in order to suppress insurrection. Utilizing this authority, Lincoln on 15 April 1861 called on the loyal states to provide a total of 75,000 men. In order for the burden to be shared equitably, the War Department assigned each state a quota of troops. Because their militia lists were obsolete, most states responded by activating their organized companies and recruiting their ranks to full strength with

individual volunteers. Patriotic fervor ran high and quotas were oversubscribed; 91,816 men eventually enlisted under this call. None, however,
were forthcoming from Virginia, North Carolina, Tennessee, and Arkansas,
which left the Union and joined the Confederacy. Rather than wait for the
passage of legislation creating additional military forces, Lincoln on 3 May
1861 increased the size of the Regular Army by ten regiments (22,714 men)
and called for an additional 42,034 volunteers to serve for three years. These
measures exceeded statutory presidential authority, but Congress ultimately
approved them retroactively. The small numbers involved have since been
criticized, in view of the enormous quantity of troops eventually needed, but
Lincoln was temporarily content.[7]

Among Union officials, only General Scott had any notion of how many
troops might be needed to crush the rebellion. Scott's strategic formulation,
which came to be called the Anaconda Plan, envisioned seizing the Mississippi
River valley, blockading the Southern coast, and ultimately squeezing the
Confederacy into submission. For these tasks, Scott estimated he needed a
land force of about 25,000 regulars and 60,000 three-year volunteers.
Although they proved to be totally insufficient, these estimates did not seem
unrealistic to the Lincoln administration in the spring of 1861, and no one had
any better estimates to offer. Scott believed the Regular Army to be the
Union's mainstay. Therefore, he decreed that it be retained in a body as a
solid nucleus of experience and a model for the volunteer units to emulate. He
rejected out of hand the alternative means of employing the regulars—as
teaching cadres to leaven the volunteer units. In an army of only 85,000 men,
the 25,000 regulars would be highly visible, as Scott intended, but if a much
larger force were required, the contribution of the regulars would dwindle into
relative insignificance. As the struggle increased in magnitude, Scott's
decision became increasingly controversial.[8]

The Confederacy did not have the luxury of beginning the conflict with a
regular army, no matter how small. As a result, the Confederate government
moved more rapidly than had the Lincoln administration to create military
forces, beginning its efforts even before the firing on Fort Sumter. On 6
March 1861, the Confederate Congress authorized President Jefferson Davis
to activate the state militias for six months and to accept up to 100,000 one-
year volunteers. At the same time, a Confederate Regular Army was created,
but it remained essentially a paper force throughout the conflict. The war
would be fought by volunteers, who initially were required to furnish their
own uniforms and horses. Davis called for 27,200 men before Fort Sumter
and asked for an additional 32,000 on 16 April. Just as in the North, strong
patriotic sentiment caused the early calls to be greatly oversubscribed.[9]

A number of former U.S. Army officers assisted the Confederacy in
organizing its forces. From the active officer corps of approximately 1,100
individuals, 286 left the Old Army by resignation or dismissal to join the

Confederate Army. Of these, 184 were graduates of West Point. In addition, 99 West Point graduates who had taken up civilian pursuits prior to 1861 offered their services to the Confederacy. Almost all of those who left the U.S. Army and took up arms for the South were Southerners by birth, but there were several exceptions, most notably Samuel Cooper of New York, adjutant general of the U.S. Army. Unlike the Union, which initially kept most of its experienced officers at their prewar rank, the Confederacy placed its trained commanders at the level where they were most needed, regardless of previous rank.[10]

Making use of a common military heritage, officers North and South proceeded to organize the thousands of patriotic volunteers. In the prewar U.S. Army, the highest permanent tactical formation had been the regiment, at full strength numbering just over 1,000 officers and men. In the war now beginning, regiments would be the building blocks from which larger formations would be constructed. Thus, the Federal volunteers were formed into infantry regiments of ten companies each, with a maximum authorized strength of 1,049 officers and men per regiment. Each regiment was commanded by a colonel, who was usually chosen by the governor of the state where the regiment originated. Officers below the rank of colonel were elected by the men. Confederate units were organized in a similar fashion.[11]

The most modern infantry shoulder weapon available to the combatants was the U.S. rifle musket, Model 1861, universally known as the Springfield from its place of manufacture, Springfield Arsenal in Massachusetts. It was a muzzle-loading, single-shot percussion rifle of .58 caliber, which fired a projectile weighing a little over one ounce. Accurate to 500 yards, it was lethal at double that range. Similar in performance was the Harpers Ferry rifle, Model 1855. Both these weapons were in relatively short supply in early 1861, and many of the militia and volunteer regiments began the war with the Model 1842 smoothbore musket. Some Confederate units were armed with flintlock muskets of an even earlier vintage.[12]

Cavalry and artillery weapons in 1861 were equally traditional. Horsemen relied foremost on the saber, with carbines and pistols as auxiliary arms. Artillerymen could draw on a variety of field guns, both smoothbore and rifled, but all were muzzle-loading. The newest and best weapons were the smoothbore twelve-pounder gun-howitzer, Model 1857 (the Napoleon), with a range of approximately 1,600 yards, and the rifled ten-pounder Parrott, Model 1861, which could fling its slightly smaller projectile almost twice as far as the Napoleon. Once again, the new guns were not universally available in 1861, causing both sides to press into service many older pieces such as the six-pounder gun and the twelve-pounder howitzer, both of which dated back to the 1840s.[13]

The doctrine that controlled the tactical employment of the weapons available in 1861 had changed little since the Mexican-American War.

Regiments still formed in close order, shoulder to shoulder, in two ranks, with one or two companies deployed slightly forward in open order as skirmishers. This system had worked well when the effective range of infantry weapons had been no more than 150 yards. Close-order formations permitted a large volume of fire while at the same time allowing officers to maintain control of their units with relative ease. As for artillery, the short range of infantry weapons allowed gunners to approach within 500 yards of a hostile line of battle and proceed to blow great gaps in the enemy's ranks. The resulting holes could then be exploited by an infantry bayonet charge or occasionally by cavalry.[14]

Unfortunately, the large-scale introduction of the rifled shoulder weapon into U.S. service beginning in 1855 made such tactics much less appropriate than in the days of the smoothbore musket. Armed with weapons having an effective range of over 500 yards, infantrymen could fire earlier at an advancing foe with much greater prospects of inflicting damage. Offensive movements, which all theorists recommended, were now potentially much more costly. As for artillery, no longer could guns be safely brought within canister range (400 yards) of an opposing line. Artillerymen thus would have to operate at greater distances from the enemy, where problems of range estimation, primitive fusing, and poor fragmentation of ammunition made them much less effective. Cavalrymen, who presented still larger targets, were even less useful than artillery on the battlefield itself and would soon be relegated to its fringes.[15]

The challenge to old tactical concepts wrought by the rifled shoulder weapon had not gone unnoticed. It had been recognized that the introduction of the new weapon required a new manual to replace Winfield Scott's *Infantry-Tactics*, whose basic form dated from 1835. In 1855, Major William J. Hardee published his *Rifle and Light Infantry Tactics*, which was officially adopted by the War Department for use with the rifle introduced that same year. Hardee accelerated the step rates of men in attack formation so as to reduce the time of exposure to defending fire, but his changes in the formations themselves were almost imperceptible. Similarly, the *Instruction for Field Artillery*, approved in 1860, and *Cavalry Tactics*, dated 1841, did not come to grips with the changing role of these arms on the modern battlefield.[16]

Little of this was apparent to the volunteers who flocked to the colors in the spring of 1861. Rather than ponder how technological change might require doctrinal change, newly chosen regimental and company officers searched wildly for manuals that would assist them in learning their jobs. No how-to-fight manuals existed. The only available tactical manuals were really no more than drill books. These were avidly studied by men innocent of even the simplest maneuvers. Some officers studied by night so as not to be embarrassed by day when giving commands on the drill field. Others openly carried the manual and referred to it before issuing an order. Seeing a lucrative opportunity, publishers rushed into print with any manual they could find, of whatever vintage. With hundreds of regiments forming under thousands of untutored officers, the demand for manuals was enormous, and volumes far less relevant than Scott's *Infantry-Tactics* saw publication once more.[17]

Armed with their well-thumbed manuals, regimental and company officers proceeded to train their men in the rudiments of soldiering. Winfield Scott strongly urged that commanders train their men as thoroughly as time would permit, but the War Department adopted no training program whatsoever, comprehensive or otherwise. For the three-month militia called up after Fort Sumter, there was hardly time for organization, much less training. Even in regiments that had enlisted for three years, training was left almost entirely in the hands of individual officers. Recruits first learned to march and execute the manual of arms. Companies then drilled individually and finally as part of a regiment. Some regiments expended considerable time on bayonet drill, probably more than was spent in target practice, and the amount of time devoted to each activity varied widely from unit to unit. Some regiments were well on their way to proficiency after only a few weeks, while others remained only armed mobs. Either way, few of the men composing the regiments formed in 1861 knew what lay ahead. In the words of a member of the 2d Wisconsin Infantry, "It is safe to say that not a man in the regiment knew anything of actual warfare, although nine companies, including mine, were organized from as many independent companies of state militia."[18] Such knowledge of war could be gained only through participation in a major battle.

In strategic terms, the requirements of the Union and the Confederacy were quite dissimilar. Desirous of restoring the Old Union, the North was forced to take offensive action to bring the seceding states back under Federal control before they marshaled their strength. In contrast, the Confederacy did not need to advance beyond its borders in order to maintain its independence, a firm defensive stance being sufficient. In the Eastern Theater, the proximity of the two capitals, Washington and Richmond, meant that the 100-mile corridor between them would likely be the scene of a major clash. Accordingly, both sides began to collect the bulk of their eastern forces along the Potomac River. Northern regiments gathered around Washington, while Virginia units occupied the line of the Potomac from Harpers Ferry in the west to Aquia Creek in the east. Once Virginia's voters ratified the state government's earlier decision to secede, Lincoln and Scott moved quickly to secure a buffer zone for Washington. Federal troops moved across the Potomac on 24 May and seized the heights south of the river as well as the city of Alexandria. Confederate forces, as yet few in number, fell back a few miles to the vicinity of Fairfax Court House and Centreville. Having secured the heights, the Federals laid out an extensive series of fortifications and initiated their construction. Behind the rising works, the green regiments resumed their haphazard training even as others were being organized throughout the North.[19]

Because General in Chief Scott was physically incapable of taking the field, commanders had to be chosen to lead the Federal armies in their inevitable advances. Scott, of course, had his favorite candidates—Robert Patterson and Joseph K. F. Mansfield—but these elderly officers did not meet with universal approval. Patterson, sixty-nine, had been Scott's second-in-command in Mexico. Initially assigned to secure Washington's line of communication through Maryland, he had been indecisive and dilatory in his movements. Nevertheless, Scott placed him in command of the troops opposing the Confederate units at Harpers Ferry. Scott wanted Mansfield, fifty-eight years old and General Zachary Taylor's engineer in Mexico, to command the army that was gathering at Washington, but Secretary of the Treasury Salmon P. Chase, who had assumed a large role in raising and organizing that army, instead favored a fellow Ohioan who had assisted him, Brev. Maj. Irvin McDowell. A forty-two-year-old West Pointer, McDowell had been commissioned in the artillery but had spent most of his career as an assistant adjutant general on the staff of the general in chief. At Chase's urging, McDowell was promoted to brigadier general along with Mansfield. Bowing to political pressure, Scott reluctantly appointed McDowell to lead the field force into Virginia but privately urged him to decline the position. Unsure that he was equal to the task, McDowell nevertheless accepted the assignment and formally assumed command of the Army of Northeastern Virginia on 28 May.[20]

South of the Potomac, the Confederacy also was picking its commanders. In mid-May, the force defending Harpers Ferry was given to Brig. Gen. Joseph E. Johnston, a fifty-four-year-old West Pointer from Virginia and former quartermaster general of the U.S. Army. Johnston had an outstanding record in the Old Army, and much was expected of him. Command of the force facing Washington passed through a succession of officers until the number of troops present justified the appointment on 31 May of the South's first bona fide hero, Brig. Gen. P. G. T. Beauregard of Louisiana, the victor of Fort Sumter. A classmate of McDowell's at West Point, the forty-three-year-old Beauregard had performed brilliantly as an engineer in the war with Mexico. His last assignment in the U.S. Army had been as superintendent of West Point. Like Johnston, Beauregard was expected to produce great victories for a public whose appetite had been whetted by his success at Charleston in April.[21]

Arriving at the front on 1 June, Beauregard quickly surveyed the strategic situation. He found Confederate forces in Virginia scattered from the mountainous regions of the western part of the state all the way to the coast at Norfolk. By mid-July, Beauregard's and Johnston's concentrations, 21,000 and 11,000 men, respectively, had become the major centers of gravity, but other units still guarded the mountains and watched the Federal troops at Fort Monroe. In addition, 3,000 troops under Brig. Gen. Theophilus H. Holmes were located at Aquia Creek, approximately thirty miles south of Beauregard. All of these forces had independent status, reporting directly to President Davis and his military adviser, Robert E. Lee.[22]

Originally located at Harpers Ferry, Johnston's troops had withdrawn from that indefensible position on 15 June and taken up a new position thirty miles southwest at Winchester in the lower Valley of Virginia. Fifty miles southeast of Winchester, beyond the Blue Ridge Mountains, Beauregard's army was concentrated around the small village of Manassas Junction, a site chosen for its strategic location. Lying between the major roads passing from Washington to Richmond, Manassas Junction was also the place where the Manassas Gap Railroad from the Valley of Virginia met the railroad route joining the two national capitals. This railroad network was the main supply route for both Johnston's and Beauregard's armies and therefore required as much protection as the Confederacy could provide. Equally important, the Manassas Gap Railroad represented a means of rapidly uniting the two Confederate forces on short notice, a possibility first noted by one of Beauregard's predecessors, Col. Philip St. George Cocke.[23]

While the Confederates pondered their defensive options, their opponents north of the Potomac came under increasing pressure to begin offensive operations. Few in the North, or the South for that matter, believed the war would be a long one. Instead, it was thought that the issue could be resolved by one great climactic battle, and the sooner that battle could be fought, the better. The Northern press began to chant, "Forward to Richmond," a call echoed first by the Northern public, then by their elected representatives. Knowing that the army was only half formed, Winfield Scott counseled delay, as did McDowell, but the press and public would have none of it: there must be an advance and it must be soon. Bowing to the inevitable, Scott in late June told McDowell to draw up an offensive plan of action for immediate adoption. The country desired a forward movement, and many militiamen wanted a fight before their three-month enlistment expired. Reluctantly, McDowell complied with their wishes and produced a plan by the end of the month. It called for a three-pronged advance against Beauregard at Manassas Junction. Without consulting McDowell, Scott set the date to begin the movement at 8 July.[24]

McDowell's plan, remarkably good for a man with so little experience, required that he face Beauregard's army alone. Patterson would have to keep Johnston occupied in the Valley in order for McDowell to have significant numerical superiority at Manassas Junction. Scott believed his friend Patterson could be relied on to play his role successfully, but others, recalling the

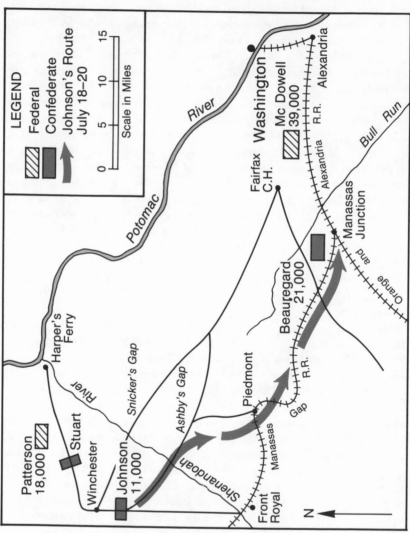

Map 4.1. Campaign of First Bull Run: Situation on the Night of 17 July 1861

War of 1812 veteran's performance in Maryland in mid-June, were not so sanguine. Certainly that operation—in which Patterson had crossed the Potomac River but had withdrawn to the Maryland shore after only three days in Virginia—had given little cause for optimism. Now, with more at stake, he crossed the stream again on 2 July and began a desultory advance that by 15 July had taken him only twenty miles beyond the Potomac. Halting at Bunker Hill, he confronted Johnston's army, barely ten miles away at Winchester.[25]

McDowell soon discovered that he would be unable to begin his campaign on the appointed date. Difficulties beset him on every hand. His soldiers were green, and experienced officers to train them were in short supply. Even worse, Scott's and Mansfield's animosity toward him led to maddening delays in the arrival of troops and supply wagons at McDowell's Virginia camps. His request for a further postponement of the advance so as to provide additional time for training was firmly denied because the enlistment period of the three-month militia would soon expire. Ready or not, McDowell had to take his army forward on 16 July. The army numbered over 35,000 men, the largest field force organized in North America to that time; yet none of its officers had previously commanded more than 500 men in action. Therefore, not long before moving, McDowell organized his forty-nine regiments and eleven batteries into brigades and divisions to facilitate their handling in the field.[26]

Brig. Gen. Daniel Tyler, sixty-two, commanded McDowell's 1st Division, consisting of the brigades of Brig. Gen. Robert Schenck, fifty-one, and Cols. Erasmus D. Keyes, fifty-one; William T. Sherman, forty-one; and Israel Richardson, forty-five. Tyler, Keyes, Sherman, and Richardson were all West Point graduates, while Schenck was a politician and diplomat with no military training whatsoever. Six of their fifteen regiments were composed of three-month militia nearing the end of their term of service. The others, who had enlisted under Lincoln's second call for volunteers, were even more inexperienced. Supporting the infantry, however, were four batteries of light artillery from the Regular Army. By virtue of his age, Tyler was considered to be McDowell's senior subordinate, although he had been out of the service since 1834. His division was the largest, numbering 12,795 officers and men.[27]

Col. David Hunter, fifty-nine, led McDowell's 2d Division. Reputedly one of the ugliest men in the Army, Hunter was also a West Point graduate, as was one of his two brigade commanders, Col. Ambrose Burnside, thirty-seven. The other, Col. Andrew Porter, forty-one, had been a Regular Army officer since 1846, with extensive service in Mexico and the Southwest. Three of their seven regiments were short-term militia, but Porter's brigade was strengthened by eight companies of U.S. Regular Infantry organized into a battalion under Maj. George Sykes, and seven companies of U.S. Regular Cavalry similarly organized under Maj. Innis Palmer. A battalion of 348 U.S.

Marines also was attached to Porter's command, but its fifteen experienced officers and sergeants led recruits even newer to the service than were the militia and volunteers. Artillery support was provided by a Regular Army battery, a volunteer battery, and two howitzers dragged along by an infantry regiment. Altogether, Hunter controlled over 6,000 men.[28]

McDowell's 3d Division was commanded by Col. Samuel P. Heintzelman, fifty-five. Heintzelman and his brigade commanders—William B. Franklin, thirty-eight; Orlando Willcox, thirty-eight; and Oliver O. Howard, thirty—all were graduates of the U.S. Military Academy; the first three had considerable field experience. Only three militia units were among their twelve regiments, but five of the others had been in existence for fewer than six weeks. The 2d Vermont had, in fact, been in Federal service for only twenty-six days. Two Regular Army artillery batteries were assigned to support Heintzelman, giving him a grand total of 9,062 men.[29]

McDowell's 4th Division, commanded by New Jersey Militia Brig. Gen. Theodore Runyon, was unbrigaded. It consisted of four three-month regiments from New Jersey and four three-year regiments—three from New Jersey and one from New York. Although they had been in service longer than many other regiments in McDowell's army, their reliability was suspect and little role was envisioned for them. This was unfortunate because they numbered 5,448 officers and men.[30]

Rounding out the army was the 5th Division of Col. Dixon S. Miles, fifty-seven. Miles was a Regular Army officer, known for his unfortunate fondness for alcohol. His two brigade commanders, Cols. Louis Blenker, forty-nine, and Thomas Davies, fifty-one, were relatively inexperienced soldiers. Davies was a West Pointer, but he had resigned two years after graduation; Blenker's only service had been in Europe's revolutionary upheavals of 1848. Between them, Blenker and Davies controlled eight regiments, whose average time in Federal service was about sixty days. Supporting them were two Regular Army batteries and a militia battery from New York. The total number of Miles' troops stood at 6,173.[31]

On 16 July, the day that McDowell's green army ponderously got into motion, Beauregard's Confederate Army of the Potomac consisted of seven brigades of varying sizes. Six were commanded by West Point graduates: Brig. Gens. Richard S. Ewell, James Longstreet, and David R. Jones, and Cols. Nathan G. Evans, Philip St. George Cocke, and Jubal Early. The seventh brigade commander, Brig. Gen. Milledge L. Bonham, although not a West Pointer, had seen service in the Seminole and Mexican-American Wars. Cocke was the oldest at fifty-two, while Jones and Evans were in only their mid-thirties. Five were veterans of the conflict with Mexico; of those five, Early had seen no combat there. Evans, Ewell, and Longstreet had had extensive service on the frontier in the Old Army. Like their Federal counterparts, however, none of them had acquired any experience in leading troop units of the size they now commanded. Bonham's 1st Brigade was the largest in Beauregard's army, with over 4,000 men; Evans' 7th Brigade was the smallest, numbering only about 1,100. Longstreet and Cocke each controlled over 3,000 men in their 4th and 5th Brigades, but Ewell, Jones, and Early had about a thousand fewer in their 2d, 3d, and 6th Brigades. Supporting the infantry were twenty-five artillery pieces and approximately 1,500 cavalry.[32]

Knowing that McDowell would most likely have Manassas Junction as his goal, Beauregard deployed his brigades forward of that point to shield it. Bonham's, Ewell's, and Cocke's units outposted Fairfax Court House, Fairfax Station, and Centreville, while the remainder deployed behind Bull Run, a stream which flowed in a southeasterly direction midway between Centreville and Manassas Junction. Normally a placid body of water, Bull Run represented a substantial obstacle to an attacker because its banks were relatively precipitous. Unfortunately, this defensive advantage was negated somewhat by the availability of numerous crossing points that provided easy access to the Confederate side. From Union Mills Ford on his right to the Warrenton Turnpike's Stone Bridge on his left, Beauregard had at least eight potential crossing places to watch, with still others both upstream and down. At none of the crossings did he erect fortifications.[33]

Believing that the most likely Federal avenue of approach would be the direct Centreville–Manassas Junction road on his right center, Beauregard weighted his right flank accordingly. When the outlying brigades retired behind the stream, the army would be concentrated in accordance with his preconceived notion of McDowell's intentions. Ewell's brigade, composed of Alabama and Louisiana regiments, would hold the army's right at Union Mills Ford and the Orange and Alexandria Railroad Bridge. Bonham's, Longstreet's, and Jones' brigades, with regiments from South Carolina, North Carolina, Mississippi, and Virginia, would guard McLean's, Blackburn's, and Mitchell's Fords on the direct approach to Centreville. Behind them in reserve would be Early's brigade of Virginians, Louisianans, and Mississippians. Upstream, Cocke's Virginia brigade would cover the widely separated Island and Ball's and Lewis' Fords. Beyond Cocke, Evans would anchor the left of Beauregard's line at the Stone Bridge with a South Carolina regiment and a Louisiana battalion. Supporting each front-line infantry brigade would be a flag signal system devised by Capt. Edwin Porter Alexander. The entire line would stretch about six miles.[34]

McDowell's Army of Northeastern Virginia began its advance on the afternoon of 16 July. The divisions of Tyler, Hunter, Heintzelman, and Miles each moved in separate columns, while Runyon's men remained behind in the Arlington defenses as a reserve. None of the troops was accustomed to marching any great distance, and most were burdened with excess baggage.

The load carried by the troops hardly mattered on the first day's march because the distance to be traveled was short, but on the following day the dilatory pace of McDowell's soldiers began to affect operations. As the hours passed and the day grew hotter, more and more men dropped out to seek water or pick blackberries along the roadside. These delays kept McDowell from meeting his timetable. He had hoped to advance rapidly enough to bag the small force of Confederates at Fairfax Court House, but these easily eluded his slow-moving columns. Their reports of the magnitude of the Federal Army, when added to other reports Beauregard had received from spies in Washington, convinced the Confederate commander that the long-awaited Federal advance had begun.[35]

By the time his leading elements occupied Fairfax Court House around 1200 on 17 July, McDowell knew that the element of surprise was lost. He wanted to continue the advance to Centreville but realized that his men were too exhausted to move further without a rest. In addition, he was unsure of the location of Heintzelman's division. With all circumstances favoring delay, he acquiesced and ordered a halt. Once his divisions were concentrated, he intended to threaten Beauregard's Bull Run position with one division while outflanking the Confederates to the east with the remainder. This, however, required a preliminary reconnaissance of the road net and terrain south of Fairfax Court House. Momentarily without his principal staff officers, McDowell took it upon himself to survey the countryside on 18 July. At the same time, he ordered Tyler, whose division was in the lead, to march to Centreville and seize the town. Once at Centreville, Tyler was to reconnoiter the roads beyond it, but under no circumstances was he to bring on an engagement.[36]

On learning that McDowell had begun his advance, Beauregard implemented the plan to concentrate his army behind Bull Run. Throughout 17 July, Bonham, Cocke, and Ewell slowly withdrew their brigades toward the stream, keeping just ahead of the lethargic Federal columns. When the day ended, they were either behind Bull Run or nearing it. As his advanced guards fell back, Beauregard sought reinforcements from the Confederate government in Richmond. Jefferson Davis responded by placing several regiments under orders to move north as soon as the necessary transportation could be collected. He also directed Brigadier General Holmes to bring his brigade north from Fredericksburg to Beauregard's assistance. The largest source of troops, of course, was Johnston's Army of the Shenandoah. Late in the day, Adjutant General Cooper wired Johnston to join Beauregard "if practicable," but the message did not reach Johnston's headquarters at Winchester until early on 18 July. Frustrated by the delays, Beauregard doubted that the reinforcements could arrive before McDowell did.[37]

The events of 18 July did not go according to plan for Irvin McDowell. First, his reconnaissance of the country clearly showed that the road net was inadequate to permit the bulk of his army to maneuver around Beauregard's eastern, or right, flank. With his initial plan of battle no longer feasible, McDowell ordered the remainder of his army to follow Tyler to Centreville. Before arriving there, he learned that Tyler had exceeded his orders and was engaged in battle at Blackburn's Ford. Riding toward the sound of the guns, he soon discovered what had happened. After occupying Centreville without a shot, Tyler had pushed Richardson's 4th Brigade down the road leading to Manassas Junction. In his efforts to discover the strength of the Confederate units barely visible beyond Blackburn's Ford, Tyler had gotten Richardson's men into a small but sharp engagement. The Federals had been roughly handled by Longstreet's and Early's brigades, losing eighty-three men in the process. Disgusted with Tyler's disobedience, McDowell ordered him to stand his ground to avoid demoralizing his troops. Once McDowell was gone, however, Tyler withdrew his command to Centreville where it joined the rest of the army. News of Tyler's rebuff quickly spread among the other divisions, lowering the morale of the troops.[38]

Uncertain what to do next, McDowell spent the next two days at Centreville completing the organization of his army, bringing forward supplies, and reconnoitering the Confederate positions behind Bull Run. He also devised a new plan of operations, announced on 20 July. Tyler's division, minus Richardson's brigade, was to move forward along the Warrenton Turnpike early on the morning of 21 July and make a serious demonstration against the Confederates in the vicinity of the Stone Bridge. Meanwhile, Hunter's and Heintzelman's divisions would march northwest by a circuitous route and cross Bull Run at Sudley Springs Ford and Poplar Ford, respectively. Once south of Bull Run, Hunter and Heintzelman would roll up the Confederate line, driving it to the southeast and away from the Manassas Gap Railroad, Johnston's route of approach. When the Stone Bridge was uncovered by the progress of the Federal flanking column, Tyler would send his brigades across Bull Run to add their weight to the attack. Miles' division, reinforced by Richardson's brigade, would provide rear-area security by holding Centreville and guarding the road to Mitchell's and Blackburn's Fords. Far in the rear, Runyon's division would protect the army's line of communication to Washington. Once again, much depended upon Patterson's holding Johnston in the Valley so he could not reinforce Beauregard.[39]

The two days McDowell spent at Centreville gave the Confederates an opportunity to significantly increase their forces along Bull Run. In the early morning hours of 18 July, Johnston finally received authority to transfer his army to Manassas. Before moving, he first had to arrange for the care of his sick, who numbered almost 1,700. In addition, he had to be relatively certain that Patterson's army would not interfere with his departure. In the event, Johnston had no difficulty disengaging from Patterson, who, confused about his mission, had withdrawn several miles to Charlestown on the previous day.

Masking his intentions with a cavalry screen under Col. J. E. B. Stuart, Johnston started his five brigades on the road to Ashby's Gap in the Blue Ridge Mountains. From there his men turned south toward Piedmont, a station on the Manassas Gap Railroad only thirty-four miles from Manassas Junction.[40]

Johnston's leading brigade, composed of five Virginia regiments, was under the command of Brig. Gen. Thomas J. Jackson. A thirty-seven-year-old West Point graduate who had been brevetted twice for gallantry in the war with Mexico, Jackson most recently had been a professor at the Virginia Military Institute. West Pointers also led three more of Johnston's brigades, those commanded by Brig. Gen. Barnard Bee, Brig. Gen. E. Kirby Smith, and Col. Arnold Elzey. Bee and Smith were the same age as Jackson but had graduated from the military academy a year earlier than he. Both had extensive Mexican and frontier service to their credit. Elzey, forty-four, had fought the Seminoles and also had been brevetted for gallantry in Mexico. Rounding out Johnston's small command was the brigade of Col. Francis S. Bartow, a Georgia lawyer and legislator.[41]

Jackson's brigade departed Winchester at 1200 on 18 July and marched seventeen miles. The other brigades followed and halted four miles behind Jackson. Early the next day, Jackson marched six miles further to Piedmont Station and entrained. Departing Piedmont at 1000, his brigade arrived at Manassas Junction during the afternoon. The other brigades reached Piedmont during the same afternoon, but the capacity of the railroad prohibited sending forward more than two additional regiments that day. These belonged to Bartow's brigade. On 20 July, Johnston himself boarded one of the trains along with two more regiments and part of a third, all from Bee's brigade. Except for Johnston's five artillery batteries and Stuart's cavalry regiment, which moved by road, Beauregard would receive no more reinforcements before the day selected by McDowell for the battle. Fully three-fifths of Johnston's army still awaited transportation at Piedmont.[42]

Johnston joined Beauregard near Manassas around noon on 20 July. Armed with a telegram from Jefferson Davis for support, he assumed command of the Army of the Potomac later that day by virtue of his pending commission as a full general. Having arrived too late to make a complete survey of the ground or of troop dispositions, he was briefed on the situation by Beauregard. The latter also persuaded Johnston to endorse his proposal to envelop the Federal force Beauregard expected would momentarily strike Blackburn's Ford. As a result, Jackson's, Bee's, and Bartow's regiments joined Holmes' brigade in reserve positions behind the Confederate right flank. Weary after several days and nights of intense activity, Johnston then retired for the evening, leaving Beauregard and his staff to prepare orders for the morning's advance. Poorly conceived and even more poorly drafted, the orders were not ready for Johnston's signature until 0430 on 21 July.[43]

McDowell's battle plan called for Tyler to get an early start from Centreville so as to clear the road for the flanking column of Hunter and Heintzelman. Much depended on Tyler. As the leading division, his troops were bivouacked in such a way that any delay in their movement would derange the timetable of the entire operation. Once at Bull Run, Tyler had to be convincing in his demonstration at the Stone Bridge or the Confederates might redeploy their units to meet the turning column if it were observed. After the Stone Bridge was uncovered by the five brigades of Hunter and Heintzelman, Tyler was to add the weight of his three brigades to the general assault. Tyler was apparently still smarting from McDowell's rebuke on 18 July. Then, he had exceeded his orders; now, he was determined not to do so.

Tyler's orders called for him to be on the road at 0230, but it was over an hour later before Schenck, Sherman, and Keyes got their green troops moving. Schenck, in the lead, was extremely cautious, and dawn was breaking by the time his skirmishers reached the vicinity of the Stone Bridge. Behind Schenck, Federal troops clogged the Warrenton Turnpike for several miles awaiting their turn to move. Finally, McDowell intervened and ordered Keyes' brigade into the fields so that Hunter and Heintzelman could turn off to the right and begin their flanking march. Around 0600, Tyler began his demonstration. Momentarily it appeared threatening, but as the hours passed, Colonel Evans, whose troops faced Tyler, became suspicious. By 0830, Evans had become convinced that Tyler's demonstration was a feint. A few minutes later he received two messages, one from pickets on his left and the other from Captain Alexander on his signal tower at Manassas Junction. Both messages indicated that a large column of Federals was marching toward Sudley Springs Ford several miles beyond Evans' left flank.[44]

Seizing the initiative, Evans left four companies of South Carolinians to amuse Tyler while he took the remainder of the 4th South Carolina regiment and the 1st Louisiana Battalion north to meet McDowell's flanking column. "Hopelessly outnumbered, he had but one thought, and that was to attack." His opponents, meanwhile, had just reached Sudley Springs Ford. The plan called for the crossing to be made by 0700, but it was more than two hours later that Burnside's brigade of Hunter's division splashed across the stream. Urged on by McDowell, the remainder of Hunter's troops, followed by Heintzelman's division, crossed Bull Run and headed south. Within a mile, Burnside's leading regiment, the 2d Rhode Island, came under fire from Evans' small force of fewer than 1,000 men and two guns, now deployed in the woods on Matthews Hill. Rather than bring up more regiments to develop the Confederate positions, Burnside initially deployed his remaining units to the right rear. Division commander Hunter did not alter Burnside's arrangements and, indeed, went forward with the 2d Rhode Island. Almost at once he received a severe wound and was carried from the field. Command of the division then passed to Colonel Porter, who brought forward his brigade to

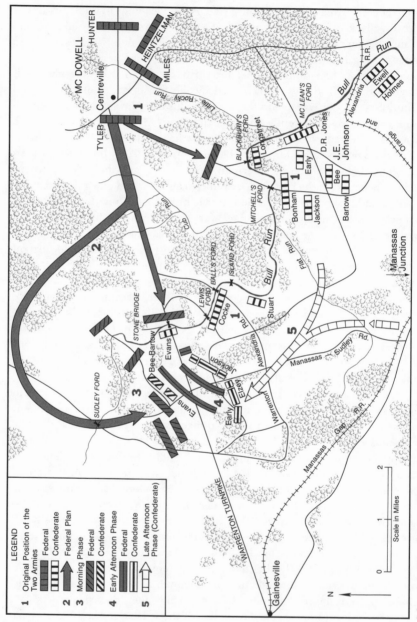

Map 4.2. The Battle of First Bull Run, 21 July 1861

extend Burnside's right. Together, the two Federal brigades dueled with Evans' handful of men for over an hour. Gradually they overlapped Evans' line and threatened to destroy his little command. Outnumbered six to one in both men and guns, Evans grimly clung to the Matthews Hill position.[45]

Five miles away on the Confederate right flank, Beauregard was preparing to implement his own offensive when he learned of the Federal approach. Believing there was still time to attack some of McDowell's units, he issued another unclear set of orders to the brigades on the right of his army. Some brigade commanders never received the orders, others received them and were confused, and at least one found himself isolated because of them. As a precaution, Beauregard at 0700 with Johnston's approval directed Bee and Bartow to take their four regiments to the left to support Evans and Cocke. Jackson's brigade also was sent slightly to the left but not as far as Bee and Bartow. Having committed his reserves before a major Federal attack materialized, Beauregard joined Johnston behind Mitchell's Ford, the place where he now expected the battle to develop.[46]

By the time Bee moved his and Bartow's regiments to the vicinity of the Stone Bridge, the hard-pressed Evans was about to lose Matthews Hill. Instantly aware of what was happening from the direction of the firing, Bee carried his command forward into the fight without hesitation. Bartow joined him, and together the four fresh Confederate regiments extended Evans' line. Thus reinforced, the Confederates held their ground, even when Franklin's brigade of Heintzelman's division joined Porter around 1100. The total Confederate force amounted to no more than 4,000 men, but the inability of the Federal commanders to use their numerical superiority made the fight an equal one until noon. At that time, Sherman's brigade of Tyler's division crossed Bull Run by a farm ford north of the Stone Bridge and came in on the Confederate flank. Sherman's attack, coupled with the arrival of more of Heintzelman's men at the other end of the Federal line, was too much for the depleted Confederate units. In danger of being overwhelmed if they stayed on Matthews Hill, they hastily withdrew across the Warrenton Turnpike and Young's Branch and finally tried to reestablish their line on the slopes of Henry House Hill.[47]

The delays that had cursed McDowell all morning now were seemingly of no consequence. When Keyes' brigade of Tyler's division followed Sherman over Bull Run and Howard's brigade crossed at Sudley Springs Ford, McDowell had a total of seven brigades west of the stream. Evans, Bee, and Bartow had fought gallantly, but their commands were now in ruins. A final assault might finish them. All McDowell had to do was to keep his brigades moving forward. Yet this proved difficult to accomplish. Burnside's and Porter's units had become disorganized by the morning's fight, and the former was given permission to rest and resupply his men in the rear. Howard's regiments were still coming forward and had not yet deployed.

Rather than remain in a central position where his subordinates could find him, McDowell dashed from place to place arranging individual regiments in line. Try as he might to press the assault, McDowell found his army slow to respond.[48]

On Henry House Hill, an open plateau 300 yards wide by a half-mile long, the retreating Confederates discovered the fresh brigade of Brigadier General Jackson. Supported by several batteries, the Virginians were deployed just below the eastern rim of the plateau, which shielded them from much of the Federal fire. Like Bee and Bartow earlier, Jackson had exceeded his orders and marched his brigade to the sound of the firing. Now he kept his men under cover, preserving them for the coming Federal assault. Arriving on the hill, Bee conferred briefly with Jackson, then rode off to rally what was left of his brigade for a charge. Before moving forward, he made the soon-to-be-famous comment, "There is Jackson standing like a stone wall." Opinions vary as to the meaning of Bee's remark. Whatever his intention, the name "Stonewall" forever after identified both Jackson and his brigade. Bee himself was never to explain his statement because he was mortally wounded a few moments later during a futile charge.[49]

Not long after Bee's misfortune, Beauregard and Johnston reached Henry House Hill. Together with Evans and Bartow, they tried to rally the disorganized remnants of three brigades and align them to the left and right of Jackson's unshaken troops. As an example, Johnston even attempted to carry forward the regimental standard of the 4th Alabama, which had lost all its field officers, but he was dissuaded by the color bearer. Colonel Bartow adopted the same tactic and paid for it with his life when he was struck down by a Federal bullet. Nevertheless, the men were momentarily steadied, and a semblance of order returned to the Confederate line stretched along the southeastern edge of the plateau. Seizing on the lull, Beauregard persuaded Johnston, the senior commander, to return to the rear and control the flow of reinforcements now rushing forward from the Confederate right. Johnston, who later claimed that he had assigned Beauregard to the front-line role, rode back about a mile and did as Beauregard had suggested.[50]

With units that Johnston sent forward and others that arrived on their own, Beauregard was able to strengthen his battle line to around 7,000 men by 1330. He was still heavily outnumbered by McDowell's forces, which now prepared to make their final push against Henry House Hill. In order to assure a successful infantry assault, McDowell directed that the regular artillery batteries of Capts. James Ricketts and Charles Griffin advance to the crest of the hill and bombard the Confederate line at close range. Both battery commanders had strong doubts about placing their guns in such an exposed position, but McDowell's orders, as transmitted by his chief of artillery, were peremptory. Assured that they would be supported by the 11th and 14th New York regiments, they obediently went forward. One of Griffin's guns, which had been disabled earlier, remained behind, but the eleven other pieces made it to the crest around 1430.[51]

The artillery tactics McDowell was employing with Ricketts and Griffin were standard practice in the war with Mexico, in which batteries posted just out of musket range decimated enemy infantry. The rifle musket of 1861, however, made such tactics virtually suicidal, especially when the promised infantry support failed to materialize in any meaningful way. For a while, Ricketts and Griffin held their own, but after a cavalry charge by J. E. B. Stuart and a volley from Jackson sent their infantry supports reeling to the rear, the batteries were isolated. Seeing their predicament, Col. A. C. Cummings of the 33d Virginia Infantry regiment, Jackson's brigade, marched his men to within fifty yards of the flank of the batteries and opened fire. Observing their approach, Griffin had wanted to fire on them but had been dissuaded by McDowell's chief of artillery, Maj. William Barry. Possibly confused by the 33d's blue uniforms, Barry believed they were the artillery's supports. A volley from Cummings' men removed all doubts about their identity and also destroyed Ricketts' and Griffin's batteries. Numbers of artillerymen, including Ricketts, went down, but the most serious blow was the loss of the horses needed to extricate the weapons from their exposed position. Only two guns were saved from the debacle; the others stood unmanned in the midst of the battle.[52]

For over an hour, the battle lines swept back and forth across the plateau with neither side able to gain a decisive advantage. Ricketts' and Griffin's guns were taken, lost, and recaptured several times. On the Federal side, Hunter's division, now under Porter, was no longer a factor in the struggle, most of its regiments having withdrawn from action. Franklin's and Willcox's brigades of Heintzelman's division and Sherman's brigade of Tyler's carried on the battle on the Henry House Hill. Keyes' brigade, with Tyler's apparent blessing, somehow wandered out of the fight, and Schenck's never crossed Bull Run, although the Stone Bridge was now unguarded and the obstructions cleared. Of those brigades that were actively engaged, not one used its strength in a concerted effort. Instead, the brigade commanders sent their regiments forward one at a time, thereby dooming their assaults to failure. Instead of bringing order out of this chaos, brigade and division commanders, as well as McDowell himself, led individual regiments into action. In this way, division commander Heintzelman received a serious wound and was forced to leave the field temporarily.[53]

As the fight for the plateau continued, each side brought up reinforcements. Howard's brigade, the last of Heintzelman's units to arrive, was sent by McDowell to the Federal right. There it was countered by two regiments dispatched by Cocke and two by Bonham, their movement to the field being directed by Johnston. Still, Howard overlapped the Confederate left, until Brigadier General Smith arrived with a brigade from Manassas Junction. The last of Johnston's units to arrive from the Valley on 21 July, Smith's three regiments had detrained at 1230 and marched directly into the fight. Ordered by Johnston to take the brigade toward the Confederate left, Smith was in the process of doing just that when he was seriously wounded. Colonel Elzey then assumed command and completed the move to the far left. There he found himself on Howard's flank. A quick volley and a charge sent Howard's men reeling to the rear.[54]

Precipitated by Elzey, the withdrawal of the units on the Federal right was hastened by the arrival of still another Confederate brigade—Early's. Summoned by Beauregard from the vicinity of Blackburn's Ford around noon, Early reached the field sometime around 1600 and added the weight of his three regiments to Elzey's drive. When Cocke appeared at the same place with another of his regiments, the Federal right flank crumbled rapidly. Sensing that the decisive moment had arrived, Beauregard ordered his entire line to charge. Recoiling from the Confederate attack, the already disorganized Federal brigades became even more intermingled. Soon all semblance of order was lost, and it was every man for himself. To one observer, it seemed as if McDowell's men suddenly and simultaneously decided they had fought long enough and were ready to go home. Seized with the idea of leaving the battlefield, they disregarded all efforts of their officers to rally them. Indeed, many officers themselves were in the forefront of the scramble to depart.[55]

As the Federal retreat gained momentum, McDowell's command simply disintegrated. On the road to Sudley Springs Ford, only Major Sykes' eight companies of regular infantry were well enough in hand to form a rear guard, and they successfully protected the disorganized mob that fled in that direction. Keyes' brigade performed a similar function for those fragments that withdrew via the Stone Bridge and adjacent fords. Beauregard and Johnston tried to hasten the retreat with several relatively fresh regiments, but most of their units were badly positioned for pursuit. A few cavalry detachments harassed the fleeing Federals, and a lucky shot from a Confederate battery blocked the bridge over Cub Run, causing the abandonment of numerous guns and wagons. Larger efforts, however, proved abortive. An attempt to drive on Centreville with Longstreet's and Bonham's brigades failed, partially because the two brigade commanders disagreed over how to proceed. Because Richardson's brigade and Miles' division blocked their way, it is unlikely they could have achieved anything even had their advance continued.[56]

It has been argued occasionally that Beauregard and Johnston missed an opportunity either to march on Washington or complete the annihilation of McDowell's army on the evening of 21 July. In support of this theory, much has been made of the utter chaos into which the Federal retreat degenerated. The scenes of abandoned guns and baggage, dazed men, and cowardly officers all have basis in fact, but they represent only one side of the story.

Beauregard's and Johnston's men had suffered as heavily as the Federals and were almost as disorganized. Further, night was approaching, and much of McDowell's army had been untouched by the fighting. Three brigades held Centreville, and Runyon's division was not far behind them. By no stretch of the imagination could the exhausted Confederates have pushed aside the remaining Federal units in the darkness and marched across the Potomac into Washington. If the losers of the battle were only too human, then so were the victors. Green troops, no matter how elated, could do only so much. Wisely, Beauregard and Johnston contented themselves with the fruits of their victory, while McDowell led his battered army into the defenses of Washington. The first major battle of the Civil War was over.[57]

Compared with what would come later, the casualty toll had not been especially heavy for either side, though both then thought it horrendous. Federal losses were finally tallied at 460 killed, 1,124 wounded, and 1,312 missing, for a total of 2,896 from an army of just over 39,000. Left behind on the field were 27 cannon; nearly 100 wagons, caissons, and limbers; 4,000 rifles; a half-million rounds of small-arms ammunition; and tons of miscellaneous equipment. This booty cost the Confederates at least 387 killed, 1,582 wounded, and 13 missing, for a total of 1,982 men from an army of about 32,000. In neither army were the losses equally distributed. Jackson's and Bee's brigades had suffered most on the Confederate side, while those of Holmes, Ewell, Longstreet, Bonham, and Jones saw little or no action. For the Federals, the brigades of Sherman, Porter, and Willcox sustained the greatest casualties; Schenck's, Blenker's, and Davies' had minimal losses. Officer casualties were severe in both armies because the inexperience of their troops forced them to place their own lives at risk even more freely than was customary. For the Confederates, Bee and Bartow were killed, Jackson and Smith wounded. Federal division commanders Hunter and Heintzelman were wounded, while brigade commander Willcox was both wounded and captured. Four colonels commanding regiments were killed, two on each side, and one Confederate regiment, the 4th Alabama Infantry, lost every one of its field officers.[58]

For the victors, Beauregard became the hero of the battle, although he had in fact provided little more than an inspirational presence in the front line. His major tactical decisions were few and had little effect on the outcome. In contrast, Johnston's adoption of a less glamorous role in the army's rear allowed him to affect the course of events significantly. Johnston spent the day directing the arrival of reinforcements and was instrumental in producing the combination on the Confederate left that precipitated the Federal collapse. Both he and Beauregard were well served by capable brigade commanders. Evans, Bee, Bartow, and Jackson all showed large amounts of initiative. Indeed, had Evans not acted as he did during the morning's fight, the battle probably would have been lost to the Confederates before they could reorient their line. Certainly Henry House Hill would not have become the focal point of the battle.[59]

From among the losers a scapegoat had to be found, and the mantle settled eventually on McDowell. Yet McDowell had done some things well. He had produced an excellent plan on short notice after Tyler and an inadequate road net had negated his initial formulation, and he had done it alone. The plan required Patterson to keep Johnston's troops occupied in the Valley, which seemed a reasonable assumption. Confused by telegrams from Scott and by his own inadequacy, Patterson failed miserably and therefore must bear much of the blame for what happened on 21 July. His failure made the two days McDowell spent at Centreville loom large in the Federal defeat because Johnston used the time to bring several thousand Confederates to Manassas Junction by rail. No doubt McDowell should have spent less time at Centreville, but the reasons for doing so seemed compelling to the com-mander of a very inexperienced army. Had Patterson fulfilled his role, McDowell's delay at Centreville would not necessarily have been fatal.[60]

Once on the battlefield, the Federal divisional structure did not prove particularly useful as a means of control. Hunter was wounded early, Heintzelman busied himself with details, and Tyler proved to be a downright hindrance. Brigade commanders generally fought creditably, but none seemed inspired except Sherman. Like Beauregard, McDowell spent most of his time arranging regiments when he should have been directing larger units. Though almost all were West Pointers, the Federal commanders seemed to have spans of vision no larger than a regimental front. This unfortunate narrowness of view was the result of their previous experience in the small frontier constabulary that was the prewar U.S. Army. A wider perspective would eventually come to many officers but not until they had been longer in command of such larger units.[61]

As might have been expected from their common military heritage, similar shortcomings permeated both armies. Each side used less than its full strength. McDowell brought no more than 18,000 men across Bull Run and probably used fewer than 10,000 of those at any one time. Beauregard gainfully employed only about 17,000 of his available 28,000. Like the Federals, most of the Confederate officers thought in terms no larger than a regiment. As a result, both sides tended to fight the battle a regiment at a time. This fault was most prevalent at brigade level but extended upward as well. Staff work for both Federal and Confederate commanders was abysmal. Crucial orders were poorly conceived, poorly written, and all too frequently went astray between sender and recipient. The art of reconnaissance was sadly neglected by both armies, but it cost the Federals most dearly in terms of lost time. As for the men, most of them equally inexperienced and only partially trained, they eagerly went where their officers sent them, no matter how inappropriate the place. With few exceptions they had little to be ashamed of on 21 July. The blind panic that gripped many Federals late in the day was unfortunate but was due more to the ineffectual leadership of their officers than to some innate inadequacy of the rank and file. Veterans, of course, would have marched faster, deployed more quickly, and been more steady in retreat, but veterans were almost nonexistent on the field of Bull Run in July 1861.[62]

The few regular formations present during the battle performed as well as their numbers and situation permitted. Although seldom called upon, George Sykes' small battalion of regular infantry fought skillfully, retained its unit integrity, and successfully covered the broken army's retreat. Less was accomplished by Innis Palmer's battalion of regular cavalry, which was scattered on peripheral duties by higher authority. The nine batteries of regular artillery also were dispersed among individual infantry brigades, and their performance was determined by the uses to which infantry commanders put them. Although the tactics that sent them to Henry House Hill were misguided, Ricketts' and Griffin's regular batteries fought there in the highest traditions of the American artillery. As for the battalion of U.S. Marines, nearly all were recruits, even greener than the volunteers, and they participated equally in the rout.[63]

While the opposing armies lay in their respective camps around Washington and Manassas pondering what had happened to them, their governments attempted to derive lessons for the future. As the defeated party, the Federals were quicker to institute changes. Upon learning the magnitude of the disaster, Abraham Lincoln called Maj. Gen. George B. McClellan from western Virginia on 22 July to assume command of both Mansfield's department and the fragments that had been McDowell's army. One of the new commander's first acts was to establish a provost guard to restore discipline. He then set to work rebuilding the army. There would be no shortage of raw material with which to work. Galvanized into action by the defeat at Bull Run, Congress on 22 July authorized the president to accept up to 500,000 three-year volunteers. The three-month militia regiments left for home by the beginning of August, but hundreds of new volunteer regiments soon were springing up to take their place. A similar process occurred in the South, where the Confederate Congress authorized the recruitment of up to 400,000 three-year volunteers on 8 August. Thus, one of the first effects of Bull Run was to show that the war just begun would require significantly larger amounts of manpower than had previously been thought necessary.[64]

Unfortunately, no major changes in the offensive tactical doctrine that would govern employment of the new masses of recruits were evident following the first Battle of Bull Run. Obviously, the rifled shoulder weapon had conferred new strength on the tactical defensive, a strength soon to be enhanced by the gradual introduction of field entrenchments as the war progressed. Bull Run allowed many officers to experience firsthand the effects of the new infantry weapon, but no lessons learned there altered accepted practice. Indeed, few such lessons could be discerned four years later at the end of the war. Throughout the conflict, commanders struggled without notable success to overcome the defensive power of the rifle musket. The use of thin lines of skirmishers to precede the traditional close-order formations became gradually more common with each succeeding campaign, but no conceptual breakthroughs occurred. Try as they might, officers could see no way to open up their formations significantly without a corresponding loss of command and control. Thus, countless more brave but foolhardy charges, like those on Henry House Hill, would be made during the war at an appalling cost in lives. At the end of the conflict, technology was still far ahead of tactical thinking.[65]

Just as in tactical doctrine, no changes in weaponry came about as a result of the first Battle of Bull Run. Infantry units on both sides eventually received variants of the Springfield rifle musket or the comparable British Enfield, but this process had been set in motion before the battle and depended on manufacturing capacity rather than on lessons learned on the plains of Manassas in 1861. Cavalry units both North and South played little role in the fight, and the changes needed in their armament would not be apparent for some time yet. Eventually, Northern industry would provide Federal cavalrymen with breechloading and repeating carbines, making them a potent striking force, but such developments were many months in the future. As for artillery, the latest American technology appeared at Bull Run in the form of the new rifled guns, which were used alongside the older smoothbores, making direct comparison possible. With their range advantage often unusable and, indeed, offset by ammunition problems, the rifled guns did not prove superior to the older weapons. Federal artillerymen, in fact, tended to prefer the bronze smoothbores, but manufacturing techniques were both simpler and cheaper with the iron rifles. As a result, when the Federal Army next took the field, rifles predominated in field batteries. Once again, the primary factors governing selection of a weapon excluded any experience derived from the first Battle of Bull Run.[66]

One technological innovation that did prove its worth at Bull Run was the railroad. Troops had been moving by rail in Europe for at least thirty years, but the value of railroads in field operations had only begun to be apparent during the Franco-Austrian War of 1859. The transfer of over 7,000 of Joseph Johnston's men from Piedmont Station to Manassas Junction in time to win the day at Bull Run furnished an even more graphic example of how railroads could affect the conduct of military operations. Before the Civil War was over, both North and South would employ railroads to move entire army corps over vast distances, dwarfing the pitiful efforts of the Manassas Gap Railroad in 1861. Railroads also made it easier to supply the much larger armies the struggle at Bull Run called into being. Their importance in both supply and movement having been recognized early, railroads increasingly became the targets of those same armies and were destroyed accordingly. Important rail centers such as Corinth, Mississippi; Atlanta, Georgia; and Petersburg, Virginia, would eventually join Manassas Junction as military objectives. The Civil War was truly a railroad war, and Bull Run was only the first of many campaigns in which victory rode the rails.[67]

Other lessons, too, were derived from the first Battle of Bull Run. Formerly lax in the extreme, training and discipline showed marked improvement in both armies after 21 July. Because no officially sanctioned program of training was ever promulgated by the war departments of either North or South, responsibility for training resided at a relatively low level throughout the war. There, experience proved to be a great teacher. For those officers present, Bull Run provided a stern object lesson in what could happen when inadequately trained and poorly disciplined troops took the field. When the veterans of the battle moved on to other commands, their experiences at Bull Run remained vivid, and they incorporated that hard-won wisdom into their training schedules. As a result, the new volunteer regiments would undergo much more rigorous drilling than had those which fought in July 1861. Target practice still tended to be haphazard, but at least the new formations would be better able to march and maneuver under fire the next time battle was joined. No matter how high they rose in rank, some officers never forgot this lesson of Bull Run. In fact, William T. Sherman, one of those who had stormed Henry House Hill, as a corps commander instituted one of the best training programs seen in the Federal Army during the conflict. Others less renowned than Sherman responded in similar fashion.[68]

In terms of organizational structure, McDowell's creation of divisions to facilitate command-and-control proved to be a step in the right direction, although its advantages were not readily apparent on 21 July. Not long after taking command, McClellan established a formal brigade structure with regiments permanently assigned to particular brigades. The Confederate brigade structure crystallized along similar lines, with regiments from the same state usually being brigaded together, unlike Federal practice. In mid-October, McClellan established a formal division structure (with McDowell as a division commander), and in 1862 he arranged the divisions into army corps. These changes, too, soon were adopted by the Confederates. Under the new Federal structure, artillery batteries were assigned to divisions rather than to infantry brigades in hopes that greater concentrations of firepower might be achieved when necessary. Confederate artillerists took this concept one step further in 1863 by grouping their batteries into battalions, which were then assigned to army corps. Federal gunners adopted a similar organization shortly thereafter. In each case, the reorganization was made to improve the potential value of artillery on a battlefield where changing technology had threatened to render artillery impotent.[69]

As for leadership, the first Battle of Bull Run had an almost instant effect in two ways on the North. An act of 22 July 1861 created military boards whose task it was to examine the "qualifications, propriety of conduct, and efficiency" of volunteer officers. These boards were a progressive step in efforts to eliminate incompetence within the officer corps. Although they were more successful in removing inefficient junior officers than senior officers from command, their effect nevertheless was salutary. Many officers voluntarily resigned rather than face a board. In the first eight months of the boards' existence, at least 310 officers either were dismissed by them or were reassigned. Fear of the boards kept an unknown number of others from accepting commissions. The second personnel action produced a similar result. This act, passed on 3 August 1861, established a retirement program for officers with either physical disability or forty years of service. Under its provisions, numerous elderly officers were eased into retirement, making their positions available for more energetic men to fill. Scott himself lingered until 1 November 1861 when, worn out from his struggles with a disrespectful McClellan, he voluntarily left the service. Ironically, his earlier call for delay in mounting offensive operations now was heeded by the Lincoln administration. McClellan would be granted the time McDowell had been denied to build an effective army.[70]

Many of those officers present at Bull Run on 21 July would go on to win far greater fame before the war ended. Sherman and Jackson are perhaps the best known, but they led a large host who would rise high in the ranks of their respective officer corps by 1865. Douglas Southall Freeman has identified at least fifty-one Confederates present on the field who were either generals already or would attain general officer status. The Federal list of Bull Run veterans who became general officers is equally extensive. Not all were uniformly successful as they climbed the ladder of rank and position, but they were forever linked by the baptism of fire they had received on 21 July 1861. Never again would they or their men be as inexperienced as on that day. If the first Battle of Bull Run proved nothing else, it showed that the raw material existed for molding capable American armies. Given suitable doctrine and training, appropriate equipment and organization, and intelligent leadership, Americans made excellent soldiers. In some respects at least—training, organization, leadership—the largest battle yet fought in North America provided the basis for improvement that would allow wise commanders eventually to bring that excellence to the fore.[71]

5

San Juan Hill and El Caney, 1–2 July 1898

GRAHAM A. COSMAS

When President William McKinley decided to use armed force to expel the Spanish from Cuba in 1898, the United States Army was in the midst of a prolonged period of organizational, technological, and doctrinal change. The standing Regular Army consisted, as it had for the previous two decades, of about 25,000 officers and men in ten regiments of cavalry, twenty-five of infantry, and five of artillery—the latter increased to seven soon after the U.S.S. *Maine* blew up. These units were scattered over the continent in more than seventy posts. The Army had no permanent tactical organizations larger than a regiment and was administered by geographical military departments and a group of staff bureaus, the whole presided over by a secretary of war and a major general commanding who spent much of their time feuding as a result of unclear lines of authority. The War Department contained no agency for contingency planning or for systematically coordinating the activities of staff and line. A generation of bare-bones budgets had left the Army without reserves of weapons and equipment for mobilization and had kept the Endicott coast defense program—the Army's major peacetime project—perennially behind schedule.

Yet within budgetary and institutional restrictions, a creative minority of officers—Civil War veterans and younger men imbued with a new sense of professionalism—were obtaining War Department, and occasionally congressional, support for piecemeal improvements copying European practices; and they were discussing more ambitious reforms designed to prepare the Army for at least limited colonial wars against major industrial nations. During the 1880s and early 1890s, the Army acquired rifled breechloading field and siege artillery and also its first bolt-action, smokeless-powder-magazine rifle, the .30-caliber Krag-Jörgensen. The Army made some progress in assembling forces for training and rapid mobilization. The 77 posts garrisoned in 1898 represented a considerable reduction from the 120 of a decade before. Most stations now contained at least three companies, and nearly half the infantry were located at regimental-size posts. Units of all arms followed regular training schedules, with considerable time devoted to marksmanship, open-order tactics, and company- and battalion-level field problems. Improvements in recruiting, pay, enlistment terms, and on-post amenities reduced desertion in the enlisted force and (assisted by the economic depression of the early nineties) enhanced personnel quality. In the War Department, Maj. Gen. Comd. John M. Schofield (1888–95) did much to improve relations between himself and the secretary of war and between the staff bureaus and the line. Unfortunately, his successor Maj. Gen. Nelson A. Miles undid much of Schofield's work. In the Military Information Division of the adjutant general's office, a rudimentary intelligence and mobilization planning agency took shape. Most important, changes in selection, promotion, and retirement systems and a network of advanced schools were by 1898 revitalizing the lower ranks of the officer corps. In summary, the Army on the eve of war with Spain was reasonably well equipped, thoroughly trained at the small-unit level, and contained at least a minority of leaders ready to use the approaching crisis to advance various reforms.[1]

The influence of reformist leaders was especially evident in War Department mobilization plans. Those plans in turn were related to an interservice effort, extensive for that time, to work out in advance how to fight a war against Spain. The Navy, through its War College and ad hoc boards, undertook operational planning as soon as the Cuban insurrection broke out in 1895. Army officers, drawn largely from the Military Information Division, joined in later, after President McKinley, his diplomatic efforts to restore peace in Cuba frustrated by Spanish intransigence and governmental instability and by the blowing up of the *Maine,* reluctantly began preparing for armed intervention. Both services envisioned a largely maritime campaign, fought for the limited objective of compelling Spain to leave Cuba under conditions compatible with U.S. strategic and economic interests in the island. They anticipated only a modest expeditionary role for the Army, requiring relatively small mobile forces rather than the mass armies of the Civil War.

The War Department, influenced by the ideas of 1870s reformer Emory Upton and by the new intellectual currents in the Army, initially proposed to provide the necessary forces by temporarily enlarging the Regular Army. In February, as part of accelerated military preparations following the *Maine* disaster, Secretary of War Russell A. Alger asked Congress for authority to augment the standing Army to over 100,000 men by adding recruits to existing units and by expanding each infantry regiment to three four-company battalions—a reorganization long desired to improve command-and-control of the infantry in open order. Alger argued that the enlistment of additional men in Regular organizations under professional officers would produce an effective force more rapidly than a muster of volunteers in new units under inexperienced commanders.

Alger's proposal ran afoul of the state militias, now called the National Guard, which had undergone a military revival of their own and had become an effective special-interest lobby. The Guard, appealing to the mythology of the citizen soldier and traditional fears of a large standing army, engineered congressional defeat of the War Department bill early in April 1898, barely two weeks before the opening of hostilities. It forced the creation of a volunteer army with regiments organized and officered by the states on the Civil War pattern and in practice formed around the existing National Guard. Eventually, McKinley called into service 200,000 of these volunteers and enlisted another 20,000 or so—including the well-publicized 1st Volunteer Cavalry (the Rough Riders)—directly under federal auspices. These numbers, which the War Department had not anticipated employing and had made no advance preparations to assemble, equip, or supply, were calculated more to accommodate the National Guard's demand for a piece of the action and to provide an outlet for patriotic enthusiasm than to meet expected military requirements.

In spite of this setback, which led to severe administrative and supply difficulties during the months of hostilities, the War Department persisted in its intention to rely as far as possible on regulars for the actual fighting. Even as McKinley and Alger were negotiating with the National Guard, they also, in mid-April, concentrated most of the Regular infantry, cavalry, and field artillery at Chickamauga Battlefield Park and at the Gulf ports of New Orleans, Mobile, and Tampa to constitute a force in readiness. As part of the legislative compromise with the state militiamen, Alger obtained authority to recruit the regulars up to a total of 60,000 men for the duration of the war and to reorganize the infantry regiments. The supply bureaus gave the regulars priority for scarce arms and equipment. For example, the Ordnance Department confined issues of the Krag-Jörgensen rifle to the regulars and the Rough Riders (who benefited from their lieutenant colonel's political prominence) and furnished the volunteers with the obsolescent single-shot Springfield. The War Department managed to assemble most of the volunteers in large federal camps by mid-June; but very few of the state regiments, even by the most optimistic reckoning, would be anywhere nearly prepared for operations for another month. Hence, not by accident, the regulars and a few of the volunteers who were ready early would fight the first decisive actions in Cuba.[2]

Where those actions would take place was not at first apparent. President McKinley had no wish to attack the 200,000 Spanish troops in Cuba if he could avoid it. He and his advisers believed that American battle casualties in any extensive land campaign would be multiplied manyfold by those from the deadly tropical diseases, notably yellow fever, prevalent in the war-devastated island. Fortunately for the Americans, Spain's expeditionary force, already fully engaged against some 35,000 Cuban insurgents, lived on imported foodstuffs. The American leaders assumed correctly that a naval blockade of Cuban ports, supplemented by destruction of as much of the Spanish fleet as ventured into the Caribbean, would induce the enemy to give up. Under these conditions, American land operations would be aimed at hastening an inevitable end, discouraging European intervention on behalf of Spain, or seizing a bridgehead in Cuba to strengthen the United States' political position in negotiations with Spain and with the rebels, who were more cobelligerents than true allies.

Influenced by these considerations, McKinley adopted an initially cautious strategy. On 23 April, as soon as Spain rejected a final American withdrawal demand, the Atlantic fleet under Rear Adm. William T. Sampson closed Havana and other Cuban ports. The Army prepared to launch a hit-and-run raid with regulars from Tampa to show the flag and deliver arms to the rebels in central Cuba. Commodore George Dewey's victory at Manila Bay on 1 May, which dramatically exposed Spanish weakness, led to a change in plans. McKinley, besides sending troops to the Philippines, now directed the Army to attack Havana, Spain's Cuban seat of government and principal fortress, as soon as it could get together the required 50,000 troops, transports, and supplies. Because mobilization barely had begun, the War Department, to the embarrassment of Secretary Alger, who tended to over-promise, inevitably had to postpone the starting date, much to the annoyance of McKinley and of Secretary of the Navy John D. Long, who saw the chance of an early end to the war slipping out of reach. The administration nevertheless remained committed to the Havana assault until late May. To lead the invasion, it transferred all the regulars from Chickamauga, New Orleans, and Mobile to Tampa, only a short voyage from Havana. When the War Department organized army corps, the regulars so assembled became the V Corps, under Maj. Gen. William R. Shafter.

While trainloads of men and stores were rolling into Tampa much faster than the newly organized corps and base staffs could dispose of them and chartered steamers were gathering in the harbor, McKinley altered plans again. This time, the change resulted from the long-delayed arrival in the Caribbean of Spain's Atlantic battle squadron, which had left its Cape Verde Islands anchorage on 29 April and had not been sighted since. U.S. Navy commanders, in common with European experts, greatly overrated the offensive capabilities of Adm. Pascual Cervera's four poorly maintained armored cruisers and three torpedo-boat destroyers. Therefore, from the time the Spanish vessels appeared off Martinique on 13 May, Admiral Sampson's fleet concentrated on finding and destroying them. After Cervera, on the nineteenth, took refuge in the harbor of Santiago de Cuba—protected by high coastal bluffs, forts, and a narrow, mined entrance channel in which Sampson refused to risk battleships—Secretary Long requested Army assistance in rooting him out. Long and Sampson wanted troops to capture the forts at the harbor mouth, assuming that if they could be neutralized, the fleet could remove the mines, steam into the bay, and duplicate Dewey's feat at Manila.

Santiago also offered the possibility of decisive land action, which McKinley had sought since early May. With 45,000 inhabitants, the city was the second most important in Cuba after Havana and was the capital of the island's eastern province. Not as strongly garrisoned or fortified as Havana, Santiago lacked road and rail connections with the capital and the more populous western end of the country where most Spanish troops were located. Its mountainous hinterland was controlled by Gen. Calixto Garcia's insurgent army, the largest and best organized Cuban force and the only one capable of more than small-unit guerrilla action. Since the beginning of hostilities, the blockading fleet and the army at Tampa had established regular communication with Garcia. They could count on him to prevent reinforcement of Santiago by the other garrisons in eastern Cuba and to assist any American landing and assault on the city.

For a variety of reasons, then, McKinley and his cabinet on 26 May decided to abandon the Havana attack for the time being and instead send the V Corps against Santiago. They would follow up the expected early capture of that city with an invasion of Puerto Rico by V Corps elements reinforced with volunteers, then move against Havana in the autumn if Spain did not capitulate. In a series of telegrams, sent between 26 and 31 May, the War Department directed General Shafter to embark the V Corps. He was to sail to Santiago under naval convoy and there assist in destroying the Spanish fleet (how was not specified), and he was to capture the city and its garrison. These orders set the Army in motion toward its first battles in the Spanish-American War.[3]

As finally organized, the V Corps included two divisions of infantry and one of dismounted cavalry. Each infantry division, as prescribed in the law creating the volunteer army, consisted of three brigades, each composed of three regiments. The cavalry division included two three-regiment brigades. An independent brigade of two regular infantry regiments and a cavalry squadron (the equivalent in that arm of a battalion) with horses, which embarked at Mobile, joined the corps a few days before it left Tampa. Directly under corps control were a provisional field artillery battalion of four batteries, two batteries of siege artillery, two engineer companies, and a Signal Corps detachment with an observation balloon. The corps was supposed to have had a third infantry division of volunteers, but Shafter took to Santiago instead the better armed and trained regular cavalry. Only three volunteer regiments—the 71st New York, the 2d Massachusetts, and the Rough Riders—accompanied the corps from Tampa, although others joined it later in the campaign. The V Corps included eighteen of the twenty-five prewar regular infantry regiments and five of the ten cavalry. Arriving at Tampa at peacetime strength, these regiments embarked before they could receive additional wartime recruits and form their third battalions. Most went to Santiago with 400 to 500 men in eight companies organized in two battalions/ squadrons. By contrast, the volunteer infantry regiments, with their three full battalions, were more than twice as large in manpower. Aside from the volunteers, it was essentially the long-service standing army that sailed for Santiago, although few junior officers, noncommissioned officers, and enlisted men, a decade after the end of the major Indian campaigns, had experienced any combat.[4]

The corps left Tampa as well armed, equipped, and supplied as it could have been at this point in mobilization. Its regular units were outfitted with the new small-arms and artillery pieces adopted during the previous ten years. The corps possessed a provisional battery of four Gatling guns with crews detailed from the infantry and commanded by 1st Lt. John H. Parker, an early and ardent machine-gun advocate. It had as well an assortment of other rapid-fire and mountain guns and an experimental dynamite gun, distributed among the infantry and cavalry. Sufficient ammunition, rations, medical supplies, and field transportation arrived at Tampa before the corps embarked. However, because of procurement and production delays, the troops lacked hot-weather clothing and had to wear the traditional blue wool shirts and trousers; the field artillery had only black powder ammunition; and the volunteer infantry still carried their old Springfields. Enough reserve Krag-Jörgensens were available with which to remedy the latter deficiency, but Shafter did not seek an exception to general War Department weapon-issue policy for the 71st New York and 2d Massachusetts.[5]

The V Corps was at least partly prepared to fight with the relatively modern weapons it possessed. American infantry tactics in 1898 were based on the squad and platoon and emphasized open, irregular order and maximum use of cover and firepower. From platoon to division, units of all sizes were to form for battle in both width and depth, with an extended firing line, supports, and reserves. In the attack, the firing line was to deploy several hundred yards from the defense and to advance by rushes until, strengthened by the support elements, it could build up fire superiority. Then the reserves would come forward for a final mass assault. Infantry still were to do most of their firing by platoon volley to ensure effective control and concentration. Nevertheless, the tactics of the 1890s, in a radical departure from the old close-order methods, decentralized the direction of troops in combat to battalion- and company-level officers and NCOs and required of them a high degree of individual judgment and initiative. Field-artillery doctrine, on the other hand, lagged behind technological change. American artillerymen still relied on direct fire, visually controlled by the battery commander; and manuals called for guns to be advanced right up to the skirmish line—a suicidal maneuver against the infantry rifles then available.[6]

At company and battalion levels, the troops assembled at Tampa had practiced these tactics at their peacetime stations; they continued to do so in their Florida camps. However, the V Corps conducted no larger battle exercises. A cavalry officer complained that in most brigades, the regiments "have never practiced attacking together"; he doubted whether "half of them have ever practiced attacking at all as regiments." Until they landed near Santiago, the divisions never maneuvered as such. Inasmuch as a brigade or division attack in extended formation was a more complex operation and required different relationships among the various command levels than did a similar close-order attack, the absence of large-unit training threatened to reduce to near chaos the execution of any ambitious battle plan.[7]

Career officers of long Regular Army service—many now holding higher-ranking volunteer commissions—commanded the divisions and brigades of the V Corps. Most were not West Point graduates, however, having entered the service as volunteers in the Civil War and remained after Appomattox. Their military education consisted primarily of experience, usually in leading small units and administering posts and geographical departments. By odd coincidence, the only academy man among the senior commanders and the only one who had led more than a regiment in combat was Maj. Gen. Joseph Wheeler of the Cavalry Division, an ex-Confederate whom McKinley appointed to the Volunteer Army as a gesture of North-South reconciliation and to encourage a shift of conservative Dixie Democrats to the Republican Party. Within the limitations of their training, these officers displayed competence and great personal courage. Yet, even in the case of Wheeler, they knew little of the planning and direction of battle with the new weapons and tactics. In addition, many regimental and company officers, after years of slow promotion, were well over forty years old; the physical hardships of tropical campaigning would weigh heavily on them.[8]

The corps commander, Major General Shafter, was representative in most respects of the officers beneath him. A Civil War volunteer from Michigan with a good record as a company officer, he transferred to the regulars and did well in frontier and Mexican-border commands. Rising slowly through the ranks, he obtained his brigadier general's star in 1897 and commanded the Department of California until the war broke out. His seniority in the Army and a general reputation for aggressiveness and common sense brought Shafter promotion to the volunteer rank of major general and his assignment to the V Corps. However, the sixty-three-year-old major general was grossly overweight, nearly to the point of incapacity for active duty. He possessed no divisional or higher command experience. On the positive side, Shafter worked diligently to prepare himself for his mission. He had some awareness of the potentialities of the new weapons; he supported

Parker's effort to form the Gatling battery. Shafter directed operations as actively as his poor physical condition allowed; his major decisions probably were the best available solutions to the problems he faced.[9]

Shafter and the other commanders worked with staffs that were primitively organized by today's standards, composed of officers largely new at their jobs. At corps and division headquarters, the commander's assistants included several aides-de-camp, often relatives or sons of friends, and a collection of officers from the various bureaus who performed work appropriate to their specialties. No functional sections existed, and no one was formally designated deputy commander or chief of staff. Ordinarily, the adjutant general informally coordinated the work of the rest of the staff and helped his general direct operations. At V Corps headquarters, the capable West Pointer Lt. Col. Edward J. McClernand performed strongly in both roles. The hastily assembled corps staff included mostly regulars with long bureau service but little experience in large tactical organizations. Lower staffs contained many officers transferred from the line and civilians recently commissioned under the Volunteer Army law. As might be expected, headquarters performance at the outset left something to be desired. Inspector General of the Army Maj. Gen. Joseph C. Breckinridge understated the case: "Nearly every officer is performing unwonted duties, even among the regulars, so there are some of the usual indicators of unfamiliar occupations."[10]

The effects of command and staff inexperience in managing large operations became evident as the V Corps embarked. Delay and confusion characterized the effort from the first loading of stores on 26 May to the last stampede of troops onto their improvised transports on 8 June. It turned out that the Quartermaster Department had overestimated the carrying capacity of the thirty-one vessels—mostly small, shallow-draft coastal freighters—it had collected for the expedition. To place on board as much of his combat force and its equipment as possible, Shafter left behind many wagons and ambulances, the cavalry division's horses, and tons of baggage and supplies. The corps commander expected this cargo, as well as more troops, to follow him within a short time on additional transports the Quartermaster Department was trying to obtain from the none-too-large American merchant marine. Shafter managed to embark about 17,000 officers and men, 300 civilian teamsters and stevedores, 16 field guns, 8 siege guns and howitzers, the Gatlings and other light artillery, over 2,200 horses and mules, almost 200 wagons, and 7 ambulances. The corps had no lack of supervision. Eighty-nine journalists, 15 foreign military observers, and Inspector General Breckinridge and his staff accompanied the first major United States overseas expedition since the Mexican War.[11]

The V Corps completed its embarkation in a great hurry (which accounted for much of the confusion) in response to War Department demands that it sail before Cervera managed to escape. Then the transports, crowded with sweltering troops, waited for several days in Tampa Bay while the Navy investigated and found false a report of Spanish warships off the Cuban coast. Shafter used the time to redistribute men and stores, correcting some of the jumble caused by hasty loading. Some units conducted disembarkation drills, the men climbing down the ships' sides on cargo nets in World War II fashion. On 14 June, the long columns of steamers and their Navy escorts at last put to sea. After an uncomfortable voyage on the overloaded, poorly ventilated ships, the expedition made its rendezvous with Sampson's fleet off Santiago on the twentieth.[12]

Santiago de Cuba, capital of the province then of the same name (now called Oriente), lies on the southern coast of the island near its eastern extremity. The city itself is about five miles from the sea, located at the landward end and on the eastern shore of its spacious bay, which is landlocked except for a narrow entrance dominated by high bluffs. In this part of Cuba, the coastline rises abruptly from the water in steep cliffs, broken infrequently by the valleys of small rivers and offering few beaches suitable for landing an army. Inland, rolling country cut up by the same rivers and streams extends for about twenty miles to the rugged mountains—the Sierra Maestra—that form most of the interior of Santiago province. Years of guerrilla warfare, which had gone on intermittently in this region since 1868, had left the countryside devastated and depopulated, with the ruins of sugar mills and plantation houses here and there and an occasional miserable hamlet garrisoned by Spanish troops. Only in the city of Santiago and its immediate environs and in the valley extending northward from the head of the bay into the mountains did anything resembling normal civilian life continue. There, also, the country was comparatively open, with patches of cultivation. Elsewhere, tropical forest and the impenetrable Cuban brush, the *manigua,* covered the land. Major troop movements were possible only along the few roads, which themselves were narrow, unpaved trails, at times running along the beds of streams.

The Spanish commander in Santiago, Maj. Gen. Arsenio Linares y Pombo, had charge of defending both the city and its province and was subordinate directly to Captain General of Cuba Ramon Blanco y Arenas at Havana. Linares' command—nominally an army corps but in fact a collection of static garrisons—included about 28,000 armed men, 13,000 of whom were in Santiago and its vicinity. Of Linares' other troops, major contingents defended Guantanamo, about 40 miles east of Santiago, and Manzanillo, 100 miles to the west. Smaller forces garrisoned a couple of minor north-coast ports. Linares' troops were deployed more to deny military and political control of territory to the insurgents than to mass for a decisive battle with the Americans. Once the United States Navy stopped sea movement around the island, the lack of roads in the interior, insufficient field transportation, and

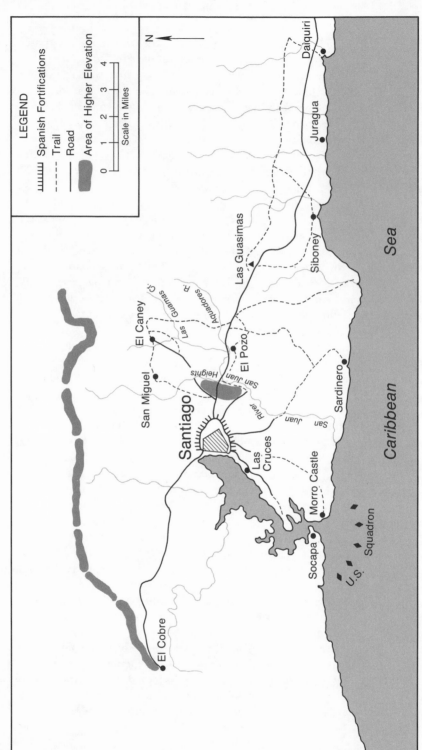

Map 5.1. Santiago de Cuba and Vicinity: The Theater of Operations

rebel opposition would have prevented the concentration of all Linares' forces at Santiago even had he chosen to attempt it, but he did not. After Shafter's fleet arrived, Linares did call in limited reinforcements from Manzanillo. On 22 June, a column of 3,500 troops from there, under Col. Federico Escario, broke through a Cuban covering force and began an epic march eastward over mountain trails, fighting its way through repeated insurgent ambushes. Reports of Escario's strength and progress were to influence significantly the timing of Shafter's major attack.

Spanish regulars, mostly infantry with small cavalry, artillery, and engineer contingents, made up about half of the force at Santiago. These troops were conscripts from the Iberian Peninsula, men largely from the poorer classes swept up by an inequitable draft. Nevertheless, the Spanish soldiers, led by officers seasoned in years of bush warfare, could put up a determined fight, especially on the defensive. Their clothing and equipment suited the climate, and they were armed with clip-fed, bolt-action Mauser rifles firing smokeless cartridges. Roughly equivalent to the regulars in leadership, equipment, and combat value were 1,000 sailors from Cervera's fleet, organized into eight infantry companies to augment the land forces. The rest of the defenders were a mixed lot. They included *Volontarios,* local militia recruited from peninsular Spanish townsmen and government functionaries; *Guerrillas,* Spanish and Cuban irregulars noted for skill and cruelty in counterinsurgency; and municipal policemen and firemen. These troops carried Remington rifles comparable to the American Springfield. Except for the *Guerrillas,* they served primarily in static defense and internal-security assignments. The garrison had the advantage of extensive fortifications that included a continuous inner line of trenches and artillery positions completely surrounding Santiago and outlying blockhouses of stone or wood banked with earth at most militarily important locations, built over the years to support a counterinsurgency strategy based largely on static defense. Usually sited for mutual support, with good fields of fire, these fortifications incorporated such modern features as slit trenches and the first barbed-wire entanglements American troops were to encounter on a battlefield. On the other hand, the Spaniards had no machine guns. Their artillery consisted of two small modern fieldpieces and sixteen obsolescent muzzle-loaders converted to breechloaders on fixed mounts in the main city perimeter. Dooming the defense in the long run, the blockaded city was short of food for both troops and civilians; disease kept up to 25 percent of the garrison always in the hospital; and the majority of the citizenry actively or passively supported the insurgents. Spain had never prepared Santiago to withstand siege or assault by a regular army; a pervasive sense that the city must fall loomed among military and civilians alike.

Linares' troop dispositions and apparent objectives reflected the attitude that his defense was at best a delaying action. He garrisoned the harbor entrance forts of El Morro and Socapa with about 400 men each and dispersed the rest of his regulars and a good many of the *Volontarios* in two "lines of observation." One of these, along the seacoast, covered the likely American disembarkation places east and west of the harbor entrance but nowhere in enough strength to do more than harass a full-scale landing. The other line— really a series of separate positions blocking roads or protecting towns— guarded the city, both shores of the bay, and the road and railway leading to the northern valley from which Santiago drew its water and a trickle of foodstuffs. This line also protected Escario's approach route from the northwest. Linares kept many of his regulars west of the bay to ward off Cuban insurgent General Garcia, who had assembled about 5,000 Cubans on that side near Aserradero. American military commentators then and since have condemned Linares for thus dispersing his forces, but his dispositions conformed to the Spanish preoccupation with denying places to the insurgents at almost any cost. His widespread troops, with the advantage of firepower and fortifications, were sufficient to hold off the poorly armed and none-too-aggressive Cubans. They at least could delay an American advance. Linares appears to have had no thought of defeating Shafter's army in a pitched battle. Instead, his aims were to inflict American losses, buy time for a decision on what Cervera should do, and perhaps force a stalemate in front of the city, or extricate the bulk of his army from Santiago with the aid of Escario's column. If these were his intentions—and the paucity of available Spanish documentation prevents an authoritative answer—Linares employed his weak force in a rational, if uninspired, manner.[13]

Primarily from Cuban rebel contacts, Shafter learned much of the foregoing, at least in outline, before he left Tampa. He began working out a campaign plan during the voyage to Cuba. After reaching Santiago, Shafter held a strategy conference on 20 June with Sampson and Garcia at the latter's headquarters at Aserradero. What he learned there confirmed the corps commander's intentions. He selected for landing places Daiquiri and Siboney, two villages about fifteen miles east of the harbor entrance that had usable beaches and small wharves built by an American-owned iron mining company. From Siboney, the closer to Santiago of the two, what passed in the region for a highway led over the hills to Santiago, about fifteen miles away. Shafter, discarding the Navy concept of attacking the harbor entrance forts, planned to advance the V Corps along this road and assault or besiege Santiago from the north and east. If successful, this maneuver, initially proposed by General Miles before the army had embarked, would capture the garrison and compel Cervera, his land base and source of coal and water gone, to surrender or run out of the bay under Sampson's guns.

Miles and Shafter believed that this strategy would produce decisive results on both land and sea while avoiding a direct assault on what they deemed to be the strongest Spanish position. Admiral Sampson and his staff, however, viewed the Army decision as a mistake and complained that Shafter had neglected to inform them of the full extent of his plans until the very eve of the first engagements. Interservice arguments punctuated the course of the campaign and continued long afterward. Whatever the merits of each side's approach—and each has its defenders—the entire situation reflected a lack of interservice coordination, both in Washington and on the scene. McKinley, Long, and Alger did not establish a joint concept of the Santiago operation or appoint an overall commander. The president's instructions to Shafter, issued through the War Department, authorized the V Corps commander to move "onto the high ground overlooking the harbor or into the interior," wording that could be interpreted as justifying Shafter's course of action. Shafter, in the end, largely fought his own war, negotiating with Sampson for Navy support as needed.[14]

Whatever their disagreements over strategy, Sampson and Shafter cooperated effectively to land the V Corps. On 22 June, 6,000 troops went ashore at Daiquiri in small boats from the transports and warships towed by Navy steam launches. Naval gunfire and an attack from the rear by the Cubans caused the small Spanish garrison to decamp without a fight. During the next three days, the rest of the corps, with its animals, field artillery, and wagons, landed at Daiquiri and at Siboney, which the first troops on shore had quickly occupied. The transports also brought about 4,000 of Garcia's insurgents around from Aserradero to Siboney, leaving about 1,000 west of the harbor to divert Spanish attention. The Cubans scouted ahead of Shafter's army and screened its front and flanks. On 24 June, Wheeler's dismounted cavalry, pushing forward more aggressively than Shafter had intended, fought the campaign's first engagement at Las Guasimas, about four miles from the coast on the road to Santiago. A cavalry brigade that included the Rough Riders, who distinguished themselves for steadiness under fire in their initial fight, drove back a larger Spanish force at a cost of sixteen American dead and fifty-two wounded. The Spaniards, conducting a rear-guard action while withdrawing from the coast toward the city, reported losses of ten dead and eighteen injured. During the next several days, the V Corps, unopposed, moved forward to within about five miles of Santiago, where it encamped in a region of comparatively open, well-watered country. General Linares, meanwhile, pulled his troops east of the harbor back to a line running from the fortified village of El Caney near the mountains, through San Juan Hill in the center, to Aguadores on the seashore about five miles east of El Morro. On 28 June, Shafter's first reinforcements from the United States, part of a brigade of Michigan volunteer infantry under Brig. Gen. Henry M. Duffield, disembarked at Siboney. Shafter went ashore with his staff the following day and established his headquarters with the leading infantry division.[15]

The corps commander delayed his movement to the front in order to organize his precarious logistical base. A shortage of lighters, an utter absence of specially designed landing craft, and the limited traffic capacity of the narrow, muddy road from Siboney dictated careful organization and management—as well as constant hard labor by engineers, stevedores, teamsters, and troops—to keep the minimum necessary quantities of ammunition and the essential ration components moving forward. Shafter felt compelled to order most heavy baggage, including regimental tentage and cooking equipment, left on the beach or the ships. He also decided against trying to bring up his siege artillery, fearing that the heavy pieces would mire down in the road and cut his tenuous supply line. Shafter sent repeated requests back to the War Department for lighters, barges, and construction crews and equipment, but these did not arrive until after Santiago had surrendered.[16]

For the soldiers, it was an austere campaign. Men slept in their small shelter tents or under the stars. They dined on canned meat, hardtack, and coffee prepared in their personal mess kits. When they could, they added mangos, limes, and coconuts picked from the trees. They sweltered in the humid heat. They welcomed and were chilled by the afternoon thunderstorms; some even were thankful at such times for their wool uniforms. Soldiers fought off nightly raids by the ubiquitous, repulsive land crabs. In spite of hardships, most of the troops remained in good health and reasonably high spirits during their first week or so in Cuba.[17]

Shafter initially planned to hold off any further advance until he could build up a substantial supply reserve at Siboney and Daiquiri and make extensive road improvements. From refugees filtering into his lines, he learned of the near-famine in Santiago and believed that, if he waited a bit, time and hunger would work in his favor. However, as the days went by, Shafter's logistical difficulties did not diminish. Further, his reading of histories of eighteenth-century Cuban campaigns and the warnings of Army medical officers made Shafter uneasily aware that, with the worst of the fever season at hand, his troops' robust health would not last. Shafter's superiors in Washington, to whom the Signal Corps had linked him by telegraph, expected early action. Finally, on 28 June, he received Cuban reports of the approach of Escario's column. These reports inflated the strength of the relief force to 8,000 men and indicated that it was escorting a cattle herd and pack trains. Shafter, on the basis of all these considerations, reversed himself and decided to advance and attack on 1 July, before the Spanish forces could be augmented to a strength superior to his own.[18]

Shafter's battle plan was the product of considerable reconnaissance by Garcia's Cubans, by Shafter's own division and brigade commanders, and by his chief engineer, Lt. Col. George F. Derby. Derby, with a half-dozen assistants and parties of American and Cuban troops, had systematically explored and mapped much of the ground in front of the army, although not that immediately at the foot of San Juan Hill. Shafter himself and many other officers obtained a wide, if superficial, view of the countryside from an open hilltop near El Poso, an abandoned sugar plantation on the Siboney road about three miles east of Santiago, where the Cubans had an advance post. The corps commander also had the benefit of limited aerial reconnaissance by his balloon detachment, which made several ascents near headquarters on 30 June.[19]

From these investigations, Shafter identified two possible lines of approach to Santiago through the almost impenetrably wooded and brush-covered flatlands that barred the way. One was the road the army had followed from Siboney. The other, farther north, was the highway connecting Santiago with Guantanamo—a thoroughfare slightly better than the road from Siboney and traversing comparatively open country. To take advantage of this latter route, Shafter decided to send the 2d Infantry Division, under Brig. Gen. Henry W. Lawton, by side trails to reach the Guantanamo highway at El Caney, a strongpoint about three miles north of El Poso, known to be defended by about 500 Spanish regulars. After taking El Caney, which Lawton, who had reconnoitered the place extensively, thought he could do in two hours, the division was to march on Santiago. This operation, contemplated by Shafter as early as 26 June and strongly advocated by Lawton and Wheeler, promised a number of advantages. It would eliminate a significant force on Shafter's flank, gain maneuvering room for the V Corps, deprive the city of food and water from the northern valley, and put troops in position to intercept the Manzanillo column.

While Lawton reduced El Caney, Shafter's other two divisions—the 1st Infantry under Brig. Gen. Jacob F. Kent and the cavalry under Major General Wheeler—were to advance directly along the road from Siboney, beginning their movement after the 2d Division was well engaged. These divisions, supported on their right, if all went well, by Lawton, were to seize San Juan Hill (variously known as San Juan Heights or San Juan Ridge), a range of low hills fronted by open fields about a mile and a half from El Poso, where the Spaniards reportedly were constructing fortifications in advance of their main Santiago perimeter. Brig. Gen. John C. Bates' Independent Brigade was to move up from Siboney, where it had been working on the road, to Shafter's headquarters to act as a reserve. A regiment of Duffield's Michigan volunteers was to advance along the seashore from Siboney, following an iron-company railroad, and make a diversionary attack on Aguadores at the extreme right of the Spanish line. Garcia's Cubans were to follow Lawton and seal off the northwest side of Santiago.[20]

Shafter, in prebattle statements and directives, specified no final objective for the advance. His purpose for 1 July appears to have been to secure a favorable position for subsequent assault or siege while blocking enemy reinforcements. On several occasions, Shafter expressed reluctance to take Santiago by storm, anticipating adverse home-front reaction to the probable heavy casualties; he indicated a preference for reducing the place by siege. He cabled the War Department on 29 June: "Expect to put division on Caney

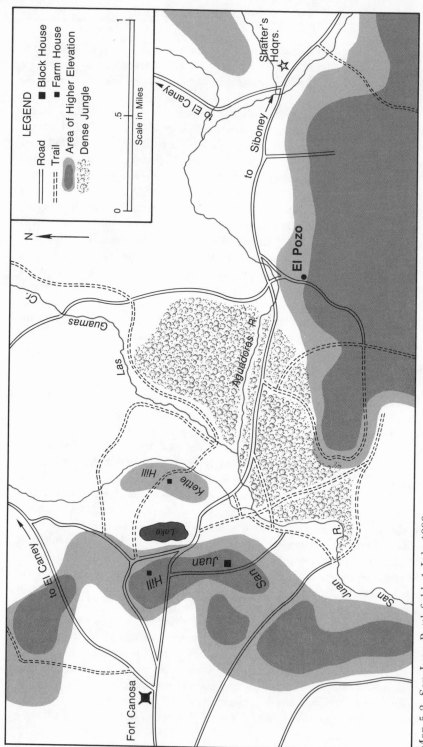

Map 5.2. San Juan Battlefield, 1 July 1898

road, between that place and Santiago, day after tomorrow, and will also advance on Sevilla [Siboney] road to San Juan River [the stream running just east of the heights], and possibly beyond." Whatever his intentions for the 1 July attack, Shafter did not spell them out for his division commanders. In particular, he neglected to clarify for Lawton the relative importance of occupying El Caney versus moving on Santiago by the Guantanamo road.[21]

During the afternoon of 30 June, after a final personal look from the hill at El Poso, Shafter assembled his division and independent brigade commanders and gave them their instructions. He issued no written operation order because, he said later, his generals "were experienced officers, who only needed to know the general plan, which was simple." Troops then began moving into attack positions. Lawton's division, with one field battery attached, followed the trails northward toward El Caney. The other two divisions, the cavalry leading, with the Gatlings and another field battery, assembled at and immediately in rear of El Poso. Two more batteries remained in reserve at corps headquarters, about a mile behind the rest of the San Juan attack force. These movements, along tracks that wandered uphill and down through the jungle, dragged on long into the night. Part of the time, the toiling columns of men burdened with packs, blanket rolls, canteens, weapons, and ammunition had bright moonlight to guide their steps; but many regiments, still on the trail after the moon set, groped their way into fireless bivouacs in pitch darkness. The soldiers found sleeping places on the ground as best they could for the few hours' rest before dawn.[22]

The village of El Caney crowned a small hill dominated from the north by the mountains that walled in the coastal plain. Its stone and wood houses were grouped around a central square with the church on one side and a military headquarters opposite. Against insurgent attacks, the Spaniards had loopholed the houses and church for riflemen and dug slit trenches protected by wire entanglements along the eastern and western sides of the town. Four wooden, earth-reinforced blockhouses, each able to hold fifteen or twenty men, covered the northern and western approaches; the northernmost blockhouse also flanked the line of advance from the east. About 500 yards southeast of El Caney, on a hillock higher than that on which the town stood, was a stone fort, really a large blockhouse, called El Viso. This fortification, surrounded by slit trenches, could bring crossfire to bear on attackers on either side of the village and was the key to the entire position. Fire from these defenses could sweep all the surrounding terrain, which was a mixture of grassland, cultivated fields, and patches of brush. Three companies of Spanish regulars of the *Constitution Regiment* and a company of *Guerrillas,* about 500 men in all, with no artillery, garrisoned the position. Their commander, Brig. Gen. Joaquin Vara del Rey, a tenacious veteran of years of civil conflict in Spain and counterinsurgency in Cuba, had the mission of holding El Caney

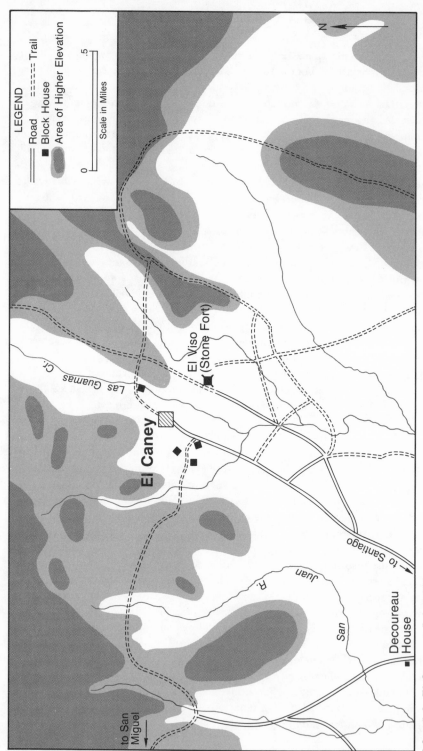

LEGEND

Road ═══

Trail ═════

■ Block House

Area of Higher Elevation

Scale in Miles

0   .5

N

El Caney

Las Guamas Cr.

El Viso
(Stone Fort)

to Santiago

San Juan R.

Decoureau House

to San Miguel

Map 5.3. El Caney, 1 July 1898

for some of the same reasons Shafter and Lawton wanted to take it: to protect Santiago's food and water supplies and keep the Americans away from General Escario's route.[23]

Around 0400 on 1 July, Lawton's troops began moving to the attack. The division's supporting battery—E, 1st Artillery, under Capt. Allyn Capron (who had lost a Rough Rider son at Las Guasimas)—unlimbered its four 3.2-inch rifles in positions prepared a couple of days before, about 2,000 yards south of El Viso. Northeast of the village, Brig. Gen. Adna R. Chaffee's 3d Infantry Brigade deployed to make the principal attack, while the 1st Brigade under Brig. Gen. William Ludlow advanced from the west to block the Spaniards' retreat toward Santiago and support Chaffee with fire. Lawton's remaining infantry brigade, the 2d, under Col. Evan Miles, remained in reserve near Capron's battery and sent patrols down the highway toward Santiago.

Lawton had promised to take El Caney in two hours; he did not deliver. Capron's guns opened the action at 0615, firing shrapnel and ordinary shell into the Spanish positions. The fire had little effect, in large part because Lawton, who acted as his own chief of artillery, failed to concentrate the bombardment on any particular target. Inspector General Breckinridge reported: "The battery opened fire with shrapnel at what appeared to be a column of cavalry moving along the road from El Caney toward Santiago, then fired a few shots at the blockhouses, then a few at the hedges where the enemy's infantry seemed to be located, and then fired a few shots into the village."[24]

As the artillery began shooting, Chaffee and Ludlow started their infantry forward. Chaffee's brigade, coming from the northeast, followed the axis of the Guantanamo road. Ludlow's men moved toward the north first, then swung to the right to engage the western defenses. The regiments of each brigade advanced in column to a point about 1,000 yards from the enemy, then formed as skirmishers, some with all their companies on line—others, as the drill manual specified, with firing line, support, and reserves. Each brigade's deployment went partially wrong. Chaffee got his 12th Infantry into line on his left, roughly opposite El Viso, and the 7th Infantry into position on the right of the 12th, facing the main part of the town. However, his third regiment, the 17th Infantry, after a bewildering series of marches and countermarches, blundered in column right into the northern outskirts of El Caney, where a close-range Spanish volley severely wounded its colonel. Chaffee eventually formed the 17th into line on the right of the 7th but facing toward the northwest, so that it took little effective part in the rest of the day's action. Ludlow, meanwhile, went in with, from right to left, the 2d Massachusetts Volunteers, a battalion of the 22d Infantry, and the 8th Infantry. The remaining battalion of the 22d, misdirected toward the north, eventually found its way into position on the left of the 8th. As a result of these maneuvers, which seem to have been aimed primarily at preventing a Spanish retreat, only the 12th Infantry and the Springfield-armed 2d Massachusetts could engage El Viso to any effect. About one-third of the men of both brigades, at the northern ends of their respective lines, were all but out of the fight.

The infantry attack soon stalled. Once deployed, men of both brigades pushed forward through alternating fields and patches of woods and brush. Between 500 and 800 yards from the trenches and blockhouses, rapid, well-directed Spanish volleys brought the advance to a halt. The action turned into a relatively static fire fight, as the Americans tried to pick off enemies seen only as gun flashes from loopholes or lines of straw hats popping out of slit trenches. Small groups tried to work their way under cover closer to the Spaniards or to better shooting positions, but such movements drew prompt fire and cost the Americans a growing toll of dead and wounded. On Chaffee's front, the 12th Infantry won some high ground overlooking El Viso, but the 7th Infantry took the heaviest casualties of any regiment in the battle in two attempts to fire volleys from a ridge crest facing the town. The 2d Massachusetts in Ludlow's brigade got into a sunken road separated from the Spanish position by open fields and tried to push forward a skirmish line. Smoke from the volunteers' Springfields—which, besides being single shot, used black powder—drew deadly enemy response. "Our own fire was not only ineffectual," the colonel reported, "but it revealed the exact location of our men and brought the concentrated fire of the enemy upon our line of smoke." Ludlow eventually ordered the regiment to cease offensive action and simply hold its position. Firing continued throughout the morning, with little visible effect on the defenders. According to the 7th Infantry commander, "though no infantry fire . . . could have been more severely or certainly delivered . . . , it seemingly had no effect upon reducing the Spanish fire delivered in our front. Continuously through the heaviest din of our fire could be heard the peculiar high-keyed ring of the defiant enemy's shots."[25]

A little before noon, firing on both sides all but ceased as commanders rested their men and replenished ammunition. General Vara del Rey, who still had telephone communication with Santiago, reported to Linares that he had repelled an assault and inflicted heavy casualties while losing seventy of his own men. Lawton had attacked with only a portion of his force and had dispersed that, bringing decisive pressure nowhere. At this point, he might have broken off the action, left a covering force at El Caney, and marched on toward Santiago, as called for in the overall plan. However, Shafter's ambiguous instructions—and evidently his own pride—led Lawton to prepare to resume the battle. Shafter left Lawton to his own devices and in mid-morning sent Bates' reserve brigade to El Caney to reinforce the 2d Division.[26]

While the attack on El Caney thus ran into difficulty, the other subsidiary action of the day, the diversion at Aguadores by General Duffield's Michigan volunteers, went according to plan. Since disembarking on 28 June, this brigade—the entire 33d Michigan and one battalion of the 34th—had guarded the base at Siboney. Early in the morning of 1 July, the 33d Michigan boarded a captured train and rode westward to a point about a mile from Aguadores, where the regiment dismounted from the cars and advanced on foot. Its objective was the place where the San Juan River entered the sea, flowing through a deep gorge crossable only on a partly destroyed railroad trestle. On the Spanish side of the gorge, two *Volontario* companies, about 270 men with a couple of small fieldpieces, held rifle pits and an old stone fort. Under instructions to simulate an attack toward El Morro, Duffield kept two of his battalions well back under cover of trees and brush and sent the third, in skirmish line, up to the river bank. For most of the day, this battalion exchanged sporadic fire with the defenders. By prearrangement, several of Sampson's warships bombarded the fort and rifle pits, their shelling directed by signals from shore. According to Navy reports, this fire was effective, but Duffield and his officers assessed the fleet's effort as unimpressive. Around 1500, the Michigan troops, who had suffered two men killed and six wounded, withdrew to their train and fell back to Siboney. They had fulfilled their orders, but they had diverted no significant number of Spaniards from the main struggle on San Juan Hill.[27]

San Juan Hill, Shafter's principal immediate objective, lay about 1½ miles west of El Poso. Rising some 125 feet above the surrounding country, the mile-long ridge consisted of two roughly equal segments, the northern one aligned generally northeast-southwest and the other on a more nearly north-south axis. Especially at the southern end, the ridge sloped steeply, at about forty-five degrees. Its crest and sides generally were free of trees and brush. Near the southern extremity of the ridge, at its highest point, stood a typical Spanish blockhouse, often called Fort San Juan, flanked by slit trenches. North of this blockhouse were a couple of other fortified buildings and additional earthworks. Almost directly east of San Juan Hill rose a smaller height topped by another building and some huge cauldrons used in processing sugar cane, which gave it its name—Kettle Hill. The valley between San Juan and Kettle Hills was generally open and featured a small lake.

The San Juan River, a waist-deep creek with steep, heavily wooded banks, flowed from north to south along the foot of Kettle Hill and about 800 yards east of San Juan Hill. Opposite the blockhouse, a similar stream, the Las·Guamas, entered the San Juan River from the northeast. A third creek, the so-called Aguadores River, paralleled the road from El Poso and joined the Las Guamas about a quarter mile above its confluence with the San Juan. The road from El Poso crossed the Las Guamas and the San Juan at fords just above where they merge, turned northward between San Juan and Kettle Hills, then angled westward again over the ridge into Santiago. East of the Las Guamas, and of the San Juan below where the Las Guamas flowed into it, thick jungle covered the ground, unbroken until one reached the El Poso clearing. West of the creeks, except for a belt of woods bordering the San Juan, fields of knee-high grass dotted with occasional trees and clumps of brush extended to the foot of the hills. Near the streams, a number of tracks branched from the main road.

On the morning of 1 July, very few Spaniards, compared to the numbers advancing upon them, occupied San Juan and Kettle Hills. General Linares believed that Garcia's main army still was at Aserradero, and he continued to be preoccupied with safeguarding his access to the northern valley and keeping open Escario's approach road from Manzanillo. Hence, he retained substantial forces west of the bay and north and northwest of the city. Linares had perhaps 4,500 men, including about half of his regulars and most of the sailors, in position to protect Santiago against attack from the east.

The Spanish commander evidently regarded the San Juan heights as an advance strong point rather than a main line of resistance. He had reason to do so. Artillery easily could bombard Fort San Juan from El Poso; and the ridge was exposed to envelopment from both flanks, especially from the northeast by troops approaching on the El Caney road. Rifles and artillery from the Spanish main defenses could sweep the open crest of the heights, limiting their usefulness to an attacker, especially as a battery position. Accordingly, as late as the night of 30 June, only one Spanish regular infantry company garrisoned San Juan and Kettle Hills. Just before the American advance began the following morning, Linares reinforced the ridge with two more companies of regulars, sixty *Volontarios,* and his only mobile artillery unit of two guns, making a total defense force of about 500 men. Linares and his staff took position about 800 yards in rear of the heights at Fort Canosa, part of the city perimeter, located on a rise where the El Caney and Siboney roads came together. There he assembled a small reserve of three additional regular infantry companies and 140 mounted *Guerrillas.* The rest of Linares' forces occupied the main line of fortifications. While not usually counted among the defenders, some of these troops, in entrenchments extending southeastward from the city, supported Fort San Juan with long-range fire. The entire inner line would join in the battle after San Juan and Kettle Hills fell. Clearly, Linares intended to fight only a delaying action on the eastern line of hills to disrupt the American advance and break its momentum.[28]

Shafter had planned to direct the action himself from a forward command post at El Poso, but several days of exertion in the humid heat prostrated the elderly, overweight general. Ill and exhausted, he remained at the main corps headquarters about a mile east of El Poso and relied on mounted messengers to bring him reports and carry orders. He stationed members of his staff, familiar with his plans, at the front to coordinate operations. In particular, he relied on his adjutant general, Lieutenant Colonel McClernand, who set up the advance command post at El Poso as Shafter's deputy. McClernand, in telephone contact with Shafter, did much to organize the San Juan attack, as did Colonel Derby, the chief engineer, and Shafter's aide, Lt. John D. Miley. Both of the latter officers went forward with the assaulting divisions.[29]

McClernand as much as anyone set the forces in motion. By dawn, Capt. George S. Grimes' Battery A, 2d Artillery, designated to support the advance, had taken position on the hill at El Poso. The Cavalry Division formed in close order just behind the battery, and Kent's infantry brigades were strung along the trail farther to the rear. According to the plan, these units were to start for San Juan Hill only after Lawton was well on the way to capturing El Caney. They waited for an hour or so, listening to gunfire from the north. Finally, according to McClernand, "it became evident that Lawton might be materially delayed." If only to prevent the enemy at Santiago from reinforcing El Caney, McClernand thought it necessary to start the movement toward San Juan. Obtaining permission from Shafter, McClernand directed the divisions to go forward and deploy—the cavalry to the right of the road, the infantry to the left.[30]

Until the divisions started forward, all information available to Shafter and his subordinate commanders indicated that few Spaniards were on the heights. The American generals accordingly deployed their troops for a lightly opposed advance rather than a set-piece assault. Shafter placed only one of his three available batteries in firing position at the start. Wheeler and Kent sent their divisions forward without detailed battle plans even for solving the difficult traffic problem of moving almost 8,000 men into combat along a road barely wide enough for a column of fours and within range of enemy fire for most of the distance between El Poso and the heights. The division commanders made no attempt to establish reserves; they simply pushed all their troops into the combat zone in a single long column. Brigade and regimental commanders received no briefings on an assault plan or on their units' missions. They advanced under such general instructions as: "Keep well closed up and . . . be in immediate readiness for action."[31]

When the Spaniards' last-minute reinforcement of their advance position precipitated an unexpected major engagement, the division commanders improvised a hasty attack. Leading their columns on horseback, they got up to where they could see the objective, made plans on the spot, and issued directives either in person or through aides and staff officers as their brigades marched up. At times, division staff gave orders directly to individual regiments and companies. Brigade commanders functioned similarly, so that there was a constant coming and going of officers carrying orders or trying to find someone to give them orders, all in dense jungle under Spanish fire. The cavalry division went into action additionally handicapped by the absence of General Wheeler and one of his brigadiers—both, like Shafter, down sick, although Wheeler recovered sufficiently to join in the battle later in the day.[32]

Grimes' gunners began the action around 0800 by shelling the San Juan Hill blockhouse. After Battery A fired a few rounds, the Spanish artillerymen on the ridge replied with their two three-inch Krupp guns, and a few cannon in the main Santiago defenses also joined in the duel. The Spaniards had the rising sun in their eyes, but they easily found the range of their adversaries from the towering grey-white smoke cloud created by the Americans' black powder. Round after round of shrapnel burst over Grimes' position and over the massed cavalry, killing and wounding several men and scattering a group of Cubans. The American artillerymen stuck by their pieces at a cost of two dead and five wounded during the day's action. In accord with artillery doctrine, they attempted counterbattery fire but had difficulty locating the Spanish guns, which used smokeless powder and hence created no revealing cloud. Before 0900, both batteries ceased fire, Grimes's because no infantry attack yet had developed for him to support and because he needed to conserve ammunition. Grimes resumed fire at the blockhouse about two hours later on orders Shafter issued at the suggestion of Miley and McClernand, who thought continuous covering bombardment would aid the advancing infantry and cavalry. Again drawing Spanish counterbattery shelling, the gunners at El Poso blazed away sporadically until some time after noon, by which time they had exhausted the 160 rounds in their limbers. Spanish shrapnel aimed at Grimes kept American commanders and staff officers from using El Poso as an observation point and endangered the long column of troops slowly filing past on the road.[33]

During the first artillery duel, dismounted cavalrymen started marching toward San Juan Heights. The 1st Brigade, composed of the 3d, 6th, and 9th Cavalry, led the way, preceded by a Cuban unit. The Cubans soon halted, however, and allowed the Americans to push through them. Cautiously, the cavalry advanced to the ford where the road crossed the Las Guamas. A Spanish outpost there fired a few shots and retreated. The troopers waded the creek about 1000 and pressed forward into the fields between it and the San Juan River, the 6th Cavalry in front, the 9th on its right and slightly to the rear, and the 3d directly behind the 6th. All three regiments deployed in two skirmish lines, with one squadron behind the other. They advanced by rushes until their foremost elements were almost at the foot of Kettle Hill, then halted to await deployment of the rest of the division.[34]

Between 1000 and 1030, the 2d Cavalry Brigade, under Col. Leonard Wood, who had replaced the ill Brig. Gen. Samuel B. M. Young, reached the Las Guamas ford. The 1st Volunteer Cavalry, commanded by Lt. Col. Theodore Roosevelt, headed the column, with the 1st and 10th regulars following. Brig. Gen. Samuel S. Sumner, Wheeler's temporary replacement, under orders from corps, turned the Rough Riders to the right and marched them northward parallel to the stream in an effort to find and connect with Lawton's division, which Shafter evidently thought might be coming on line with the main advance at about that time. The cavalry commanders realized almost at once that Lawton was nowhere in the vicinity. Wood's brigade went into line along and just beyond the Las Guamas in rear of the 1st Brigade, with the Rough Riders on the right, the 1st Cavalry on the volunteers' left, and the 10th Cavalry behind and to the right of the 1st. Each of these regiments deployed more or less in two squadron skirmish lines.[35]

Until the Rough Riders crossed the Las Guamas, the Spanish defenders on the ridge remained largely invisible to the Americans and contested the advance only with periodic shelling of Grimes' battery. The enemy riflemen opened fire just as Wood's regular cavalry were beginning to deploy and in response to perhaps the oddest event of the battle: the arrival of the Signal Corps observation balloon at the Las Guamas ford.

Lt. Col. Joseph E. Maxfield and his twenty-four-man detachment had brought their old, much-patched balloon, with its auxiliary equipment and tanks of inflating hydrogen, up to corps headquarters on 29 June and had made several flights the next day. On the morning of the attack, Maxfield planned to raise his captive balloon near El Poso, but the initial Spanish bombardment drove him off. The balloon made one ascension east of El Poso between 0900 and 0930, during which the observers in the basket saw only a few Spaniards on San Juan Hill and no sign that the enemy were reinforcing the position. Colonel Derby, under whom Maxfield worked, then ordered the signal officer to tow his balloon farther forward. Maxfield complied only under vehement protest, though in Derby's defense it must be noted that no firing, beyond the brief artillery exchange, had yet occurred. The detachment guided its craft, hovering barely above the treetops, to a small meadow just beyond the Las Guamas, in the process temporarily blocking the march of the 1st and 10th Cavalry. When the signalmen tried to raise their balloon, they found that the guide ropes had become entangled in branches and undergrowth, completely immobilizing the craft. Derby and Maxfield, who had ridden forward in the basket, tried to observe from their treetop-level position. They did so only briefly. The Spaniards suddenly opened fire at the balloon, and rifle bullets and shrapnel soon punctured the bag and brought it down, leaking gas and rapidly collapsing, into the creek bed. Using the balloon's former position as an aiming point, the defenders of San Juan Hill from then on kept up a steady harassing fire on the ford and the road leading to it. The balloon detachment, at considerable risk to themselves, managed to recover their equipment and haul it to the rear. To show for this—the first and, according to the corps chief signal officer, probably the last balloon ascension on a skirmish line—Derby and Maxfield obtained two significant pieces of information. They confirmed for the first time that day that the Spaniards were holding San

Juan Hill in some strength, and they spotted a trail, branching left from the main road before it reached the Las Guamas, that led to the banks of the San Juan River and offered an alternative route of advance for the approaching infantry.[36]

As though the balloon's appearance at the ford had signaled them, the Spaniards on San Juan and Kettle Hills directed musketry and artillery at the road and at the Americans in the meadows and on the fringe of the jungle. Troopers of the 1st Cavalry Brigade, closest to the hills, unable to spot targets for effective return fire, hugged the ground and sought cover in the tall grass and brush. They discovered, as other Americans attacking San Juan Hill were to do, that the Spaniards had placed their trenches such that they could not aim directly at enemies close under the foot of the steep slopes. Nevertheless, unaimed volleys killed some cavalrymen and wounded others in both brigades. Many of the wounded crawled or were carried to an aid station that 3d and 6th Cavalry surgeons had set up under the high bank of the Las Guamas. As the troopers lay in the field, their division's dynamite gun and Hotchkiss mountain battery unlimbered just west of the Las Guamas and opened fire. The compressed-air-powered dynamite gun suffered a breech failure after a couple of shots. The Hotchkiss battery drew a heavy answering fusillade from the trenches and blockhouse and withdrew after twenty to thirty minutes.[37]

For the rear regiments of the cavalry and for the infantry now coming up alongside them, the approach march became a hazardous ordeal. Most companies early in the advance dropped off packs and blanket rolls at the roadside with a couple of guards, often the most recent recruits. They went into action carrying rifles, 200 rounds of ammunition, canteens, haversacks, and first-aid packets. Walled in on both sides by the *manigua,* unable to see the objective or anything else except the troops immediately in front and behind, soldiers toiled along in column of twos and fours and at times in single file. They moved, halted, and moved again in oppressive heat unrelieved in that enclosed space by any breeze. Company officers could do little but try to keep their men together and moving forward. The more provident took advantage of halts to let their troops sit down and rest, if only for a few moments. Even then, the march drained men's strength. "Every scrap of shade along the road," a participant recalled, "was occupied by some panting soldier." Officers and enlisted men alike dropped out from heat stroke and exhaustion; the less severely afflicted rested for a while, then staggered after their units. Aides and staff officers, mounted and on foot, ranged up and down the column urging everyone to hurry up. A few company commanders, afraid their regiments might leave them behind, pushed their men past the units in front, adding to the congestion.

The column advanced under constant unaimed musketry and shelling and also under aimed rifle fire from Spanish sharpshooters hidden in trees

along the road. These riflemen shot at officers; they also attacked indis-
criminately any passing Americans, even the wounded and medical personnel. Bullets and shrapnel constantly tore through the brush, periodically
dropping a man in the slow-moving files. Casualties were not heavy enough to
halt the advance or to disorganize units, but the troops underwent the strain of
being shot at and hit long before they could see or attack the enemy. American
fighting men here experienced for the first time the enlarged lethal zone of the
twentieth-century battlefield. The regulars stoically endured this punishment.
One of Kent's staff officers observed: "A to me remarkable feature . . . was
the absence of cries or groans. Men received their death wounds, but beyond
the dull thud of the bullet when it struck human flesh, followed briefly,
perhaps, by the exclamation of the victim, there was no other lamentation
when our men suffered injuries from shot or shell, and fell or dragged
themselves into the bushes." Straggling did occur, however, by men helping
wounded comrades and by others for whom, as Lieutenant Colonel McClernand put it, "the firing was probably hotter than some like." McClernand
late in the afternoon asked Shafter for a troop of mounted cavalry to round up
soldiers who had drifted to the rear.[38]

With the outbreak of heavy Spanish fire and Derby's report from the
balloon of sizable enemy forces on the San Juan heights, Shafter and his
representatives at the front realized they were fighting a major engagement.
They attempted to coordinate and support the attack that had now become
necessary. Besides ordering Grimes to resume fire, the corps commander
directed Lieutenant Colonel McClernand to "get those Gatling guns to work
if you can," and he started the two reserve light batteries toward El Poso. At
an undetermined time during the morning, Shafter also sent forward
instructions for Kent and Sumner to "fight all their men if they can do so to
advantage"—an order McClernand interpreted to the division commanders
as authorizing an assault on the ridge.[39]

Before such an assault could begin, Kent's infantry division, coming up
behind the cavalry, had to get into line. General Kent, impatient with the slow
progress of deployment, pushed his leading brigade, the 1st, under Brig. Gen.
Hamilton S. Hawkins up alongside the cavalry shortly before the heavy firing
started. Kent, Hawkins, and their staffs, at the head of the division column,
reached the Las Guamas ford around 1100, while the balloon still floated
overhead and Wood's cavalry were filing off toward the north. The infantry
division was debouching from the jungle almost in line with the southern end
of the enemy-held ridge, presenting what seemed to Kent and Hawkins an
opportunity to envelop the Spaniards' right flank. After a look at the hill and a
consultation with Derby, who told them of the newly discovered trail, Kent
and Hawkins sent two regiments, the 6th and 16th Infantry, off to the left of
the main road with orders to extend their line still farther to the left and
enfilade the hill. Without informing Hawkins, Kent directed the third

regiment of the brigade, the 71st New York, into the side trail, from which it could deploy to prolong the regulars' line.[40]

The two regular regiments—the 6th in front and the 16th behind and slightly to its left—crossed the Las Guamas into the angle between that stream and the San Juan River. This area, not previously reconnoitered, was covered with heavy brush and a field of head-high grain, which restricted vision and made control of battalions, even of companies, extremely difficult. Under unaimed fire as they had been on the road, the regiments made a confused effort to examine the terrain ahead of them. Then they groped forward to the San Juan—here waist deep, with steep, wooded banks—and struggled across it, companies becoming broken up and intermingled in the process. Another short push through the *manigua* brought the leading companies into a sunken trail that bordered the open meadow below the ridge. This track paralleled the San Juan River and then turned northwest. It formed a continuous, ready-made trench angled toward the enemy position at its northern end. A fence of several strands of barbed wire fastened to tree trunks ran along the ridgeward side of the road.

The regiments worked their way into this position and spread out, the 6th generally on the right and the 16th on the left but with elements of each regiment mixed into the other's line. Right-wing companies of the 6th edged along the track to a point close under the ridge, actually between the blockhouse and Kettle Hill. Here, for the first time since leaving El Poso, the infantrymen could see and fire at the Spaniards. For about an hour, they engaged the trenches and blockhouse. During this fire fight, the 6th Infantry attempted a further advance. Col. Harry C. Egbert, the regimental commander, seeking a more advantageous firing position, ordered a movement across the fence into the meadow. His troops, who had few wire cutters, sawed strands with bayonets, hammered them loose from the trees with rifle butts, or crawled under the barrier. A black Cuban soldier, who had attached himself to the regiment and was killed later in the attack, cut a number of gaps with his machete. Once through the fence, companies of the 6th Infantry and some elements of the 16th tried to open out as skirmishers, but restricted frontage caused portions of the line to bunch up two or three men deep. The companies poured volley and individual fire into the hilltop. This blast from a line partially concealed in the tall grass initially shook the Spaniards, but they soon rallied and concentrated their own musketry and artillery on Egbert's troops. During about ten minutes in the field, the 6th Infantry lost almost one-fourth of its 463 officers and men before being forced back into the road.[41]

Instead of outflanking San Juan Hill, the 6th and 16th Infantry had come into action directly in front of it. Kent's planned envelopment now depended on the troops moving down the trail to the left of the main road. On this narrow, brush-walled track, Spanish rifle and artillery fire proved too much for the cohesion and discipline of the 71st New York, the first regiment to follow the route. When shrapnel killed and injured several men in its leading battalion, the 71st halted in milling confusion; its officers could not restore order. Unable to get the volunteers moving again, Kent and his staff finally herded them off the path and had them lie down in the brush. The 71st remained along the trail for the rest of the action, except for individuals who got up and joined other regiments as they passed. These bold spirits often appropriated the Krag-Jörgensens of regular casualties as they went forward—an indication that lack of confidence in their Springfields had contributed to the volunteers' demoralization. Later in the afternoon, division staff officers regrouped the New Yorkers and brought them up to San Juan Hill to reinforce the line.[42]

After the 71st New York disintegrated, Kent hurriedly called up his all-regular 3d Brigade, under Col. Charles A. Wikoff, which was behind the 1st in the division column. Wikoff's command reached the turnoff to the trail about 1220 and headed down it on the double, the 13th Infantry in the lead, followed by the 9th and 24th. Running over and past the prone New York troops, the 13th emerged from the jungle on the edge of the San Juan River just below its junction with the Las Guamas. The same sunken road and barbed-wire fence that Hawkins' men had encountered bordered the west side of the stream here, with grassland beyond extending to the ridge. Heavy and accurate fire from the fortifications and from sharpshooters in trees to the front and left flank hit Wikoff's troops as they crossed the stream and deployed. Colonel Wikoff himself fell mortally wounded; two replacement brigade commanders went down within ten minutes.

Nevertheless, in relatively open ground, the 3d Brigade went into action rapidly and in good order. The 13th Infantry, in contact on its right with the 16th, formed a line in the shelter of the high west bank of the creek. Hacking gaps in the wire, the regiment went into the field as skirmishers, its 1st Battalion on the right and the 2d on the left. Its line advanced about 100 yards, found cover in an undulation of the ground, and opened fire. "Some of the best shots," a company commander recalled, competed "in picking off individuals exposing themselves on the enemy's works." The two other regiments of the brigade became entangled during the approach march, so that a battalion of the 9th Infantry came into line next some distance to the left of the 13th. A battalion of the 24th then filled the gap. These battalions extended the left of the firing line in the meadow. The remaining battalions of the 9th and 24th were not engaged before the final advance began.[43]

Until the infantry went into action, the Spanish defenders of the ridge had hardly considered themselves under attack; but with the deployment of the 3d Brigade, the equivalent of four infantry regiments—almost 2,000 rifles—were firing at the San Juan blockhouse and the trenches around it. Kent's enveloping maneuver was beginning to take shape. Additional American firepower almost simultaneously came into play. The two reserve batteries

Shafter earlier had sent forward—F, 2d Artillery, and K, 1st Artillery—unlimbered alongside Grimes on the El Poso hill and opened fire about 1300. They had time, however, to fire only one round from each gun before American infantry reached the crest of San Juan Hill.[44]

Much more decisive was the intervention of Captain Parker's Gatling battery. Parker's detachment of forty men and four guns on mule-drawn wheeled carriages reached the Las Guamas a little before noon. On orders from Colonel Derby, the battery waited for an hour or so until the infantry could deploy, the crews lying down under the guns for protection from the fire sweeping the ford. About 1300, Derby sent Parker into action. Leaving one of his guns in reserve with Lieutenant Miley, Parker galloped the other three forward to a previously selected position west of the creek. His battery unlimbered about 1315 and for the next eight minutes directed streams of bullets at the enemy trenches 800 yards away. This sudden increase in the volume of American fire had dramatic effects. The Spaniards at first concentrated their own musketry on the Gatling detachment, killing one crewman and wounding another, but their fire soon died away. Infantrymen on the line in front of the ridge could see Spaniards emerging from their trenches and running for the rear.[45]

Parker's Gatlings delivered the final blow to an already-crumbling defense. Around noon, the Spanish gunners had run out of shrapnel, their most effective projectile. Casualties increased under the steadily intensifying American fire, especially in the company of the *Puerto Rico Regiment* holding the blockhouse and its flanking entrenchments. General Linares, observing the action from Canosa, was especially concerned about the extension of the American line toward his right, which threatened to enfilade the withdrawal route of the San Juan Hill defenders. Whether directed or spontaneous, a retreat from the ridge began. Linares committed his reserves to cover it and to check any further American advance. The final V Corps assault on the heights thus went in against defenders who already were pulling back. The Spaniards remained longest in the center of the ridge, near where the road crossed it. There, forty *Volontarios,* fighting with outmoded Remingtons, made a stand to cover the removal of the artillery.[46]

The exact timing and sequence of events of the climactic American assault remain a matter of dispute, as does the question of who actually ordered the movement. It apparently began with the cavalry, some of whom had been holding their ground close to the hills for almost three hours. General Sumner, who seemed uncertain what he was supposed to do but was convinced that his division would be slowly shot to pieces unless it either retreated or advanced, sent a message to McClernand through Lieutenant Miley requesting permission to attack. McClernand, for the corps commander, told Sumner to go ahead, although he considered the authorization unnecessary because, according to him, Shafter's directive about fighting all the troops constituted an attack order. Kent's division simply assaulted without further direction from the corps.[47]

The cavalry started forward just before the Gatlings opened fire. They moved initially toward the northwest, across the San Juan River, up Kettle Hill, and through the low ground between it and the San Juan heights. As the skirmish lines worked their way through barbed-wire fences and patches of trees and brush, organizations became increasingly intermingled. The second-line squadron of each regiment gradually merged with the first. Adding to the jumbling of units, Wood's 2d Brigade evidently began moving before the 1st Brigade and overran part of its line. The cavalrymen thus fought as separate troops (companies) and often as ad hoc groups of men from different regiments, who followed whatever officer collected them and led them forward. Lieutenant Colonel Roosevelt, among others, distinguished himself in these improvisational tactics. A regular who saw Roosevelt in action, the famous teeth grinding and the shrill voice exclaiming "God damn 'em" when exhorting men to charge the foe, said of the future president, "He was an inspiration. Men were bound to follow him."[48]

Firing as they went and at first taking heavy fire in return, the right wing of the cavalry swept over Kettle Hill and killed or captured the few Spaniards who remained on its crest. The leftmost troops, meanwhile, moved up onto the main San Juan ridge; some joined the infantry assaulting the blockhouse. Hastily re-forming a line, the men on Kettle Hill pushed on across the valley in front of them and completed the capture of northern San Juan Hill, again all but abandoned by the enemy before the cavalry reached the Spanish trenches.[49]

If any one man set the infantry assault in motion, it was General Hawkins. Hawkins, near the junction of the 6th and 16th Infantry, also believed that he had to go forward or fall back. He ordered the two buglers accompanying him to sound the advance and sent aides along his own line and that of the 3d Brigade with the same message. In the 3d Brigade, temporarily without a commander due to casualties, the adjutant, on his own, notified all the troops he could reach "that the movement was to be forward over the field at once." Some company commanders, however, insisted that they received no order to advance and did so either from tactical necessity or because they saw units on their flanks going forward.[50]

The 3d Brigade regiments and the 16th Infantry, which had about 800 yards of open field to cross, initiated what came to be called the charge. To the right of the rest of the line and nearer the ridge, the 6th Infantry went through the barbed wire fence into the meadow a second time and joined the assault when Colonel Egbert (wounded just as the charge began) and his captains saw the other regiments in motion. More or less in line, different companies moved at various paces. Some ran ahead without halting; others walked or jogged, pausing periodically to fire, re-form, or simply rest. Spanish fire, at first heavy, soon slackened, so that American casualties grew fewer as the troops approached the ridge, especially as they got into the sheltered ground immediately at the foot of the abrupt slope. By the time the foremost units reached that point, the San Juan defenders were already in retreat. According to Capt. J. B. Goe, 13th Infantry, "When the line reached the base of San Juan Hill the battle was practically won, for our fire, together with that of the artillery and Gatling guns, had driven most of the enemy out of the blockhouse and trenches . . . although the enemy directed a heavy fire from other positions . . . upon us when we reached the top of the hill."[51] Goe and other captains, seeing the crest deserted, actually halted for a time under the hill and tried to re-form their companies before climbing on up.

Companies of the 6th and 16th Infantry, many starting from positions far forward in the sunken road, first approached the crest. They halted temporarily just below it when shells from the El Poso batteries exploded ahead of them. In a moment of confusion and hesitation that enraged the commanders of the leading companies, the foremost men drifted part way back down the slope. This pause allowed the 3d Brigade regiments to catch up, so that companies of the 6th, 9th, 13th, 16th, and 24th regiments all swarmed over the objective more or less simultaneously about 1330. The first troops on the hill quickly dispatched or rounded up the few unwounded Spaniards still there. An injured Spanish officer shot dead one of General Hawkins' aides and was promptly riddled by angry Americans. No one counted the enemy casualties strewn over the hilltop, although officers reported seeing a trench heaped with dead and injured. A foolhardy 13th Infantry soldier tore down the red and yellow Spanish flag from the blockhouse and ran out into the open to show it to his friends. He drew a fusillade that wounded him and several other soldiers. The troops then decided the flag brought bad luck and tore it to pieces. The first officers on the ridge, soon joined by General Hawkins, organized men to fire at the enemy and gather up the weapons of the Spanish prisoners and casualties. They also waved flags and otherwise signaled frantically to stop the continuing fire of the American lines still crossing the field and climbing the hill.[52]

While the 1st and 3d Brigades were deploying and moving to the attack, Kent's 2d Brigade, last in the divisional column, reached the Las Guamas. Kent directed the two leading regiments, the 10th and 2d Infantry, under the brigade commander, Col. Edward P. Pearson, down the side trail after Wikoff's troops. He pushed the third regiment, the 21st Infantry, straight ahead to support Hawkins. Pearson's two regiments made an abortive attempt to form a firing line east of the San Juan River to assist the 3d Brigade in front of them, then crossed the stream and deployed at about the time the rest of the division was charging the hill. Crowded out of the line of advance toward the blockhouse, Pearson's regiments—the 10th in front and the 2d in echelon to its left rear—passed to the south of Fort San Juan and occupied a ridge about 800 yards farther west, reaching this position about 1430. The 21st Infantry, meanwhile, followed the route of the 6th and 16th to the blockhouse, then moved left to join its parent brigade. Pearson's position formed a crescent, with Spanish fortifications 400 to 1,000 yards distant to its front and on both flanks. Under constant, at times heavy, crossfire, the 3d Brigade held this height for the rest of the day, forming the left of the entire American line.[53]

While the ridge east of the main Spanish perimeter now had fallen, fighting went on through the remaining daylight hours. The Spaniards successfully extricated their surviving troops from the San Juan heights, although the artillery, among the last to go, came under enfilade fire from Americans on the ridge west of the blockhouse and lost eighteen out of fifty men. One Krupp gun, the mules carrying it having been slain by the same fusillade, lay abandoned in the road between the lines. A suicidal mounted charge by the *guerrillas* of Linares' Canosa reserve and heavy Spanish infantry fire kept the attackers away from the weapon until gunners could retrieve it during the night. The three companies of the *Talavera Regiment* at Canosa and the troops that had rallied after retreating from San Juan Hill, reinforced late in the afternoon by 100 armed convalescents from the military hospital and a company of sailors, kept up steady fire on the American-held crest, volleying at any unit that tried to push forward. Troops all along the eastern side of Santiago joined in the firing. Some of the artillery, lacking other ammunition, sent solid shot into the American lines. One of these projectiles buried itself in the dirt at the feet of General Wheeler's staff. Under Linares' personal leadership, the Spaniards maintained a brave front. Once or twice, units advanced out of their earthworks and appeared to threaten a counterattack, but they quickly sought cover as American fire converged on them. The defenders held their second line at heavy cost in casualties. Two *Talavera* companies at Canosa, which had entered the action with 150 men each, ended the day 30 and 50 strong. Spanish officers set a heroic example for their troops and suffered accordingly. Linares himself received a severe arm wound. Many members of his staff and other high-ranking officers, including the artillery commander and the chief engineer, were killed or injured. Cervera's chief of staff, Capt. Joaquin Bustamente, fell mortally wounded as he led the sailors from the squadron in an abortive counterattack.

The Americans, for their part, spent the afternoon consolidating their position on San Juan Hill. General Kent and his staff reached the crest soon after the blockhouse fell. The cavalry commander, General Wheeler, who had risen from his sickbed to get into the action, also came up; by virtue of seniority and experience, he more or less took charge of the whole line. With their troops tired and disorganized from the initial assault and with no available reserves, the commanders on the ridge had no thought of further advance. They re-formed brigades and regiments, saw to the collection of dead and wounded, and sent requests to the rear for ammunition, entrenching tools, and rations. Skirmishers kept up fire on the Spanish line as the infantry and dismounted cavalry began digging in, at first using bayonets, meat cans, and other improvised implements. During the afternoon, Battery K, 1st Artillery under Capt. Clermont L. Best moved forward from El Poso to San Juan Hill and tried to go into action on the skirmish line north of the blockhouse. Spanish musketry and shelling drove the battery off the crest after about fifteen minutes. Parker's Gatlings did better. They gave effective support to the cavalry division and temporarily silenced a Spanish cannon. Around 1930, the firing died down. After dark, the regiments set up outposts. With picks and spades now reaching the front, they began digging in. Pack trains brought up limited quantities of food and cartridges.[54]

At about the time the American pressure on San Juan Hill began to intensify, Lawton renewed his attack on El Caney with increased forces and greater concentration of effort. Around 1230, Capron's battery, at Lawton's direction, began a steady bombardment of El Viso and its surrounding trenches. This shelling, kept up for about two hours, breached the fort's stone walls and demoralized the defenders. Lawton committed Colonel Miles' 2d Brigade, which had stood idle throughout the morning, on Ludlow's right directly west of the fort. He deployed the two regiments of Bates' brigade, just arrived from El Poso, to add still more firepower from a position southeast of El Viso.

Miles' brigade, deploying just as Capron resumed fire, especially added to the pressure on the key enemy position. Miles attacked with two of his regiments, the 4th Infantry on the left and the 25th on the right. (His remaining regiment, the 1st Infantry, stayed in reserve near the battery.) The 4th and 25th each advanced in drill-book style, one battalion in the fighting line with two companies skirmishing and two in support and a second battalion following in reserve. Defying heavy fire, the 4th Infantry maneuvered to within about 200 yards of the village and blockhouses and poured in volleys. Directly in front of El Viso, the black soldiers of the 25th carried their skirmish line to within 150 yards of the enemy; the regiment's marksmen shot at Spaniards in the rifle pits and at doors and loopholes.[55]

While rifle and artillery crossfire swept the El Viso knoll, the 12th Infantry of Chaffee's brigade worked its way to a position close to the east side of the fort and partially sheltered from fire. The regimental commander, Lt. Col. Richard Comba, assembled an assault force of several companies. Between 1400 and 1500, as the defenders' fire diminished, the 12th Infantry troops rushed the knoll and overran El Viso. As they did so, the 25th Infantry saw a Spanish officer carrying a white flag emerge from a door in the side of the fort facing them. The continuing crossfire cut him down before the Americans could respond to his surrender signal. Soldiers of the 25th then advanced onto the hill and seized a Spanish flag, giving rise to a dispute between that regiment and the 12th over credit for capturing the position. According to a participant, the rifle pits around El Viso "were open graves, while the interior of the fort, with its walls, floor and ceiling bespattered with human blood, was a real 'Chamber of Horrors.' " Lieutenant Colonel Comba reported finding one Spanish officer and ten enlisted men dead in the works and taking prisoner two officers and twenty-one troops, including a dozen wounded.[56]

Belatedly, as El Viso was falling, Shafter tried to disentangle Lawton from El Caney. Around 1400, he sent the division commander a note—more a suggestion than an order—urging him not to "bother with little block-houses. . . . Bates's brigade and your division and Garcia," Shafter continued, "should move on the city and form the right of the line going on the [Siboney] road. Line is now hotly engaged." Lawton ignored this communication, claiming his troops were now too heavily committed to withdraw. He continued the reduction of the small place that so unreasonably defied him.[57]

The fight went on for another two hours after the capture of El Viso. Capron moved his guns closer to the town and began blowing apart the lesser blockhouses Shafter had mentioned. Infantry of Miles', Bates', and Chaffee's brigades took position on the El Viso knoll and from the higher ground picked off the now-exposed defenders in the village and its flanking trenches. Ludlow's troops west of the town noted a gradual slackening of the Spanish fire against them. However, none of the encircling American units ever physically stormed El Caney. Instead, the survivors of the garrison tried to withdraw along a trail running northwest into the mountains to another village from which they could work their way back to Santiago. They carried along many of their wounded, including General Vara del Rey, shot in both legs. This column passed across the front of Ludlow's left wing regiments, which shot down dozens of Spaniards and killed, among others, the valiant enemy commander. Vara del Rey's second in command, Lt. Col. Juan Punet, finally extricated about eighty men and by a long, roundabout march brought them into Santiago. The rest of the 500 soldiers of the garrison scattered into the hills, came out of dwellings and blockhouses with their hands up, or were found dead and wounded by infantry and cavalry who searched the town after firing ceased around 1630.[58]

The aftermath of the battle was, for Lawton, the culmination of a bad day. Bates' brigade, only briefly engaged, left El Caney soon after nightfall. At Shafter's direction, it marched to El Poso and then to San Juan Hill, where it took position on Pearson's left around midnight. Lawton's troops spent several hours resting and collecting their dead and wounded. Around 2230, the division started down the road to Santiago, leaving a few infantry companies behind to finish policing the battlefield. Lawton, although he had available a fresh infantry regiment and some mounted cavalry, had made no attempt to reconnoiter and secure his route while it was still daylight. His

column moved along blindly in the darkness until it reached a ruined
plantation, the Ducoureau house, about a mile from El Caney. There, it
collided with a Spanish picket in a quick flurry of shots. Lawton, uncertain
what was in front of him, sent a messenger back to corps for orders. Shafter,
playing it safe, directed Lawton to abandon the route for which he had fought
all day and march to San Juan Hill, as Bates had done, via El Poso. Lawton's
dead-tired, hungry troops began their long walk about 0300 on 2 July. Five
hours later, the leading brigade—Chaffee's—filed onto the ridge on the right
of Wheeler's cavalry.[59]

On 2 July, the fighting on the San Juan ridge took on the distinctively modern
form of continuous exchanges of fire from entrenched positions. The Spaniards held their main line of resistance and reinforced the much-reduced
defenders of Canosa with regulars transferred from west of the bay. Shafter,
with Bates now on the extreme left of his line, used Lawton and Garcia to
extend his right wing almost completely around the north side of Santiago.
Before dawn, the Americans emplaced three field batteries on San Juan Hill
north of the blockhouse and tried to bombard the city. Spanish musketry and
artillery, as they had the day before, forced the batteries to withdraw after
about an hour of fighting, during which the artillery used canister and
shrapnel with the fuses cut short against enemy riflemen who worked their way
close to the gun positions. For the rest of the day, both armies kept up
intermittent fire and suffered casualties, about 150 in the V Corps. The
fighting died down at nightfall, then erupted again briefly around 2200, as
each army volleyed noisily against what it mistakenly thought was an assault
by the other. In this new phase of the battle, according to Col. Charles
McKibbin of the 21st Infantry, "The troops were subjected to the severest
strain, under a continuous fire, exposed to a fierce tropical sun, which
exhausted and prostrated the men by scores, and to the drenching show-
ers. . . . It being impossible to make fires, officers and men for forty-eight
hours subsisted on . . . hard bread and raw bacon. Sleep was impossible."[60]
    By the end of the second day's action, Shafter had accomplished his
minimum objective: he had secured a line from which to assault or invest
Santiago. He had done so, however, at considerable cost. Fifth Corps
casualties in these engagements amounted to over 220 officers and men killed
and 1,300 wounded. Eighty of the dead and 360 of the injured fell at El Caney.
In most regiments, the officer casualty rate was about double that for enlisted
men—an indication of the extent and the price of leadership from the front.
About 50 Spanish officers and 500 troops died or were wounded at San Juan
and El Caney; another 100 or so were captured, most of them at El Caney.[61]
    The hard fighting left the V Corps shaken in confidence and afflicted with
pessimism. Americans of all ranks had found Spanish tenacity and firepower
in defense unexpectedly formidable. Unanimously, they considered the

Santiago inner defenses too strong to storm with the troops on hand and believed that, even substantially reinforced, the V Corps would lose as many as 3,000 men taking the city by assault. Shafter and his division commanders, worried about supplies and fearing counterattack by the Manzanillo column, now reportedly nearing Santiago, held a council of war on the night of 2 July to consider retreat—although none of them later would own up to originating the idea. Tentatively, they decided to hold on. Lower-ranking officers were depressed by the loss of friends, and they anticipated catastrophe. Even the ebullient Roosevelt was affected. He wrote his friend Henry Cabot Lodge: "We have won so far at a heavy cost; but the Spaniards fight very hard and charging these entrenchments against modern rifles is terrible. We are within measurable distance of a terrible military disaster." Many soldiers believed the battle had been inexcusably botched. A 16th Infantry officer wrote in his diary: "Gen Shafter is a fool and I believe should be shot. . . . We are now and have been handled by incompetent men and I sincerely hope that they may be made [to] suffer some day."[62]

The conduct of the campaign and battles came in for extensive contemporary analysis, criticism, and second guessing, much of which has passed relatively unaltered into the historical literature. Navy writers such as the authoritative French Ensor Chadwick have condemned Shafter's refusal to attack the harbor entrance forts and argued that the original Navy concept of operations, if followed, would have brought an easier, less costly victory for both services. Critics of the land campaign accuse and usually convict Shafter of having neglected reconnaissance, of having wrongfully and dangerously divided his forces by simultaneously attacking San Juan and El Caney, of having misused his artillery, and of having failed to take advantage of naval gunfire support at San Juan Hill.[63]

Certainly Shafter's conduct at many points reflected inexperience in corps command. His inability to disengage Lawton from El Caney and his vacillating abandonment of the line of advance Lawton's division had won indicated less than perfect control of operations on 1 July. Yet there is a case for the defense. Shafter's division of forces between El Caney and San Juan, although it violated the theoretical principle of concentration, had little practical effect on the fighting of either battle. Each of the two attack columns possessed more than sufficient men and firepower, if properly handled, to accomplish its mission. Each did so in a relatively short time once it brought its full strength to bear, which did not happen on either battlefield until around midday. At El Caney, General Lawton certainly bears much responsibility for the delay in developing an effective attack and then the abandonment of fruits of belated victory.

Critics of the San Juan action start from the assumption that it was a planned, deliberate assault on heights known to be strongly held. The battle, however, was essentially a meeting engagement between forces marching to deploy and a belatedly strengthened enemy outpost. Shafter and his subordinates can be faulted for having neglected last-minute reconnaissance and perhaps for having failed to keep a fresh brigade or two in reserve at El Poso rather than pushing everyone into the traffic jam on the road, but they can be credited for having reacted effectively to an unexpected situation. Once they deployed their men, after all, Kent and Sumner cleared the ridge in about an hour. Misuse of artillery and neglect of naval gunfire reflected as much the then-current Army emphasis on direct fire and cannon on the skirmish line as it did individual incompetence. Whether the Navy campaign plan would have worked out better than the one actually followed cannot be decided conclusively after the fact. Even Chadwick, it might be noted, believed in retrospect that a combination of Shafter's inland approach with an attack on the harbor forts would have been the best course of action. In summary, the higher direction of the V Corps at Santiago, while it had its lapses, was far from totally incompetent. The small-unit cohesion and high level of training of the regulars and the courageous personal leadership by officers of all ranks overcame the mistakes that were made.[64]

The Army's subsequent campaigns in Puerto Rico and the Philippines went much more smoothly, both logistically and tactically, than that at Santiago. In both of these later operations, Army forces had clearly defined objectives and were able to work at their own pace rather than in hasty response to the requirements of naval strategy. Both expeditions embarked from more commodious bases than Tampa, possessed adequate shipping and landing craft (the Puerto Rico expedition benefited in this respect from War Department efforts to help Shafter), and landed at harbors significantly more suitable than Daiquiri and Siboney. They were much better outfitted with land transportation than the V Corps had been, they fought over country with more extensive road networks, and they were able to procure additional transportation, as well as some supplies, on the spot—something the V Corps could not do in the war-ravaged Santiago region. Tactically, the forces in Puerto Rico and the Philippines faced much weaker opposition than that encountered at Santiago; combat in Puerto Rico, in fact, consisted only of minor skirmishes. Both forces, nevertheless, reconnoitered thoroughly, outflanked fortified positions whenever possible, and showed that they could prepare systematically for large-scale operations and conduct them efficiently. In the Philippines, the VIII Corps, which captured Manila and then fought the Filipino insurgents, achieved a high level of tactical and logistical competence. It did so with volunteer troops armed with the old Springfields and with commanders and staff officers generally similar in training and experience to those at Santiago. Army performance in these other theaters indicates that the troubles at Santiago probably stemmed more from the particular circumstances of that campaign than from inherent service deficiencies in organization, training, or doctrine.[65]

At the time, the Army learned relatively few tactical lessons directly from San Juan and El Caney, and some it did learn were incorrect in light of later developments. All participants at Santiago were united in condemning the use of black powder and the Springfield rifle—the latter more because of the rifle's high trajectory than for its lack of a magazine. Even the conservative Ordnance Department, however, had abandoned black powder before the war and issued it to the artillery and volunteers at Santiago only for lack of anything else. Employment of the Springfield was also a stopgap. The inability of batteries to stay on San Juan Hill under Spanish musketry did not shake the predominant faith in direct-fire artillery tactics. Instead, officers of other arms criticized the artillery at Santiago for not having followed the doctrine aggressively enough, or they complained that the V Corps had had too few guns. Captain Parker pointed out the enormous potential of the machine gun, but he emphasized its offensive value as a substitute for conventional artillery and gave little consideration to what would have happened at San Juan Hill if the Spaniards also had had Gatlings. Probably the transport and landing-craft deficiencies of the expedition, its supply difficulties on shore, the epidemics that followed the surrender of Santiago, and the administratively messy evacuation of the corps to quarantine camp at Montauk Point had more long-range impact on the development of the Army than did any tactical occurrence. These logistical deficiencies, combined with administrative breakdowns and epidemics in the large volunteer camps in the United States, created a political furor that focused public attention on Army reform and provided strong talking points for Secretary of War Elihu Root's drive to create a general staff, reorganize the War Department bureaus, and reform the National Guard.[66]

The Spanish-American War and the overseas commitments that resulted from it brought permanent change to the Army. The service remained at a strength of 100,000 men—many of them engaged in counterinsurgency in the Philippines—for three years after the end of hostilities against Spain. The Army emerged from the war with much-enlarged equipment stockpiles, an ocean transport fleet, and commanders and staffs seasoned by campaigning experience. To this foundation, Root between 1899 and 1903 added a general staff, an enlarged officers' school system, expansible organization for the regular force, and the beginnings of effective integration of the National Guard into the military establishment. Under Root and his successors, regulars and National Guardsmen routinely conducted divisional and larger maneuvers. Shortly before World War I, Maj. Gen. Leonard Wood, as chief of staff, finally achieved the organization, at least on paper, of peacetime Regular Army divisions. Adoption of a new three-inch fieldpiece with a recoil-absorbing carriage laid the technological foundation for a shift from direct- to indirect-fire artillery tactics in response to the lessons of the Russo-Japanese War. The War Department rearmed the National Guard with the Krag-

Jörgensen and, in due course, with the successor rifle to the Krag, the 1903
Springfield. Guardsmen would not have to undergo again the experience of
the 71st New York at San Juan and the 2d Massachusetts at El Caney. Army
reformers often cited the events of the Spanish-American War as justifications
for these and other improvements, but the service generally, in the years
before World War I, simply moved at an accelerated pace along lines
established before 1898. The nation went to war with Germany in 1917 with
an army fairly well prepared to fight a larger version of the conflict with
Spain.[67]

The Santiago battles were too brief and too successful to teach the Army
much more about modern warfare than it already knew or thought it knew.
San Juan Hill and El Caney, in fact, decided the Santiago campaign and to a
large extent the war. On 3 July, Admiral Cervera, concluding that his position
in the city had become untenable, took his squadron out to sea to its
destruction. The city garrison—down to 190 rounds of ammunition per man,
its food shortage worsened by Escario's arrival the day of Cervera's disaster,
and cut off from escape or additional relief—capitulated on 17 July after a
siege and much tedious negotiation. Its surrender included all the other
Spanish troops in Santiago province. Then followed the easy victories in
Puerto Rico and at Manila. With Cervera's fleet and most of their colonial
empire lost, the Spaniards sued for peace. On 12 August, they signed an
American-dictated armistice under which the United States gained effective
control of Cuba, Puerto Rico, Guam, and Manila. In the Spanish-American
War, the first battles were, for all practical purposes, the last battles.[68]

6

Cantigny, 28–31 May 1918

ALLAN R. MILLETT

On the eve of its greatest challenge since the Civil War, the United States Army found itself caught in organization and operational doctrine between its North American past, its imperial present, and its European future. An army of many missions, its major posts in the trans-Mississippi West and abroad in the newly gained possessions of Hawaii, the Philippines, and the Canal Zone reflected the Army's multiple tasks. The worst but least likely contingency was a major war with another industrial nation. If the enemy was Great Britain, the war would probably include an overland invasion from Canada, the seizure of an enclave in the northern Atlantic states, and a campaign for Caribbean bases. A war with Germany would involve the same problems, less the Canadian invasion. A war with Japan, however, would begin thousands of miles away in the Philippines or, perhaps, Hawaii, which would mean that the Navy would have to bear the principal responsibility for victory or defeat. From its birth in 1900, War Plan Orange, the contingency plan for war with Japan, assumed it unlikely that the Philippines could be held. Hawaii and the Canal Zone, however, seemed defensible.

In reality, the planners of the War Department General Staff paid just as much attention to major military operations in the Western hemisphere against Latin foes, principally the Cubans and Mexicans. War Plan Tan examined the problems of supporting an incumbent Cuban government against an insurgent army, while War Plan Green developed the strategy for intervention in Mexico, a distinct possibility after the Mexican Revolution in 1910. The likelihood of military operations against the Mexicans kept much of the Regular Army, in fact, mobilized along the border after 1913. When Woodrow Wilson sent the Army's 4th Brigade from Texas to Vera Cruz in April 1914 to hold the port, seized by a landing force of marines and sailors, many Army officers thought it was only the first step in War Plan Green, a modern version of Winfield Scott's 1847 campaign against Mexico City.[1]

Except for minor expeditions to the Caribbean and peacekeeping along the Mexican border, the War Department General Staff knew it did not have enough troops. From 1903 until 1916, it turned its attention to designing a system of manpower mobilization that reconciled wartime force estimates with the vagaries of the American political system. The latter virtually insured that the nation would not adopt compulsory peacetime military training on the European model. One option was to increase the size of the Regular Army, and that did occur beween 1901 and 1916. Largely driven by the estimated demands of imperial defense, Congress raised the Army to a paper strength of 100,000 officers and men in 1901, then funded real-strength increases in small increments toward and past this goal. In 1915, for example, the Army had 4,798 officers and 101,195 enlisted men, a host four times larger than the pre-1898 Army, but only one-tenth the estimated needs for a major war. In the National Defense Act of 1916, Congress increased the size of the U.S. Army to 175,000, but this increase was to be accomplished over a five-year period. When it went to war with Germany, the United States had only 5,971 officers and 121,797 enlisted men in the Regular Army.

The nation, however, did have a land-force reserve, the National Guard of the United States, built on the states' volunteer militia. After the war with Spain, the National Guard reform movement had borne limited results. The Militia Acts of 1903 and 1908 had traded federal financial support for greater War Department control over militia organization, training, and employment. In sum, the legislation helped steer the militia toward a primary role of wartime mobilization and the creation of organized units ready for the battlefield. A coalition of National Guard officers, in fact, took control of the National Guard Association of the United States and used its political influence to improve the Guard's readiness, a movement that culminated in the National Defense Act of 1916. This act, which required guardsmen to take a dual federal and state oath, removed the constitutional uncertainty about the Guard's obligation to serve beyond the continental United States or to mobilize without a declaration of war. It did not, however, change the Guard's voluntary character. Without further incentives such as federal drill pay, the Guard remained far short of its authorized strength of 450,000. In April 1917, the National Guard numbered 174,008 officers and men.[2]

U.S. Army tactical structure showed substantial recognition that the Army had changed from a frontier constabulary and coast-defense organization to a more balanced force capable of meeting a modern enemy in the initial stages of a major land war. The General Staff's periodic proposals, finally accepted by Congress in 1916, placed major emphasis on the "Mobile Army." The proposed increases were based on estimates developed for garrisoning overseas possessions and creating a field army in the United States, either to reinforce possessions or to conduct operations in the Western hemisphere. Not surprisingly, the General Staff sought increases in all the combat arms, but in proportional terms it wanted the most important increases in the infantry and field artillery. While the cavalry would expand from fifteen to twenty-five regiments after 1916, the infantry was to increase from thirty to sixty-five regiments.

The most dramatic changes, however, occurred in the artillery. A major artillery reorganization in 1907 reflected an increased emphasis on the field artillery, re-established as six regiments of thirty-six firing batteries. Two regiments were designated pack or mountain artillery, which meant that their weapons were light and designed for mule transportation over rough terrain along the Mexican border and in the Philippines. The massing of batteries supported a plan to create an artillery brigade whenever the Army fielded a full division. The coast artillery, however, remained the dominant artillery branch. It mustered 170 companies to man coastal guns in the United States and abroad. The 1915 artillery establishment numbered around 5,700 officers and men in field artillery units and nearly 20,000 in the Coast Artillery Corps.[3]

The National Defense Act of 1916 did not immediately change the balance of field to coast artillery, but it did reflect a heightened appreciation for artillery in land combat. The legislation increased the coast artillery companies from 215 in 1915 to 263, fewer than artillery planners thought advisable. The field artillery, on the other hand, was supposed to expand from six to twenty-one regiments, the largest proportional increase of any of the Army's combat arms. In April 1917, the field artillery had already expanded to nearly 8,500 while coast artillery strength remained stable. The General Staff had examined the reports of its own observers and analysts of the Russo-Japanese War (1904–05) and the fighting in the Balkans before the First World War. In summarizing the lessons learned from the twentieth century's first wars, the chief of ordnance in 1915 made a prescient case for expanding the field artillery, a case then viewed as heresy by cavalry and infantry officers: "It appears that although field artillery has played an important role in all modern wars, its use has now been extended to the point where it becomes a question as to whether it does not actually make the main attack, which is rendered permanently effective by the infantry advance, instead of, as formally considered, being used to prepare the way for the main attack to be made by the infantry."[4]

The trends identified by the chief of ordnance, which included the adoption of heavier field artillery guns and howitzers, did not fit well with the Army's prevalent view of waging war, which emphasized mobility and infantry firepower. In strategic and tactical terms, the Army's officer corps since the Napoleonic era had stressed the importance of offensive operations, an emphasis reinforced by its limited forces and the vastness of the North American continent. A century of warfare with the Indians probably reinforced this disposition, but it also reflected the realities of meeting a foreign invader, conducting operations in Mexico, and buying time for the nation to mobilize. In analyzing and war-gaming land campaigns with Great Britain and Mexico, for example, the faculty of the Army War College stressed the importance of strategic mobility, particularly the use of railroads and steamships to support the Army. The same emphasis came in massing forces to meet a Japanese invasion of the Philippines, Hawaii, Alaska, and California. The principal text Army officers consulted on the nation's wars, Capt. Matthew F. Steele's *American Campaigns* (1909), exalted maneuver at the strategic level and applauded the leadership of such offensive-minded, maneuver-oriented commanders of the Civil War as Grant, Sherman, Jackson, and Lee. The Army's fascination with Germany's campaigns between 1864 and 1871 further reinforced the officer corps' commitment to offensive operations. At the Army School of the Line and the Staff College at Fort Leavenworth, the hotbed of operational instruction and doctrinal analysis, the Army's most promising junior line officers learned that the essence of battlefield success was the use of surprise, maneuver, and the envelopment. One officer who attended both Leavenworth and the Army War College thought that strategic and tactical mobility in theory had so mesmerized the officer corps that it overlooked the fact that "somebody has to take the enemy head on . . . to go up against it—a sad but unavoidable fact that helps materially . . . to make war hell."[5]

As codified in the Army's *Field Service Regulations (FSR),* the bible for field commanders and largely the work of the Leavenworth faculty, offensive action by infantry "gives the entire battle its character. . . . *Decisive results are obtained only by the offensive.*" Although artillery fire could reduce the enemy's resistance, the success of any attack depended ultimately on the infantry's ability to deliver high volumes of aimed fire and distribute it against all the enemy forces in its zone of action. In fact, argued Col. John F. Morrison, the Army's foremost tactical theorist and instructor in the prewar schools, untrained infantry exaggerated the effectiveness of artillery fire, which could be neutralized by properly extended combat formations and rapid movement through the artillery's beaten zone. On the other hand, musketry could cause casualties and suppress enemy fire and movement at ranges up to 1,200 yards. Although a defender might have the advantage of prepared positions or natural cover, experienced infantry could still move forward by bounds. Movement would be possible as the infantry increased the volume and accuracy of its rifle fire as it reduced the range to its targets. Naturally, the skilled commander would seek an open enemy flank so he could deliver his fire along the long axis of the enemy's position and increase its physical and moral effect. The U.S. Army did not disregard elan; however, it was an army not of bayonet thrusters of the Grandmaison school but of keen marksmen.

Morrison and the *Field Service Regulations* recognized that artillery and machine-gun fire might contribute to the attack, but indirect fire would never replace musketry as arbiter of the battlefield. Capt. Oliver L. Spaulding, Jr., the Army's foremost writer on artillery affairs and a protégé of Morrison, agreed that the major role of artillery was to allow the infantry to advance to within effective rifle range. Like its European contemporaries, the American artillery had adopted light fieldpieces capable of rapid fire, the optimum weapons to keep opposing defenders under cover while friendly infantry advanced. Artillery fire, if properly massed and timed, might crush the defenders of a fixed objective, but it would probably be more effective protecting the flanks from counterattacks and delivering counterbattery fire. Spaulding saw the possibility that the artillery might have to surrender some mobility in order to increase the weight of its fire, but before 1917, the theory of artillery employment fit the Army's general concept of land warfare, which saw battle as a struggle of widely maneuvering, semi-independent divisions of infantry with minimal cavalry and artillery support.[6]

The Army's emphasis on mobility and infantry firepower for offensive operations shaped its training. In addition to extensive marksmanship programs, infantry regiments stressed small-unit tactics, physical training, individual infantry skills, long hikes under full field equipment, and scouting and patrolling. When the "Mobile Army" took the field for large-unit maneuvers, a common feature of training after 1910, it exercised in conformity with the *FSR*'s maneuver warfare doctrine. After 1913, most units of the "Mobile Army" deployed along the Mexican border where they trained hard for possible war. The largest concentrations of these troops outside the cavalry regiments patrolling the border were the 8th Brigade (El Paso) and the 2d Division (Texas City and the lower valley of the Rio Grande). These exercises gave Army officers more practical experience than they had had since the pacification of the Philippines and the subsequent Moro campaigns. Successive commanders of the 2d Division, including Maj. Gens. J. Franklin Bell, Frederick Funston, and William H. Carter, reported to Chief of Staff Leonard Wood that the division had reached a peak of skill unusual for peacetime. The commander of the 8th Brigade, Brig. Gen. John J. Pershing, observed equally favorable results from his training program. The crisis of 1916, however, disrupted the training. While Pershing's Punitive Expedition plunged into northwestern Mexico after Pancho Villa's guerrilla horsemen, the 2d Division assumed a border-security mission and had to provide many skilled officers and noncommissioned officers to organize and train the 100,000-some National Guardsmen mobilized by Woodrow Wilson.[7]

The Army's weaponry reflected its commitment to maneuver warfare, and it entered the First World War lightly armed by 1917 standards although not by 1914 standards. The infantry's .30-caliber Springfield magazine rifle, Model 1903, was among the best in the world for long-range shooting. The standard machine gun was less impressive. Army doctrine assumed that machine-gun design would continue to follow two paths, the development of heavy machine guns on the Vickers-Maxim model for defensive purposes and the adoption of light (fewer than thirty pounds) machine guns or automatic rifles for infantry offensive missions. The U.S. Army went light and chose an Ordnance invention, the Benét–Mercié gun, noted for its inaccuracy and tendency to jam. Only the war emergency galvanized the Army's machine-gun program, which eventually produced the superb family of .30-caliber weapons invented by John M. Browning: the water-cooled heavy machine gun M1917, the air-cooled light machine gun M1919A1, and the Browning automatic rifle M1918. None of these weapons appeared on the Western Front until the war's end, and most American infantry in France fought with the French Chauchat automatic rifle and the Hotchkiss heavy machine gun. The standard field artillery piece was the high-velocity, flat-trajectory 3-inch gun, M1902, which resembled the famous French 75-mm artillery piece. The artillery's prime movers still ate oats, not gas. Of the special weapons of the Western Front—heavy field howitzers, mortars, hand and rifle grenades, poison gas, flame-throwers, and 37-mm man-portable artillery—Americans knew little except what they read in military journals.[8]

In field service, the U.S. Army's line officers, however, had a wealth of experience by 1917. About a third had served in the Spanish-American War and the Philippine Insurrection (campaigns that did not impress their European colleagues), and many others had seen arduous field service in the Moro country and along the Mexican border. The experience, however, was concentrated. In April 1917, the Army had 5,791 officers, of whom only 3,885 had had more than one year's service and were available for general assignments. Moreover, the amount of formal military education in the officer corps was limited. Of the officers available for line service, about half were West Point graduates, but only 379 were graduates of the Staff College or the Army War College, the assumed *sine qua non* for high command or general staff service. The National Guard and the Reserve Officer Corps (created in 1916) provided another 6,000 officers with some military experience, but many of the volunteer veterans of 1898–1901 had become too old for combat service as company grade officers. Throughout World War I, the Army suffered from uneven leadership by its junior officers, largely because so many of them did not have the time to learn and live on the Western Front. The senior officers of the American Expeditionary Forces (AEF) were predomi-nantly (over 80 percent) West Point graduates, but more than half of these career professionals, who ranged from thirty-five to sixty years in age, had no postcommissioning schooling. Of the AEF's generals, only one, John J. Pershing, had ever commanded even a brigade in action, a fact not lost on the British and French. The Allies did not think a tour at Leavenworth counted for much, and even Pershing did not think division commanders should be over forty years old. In April 1917, officers of comparable youth were mere majors and captains. In sum, the Army officer corps was a question mark.[9]

Serious students of German military affairs for a generation, the officers of the U.S. Army, especially the school-trained elite, knew in 1917 that they faced the world's premier combat force, the Imperial German Army. While sailing toward France, one American general overheard two of his staff officers discussing the coming campaign. The officers were "Leavenworth instructors who by their studies at that school have in my opinion been [so] impressed with the efficiency of the Germans as soldiers that they have plainly weakened their own courage in the face of the Germans. The impression the average man derives from hearing them is the hopelessness, the utter folly of our resisting or fighting the Germans at all."[10] However irritating, military Germanophilia had merit. Outnumbered, faced with a three-front war (largely of its own making), pressed by a naval blockade, the German Army had expanded from 840,000 (1914) to 6 million (1917). In the war's fourth year, the Germans—fielding 241 divisions—still held the Allies at bay, and by the end of the year, they and their Austro-Hungarian collaborators had eliminated the Russians and Italians as threats. Although the German Army had already suffered more casualties by 1917 than both sides in the American Civil War, it was still a dangerous, professionally adept force. And, unlike its British and French counterparts on the Western Front, it had established a pattern of doctrinal adaptation to the new conditions of war.

In organizational terms, the Germans recognized the dynamic relationship between firepower and maneuver. Although the *Grosser Generalstab* tripled its peacetime infantry establishment, it increased its artillery establishment by a factor of five and equipped it with heavier howitzers and mortars. The basic combat formation, the division, had been reduced to around 12,000 men for greater mobility, largely by dropping one infantry regiment and most of its cavalry. In 1917, the combat power of the German division centered in an infantry brigade (8,500 men) of three regiments and an artillery command of three battalions (thirty-six field guns and howitzers and 1,300 men). Each infantry battalion contained a headquarters, a machine-gun company, a light-mortar detachment, and four infantry companies numbered consecutively by regiment. (The I Battalion would, for example, be composed of the 1st, 2d, 3d, and 4th Companies; the III Battalion, the 9th, 10th, 11th, and 12th Companies.) The German division was light on division support troops (engineers, communicators, drivers, clerks), who numbered only 1,600.

The Germans had made the machine gun their national weapon. Each infantry company had three to six Spandau light machine guns, and each machine-gun company contained twelve Maxim heavy machine guns. Every infantry battalion, therefore, if fully supplied, could point thirty-six machine guns at its foe, a fact the British learned with horror on the Somme. On the other hand, the dramatic increase in infantry firepower also reduced the number of riflemen available for attacks in the standard infantry battalion. To compensate for the diminished mobility and elan of the average infantry battalion, the Germans in 1916 created special assault detachments, storm troops *(Stosstruppen)* of battalion strength. With the exception of flame-throwers and light man-packed cannon, the assault battalion had much the same armament as the average battalion, but its riflemen were specially picked and trained and their numbers kept up to full strength.[11]

If the Germans had any secret weapon, it was not their arms or their organization. German prowess rested on tactical doctrine and the rigorous training necessary to make doctrine work. Although the German Army by 1917 had not completed its major offensive reform—the adoption of infantry infiltration attacks with short, intense barrages—it had already developed a system of flexible defense that confounded the Allies. German defensive doctrine rested on the organization of defenses in depth with as few troops forward as possible; but these troops were concentrated in strongpoints amply provided with machine guns. In an infantry regiment's sector, only one battalion would man both the outpost zone (up to a kilometer in depth) and the positional defenses of the battle zone, as much as two kilometers deep. The frontage was normally a kilometer wide. The other battalions occupied the support and rest positions. The support battalion stood ready to mount immediate counterattacks in the battle zone, positioned so that it did not draw direct fire; the rest battalion occupied positions outside of most Allied artillery fire, but it too had to remain prepared for counterattack missions.

In addition to the standard deluge of shells that German artillery could drop upon attacking troops, the counterattack was the key to the flexible defense. German doctrine insisted that front-line commanders mount both immediate and deliberate counterattacks, thus taking advantage of the disruption caused by machine-gun fire and artillery barrages. The management of counterattacks rested with the commander of the combat battalion in the battle zone, not the reinforcing unit. In fact, battalion commanders could deal directly with division headquarters in arranging counterattacks. And the Germans proved in 1917 that the doctrine worked. Its success derived in part from conceptual soundness and partly from the German command system's effectiveness in ensuring that the doctrine was taught to the officers and men who had to make it work.[12]

For all the popular enthusiasm that swelled with the declaration of war against Germany on 6 April 1917, the War Department General Staff estimated that the United States could not soon fight on the Western Front. The General Staff had concluded that the war would be won or lost in France. Allied diplomatic and military missions to the United States reinforced this judg-ment. Army planners believed that the wartime army for such an enormous mission would require no less than 1 million men and might reach 4 million. To raise, organize, arm and equip, train, and deploy such a force might take two years. The planners were confident that a combination of volunteering and conscription, administered on a national basis, would provide the men, but they doubted that American industry could convert rapidly to wartime production. For all the heroic rhetoric, the realities of military mobilization in 1917 meant that the United States could provide only token aid to the Allied cause for months to come.[13]

From the Allies' perspective, their cause needed even symbolic support because their offensives of 1917 had again foundered in the shell-churned mud of the Western Front. Even though ill informed about Allied casualties and the mutinies in the French Army, the people of France and Britain—so their governments reported in Washington—had reached new depths of despair. The Allied cause required an American presence in France as quickly as possible, and that presence should include some combat troops, an augury of the millions of men to follow. The War Department responded by forming the 1st Expeditionary Division (redesignated the 1st Division) on 24 May; the division was built around four infantry and three artillery regiments drawn from the Regular Army. In early June, the extemporized division moved toward its embarkation port at Hoboken, New Jersey. On 14 June, the first contingents sailed for Europe, and a month later all the major elements of the division had departed.

The War Department also sent Major General Pershing to France, but the new commander in chief of the American Expeditionary Forces was no mere symbol. Hardened by field service in Cuba, the Philippines, and Mexico and by the accidental deaths of most of his family members in 1915, Pershing was far more than a simple soldier. He had served on the General Staff, observed the Russo-Japanese War, and developed personal connections with Washington's political elite. He had studied European military developments and spoke some French. And he had in abundance the qualities Secretary of War Newton D. Baker thought essential: a willingness to accept political guidance, staunch nationalism, organizational ability, physical vigor, enormous determination, and great pride in the latent abilities of the American officer corps. In his instructions to Pershing, Baker stressed that the AEF must retain a distinct national character and that Pershing should not commit the AEF to battle until he thought it was combat ready. To shape the size and timing of the American expedition to France, Pershing and a small staff sailed on 28 May.[14]

Within three months of arriving in France, Pershing's General Headquarters, American Expeditionary Forces (GHQ AEF), had completed its first major task: drafting a plan for forming an army in France and deploying it against the Germans. Pershing reported to Baker that the AEF should reach a minimum strength of 1 million men, which would require a troop base of 3 million. Reaching similar conclusions, the administration had already persuaded Congress to pass the Selective Service Act in May 1917 and had begun the organization of a wartime draft for a "National Army." If it could

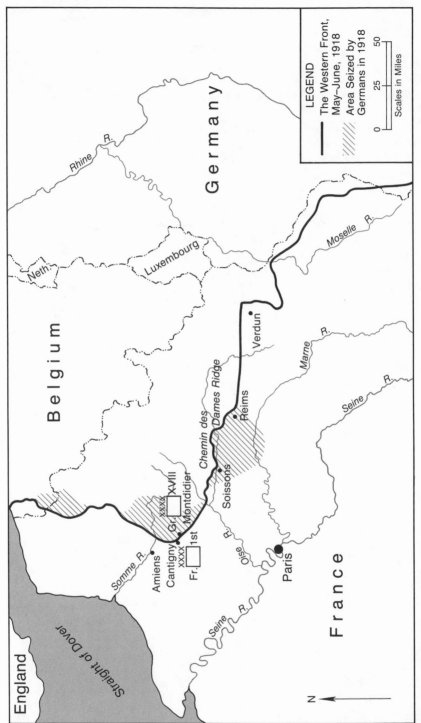

Map 6.1. The Western Front, May 1918

LEGEND

The Western Front, May–June, 1918

Area Seized by Germans in 1918

Scales in Miles

0   25   50

overcome materiel shortages, the AEF should be ready for a minor offensive in 1918 and a major campaign in 1919. Pershing's planners selected the fortress city of Metz, an important German railway complex, and the neighboring Saar basin (rich in coal and iron ore) as the AEF's strategic objective area. Selection of the Lorraine sector for the AEF's offensive action allowed Pershing to develop a training-camp system and logistical complex south of the operational triangle (Verdun to the east, the English Channel to the north, and the mouth of the Seine to the west) already dominated by the British Expeditionary Force (BEF) and the French army. The pattern of deployment reflected ''The Chief's'' unshakable commitment to one overriding consideration: the importance of creating an American field army for independent offensive operations.[15]

As part of GHQ AEF's General Organization Project, the U.S. Army changed the structure of its notional division. Under the influence of Allied advisers and the first reports of its own military missions to France, the War Department in July 1917 cut the size of the division from 28,256 men to 19,492, largely by eliminating one of three infantry brigades (three regiments) and reducing the two remaining brigades from three to two regiments. The divisional cavalry regiment also disappeared. The artillery brigade retained three regiments with seventy-four guns and added a battery of twelve trench mortars. In firepower terms, the major change came in the addition of a machine-gun company to each of the twelve infantry battalions, but each infantry battalion dropped one of its four rifle companies.

Pershing's staff did not think the War Department division of July 1917 had enough manpower—especially in riflemen—to conduct offensive operations in France, and in less than a month, GHQ AEF designed another division. The AEF division, the wonder of the Western Front, ballooned up to 27,124 officers and men. As approved in August 1917, the standard AEF division (which varied little throughout the rest of the war) was infantry rich and represented a compromise between Allied advice about trench combat and the American devotion to maneuver warfare. The number of infantrymen almost doubled (from 7,344 to 12,288) by increasing the size of each rifle company to 250 and returning the fourth rifle company to each of the division's twelve infantry battalions. The infantry battalion lost its organic machine-gun company, but each regiment gained an organic machine-gun company and detachments of 37-mm man-portable cannon and 3-inch mortars. The machine-gun companies were reorganized as one battalion of three companies for each of the two infantry brigades. The machine-gun establishment added a third divisional machine-gun battalion of four companies, which meant that the American division entered combat in 1918 with fourteen machine-gun companies, each with twelve or sixteen guns. AEF planners did not have to be shot with Maxims to appreciate the role of machine guns on the Western Front.[16]

Under French influence, the internal organization of the American rifle company underwent dramatic changes. In 1917, the French infantry company numbered 172 soldiers, but only 68 were primarily riflemen; in the American company, 200 were riflemen, organized in 8-man squads. After much experimentation, the 1st Division as a tactical laboratory for the AEF created an infantry company that added French weapons—the Chauchat automatic rifle, hand grenades, and rifle grenades—and the tactics to exploit their destructiveness without reducing the number of riflemen and the traditional emphasis on musketry. In addition to the company headquarters (two officers, twenty enlisted men), the company had four platoons, each organized as a headquarters and four sections. The first section (twelve enlisted) contained the company's "hand bombers" or grenadiers; the second section (nine enlisted), rifle grenadiers; the third section (seventeen enlisted), riflemen; and the fourth section (fourteen enlisted), automatic riflemen. The first, second, and fourth sections included rifle-armed ammunition carriers who could perform riflemen's functions, and the company's full establishment armament included 235 rifles, combined with 16 automatic rifles. In tactical terms, the standard infantry formation was two platoons in the assault and two in support, which gave the company commander some latitude for maneuver. The standard platoon formation had the same boxlike character. The 1st Division adopted three variations of the standard two sections in a first line, two in the second, in order to both mass fire to the front and provide riflemen for enveloping enemy positions such as machine-gun nests. Nevertheless, the emphasis in the first line was on hand grenadiers and automatic riflemen, the emphasis in the second on riflemen and rifle grenadiers.[17]

The AEF organizational project had other characteristics that could not be explained in precise operational terms. The division's size represented not just GHQ AEF's estimates on the requirements of sustained offensive combat but also a fear that the U.S. Army could not provide enough division commanders and staffs to control a larger number of smaller divisions. From the summer of 1917 to the Armistice, British and French generals expressed concern about the ability of American officers to command divisions, corps, and armies. Their pessimism was directly related to proposals that American units be "amalgamated" into manpower-starved Allied formations in sizes ranging from battalions to divisions. Pershing found such proposals anathema to his mission and his professional pride, and his staff unanimously supported his position. When the War Department wavered on amalgamation (as it did several times), Pershing stiffened its resolve to form an independent army, but his stand required that American divisions perform well in their first battles. Thus, GHQ AEF took control of divisional training and used the 1st Division as a model.

The 1st Division had many shortcomings. One was its ability to communicate. The organic field signal battalion had only 262 officers and men, which might have been adequate had it not been for the primitive state of the AEF's communications techniques. Because field radios (using either continuous wave or voice) were undependable and immobile, the division depended principally on runners and telephones, both vulnerable to enemy action. The division exploited every known means of message transmission: carrier pigeons, panel messages for observation aircraft, visual communications by flags and signal lamps, and buzzer codes sent over telephone lines. But its ability in command-and-control ("liaison" in World War I usage) seldom met a commander's needs in action. The only alternative, Pershing's staff reasoned, was elaborate planning and rigidly prescribed schemes of fire and maneuver.

The communications problem had a direct effect on the most important element of warfare on the Western Front, infantry-artillery coordination. GHQ AEF's design of the AEF division was supposed to maximize infantry-artillery cooperation, and its own general staff college in France in late 1917 stressed that artillery considerations should shape all offensive planning. Normally, a division would require reinforcing fires from corps and army heavy artillery in order to conduct a successful attack, even assuming some degree of tactical surprise. Although AEF doctrine stressed the difference between open and trench warfare, it did not compromise on the essential element of artillery superiority. The problem was that open warfare required an ability to spot and adjust artillery fire, and such a capability was difficult to maintain in a division on the move. Ground observation posts were hard to find, man, and link with guns, so spotter aircraft carried the burden. But aircraft needed overhead air cover, accurate knowledge of the ground situation, and secure radio links back to the artillery. The 1st Division did not neglect infantry-artillery liaison on the ground, however. Before its first battle, the division's standing operating procedure (SOP) for artillery liaison placed officer-led artillery liaison teams with each infantry regiment and NCO-led teams with each battalion. Even before Cantigny, these teams had swelled to seventy officers and men for each infantry regiment, but the function of the artillery liaison teams centered on reconciling infantry movement and needs with preplanned fires, not adjusting fire on targets of opportunity. The fragile nature of dependable communications limited the flexibility of providing artillery fire, a major consideration in planning any attack.[18]

Whatever the doctrinal emphasis on infantry-artillery cooperation, the circumstances of the 1st Division's training in France limited the division's ability to develop as a combined-arms team. In accordance with a Franco-American agreement to arm the AEF with French artillery pieces, a decision designed to free scarce shipping for men and to exploit France's developed ordnance industry, the 1st Artillery Brigade (5th, 6th, and 7th Field Artillery regiments) went to the French artillery training center at Le Valdahon rather than the division's training area near Gondrecourt. From August to October

1917, the brigade learned to fire its new weapons, French 75-mm guns and 155-mm Schneider howitzers. It had much to learn about World War I artillery procedures, and it learned well, but it did not see any of the division's infantry until the 1st Division rotated its infantry regiments into the line in the Sommerviller sector in October and November 1917. For its introduction to the trenches, both the artillery and infantry battalions remained firmly under French control. In the meantime, the infantry of the 1st Division underwent a rigorous training schedule that stressed weapons proficiency, individual and small-unit tactics, and physical conditioning. The 1st Division had all the disadvantages of being "Exhibit A," as its operations officer, Lt. Col. George C. Marshall, characterized it. Pershing and his staff kept it under continuous pressure to train hard and behave with the highest discipline. They also wanted it to prepare for open warfare. The division's French advisers, on the other hand, stressed trench-warfare techniques.[19]

In both styles of combat, the division had much to learn, for its regular Army status meant little in military experience. Two-thirds of its enlisted men were wartime volunteers, and only 40 percent of its NCOs had had prewar service. Only half the company commanders were prewar officers, and all the platoon commanders were either brand-new officers from officer candidate schools or newly commissioned NCOs. The division felt the ravages of the AEF's expansion: officers and NCOs left its ranks for school training, staff assignments, and service in the burgeoning AEF services of supply.

By December 1917, however, the division's senior officer ranks stabilized with the assignment of an elite group, some personally selected by Pershing to compensate for the division's inexperience and the likelihood that it would be the first to fight. Pershing replaced Maj. Gen. William L. Sibert, a much-loved engineer, with Maj. Gen. Robert L. Bullard, an experienced infantryman with combat experience in the Philippines. A lean, articulate, ambitious Alabaman, Bullard completely approved of Pershing's open warfare doctrine, but he also gloried in his ability to get along with the French (rather too well, some thought) in their own language. The infantry brigade commanders were Beaumont B. Buck and George B. Duncan; both became division commanders. The artillery brigade commander, Charles P. Summerall, already had a reputation for great technical skill, absolute fearlessness, and uncompromising discipline and performance standards. The quality of the regimental commanders was no less impressive. In the infantry, Cols. John L. Hines, Frank Parker, and Hanson Ely later commanded divisions and corps, and Col. Hamilton A. Smith of the 26th Infantry would have had he survived Soissons. The artillery regimental commanders, especially Col. Lucius R. Holbrook of the 7th Field Artillery, were no less able. Bullard's two principal staff officers, Col. Campbell King (chief of staff) and Marshall, were polished products of the Army school system, accomplished field soldiers, and highly regarded by GHQ AEF. In fact as well as in division lore, the 1st Division's officers were first rate.[20]

The pressure on the 1st Division accelerated during the winter of 1917-18, for the Allied cause appeared to be on the brink of disaster. Victories in Russia and Italy had allowed the Germans to assign scarce divisions to the Western Front for a great offensive in 1918. As yet, the American reinforcement had made no significant improvement in the Allied situation. Slowed by materiel shortages and clumsy Home Front mobilization, the War Department's ambitious thirty-division program had produced only four combat divisions and fewer than 200,000 men in France. Talks of amalgamation filled conference rooms in London, Paris, and Washington, and the British bombarded the War Department with various schemes to send shipping for American soldiers, provided they were infantrymen and machine-gunners available to the BEF for emergency use.

When the 1st Division returned to the front in January 1918 for further seasoning in the trenches, its senior officers knew that Pershing regarded it as the prime example of what the AEF might produce in combat effectiveness—in time. Over the next three months, this impression was reinforced by constant visits from French and American senior officers and staff entourages. Plagued by miserable weather and German shelling, the division's principal problems in the Ansauville sector were administrative and logistical, not tactical. Its limited fights were small-unit affairs in the trench-warfare mode, and its most elaborate raids did not go well. The division unquestionably could hold defensive positions, but its offensive potential remained untested. French observers worried about the division's staff work, its consumption of supplies and engineering materials, the conditions of its horses and trucks, and its artillery planning. Allied criticism focused on the division's size and its numbers of infantrymen, which implied continued skepticism on the GHQ AEF's emphasis on open-warfare offensive capability. As the organizational and doctrinal debate continued, so did the war.[21]

On 21 March 1918, the German Army unleashed its long-expected offensive in the valley of the Somme against the British Fifth and Third Armies, not against the French in the Champagne region where most intelligence experts had expected the attack. Utilizing the combination of short, crushing bombardments and infantry-infiltration assaults, forty-seven German divisions opened a salient forty by fifty miles in the BEF's position. As his troops fought for their lives and the critical transportation junction of Amiens, General Sir Douglas Haig requested French reinforcements as planned, and French headquarters dispatched its First Army to hold the southern half of the salient. In the crisis, the Allies finally agreed to place operations in the hands of a supreme commander, General Ferdinand Foch, who met with Pershing on 28 March. Although his staff correctly judged that the Allies could halt the Germans without American help, Pershing volunteered the AEF for emergency service under Allied commanders. In an emotional conversation with Foch, French army commander General Henri Philippe Pétain, and Premier Georges Clemenceau, Pershing promised that "all we have is yours." For all practical purposes, Pershing meant that he would add the 1st Division to the growing French presence in Picardy where the Allies had halted the German offensive. On 1 April 1918, the 1st Division began to move to an assembly area north of Paris where it would conduct one last maneuver and then join the French First Army. The division had started on the road to Cantigny.[22]

Having completed a full-division exercise in open warfare, the 1st Division started to hike toward the front on 17 April, but this hike was not like the winter's training marches or tortuous struggles to the Saint-Mihiel trenches. The weather had turned fair, and daylight lingered well into the evening, bathing the blossoming French countryside with a yellow twilight glow until late evening. The farmlands north of the Seine were unscarred, and the families who gathered to wave to the Americans seemed more friendly than the dour peasants of eastern France. Some conditions had not changed, however. The "doughboys" of the 1st Division went to war burdened with packs and equipment that staggered mules. The files of marching infantry did not move rapidly as pack straps cut into shoulders, backs ached, and shinsplints sent shooting pains through lower legs. The smell of sweat hung around the columns of men in olive-drab woolen uniforms with choke collars and leg wrappings; officers had no need for their raincoats, and the men's overcoats went into the massive packs that towered over their shoulders. With their shallow helmets riding precariously on their heads, the men moved northward, aware of a high sense of drama and the division's reinforcing mission. What they did not know was that the 1st Division was marching toward war in temporary disfavor with GHQ AEF.[23]

Although Pershing and his staff believed the 1st Division could handle any combat mission, they expressed displeasure with several aspects of the division's movement to Picardy. For one thing, General Bullard had hospitalized himself (then discharged himself as well) with a severe case of neuritis. Pershing's staff argued that Bullard should be replaced, but Pershing allowed the weakened division commander to rejoin his troops. GHQ AEF also had to respond to the complaints of the 26th ("Yankee") Division that the 1st Division had left its sector at Ansauville unpoliced. Amid rumors of relief and disgrace, AEF inspectors interviewed the alleged villains, largely officers of the 1st Artillery Brigade and the 26th Infantry, before concluding that the 26th Division and the French were more culpable than the 1st Division in the turnover of position.

Pershing demonstrated his concern about the 1st Division's performance by assembling its senior officers for a brief talk on 16 April. No orator, he nevertheless impressed his listeners with the importance of winning the AEF's first battles, at whatever the cost. His concern increased four days later when German storm troops assaulted and punished a front-line regiment of the 26th Division at Seicheprey. Although the French high command did not regard the Seicheprey affair as important, GHQ AEF concluded that the Yankee Division had given the Germans reason to believe their own propaganda regarding American ineptness. Feeling the pressure, 1st Division commanders studied their training and found it flawed. The infantry had not had enough marksmanship training; only the 28th Infantry had a majority of trained riflemen. Artillery-infantry coordination left much room for improvement. Tactical instructions had been too complex, complicated by high personnel turnover. The division staff blamed its French advisers for much of the confusion in training because they refused to approve AEF open-warfare techniques. Confident of the troops' morale but skeptical of their state of training, the division's commanders moved their units into the line on the night of 24–25 April.[24]

Roughly five kilometers west of Montdidier, a major road junction in German hands, the Cantigny sector had seen active fighting between French First Army divisions and the lead elements of the German *Eighteenth Army* until 23 April. The battle had been fluid as the Germans seized the terrain they needed to hold Montdidier and to create the impression that they would continue the drive towards Amiens. A new battlefield, the sector had many shell holes and unburied bodies but few prepared positions. An area of gently rolling terrain broken by thick wood lots, shallow ravines, and small farm towns, Cantigny offered few critical terrain features, but one was a low ridge some 300 meters from the division's outpost line. The town of Cantigny, broken and deserted during the spring fighting, marked the south edge of the ridge. A shallow ravine south of the town was a true No Man's Land, but the French had held advanced positions further south in the Bois de Cantigny and the Bois de Fontaine. The Germans also held part of the Bois de Fontaine to protect their position at Fontaine-sous-Montdidier, which anchored the southern part of the combat zone confronting the 1st Division. The rest of the German position ran through Hill 104 in the center through the Bois de Framicourt and Bois de Lalval to the north, a kilometer east of Cantigny. The Germans had pushed west of the Cantigny-Grivesnes road in order to seize the ridge, but again the open terrain and the French had conspired to make a further advance unattractive. The result was that Cantigny rested in a salient about 1,000 meters deep and 1,500 meters wide.[25]

Under the direction of the French First Army (Gen. Marie Eugene Debeney) and the X Corps (Maj. Gen. Charles A. Vandenberg), the 1st Division established a defense in depth with the 1st Infantry Brigade forward, both regiments abreast (battalions in column), and the 2d Infantry Brigade in reserve. The 1st Artillery Brigade occupied positions in echeloned depth,

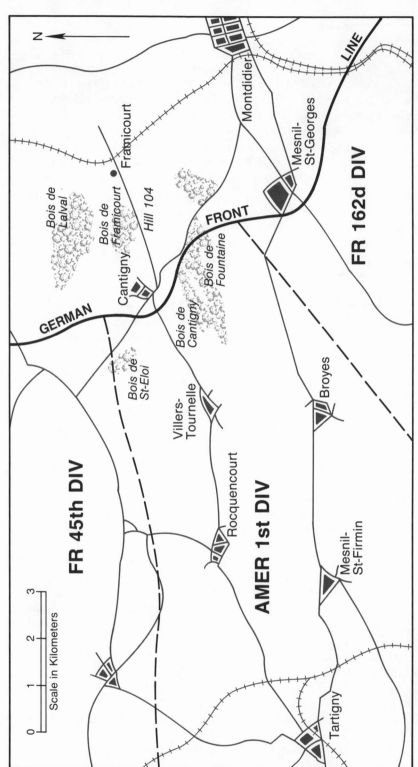

N

Bois de
Laval

Bois de
Framicourt

Framicourt

Hill 104

Cantigny

Bois de
St-Eloi

GERMAN

FRONT

Bois de
Cantigny

Bois de
Fountaine

Montdidier

Mesnil-
St-Georges

LINE

FR 162d DIV

Villers-
Tournelle

Rocquencourt

Broyes

Mesnil-
St-Firmin

FR 45th DIV

AMER 1st DIV

Tartigny

3

2

1

Scale in Kilometers

0

Map 6.2. Cantigny-Montdidier Sector, May 1918

seeking as much cover and concealment as possible. The entire position needed extensive engineering work. The infantry positions were primarily shell holes linked by shallow lateral trenches; communications trenches extending to the rear did not exist. Because the Germans enjoyed superior ground and air observation in the sector, daytime movement and digging were invitations to disaster. Even nighttime entrenchment had limitations because the white, chalky soil had to be camouflaged. Carrying parties with food, water, and ammunition for the front-line troops could move only at night and often went astray. Deepening heat and the noxious smells of gas and decaying flesh made life in the forward positions tests of endurance. German artillery and air attacks made the division's ordeal memorable. One gas attack eliminated nearly a full battalion of the 18th Infantry; shells and bombs forced the division staff to work deep in the cellars of a nearby chateau; and the demands of command and logistics so exposed the Americans that their casualties doubled those of the French division they had replaced. The 1st Artillery Brigade returned the German shelling, but its effects could not be easily gauged. Bullard and his staff did not relish the division's defensive posture, which tested the soldiers' capacity to suffer but not to fight.[26]

Responsible for the sector northwest of Montdidier, the German *26th Reserve Corps* wanted to pin the French X Corps on the defensive, if only with artillery fire, for the German corps was replacing its first-class assault divisions with less formidable troops. The best divisions moved south for the next major offensive, planned for the Chemin des Dames sector at the end of May. As part of the redeployment, the German *30th Division* surrendered its Cantigny position to the *82d Reserve Division.* Originally formed from men recruited in northwestern Germany and Silesia, the *82d* had spent most of the war on the Eastern Front. Suffering heavily in a 1915 offensive against the Russians, its ranks had been filled with healed veterans, young recruits, dismounted cavalry, overage *landwehr* men, and railway guards. Nearly inactive for about two years, the division had left the Eastern Front for retraining in November 1917. Even after extensive exercises, it did not impress German inspectors, who barely approved it for defensive service on the Western Front. After short service in a quiet sector in the Woëvre region, it moved to the *26th Reserve Corps* area in Picardy, entering the line in mid-May. The division deployed its three infantry regiments abreast with battalions in the standard three-deep defensive posture. The *270th Reserve Infantry Regiment (RIR)* manned the positions along the Cantigny-Grivesnes road in front of the Bois de Lalval; the *272d RIR* held the middle with its left-flank company on the edge of Cantigny and the bulk of the regiment deployed back through the Bois de Framicourt to positions east of the Trois des Doms creek; the *271st RIR* held Cantigny and the southern edge of the salient back to Hill 104 and the approaches to Fontaine-sous-Montdidier The division's artillery took positions principally in the northeastern woods, while infantry mortars and machine guns covered Cantigny ridge.[27]

Both Generals Oskar von Hutier (German *Eighteenth Army*) and Debeney wanted action in the Montdidier section, although neither anticipated a major offensive. Debeney and Vandenberg designed an ambitious plan, a X Corps attack by three divisions, that would bring Allied artillery in range of Montdidier. The 1st Division's attack mission might with luck take the division as far as Fontaine-sous-Montdidier, Hill 104, Trois des Doms creek, and the far edge of the Bois de Framicourt. Cantigny was not in the division's zone. Calculating the division's fire-support needs, George C. Marshall's G-3 planners requested and received substantial French corps and army artillery reinforcements. The French also provided twenty-four heavy Schneider tanks and a flame-thrower section. No sooner had the 1st Division issued a general field order for this operation on 15 May than Debeney, fearing a German attack to the north, called off the offensive. Vandenberg and Bullard then proposed a more limited attack—elimination of the Cantigny salient—which received Debeney's and Pershing's enthusiastic approval. On 20 May, the 1st Division published Field Order 18 for a one-regiment attack on Cantigny.[28]

The rationale for the attack rested more on psychological than operational advantage. Although elimination of the Cantigny salient would curb observed German artillery fire and improve the division's defensive posture— and add some small margin of future offensive advantage—Pershing and Bullard saw the attack as a way to demonstrate the skill and elan of the AEF. As yet, the Americans had mounted no offensive operation more ambitious than a trench raid. Pershing's approach to the AEF's organization and deployment rested on his commitment to building an independent army for offensive operations, a policy that justified holding back the AEF. The American policy of keeping most of its divisions in the United States until they were prepared for offensive operations reflected the same position. (This policy had already been modified by the crisis of 1918 but remained fundamentally intact despite the first rush of reinforcements to Europe.) Because the 1st Division had not shown it could mount an attack, Cantigny became one more test for "Exhibit A."[29]

For planning the Cantigny operation, Bullard delegated principal authority to his G-3, Lieutenant Colonel Marshall, and to his artillery commander, Brigadier General Summerall. General Buck of the 2d Brigade followed the planning but received little latitude in designing the attack. Colonel Ely of the 28th Infantry, whose fresh regiment received the Cantigny mission, had even less initiative. Basically, Marshall organized the ground advance and Summerall the massive artillery support. Both learned from personal experience that visual reconnaissance had its limits by visiting the front under fire, but both received detailed enemy information from French sources, German prisoners, and extensive aerial photographs.

From Marshall's perspective, the key to the operation was surprise, which meant the rapid movement of the 28th Infantry through the entire zone of the German "combat" battalions to defensible positions east of Cantigny. Speed of movement, crucial to exploiting Allied artillery and avoiding the inevitable German barrages, dictated a wide attack formation. The 28th Infantry would hit Cantigny with all three battalions abreast and all companies committed but one. Marshall designated two companies of the 18th Infantry as a reserve for the 2d Brigade because the 26th Infantry was already fully deployed in and south of the Bois de Fontaine. From north to south, the 3d Battalion, 28th Infantry, would attack objectives along the Cantigny-Grivesnes ridge road and establish liaison with the French division on the left flank; the 2d Battalion with twelve French tanks and a flame-thrower section would clear Cantigny; and two companies of the 1st Battalion would pass along the town's south edge and establish positions east of the town on ground commanding the road from Fontaine-sous-Montdidier. A third company of the 1st Battalion would proceed from the Bois de Cantigny and block the southern approaches to Cantigny, its exposed position supported by fire from the woods by Maj. Theodore Roosevelt, Jr.'s, 1st Battalion, 26th Infantry. (The fourth 1st Battalion company was regimental reserve.) Each infantry battalion would have an attached machine-gun company, and these companies would establish strong points in each battalion sector, supported by one infantry platoon. To clear obstacles, eliminate German bunkers with explosives, and build strong points, Marshall attached one full engineer company to the 28th Infantry. Regimental 37-mm guns and mortars would go forward to support the consolidated defense.[30]

Working with French corps artillery planners, Summerall's staff fashioned a plan designed to crush German infantry resistance and neutralize all German artillery within range. Division planners recognized that the 28th Infantry's advance would not force any German batteries to displace. Although Marshall massed sixty-four machine guns to fire along the regiment's flanks, the artillery bore the principal responsibility for gaining fire superiority. French reinforcements were critical, and the French kept twelve of the fifteen artillery groups (thirty-seven batteries) they had committed to the original attack in the fire plan for the Cantigny operation. The French artillery contribution was eighty-four 75-mm guns, twelve 155-mm GPF guns, and twelve 220-mm mortars. Because the 1st Division's artillery brigade numbered only nineteen firing batteries, the French contribution was almost double the American, and the heavier French guns, howitzers, and mortars provided the margin of fire superiority.

Organized into six groups by mission and firing characteristics, the artillery covered the planned battlefield with prearranged concentrations and a massive rolling barrage. One Franco-American group of seventeen 75-mm batteries commanded by Colonel Holbrook would provide the rolling barrage,

while fifteen French 75-mm batteries would provide fires to cover both
exposed flanks of the 28th Infantry from the Bois de Lalval to Fontaine-sous-
Montdidier. A group of nine French and American 155-mm howitzers and
guns had the primary responsibility for counterbattery fire, but they would
also reinforce the 75s' concentrations and provide destruction fires upon
Cantigny itself. The remaining two French groups of heavy howitzers and
trench mortars would also pulverize Cantigny and other German positions
and fire counterbattery missions. The planned concentrations also covered
counterattack routes in an arc east of the town, and the division could call on
corps for more heavy artillery support. Beginning on 20 May, all the artillery
would move forward where necessary to extend its range, paying particular
attention to camouflage. The 1st Artillery Brigade trucked forward six days'
supply of ammunition, the French three days'; in all the artillery stockpiled
200,000 rounds of ammunition. Marshall and Summerall intended to use the
shells in much the same fashion as did the noted German artillerist, Georg
Bruchmuller. The artillery preparatory fires would begin at H-1 hour but fall
in full force only five minutes before the attack. At H-hour, a rolling barrage
two kilometers wide and one and one-half kilometers deep would convoy the
infantry to Cantigny while the heavy guns unleashed full destruction fire.
Smoke shells would help to mask the Americans, but the Allies' limited gas
shells would fall well clear of Cantigny on suspected German artillery
positions and counterattack assembly areas. As the planning developed, both
Marshall and Summerall recognized that a key to the operation would be the
effectiveness of Allied counterbattery fire.[31]

During the planning, the 1st Division's requirements became more
complex and forced a week's postponement. The logistical estimates on
evacuating casualties, providing supplies, and protecting the 28th Infantry in
the forward trenches made necessary extensive nighttime engineering by both
the 28th Infantry and the 1st Engineers. The division also made another
organizational adjustment. Influenced by French advice, Bullard reduced
every rifle platoon from fifty to forty men, a show of initiative that shocked
GHQ AEF. The change meant that each company now had a fifth platoon,
which, according to Allied practice, could be held out of action to provide the
nucleus for rebuilding a shattered infantry company. Bullard originally
intended to use the extra platoons to form a fourth (reserve) battalion for each
regiment, but Pershing's displeasure at the reform persuaded the division staff
to reconsider its plan. Although the 28th Infantry assaulted Cantigny with
forty-man platoons, each company retained its fifth platoon as a carrying
party, burdened with extra tools, empty sandbags, water, and ammunition.
The reorganization encouraged Marshall to press for a full rehearsal of the
attack, which Bullard approved. Key officers from the 28th Infantry went to
the rear to study aerial photos and terrain models; Marshall then set up a
rehearsal area and walked through the attack with officers, guides, signalers,

and liaison personnel. On 22 May, the division withdrew the 28th Infantry from the front and held two full rehearsals, complete with critiques. Both rehearsals included simulated artillery fire, and the last incorporated the French tanks and flame-thrower teams. Satisfied that he and his staff had done everything possible, Bullard on 26 May designated the morning of 28 May for the attack. That night the 2d Battalion, 28th Infantry, started the regiment's return to the jump-off trenches.[32]

Poised for the attack, Bullard and his staff faced a crisis, for they had reason to fear that their operation had been compromised and fatally weakened by two sudden turns of events. The first was two unexpected German raids by three platoon-sized *jagdkommandos*. One raiding force struck the lines of the 26th Infantry in the Bois de Fontaine; repulsed with heavy losses, the Germans, nevertheless, carried off two American enlisted men. The other raid, mounted by the *272d RIR*, struck the lines of the 2d Battalion, 28th Infantry, which had just returned to the trenches fully informed on the next day's attack. Shaken by a violent artillery barrage, the Americans nevertheless halted the raid short of their own positions, but the troops saw one American run out to meet the Germans. Whether the man was a spy (unlikely) or a panic-stricken replacement was uncertain, but rifle fire dropped both the American and his German captors. The Germans fell back without a live prisoner of war from the 28th Infantry, but the raid heightened the division staff's anxiety, for it feared that the Germans might also have found an engineer lieutenant missing in the same sector. More sober assessment of the raid, assisted by the interrogation of two German POWs from the *272d RIR,* suggested that the Germans did not know of the impending attack. In fact, the division G-2 discovered that the *272d RIR* was in the process of rotating its combat battalions and that the American picture of the enemy situation was remarkably accurate.[33]

A second development was more serious. On 27 May, the division learned that the German *First* and *Seventh Armies* had plunged through the weak Allied positions along the Chemin des Dames ridge and seemed headed for the Marne River and the approaches to Paris. Hurried conversations with French artillery liaison officers confirmed the staff's worst fear: that the X Corps would withdraw its heavy artillery after one day of support. Marshall quickly designed a compensatory attack from Cantigny toward the Bois de Framicourt by two companies in order to capture a battery of German 150-mm howitzers but left Ely to decide whether or not to mount the attack. Marshall suggested that another company of the 18th Infantry might be used for this mission if the 28th Infantry could not spare the troops. The critical judgment, however, was Bullard's. Consulting with Summerall, he decided to go ahead with the attack, a decision seconded by Pershing, who visited the division PC (Post of Command) the same day. On the afternoon of 27 May, the division confirmed that the attack would begin as planned the next morning. As soon as it became dark, the two remaining battalions of the 28th Infantry started their slow march to the trenches.[34]

As the 28th Infantry watched the eastern sky begin to glow, the guns of the 1st Artillery Brigade and the French reinforcing batteries began preparatory fires promptly at 0445. For the men, the night had been a mixture of last-minute inspections, equipment and mission checks, and quiet anxiety. Officers paced the trenches, ensuring that their men had shaved and come to the front with adequate ammunition (220 rounds per man), water (two canteens), and emergency rations. Morale lifted as the first Allied shells screamed overhead. The Germans, however, immediately responded, sending observation balloons skyward with artillery spotters. Some German shells fell along the jump-off trenches, but most fell to the rear on suspected American assembly areas. One barrage, for example, dropped in a quarry near the 28th Infantry's PC and destroyed most of two sections of Company D, 1st Engineers. The German fire did not intensify, because, as Summerall had hoped, the *82d Reserve Division* staff thought the American shelling was merely retaliation for the trench raids. When the Allies began their "fires for destruction" at 0545, they quickly suppressed the German batteries with high explosives and gas; the heavy shellfire on Cantigny itself and on the ridge line seemed to lift the buildings and ground into the air until no one could see the German positions through the smoke and dust. The noise of the bombardment deafened the men in the jump-off trenches, but the violence of the artillery preparation sent their spirits soaring. When the first wave of troops went over the top at 0640, spurred by officers' whistles and sergeants' shouts, the men were smoking, laughing, and shouting back and forth with real (if strained) enthusiasm. The inexorable weight of the attack received further support from the forward movement of the French tanks with the 2d Battalion and the precise fall of the first shells of rolling barrage. With rifles at high port and bayonets fixed, the leading companies crossed No Man's Land in ten minutes and reached the German positions. The second and third waves of the regiment, marching in platoon columns, followed, although they tended to lose their interval as the third-wave troops understandably increased their pace in order to escape the anticipated German barrage. A few minutes after 0700, Ely, Buck, and Bullard knew that the initial assault had been a surprise and a success.[35]

Working from a PC just to the rear of the jump-off trenches, Ely did not yet have a clear picture of the tactical situation. His immediate reports drew their optimism from the 2d Battalion's easy capture of Cantigny, not from the experiences of the 1st and 3d Battalions on the attack's southern and northern flanks. The 2d Battalion's attack warranted optimism, for its three assault companies, flanked by Company D, 1st Battalion, and Company M, 3d Battalion, met little resistance. The assault had come so quickly that the German observers had not called in the defensive barrage, and the tanks and infantry had silenced the surviving machine-gun nests. The Allied artillery fire had virtually destroyed three German companies in Cantigny (the *12th Company* of the *272d RIR* and the *1st* and *2d Companies* of the *271st RIR*). Flame-thrower and demolition teams caught scattered Germans in cellar sanctuaries; those who did not surrender perished. (In their excitement, the Americans also shot some Germans in the act of surrender.) The remnants of the *III Battalion, 272d RIR,* fell back toward the Bois de Framicourt; the disorganized survivors of the two companies of the *I Battalion, 271st RIR,* ran east toward Hill 104, held by the same regiment's *II Battalion.* The fire of the French tanks proved critical to the Germans' panic and to the fact that the *1st Company, 272d RIR,* attached to the *III Battalion,* did not mount an immediate counterattack from its position south of the Bois de Framicourt.

The five center companies of the 28th Infantry, followed by Company G, cleared Cantigny and established defensive positions east of the town. Engineers, machine-gunners, the 37-mm cannon detachment, and the mortarmen established three strong points as planned in an arc that ran from Cantigny cemetery to the north through a wood lot northeast of the town to the Chateau de Cantigny on the town's southeastern border. Drawing his information primarily from Lt. Col. Robert J. Maxey, commander of the 2d Battalion, and from artillery and machine-gun liaison officers, Ely reported that he had secured all his objectives with fewer than a hundred casualties. Quickly interrogating the German officers and NCOs among the 180 POWs taken in Cantigny, Ely's intelligence officer verified the victory and his commanding officer's understanding of the situation. The appearance of the POWs, "sorry looking rats, covered with blood & dust, most of them wounded & all badly shaken," heightened American optimism. A French airborne observer sent additional positive reports.[36]

Ely did not grasp that his attack had created a salient within a salient. His 1st and 3d Battalions had not, in fact, taken all their positions in good order. The 1st Battalion's situation was the least precarious, but it was not good. Attacking from its isolated position in the Bois de Cantigny, Company A had taken its blocking position on the road to Fontaine-sous-Montdidier, but enfilading machine guns had dropped all three of the company's officers and some men. Part of the company had fallen back to the woods; others had moved north to the position of Company B, which had also taken casualties, including officers, while moving through the ravine on Cantigny's southern edge. When the *2d Company, 271st RIR,* mounted the first German counterattack about 0800 against this position, it was easily repulsed—largely, the German company commander thought, because his flares for artillery had gone unseen. In any event, Ely had Company L, 18th Infantry, to shore up this flank, supported by the 1st Battalion, 26th Infantry, in the Bois de Fontaine. The 3d Battalion's position was much weaker. On the extreme left, German machine-gun fire had so punished Company K that it had not

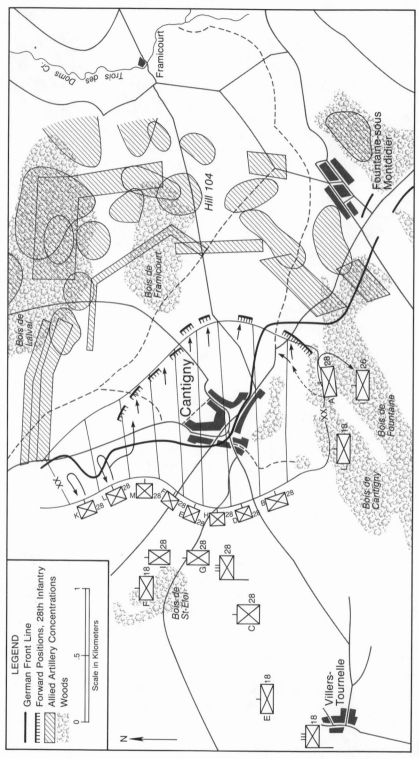

Map 6.3. The Battle of Cantigny

advanced much beyond the American wire, and its scattered elements had taken refuge in the jump-off trenches and shell holes in No Man's Land. Company L had not fared much better. Enfilade fire had driven part of the company back from the German lines or south into the zone of Company M. When he learned that his flank was in the air, the battalion commander, Maj. J. M. Cullison, had sent his reserve, Company I, into positions around Cantigny cemetery where it had joined the orphans from Company L. Either because the 3d Battalion commander had not fully appreciated his peril or because his runners had not gotten through to the regimental PC, Ely did not understand the situation north of Cantigny until the afternoon of 28 May. But by that time, his whole regiment was in trouble.[37]

Concerned that the American attack would continue east and south toward Hill 104 and Fontaine-sous-Montdidier, the commander of the German *26th Reserve Corps* ordered the *82d* and *25th Reserve Divisions* to mount deliberate counterattacks on the evening of 28 May. Meanwhile, the support battalions of the *272d RIR* and *271st RIR* attempted to attack the American positions, but Allied artillery fire broke up the assaults before they began, and the German support battalions did not venture far from their positions along the Bois de Framicourt and Hill 104. In the meantime, the *82d Reserve Division* ordered its rest battalions *(I Battalion, 272d RIR,* and *III Battalion, 271st RIR)* to counterattack assembly positions in the Bois de Framicourt and behind Hill 104. The *25th Reserve Division* moved the *II Battalion, 83d RIR,* to an assembly area in the Bois de Fontaine. Harried by Allied artillery, the Germans moved forward in small groups to avoid casualties, a process that saved lives but took time. The march was especially arduous for the *I Battalion, 272d RIR,* because its troops had just finished a five-kilometer hike to their rest position the night before. Throughout the afternoon of 28 May, French aerial observers and 28th Infantry outposts reported the German movement, and Ely asked for more aerial reports and fire support. Working from Ely's PC, Colonel Holbrook and Lt. Col. Frank S. Bowen, the division machine-gun officer, directed massed fires against suspected German assembly areas. Bullard and his staff followed the operation carefully through reports from General Buck and telephone messages that reached the headquarters of the 1st Field Artillery Brigade. They and General Pershing, who visited the division PC during the morning of 28 May, agreed that the operation would face a crisis that evening. Thus far, however, they left the management of the battle to Buck and Ely.[38]

As the afternoon waned, the Germans intensified their artillery fire on the American positions, and the 28th Infantry's casualties mounted at an alarming rate. Sited on open slopes, the infantry's trench lines could be seen easily by German aerial spotters, who called down heavy howitzer and mortar fire on the Americans. Long-range machine-gun fire also reached the 28th Infantry positions. Although the three strong points drew the most fire, they survived because they were placed in covered positions that the engineers had strengthened; the infantry positions were less secure. The worst part of the German bombardment was the heavy mortar shells, which the Americans could see arcing toward their holes. Individual American soldiers, including some officers, broke for the rear or became crazed with shellshock. Carrying parties and stretcher bearers fell in the shellfire, and officers and NCOs, moving from position to position, bore a disproportionate share of the casualties. Lieutenant Colonel Maxey of the 2d Battalion received a fatal wound, and his command passed to Capt. Clarence R. Huebner, a sturdy fighter who would later command the 1st Infantry Division in World War II. Ely estimated that by late afternoon one-third of his front-line troops had become casualties.

Between 1800 and 2000, the Germans launched the first major counterattacks on Cantigny, all of which failed. Instead of one massive assault, the Germans came on in one small and three battalion-sized attacks. The first attack came from the remnants of the *III Battalion, 272d RIR,* and two companies of the *II Battalion* under the direction of the captain commanding the *III Battalion,* who either advanced on his own or thought he was mounting the major attack from the Bois de Framicourt. In any event, his attack began an hour too early. American artillery drove the Germans back to the woods, but the German shells that fell on Cantigny inflicted more casualties on the 1st and 3d Battalions, and Ely learned that some of his men had abandoned the front-line trenches. He requested more artillery on the Bois de Framicourt and ordered up his sole reserve, Company C, 28th Infantry, to strengthen the 1st Battalion's position on the south flank. He readied Company F, 18th Infantry, to reinforce the 3d Battalion and ordered Company L, 18th Infantry, to move from the Bois de Cantigny to an assembly area in the Bois St. Eloi near his own PC, replacing Company C, 28th Infantry. This commitment required General Buck's approval, and the brigade commander gave Ely control of the two brigade reserve companies. Buck also alerted Company E, 18th Infantry, in an assembly area north of Villers-Tournelle but warned Ely that Companies E and L, 18th Infantry, should be used only for counterattacks. In the meantime, Company F, 18th Infantry, marched rapidly through desultory shellfire into the positions of the 3d Battalion. Because the company thought it was counterattacking an enemy position, it moved rapidly and in assault formation. Fortunately, it did not open fire on the already hard-pressed men of the 3d Battalion, and the momentum of its "attack" carried the Americans back to their original trenches just in time to face the major German thrust.

As the situation shifted in the 3d Battalion sector, the German attack by the *II Battalion, 271st RIR,* moved toward Cantigny from Hill 104, but the 2d Battalion halted the first waves with rifle and machine-gun fire while artillery dispersed the succeeding waves. The planned German H-hour was 1845, but the northern and southern portions of the counterattack did not get under way until fifteen minutes later. The delay was fatal for the Germans, who lost the effects of their own rolling barrage. Jumping off at 1900, the *II Battalion, 83d RIR,* advanced along the Cantigny–Fontaine road right into the American defensive barrage; the attack ended 500 meters south of Cantigny as the Germans dived into shell holes and continued the attack by fire only. The attack by the consolidated companies of the *I* and *II Battalions, 272d RIR,* led by the *II Battalion* commander, fared no better. Compromised by the first, premature attack from the Bois de Framicourt 1½ hours earlier, the *272d RIR*'s main assault from the Bois de Lalval met intense flanking machine-gun fire and the full force of the 1st Division's defensive barrage. The attack collapsed immediately, and the surviving German infantry returned to the Bois de Framicourt. Just before 2000, Buck learned from a forward observation post that the Germans had retreated. Ely agreed but reported that his regiment's casualties from artillery fire had reached critical levels and that he needed either relief or permission to withdraw. Learning that Ely had not yet used the two reserve companies of the 18th Infantry and did not need them for counterattack, Bullard allowed Buck to release them for Ely's use. He did not think the division had time to withdraw the 28th Infantry that night, but he moved two 18th Infantry battalions forward either to counterattack or later relieve the 28th Infantry. The 28th Infantry, now stiffened with three 18th Infantry companies, would have to hold Cantigny for at least another day.[39]

On its second day, the Battle of Cantigny lost its last vestiges of tactical sophistication and became a contest between the wills of the opposing commanders and troops and the weight of their supporting artillery. Following German doctrine and the orders of its superiors, the *82d Reserve Division* mounted two early-morning attacks from the Bois de Framicourt. Even reinforced by a company from the uncommitted *270th RIR,* the companies of the *272d RIR* had lost too many officers and men on 28 May to mount an effective assault. After its half-hearted efforts, the *272d RIR* numbered only about twenty effectives per company, one of which was now commanded by a corporal. The *271st RIR,* now concentrated around Hill 104, kept the Americans under fire but did not advance. Watching the battle closely, General von Hutier had begun to suspect that the Americans did not plan to advance beyond Cantigny. The area around Hill 104 seemed secure enough, now covered by the relatively undamaged *270th RIR* of the *82d Reserve Division.* Allied counterbattery fire had slackened. The most worrisome situation was the security of the Cantigny–Fontaine road. To insure that the Americans did not improve their position, von Hutier ordered another counterattack on Cantigny for the late afternoon of 29 May, an attack supported by massive heavy artillery and mounted from east and south of Cantigny by the *83rd RIR* of the *25th Reserve Division.*[40]

For the 1st Division, the fighting of 29 May required a major shift of artillery employment, for on the evening of 28–29 May, the division lost two full regiments of French artillery from its artillery groupment. The planners of the 1st Artillery Brigade conceded that their guns could not completely suppress the German heavy guns, and they concentrated their fire instead on areas the Germans might use for infantry counterattacks. They faced a test of this decision around 1630 on 29 May when the *83d RIR* attacks began. Amid the deluge of 75-mm shells, the Germans made no appreciable advance. Their own artillery fire, however, pulverized the 28th Infantry's positions. Several Allied 155-mm short rounds also fell among the American infantry, which did not improve morale. Alarmed by pessimistic reports from the front, Ely left his own PC—which had drawn fire and its share of wounded and dispirited soldiers—to confer with Colonel Parker, 18th Infantry, at the latter's PC at Villers-Tournelle. To the two colonels, the situation appeared desperate. Front-line observers sent messages that German tanks had been spotted in the Bois de Lalval and that men of the 1st and 2d Battalions had again retreated from their trenches back into Cantigny. A French aerial observer radioed, however, that the American lines were holding and that the German attack had dissolved. Ely still wanted to throw at least another battalion of the 18th Infantry into the battle. "Front line pounded to hell and gone, and entire front must be relieved tomorrow night [or] he would not be responsible." Bullard, however, refused the request for reinforcements but agreed to speed arrangements for a relief. He also ordered Ely to get his troops back to the forward trenches. Observing this movement, the Germans believed the Americans had mounted a counterattack of their own. Their infantry hastily took up defensive positions, and more artillery rained on Cantigny. As night finally came, the shelling diminished, but the battlefield had become a maze of holes sheltering the remnants of the German and American regiments that still faced one another.[41]

On 30 May, the fighting slackened, but the Germans probed the 28th Infantry position once more about 0345. They found Company A, 28th Infantry, a forlorn handful of men, gone from the Cantigny–Fontaine road, for Bullard had allowed Ely to withdraw Companies A and B back to Cantigny. First Battalion, 26th Infantry, which had already had its share of action in the southern woods, covered the road by fire, an option the Americans should have chosen earlier. German artillery fire still ranged across the Cantigny position and deeper American assembly areas—and German aircraft occasionally swooped down as they had the day before to bomb and strafe—but no more counterattacks came against the 28th Infantry's lines. The division intelligence section gauged the enemy activity: "Artillery active. Infantry nervous. Aviation very active."[42] General von Hutier, however, had decided that the Americans were not marching toward Montdidier, and he allowed the *26th Reserve Corps* to stop the counterattacks. Instead, he wanted the corps to use its artillery fire to simulate the opening phases of a major German offensive. This ruse was superfluous, for General Vandenberg, French X Corps, had ordered a general reorganization of his front, which now included Cantigny, a move that Bullard and his staff were already planning.

The 1st Division's final consolidation of the Cantigny attack began on the night of 30–31 May when battalions of the 16th Infantry, released from X Corps reserve, replaced the 28th Infantry at the front and the two 18th Infantry battalions positioned in support. The relief was finished the following night. When the 28th Infantry and its attachments finally took a careful personnel check, Bullard learned that 38 officers and 903 men had been killed or wounded. His principal adversary, the *82d Reserve Division,* suffered catastrophic losses in two infantry regiments: 1,437 officer and enlisted casualties, of whom 488 were missing. (Of the German missing, the Americans captured 285.) The Germans also lost 324 men in the *25th Reserve Division*'s *83rd RIR.* Their engaged artillery batteries suffered—as did the 1st Division's—but these losses paled beside those of the infantry regiments. Quite properly, the 1st Division reported that it had destroyed the offensive capability of two German infantry regiments. It did not add that the 28th Infantry was not exactly combat fit after its three days in Cantigny, for the reinforced regiment had lost half its officers and a third of its enlisted men. Nevertheless, the operation ended with little doubt about the victor. While the German *Eighteenth Army* started an investigation of the loss of Cantigny, the 1st Division initiated action to make awards for valor to its soldiers.[43]

As a test of the 1st Division's offensive capability, the Battle of Cantigny accomplished its psychological purpose. General Bullard assessed the operation: "The moral effects to flow from this proof of the reliability in battle of the American soldiers far outweigh the direct military importance of the actions themselves." Pershing's inspector-general, Maj. Gen. André W. Brewster, thought the battle also showed that Bullard and his staff could plan and control an operation with the highest professional skill. When Pershing himself next visited the division, he told the troops publicly and Bullard privately that the division had set the standard for the AEF and had inspired the French and American home fronts. Pershing told the War Department that Cantigny should quell talk of amalgamation because the division had fought well in professional terms: "It is my firm conviction that our troops are the best in Europe and our staffs the equal of any." Pershing's liaison officers with the principal French commanders reported that they were more than satisfied with the 1st Division's performance. As a test of fighting spirit, Cantigny had presented a formidable challenge, and the 1st Division had proved more than ready.[44]

Given its limited objectives, deliberate planning, and set-piece design, the Battle of Cantigny did not provide a full test for Pershing's open-warfare doctrine, but it did provide lessons on the critical relationship between artillery superiority and infantry advances. Cantigny, of course, was but one of a series of pyramiding experiences for the AEF in the early summer of 1918. At the time of Cantigny, in fact, Pershing's attention had already shifted to the German offensive toward the Marne River, and the next American battles, fought by the 2d and 3d Divisions, AEF came as part of the defense of the Marne River line east and west of Chateau Thierry.

Fought by the two best-prepared divisions in the AEF—the 1st and 2d— two engagements in the Aisne-Marne sector in June and July 1918 dramatically demonstrated the limits of American open-warfare doctrine. The first engagement, the twin fights by the 2d Division for Belleau Wood and the town of Vaux (7 June–1 July), again proved that American infantrymen had great courage and capacity to suffer but lacked tactical sophistication. Plagued by poor planning and inadequate artillery support, the engagement cost the 4th Infantry Brigade (U.S. Marine Corps) 126 officers and 5,057 men and the 3d Infantry Brigade 68 officers and 3,184 men. On the first day's assault on Hill 142 and Belleau Wood, the Marines lost more men than the 28th Infantry had lost in three days at Cantigny. Most casualties came from machine-gun and artillery fire on American infantry formations advancing across open terrain. If the 2d Division's battle for Belleau Wood–Vaux had some similarities to Cantigny (both were limited, local counterattacks), the corps counteroffensive at Soissons (18–21 July) was a classic open-warfare operation for the now-veteran 1st and 2d Divisions. Advancing about six miles, the two divisions captured 143 German guns and 6,500 POWs. No doubt the Americans punished the elements of the seven under-strength German divisions they attacked, but their own losses were appalling: 12,200 officers and men, most of them from the infantry brigades of the two American divisions. Although all the regiments suffered catastrophic losses, the 1st Division's 26th Infantry held the dubious honor for sacrifice, mustering 200 effectives from the 3,000-some soldiers it took into battle on 18 July. The senior active officer was a captain, the regimental adjutant.

GHQ AEF concluded that its divisions had not mastered open-warfare tactics, and it attempted to assess the lessons of the Aisne-Marne operation and spread those lessons throughout the AEF. In August 1918, the Training Section (G-5) of GHQ AEF began to publish a series of "Combat Instructions" and "Notes on Recent Operations," brief pamphlets to be distributed down to the company and battery levels. For the infantry, the guidance was pertinent and accurate. American attacks did not exploit fire and maneuver but placed undue emphasis on the problems of direction, frontages, and formations. Infantry commanders did not correctly employ their supporting arms—machine guns, 37-mm cannon, and mortars—and they did not maintain adequate liaison with supporting artillery. Attacks were too stereotyped and did not consider the proper use of terrain to provide concealment, cover, fields of fire, and observation posts. Plans of attack tended to be too rigid and often reached subordinate units too late to allow further planning by small-unit leaders. Instead of exploiting gaps in German positions, attacking units spent too much time reducing remaining strong points that could be handled by reserve units. In sum, Pershing reluctantly agreed with his French allies and German opponents that AEF commanders wasted lives by failing to use their infantry properly, primarily by not providing it adequate fire support. Courage and rifles alone could not conquer German machine-gun nests and artillery barrages. Although individual units did, in fact, show a level of skill that approached the Germans' by 11 November, Pershing's headquarters found the same persistent flaws in offensive operations right up to the Armistice.[45]

American artillery units bore an equal responsibility for the AEF's uneven performance, a responsibility fully acknowledged by Maj. Gen. Edward F. McGlachlin, Pershing's Chief of Artillery and commander of the First Army's artillery. McGlachlin's staff also published operational analyses during 1918 that correctly evaluated the shortcomings of AEF artillery planning and operations. Division artillery had one primary mission: to support attacks by firing at German positions that faced the infantry. Its secondary mission was counterbattery fire, but this task rested primarily with corps and army artillery whose heavier guns and longer ranges made it a better instrument for battling German artillery. Division artillery, however, did not meet the infantry's needs for many reasons. Firing batteries did not displace forward rapidly enough; infantry and artillery officers did not correctly identify friendly infantry positions at the front; observed and adjusted fire was virtually nonexistent; and preplanned and scheduled concentrations did not usually fit the fluid situations of open warfare. Infantry-artillery cooperation was critical to tactical success, but too often it did not exist. American artillery fire affected the battle through mass (e.g., 4,000 guns supported the first day's attack of the Meuse–Argonne offensive), not skill. Profligate use of shells in the best Western Front tradition could not compensate for the shortcomings of artillery operations.[46]

As General Pershing and the AEF learned to their frustration, ground combat on the Western Front had produced a grim pattern that none of the belligerents (including the Germans) had yet fundamentally changed. Reforms on the battlefield could only improve attacks within the system, not destroy the system itself. Basically, the infantry could move forward only when it was supported by massed artillery fire delivered from semipermanent positions behind the original line of departure. Firing preregistered concentrations on obvious, tactically significant targets (e.g., known enemy positions, road junctions, the forward edges of woods), the artillery could reduce enemy resistance in the forward defensive zone, which the infantry could normally seize with the assistance of a rolling barrage. Static ground observation posts and aerial observers gave the artillery some capacity to fire on targets of opportunity. Prepositioned dumps of artillery shells provided the ammunition for such saturation fires.

Problems quickly developed, however, as the infantry moved out of range of the division artillery or encountered strong points that did not fit neatly into the artillery's fire plans. Even if artillery liaison teams were far enough forward to see targets, they seldom had working telephone communications back to their fire-direction centers, and other means of communication were notoriously slow or malfunctioned. (One can imagine the anxiety of a commander submitting an urgent-fire request by either exhausted runner or carrier pigeon.) Only an efficient, portable radio could provide the vital infantry-artillery link, and such a radio did not yet exist. The division artillery might have eased the liaison problem if it had closed the distance between the firing batteries and the infantry, but moving the artillery forward presented nearly insurmountable problems in the heat of battle. Batteries on the move presented lucrative targets for the Germans; shell-churned roads made battery movement slow; horse-drawn caissons seldom supplied adequate ammunition. As a result, artillery battalions were reluctant to displace until the front had stabilized. Meanwhile, the infantry tried to continue the attack despite the reduction of artillery support. As the numbers of shells fired dropped, infantry casualties climbed until the attack stopped, usually in about four days' time for a division on the offensive. In another four days, infantry-artillery cooperation was reestablished, and the attack continued in the face, of course, of reorganized German resistance. Only in the last two weeks of the war did the Meuse–Argonne offensive of the U.S. First Army show signs—against weak German resistance—of breaking free from this operational pattern, largely because more experienced infantry units mounted surprise night operations. Senior American officers, including Pershing, understood the limitations of open warfare. They simply could not find the means in 1918 to correct the shortcomings.

Amid the flurry of redeployment and demobilization, Pershing's GHQ AEF and the War Department General Staff conducted a series of studies of the AEF's performance and the implications of its experience for postwar military policy and Army organization. Although Pershing believed that his army had provided the margin of victory for the Allies, he and his senior officers knew that the AEF had not fought up to its potential, largely because its state of training in 1918 had not matched the demands of the battlefield. No doctrinal problem caused more comment than fire support for infantry in the attack. Pershing's "Superior Board on Organization and Tactics" identified artillery-infantry teamwork as the critical ingredient in future land warfare, and two different artillery boards reported that the artillery had to modernize rapidly if it was to meet the infantry's needs for fire support. Among the boards' major recommendations was a blueprint for postwar development:

motorizing and mechanizing artillery in order to improve its battlefield mobility, the change of division artillery to a mix of guns and lighter howitzers, the addition of an organic air-observation squadron to the division, the provision for more artillery liaison officers available for constant service with infantry units, improved communications, and the creation of an independent system for collecting target information. Additional studies added an emphasis to the artillery reports: the Army needed to educate its infantry officers on the intricacies of integrating artillery fire and the support of crew-served infantry weapons (machine guns, mortars, 37-mm cannon) in offensive operations. The implication was that the day of the independent rifleman had passed.[47]

In the postwar debate on military policy that finally produced the National Defense Act of 1920, questions of operational doctrine surfaced periodically among the incrusted arguments about Army organization and peacetime military training. Yet amid all the verbiage of the testimony and the final legislation rested some successful reforms based on the AEF's combat experience. To further the institutional interests of their respective arms, a chief of infantry and chief of field artillery joined the War Department's central staff in Washington. (The latter office had actually been created in 1918 by executive action.) The institutionalization of the Officers Reserve Corps and the Reserve Officers Training Corps promised to provide wartime officers of improved skill. Congress rejected airmen's pleas for a separate air force and placed the infant tank force under infantry control, largely because the senior commanders of the AEF testified that tanks and aerial artillery observers provided essential assistance to the division. Congress also allowed the president to organize Army tactical corps and divisions in peacetime if he so chose, a policy that could enhance all types of integrated arms training. The consensus of the Army officer corps on the nature of war had not changed appreciably—victory in land warfare required offensive operations to destroy the enemy's armed forces—but the instruments of land warfare had changed during World War I. The question was not whether a revolution in warfare had occurred, but what the extent and implications of that revolution were.[48]

After 1921, however, Congressional budget cutting deprived the Army of both the men and material it needed to test new operational concepts in the field. Regular infantry and artillery regiments, burdened with housekeeping and administrative duties and maintained with limited strength, concentrated on individual and small-unit training. Congress expected the Army to train with surplus arms and equipment. In the face of declining budgets, the War Department General Staff stressed manpower funding rather than training and force modernization, for the Army's senior officers believed that manpower mobilization organization and peacetime training for reserve components represented a better investment than equipment modernization beyond the research and development phase. Postwar military economizing (the

Army received about 14 percent of the federal budget) forced the Army to live with the forces that still had all the technical limitations of the AEF, e.g., horse-drawn field artillery, primitive field radios, relatively immobile heavy artillery, and World War I–model tanks. With such forces, tactical training by the Army and the National Guard could not reflect the hard-learned lessons of the Western Front.[49]

In official doctrine as written into the *Field Service Regulations* and the instruction at the Infantry School and the Field Artillery School, the Army demonstrated, however, that it had learned the importance of infantry-artillery cooperation, the war's major legacy. Published in 1923, the first postwar revision of the *Field Service Regulations* stressed that effective infantry offensive action demanded constant fire superiority, furnished primarily by artillery and machine guns. Aircraft, tanks, gas, and smoke also improved the chances of infantry attacks. Differentiating for the first time between types of operations (e.g., river crossings, attacks on fortified positions, fighting in built-up areas), the *Field Service Regulations* identified the critical element in attack planning as the assessment of the role of fire support. While attacking infantry should seek surprise, it should not do so at the expense of fire support. As taught at the Infantry School and spread throughout the Army in the classic *Infantry in Battle* (1934), the doctrine of artillery-infantry cooperation was unequivocal: *"Infantry unsupported by artillery or tanks has practically no chance of success in a daylight advance over bare, open terrain against hostile machine-gun fire."*[50] During the "golden age" of the Infantry School in the early 1930s, three of its prominent leaders—Campbell King, George C. Marshall, and Clarence R. Huebner—had personal experience drawn from Cantigny to verify this doctrine. Similar conclusions reached the Army through the writing of Lt. Col. Oliver L. Spaulding, Jr. Serving in the 2d Division in France, Spaulding also had seen the wreckage of infantry regiments that had attacked with inadequate artillery support. While he believed the war had not ended the infantry's principal role on the battlefield, he thought the great lesson of the war was the importance of fire support, and he advocated combined-arms training for all line officers. Spaulding identified infantry-artillery cooperation as the war's principal tactical development.[51]

The reorganized division of the postwar Army showed increased attention to fire support and declining confidence in the battlefield power of unsupported riflemen. In fact, the postwar division was closer to the War Department model of 1917 than to Pershing's massive AEF division in structure and strength. To number 22,000 officers and men at full strength, the division would still build its combat power around one artillery and two infantry brigades. The artillery brigade retained two regiments of 75-mm guns, but dropped its 155-mm howitzers. The infantry changed substantially. The four infantry regiments of the division (three battalions each) fell from twelve to nine rifle companies (three per battalion), but each battalion now included a weapons company of machine guns. Each regiment included additional machine guns, mortars, and cannon in its regimental headquarters. In addition, the size of each rifle company dropped from four platoons to three. New additions to the divisional organization were supposed to improve fire support (a light-tank company) and infantry-artillery coordination (an aviation observation squadron). Even before the Army moved to motorization, it had recognized that mobility and increased fire support demanded a leaner combat division.

Cantigny stands in a continuum of battlefield experiences in World War I. It was a test of the changes the American Expeditionary Forces had already made in doctrine and organization before mounting major offensive operations, and these changes stemmed from lessons learned by both Allied and German forces. Given the conditions of the Western Front and the absence of motorized and mechanized forces, the Germans developed the best wartime doctrine by tying infantry infiltration tactics with short, intense, surprise bombardments. As a concept, the "von Hutier tactics" appealed as much to the AEF as to the Germans. Pershing's problem was that the rapid expansion and commitment of the AEF in 1918—a full year ahead of planning— prevented the orderly training that Pershing would have preferred. The sheer expansion of the American Army prohibited the high degree of professionalism implicit in infantry-artillery cooperation. (For example, the AEF in 1918 had more artillery *regiments* than the entire field artillery had *officers* of more than one year's service in April 1917.) Given an adequate level of training and time to plan, the AEF could fight well on the offensive—as Cantigny proved—as long as the physical movement of the infantry remained within the supporting ranges of corps and division artillery. Cantigny also proved once again that infantry on the Western Front could not fight—they could only die—without massive, accurate, properly timed artillery support. The challenge for military planners, American and European alike, in the postwar period was to find an escape from the infantry-artillery yoke by creating a new form of mobile warfare that retained a high level of firepower. In the post–World War II fascination with the origins of armored warfare, military analysts overlook the fact that the interwar Army also made significant advances in improving the offensive effectiveness of the artillery-infantry team. Two of these improvements were the development of centralized-fire direction centers, crucial to rapid and flexible shifting of massed fires, and the creation of radio-equipped forward observer teams that could call observed fire down on targets of opportunity. These improvements in infantry-artillery cooperation proved as important as the development of armored forces, for they later provided a margin of American tactical excellence in every theater, in every type of terrain, in all weather conditions, and against every enemy. Built on the lessons of World War I, the doctrinal attention to infantry-artillery cooperation was validated in World War II.

7

Buna
19 November 1942–2 January 1943:
A "Leavenworth Nightmare"

JAY LUVAAS

NEW GUINEA PINCERS CLOSE ON FOE . . . ALLIES IN JUNCTION

AUSTRALIANS AND U.S. TROOPS CONVERGE FOR ATTACK ON BUNA

JAPANESE CAUGHT IN TRAP

These headlines in the late city edition of the *New York Times,* 16 November 1942, served notice that unidentified Australian and United States units "have joined forces and are moving in for an attack on the Japanese at Buna" and are "pressing forward in a semi-circular manoeuvre against the Japanese beachhead. . . . This week may see our troops besieging the Buna beachhead—if the strength of the enemy defenses and resistance necessitates a siege." The next day headlines trumpeted: *"MACARTHUR AT BUNA FRONT LEADS ASSAULT ON JAPANESE."* Establishing field headquarters in "a fighting zone for the first time since he was with his . . . troops in the defense at Bataan," General Douglas MacArthur was leading his forces in a rapid advance "and driving the Japanese into a trap protected by the sea and jungles." The "nutcracker movement . . . might finish off the fight within days or even hours," for this time "MacArthur is on the offensive—with plenty of men, weapons and food at his command to score his first victory over the Japanese."[1]

Headlines in the following weeks stressed minor air and naval successes as the ground attack somehow got bogged down. Most readers did not know that most of the American troops had come from the U.S. 32d Infantry Division, an old National Guard outfit, and not until the campaign was over were names of the other commanders released. Meanwhile, the press (and probably the public) devoted most of its attention to the battle for Stalingrad and the expanding campaign in Tunisia. To military men concerned with matters of doctrine and training, however, the fight for Buna demanded close attention.

Doctrine in the U.S. Army in 1942 had been essentially derived from a study of its experiences on the Western Front in 1918. Not since the Civil War had American commanders functioned in the operation of large units in combat, and most of the manuals after 1918 were written with the special conditions of stabilized warfare in mind. The first postwar revision of *Field Service Regulations,* which appeared in 1923, had remained in force until the publication of the *Tentative Field Service Regulations: Operations* (more popularly known as FM 100-5) in 1939. This in turn was superseded by the 1941 *Field Service Regulations,* which contained the doctrines and basis of instruction for the American troops that had assumed the offensive in New Guinea.[2]

The differences between the 1923 *Field Service Regulations* and the 1941 version were significant. While both stressed the combined employment of all arms, the infantry in 1923 were considered of paramount importance, and the special missions of the other arms were to be "derived from their powers to contribute to the execution of the infantry mission."[3] The 1941 edition still considered infantry as the main arm of close combat but placed greater emphasis on the combined action of all arms: "No one arm wins battles."[4] The role of cavalry had not changed since World War I, but the tank was no longer regarded primarily as an infantry-support weapon, transporting firepower across no man's land to close with intrenched enemy units protected against the effects of ordinary infantry fire. By 1941, there were armored divisions to conduct offensive operations against hostile rear areas either through penetration or envelopment. There were also special tank units of GHQ reserve to assist rifle units in reaching objectives, but the *Regulations* warned that "tanks should not be tied too closely" to infantry because that would sacrifice mobility and expose infantry to concentrated artillery fire.[5]

There were other striking differences. The 1923 *Regulations* contained sections that could almost pass for a description of a typical assault in the Meuse-Argonne, with zones of action and sectors, artillery missions, fire superiority, and entrenchments. In 1941, more attention was paid to a war of movement as well, although the emphasis was still on the attack and defense of organized positions. The 1939 *Regulations* gave brief coverage to special operations, including combat in towns, mountainous terrain, and guerrilla warfare, obviously in reponse to recent military operations during the Spanish Civil War and perhaps in China.[6] This section was expanded again in 1941 to include attack on a fortified locality, mountain operations, combat in snow, desert operations, partisan warfare, and jungle operations—obviously an attempt to digest the lessons of some of the 1940-41 campaigns. Although only two pages were devoted specifically to jungle operations, the 1941 *Regulations* correctly anticipated many problems that soon would surface in New Guinea. Movement would be restricted, direction hard to maintain, and control and maneuver would pose special problems. Troops could expect close fighting in the jungle, with artillery and other supporting weapons playing only limited roles. Air observation would be difficult and signal communication often inadequate.[7]

These observations were supplemented in December 1941 with the appearance of the FM 31–20, *Basic Field Manual: Jungle Warfare*. In addition to providing practical information on preparing for jungle service—personal hygiene, poisonous plants, snakes, and insects—this manual applied current doctrine on the march, in attack and defense, and in special operations, thus increasing the importance of initiative and troop-leading ability of lower commanders. "Each lower unit must consider itself as a self-contained unit with a definite task to accomplish, without expectation of direct assistance from adjacent units."[8] The new manual mentioned the importance of prepared fire lanes in the jungle but did not anticipate the existence of any system of formidable pillboxes or defenses. The jungle obviously was viewed as something to pass through, not defend, and neither fixed defenses nor a definite line separating the combatants was expected—certainly nothing comparable to no man's land. Had more careful attention been paid to the manual's advice on the jungle's natural defenses, many American lives might have been spared at Buna.

Although the basic large unit at Buna was the U.S. 32d Infantry Division, it never was able to function in battle in the way envisaged in *A Manual for Commanders of Large Units*.[9] The division was forced to leave some supportive units behind in Australia because of transportation difficulties, it advanced across the Owen Stanley Mountains in separate battalions, and it fought against the Japanese at Buna mostly as individual battalions and companies. Because of the difficult terrain, Buna was predominantly an infantry battle. Only where the ground was open and dry could tanks give effective support. Moreover, the only available tanks were Australian and had not been designed for infantry support.[10] Artillery rendered more effective support, but the terrain restricted its role as well. At Buna, the artillery consisted of eight twenty-five-pounders, two 3.7-inch mountain howitzers, and one 105-mm howitzer—the only U.S. fieldpiece used in the battle. Cooperation between the arms was further hampered by the fact that neither the Australian tank crews nor the artillerymen had ever worked together with American infantry.[11]

The United States Infantry Division in 1942 comprised three infantry regiments each containing three battalions and four field-artillery battalions. The basic tactical unit was the battalion, which normally included a headquarters and a headquarters detachment, three rifle companies, and a heavy-weapons company. Thus, a battalion was designed to function as a complete infantry unit; organically it included no weapon that could not be advanced by infantry over a distance of several hundred yards. It was designed to handle a frontage of 500 to 1,000 yards.[12]

The basic infantry unit was the company, comprising three rifle platoons and a heavy-weapons platoon. At full strength, therefore, a rifle platoon would consist of thirty to forty infantry armed with the M1, a semiautomatic rifle capable of about twenty to thirty aimed rounds a minute, and an automatic-rifle squad of eight men and two Browning automatic rifles (BARs), which were capable of a large volume of concentrated fire for short periods of time. It was assumed that the BAR would be of greatest value in defense, but it was mobile enough to accompany infantry in the attack. The heavy-weapons platoon contained one 60-mm mortar section and one light-machine-gun section; all were armed with either pistols or the M1.[13]

The heavy-weapons company added the firepower of two .30-caliber heavy machine gun platoons and one 81-mm mortar platoon to the capabilities of the battalion by providing close support and protection to the rifle companies. In the attack, the heavy-weapons company was expected to assist the advancing echelon with concentrated fire against key enemy positions such as crew-served weapons and organized strongholds and to provide long-range fire or to cover the flanks of attacking units. On defense, the heavy machine gun could give close support to the main line of resistance and protect the battalion against low-flying enemy aircraft; the mortar could sweep reverse slopes, wooded areas, ravines, and other defiladed areas and contribute to a concentrated fire along the entire front. Neither the heavy machine gun platoons nor the 81-mm mortar platoon was as mobile as the rifle companies, and in the jungle their effective ranges—2,000 yards for the machine gun and over 3,000 yards for the mortar—were sharply reduced by limited observation.[14]

"The infantry mission in the attack is to close with the enemy and capture or destroy him; in defense, to hold its position and repel the hostile attack."[15] Doctrine stressed alternate fire and movement at every level and close coordination between them, for it was recognized that the offensive power of infantry "decreases when its freedom of maneuver is restricted."[16] In preparing for an attack, a base of fire would be established, utilizing heavy machine guns, mortars, and supporting artillery. Rifle units would join in the fire fight as they came under enemy fire; this combined fire would create conditions favorable for the attack. Rifle units of the attacking echelon were to "exploit these conditions by alternate fire and movement," some of them firing to hold down enemy fire while others advanced from one cover or firing position to another. Enough rifles were to remain in action to smother enemy fire; "units most favored by terrain or fire support push forward while those most exposed support the advancing elements by fire."[17] When the enemy's

[handwritten margin note: contrast to DePuy's assertions]

fire had slackened, the signal would be given for the advance, which would be executed by small groups or individual rushes, and every lull in the fight would provide an opportunity to push more groups to the front. A unit that was held up was to send its reserves in a flanking movement; penetrations were to be exploited by reserves rushed forward from the next higher unit. "As one terrain feature is occupied, the advance to the next line is organized. Fire bases are rapidly organized. While the enemy's resistance remains unbroken, no movement is made without covering fire. . . . When tanks lead the advance . . . rapid action is required. The advance is as rapid as possible in order to exploit promptly the action of the tanks. . . . Rapid dashes are made from cover to cover with minimum periods of exposure."[18]

When no further advance was practicable, the captured terrain would be organized, combat outposts established, and troops regrouped to continue the attack, usually at daybreak the following morning. If tanks were used to lead the advance, the infantry was to move forward rapidly to exploit success. "Rapid dashes are made from cover to cover with minimum periods of exposure, and a portion of the heavy weapons moves forward behind the leading rifle companies to establish a base of fire on the next objective."[19]

Officers were expected to learn their trade in troop schools where they received basic instruction, in the various branch schools, "and by individual application and study."[20] In the final years before the war, a conscious effort was made to move from peacetime theoretical training in tactics toward greater realism by using historical examples to depict actual conditions that might be encountered in a campaign. "We must be experts in the technique— and the *special* tactics—of handling hastily raised, partially trained troops . . . when discipline is poor, officers green and information of the enemy invariably lacking," insisted Col. George Catlett Marshall, who for several years had been head of the Academic Department at the Infantry School at Fort Benning and who was destined to be appointed chief of staff the day war broke out in Europe on 1 September 1939. "All these things are far more difficult to learn than the related ponderous technique and formal tactics of Leavenworth."[21] In his introduction to the 1941 *Field Service Regulations*, Marshall specified that "set rules and methods must be avoided" because "they limit imagination and initiative which are so important in the successful prosecution of war."[22]

But problems of leadership intensified in the case of the 32d Infantry Division, whose officers and men had come recently from the National Guard and induction centers of the first peacetime draft in the nation's history. Early in August 1940, the Army was expanded to protect the United States and the Western Hemisphere. In September, four National Guard divisions were called up, and in October, the 32d Division from Wisconsin and Michigan was activated. Like all National Guard divisions, "the 32d had to go through a difficult period of personnel changes incident to the separation of officers and men who could not meet the physical requirements, were over age, or had dependents who created hardship cases."[23]

The 32d was greatly under strength when it was called up: of eighteen National Guard Divisions mobilized, only four required a higher percentage of draftees (46 percent) than the 32d to bring them up to assigned strength, and it took time to absorb and train these recruits before the division could get on with the task of meeting the standards required for combat efficiency.[24] In 1940, it was still widely assumed that once the twelve months of service had elapsed, everyone would go back to peaceful pursuits. "It was largely an army of amateurs in which many officers were occupied chiefly in learning how to be officers, and the men were being trained with scant equipment, and without realization, on their part, of the dead seriousness of the task ahead. The vast majority . . . did not conceive [of] themselves as future fighters."[25]

The 41st Division, which also sent a regiment into the battle in the latter stages, was probably more fortunate than most with its opportunity to train. Called up in September, it needed only 4,300 draftees (as opposed to the nearly 8,000 the 32d needed) to bring it up to wartime strength of 18,300, and within a month it was busy training.

General Marshall injected the idea of combining different arms and services—a battalion of artillery, an infantry regiment, and an engineer company—to form combat teams so that the commanding officer "could go into the field with a little army of his own, self-sufficient to live and fight for days and weeks at a time. This objective was to be fulfilled in later days of hard fighting in the jungles . . . of the Pacific."[26]

Both divisions participated in extensive maneuvers in 1941—the 41st in California and also in the Fourth Army maneuvers in Washington and the 32d in the famous Louisiana maneuvers, the greatest peacetime exercise in the history of the U.S. Army. The 32d also sent a regimental combat team consisting of the 128th Infantry, a battalion of field artillery, and engineer, medical, and signal troops to the Carolina maneuvers, where its performance was judged "of the highest order."[27] Early in 1942, both divisions were converted from the traditional *square* division, based on four regiments organized into two brigades, into the new *triangular* division, built around three infantry regiments, which further complicated administrative and training problems.

Initially, the 32d had been alerted to go to Northern Ireland; its engineer regiment had already been shipped when orders were received to leave Fort Devins, Massachusetts, for a San Francisco port of embarkation, from where it sailed for Australia on 22 April 1942. Three thousand filler replacements fresh from basic training and the 114th Engineer Combat Battalion, which had been activated only a few weeks earlier, sailed with the division; yet it was still short 4,788 enlisted men.[28] The 41st, regarded as one of the best National Guard divisions, landed at Sydney on 6 April and by the end of the month was

engaged in training, including thirty-mile marches on each of three consecutive days.[29] It moved to Rockhampton in July, and in the semitropical
climate, battle training became more realistic. Each battalion had amphibious
training under the Australian Army. By the time Lt. Gen. Robert L.
Eichelberger and his I Corps staff arrived in Rockhampton in July, introduc-
ing field tests conducted by corps officers every twelve weeks on all kinds of
tactical problems, the 41st Division was about ready for combat.

This was not the case with the 32d, which arrived at Adelaide in southern
Australia on 14 May. Training conditions at Adelaide were unfavorable: the
winter was cold and rainy, ammunition was in short supply, and there was no
opportunity to train for jungle warfare. It took time to absorb the large
number of inexperienced replacements who had joined the division in San
Francisco, and it took time to build camps near Adelaide and later near
Brisbane. Since February, the division had moved from Louisiana to Fort
Devins and thence to San Francisco, Adelaide, and finally Brisbane, each
move consuming nearly a month. With the time and turmoil of each move,
the division had scarcely five solid weeks of training when it was ordered to
New Guinea. There also had been a substantial turnover of battalion and
regimental commanders, which may have influenced the division commander,
Maj. Gen. Edwin F. Harding, to believe it "good policy" to retain as many of
the original National Guard officers "as could do a job," even if some
admittedly lacked drive and energy.[30]

When Eichelberger, as commander of the I Corps, first visited the 32d in
September, he was astonished to learn that the troops had had no jungle
training and obviously needed further hardening before they could hope to
meet Japanese veterans "on equal terms."[31] Because early training in
Australia had been under Australian control and the emphasis had been on
defense of the mainland, there had been little advanced training of any kind,
just "more of the same thing they had had back home."[32] Harding admitted
that he was familiar with the *Jungle Warfare* pamphlet, but he considered it
"old stuff—based on old campaigns," and in any case, neither the pamphlet
nor the time available contributed much to a realistic training system.[33] One
soldier subsequently confessed to Eichelberger that in twenty months of
service, he had had only one night problem. Only artillery training seems to
have been adequate.[34]

Why then was the 32d instead of the 41st picked to go to New Guinea?
Harding recalled a conference with Eichelberger and his chief of staff, Brig.
Gen. Clovis E. Byers, about 7 September in which Eichelberger indicated that
the 32d "was a little better trained." At that time "Eichelberger didn't seem
to be getting along with [General] Fuller," and Harding claimed that his
division was "at least as ready to go as the 41st.[35] Eichelberger mentioned
nothing of this but pointed out that in July, when both divisions had moved to
new camps in Queensland, the 41st had set up "a good camp" at Rock-

hampton, "excellently situated for jungle training," whereas the 32d occupied "a poor camp" near Brisbane. He had already decided to transfer the 32d to Rockhampton so that his two divisions could train together when the call came, and he selected the 32d to go to New Guinea because it would have to be moved anyway and he did not wish to interrupt the training program at Rockhampton, which was "under way and getting good results."[36]

The situation in New Guinea had become critical. During the weeks and months following the surprise attack at Pearl Harbor, there had been no stopping the Japanese military forces. Evening newcasts reported one impending disaster after another. By Christmas, Japanese forces had seized Hong Kong, Guam, Wake Island, and the Gilberts; Japanese aircraft had sunk the powerful British battleships *Repulse* and *Prince of Wales* in Malayan waters; and Japanese troops were advancing steadily in Malaya, Borneo, Burma, and the Philippines. In February, 80,000 British troops surrendered at Singapore. In March, General MacArthur left the Philippines for Australia to assume supreme command of all Allied forces in the newly established South-West Pacific Area (SWPA). But until the arrival of veteran Australian divisions from the Middle East and freshly trained infantry from the United States, there was little he could do to stem the tide. Already the Japanese had captured the Australian forward base at Rabaul in New Britain, invaded Java and Timor in the Netherlands East Indies, and occupied Lae and Salamaua in northeast New Guinea.

MacArthur's first priority was to defend Australia so that it could serve as a base for future offensives against the Japanese in New Guinea and the Bismarck–Solomon Islands. Where his Australian predecessors had planned originally to defend their country on the mainland of Australia, MacArthur preferred to wage the battle in New Guinea, where he could establish advance airdromes and impede the development of the Japanese bases at Lae and Salamaua.

Early in May, the Japanese made a first effort to seize Port Moresby, a key point near the southeastern tip of New Guinea that was vital both to the security of Australia and to any future Allied offensives against Japanese bases to the north. On 5–8 May, in a battle fought entirely between carrier aircraft over the Coral Sea, the Allies turned back the Japanese carriers and transports. The next week, the 14th Australian Infantry Brigade group was sent to reinforce Port Moresby, and later the Australians mounted guerrilla raids. The naval battle at Midway on 3–6 June also influenced the situation in New Guinea. With the naval balance in the Pacific now restored and the initiative passing to the Allies, the Japanese had to resort to a difficult land campaign when they renewed their efforts against Port Moresby in July. On the night of 21–22 July, a substantial Japanese force landed near Gona. Within hours, they had seized Buna about nine miles farther down the coast and were advancing inland along the Kokoda Trail, a treacherous and sparsely traveled track that twisted and turned through jungle, over towering mountains, and across precipitous slopes and broken ridges. The smaller Australian infantry force was driven back along the Kokoda Trail. In fierce fighting for the Kokoda plateau, the Australians, who could reach the scene only after a grueling climb over the Owen Stanley range, lacked the strength to expel the Japanese. Japanese reinforcements were temporarily diverted when the 1st U.S. Marine Division struck at Guadalcanal on 7 August. By 22 August, however, the Japanese had landed substantial reinforcements at Buna, and the offensive was renewed.

This was actually part of a two-pronged pincers movement directed against Port Moresby, for on the night of 26 August a force of nearly 2,000 Japanese landed in the Milne Bay area, where MacArthur had sent Australian infantry and a company of the 46th U.S. Engineers to construct an air base two months before. For the next five days, the Japanese tried desperately to seize the three airstrips, but the 7th Australian Infantry Brigade, which outnumbered the Japanese by four to one, defeated the invading forces at comparatively light cost.[37]

The same day that the Japanese landed at Milne Bay, Maj. Gen. Tomitaro Horii, who now had over 13,000 army and naval troops at his disposal, renewed his attack along the Kokoda Trail. Against this force, the Australians could assemble only three battalions, one of them sadly depleted. Outnumbered, continually outflanked, sick, exhausted, and dangerously short of food and supplies, the Australians fell back through the gap and across the Owen Stanley barrier, "fighting tenaciously and gallantly under conditions of extraordinary hardship and difficulty."[38] At Imita Ridge, within view of the sea on the Australian side of the mountains, the Australians prepared to make a last-ditch stand. The threatened attack never came. The Japanese thrust along the Kokoda Trail, with all supplies and heavy artillery ammunition having to be carried through deep forests and ravines, clinging mud, and over steep precipices, came to a natural halt before the Imita Ridge. Before General Horii could strengthen his position, reorganize his forces, replenish stores, and recover the health of his men, he was ordered back to the Buna–Gona area by *Imperial General Headquarters* because of the deteriorating situation on Guadalcanal. Accordingly, on 18 September, Horii began his own withdrawal across the hostile Owen Stanleys.

This coincided with a change in the Allied command. All Australian and American units in Australian New Guinea belonged to the New Guinea Force, which had been commanded since 18 August by Maj. Gen. Sydney F. Rowell. MacArthur, who erroneously kept insisting that Australians outnumbered Japanese in the Owen Stanleys and that "the real reason for the unsatisfactory position there was the lack of efficiency of the Australian troops"—and by inference, the lack of energy on the part of General

Rowell—urged General Sir Thomas Blamey, commander of the Allied Land Forces, to go to the front and "energize the situation."[39] Rowell, a proud and sensitive man, resented this intervention, and relations between the two Australian commanders so deteriorated that Blamey felt compelled to relieve him. Lt. Gen. Sir Edmond Herring, a fortunate selection, was sent to replace Rowell. Ironically, before Rowell's departure, the Australians had gone over to the offensive on Imita.[40]

On 1 October, GHQ issued the first comprehensive plan for the pursuit of the Japanese and the ultimate destruction of the Buna–Gona beachhead. "One axis would engage the enemy in a frontal action along the Kokoda Trail; the second would involve a wide flanking movement over the Owen Stanleys east of Port Moresby against the enemy lines of communication and supply; and the third axis of advance would consist of large-scale infiltration from Milne Bay along the northeastern coast of Papua."[41] All three approaches would eventually converge on fortified beachheads at Buna, Gona, and Sanananda, where it was expected that a final assault would have to be made against the Japanese coastal stronghold.

By this time, two regimental combat teams from the 32d Division, comprising the 126th and 128th Infantry regiments—each with a platoon of the 114th Engineers, a collecting company, a platoon of the clearing company of the 107th Medical Battalion, and a detachment of the 32d Signal Company—had arrived in Port Moresby, where they came under the control of the New Guinea Force. Because of transportation difficulties, the infantry howitzers—about two-thirds of the 81-mm mortars, and the battalion of field artillery that normally would have been included in a regimental combat team—had been left behind.[42] Harding had picked the 126th to go first because he considered it the best-led, best-trained regiment in his division, and in the interests of saving time, Company E plus one platoon from Company A, 114th Engineer Battalion, was flown to Port Moresby on 15 September and thus became the first U.S. Infantry to set foot in New Guinea. In the rush to get ready, the men had had to spray their fatigues with green camouflage dye, still wet when they boarded the collection of Douglas and Lockheed transports at Amberly Field near Brisbane. The rest of the regiment was shipped by sea because the loading had already begun before Maj. Gen. George C. Kenney, commanding the Allied and the Fifth Air Forces, suggested that his planes could transport the rest of the regiment. Kenney did manage to assemble enough civil transports and bombers to fly the entire 128th regiment to New Guinea on 25 September—the greatest air lift the U.S. Air Force had undertaken up to that time and the first major move of American troops by air in World War II.[43]

From Port Moresby, several trails led to the Buna–Gona area. The Australian 7th Infantry Division pursued General Horii's detachment across the Owen Stanleys and down the Kokoda Trail. The debris of the retreating

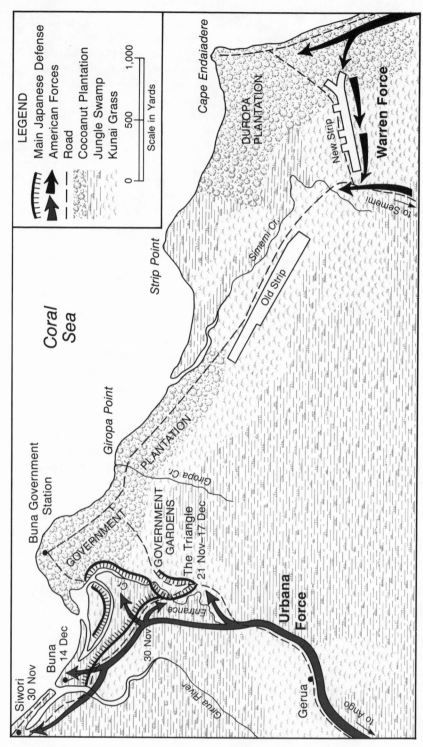

LEGEND

	Main Japanese Defense
	American Forces
	Road
	Cocoanut Plantation
	Jungle Swamp
	Kunai Grass

Scale in Yards

0   500   1,000

Coral
Sea

Cape Endaiadere

DUROPA
PLANTATION

New Strip

Warren Force

to Sememi

Strip Point

Simemi Cr.

Old Strip

Giropa Point

Buna Government
Station

GOVERNMENT

PLANTATION

Giropa Cr.

GOVERNMENT
GARDENS

The Triangle
21 Nov–17 Dec

Siwori
30 Nov

Buna
14 Dec

30 Nov

Entrance

Urbana
Force

Girua River

Gerua

to Ango

Map 7.1. American Operations before Buna

Japanese made it obvious that terrain, lack of rations, fatigue, and disease had taken their toll; it was slow and heavy going. Confined to one line of advance in country that did not lend itself to quick or wide encircling maneuvers and able to maintain at most three battalions in contact with the Japanese at any one time because of a shortage of native carriers, the 7th Division encountered heavy fighting in one rear-guard action after another. Pushed to the limit by the physical conditions along the trail—and by constant pressure from Blamey in Port Moresby and MacArthur back in Brisbane—the 7th Division advanced persistently. One battalion diarist noted, "Many men in such condition that it was pitiable to see them struggle on will power in many cases fighting against bodily exhaustion. . . . Frequently a day's hard march found the unit bivouacked for the night no further than one mile from the previous bivouac area." By 1 November, the leading units reached the Kokoda valley, leaving "the pouring, dripping, misty ranges" behind and discovering sun at their backs and vegetables in native gardens.[44] The next day the airfield was recaptured, and soon the supply situation improved dramatically. By mid-November, the Australians had fought their way around Japanese strongholds at Oivi and Gorari and were in position to cross the Kumusi River at Wairopi when the time came to close on Buna. General Horii himself drowned trying to escape.[45]

The second route, if indeed it can be called that, over the Owen Stanleys was the primitive Kapa Kapa track leading from a coastal village some 40 miles southeast of Port Moresby to Jaure on the headwaters of the Kumusi. The 2/126th Infantry was sent over this track to envelop any Japanese force seeking to maneuver around the right flank of Australians advancing along the Kokoda Trail. The intention originally had been to march the two regimental combat teams over the mountains, but the dramatic success of the air lift from Australia—and the existence of an airstrip at Wanigela Mission near Collingwood Bay that had been cleared by local Australian officials during the summer—convinced senior commanders that most of the division could be moved and supplied by air.

Although the *Regulations* specified that "all troops must be thoroughly acclimated before initiating major operations" in the jungle, what happened to the 2d Battalion of the 126th during the next few weeks revealed how unprepared the men of the 32d Division actually were.[46] An advance echelon of about 250 soldiers and 100 New Guineans began the march on 6 October, followed by the companies at one-day intervals beginning a week later. The men had no trail discipline whatsoever; they discarded essential articles, drank contaminated water, and needlessly exposed themselves to dysentery, leeches, and insects. Moreover, they were forced to eat cold rations and endure heavy rains and stifling heat. They "climbed, scrambled, clawed and suffered" across the hostile mountain barrier. "It was one green hell to Jaure," one sergeant later recalled. "We went up and down continuously. . . . It would take five or six hours to go a mile, edging along cliff walls, hanging on to vines, up and down, up and down." In his diary, he despaired: "God, will it never end?"[47]

It took two weeks to reach Jaure and another two weeks to get to Bofu, within striking distance of Buna. Among the casualties of this march was the battalion commander, Lt. Col. Henry A. Geerds, who suffered a heart attack and had to be evacuated, and Harding's best regimental commander, Col. L. A. Quinn, whose plane crashed as he personally flew over the troops to supervise the airdrop of supplies.[48] Some writers have attributed this "fiasco" to the "impatience and ignorance" both of the reconnaissance party and the senior commanders.[49] But in fairness to those who ordered the march, it must be remembered that the purpose was not merely to negotiate the mountains but also to guard against any enemy attempt to envelop the Australians on the Kokoda Trail by advancing down the Kumusi River. No general officer had actually seen the terrain. The rest of the division went by air. A missionary named Abel had emerged at Port Moresby with news that there was a decent airstrip in the upper valley of the Musa River and that a trail suitable for marching led to Pongani on the coast, about forty-five miles distant. On 8–10 November, most of the 1st Battalion of the 126th landed at "Abel's Field" while the rest of the regiment flew directly to Pongani, where units from the 128th regiment, having previously landed at Wanigela and worked their way through swamps and along the coast with the aid of small fishing boats, had cleared ground for yet another airstrip.[50]

By mid-November 1942, the Australian 7th Division and the two American regimental combat teams had completed the difficult approach march to the Buna–Gona beachhead. With a primitive yet complicated logistical system somewhat reminiscent of the eighteenth century, when armies could move only from one fortified depot to another, separated by a four- or five-day march, supplies and rations had been carried, shipped or airdropped to a series of predetermined sites. The men carried sufficient food to move from one dropping zone to the next. Places with code names taken from cities in Michigan and Wisconsin and activities dear to the natives of those states— "Horse," "Beaver," "Fish," and inevitably "Whiskey," "Gin," and "Saloon"—became scenes of feverish activity. At times the supply route would be knee deep in water. Radio contact frequently broke down. Shoes deteriorated with constant soaking, and a number of small craft carrying men, supplies, and ammunition were sunk by Japanese aircraft.[51] This prompted an order that coastal shipping could move only between 1700 and 0800 to be safe from air attack, but the reefs were even more treacherous in the dark, and this restriction doubled the number of days needed to move troops along the shallow and constricted waters.[52] To airdrop food and ammunition without parachutes was likewise "a costly enterprise," for only about 50 percent of the goods delivered by this method reached the right place unbroken.[53] Accordingly, on 3 November, the 32d Division was ordered not to move beyond the line Oro Bay–Bofu–Wairopi until ten days' supplies could be built up behind each advancing column. MacArthur anticipated that the attack on Buna would occur on 15 November.[54]

The reasons for this delay were logistic, but the American troops and their leaders, believing that Buna would be a pushover, were convinced that MacArthur's order was politically inspired. If green American soldiers were to capture Buna, it might be construed as a slap in the face to Australians who had fought their way along the Kokoda Trail. At this stage in the campaign, many Americans did not hold Australian soldiers in very high regard. In private conversation, MacArthur intimated that the Aussies were "not even good militia," an attitude that permeated his staff and perhaps filtered down to the troops. "The Australian command was well aware of these criticisms," General Eichelberger later recalled, and had it not been for his own warmth, candor, and unfailing sense of humor, combined operations in Papua would have experienced still greater difficulties.[55]

Most American soldiers considered the campaign almost over as they stopped to resupply before their entry into Buna. Natives reported the Japanese falling back, patrols made little contact with the enemy, and pilots flying over the area reported that they could see no signs of enemy troops and had encountered no Zero fighter aircraft within the past month. "Why don't the ground troops get going. . . . There is nothing around Buna but a few sick Japs."[56] Actually, the Japanese were there in imposing strength. One authority estimates that from first to last, some 18,000 Japanese army and naval personnel were employed in the Kokoda and Buna–Gona operations, and there seems to be general agreement that some 5,500 were dug in at Buna and Sanananda at the time the Allies closed in.[57] Most of these were veteran troops. The first to land in New Guinea in July belonged to the *South Seas Detachment,* some 5,000 men who had been detached from the year-old *55th Infantry Division* several days after Pearl Harbor for the purpose of capturing Guam, after which it was sent to Rabaul and then on to New Guinea in March. At full strength, it consisted of the headquarters, *55th Infantry Group,* the *144th Infantry,* a company and one squad of antitank guns of the *55th Cavalry,* the *1st Battalion* of the *55th Mountain Artillery,* and supporting ordnance, signal, transportation, and medical units.

In May, the *Seventeenth Army* had been activated by *Imperial General Headquarters,* and the *South Seas Detachment* was placed under the command of this army and given the mission of capturing Port Moresby. This land drive against Port Moresby was stalled in September due largely to logistic difficulties—despite 20,000 steps built on the trail over the Owen Stanleys, it was still impossible to take pack horses that last half of the way—and the Japanese situation on Guadalcanal had become critical. Thus, the transportation of the main forces of the *South Seas Detachment* to Buna was delayed, and the troops confronting the Australians at Imita Ridge were ordered to withdraw to the Kokoda section. The *41st Infantry,* which had been sent to reinforce the detachment in August, was ordered back to the Buna–Gona area to help build defenses. In an effort to hold the Solomons and Eastern New Guinea, *Imperial General Headquarters* on 15 November created a new command, *Eighth Area Army,* to comprise the *Seventeenth Army* in the Solomons and the new *Eighteenth Army* formed of all Japanese troops in New Guinea. Lt. Gen. Hatazo Adachi was given command of the *Eighteenth Army.*

Although officially designated an army, this was no organic force prepared to operate as a large unit in the field. In addition to the survivors of the retreat along the Kokoda Trail, who were short of small arms, food, and medical supplies and were "riddled by battle casualties and disease," it included 300 replacements for the *144th regiment,* who landed on 17 November.[58] These men were veterans of the campaigns in the Philippines, China, and Malaya, and the *3d Battalion* of the *229th Infantry,* which reached Buna about the same time, included many who had seen service in China, Hong Kong, and Java. The *Naval Force* was a marine battalion that had fought in China, Malaya, Singapore, and some of the Pacific islands. The arrival of these fresh and experienced troops increased the Japanese strength in the Buna–Gona area to about 6,500 men to defend works that had been under construction since 23 September. Of these, about 2,500 manned the Buna defenses.[59]

The Japanese defenses were formidable. Located on dry ground and with good lateral communications along the beach, they dominated the rather narrow corridors that constituted the only natural approaches from the land side. In the weeks before the battle, the Japanese had constructed a series of bunkers and pillboxes using coconut logs for a framework of columns and beams and to strengthen the sides, which were often reinforced by steel oil drums and sand-filled ammunition boxes. An Australian war correspondent described the Japanese defenses he inspected that December.

> Every weapon pit is a fortress in miniature. Some are strengthened by great sheets of armor and by concrete, but the majority are merely huge dugouts—several are 150 feet long—protected from our fire and bombs by sawn logs and felled trees which form a barrier, six, ten and sometimes 15 feet thick. The logs are held in place by great metal stakes, and filled in with earth in which the natural growth of the jungle has continued, providing perfect camouflage. Many of the pits are connected by subterranean tunnels or well protected communication trenches. . . . From every trench or pit or pillbox all approaches are covered by wide fields of sweeping fire along fixed lines. . . . [The] wily enemy . . . has established concrete gunpits and dug grenade-proof and mortar-proof nests beneath the roots of giant jungle trees. He has put keen-eyed snipers in hundreds of treetops. He has mown

down the grass and jungle to give lanes of sweeping fire to his many machine guns. From such positions companies can hold up battalions and battalions could resist divisions. . . . These pockets cannot be bypassed because of neck-deep swamps of black, sucking mud. They must be assaulted at whatever cost, and destroyed one by one.[60]

These were no "hasty field intrenchments," although MacArthur's chief of staff once used that term in talking with Eichelberger during the battle.[61] Organized in depth and usually invisible from more than a few feet away, the Japanese defenses at Buna were "almost impregnable."[62] American survivors of the battle must have smiled grimly, viewing the defense system, as they recalled their optimism only a few weeks before.

On 16 November, the Allies resumed their advance. On the extreme left, the Australian 25th Brigade crossed the Kumusi and moved through the tropical lowlands toward Gona, about forty miles distant. By the twenty-first, patrols had penetated to within two miles of the Japanese position, which was defended by a makeshift force of at most 1,000 men—patients from a field hospital, a road construction unit, a military laborers unit, and a water supply and purification unit, plus 69 infantry from the *41st Regiment* and 60 men from a health unit. At times, the Japanese lines were stretched so thin that it was necessary to assign a single man to guard a fifty-meter front. Some idea of the fierce resistance is suggested by the experience of 80 men of the *Yamasaki Unit,* which had been dispatched from the *South Seas Detachment* on 24 November: in one day, 6 December, every man in this unit was killed in action.[63] It took the 25th, which was later reinforced by the Australian 21st Brigade, a month of "wearing operations" and heavy casualties before Gona was finally secured in late December.[64]

The Australian 16th Brigade advanced on a parallel track a few miles to the east until it bumped into an entrenched outpost a short distance beyond Soputa. On 20–21 November, there was sharp fighting along the Sanananda track, but when a detachment of about eighty Australians managed to work their way around the Japanese position and fight back repeated counterattacks two miles to the rear, the Japanese withdrew to their main positions astride the junction of the tracks leading to Sanananda and Cape Killerton, where they had erected two fortified positions about 1,500 meters apart. Here, in what they called "the Central Position" (midway between Girua and Soputa), were roughly 4,000 Japanese troops, including the main body of the *41st Infantry,* now only about 200 strong; what was left of the headquarters of the *South Seas Detachment;* a mountain artillery battalion; about 300 troops from the *47th Field Artillery Anti Aircraft Battalion (F.A.A.A.)* and a like number from the *15th Independent Engineers;* and three medical units with a total strength of 2,500, mostly patients.[65] The 16th Brigade, however, was in no shape to continue the offensive. The men were tired, hungry, and many were sick, and the brigade

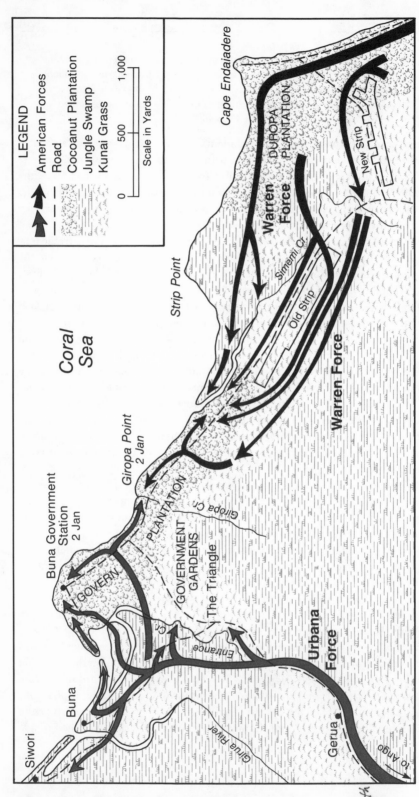

Map 7.2. Lines of Advance of Warren and Urbana Forces, 18 December 1942–2 January 1943

LEGEND

American Forces
Road
Cocoanut Plantation
Jungle Swamp
Kunai Grass

Scale in Yards

0   500   1,000

Coral
Sea

Cape Endaiadere

DUROPA
PLANTATION

Warren
Force

New Strip

Simemi Cr.

Old Strip

Warren Force

Strip Point

Giropa Point
2 Jan

Buna Government
Station
2 Jan

Buna

Siwori

Girua River

GOVERN.
PLANTATION

(GOVERNMENT
GARDENS)

Giropa Cr.

The Triangle

Entrance

Cr.

Urbana
Force

Gerua

to Ango

had already lost one-third of its number in continuous fighting along the Kokoda Trail. The only reinforcements near at hand were Americans of the 126th Infantry.[66]

A conventional narrative of the battles about to unfold would have to devote equal time to the Australians, who had fought their way from the Owen Stanley Mountains to the beachheads; who had captured Gona, participated in the fighting on the American right flank at the New Strip and Cape Endaiadere; and who were engaged in desperate fighting along the Sanananda and Killerton tracks. For an analysis of the first battle fought in the Pacific by the U.S. Army after the fall of the Philippines, however, it is necessary only to focus on the fighting of the 32d Infantry Division at Buna, as long as it is remembered that the Papuan campaign was a combined operation, that Buna was only one of three fortified beachheads under assault, and that the 32d Division came under immediate control of the New Guinea Force, commanded by an Australian.

The main Japanese defense line ran from the mouth of the Girua River, a short distance west of Buna Village, to the Duropa plantation half a mile south of Cape Endaiadere. The Buna garrison unit included the *3d Battalion* of the *229th regiment,* one mountain artillery battery of the *38th Division,* one battery of the *47th F.A.A.A. Battalion,* and replacements of the *144th Infantry*—about 1,600 men. There was also a naval defense force of about 900 men. Both Japanese flanks were secure and it was open to frontal assault only along two narrow and heavily fortified corridors. This necessitated establishing two separate fronts, soon to be known as Warren front and Urbana front, named after the Ohio hometowns of two of the American generals involved. Although only two or three miles apart by air, the fronts were separated on the ground by impassable swamps and thick jungle. The Americans did not enjoy lateral communications: liaison between the two forces involved tortuous native trails, "narrower than your two arms outstretched," and distance was more a matter of hours than of miles—six or seven hours to walk from one flank to the other and then, during rains, "the traveler walked up to his hips in water."[67] Any extensive movement of troops necessitated a two-day march by way of Simemi and Ango, whereas the Japanese had a road from Simemi Creek to Buna Mission and could reinforce either flank in a matter of minutes. The Japanese position, and hence the battleground, was about three and one-half miles long and three-quarters of a mile deep.[68]

On 15 November, General Harding issued Field Order No. 1. The 2d Battalion of the 128th Infantry was to move along the coast and take Cape Endaiadere; the 3d Battalion would assault the airstrip; and the 2d Battalion would help the engineers construct an airfield at Dobodura while serving also as a division reserve. The 126th Infantry, which had reunited at Natunga, was directed to close on Inonda, where it would receive orders to move against

Buna.[69] There were at this time only about 7,000 officers and men of the entire division in the combat area. As Harding wrote his orders, the 127th Regimental Combat Team was about to embark on a Liberty ship back at Camp Gable near Brisbane, and most of the supporting units, including many engineer and artillery units, were not present. The division therefore could not be committed as an organic whole, even had the terrain permitted.[70] Accordingly, the 128th Infantry, minus one company that had been left at Pongani, moved out on 16 November. The 1st Battalion, commanded by Lt. Col. Robert C. McCoy, advanced from Embogo along the coast to Boreo, a distance of perhaps six miles. Lt. Col. Kelsie E. Miller's 3d Battalion followed the trail from Embi to Dobodura, which it reached the following day. Progress on 17 November was much slower on the right, where the 1st Battalion moved only a short distance along the shore. As planned, Lt. Col. Herbert A. Smith's 2d Battalion and a company of engineers reached Dobodura and began clearing a landing strip.

Harding's plan suffered a serious setback when Japanese aircraft struck three luggers and a landing barge as they rounded Cape Sudest on the evening of the sixteenth. Allied fighter aircraft had departed in order to reach the Port Moresby landing fields before dark, and eighteen Zero-type fighters strafed the ships and destroyed the ammunition aboard, killing twenty-four and forcing Harding, Brig. Gen. Albert W. Waldron, his division artillery commander, and two observers sent out from Army Ground Forces to swim for shore. This action cost Harding the loss of a number of 81-mm mortars and heavy machine guns, which were difficult for troops to carry along jungle trails, and two Australian twenty-five-pounders, roughly the equivalent of the American 105-mm in range and deadliness. The next day, Japanese aircraft sank two of the remaining three luggers. With no replacement vessels in sight and short of artillery, heavy mortars, machine guns, and other essential material, Harding's entire supply plan had been disrupted, and he was forced to adjust his dispositions for the attack. Brig. Gen. Hanford MacNider, who was to command the attack of Warren Force (the original name given the mixed Australian and American force built up at Wanigela in October), was ordered to hold up his advance until the one remaining lugger could deliver its supplies, and the troops left behind at Pongani were now forced to follow McCoy's coastal column on foot instead of moving to Embogo by boat. In the words of the official history, the loss of the coastal boats "was a catastrophe of the first magnitude."[71]

On the left flank, the friction of war caused other serious adjustments. Harding's original intent had been to bring the 126th Infantry to Buna from Inonda by a route "to be specified later."[72] Whatever Harding may have had in mind most certainly was not what occurred next. Instead of bringing the 126th Infantry to the front by way of Dobodura and Ango, Harding felt it necessary to change his plans when he lost radio contact with the Australians

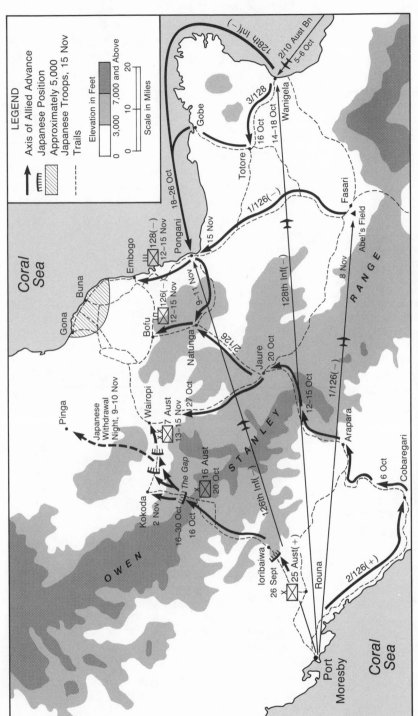

Map 7.3. Allied Advance across Owen Stanley Range, 26 September–15 November 1942

during the early stages of his advance. He ordered Col. Clarence M. Tomlinson, who was then awaiting instructions at Inonda, to move his regiment to the left by way of Popondetta and Soputa to forestall any Japanese attempt to threaten the American left flank. This brought the 126th Infantry on the Sanananda track behind the Australian 16th Brigade, and on 19 November, when the New Guinea Force decided to attack the Japanese concentrations west of the Girua River with all forces available, the 126th Infantry, despite Harding's protests, was placed under control of Maj. Gen. G. A. Vasey, commanding the Australian 7th Division. Advance units from the 126th Infantry began to reach Soputa on the afternoon of 20 November.

By this time, Harding's initial attack had already taken place. Harding set H-hour as 0700 on 19 November. The 1st Battalion of the 128th moved against Cape Endaiadere, and the 3d Battalion advanced from Simemi, both with enough rations and ammunition for only one day because of the sinking of the supply luggers. Three companies of the 2d Battalion, 128th Infantry, were ordered forward from Dobodura to Ango Corner, to cover the junction of the tracks from Dobodura and Soputa pending arrival of the 126th Infantry. When Harding learned the next day that the 126th had been diverted to Australian control, he was forced to commit the 128th, his only available reserve, to continue the advance along this axis to Buna, a task for which he originally had assigned an entire regiment.

The 1st Battalion ran into a fortified outpost line about halfway between Boreo and the Duropa plantation. McCoy was advancing in a column of companies in pouring rain along a narrow path about twenty yards from the beach, when the advance patrol of Company G ran into heavy machine-gun and rifle fire. The troops deployed and attacked, but the thick jungle growth concealed the enemy, whose weapons gave off no flash and muffled and distorted the sounds, so that it was difficult to determine the source of the fire. Nor was it easy for the Americans to set up their mortars, and to make matters worse, the Japanese rotated their weapons among several concealed positions, creating the illusion that the fire was coming from all directions. Often the Japanese would let the green troops advance to within a few feet of a machine-gun post before opening fire; other times they would permit them to pass by before firing on the rear elements. According to one officer, "our troops were pinned down everywhere. . . . It was dangerous to show even a finger from behind one's cover, as it would immediately draw a burst of fire." The Americans, who had approached the battle confidently and with light hearts, were stunned by this unexpected resistance. Out of rations and rapidly running out of ammunition, the 1st Battalion ended the day "a badly shaken outfit."[73] When Japanese outposts fell back a few yards because of the pressure, the green American troops were in no position to push ahead.

The 3d Battalion on the left had even rougher going. The route from Simemi brought Colonel Miller's men into a narrow corduroy causeway leading to a bridge across Simemi Creek between the Old Strip, west of the creek, and the New Strip east of it. Both strips were heavily fortified: the Old Strip was bounded on the southern edge by a formidable swamp, while bunkers, fire trenches, and barbed wire protected the northern edge; the bridge was protected front and rear by bunkers and gun emplacements, and the New Strip even contained some concrete and steel pillboxes.[74] Confined to the causeway by oozing swamps on both sides, the men of the 3d Battalion ran into heavy mortar and machine-gun fire about 500 yards southwest of the New Strip. Miller's men were thus forced to attack through swamps that were sometimes waist deep, and they could carry only light weapons, so there were no 81-mm mortars to return the fire. The hand grenades, which were Mills bombs obtained from the Australians, were ineffective when wet, and the men were running low on .30-caliber ammunition. Miller's battalion was, in his own words, "stopped cold."[75] On the far left, a patrol from the 2d Battalion pushed to within one mile of Buna, where it was held up by an estimated eighty Japanese. The rest of the battalion was reported in position to support an attack.[76]

The attacks were renewed at 0800 the next day. After a brief bombardment from several light bombers and unobserved fire from two Australian mountain guns located some 600 yards north of Hariko, McCoy's battalion attacked on a two-company front.[77] Company C moved along the coast to infiltrate and knock out several Japanese machine-gun nests, and the entire command moved forward several hundred yards, but on the left, near the airstrips, Miller's men made no progress whatever. That evening, both battalions received rations that had been airdropped at Hariko and Simemi, and Lt. Col. Edmond J. Carrier's 1st Battalion of the 126th Infantry, which had landed at Abel's Field instead of Pongani with the rest of the 126th, moved into the rear of McCoy's position after a twenty-five-mile march from Pongani with full pack. They were followed by Maj. Henry G. Harcourt's Independent Company, an Australian unit, which arrived at 0700 on the twenty-first. Despite the lack of progress, a communique from MacArthur's headquarters in Australia claimed that American ground forces "have rapidly closed in and now pin the enemy down on the narrow coastal strip." MacArthur ordered an all-out attack along the entire front from Gona to Buna for the twenty-first.[78]

Once again, McCoy's battalion would advance on the extreme right, with Carrier's 1st Battalion of the 126th keeping pace on his left; what was left of these two battalions occupied a frontage of about 300 yards, less than a third of the distance specified in the *Field Service Regulations*. Harcourt's Independent Company guarded the left flank against Japanese attacks from positions at the eastern end of the New Strip. Miller would try once again with his battalion to take the bridge, and on the far left Lt. Col. Herbert A. Smith would advance from Ango to Girua and on to Buna. The attack began poorly. The bombing run occurred at 0800 as scheduled, but coordination with ground forces had been faulty, and neither McCoy nor Miller had been notified in time; in fact, their final orders for the attack were not received until forty minutes later. A second air strike planned for 1245 did not materialize, and a third, executed shortly before 1600, may have produced more American casualties than Japanese.[79]

"This is the big show," MacNider was warned. "Take Grand Rapids (Buna) today."[80] But when the attack finally went in, it was nearly stopped in its tracks. Along the coast, the 1st Battalion made little headway, the 3d Battalion lost forty-two men trying in vain to take the bridge, and Harcourt's Independent Company halted within sixty yards of the New Strip. On the far left, where the track from Ango forked—the right branch leading to Buna Mission and the left to the village—the enclosed "Triangle" served the Japanese as a well-fortified redoubt. As Smith's 2d Battalion of the 128th neared the Triangle, his advance elements encountered machine-gun and rifle fire from the elaborate network of bunkers. Quickly sending Company G into the swamps to the right and Company F to the left while Company H fought a holding action along the trail, Smith tried to envelop the enemy position. "Am pushing forward slowly, advance delayed by shoulder deep swamp more than enemy fire," he advised division headquarters early in the afternoon.[81] The day ended with his two flanking companies still deep in the swamps and Company G, on the right, in real difficulty. But help was at least on the way. That afternoon, Harding requested the return of one of the two battalions of the 126th Infantry that had been sent to reinforce the Australian 16th Brigade along the Sanananda track. While this "is primarily for Smith's protection," he explained to General Herring, if made promptly, it "should enable us to take Buna tomorrow."[82] The transfer, however, was not made promptly. The 2d Battalion, gaunt survivors from the ordeal along the Kapa Kapa track, had to cross a flooded river and could not join the troops bogged down at the Triangle until the morning of 23 November.

The situation then facing the 32d Division explains the confusion and disorder of the next several weeks. The terrain channelized the attacks, and circumstances had scrambled the units. Two battalions of the 128th and one of the 126th, plus some Australians, now made up Warren Force. The 2d Battalion of the 128th and now the 2d Battalion of the 126th—ironically both commanded by officers named Herbert Smith—were fighting to envelop the Triangle, while the 3d Battalion of the 126th Infantry had joined the Australian 16th Brigade along the Sanananda track and was poised to attack Japanese positions the next day. This mixing of units was caused by transportation difficulties, enemy action, and orders from the New Guinea Force; it led to confusion, additional administrative details, and problems in supply and evacuation. It also "had its effect on morale . . . because a unit separated from its parent organization invariably believes that it is discriminated against in supplies provided and tasks assigned."[83]

The identity crisis in front of the Triangle was quickly solved: Harding designated Smith of the 126th *Red* Smith, and the commanding officer of the 2d Battalion, 128th Infantry, *White* Smith. On Warren front, the command situation was blurred somewhat for more basic reasons. The commander of the 128th regiment, Col. J. Tracy Hale, was the senior National Guard officer in the division. Because Hale lacked drive, Harding had given command of Warren Force to General MacNider, and MacNider had largely ignored Hale in the advance from Wanigela. But MacNider was wounded by a Japanese rifle grenade while inspecting the front on 23 November, and Harding was reluctant to bypass Hale again because of the adverse effect it might have on other National Guard officers. Therefore, he gave Hale command of Warren Front but placed Lt. Col. Alexander J. MacNab, executive officer of the 128th, in operational command of the drive along the coast.[84]

The 21st was not an entire loss, however. The airstrip at Dobodura was completed on that day, and the artillery situation improved with the arrival by boat of two Australian twenty-five-pounders and 200 rounds of ammunition, although one of the guns could not be used for several days after a Japanese air attack damaged the sights. On 23 November, two additional twenty-five-pounders were flown into Dobodura, which was another first, for, unlike the mountain guns, the twenty-five-pounders could not be disassembled.

For the next two days, MacNab's drive along the coast on the right made little progress—100 yards at most on the coastal flank and center and nothing on the left—while American infantry on the Urbana front, as the area crossed by the Ango track came to be known, pushed deeper into the swamps, seeking a soft spot in the Triangle. Company F on the left made some progress along Entrance Creek, and Company G, on the extreme right, waded to a stretch slightly above marsh level that seemed within 200 yards of the Japanese position, but because its line of supply was "neck deep in mud and water," White Smith asked permission to withdraw the company.[85] An error by the decoding clerk at division headquarters lowered the water to "knee deep," and Harding ordered the attack to proceed: "This is war, not a maneuver."[86] The "air show" preceding the attack on 24 November was "a fizzle": no bombers were available and the four fighters that did appear strafed White Smith's command post.[87] The attack of Companies E and G was supported by unobserved artillery and heavy mortar fire but failed to make a dent in the Japanese defenses. A mix-up in orders caused Company E and the weapons platoon of Company G to fall back prematurely, and Smith abandoned further efforts to outflank the Triangle on his right. While casualties in the area of the Triangle thus far had not been heavy—two killed, ten wounded, and one missing since 21 November—the terrain made it extremely difficult to hold

supply lines open, and wet, muddy weapons often malfunctioned. All of the
hand grenades and half the light mortar rounds were ineffective.[88]

On 27 November, General Harding sent his chief of staff, Col. John W.
Mott, to assume command of Urbana Force, and White Smith returned to his
battalion. Mott relieved the commanders of Companies E and G and ordered
the companies back to the positions they had abandoned three days before,
but by now it was apparent that the best opportunity to outflank the Triangle
was on the left.

The next serious attack occurred on 30 November. Beginning with the
biggest air strike thus far in the campaign—a total of fifty aircraft, fighters
followed by bombers—and for the first time supported by eight twenty-five-
pounders and a dozen heavy mortars, the two front-line battalions on Warren
front renewed their attack. McCoy's battalion, now reorganized into two rifle
companies and one heavy-weapons company, attacked up the coastal track in
column of companies on a 350-yard front. (The attack was to have been
preceded by two Australian Bren-gun carriers, but they failed to arrive on
time because of problems in shipping.) The Japanese defenses, however, had
not been neutralized, and the enemy quickly emerged to block the lead
company. Carrier's 1st Battalion of the 286th Infantry on the left was also
stopped by enemy fire, while the Independent Company was halted near the
New Strip and forced to dig in. Company I of Miller's 3d Battalion of the
128th Infantry remained to block the bridge; the other companies had been
sent to the right as a reserve. On the Urbana front, Mott made his main effort
with a night attack on the left. Using telephone wire to find the jump-off point,
three companies of the 2d Battalion, 126th Infantry, attacked the Japanese line
of machine gun posts. "All hell broke loose. . . . Machine gun tracers lit the
entire area, and our own rifle fire made a solid sheet of flame. Everywhere
men cursed, shouted, or screamed. Order followed on order. . . . Brave men
led and others followed. Cowards crouched in the grass literally frightened out
of their skins."[89] Company F managed to secure the crossing over Siwori
Creek, cutting the Japanese land communications between Buna and Sanananda, and other troops got within 100 yards of Buna Village, although the
enemy position between the Triangle and the coast remained intact.

In Port Moresby, MacArthur received reports from the front with
growing impatience. To him, light casualties meant one thing: there had been
little serious fighting.[90] While the two American regiments thus far engaged
had suffered 492 battle casualties, this statistic alone could not have conveyed
an accurate picture.[91] MacArthur could not have appreciated how many
riflemen were too sick and worn out to fight aggressively or even the extent to
which terrain and shortages of ammunition and supplies had limited tactical
possibilities. He did hear from Blamey and Herring about the poor morale
and discipline of the American soldiers, "a bitter pill . . . to swallow."[92]
MacArthur sent his chief of staff and his G-3 to the front; both confirmed his

conviction that leadership in the 32d Division was unaggressive, although
Harding stood behind his regimental officers.

On 29 November, Lieutenant General Eichelberger, who was at Rockhampton training the 41st Division, was summoned to Port Moresby. When
he reported to MacArthur, the commanding general of the I Corps was told in
a grim voice: "Bob, I'm putting you in command at Buna. Relieve Harding
. . . remove all officers who won't fight. Relieve regimental and battalion
commanders: if necessary put sergeants in charge of battalions and corporals
in charge of companies—anyone who will fight. Time is of the essence; the
Japs may land reinforcements any night. . . . *I want you to take Buna, or not come
back alive.*"[93] Unlike Harding, who had spent most of his career with troops,
Eichelberger's career since serving on the staff of the American Expeditionary
Force in Siberia in 1918–20 had been spent mostly in military intelligence or
in the adjutant general's department. Not until war clouds began to gather in
1937 did he transfer back to the infantry. In 1938, he had attended the
Infantry School at Fort Benning and then commanded the 30th Infantry
before being promoted to brigadier general and appointed superintendent of
the military academy. Soon after Pearl Harbor, he was promoted again and
given command of an infantry division then being organized at Fort Jackson,
and in June 1942, he was named commander of the I Corps, which originally
was to have been trained in amphibious warfare for use in the forthcoming
North African landings. In late August, however, he found himself flying
instead to Australia, where his mission was to supervise the training of the 32d
and 41st Divisions. It was not anticipated, at least at this early stage, that
operations would be on a scale large enough to require the intervention of a
corps commander.

Eichelberger reached the 32d Division command post and assumed *how did*
command on 30 November. The next morning he visited the Urbana front. *he move*
He never forgot the sight that greeted him—no front-line discipline; no *so quickly?*
thought of going forward; men loitering about in rear areas, many without
permission. When he told Mott how conditions looked to him, Mott's temper
flared as he explained what hunger, fatigue, and fever had done to his men.
Harding supported his subordinate, and, when the two of them lost their
tempers a second time the next day, Eichelberger relieved them. He placed
General Waldron in charge of the division and Lt. Col. Melvin McCreary,
another artillery officer, in command of Urbana Force. With Waldron's
approval, he also replaced Hale with Col. Clarence Martin, the I Corps G-3.

Eichelberger's arrival struck his immediate superior, General Herring, *New Guinea*
as "a very pure breath of fresh air" that "blew away a great deal of the *Force Cmdr*
impurities that were stopping us getting on with the job."[94] Almost immediately, he set about putting aggressive leaders in charge of things at the front.
Col. John E. Grose, I Corps inspector general, was given command of

Urbana Force. The next day, however, Colonel Tomlinson, who commanded the 126th Infantry, moved his command post from the Sanananda track to Urbana front, leaving one battalion, the third, to man the defensive position it had captured and fortified some 1,500 yards behind the main Japanese defenses and perhaps 300 yards in front of the enemy's second line.[95] Grose, who had been promised command of the 127th, which was due to arrive shortly, suggested that while he attended to supply matters, Tomlinson be given command of the Urbana Force. But within two weeks Tomlinson, an aggressive leader whose "work in spots has been quite good," was so exhausted that he asked to be relieved and Grose took over.[96]

Carrier, suffering from a heart attack, was replaced by Major Chester Beaver on 13 December, and Major Gordon Clarkson, who fewer than five years earlier had been a first classman at the military academy, took over the 1st Battalion of the 128th. "I raised him from a pup in the 30th Infantry," Eichelberger explained to General Richard K. Sutherland. "He is full of fight and will do what I tell him to do. I do not intend to let the Japanese sit down and sleep."[97] Several field officers exchanged jobs to their mutual benefit. Sometimes the change was perceived within the man. White Smith, "who was on the borderline of being relieved . . . developed into quite a fighter."[98] So too did Red Smith of the 2d Battalion, 126th Infantry, who was severely wounded on 7 December leading his men on the front lines. Such men, when they returned to duty, would give the 32d "something solid to build on."[99] "Eventually," Eichelberger hoped, "the 32d Division will be a fighting organization which will not wring every drop of blood out of those who are responsible for trying to make it advance."[100]

"The morale of a unit is that of its leader. . . . The presence of a commander with the troops in action, as often as possible, is essential to morale."[101] If ever a commander gave truth to this assertion, it was Eichelberger at Buna. He analyzed the situation quickly, reorganized and regrouped badly intermixed forces, improved the supply problem, which had become less acute once the airstrip was operational at Dobodura, and provided dynamic leadership that would infuse new life into units at every level. He insisted on frequent visits to the front to see and be seen, yet he was the only American general officer in the combat zone who did not become a casualty.[102] "Somebody has got to plead for my immortal soul," he confessed in a letter to Sutherland, "because strange words of profanity have rolled out of my face that I never knew I understood."[103] He gave pep talks to troops trudging up the line and direct orders to subordinates who seemed cautious or indecisive. An aide was severely wounded by a sniper while standing only a few feet from the general. Members of his staff pleaded with him in vain to remove his stars, which could easily identify him to snipers, before another visit to the front. His activities during the day "could well be classified, from an academic viewpoint, as interference, but were, as a practical matter, assurances of maximum

effort. . . . His three stars were in evidence to the tired, dirty doughboys that the high command was taking a very personal interest in the fight."[104] For this reason, Buna was used for years as a case study of the corps commander in modern battle in the leadership course at the Command and General Staff College, Fort Leavenworth.[105]

Because jungle fighting "is usually and necessarily carried on independently by small clusters of men" who need to understand "where they are going, and more important why," Eichelberger halted all offensive action for two days while he unscrambled his units and tightened the chain of command.[106] Meanwhile, Waldron planned a divisional attack scheduled for 5 December. It was to be a frontal attack on both the Warren and Urbana fronts, preceded by an air strike and artillery bombardment. On Warren front, the infantry were deployed from right to left in this order: 3d Battalion, 128th Infantry, in the coconut grove; 1st Battalion, 128th Infantry, against the eastern end of the New Strip; the Australian Independent Company to exploit any openings in the center of the strip; and on the far left, the 1st Battalion of the 126th to operate against the western end of the New Strip and bridge. The main thrust was to be along the coast, where five Australian-manned Bren-gun carriers, which had finally arrived the previous day, were to lead the attack accompanied by Company L, with Company I following in column on the left rear. On Urbana front, the plan called for the Cannon Company, 128th Infantry and the 2d Battalion of the 126th to attack designated points in the Japanese perimeter around Buna Village, with Company F, which had already taken heavy losses in previous attacks, in reserve.

At 0820, six medium bombers strafed and bombed the Japanese position between Cape Endaiadere and the Old Strip, and beginning at 0830 there was a brief artillery barrage. Neither did much damage. The lightly armored, open-topped Bren-gun carriers failed in their role as tanks. The four-man crews were exposed to deadly sniper and machine-gun fire, and within a half-hour, all five vehicles were out of action. Left to its own resources, the infantry, suffering heavy casualties both from hidden, well-placed pillboxes and from the intense heat, gained only forty yards. Company A of the 128th Infantry made some progress across the eastern end of the New Strip but was halted "by rifle grenade, mortar and machine gun fire from three directions."[107] Company B, to the immediate left, ended the day consolidating at the eastern end of the strip. Meanwhile, on the far left, efforts to carry the bridge between the strips failed again, although seven Japanese pillboxes were knocked out. An attempt later in the day to cross Simemi Creek failed because of reported quicksand and the deep water. "We have hit them and bounced off" was the best Colonel Martin could report to the 32d Division command post that night.[108]

Things went better that day on the Urbana front, where, after aerial and artillery bombardment, the attack was launched at 1030. Although it did not gain the objective, the Cannon Company of the 128th, reinforced by a platoon of Company F of the 126th, managed to get within fifty yards of Buna Village, and in the center, Eichelberger personally threw in his only reserve, Company F, in a futile effort to take the village. It was thought "that we needed little more than our bayonets to do it," commented the company commander, a lieutenant. "Well, off we went, and within a few minutes our rush forward had been definitely and completely halted. Of the 40 men who started with me, 4 had been killed, and 18 were lying wounded. We were within a few yards of the village, but with . . . no chance of going a step further."[109] On the right, however, a platoon of Company H, led by S. Sgt. Herman J. F. Bottcher, actually pushed through to the sea and dug in, completing the encirclement of Buna Village and severing communication between the village and Buna Mission. General Waldron, who was at the front leading the men by personal example, was wounded by a bullet and a grenade or mortar shell that exploded nearby: "It felt as though my whole right side had been blown off."[110] Brigadier General Byers took over command of the 32d. "One finds a lot of philosophy in life," Eichelberger mused that night in a letter to his wife. "Saturday the fifth of December will always remain with me as long as I live. I tried to do so much and . . . I did not do all I had hoped for. . . . Some want to run away and some seem to have inherited the spirit of 'the fighting races.' "[111] To Sutherland, he wrote that most of the troops had fought hard and that there was "much to be proud of during the day's operations."[112]

The attack on 5 December represents a watershed in the Buna battle. It convinced Eichelberger that the Japanese position was too strong to be breached by frontal attack: he would await the arrival of Australian reinforcements and tanks, which had been promised two days earlier, before making another major effort. Meanwhile, he ordered "continued pressure and advance by infiltration," attempted new methods to reduce pillboxes, insisted upon more aggressive patrolling, particularly at night, and built up supply and ammunition reserves.

The total effective strength of Warren Force after the fighting on 5 December was 2,067 officers and men; for Urbana Force, 1,188. With some rest, however, they were considered in satisfactory combat condition, and with the arrival of the first elements of the 127th Infantry regiment on 11 December, morale improved noticeably. After this date, G-3 situation reports indicate that the morale of the men was good and that the front-line troops were growing increasingly aggressive.[113] Americans were finally learning how to fight *in* the jungle, instead of thrashing around against it. The Buna campaign became known as a "Leavenworth Nightmare."[114] Eichelberger reflected in one of his letters to Sutherland: "Some day the Leavenworth boys will get on their platform and describe a Japanese position which initially had a left flank resting on the ocean, a right flank resting on unfordable tidal streams, a rear on the ocean and an impassable swamp across most of the front."[115] The proverbial "school solution" did not seem to fit the terrain, yet MacArthur urged the conventional concentration of force:

> Where you have a company on your firing line, you should have a battalion; and where you have a battalion, you should have a regiment. And your attacks, instead of being made by two or three hundred rifles, should be made by two or three thousand . . . so that their fire power can beat the enemy down. . . . Attrition will have to apply. It will be an eye for an eye and a tooth for a tooth—and a casualty on your side for a casualty on his. . . . Your battle casualties to date compared with your total strength are slight so that you have a big margin still to work with.[116]

The man on the spot, however, had a long line of communications that soaked up precious manpower in engineers, supply, and hospital troops. His rifle companies were down to an average strength of about sixty-five men, and on several occasions he had committed his last reserve. The Americans were far from outnumbering the enemy, as MacArthur had asserted; Eichelberger claimed that the Japanese, had they been at all aggressive, could have utilized interior lines and counterattacked with superior numbers.[117] "At one time I was attacking Buna Village with fewer men than were inside,"[118] Eichelberger reported.

His greatest difficulty, however, was not lack of numbers but "the lack of maneuver space in the narrow corridors in which we have had to operate."[119] Each corridor was heavily protected by fire from automatic weapons. He could not afford to continue the "pallid siege," with the capacity of the Japanese to reinforce the Buna garrison and the fever certain "to reduce our men to nothing. . . . Another month and the Japanese could have come out and whipped our men with clubs!"[120] Because it was "a major operation" for the Americans to move from one front to the other, Eichelberger decided to treat the Warren and Urbana fronts as separate operations in which he would try "to pull the strings," but the problems inherent to each required somewhat different solutions.[121]

He would hold onto Warren front, using more aggressive patrols and infiltration rather than frontal infantry assaults. And instead of concentrating artillery and mortar fire before every attack, allowing the Japanese to find relative security in their bunkers and still scramble out to their firing positions before the American infantry appeared, the firing would be at irregular intervals and only on specific targets located by the patrols. Australian forward observers, especially those who hovered over enemy lines in the Wirraway airplanes, increased the artillery's accuracy. The effectiveness of the artillery was further increased once sufficient ammunition was available for the one 105-mm howitzer, which had a high trajectory and could fire shells with delayed-action fuses. As Waldron described it, when one of these shells hit a Japanese installation, "the whole fortification seemed to explode."[122]

While Warren Force maintained fluid pressure on the Japanese dug in along the New Strip and throughout the Duropa coconut plantation, Urbana Force made every effort to capture Buna Village. The savage fighting on this front struck an Australian newspaperman as the fighting of 1917–18 all over again in a tropical setting. "It's the same old picture of trench fighting, or dugouts and pillboxes, of stomach-twisting bayonet charges behind lifting artillery barrages, of nerve-wracking night patrols . . . of deadly sniping and awful moments of suspense waiting for the zero hour."[123] Even the nightly artillery bombardments resembled that war of attrition. "The blasted war's gone old-fashioned on us all of a sudden," commented General Vasey, who commanded the Australian 7th Division.[124] There was, however, one new wrinkle: "Zero hour" came also to mean that last hour of daylight, after American fighter cover had disappeared to airfields on the other side of the mountains, when Japanese Zeros were free to strafe and dive-bomb without fear of molestation.

On 7 December, the anniversary of Pearl Harbor, Sergeant Bottcher's men fought off fierce counterattacks on both sides of his narrow corridor. The following day, Companies E, F, and G of the 126th Infantry, following a mortar and artillery barrage and unsuccessfully using two flame-throwers, failed to capture the village in twelve futile attacks. The 127th Infantry, which had landed recently at Dobodura, arrived on 11 December to relieve Companies E and G of the 126th and continue the probing attacks against the village. Two days later, the Japanese, now reduced to about 100 men, evacuated the position after 400 rounds of mortar fire heralded still another assault. "We shall reorganize and push on," Eichelberger assured Sutherland.[125]

The next objective was the coconut grove, southeast of Buna Village and the only position west of Entrance Creek still in enemy hands. This task fell to White Smith's 2d Battalion of the 128th Infantry, which now numbered but 350 men and was stretched along a 1,750-yard front from the Triangle to a point below Musita Island. Smith could spare fewer than 100 men for the assault. A bombardment of 100 mortar rounds had failed to knock out any of the bunkers, and Smith's men got bogged down on the evening of the fifteenth and penetrated only a few yards into the grove; Eichelberger "had to call them a lot of nasty names to get results." On the morning of 16 December, however, they fought their way into the grove, and some heroic infantry from Company E cleared out a troublesome bunker with hand grenades. Smith ordered the others to press the attack, and by noon, the elaborate trench system and bunkers had been captured at the modest cost of four killed and thirteen wounded. What especially pleased Eichelberger was that this bat-

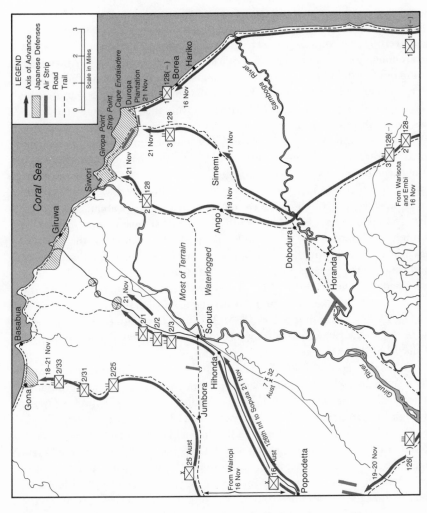

Map 7.4. Closing in on the Japanese Beachhead, 16–21 November 1942

LEGEND

Axis of Advance
Japanese Defenses
Air Strip
Road
Trail

Scale in Miles
0 1 2 3

Coral Sea

Basabua
Gona
Giruwa
Siwori

Giropa Point
Strip Point
Cape Endaiadere
Duropa Plantation 21 Nov
1 128(–)
Borea
Hariko
16 Nov

21 Nov
3 128

2 128
21 Nov

17 Nov
Simemi

19 Nov
Ango

Most of Terrain
Soputa Waterlogged

Dobodura

Horanda

From Warisota and Embi
16 Nov
3 128(–)
2 128

Samboga River

2/33 18–21 Nov
2/31
2/25

21 Nov
2/1
2/2
2/3

Jumbora
Hihonda

7 Aust 32

126th Inf to Soputa 21 Nov
16 Aust
From Wairopi 16 Nov
25 Aust

Popondetta

Girua River

126(–)
19–20 Nov

1 128(–)

talion "has found its soul. It will now be worth something. As a matter of fact
the boys are coming to life all along the line."[126]

On 18 December, the attacks were renewed along both fronts. Urbana
Force tried simultaneous attacks against the island, which served as a sort of
outwork for Buna Mission, and the Triangle, a redoubt protecting the mission
from being approached from the southeast. Company L from the fresh 127th
Infantry worked a couple of platoons onto the island, but these withdrew to
the mainland when they ran into heavy fire. And after a bombardment by
seventeen 81-mm mortars, which Colonel McCreary had placed in battery
close enough to hit every target in the Triangle, three attacks by 107 men from
Companies E and G of the 126th regiment cost 40 casualties and failed to get
even a toehold in the Triangle. The next morning these battle-weary troops
were replaced by Company E, 127th Infantry, and the entire 126th—all 240—
was placed in reserve. The 127th resumed the attack against the Triangle on
20 December, but despite a heavy artillery and mortar barrage, the attacks
failed.[127] Eichelberger then attempted to bypass the Triangle and establish a
bridgehead on the east bank of Entrance Creek. Efforts to get troops across the
tidal river, which was fifty yards wide where the bridgehead was to be formed,
failed repeatedly throughout 21 December, but that night about seventy-five
men from Company K crossed with the aid of a heavy rope carried by
swimmers. Company K, which suffered fifty-four casualties in the attempt,
was joined the following day by Company I, which crossed on an improvised
footbridge. "The Japanese were fighting every inch of the way," Eichelberger
explained to Sutherland, "and I find that no matter how great my enthusiasm
. . . it is hard to make troops in their first fight cross an unfordable stream in
the face of the enemy in the dark."[128] That same day engineers had replaced
the bridge to the island, permitting its capture by two platoons of Company F
of the 127th Infantry the following morning.[129]

With the capture of Musita Island, the Americans now had two axes of
advance against Blue Mission: from the island, where a beachhead might be
established on the shore, and from the bridgehead across Entrance Creek,
through Government Gardens to the sea. On 24 December, five companies of
the 127th Infantry, now commanded by Colonel Grose, attacked the Government Gardens, an area overgrown with kunai grass, which grows to a height
of six feet, behind which was a swamp some 125 yards wide and a coconut
grove known as Government Plantation. The entire area was well fortified,
and the attack soon ran into trouble. "I think that the all time low of my life
occurred yesterday," Eichelberger wrote of Grose's attack.

> It was a well ordered, well prepared attack but when the rolling barrage
> started his troops bogged down almost at once. Instead of pushing through
> with a power drive as I had instructed, he took counsel of his fears and
> thinking his whole force had bogged down, delayed his advance. When he

found the platoon of L Company had gone thru he pushed K Company in. K Company did not acquit itself with credit and only one officer and eight men went through. As a consequence the platoon of L Company which reached the beach, led on partly by the Japanese pressure . . . retired. Prior to that attack E, I and K companies had been badly handled by the Japanese and were not in good shape even for troops that had not been under fire before the last few days.[130]

The attack was renewed on Christmas Day with eight companies. Company F got within 250 yards of the sea and established a defensive perimeter, where it was joined on the twenty-seventh by Company B, and early on 28 December, other units linked up with the troops on the beach to establish a broad corridor from Entrance Creek to the coconut plantation. This placed the Japanese troops in the Triangle in an untenable position, but they succeeded in slipping away without detection.[131]

On 18 December, Warren Force began the final phase of its operations. The slow progress of American troops had already convinced General Blamey that "the American troops cannot be classified as attack troops" and were not even equal to the Australian militia.[132] On 8 December, he decided to send Australian reinforcements to break the impasse at Buna. Brig. Gen. George F. Wootten and two battalions, the 2/9th and the 2/10th of the 18th Australian Infantry Brigade, plus two troops of tanks from the 2/6 Australian Armoured regiment were sent forward from Milne Bay in the first landing craft to reach the combat zone. Because of Wootten's rank, Eichelberger offered to place him in command of Warren Force, with Colonel Martin as second-in-command. The tanks were American M3 Light, or General Stuart, tanks mounting a 37-mm quick-firing gun and two .30 Browning machine guns.[133]

The initial objective was to capture the area extending to the mouth of Simemi Creek on the coast and the entire New Strip, which would be attacked simultaneously from the east and south. Following a brief but intensive air, artillery, and mortar bombardment, seven tanks (with an eighth in reserve) moved forward, with the plucky Wirraways flying overhead to provide noise cover until the tanks were in position to attack. As planned, the tanks and infantry attacked promptly at 0700, the 2/9 Battalion working with the tanks and the 3d Battalion, 128th Infantry, mopping up behind. Within an hour, despite heavy casualties and the loss of two tanks, the Australians penetrated to Cape Endaiadere and then turned west along the coast to join in the fight developing for the New Strip. "Behind the tanks went the fresh and jaunty Aussie veterans, tall, mustached, erect, with their blazing Tommy-guns swinging before them. Concealed Japanese positions—which were even more formidable than our patrols had indicated—burst into flames. . . . Steadily tanks and infantrymen advanced through the spare, high coconut trees, seemingly impervious to the heavy opposition."[134] A third tank was lost attacking a strong point at the spur of the New Strip. At a cost of one-third of the Australians engaged, the Duropa plantation, "a mass of fortifications which the infantry alone could probably never have stormed," was taken.[135]

During the next two days, the Australian infantry and units from the 3d Battalion of the 128th advanced to the mouth of Simemi Creek, while the 1st Battalion of the 128th and the 1st Battalion of the 126th closed in on the New Strip. By noon on the twentieth, they had reached the bridge, and on the twenty-first, the Australian 2/10 Battalion, which had arrived by boat two days earlier and was put into line along the creek bank north of the bridge, began its undetected crossing at a ford several hundred yards below the bridge. Not until 23 December did the Australian battalion manage to clear the area on the far side of the bridge, permitting the two American battalions to cross. A platoon from Company C, 114th Engineer Battalion, repaired the bridge sufficiently to permit four tanks to cross the next day, and on Christmas Day, the three Allied battalions west of the creek began the mopping-up operations. The tanks were less effective here because of the heavy fortifications and the presence of dual-purpose three-inch Japanese artillery, which knocked out the thinly armored General Stuarts, and it was not until Australian infantry captured the two guns the next day that further progress was possible. The infantry got effective support from another arm, however: one of the twenty-five-pounders was hauled from its battery position near Hariko on the coast and sited forward of the bridge between the airstrips, the first time that an accompanying gun could come into direct action. With an observation post officer high in a seventy-foot banyan tree some 1,300 feet ahead of the gun, the first shell fired (armor piercing to lessen the danger to Allied infantry) hit a one-foot-square embrasure and knocked out a 75-mm gun.[136] On 29 December, four new tanks arrived to spearhead an attack against Giropa Point, but supporting infantry lagged so far behind that the Japanese infantry let the tanks pass overhead and then filtered back into the first line to fight off the infantry. In an hour and a half, the tanks had exhausted their ammunition and the attack had to be called off.

On 30 December, a fresh Australian unit, the 2/12 Infantry Battalion, arrived along with additional tanks, and on the first day of the new year this force, followed by the 1st Battalion, 128th Infantry, captured the enemy defenses on Giropa Point. The following day, these forces made contact with Urbana Force–Company B of the 127th, which had fought its way to the sea a week before and was stubbornly defending the east flank of the corridor. On 2 January, Urbana Force finally overran Buna Mission—"a grand day," Eichelberger reported to Sutherland.[137] To his wife, he was somewhat more introspective: "To see those boys with their bellies out of the mud and their eyes in the sun, closing in unafraid on prepared positions, made me choke, and then I spent a moment looking over the American cemetery which my orders of necessity have filled from nothing. Not large, perhaps, but you can understand."[138]

The campaign was not yet over, although the conspicuous return of GHQ to Australia may have indicated to some that it was. Much serious fighting remained for the 127th Infantry and the recently arrived 163d west of the Girua as the Allies closed in on Sanananda. Gona had fallen to the Australians before Christmas, and the final offensive against Sanananda began on 15 January and ended a week later with Herring's Order of the Day announcing the end of the "long and tedious campaign."

For the Americans fighting in what Eichelberger termed "a miniature war," it had been a costly campaign: 2,848 battle casualties as opposed to 5,698 for the Australian ground forces. This may not seem like much compared with losses in the greater battles that followed, but there were 2,701 more casualties in the Papuan campaign than on Guadalcanal, where more troops were involved and the fighting was of longer duration. Of the 14,646 American troops committed in the combat area, nearly two-thirds—8,659—suffered from infectious disease: nearly half the 11,000 troops of the 32d who served in New Guinea came down with malaria. Of perhaps 18,000 men that the Japanese had sent to New Guinea, only about 4,500 were evacuated: 350 were taken prisoner, and the rest died or were killed.[139]

Whatever mistakes were committed at Buna, there seems to be broad agreement that prewar doctrine was not at fault. This is explicit in the Buna Forces after-action report, in which the G-2 concluded that "failures were in execution, not in the fundamentals of standard training and operation," and the G-3 stated that "no new principles of warfare were discovered during the Buna Campaign," although "the nature of the terrain and the disposition of the enemy necessitated some novel applications of well known principles."[140] Col. H. F. Handy, an observer from Headquarters Army Ground Forces, ended his detailed report of American operations at Buna by declaring, "My faith in our teachings and our tactical doctrines remains unshaken. I am convinced that they are essentially sound, and that our chief danger lies in failing to apply them."[141] That this reaction was not limited to American experiences in Papua is indicated by Maj. Gen. O. W. Griswold, commanding general of XIV Corps, who wrote six months later of his own operations on New Georgia in July 1943: "From combat experiences to date, I am convinced that our tactical doctrine, as set down and prescribed at home, is eminently sound for this Theatre."[142]

There had clearly been difficulties in applying the doctrine, both in training and on the battlefield. Even where prewar manuals had correctly anticipated many of the features of jungle fighting, the men of the 32d were not adequately trained for what lay ahead. They had had no realistic training in patrolling, and as a result, the selection and organization of patrols appeared to be "rather haphazard" and resulted in "meager and inaccurate information."[143] According to the after-action report, "with few exceptions our patrols were neither determined, aggressive nor resourceful. They were consistent in their overestimate of enemy strength and prowess. This led to 'hiding out' and 'fairy stories.' . . . Had the men of the command been instilled with the resolute confidence that comes from severe, realistic training, the problems of scouting and patrolling would have been much less difficult.''[144]

Until Eichelberger arrived at the front, almost no patrolling was done at night. He saw to it that orders were issued that each company "for TRAINING PURPOSES, would send out one patrol commanded by an officer each night, the patrol to stay out for two hours.''[145] The troops could have been exposed to such training before they were sent to New Guinea.

The troops lacked camouflage discipline and had not been taught even "the most rudimentary, common sense principles of security and concealment.''[146] It was weeks before they learned to conceal supply tents, ammunition stocks, and infantry bivouacs from air observation and attack or not to congregate in clearings while unidentified aircraft hovered overhead. This too was a consequence of poor training. As was pointed out in the after-action report, "It is not enough that the principles of using cover and concealment be taught—the application must be drilled into the soldier until it becomes automatic.''[147]

Although General Harding had tried to devise a realistic moving target for training purposes in Australia, Japanese diaries captured at Buna reveal that the American riflemen lacked fire discipline. "In the jungle it seems they fire at any sound. . . . From sundown until about 10 P.M. they fire light machine guns and throw hand grenades recklessly. . . . They hit coconuts that are fifteen meters from us. There are some low shots but most of them are high. They do not look out and determine their targets from the jungle. They are in the jungle firing as long as their ammunition lasts. Maybe they get more money for firing so many rounds.''[148] While this obviously reflected the nervousness to be expected in green troops, Army Ground Forces observers were convinced that most of this could be remedied by proper training in combat firing with emphasis on fire discipline rather than on volume of fire.[149] Unlike the Australians, who in their exercises and demonstrations "made highly realistic use of live ammunition and of prepared mines to simulate shell fire and bombing," American infantry had never been fired over, and one of the lessons learned at Buna was that "infantry must have had experience of their own artillery firing over their heads and as close in as safety regulations permit," while "artillery must have the experience of firing close to their own infantry, so as to be impressed with the accuracy necessary.''[150] For lack of this training, the effect of an artillery barrage often was wasted because the enemy had time to recover before the infantry was ready to advance. It was also pointed out that units had not been properly trained in the use of mortars in jungle country.[151]

Part of the problem was that those concerned about training troops for
the jungle could not anticipate all of the problems they would face. ''When
you arrive up in this jungle,'' Eichelberger wrote the commander of the 41st
Infantry Division back in Australia,

> you will find rising up in front of you, to haunt you, the spectre of all those
> things you have failed to teach your men. You read about snipers in
> trees. . . . Our men are now climbing trees and becoming snipers. . . . Our
> men creep forward at night. . . . A battalion of the 126th Infantry, serving
> under the Australians, was held up by what was reported to be one machine
> gun. . . . It turned out to be an area heavily defended [Sanananda] . . .
> about one thousand yards deep and three hundred yards across, full of trees.
> How would you take that out? Our battalion was ordered to advance in a
> column of platoons, first platoon firing Tommy guns from the hip, second
> throwing grenades, and was stopped by twenty-five percent losses. The
> Australians tried it and they had even greater losses. Now they are trying to
> whip the Japanese by the attrition method. . . .
>
> You can figure out any number of combinations and I would so train
> my troops, because just as sure as night follows day you are going to be up
> against it some day.[152]

Eichelberger had never anticipated having to fight along narrow corridors
where maneuver ''is terrifically restricted.'' ''In our training in the future,''
he wrote Sutherland, ''we should train for conditions as I have seen them.''[153]
These conditions explain the reactions of one observer:

> The application of tactical principles used in jungle warfare in New Guinea
> is radically different from those taught in our service schools. There is
> practically no distribution in depth and little chance for maneuvering except
> infiltration by patrols. Very small reserves were held out and these were
> close to the front line.[154]

Buna was probably about what one should expect of a first battle. If not a
signal victory for American doctrine as laid down in the prewar manuals, it
was nonetheless a victory, and from all of the information, suggestions, and
''lessons learned'' that flowed back to Army Ground Forces from participants
and observers, there was no serious question concerning the validity of the
current doctrine. Those who trained at Fort Benning while Marshall headed
the Infantry School or who had taken the pains to read *Infantry in Battle,* which
was published under his direction, might have remembered the opening
sentence in the book that represented his own view of doctrine: ''The art of
war has no traffic with rules, for the infinitely varied circumstances and
conditions of combat never produce exactly the same situation twice.''[155] At
Buna, much that went wrong could be attributed to the ''varied circumstances
and conditions'' of combat fought over extremely difficult, hostile, and
unhealthy terrain by troops who lacked adequate preparation, discipline, and

often necessary equipment: even the special jungle kit developed by July 1942 did not reach the troops in New Guinea until the later stages of the fighting.[156]

Inspired leadership is always a problem in new units exposed to combat for the first time, and this may be particularly true of a National Guard division, in which years of loyal peacetime service, age, and limited opportunities for professional growth—to say nothing of political considerations—make it difficult for sensitive commanders to make desired changes until forced by circumstances. Harding was too kind in this regard: mindful of what his National Guard officers had given the division in time of peace when public opinion and the government alike had neglected the military establishment, he stayed with his regimental and battalion commanders too long. He kept Hale in command of the 128th Infantry after it was apparent that the situation required more aggressive and effective leadership. Although more tough minded, Eichelberger too was concerned about National Guard officers' reactions to changes in command. When he named the division G-3, Lt. Col. Merle H. Howe, to command the 127th Infantry in the latter stages of the battle, he wrote Sutherland: "I will be glad to see him there for he is not a regular officer and I do not want to give the impression that I favor the regular army."[157]

While Eichelberger pondered his next moves at Buna, his old Leavenworth classmate Lt. Gen. Dwight D. Eisenhower was having similar problems in North Africa. "I have no great fault to find with our training doctrine or methods," Eisenhower wrote still another Leavenworth classmate. "Generally they are sound. It is in the application of them that we fail."[158] Eisenhower shared Eichelberger's opinion that "basic individual and small unit training has left much to be desired." He, too, discovered "quite a number" of officers "that have failed to prove their worth in active operations."[159] Perhaps not too much should be made of the fact that the 32d was a former National Guard outfit, for its experience with respect to leadership and inadequate training may not have been unique.

Buna was a first battle rich in lessons learned. Observer and after-action reports have fascinating and instructive things to say about the performance and handling of individual weapons, the special tactics of jungle warfare, proper functioning of the chain of command on the battlefield and in rear areas, map and aerial-photo reading and procurement, aerial observation, the nature of Japanese defensive positions, the function of artillery in a jungle environment and the units of fire that must be maintained, movement and supply of troops by air, effects of the jungle and tropical climate on equipment, and measures necessary to protect the health of the soldier in the world's most heavily infested malaria region.

It was many months before the 32d Division recovered enough to fight again. "You are dead right in returning the 32d Division to the mainland," Eichelberger reassured Sutherland, "for it will need building up from the bottom. So many of the brave men have died or been injured, but when men like Major Smith . . . return to duty there will be something solid to build on and these men have had their baptism of fire.''[160] Under the direction of I Corps, which was still basically a training command, the weaknesses revealed at Buna were stressed in a new training directive, ''Training Memorandum No. 3, I Corps, USAFFE, 14 February 1943.'' Survivors and replacements were to be taught the techniques of scouting, patrolling, cover and conceal-ment, night operations, combat firing, sniping, swimming, and hand-to-hand combat, as well as preparations for amphibious landings.[161]

''We are fortunate to have General Eichelberger and Clovis Byers with us,'' the I Corps deputy chief of staff wrote during the rehabilitation and retraining of the 32d Division after it had returned to Australia; ''they are putting the same punch into the Corps to accomplish the training that brought success at Buna.''[162] The division's survivors had learned much about combat in jungles, Japanese defensive methods, ''and about the importance of sanitation, weapons maintenance, discipline and teamwork.''[163] When the 32d next went into combat, in the Saidor area in January 1944, its performance was ''a great improvement'' over the Buna campaign.[164]

Finally, Buna was a successful first battle because it represented a first essential step down that jungle road to Tokyo. Possession of Buna and Sanananda gave MacArthur the necessary sites for airstrips so vital to any further advance along the New Guinea axis. For these airfields, as well as the lessons learned in capturing them, the trial by combat of the 32d Division probably was worth the human cost—at least in retrospect.

8

Kasserine Pass, 30 January–22 February 1943

MARTIN BLUMENSON

When World War II opened in Europe in September 1939, the U.S. Army lacked the capacity to wage modern warfare. Although many dedicated individual professional soldiers had during the 1920s and 1930s conscientiously studied to be ready for the next war, decline, neglect, and stagnation marked America's military forces. As the Army's strength decreased, its potential to function decayed. Whether this "tragically insufficient" establishment was capable of restoring itself quickly in a time of emergency became questionable.[1] The Army, which had shrunk in size between 1919 and the mid-1930s, was unable to absorb new techniques of waging war. Equipment deteriorated continuously as World War I stocks were used up. Personnel shortages brought Regular Army training to a standstill in 1934. The Army still "had ample time to rebuild itself, but no money." Without adequate funds, raising a credible Army and concluding contracts for modern materiel were impossible. Several years later, the Army received "more money, but time . . . was lacking."[2]

Several circumstances accounted for the Army's weakness. Victory in World War I had bred complacency and inhibited imaginative ideas and experiments in doctrine, organization, and materiel. A revulsion against war in general and disillusionment with World War I in particular, together with faith in the oceans as bulwarks of protection, had prompted retreat into national isolation and desire to avoid foreign entanglements. Because of the great economic depression, congressional appropriations had dwindled, manpower had declined, and the development and procurement of weapons and equipment had languished. Even after World War II began in Europe, the American public had remained lethargic toward military issues. A "large and expensive combat-ready military structure" could not be supported, and "for two decades after 1920 the Army and the National Guard together were quite incapable of waging war."[3] As Japanese aggression in Asia and as German and, to a lesser extent, Italian preparations for war and expansion in Europe created international tensions, President Franklin D. Roosevelt and Congress gave some attention to military problems and allowed increased expenditures. Yet General Malin Craig, the U.S. Army chief of staff, wondered whether a renascence might be too late. In the summer of 1939, he warned that at least two years were required to transform funds into military power. "Time is the only thing," he said, "that may be irrevocably lost."[4]

At the outbreak of the war in Europe, the U.S. Army was still seriously undermanned and underequipped, practiced obsolete procedures with out-moded weapons, and from 1933 ranked seventeenth in size among the armies of the world. The actual strength of the Regular Army in 1939 totaled fewer than 190,000 troops, who were scattered, usually in battalions, among 130 posts, camps, and stations. Although Craig's successor, General George C. Marshall, predicted the impossibility of expanding and modernizing the establishment overnight, that was exactly what the Army would have to do.[5] How well the Army had performed the task of rehabilitating itself would become apparent in February 1943 during a series of engagements in Tunisia that came to be known as the Battle of Kasserine Pass.

Rapid demobilization after World War I had left the Regular Army with 130,000 men on 1 January 1920.[6] The National Defense Act of that year authorized 280,000 active-duty soldiers, but Congress reduced the number to 150,00 regulars in 1922, to 135,000 in the following year, and to 118,750 in 1927. The National Guard, with a ceiling of 450,000 members, rarely totaled half that number, while about 100,000 officers and men, receiving at best indifferent attention, formed the Organized Reserve Corps.[7] Consisting of 110,000 men in 1936, the standing Army lacked airplanes, tanks, combat and scout cars, antiaircraft artillery guns, searchlights, fire-control equipment, .50-caliber machine guns, and other vital materiel. The United States "on its own initiative had rendered itself more impotent than Germany under the military limitations of the Treaty of Versailles."[8] Authorized a 165,000-member Regular Army in 1937, and a 210,000 level in 1939, the U.S. Army was without a single division prepared for combat.

The experience of the American Expeditionary Forces (AEF) in France in 1918, particularly the final phase, largely determined Army doctrine during the interwar years. Offensive operations had featured large and heavy artillery preparations, barrages timed to move forward on successive lines ahead of the infantry assault, use of tanks to assist infantry through the barbed wire and across enemy trenches, and massive advance of infantry to engage in hand-to-hand combat with the enemy. The National Defense Act of 1920 confirmed refighting "the *old* kind of war" in the future.[9] Proficiency in the rifle and bayonet used in open and fluid rather than in static warfare and the efficacy of the "headlong attack" were basic doctrinal beliefs.[10] Infantry advancing to "engage and destroy the enemy by physical encounter" was the key to victory in battle. Despite the emergence of machine guns, automotive transportation, tanks, planes, and other developments, the rifle remained the most important weapon. Doctrine relegated aircraft, tanks, machine guns, and artillery to employment as auxiliary arms for the infantry and at the same time proclaimed adherence to offensive and aggressive tactics.[11]

Tanks had formed a separate component in the AEF, and four battalions, all using French and British models, participated in battle, but the National Defense Act of 1920 placed tanks under infantry control. This reinforced the idea of gearing tanks' forward movement to the pace of the infantry soldier. Tanks became in effect self-propelled artillery pieces to assist the infantry advance. The Army built thirty-five between 1920 and 1935, most of them test models, and the first standard model adopted in 1938 represented no doctrinal change. Tanks continued as infantry-support weapons.[12] The horse cavalry continued to have an eminent place in doctrine, not only for reconnaissance and communications but more especially for pursuit. In search of traditional mobility but prohibited from developing tanks, the cavalry experimented with light armored cars but made little progress because of endemic penury and meager manpower.[13] All the combat arms tried to gain mechanized vehicles— those used in combat—and motorized vehicles—those used for transportation—but the efforts withered. Motorization for artillery was deemed to be "madness." Attempts to organize and establish a mechanized force in 1928 and again in 1930–31 failed.[14]

The Army Air Corps, practicing a variety of functions and missions, turned increasingly to strategic bombardment and neglected close tactical support of ground forces. "Air Corps infatuation with the heavy bomber and strategic air power" resulted in "a reasonably good bomber . . . but no similarly adequate fighters and attack planes to support surface battles."[15] The doctrinal coordination of ground and air action was primitive. The artillery gave thought to centralizing the control of gunfire, both for direct and indirect firing, and also to the use of forward observers. Lack of resources, particularly communications equipment and manpower, inhibited solid development of these new techniques.[16] Except for conversations among thoughtful officers and some small tactical experimentation in the field, doctrine remained relatively unchanged between the wars. Lacking the means to try new procedures, the Army kept alive its stress on offensive and aggressive operations. As late as the summer of 1939, the Army was "still attuned to the combat styles of 1918."[17]

Realistic exercises to train and test individual soldier, unit, and combined-arms proficiency, to practice procedures in the field, to disseminate knowledge, to stimulate air-ground cooperation, to give officers experience in handling large organizations—in short, to achieve war readiness—were out of the question for most of the interwar period because of the stringent economy in defense expenditures, the low peacetime strengths of the Regular Army, the National Guard, and the Organized Reserve Corps, and the dispersal of the few divisions in existence.[18] In overseas posts—Hawaii, Panama, and the Philippines—units could concentrate for periodic war games, but the three regular infantry divisions in the continental United States were so scattered that it was difficult and costly to bring together divisional components for training. Not until the latter part of the 1930s did maneuvers involve at least a corps headquarters and two or more divisions.[19] The imposition of nonmilitary duties also detracted from serious attention to training. The Civilian Conservation Corps (CCC), created in 1933 to give work to unemployed young men, came under Army administration, and this responsibility diverted officers and men from drill.[20] Units of an under-strength National Guard and members of the Organized Reserve Corps gathered once a week in armories and spent two weeks of the summer in the field every year to work with obsolete equipment in very short supply. The training was rudimentary. The primary function of the National Guard was to be ready at the behest of state governors to help maintain public order during natural disasters and civil strife. While duty of this sort built unit cohesion, it was less than valuable as wartime preparation.

The War Department created four field armies in 1932, and, although they "existed only on paper," the department gave them primary responsibility to train the units in their areas.[21] Four years later, in 1936, no corps headquarters troops and few army headquarters troops existed. As late as 1939, the First Army had two officers serving as permanent headquarters staff members. No wonder that the First Army, in a major exercise in 1935, could do no more than test the assembly of 36,000 troops. The Third Army staged an exercise in 1938 involving 24,000 troops, and the outcome, according to its commander, proved the continuing usefulness of the horse cavalry. In 1939, the First Army conducted a series of exercises for about 50,000 troops, actually a collection of individual organizations without supporting units. At 23 percent of authorized war strength, the force had no 155-mm howitzers, was short in antitank weapons, had on hand 6 percent of its infantry mortars, 33 percent of its machine guns, and 17 percent of its trucks. One river crossing used up more than half the engineer pontoon equipment available to the entire U.S. Army. The outcome of the maneuver, according to the commander, proved the continuing utility of the World War I square-type infantry division.[22]

That these exercises proved the validity of concepts already outmoded indicated the nature of the maneuver problems and the methods in the field for solving them. By 1939, the Army had virtually forgotten how to conduct training on a broad scale. Very few officers could handle organizations larger than a battalion. Advanced officers' courses in the branch schools were generally stereotyped and routine, although the temporary association of young officers, presumably the best of their generations, provoked discussion among them and stimulated professional reading.[23] The two-year course at the Command and General Staff College stressed solving military problems by the "school solution," and although the practice stifled initiative and originality, it did produce officers who were "standard" in thought processes, who were at home and at ease in any headquarters and unit. Early in the postwar period, the college taught what was called the latest tactical doctrine of World War I. New tactics and techniques of the separate arms, as well as of the combined arms, found places in the curriculum by 1929, mechanization and motorization were taught beginning in 1935, and the employment of the mechanized division received attention in the following year, all on a highly theoretical basis.[24] The Army War College offered lectures by military and civilian experts, expected students to read and to do research, and had them solve more or less realistic problems derived from history and theory, individually as well as by committee. The final exercise, visiting the principal Civil War battlefields in Virginia and Pennsylvania in order to follow the operations of the armies, corps, and divisions, indicated a persistent concern with the past.

Standard weapons and equipment were of World War I vintage: the Springfield Model 1903 rifle throughout the Army (although the M1 Garand semiautomatic rifle was in limited production by 1939), the 75-mm and 155-mm howitzers for the artillery; the .50-caliber machine gun for antitank and antiaircraft use (although the 37-mm gun was being produced by 1939), and the Stokes three-inch trench mortar for the infantry (although 60-mm and 81-mm mortars were being developed by 1939). About a thousand tanks were left over from World War I, and in 1934, only twelve postwar tanks were in service. All the tanks on hand were lightly armed and armored. Walter Christie built a tank with a new suspension system and with interchangeable wheels and tracks, but the Army purchased only a few experimental models.[25]

The organization of the War Department General Staff fostered compart-mentalization and inhibited the use of combined arms. Chiefs of infantry, cavalry, and artillery presided over more or less autonomous branches and discouraged interaction and mutual experimentation. The basic combat organization was the infantry division, nonmotorized, structured as in World War I with two brigades, each of two regiments of four battalions each. Toward the end of the 1930s, some students and faculty members at the Army War College recommended reducing the size of the division in order to enhance mobility and flexibility. At least one student committee suggested abolishing the brigade level of command. From 1936 on, Lesley J. McNair, first at Fort Sill, later at Fort Leavenworth, worked out a blueprint to streamline the square-type division to triangular shape, not only to attain mobility and flexibility, but also to gain personnel for corps and army headquarters troops and support units. Nothing would come of this before 1939.*

A start toward mechanization occurred in 1928 with the formation of an experimental organization composed of two tank battalions, an armored cavalry troop, an infantry battalion, an artillery battalion, engineer and signal companies, a medical detachment, an ammunition train, and a squadron of observation planes. The provisional force was broken up after three months for lack of funds. While the infantry branch did little to further armored warfare, the cavalry developed "combat cars" (light tanks) and in 1932 activated the 7th Cavalry Brigade (Mechanized).[26] In the summer of 1939, the combat forces of the U.S. Army consisted of three embryonic infantry divisions at half strength and six others consisting of skeleton cadres; two cavalry divisions, each totaling about 1,200 men; the 7th Cavalry Brigade (Mechanized) at half strength; several assorted regiments; and 17,000 airmen using obsolete planes.[27]

The U.S. Army chiefs of staff in the 1920s and 1930s—Generals Peyton March, John J. Pershing, John Hines, Charles P. Summerall, Jr., Douglas MacArthur, and Malin Craig—struggled to modernize the Army. Their efforts were in vain because of the lack of general public interest and the scarcity of funds. On the intermediate and lower levels, military life during the greater part of the interwar period was generally one of stultification. The prerogative of seniority brought older officers to important positions, and many lacked energy and stamina, looked with satisfaction on the achievements of World War I, and were cautious and conservative in their outlook. Yet a group of younger professionals was studying the art of war, reading military journals and books, and seeking to prepare themselves for combat; a surprising number would attain prominence in positions of great responsibility during World War II. It was a wonder that these officers serving "in the dullness of a skeletonized army" emerged in the 1940s as brilliant administrators and leaders.[28]

The state of affairs on the other side was quite different. The Germans after World War I, restricted by the Treaty of Versailles to an army of 100,000 men, turned this force into a professional cadre capable of quick expansion in time of war. Seeking military reasons for their defeat, maintaining their tradition of studying the lessons of the past to apply them to the future, and determined to be ready for modern warfare, the Germans, who had had but a few tanks in the Great War, restored mobility to the battlefield. They developed armored warfare according to the precepts of J. F. C. Fuller and B. *debatable* H. Liddell Hart and created a doctrine of *blitzkrieg* (lightning war) founded on the principles of the so-called Hutier tactics, that is, to exploit quickly penetra-

---

* The 2d Infantry Division was triangularized in 1937 for field tests, but on completion of the exercises it returned to its original organization.

tions of the enemy line by avoiding centers of resistance and striking deeply into the rear in order to paralyze communications. Civil flying and glider enthusiasts formed nuclei for a resuscitated air force, which concentrated on lending close tactical support to the ground forces.

The rise to power of Adolf Hitler in 1933 gave immediacy to a well-integrated program of militarization beyond Versailles Treaty limits. A gigantic industrial renascence, in large part intended to overcome economic depression, provided weapons and equipment for an army increasing in numbers and in skill. By 1936, the German Army and Air Force were strong and well trained; intervention in the Spanish Civil War tested doctrine, weapons, equipment, and organization and gave experience to those who took part. The apparently united will of the German people to restore the former power of Germany complemented astounding progress in the art of war. Although German military leaders felt themselves unready for general war before 1942, the successes of Hitler's diplomacy in the 1930s—in the Rhineland, Austria, and Czechoslovakia—stilled their reservations. German victories in Poland, Denmark, Norway, and Western Europe in 1939 and 1940 were astonishing. The German invasion of the Soviet Union in 1941, although promising quick success, bogged down because of the enormous distances, contradictory objectives, and, eventually, the winter weather.

The Italians shared with Benito Mussolini dreams of restoring the glory of ancient Rome. Although the Italian ground forces succeeded in Ethiopia against a primitive foe, Italian participation in the Spanish Civil War and the later 1941 thrust from Albania into Greece showed deficiencies in organization, weapons, equipment, and leadership, perhaps partially the result of a lack of the natural resources, particularly oil, required for modern war. A few elite units were first rate, but many Italian formations reflected the general corruption of the state system. The Italian Army in North Africa, specifically in Libya, had light, under-powered tanks and trucks, World War I artillery pieces, old-fashioned antitank and antiaircraft guns, and obsolete rifles and machine guns.[29]

The Germans and Italians fought a coalition war under the disadvantageous lack of a coalition machinery to translate policy on the highest level into strategy. The two allies cooperated through loosely organized, complicated, and often poorly defined and ineffective diplomatic and special liaison arrangements. Although the two dictators, Hitler and Mussolini, occasionally met, they fought parallel wars. German aid, in the form of troops, weapons, equipment, supplies, and leadership, was necessary to sustain the Italian effort, and this bred German feelings of superiority, disdain, even contempt for Italy as well as an Italian sense of inferiority and jealousy. The Axis war was poorly directed, and the inability to synchronize activities was made evident in the Battle of Kasserine Pass.

On 1 September 1939, on the same day that Germany invaded Poland, Gen. George C. Marshall became U.S. Army Chief of Staff.[30] He immediately implemented policies to retire older officers, reassign those who were incompetent, and bring younger and more energetic men to responsible positions.[31] A week after the German invasion, President Roosevelt raised the authorized strength of the Regular Army to 227,000 men and the National Guard to 235,000 and permitted members of the Organized Reserve Corps to volunteer for active duty. The War Department that fall, in accordance with McNair's plans, reduced the size of the infantry division and reorganized it from a square to a triangular type, giving it three infantry regiments consisting of three battalions each. The gain in manpower as a result of triangularization, as well as the influx of men into the Regular Army and National Guard, enabled the War Department to hold genuine corps and army maneuvers in the spring of 1940, the first full-fledged corps maneuvers since 1918.

The task of attaining war preparedness began seriously in 1940 as larger and more realistic exercises and maneuvers developed and refined new doctrine, techniques, and equipment. In January 1940, the Fourth Army Headquarters laid out an unprecedented amphibious exercise involving Army, Navy, and Air Corps elements. Fourteen thousand participating troops of the 3d Division moved by water from Tacoma, Washington, landed on the shore of Monterey Bay, California, and "captured" San Francisco.[32] Maneuvers in Georgia and Louisiana in April and May 1940 tested new types of corps headquarters directing triangular infantry divisions. At the same time, the 7th Mechanized Cavalry Brigade and the infantry's Provisional Motorized Tank Brigade came together to form an improvised armored division. Recommendations from these exercises included combining the regimental artillery battalions of an infantry division under the central control of a division artillery, expanding the mechanized brigade into an armored division, and creating a second armored division.[33]

Spurring these developments was the phenomenal success of the German *blitzkrieg* in France in May and June, which produced consternation, then defeatism and apathy, in the War Department. How could the German tanks be stopped? Marshall dispelled the gloom with two positive decisions. He established the Armored Force, whose mission was to match the power of German mobile forces. He directed his planners to provide antitank defense of an offensive nature to halt the enemy's massed armor.[34]

The Armored Force, under Brig. Gen. Adna R. Chaffee, came into being in July 1940. The I Armored Corps, with two divisions under its command—the 1st at Fort Knox, Kentucky, the 2d at Fort Benning, Georgia—supervised training. Both armored divisions were formed with a reconnaissance battalion and an armored brigade, the latter consisting of two regiments of light tanks armed with the 37-mm gun, a regiment of medium tanks armed with the short-barreled 75-mm gun, an infantry regiment of two battalions, a field-artillery regiment, plus an additional field-artillery battalion, an engineer battalion, and signal, ordnance, quartermaster, and medical units.[35]

Activated on 15 July 1940 with Regular Army personnel later augmented by draftees, the 1st Armored Division, which would see action in the Battle of Kasserine Pass, pioneered the development of tank gunnery and used forward-observer fire-direction techniques developed after World War I. By 1941, although shortages of all sorts existed—for example, only sixty-six medium tanks produced in the United States were on hand—the 1st Armored Division was able to participate in the Louisiana and Carolinas maneuvers. The units engaged in simulated battle during daylight and night hours, practiced maintenance, performed logistics and administration, and lived in field conditions.[36]

Both armored divisions participated in the Louisiana maneuvers in September 1941. Involving 400,000 troops, pitting for the first time one field army against another, featuring armored and paratroop forces, assembling the unheard-of number of more than 1,000 aircraft, the exercises demonstrated "an unusual amount of experimentation."[37] The foremost purposes were to fight large-unit battles, to test motorized and mechanized techniques, to foster air-ground cooperation, and to practice medical evacuation, demolitions, reconnaissance, and intelligence.[38] In the Carolinas in October and November, the training exercises were a major test of the 1st and 2d Armored Divisions. A total of 865 tanks and armored scout cars opposed 4,320 guns effective against tanks. The results were inconclusive, and no firm doctrine could be enunciated and written, mainly because of shortages in authorized strength and weapons in all the participating units. Missing were 10 percent of the mortars, 40 percent of the 37-mm guns, 18 percent of the 155-mm howitzers, and 87 percent of the .50-caliber machine guns.[39]

Clearly, features of the armored division required modification. When Chaffee took ill, Lt. Gen. Jacob L. Devers replaced him as chief of the Armored Force on 1 August 1941. An artilleryman, Devers improved firepower. Maj. Gen. George S. Patton, Jr., commanding the I Armored Corps, stressed mobility. Together they gave the armored divisions better balance.[40] On 1 March 1942, as Maj. Gen. Orlando Ward, who had commanded the 1st Armored Brigade in the Louisiana and Carolinas maneuvers, took command of the 1st Armored Division, a drastic reorganization of the Armored Division was under way. In order to gain flexibility, the brigade headquarters was eliminated and replaced by two combat commands. Each combat command had its own intelligence and operations capabilities but depended on the division for logistics and administration. Three separate self-propelled field-artillery battalions operated under the division artillery. The division trains controlled the service elements. A higher proportion of infantry to tanks was achieved by increasing the number of battalions in the infantry regiment to three and by reducing the number of tank regiments from three to two regiments of three battalions each. A total of 14,620 troops manned the division, which was equipped with .30-caliber carbines, self-propelled and towed antitank guns, self-propelled assault guns, .30- and .50-caliber machine guns, 105-mm self-propelled howitzers, 60-mm and 81-mm mortars, light and medium tanks, armored and scout cars, and half-tracks. Unfortunately, much equipment was lacking.[41]

Before the 1st Armored Division could train in its new form, it received a massive infusion of recently inducted replacement troops, bringing the division to authorized strength, and went to Fort Dix in April 1942 for shipment overseas. Overage officers were relieved and replaced, and the division sailed for Northern Ireland in May and trained there for five months. The stress was on small-unit training and gunnery. The work improved tank-artillery cooperation, but tank-infantry and air-ground cooperation remained weak.[42]

In November 1942, the 1st Armored Division embarked in ships again, this time for a voyage to North Africa and the eventual engagement of Kasserine Pass. It would go into battle with two battalions of light tanks armed with the 37-mm gun, three battalions of medium tanks armed with the low-velocity 75-mm gun, and one battalion of early-model Sherman medium tanks. The "relative weakness in armor and fire power when compared with the German tanks was not suspected until they met in Tunisia."[43]

To stop German massed armor, the War Department created the tank destroyer, so named to connote offensive and aggressive characteristics as opposed to the defensive and passive meaning of "antitank." A "marriage of the artillery gun to truck and tractor," the tank destroyer was to embody an aggressive spirit and to destroy enemy tanks by maneuver and fire.[44] To create an ideal tank destroyer with mobility and punch, quickly and easily fired and giving the crew protection against small-arms fire, was a difficult task. From a 37-mm gun mounted on a quarter-ton truck or jeep, the tank destroyer evolved to a 57-mm then 75-mm, 76-mm, and finally 90-mm gun mounted on a carriage resembling a tank.

During maneuvers in August 1940, the employment of antitank guns, manned by antitank companies in the infantry regiments, was passive; they were deployed in cordon defense. A year later, bringing the companies together under central control proved a more satisfactory practice for offensive, aggressive movements in large-scale exercises. Yet observers noted tendencies to commit the guns prematurely and to fragment their strength. In November 1941, the War Department projected activating fifty-three tank-destroyer battalions, and a month later, eight infantry antitank battalions were redesignated tank-destroyer battalions. Tank destroyers became a provisional branch with a Tactical and Firing Center to supervise organization and training. Not until August 1942 when Camp Hood, Texas, opened, did a thoroughly rounded program begin. A tank-destroyer field manual published in June 1942 developed the motto "Seek, Strike, Destroy." The first officers candidate class graduated in October. By then, tank-destroyer battalions were attached and later assigned to divisions. The War Department planned to activate a total of 222 battalions.

The antitank rocket launcher called the bazooka, a grenade with a new tail assembly, came into existence in mid-1942. It was recommended for issue to tank-destroyer battalions. Training in its use started in December 1942. That was too late for the units already overseas, and bazookas were issued to troops already in Tunisia and to soldiers aboard ships. However, no one really knew how to operate and employ them.[45]

By far the most important entity dealing with mobilization, organization, and training came into being in July 1940. This was General Headquarters, U.S. Army, known as GHQ, modeled on Pershing's AEF headquarters. U.S. Army Chief of Staff Marshall named Brigadier General McNair, then commandant of the Command and General Staff College, to be his chief of staff at GHQ and gave him a free hand to fashion the combat units into a proficient fighting force. GHQ was inserted structurally between the War Department General Staff and the four field armies, which had formerly conducted training. Although army commanders were initially reluctant to relinquish their training function, McNair quickly established a standard system progressive in nature, that is, a regular training cycle from the recruit through the unit to combined-arms teams.

After the German spring campaigns in Denmark and Western Europe in 1940, the president raised the Regular Army to 280,000 men, then to 375,000. In September, authorized to do so by the Congress, he enlarged the Regular Army to 500,000 troops and called the 270,000 men of the National Guard into active federal service for a year. The Selective Service Act in the same month permitted the induction of 630,000 draftees into uniform. This gave the Army a strength of 1.4 million troops.[46] The absence of sufficient housing, mess, and training facilities in the camps, posts, and stations made it impossible to transfer the eighteen National Guard divisions to federal status at once, and they came on active duty over the space of a year. By mid-1941, almost 1.5 million men had been mobilized, assigned to units, and were engaged in all forms of training.[47] The National Guard divisions were restructured into triangular shape and brought to full authorized strength. Commanders and staff officers who owed their appointments to state politics and who were less than qualified on grounds of military education or physical conditioning were removed and replaced by Regular Army officers. Complicating the massive mobilization and training experience were the activation of new divisions and other units, revisions in tables of organization and equipment, the adoption of newly developed weapons—examples were the tank destroyers, the replacement beginning in 1940 of World War I-type 3-

inch mortars by the 60-mm and 81-mm mortars, the issue of the M1 semiautomatic Garand rifle after 1941—and the acceptance of new combat doctrine. That the entire process did not collapse into chaos bordered on the miraculous.[48]

McNair set into motion, inspected, and critiqued a variety of exercises to test proficiency and identify failures in the training programs. For example, the critique of a First Army maneuver in August 1940 noted such important errors as improper use of combat teams and motor transportation, inability to reconnoiter and maintain contact between adjacent units, and deficiencies in signal communication, antitank guns, ammunition supply, and medical evacuation. All National Guard units, in particular, reflected inadequate training. Many officers and men were physically soft and undisciplined; many headquarters, particularly signal, military police, ordnance, engineer, and medical, were nonexistent; and weapons and equipment were in extremely short supply. GHQ maneuvers in Tennessee in early 1941 showed the troops still road bound, ignorant of field manuals, unable to reconnoiter properly, and generally deficient in basic- and small-unit training; leadership was weak and unable to coordinate with adjacent and supporting units and with units of other branches.[49]

The apex of McNair's training efforts came at the Louisiana and Carolinas maneuvers in 1941. Testing army aviation, GHQ found it poorly coordinated with ground action. Ground troops underestimated air potential, were weak in liaison and communications, had inadequate combat intelligence, and were guilty of dispersed and fragmented efforts. There was a general lack of discipline, an unwillingness to move off the roads, and a reluctance to break column formations.[50] Yet the results of the Louisiana maneuvers of 1941 confirmed "the soundness of existing policies."[51] The major lesson of the Carolinas maneuvers was "the crying need for infantry support, both within the [armored] division and between infantry and armored divisions."[52] Both maneuvers accelerated the creation of independent tank battalions to work with infantry. A light plane, the Cub, for artillery spotting began to be built in 1942. What no one seemed to notice was how the air service had thwarted the War Department's efforts to create air support of ground forces. No procedures or command relationships existed for large-scale air-ground operations.[53]

At the end of November 1941, just a few days before the Japanese bombed Pearl Harbor and brought the United States into the war, McNair judged whether the troops were ready for combat. They "could fight effectively," he said, but "losses would be unduly heavy." Against the Germans, he added prophetically, the results "might not be all that could be desired."[54] There had simply not been enough time for training. At the time of Pearl Harbor, 1,638,000 men were in Army uniform, but only a single division and a single antiaircraft artillery regiment were on full war footing.[55]

"Though a large Army was not ready for combat . . . the United States entered the war . . . with a training program carefully thought out and in full operation."[56] GHQ training principles included progression through a four-phase sequence, tests in each phase, unit training with frequent review, free maneuvers, immediate critiques, the goal of general combat proficiency, integration of the tactical units, a stress on the responsibilities of commanding officers at all levels, and an emphasis on battle realism.[57] In line with the last principle, GHQ established the Desert Training Center in California and Arizona early in 1942. There, in a primitive environment, troops lived, moved, and fought under simulated battle conditions.[58]

Beginning in December 1940, the War Department abolished the traditional two-year course at Leavenworth and instead offered short, special, and refresher instruction to selected commanders and staff officers who were scheduled to assume positions of major responsibility in new units. The Army discontinued the War College course and assigned faculty and staff members to the War Plans Division of the War Department General Staff and elsewhere.[59] GHQ itself went out of existence in March 1942. The War Department abolished the branch chiefs and formed the Army Ground Forces under McNair to continue training combat forces. Earlier maneuvers had focused on testing equipment and training, but large-scale exercises in 1942 tested doctrine, particularly infantry-armor coordination, which improved, and air-ground cooperation, which remained disappointing.[60] Unfortunately, the two major units that would fight at Kasserine Pass, the 1st Armored Division and the 34th Infantry Division, did not take part in the 1942 exercises, for they were in Northern Ireland. As late as July 1942, the 1st Armored Division was still awaiting delivery of much equipment, and the 34th Division, which had just started training for amphibious landing, had few antiaircraft guns and no tanks.[61] The tank destroyers with these divisions had light 37-mm guns and light armored cars. Antiaircraft artillery units were shipped overseas after attaining only "minimum proficiency in their weapons and before receiving combat training with other ground arms or with aviation." Because of the wide dispersion of training centers and the insufficiency of planes to tow targets for firing practice, antiaircraft personnel were quite simply "improperly trained."[62]

The 34th Infantry Division, the first American division to go to Europe, originated in the National Guard. It was chosen for overseas service presumably because it was deemed to be well trained. Among its major organic components was the 168th Infantry regiment, which had had a typical prewar military upbringing and would be involved in the Battle of Kasserine Pass.[63] The 168th had participated as an Iowa volunteer unit in the Civil War, specifically in Grant's campaign against Vicksburg and in the later movement of the Union Army through the Carolinas. Mobilized again in 1917, the regiment fought in France as part of the 42d Rainbow Division. Members in the 1920s and 1930s were proud of the unit's combat history and had a special feeling of cohesion. Of northern European stock, the men were from the towns of Atlantic, Council Bluffs, Glenwood, Red Oak, Villisca, Shenandoah, and Carlinda, agricultural communities in the gently rolling hill country of southwestern Iowa. In these towns, citizens had purchased shares to construct armories for the companies of the regiment, and the state government paid rent to the owners. An armory contained offices, a drill hall resembling a basketball court, supply rooms, and facilities for reunions, dances, banquets, and patriotic celebrations.

Guardsmen were, for the most part, unmarried men from eighteen to thirty-five years of age. They received one dollar for attending a training session, and the pay was important in attracting members during the Depression. They met every Monday evening and practiced close-order drill and the manual of arms. They occasionally performed small-unit maneuvers on a football field or in a city square. They received summer training at Camp Dodge, Iowa. The annual inspection in each armory was usually linked to a military ball, the highlight of the social season. Maj. Walter Smith inspected the southwestern Iowa units in 1939 and called them a "very very fine organization." Other regiments in northern and northwestern Iowa, in Minnesota, and in North Dakota came together with the 168th to form the 34th Division, commanded in 1939 by Maj. Gen. E. A. Walsh of Minneapolis. In the summer of 1940, the division trained at Camp Ripley, Wisconsin. Upon the troops' return to their armories, revised National Guard programs and schedules doubled their training time. The average guardsman in the 168th had eighteen months of service. Two-thirds were high school graduates; about one-third had some education beyond high school. Captains were between thirty-four and forty-five years of age, and many of them, and more senior officers, had served in World War I. Quite a few men joined the regiment in 1941 to avoid the draft.

The 34th Division was called into active federal service in February 1941. On 2 March, the men of the 168th Infantry had farewell dinners in the armories in their home towns, paraded, then marched to the train stations. They traveled to Camp Claiborne, Louisiana, which was still under construction. Living in tents, the men engaged in close-order drill and small-unit tactics, including night attacks. Some went to schools for special training. Equipment and weapons were in such short supply that stovepipes simulated mortars, trucks carried signs to denote their use as tanks, and broomsticks served as rifles. The heaviest infantry weapon was the 37-mm gun. In April, draftees from all over the country arrived to bring the 34th Division regiments up to strength. The division participated in two maneuvers in Louisiana in June and August.[64] A Regular Army officer, Maj. Gen. Russell P. Hartle, took command in August. In January 1942, when Hartle assumed command of the V Corps, Maj. Gen. Charles W. Ryder, a West Point graduate, succeeded him as division commander, and the division sailed for Northern Ireland. The following month, the division was triangularized. The men continued training, practicing amphibious landings in Scotland later that year.

In November, the division participated in the North African invasion, coming ashore near Algiers. Of the soldiers then constituting the 168th Infantry, about 30 percent were from the local armories in southwestern Iowa. Two hundred of these men were reported missing in action on 17 February 1943, a day of severe fighting during the Battle of Kasserine Pass.

In summary, the entire mobilization process, including the organization and training of the U.S. Army, was hasty, largely improvised, and saved from disaster by the stability and intelligence of leaders like Marshall and McNair. This crash program gave the field forces a semblance of preparedness. Yet maneuvers revealed many deficiences in basic soldiering skills and, among a large proportion of officers, basic command skills. Shortages of weapons and equipment and the need to improvise had hampered instruction. There was insufficient time to permit individuals and units to acquire and become proficient in the doctrine, weapons and equipment, and skills required for the modern warfare of the 1940s. Organizations and men were still largely in tune with the time and space factors that had prevailed in the previous war. They had yet to adjust to the accelerated tempo and increased distances of the battlefield—in particular, the necessary speed of reaction so well understood by their adversaries. American leadership and manpower had the potential to excel, but it would take the reality and the adversity of Kasserine Pass to develop an inherent capacity for excellence.

Deployment of American forces began shortly after Pearl Harbor, when Roosevelt and British Prime Minister Winston S. Churchill confirmed a strategy unofficially reached during Anglo-American staff conversations in 1941. The Allied leaders endorsed a Europe-first endeavor and established machinery to direct the coalition military effort.[65] The president and prime minister worked through the British Chiefs of Staff and the American Joint Chiefs of Staff sitting together to form the Combined Chiefs of Staff (CCS). The CCS issued directives to the theater commanders who were supreme Allied commanders or Allied comanders in chief—the terms were inter-changeable—and who would exercise a unified command over the forces of both nations.

American strategists generally favored a massive blow against the German-occupied continent of Europe and a direct thrust into Germany. To these ends, the 34th Infantry Division, the 1st Armored Division, and later the 1st Infantry Division went to Northern Ireland, where they trained under the V Corps headquarters. The European Theater of Operations, U.S. Army, under General Eisenhower provided overall direction, and the II Corps headquarters under Lt. Gen. Mark W. Clark, who had been McNair's closest associate, served as the theater training command. The British preferred an invasion of French Northwest Africa, where German and Italian troops were absent as a result of the armistice terms of 1940. The French had pledged to resist invasion, but if, as the Allies hoped, they quickly came over to the Allied side, they would offer only brief resistance to the untried Americans. The landings in the French territories would also threaten the Axis forces based in Libya and fighting the British in Egypt.

North Africa became an active theater of operations in 1940 when Italian forces attacked the British. The ensuing campaigns were of a seesaw nature, with first one opponent, then the other achieving temporary success. In 1941, to help Mussolini, Hitler sent General Erwin Rommel's *Afrika Korps* of several German divisions to North Africa. Subsequently, Rommel took command of *Panzer Grupp Afrika,* which consisted of the *Afrika Korps* augmented by several mobile Italian divisions; in 1942, he took charge of *Panzerarmee Afrika,* all the German and Italian combat units. Mussolini and his *Comando Supremo* directed the operations in North Africa through an Italian theater commander. To facilitate Rommel's access to the German high command and to smooth Italo-German coordination, Hitler dispatched Field Marshall Albert Kesselring to Rome. At first commander of the German air forces in Italy, Kesselring was the ranking German officer in the Mediterranean area and, as such, virtually a theater commander. With Kesselring's support, Rommel attacked in May 1942. By June, he was at El Alamein, Egypt, sixty miles short of the Nile. This was the situation in mid-1942 when Roosevelt accepted Churchill's suggestion to invade French Northwest Africa. Eisenhower, named Supreme Allied Commander, and Clark, his deputy, formed a new Allied Force Headquarters (AFHQ) in London and began to plan landings, code-named TORCH, on the shores of Morocco and Algeria.

In August 1942, Rommel attacked from El Alamein only to be stopped by General Sir Harold Alexander, commander of the British Middle East Forces with headquarters in Cairo, and General Sir Bernard E. Montgomery, commanding the British Eighth Army in Egypt. After receiving 300 brand-new American Sherman tanks, the British took the offensive on 23 October and forced Rommel to withdraw. As the British pursued, Rommel conducted a retrograde movement across Libya. During that retreat, TORCH was launched. The invasion took place on 8 November 1942. A task force under Ryder and consisting of the 34th Division, part of the 1st Armored Division, and British elements made the easternmost landing near Algiers, where fighting ended on the first day. Another task force under Maj. Gen. Lloyd R. Fredendall's II Corps and containing the 1st Infantry Division and British units invaded in the center near Oran, where combat terminated on the second day. A wholly American task under Patton, sailing directly from the

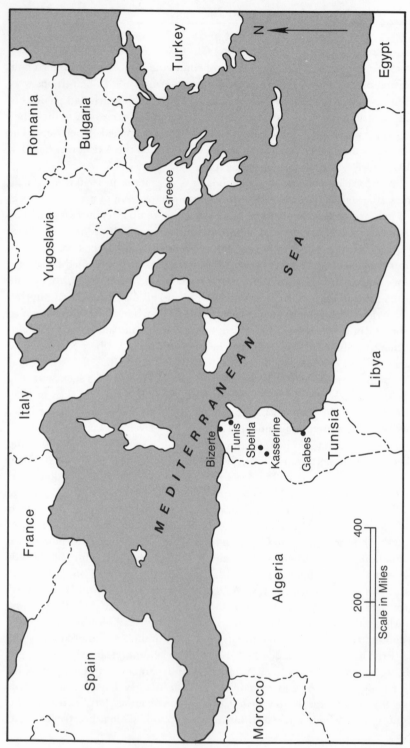

Map 8.1. North Africa

United States, landed in the west near Casablanca and battled French forces vigorously for three days.

These events introduced American troops to combat on the Atlantic side of World War II. But this hardly constituted the first battle, for the French were not the enemy. Most French commanders and units offered reluctant opposition. French organization, doctrine, and war materiel had not been updated since 1940. Curiously, resistance met by the Americans had been more intense and of longer duration in Morocco. The future participants in the Battle of Kasserine Pass were those who had engaged in almost no active operations. They saw their performance against the French as more than adequate for success against the Germans and Italians. Confident of their underpowered light tanks with 37-mm guns, trusting the power of the 57-mm and 75-mm guns on their Shermans, they believed themselves to be blooded and tried in action.[66]

The French authorities in North Africa, after agreeing to a truce, joined the British and Americans who, by then, in accordance with prior plans, had turned eastward from Algeria, entered Tunisia, and were driving toward Bizerte and Tunis, their ultimate objectives. On the way they quickly ran into opposition. Axis troops had entered Tunisia from Italy shortly after TORCH, and eventually a field-army-size force, under General Juergen von Arnim, built up an extended bridgehead covering Bizerte and Tunis in the north-eastern corner. Von Arnim sought to prevent the Allies from overrunning Tunisia and also to permit Rommel's army to finish withdrawing from Libya into southern Tunisia. The Axis would then hold the eastern seaboard of the country. To guarantee their security on the eastern coastal plain, von Arnim and Rommel needed to control the passes in the Eastern Dorsale, a mountain range running generally north and south. Through that chain were four major openings—Pichon and Fondouk in the north and Faid and Rebaou in the south. Von Arnim seized Pichon in mid-December 1942. Toward the end of January 1943, as Rommel settled into the Mareth Line in southern Tunisia, the Axis desire for the other passes initially spurred what developed into the Battle of Kasserine Pass.

The Allies deployed in Tunisia with the bulk of their strength in the north.[67] Because of bad weather and supply deficiencies, Eisenhower on 24 December called off the offensive toward Bizerte and Tunis. Early in January 1943, to counter Rommel's growing presence, he began moving Fredendall's II Corps headquarters and American units to southern Tunisia in order to buttress poorly equipped French troops holding the Fondouk, Faid, and Rebaou Passes and the town of Gafsa, an important road center.

Allied command lines were less than firm. General Sir Kenneth A. N. Anderson, at the head of the British First Army—with the British V Corps, several British divisions, and some American and French units in the north—

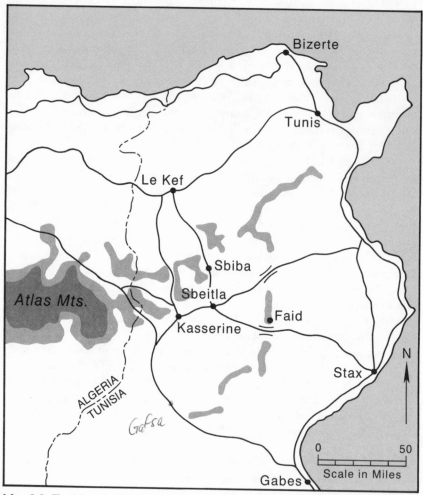

Map 8.2. Tunisia

was the overall tactical commander in Tunisia, but Americans found him difficult to work with. Fredendall exacerbated the problem because he saw his role as autonomous. The French, who had General Louis-Marie Koeltz's XIX Corps in the center, a division in the north, another in the south, and miscellaneous detachments scattered virtually everywhere, refused to serve under direct British command. As a consequence, General Alphonse Juin, commander of the French land and air forces in French Northwest Africa, exercised loose direction and provided liaison and guidance to all French formations.

Fredendall had small packets of troops dispersed over a very large area— one battalion of the 1st Infantry Division at Gafsa, another blocking the Fondouk road to Sbeitla, Combat Command A (CCA) of the 1st Armored Division at Sbeitla, Combat Command B (CCB) near Tebessa. He could bolster the French garrisons holding the Faid and Rebaou Passes, keep his forces concentrated in a central location and ready to counterattack, or strike toward the east coast to sever the contact between von Arnim's and Rommel's armies. He sought to do the latter by raiding a small Italian detachment at Sened on 24 January. The action was highly successful as a morale builder but had no real result except to squander Fredendall's meager resources.

The Axis command correctly read the situation and continued planning to take control of the Eastern Dorsale. Rommel established his headquarters in southern Tunisia on 26 January, and two days later *Comando Supremo* in Rome approved a cautious push to take the Fondouk and Faid Passes and to advance on Gafsa. With Rommel's *10th* and *21st Panzer Divisions* temporarily under von Arnim's control, von Arnim attacked on 30 January to open the Battle of Kasserine Pass. Just before dawn, thirty tanks struck 1,000 French troops in the Faid Pass while another contingent of German tanks, infantry, and artillery drove through the Rebaou defile ten miles to the south, overran several hundred French defenders, and came up behind the French holding Faid. Encircled and outnumbered, the French fought gallantly for more than twenty-four hours until they were overwhelmed.

Five hours after the German attack started, Anderson instructed Fredendall rather vaguely to restore the situation at Faid. Because Ward, the 1st Armored Division commander, was at Gafsa supervising the Sened raid and other useless actions, Fredendall communicated directly with the CCA commander at Sbeitla, Brig. Gen. Raymond McQuillin, who was old in appearance, mild in manner, and cautious in outlook. McQuillin sent out two small reconnaissance units toward the Faid and Rebaou Passes to determine what was happening. At noontime, even though the French at Faid were still resisting, the reconnaissance elements erroneously reported the Germans in control at both passes. McQuillin decided to counterattack. As he moved his assault forces forward, German planes bombed and attacked his units and disrupted the advance. American aircraft dispatched to intercept the Germans dropped bombs on the CCA command post by mistake, and American antiaircraft gunners shot down an American plane. McQuillin then waited for nightfall. During the hours of darkness, he pushed his forces about halfway to Faid and Rebaou.

On the morning of 31 January, more than twenty-four hours after the German attack, McQuillin committed a small-tank infantry force under Col. Alexander N. Stark, Jr., to strike to Faid and another such force under Col. William B. Kern to go for Rebaou. Late getting under way, the effort was badly coordinated and too weak to attain the objectives. Heavy German defensive fires, together with effective bombing and strafing from the air, knocked out several tanks and induced terror, indecision, and paralysis among the American units. McQuillin's effort petered out. As Fredendall, the II Corps commander, was thinking on 1 February of moving CCB from Tebessa to Sbeitla, Anderson, the First British Army commander, instructed him to dispatch CCB toward Fondouk, where von Arnim had struck Koeltz's French elements, seized the pass, and threatened a serious penetration. Fredendall complied. McQuillin tried again that day to reach Faid but failed because, he said, of the disgraceful performance of Stark's infantry. Von Arnim, now in control of the four major passes, called off further endeavor. With the *10th Panzer Division* at Fondouk and the *21st* at Faid and Rebaou, von Arnim, instead of returning both divisions to Rommel, hoped to keep them for use in the north. The front in Tunisia now became quiet, and the first or preliminary phase of what would develop into the Battle of Kasserine Pass ended.

On the Allied side, Eisenhower questioned Fredendall's competence, Anderson doubted the battleworthiness of American troops, Fredendall wondered whether Ward was proficient, McQuillin castigated Stark, and so it went down the line. American ineptitude and failure to rescue the French defenders at Faid had shocked the French. Additional American units—parts of Maj. Gen. Terry Allen's 1st Infantry Division and of Ryder's 34th Division—moved into southern Tunisia but they were split into small parcels and physically separated. During the second week of February, Fredendall's combat units were deployed as follows: At the front, in blocking positions on two hills covering the roads west from Faid and Rebaou to Sidi bou Zid and Sbeitla were two forces. On the hill called Djebel Lessouda north of the Faid road was Lt. Col. John K. Waters of the 1st Armored Division. He commanded about 900 troops—a company of fifteen tanks, some reconnaissance elements, a tank-destroyer platoon, and a battery of self-propelled 105-mm howitzers—as well as the 2d Battalion (less a rifle company) of the 168th Infantry. In support of Waters, Lt. Col. Louis Hightower, a few miles away at the village of Sidi bou Zid, commanded fifty-one tanks, twelve tank destroyers, and two artillery battalions of the 1st Armored Division.

On Djebel Ksaira, overlooking the road from Rebaou, was Col. Thomas D. Drake, who had taken command of the 168th Infantry in January. He had about 1,000 men of the 3d Battalion (plus a rifle company of the 2d) of the 168th, plus 650 miscellaneous troops—a medical detachment, the regimental band, 200 engineers, an attached cannon company, several antiaircraft guns, and a few artillery pieces. Supporting Drake was the Reconnaissance Battalion of the 1st Armored Division near Sidi bou Zid. Drake received 200 replacement troops on 12 February, but some lacked weapons, quite a few had never fired a rifle, and none had entrenching tools or bayonets. On the following day, Drake accepted several truckloads of brand-new bazookas; no one on the hill had ever fired this antitank weapon, and Drake planned to figure out how to operate them and to start a training program on 14 February. Behind and west of Waters and Drake were elements of McQuillin's CCA at Sbeitla and Sidi bou Zid. Ward had his division reserve at Sbeitla, a battalion of infantry under Kern, a battalion of tanks, and a company of tank destroyers. CCB was near Fondouk, 100 miles from Sbeitla; Col. Robert I. Stack's Combat Command C (CCC), consisting primarily of the 6th Armored Infantry, was twenty miles away in the same direction.

West of Sbeitla, Stark's 26th Infantry of the 1st Infantry Division and a 1st Armored Division tank battalion under Col. Ben Crosby were at Feriana guarding the road from Gafsa and protecting the airfields at Thelepte, but who controlled them was unclear. Arriving at Gafsa to augment French units presumably under Fredendall's command were a U.S. Ranger battalion, some artillery and tank-destroyer units, plus about a battalion of the 1st Derbyshire Yeomanry, a British armored-car regiment dispatched by Anderson to bolster the inexperienced Americans. Fredendall's II Corps reserve consisted of several artillery and tank-destroyer battalions near Tebessa, where the corps headquarters was located, plus the 1st Battalion, 168th Infantry.

Ultra-secret intercepts indicated an apparent enemy plan to strike through Fondouk to destroy the French in the center of the Allied front, then to turn north and rip into the British flank. Although other sources of intelligence pointed to Axis offensive preparations in the south, Eisenhower's G-2 at AFHQ, a British officer, as well as Anderson, became convinced of an imminent Axis thrust in the north. To preserve these positions, which pointed toward Bizerte and Tunis, Anderson instructed Fredendall to be ready to abandon Gafsa in the south. Together with Koeltz, Fredendall was to prepare to withdraw about fifty miles to the Western Dorsale and there to plug the passes, especially the two important defiles at Kasserine and Sbiba. Contrary to Allied expectations, Kesselring, von Arnim, and Rommel, with *Comando Supremo* approval, decided to launch two attacks, both in the south. Von Arnim was to head for Sidi bou Zid, Rommel for Gafsa. The concept, however, was somewhat fuzzy. Von Arnim wished simply to throw the Allies off balance and to retain possession of the *10th* and *21st Panzer Divisions*. Rommel hoped to recover control of his two panzer divisions and to go all the way to Tebessa and, if possible, beyond. If the attacks went well, Kesselring promised to give Rommel control of at least one of the panzer divisions and permission to go as far as he could.

The second phase of the Kasserine battle started very early on the morning of 14 February, before Drake could institute his bazooka-firing training program on Djebel Ksaira. During a raging sandstorm, more than 200 German tanks, half-tracks, and guns of both panzer divisions came through Faid. One task force swung around the northern side of Lessouda and encircled the hill; another swung around the southern side of Ksaira and surrounded the height. Waters' and Drake's forces, Fredendall's blocking positions, were thus marooned. A series of American mishaps, due largely to inexperience, then permitted the Germans rather easy and quick success. The bad weather relaxed the Americans' security arrangements, and they were unable to react quickly and firmly. Until the storm lifted, men on the hill had difficulty identifying the German elements and held their fire. At 0730, as the weather cleared, McQuillin initiated planned countermeasures. He limply told Hightower to clear up the situation. As Hightower prepared to drive to Djebel Lessouda and relieve the American defenders, enemy aircraft struck Sidi bou Zid and temporarily disrupted McQuillin's command post and Hightower's preparations. Throughout the rest of the day, German planes harassed the Americans. Despite repeated requests for air support, only one flight of four American aircraft appeared briefly over the battlefield.

Hightower went into action with forty-seven tanks. Although outnumbered, he fought bravely against the more effective German tanks. By mid-afternoon, all but seven of his tanks had been destroyed. During the engagement, some American artillerymen panicked and abandoned their guns. The 1st Armored Division Reconnaissance Battalion, ready to rescue Drake's men on Djebel Ksaira, was unable to even start its counterattack because some of the German tanks surrounding Drake had thrust forward toward Sidi bou Zid and captured a reconnaissance company. The rest of the American reconnaissance units then pulled out and headed for Sbeitla.

With his command post in Sidi bou Zid directly threatened, McQuillin, covered by Hightower's engagement, decided to withdraw to Sbeitla. He phoned and asked Ward to provide a shield by blocking the main road from Faid to Sbeitla. Ward sent Kern and his infantry battalion to take up defensive positions eleven miles east of the town at a road intersection that became known as Kern's Crossroads. Around noon, McQuillin started to move his artillery units and command post out of Sidi bou Zid. German dive bombers attacked them and prompted confusion. As a consequence, for several hours McQuillin lost communications with his subordinate units. That afternoon a swirling mass of American troops—McQuillin's command post, mis-

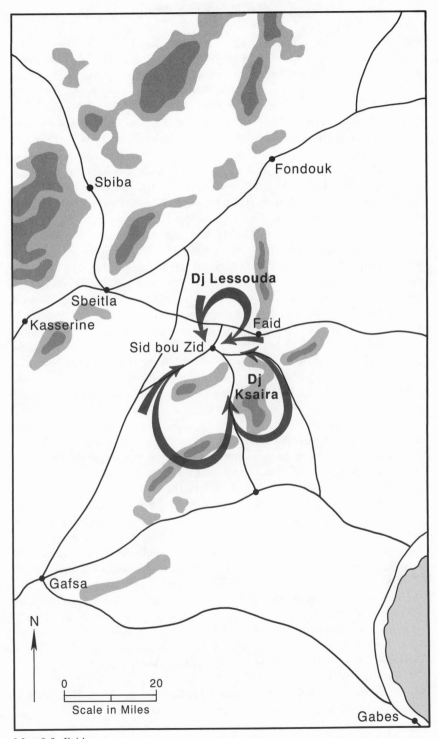

Map 8.3. Faid

cellaneous elements, Hightower's remnants, artillery pieces, tank destroyers, engineer trucks, and foot soldiers—fled toward Sbeitla. McQuillin re-established his command post there and began to assemble and reorganize his units.

Initial estimates of losses on that day were shocking: 52 officers and more than 1,500 men missing. The final numbers of casualties on 14 February were much smaller: 6 killed, 32 wounded, and 134 missing. But between Faid and Kern's Crossroads on the Sbeitla plain, forty-four tanks, fifty-nine half-tracks, twenty-six artillery pieces, and at least two dozen trucks were wrecked, burning, or abandoned. An artillery commander, Charles P. Summerall, Jr., took his men out during the night to recover guns, trucks, and ambulances; on the following morning, he had eight instead of his normal twenty-four pieces—the others were lost—backing the troops at Kern's Crossroads.

Rommel urged von Arnim to continue his attack during the night in order to exploit his tactical success, but von Arnim was satisfied to await the American counterattck he figured was inevitable. Ward at Sbeitla was indeed planning a counterattack. He, as well as McQuillin and Fredendall, radioed Waters and Drake to sit tight on the heights and await rescue. To strengthen Ward, Fredendall sent him some artillery and tank destroyers from Feriana. Fredendall asked Anderson to return Brig. Gen. Paul Robinett's CCB to Ward's control. But because Anderson expected the main German effort to strike in the Fondouk-Pichon area, he held the bulk of Robinett's force and released Lt. Col. James D. Alger's tank battalion, which arrived in Sbeitla on the evening of 14 February. With Alger merely replacing Hightower's destroyed battalion, Fredendall ordered Crosby to move his battalion from Thelepte to Sbeitla during the night.

Anderson had three major concerns: the American losses in the Faid–Sidi bou Zid region, the dispersal of the Allied units in the south, and the increasing vulnerability of his positions in the north. Telephoning Eisenhower, Anderson suggested evacuating Gafsa in order to concentrate strength in defense of the Feriana-Sbeitla area. Eisenhower agreed but asked Anderson to withdraw over two consecutive evenings. Anderson then instructed Fredendall to move the French troops out of Gafsa that night, 14 February, and the Americans on the following night. The French pulled out of Gafsa; so did most of the civilian population and American supply and service units. Around midnight, Anderson changed his mind and ordered Fredendall to withdraw the American combat troops. As the considerable movement reached Feriana, forty miles away, many rear-area troops became nervous. Some began to destroy depots and supply points in Feriana and Thelepte. Uncertain that Ward could hold Sbeitla, Anderson on the evening of 14 February instructed Koeltz to cover the Sbiba Pass in the Western Dorsale. He was to move French troops and the 34th Division to Sbiba. To block the Kasserine Pass if Ward had to pull out of Sbeitla, Anderson told Fredendall to have Ward fall back to the west for twenty miles and defend at Kasserine. Fredendall sent engineer troops to Kasserine to start building defensive positions.

In Algiers, Eisenhower ordered American units in Algeria to start for Kasserine Pass, a movement requiring several days' travel. News of their departure, he surmised, would perhaps hearten the troops in Tunisia. While Eisenhower, Anderson, and Fredendall prepared to withdraw to the Western Dorsale, Ward looked forward confidently to his counterattack on 15 February. Stack's infantry and Alger's tanks were to marry up at Kern's Crossroads, drive to Sidi bou Zid, then rescue the troops on the heights of Lessouda and Ksaira. While Alger, who had yet to lead his troops in combat, studied the terrain from a hill on the morning of 15 February and Stack readied his infantry for the advance, a flight of German bombers struck their formations and prompted enormous confusion.

The counterattack finally started at 1240 in great precision across the Sbeitla plain. Alger's tank battalion led, his three tank companies advancing in parallel columns with a company of tank destroyers, half-tracks mounting 75-mm guns, flaring out on the flanks and protecting two batteries of artillery. Behind rode Stack's infantry in trucks and half-tracks with several antiaircraft weapons as protection. Unfortunately, steep-sided *wadis*—dry stream beds— crossed the plain irregularly and disturbed the careful spacing of the attacking troops. As the tanks crossed the first ditch, German dive bombers jumped them. They bombed and strafed again at the second gully. At the third depression, German artillery began firing. Finally, German tanks emerged from hiding and started to encircle the entire American force. The Americans, fighting bravely and desperately against superior German weapons and experienced German troops, tried to beat back the German wings threatening to surround them. At 1800, Stack ordered all units to disengage and return to Kern's Crossroads. The infantry and artillery escaped relatively unscathed. The tanks were completely destroyed. Alger was taken prisoner, 15 of his officers and 298 enlisted men were missing, and fifty of his tanks had been knocked out. In two days of battle, the 1st Armored Division lost ninety-eight tanks, fifty-seven half-tracks, and twenty-nine artillery pieces.

Just before darkness, a pilot dropped a message from Ward to the troops on Lessouda. They were to get out during the night. Waters having been captured, Maj. Robert R. Moore, who had taken command of the 2d Battalion, 168th Infantry, fewer than two weeks earlier, displayed magnificent leadership and marched out about one-third of the 900 troops on Lessouda to Kern's Crossroads. The other men, together with vehicles and equipment, fell into German hands. Drake on Djebel Ksaira received a message from McQuillin on the afternoon of the following day, 16 February, to fight his way out. That night, Drake led his men off the hill and across the plain. German troops intercepted them and captured almost all. Only a handful reached safety. The two battalions of the 168th Infantry involved on Lessouda and Ksaira sustained losses of about 2,200 men. Two hundred of the soldiers reported missing were from the southwestern Iowa National Guard units. Meanwhile, when Rommel's attack forces, an Italo-German group of 160 tanks, half-tracks, and guns, learned on the afternoon of 15 February that the Allies had abandoned Gafsa, they advanced to the town, entered, and patrolled toward Feriana. That brought the second phase of the battle to a close.

In southern Tunisia, Rommel completed his long retreat across Libya and gathered his troops to the Mareth Line on that day. He could not understand why von Arnim did not push immediately into and through Sbeitla. Von Arnim cautiously wanted first to mop up in the Lessouda, Ksaira, and Sidi bou Zid area. Then he would take Sbeitla, turn north, and sweep clear the western exits of the Fondouk and Pinchon Passes. The absence of an overall commander of the two separate German forces in Gafsa and in Sidi bou Zid, together with the lack of firm objectives at the outset of the attack, now delayed the German course of action. Kesselring, visiting Hitler in East Prussia, learned what had happened and telephoned his chief of staff in Rome. He directed him to relay an order for a push to Tebessa with Rommel in command. This first required *Comando Supremo* approval, and when approached, the Italian high command hesitated.

In the meantime, on 16 February, Anderson and Fredendall ordered Ward to go over on the defensive and to concentrate "on guarding the Feriana, Kasserine, Sbeitla areas." Ward's chances of doing so improved when CCB, after an all-night movement, reported at Sbeitla. Ward put CCB south of the town, beside CCA, which pulled back from Kern's Crossroads. For the first time, the 1st Armored Division was operating in combat as a single unit. That afternoon, when small German forces probed toward Sbeitla, Crosby's tank battalion and a provisional company of a few tanks and tank destroyers under Hightower halted them and permitted Ward to set up a coherent defensive line covering the town. On the same afternoon, Anderson moved to strengthen the defense of the Sbiba Pass. From the northern sector, he sent a brigade of Maj. Gen. Sir Charles Keightley's British 6th Armoured Division southward. Koeltz moved the 34th Division (less the 168th Infantry) west from the Pichon area. That evening, *Comando Supremo* gave von Arnim permission to attack Sbeitla, and he jumped off at once. After nightfall, preceded by reconnaissance units, German tanks approached Sbeitla in three columns, firing as they advanced. Shells dropping into Sbeitla prompted McQuillin to shift his CCA headquarters to a location west of the town. Many American troops misinterpreted the movement and believed a wholesale evacuation was in progress. A good part of the CCA defenders panicked and fled. Why?

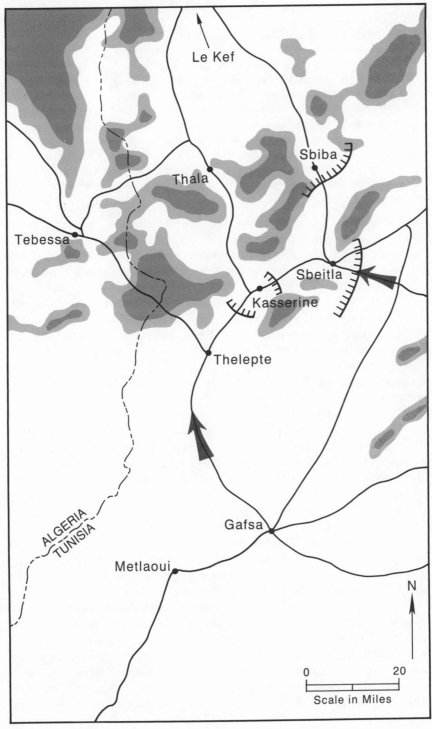

Map 8.4. Sbeitla

Night fighting was a new and terrifying experience for most of the men. The solidity of the defensive line was more apparent on a map than on the ground. Because of the darkness, the troops were not well placed. Because of the haste of the withdrawal, they were not well dug in. The harrowing events of three days of defeat had exhausted many soldiers, morally and physically. Uncertain and nervous, fatigued and confused, hemmed in by widespread firing that seemed to be all around them, believing that the Germans were already in Sbeitla, demoralized by the piecemeal commitment and intermingling of small units, no longer possessing a firm sense of belonging to a strong and self-contained organization, and numbed by a pervading attitude of weariness and bewilderment, many men lost their confidence and self-discipline.[68]

A churning mass of vehicles surged through the town and departed. When engineers demolished an ammunition dump, they intensified fear and prompted additional departures. Around midnight, concerned over his ability to hold Sbeitla, Ward telephoned Fredendall and suggested reinforcing Kasserine in strength.

At 0130 on 17 February, Anderson, talking with Fredendall on the telephone, authorized Ward to withdraw from Sbeitla. Anderson asked that Ward hold all day in order to give Koeltz more time to install blocking positions at Sbiba. Fredendall thought that that was too much to ask of Ward, and Anderson finally agreed that Ward was to hold the town until 1100 on 17 February and longer if he could. At dawn, on 17 February, Fredendall issued a directive. Ward and the 1st Armored Division, when forced to leave Sbeitla, were to retire through the Kasserine Pass toward Thala. Anderson Moore's 19th Engineers were to organize the Kasserine Pass defensively and to cover Ward's withdrawal. Stark's infantry regiment was to defend Feriana until compelled to pull back toward Tebessa. Air force personnel were to abandon the Thelepte airfields. At Sbeitla, the Germans lessened their pressure as they turned to round up Drake's men coming off Ksaira. The 1st Armored Division settled down and held, although rear-area units, preparing to leave, blew up dumps and destroyed supplies.

From Gafsa, the Italians and Germans of Rommel's force advanced in strength and entered Feriana. About 3,500 men at the nearby Thelepte airfields were streaming toward Tebessa after having burned 60,000 gallons of gasoline, thirty-four disabled aircraft, and facilities. Stark retired to Tebessa. The *Afrika Korps* entered Thelepte at noon and salvaged twenty tons of aviation gas, thirty tons of lubricants, plus ammunition and assorted supplies. Fredendall moved his command post out of Tebessa and for about six hours had no communications with his subordinates. Increasingly nervous supply and service units in and around Tebessa began to head for the west in search of safety. At Sbeitla, the Germans attacked that afternoon, and, although CCB held relatively well, panic in the town turned the place into a nightmare.

In accordance with new instructions, CCA, harassed by German planes, pulled back and moved north to Sbiba. That evening, the troops dug hasty defenses to block the Sbiba Pass and allow Koeltz's arriving forces to take positions. CCB withdrew to Kasserine. The Germans entered Sbeitla at 1700.

After four days of fighting in the Faid–Sidi bou Zid–Sbeitla area, the Americans had lost more than 2,500 men, 100 tanks, 280 vehicles, and 30 guns. Mounting uncertainty and nervousness infected Allied forces as far away as Algiers. The Germans, holding Gafsa, Feriana, Thelepte, and Sbeitla, threatened the Sbiba, Kasserine, and other passes in the Western Dorsale. If they pressed forward, they would menace Tebessa, Le Kef, Bone—indeed, the entire Allied front in Tunisia. Thus ended the third phase of the Battle of Kasserine Pass.

On the evening of 17 February, von Arnim left the *21st Panzer Division* at Sbeitla, sent a task force north toward Sbiba, and dispatched the *10th Panzer Division* to take positions in reserve behind the Pichon and Fondouk passes. When Rommel telephoned that evening and suggested a lightning thrust to Tebessa, von Arnim was uninterested, although he permitted reconnaissance elements to probe beyond Sbeitla toward Kasserine the next day. Rommel, still lured by the prospect of exploiting success, sent a message to Kesselring on the afternoon of 18 February. He proposed an attack to Tebessa with the *10th* and *21st Panzer Divisions.* Kesselring was in accord and passed the recommendation to *Comando Supremo.* That night, *Comando Supremo* approved but stipulated a shorter hook or envelopment to Le Kef. Rommel was to control the two panzer divisions and the *Afrika Korps,* of which the Italian *Centauro Division* was a part, but he was to have no authority over von Arnim. Instructing the *21st Panzer Division* to strike to Sbiba, the *Afrika Korps* to advance to Kasserine, Rommel recalled the *10th Panzer Division* to Sbeitla. Depending on which attack succeeded, he would commit the *10th* to Sbiba or to Kasserine.

On the Allied side on 18 February, the shock of defeat was visible among the troops. Everyone was tired. Units were mauled, dispersed, and mixed; had no specific missions; lacked knowledge of adjacent formations. The troops seemed to be slipping out of control. Eisenhower sent artillery and tank destroyers from Algeria to Tunisia. A shipment of 295 new Sherman tanks had just arrived, but unwilling to risk losing them all, he released 30 to the British and 30 to the 1st Armored Division. Alexander had come to Algiers on 15 February in accordance with agreements reached at the Allied Casablanca Conference in January and prepared to take command of the ground forces in Tunisia—Anderson's First Army and Montgomery's Eighth—which were approaching the Mareth Line. Alexander conferred with Eisenhower, then toured the British front on 16 February, visited the French sector on 17 February, and traveled on 18 February to the II Corps area. He was horrified to see the state of confusion and uncertainty and was upset by the absence of a

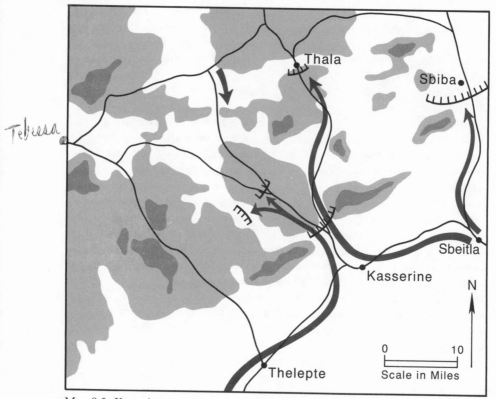

Map 8.5. Kasserine

coordinated plan of defense. Instead of waiting to take command of the ground forces on 20 February, he assumed command on the nineteenth and ordered everyone to hold in place. There was to be no withdrawal from the Western Dorsale.

Moore's 19th Engineers had been laying mines between the village of Kasserine and the pass, five miles beyond. On 18 February, having covered the withdrawal of CCB through the village and the pass, Moore moved his men through the pass and organized defensive positions. Just beyond the pass, on the western side, the road splits: one route leads to the west toward Tebessa; the other, the main road, goes north to Thala. Moore, with about 200 engineers and infantrymen armed with small arms and automatic weapons and supported by two batteries of U.S. 105-mm howitzers, a battery of French 75s, and a battalion of tank destroyers in the rear, covered the road to Tebessa. An infantry battalion defended the road to Thala.[69] Most of the troops were inexperienced and nervous. On the evening of 18 February, Anderson instructed Koeltz to dispatch a brigade of Keightley's 6th Armoured Division from Sbiba to Thala. Brig. Charles A. L. Dunphie's 26th Armoured Brigade moved. He was thus in place to help the American battalion defending the road from Kasserine to Thala. Or he could move back to Sbiba if the main German threat developed there.

Meanwhile, CCA of the 1st Armored Division, having given Keightley's and Ryder's forces, as well as the French, time to set up defensive positions at the Sbiba Pass, drove through Sbiba to Tebessa. On 19 February, CCA arrived at the three minor passes south and west of Kasserine to bolster remnants of a French division, two American battalions (one of Rangers, the other of infantry), the Derbyshire Yeomanry, and CCB. When German reconnaissance units probed the Kasserine Pass on the evening of 18 February, some of Moore's engineers fled. That night Fredendall put Stark in command of all the units defending the pass. Stark arrived on the morning of 19 February as the Germans attacked in earnest. Seeking surprise, an infantry battalion of the *Afrika Korps* advanced through Kasserine Pass without artillery preparation. When the troops met opposition, a panzer grenadier battalion backed by 88-mm cannon reinforced them. A unit of British mortars and some reconnaissance elements had just arrived at the Kasserine Pass, and they helped the Americans hold off the Germans. When Moore asked for more infantry to support his engineers, Stark seized on a battalion of the 9th U.S. Infantry Division that had just arrived from Algeria. Stark sent two rifle companies to Moore—one for each flank of Moore's defenses—and kept one for the Thala road, thereby splitting the battalion.

Rommel himself came to Kasserine, was impressed by the opposition, and decided to make his main effort toward Sbiba. But he wished the attack at Kasserine to continue. After clearing the pass, his troops were to strike westward toward Tebessa in order to stretch the Allied defenses. The *21st*

Panzer Division had attacked Sbiba that morning, but Koeltz, Keightley, and Ryder had stopped the thrust. Rommel then changed his mind and decided to concentrate in the Kasserine area. He ordered the *10th Panzer Division,* which was on its way to Sbeitla, to continue on to the Kasserine Pass. The division was at half strength, for von Arnim had refused to release some units, particularly the heavy panzer battalion, which had about two dozen enormous Tiger tanks. Because the *10th* was moving slowly, an impatient Rommel brought up the *Centauro Division.* He now wished the *Afrika Korps* to open the pass and to drive westward toward Tebessa. The *10th Panzer Division,* after going through the Kasserine Pass, was to strike at Thala. That evening, the 16th Infantry of the 1st Division marched from the Sbiba area to the Kasserine area. Fredendall sent it to bolster the minor passes south and west of Kasserine. He gave General Allen, the 1st Division commander who was with the regiment, the job of coordinating the defenses of these passes. Fredendall then ordered CCB of the 1st Armored Division to back up the engineers on the Tebessa road at Kasserine Pass where the defenses seemed on the verge of collapse. Dunphie, commander of the 26th Armoured Brigade at Thala, asked permission to reinforce Stark, but Keightley wanted him to be on hand if he was needed at Sbiba. Dunphie nonetheless sent eleven of his tanks from Thala to buttress Stark's positions that night.

On 20 February, the *21st Panzer Division* attacked Sbiba again and made no progress. But at Kasserine, the shrieks of the *nebelwerfer,* multiple rocket launchers that had been recently introduced by the Germans, unnerved Moore's engineers holding the Tebessa road. They fell apart, and by afternoon—having lost eleven men killed, twenty-eight wounded, and eighty-nine missing in three days (and many more had temporarily vanished)—they no longer existed as a coherent force. Fortunately, Robinett's CCB arrived and blocked the road. On the main route to Thala, although jittery, the defenders held. Rommel then became even more impatient for a quick victory at Sbiba and Kasserine. He was apprehensive over the Mareth Line positions, for Montgomery had just that day attacked his outposts in southern Tunisia. Late in the afternoon, on Anderson's order, Keightley dispatched Brig. Cameron Nicholson, his assistant division commander, from Sbiba to Thala with miscellaneous troops. No longer confident of Fredendall's ability, Anderson wished Nicholson to command, as Fredendall's representative, all the British, American, and French fighting on the west side of Kasserine Pass. What actually developed was that Fredendall and Robinett commanded the forces blocking the Tebessa road, and Nicholson and Dunphie took control of the units defending the Thala road.

On 21 February, Rommel let the attacks in the Sbiba area continue but looked for decisive success at Kasserine. He decided to make his main effort to Thala and to head for Le Kef beyond. Furious fighting on both the Tebessa and Thala roads resulted in a slight German advance toward Tebessa and the prospect of German tactical success at Thala. By now, Stark's force on the Thala road had virtually evaporated, and Dunphie emerged as the chief Allied protagonist. Committing his tanks and infantry against a strong thrust directed by Rommel himself, who took control of the battle for several hours, Dunphie lost the bulk of his armor and had to withdraw to the final line of defense before Thala. The Germans followed, and fierce combat erupted after darkness and ended in a draw. Both sides retired 1,000 yards—Dunphie to the north, the Germans to the south. The final defensive line was virtually uncovered, and Rommel seemed about to enter Thala. Expecting just that, Anderson asked Koeltz, who had again stopped the Germans at Sbiba, to send a battalion of infantry and whatever else he could to Thala. Because Ryder was making some local adjustments, Koeltz requested Keightley to dispatch elements. That night, a battalion of British infantry and some tanks traveled along a mountain trail to reinforce Nicholson and Dunphie.

Meanwhile, Allied units were coming from Algeria. A battalion of French infantry moved from Constantine and arrived at Sbiba. Fifty-two Sherman tanks and crews were en route to Tebessa. A provisional British unit with twenty-five new Churchill tanks reached Sbiba. The 47th Infantry of the 9th U.S. Division was on the way from Oran to Tebessa. Most important, Brig. Gen. S. LeRoy Irwin's 9th Division Artillery, with three artillery battalions and two cannon companies, traveling from western Algeria, got to Tebessa on the afternoon of 21 February. Ordered to Thala at once, Irwin's guns were in position by midnight. Nicholson placed Irwin in charge of all the artillery at Thala, and Irwin sited his forty-eight pieces, plus thirty-six other guns of various calibers, to cover the all-but-abandoned final line of defense, manned now by British infantry reinforced by stragglers rounded up by Stark, about twenty tanks of Dunphie's brigade, plus the British infantry battalion and a few tanks, some of them new Shermans released by Eisenhower, coming from Sbiba. Less than a mile away were at least fifty German tanks, 2,500 infantry, thirty artillery pieces, and other weapons, including the notorious *nebelwerfer.*

The *10th Panzer Division* was ready to start what Rommel expected would be the advance into Thala on the morning of 22 February, when Irwin's guns opened up. Expecting a counterattack, the Germans postponed their effort. Nicholson launched a foray and, although he lost five tanks, bluffed the Germans. Rommel came up the Thala road, noted the increased volume of Allied shelling, and gave permission to delay the offensive. Now Robinett and his CCB seemed about to be overwhelmed. During the previous night, approximately a battalion of German and Italian troops had infiltrated the American positions. Intending to strike toward Tebessa, they became lost. On the morning of 22 February, they arrived in the rear of the miscellaneous Allied troops—American, French, and British—guarding the Bou Chebka Pass, one of the minor defiles south and west of Tebessa. The Axis force captured several American howitzers and antiaircraft guns and prompted considerable anxiety over the security of that pass and two others nearby. It took most of the day to track down, disperse, and capture the Italo-German unit.

Under the impression that Allied defenses were caving in, Fredendall went to the commander of the under-strength French division in the area and asked him to defend Tebessa. While Fredendall was gone, someone at the II Corps headquarters decided to move the corps command post to avoid being overrun. When Fredendall returned, he found his headquarters half abandoned; many clerks and radio operators were on the way to Le Kef and Constantine. Feeling unable to maintain control, Fredendall, having already passed responsibility to Allen for the minor passes, now instructed Ward to coordinate the defenses on the Tebessa road. Learning that the 47th Infantry of the 9th Division was about thirty miles south of Constantine, Fredendall asked the regiment to remain where it was in order to protect Constantine in case the Axis forces broke through Thala and Tebessa.

During the night of 22 February, Anderson, whose British First Army headquarters was nine miles north of Sbiba, shifted his command post behind Le Kef. Koeltz almost pulled his headquarters back too, for von Arnim had attacked half-heartedly in the Pichon area. But Koeltz drew Keightley's and Ryder's divisions out of Sbiba and faced them toward Thala to meet the expected breakthrough there. Sbiba lay open to German entry. However, nothing happened at Sbiba or at Kasserine. After conferring with Kesselring, who came to Tunisia on the afternoon of 22 February, Rommel called off his attack. He had been unable to secure von Arnim's cooperation. He thought it impossible to obtain a decisive victory before Montgomery attacked the Mareth Line. His units were fatigued, and Rommel himself was extremely tired and discouraged. That night, Rommel ordered his forces to withdraw to the Eastern Dorsale and the east coast. They did so early on the morning of 23 February, leaving a profusion of mines and destroyed bridges in their wake. There was no Allied pursuit of the departing enemy. According to Koeltz, the Allied units "were in such disorder and their commanders so shaken" that no immediate reaction was possible.[70] The Battle of Kasserine Pass was over.

On the afternoon of 23 February, some Allied units moved forward cautiously. They found no enemy. Not until two days later did the Allies understand that Rommel's offensive had ended. They then advanced to the east and several days later were again in Sbeitla and Sidi bou Zid, in Thelepte, Feriana, and Gafsa.

German losses in the Kasserine operation totaled almost 1,000 casualties—200 men killed, almost 550 wounded, 250 missing—and 14 guns, 61 motor vehicles, 6 half-tracks, and 20 tanks were destroyed. Italian losses are unknown. The II Corps took 73 Germans and 535 Italians prisoner. The Germans reported capturing 4,000 prisoners, 62 tanks and half-tracks, 161 motor vehicles, and 36 guns. But American losses were much higher. About 30,000 Americans engaged in the Kasserine fighting under II Corps, and probably 300 were killed, almost 3,000 wounded, nearly 3,000 missing. It would take 7,000 replacements to bring the units to authorized strengths. The 34th Division under the French XIX Corps at Sbiba sustained approximately 50 men killed, 200 wounded, and 250 missing. II Corps lost 183 tanks, 104 half-tracks, 208 artillery pieces, and 512 trucks and jeeps, plus large amounts of supplies—more than the combined stocks in American depots in Algeria and Morocco. The series of operations known as the Battle of Kasserine Pass—from the start at Faid through Sidi bou Zid and Sbeitla to the final act at the Kasserine defile—was a disaster for the U.S. Army.

U.S. forces at Kasserine displayed several strengths. The battle confirmed the leadership of certain individuals—among them Ward, Robinett, Hightower, Alger, Waters, and Stack in the 1st Armored Division; Ryder, Drake, and Moore in the 34th Division; Summerall the artilleryman; and many at the small-unit level whose names escaped notice. New weapons and equipment coming to the field of battle, although at first poorly managed, turned out to be superior. The .50-caliber antiaircraft machine gun, used particularly well by CCB along the road leading to Tebessa, spelled the doom of the German dive bomber. The Sherman tank proved to be battleworthy. The bazooka would be used with success later. When relatively inexperienced American troops fought alongside seasoned allies, notably as at Sbiba, they stood firm and controlled. If the British were largely responsible for stopping the Germans on the road to Thala, the Americans had, after initial unsteadiness, settled down and blocked the road to Tebessa. Instead of being disheartened by their inexperience, they displayed a remarkable recovery and an ability to learn. Subsequent operations in Tunisia revealed their competence and confidence. They quickly came to regard their allies with understanding and to work with them closely despite differences in national outlooks, habits, and methods.

The weaknesses the Americans showed were those usually demonstrated by inexperienced troops committed to battle for the first time. Beforehand, they were overconfident, as CCA was at Sidi bou Zid; once committed, they were jittery, as were Moore's engineers. They lacked proficiency in newly developed weapons such as bazookas. They had difficulty identifying enemy weapons and equipment. They were handicapped by certain poor commanders—Fredendall, who was arrogant, opinionated, and perhaps less than stable; McQuillin and Stark, known as Old Mac and Old Stark, whose reactions were slow, cautious, and characteristic of World War I operations. Units were dispersed and employed in small parcels instead of being concentrated. Air-ground cooperation was defective. Replacement troops were often deficient in physical fitness and training. Some weapons were below par—the light tank was suitable only for reconnaissance; the tank destroyer was insufficiently armed and armored; the 37-mm gun was too small. Higher commanders shirked the responsibility or lacked the knowledge to coordinate units in battle, to delineate firm unit boundaries, to mass defensive fire, and to provide military police to handle traffic and prisoners of war. Commanders were in general imprecise in their orders. Command lines among the Allied forces had been tenuous, and mutual lack of confidence and bitterness marred relations. In addition, "American troops in North Africa enjoyed very little direct support from aircraft and suffered many attacks at the hands of friendly fliers, all because no solutions had been developed for the problems identified in the 1941 maneuvers of Louisiana and Carolinas."[71]

The strengths of the Axis as perceived by the Americans consisted of combat troops' experience; the superiority of certain items of equipment, notably the German tanks; the effectiveness of the *nebelwerfer;* and the close coordination of tactical air support with ground operations. Axis weaknesses were a lack of trust between Germans and Italians, the absence of an effective coalition machinery to provide overall theater direction, and, although it was scarcely remarked on at the time, the petty jealousies among commanders, notably between von Arnim and Rommel. Had Axis forces been closely coordinated by an overall commander in pursuit of bold objectives enunciated by a self-confident coalition, the Axis would, no doubt, have attained a strategic victory instead of merely a tactical success.

As a consequence of the Battle of Kasserine Pass, the U.S. Army instituted many changes. Officers worked to improve fire-direction control, to obtain better battlefield intelligence, and to gain more effective air support. Four months after Kasserine, in July 1943, the Army Ground Forces lengthened the thirteen-week basic training cycle to seventeen weeks and stressed physical conditioning, mine laying and removal, patrolling, reconnaissance, and other combat techniques. The Army concentrated on producing the Sherman tank and procuring larger caliber guns, notably those of 76-mm and 90-mm. Commanders decided to employ units as units instead of parceling them out in small segments. Fredendall, McQuillin, and Stark were removed from positions of leadership. Emphasis was now placed on efficiency, discipline, and self-control. The Army tightened its procedures and became more military in the best sense of the word.

More specifically, the War Department made changes in the infantry division.[72] In March 1943, the infantry squad was authorized ten Garand rifles, one automatic rifle, and one Springfield 1903 Model rifle, a considerable increase in small-arms firepower. The cannon company with six self-propelled 75-mm howitzers and two self-propelled 105-mm howitzers had been used at the infantry battalion level, but in March 1943, the War Department abolished the cannon companies in infantry battalions and replaced them with the increased firepower and greater flexibility of three cannon platoons at the infantry regimental level with six towed 105-mm howitzers. The experience of the 1st Armored Division in North Africa was considered too fragmentary to give guidance on reorganization. Furthermore, deployment of the armored division in the Battle of Kasserine Pass was defensive and not in line with the aggressively offensive mission for which the armored divisions had been intended. Nevertheless, on 15 September 1943, while the 1st and 2d Armored Divisions, both overseas, remained as constituted under the 1942 tables of organization and equipment, other and newer armored divisions were restructured and lightened. The regimental echelon was abolished, and the battalion became the basic unit. All battalions were alike and therefore interchangeable. Three battalions of tanks, infantry, and artillery increased flexibility and doubled the proportion of infantry to tanks. Three combat commands, all of which could fight, now became standard.

The 37-mm gun had been a failure in North Africa, and the War Department recognized this fact. But while the weapon was "definitely abandoned" in favor of the 57-mm gun as the result of experience in Tunisia, the 37-mm gun had to be retained until enough 57-mm guns could be produced to replace the lighter model.

The tank destroyer, "armed with unsatisfactory and makeshift expedients," was a disappointment. In general, the weapon lacked suitable armor protection and firepower. Creation and development of the weapon, as well as training for its use, had come too late for Kasserine Pass. When "it became clear from the limited operations in Tunisia . . . that tank destroyer units would not be requested by theater commanders in anything like the numbers that were becoming available," McNair recommended in April 1943 further reducing the number of tank destroyer battalions to be activated. The maximum projection of 222 battalions had already been cut to 144; now it was curtailed to 106.

In May 1943, when Ward, having been relieved as commander of the 1st Armored Division, assumed command of the Tank Destroyer Center at Camp Hood, he shifted the principal training emphasis to gunnery, developed the capacity for indirect fire, and stressed teamwork and operating in simulated battle conditions. The field manual was rewritten in June 1943 in light of the lessons of the battle. There was a shift toward using towed three-inch tank destroyers, which were now beginning to be regarded as defensive weapons. Not until the European campaign of 1944 was a proper role found for tank destroyers. They were recognized as defensive weapons and, instead of the earlier offensive orientation, they operated with "aggressive spirit."[73] While tanks became the primary antitank weapons, tank destroyers became highly mobile supporting artillery. They functioned as auxiliary artillery, together with tanks and antiaircraft artillery. The Tunisian operation led to increased numbers of field artillery, tank, and combat-engineer battalions.[74]

The antiaircraft training cycle, which had been increased from thirteen to eighteen weeks before Kasserine Pass, was again lengthened in July 1943, this time to twenty-two weeks.[75] Yet the "most disappointing aspect of the 1943 maneuvers . . . was air-ground cooperation."[76] Planes frequently attacked friendly forces because of failure to display panels on the ground or to properly use pyrotechnics, and antiaircraft artillery continued to shoot down friendly planes. Close coordination of ground units and tactical supporting air units would be successfully resolved only after the Normandy invasion, when tactical air commands worked closely with each field army and when special radios enabled pilots to talk directly with the ground units they were assisting.[77] By the late summer of 1943, Army authorities agreed that combined-arms training had never been satisfactory. Infantry and armored officers had had inadequate training in each other's operations; higher commanders and staffs were inexperienced in coordinating operations and had a tendency to use units "in such driblets that their effectiveness was lost." Not enough weapons and units had existed in 1942, or even in 1943, for effective combined-arms training.[78] Until late in 1943, armored and infantry divisions were unable to train together, and nondivisional units had only "limited opportunities for combined [arms] training."[79]

As Army Ground Forces noted in March 1943, divisions in the United States had received only 50 percent of their authorized equipment in certain critical items, while nondivisional units had received a mere 20 percent. Thus, "shortcomings shown by American troops in combat in North Africa . . . were attributed . . . in large measure to lack of opportunity to train with enough weapons and ammunition."[80] Although Army Ground Forces had tried to issue full allowances to units in training, continuing shortages of equipment and supplies had made the practice impossible.[81] On the other hand, a major confirmation of prewar outlook was the role of the division organized to fight as a self-contained organization.

The vision of how the U.S. Army was to fight in World War II was essentially sound. As McNair remarked in June 1943, a defensive attitude stimulated by the Battle of Kasserine Pass was "undermining the offensive spirit by which alone we can win battles."[82] The late date and the short duration of the mobilization and organization process, of the development and procurement of weapons and equipment, and of the training cycle, together with necessary haste and improvisation, made impossible adequately preparing troops for the exigencies of what was to them the new and sobering reality of war. Americans at Kasserine "paid in blood the price of battlefield experience."[83] For Americans who had been imbued with an aggressive and offensive notion during training, the defensive Battle of Kasserine Pass imposed a role for which they were psychologically ill equipped. Yet the underlying cause of the American failure was discrepancy in numbers between the Allies and the Axis. The Axis built up its strength in Tunisia faster than the Allies could, and the presence in the field of two Axis armies against a single Allied army (before Montgomery arrived) gave the Axis an indisputable advantage. Another trump card was the German and Italian troops' prior battle experience. Still another was superior Axis equipment, particularly tanks and guns. The close coordination of ground-air units by virtue of doctrine, training, and experience also was vitally important.

The Americans made many mistakes in this first large-scale engagement of the war in Europe, but they learned from their errors and made adjustments that enabled them to go on to victory in Tunisia and beyond. The defeat at Kasserine showed the Army what troops had to learn and to do. That they quickly became proficient in the warfare of the 1940s confirmed their spirit, their flexibility, their strong sense of purpose—their will to win.

9

Task Force Smith and the 24th Division: Delay and Withdrawal, 5–19 July 1950

ROY K. FLINT

Standing on a low hill north of Osan, Korea, Lt. Col. Charles B. Smith peered north through a summer rain in the direction of the town of Suwon from which North Korean troops were expected to come. It was late afternoon on 2 July 1950. Here he was, in command of Task Force (TF) Smith, half of his battalion and an artillery battery, looking for a piece of ground from which he could fight the advancing North Koreans. A veteran of the 7 December 1941 attack on Pearl Harbor and now commander of the 1st Battalion, 21st Infantry regiment—the Gimlets—of the 24th Infantry Division, Smith had been catapulted into another war, a war he had not expected and one for which his unit was not fully prepared. Literally and symbolically, Smith was leading the United States into war for the second time in ten years.[1]

The first American battle in Korea began with the fight at Osan where Task Force Smith first engaged the North Koreans. It ended after two weeks of delay and withdrawal with the loss of Taejon, when the 1st Cavalry Division finally relieved the 24th Division. During those weeks, the 24th suffered heavy casualties and gave up more ground than it should have in nearly every engagement. Veterans of the division are quick to admit failure, but in truth, the poor performance of the 24th was more the result of inadequate preparation during the prewar years in Japan than of any specific lapse on the battlefield. The tactical defeats endured by the officers and men of the 24th Division were rooted in the failure of the Army—and not just the divisions in Japan—to prepare itself during peacetime for battle. After the Korean War, the Army reformed its readiness procedures to ensure that it was combat ready and organized for commitment on a moment's notice anywhere in the world. But in 1950, the 24th Division was part of another kind of army.

Brad Smith was in Korea because war had broken out on 25 June 1950. Before dawn that day, North Korean artillery had opened fire across the 38th parallel and, unlike the frequent border incursions of the recent past, had continued to fire until well after daybreak. The South Korean troops targeted were dug in on the Ongjin Peninsula and in the Kaesong area in the west *(see Map 9.1)*. About thirty minutes after the preparatory fires began, the North Korean *1st* and *6th Infantry Divisions,* the *3d Constabulary Brigade,* and one regiment of the *105th Armored Brigade* crossed the border to fix the South Korean defenders in place while the main effort was prepared. An hour later at 0530, clanking North Korean T-34 tanks signaled the main attack just north of Uijongbu astride the shortest route between the 38th parallel and Seoul, the capital of the Republic of Korea. Here, the rest of the *105th Armored Brigade* spearheaded the North Korean *3d* and *4th Infantry Divisions* in a drive to capture Seoul. Farther east, in the mountains of central Korea, two more infantry divisions, the *2d* and the *7th,* struck the South Koreans. A fourth prong of the attack pointed down the east coast of Korea. There the *5th Infantry Division,* a motorcycle regiment, and an independent infantry unit supported by previously infiltrated guerrillas crossed the 38th parallel heading for Samch'ok. At 0600, motorized junks and sampans landed amphibious assault troops on the east coast, north and south of Samch'ok.

Shocked by the North Korean attack, the United States government turned to the United Nations to mobilize an effective political response. During the week following the invasion, deliberations in the UN and in Washington moved the world toward war. UN resolutions committed the organization to stop North Korean aggression. By week's end, General of the Army Douglas MacArthur, Commander in Chief of the U.S. Far East Command, reported little hope of saving Korea unless the United States entered the fight. On 30 June, he recommended the commitment of combat elements of the Eighth U.S. Army, stationed in Japan; without hesitation, President Harry S. Truman approved. With that, MacArthur began to move Smith's battalion of the 24th Infantry Division to Korea.

When the United Nations and the United States decided to come to the aid of South Korea, the situation could not have been more bleak. Not only were U.S. forces only marginally ready for war, but a week after American units first engaged the North Koreans at Osan, intelligence estimates pitted the U.S. 24th Division and the weakened South Koreans against nine North Korean divisions, numbering 80,000 men and 100 to 150 tanks. Intelligence officers believed that the North Koreans could threaten the port of Pusan within two weeks.[2] In light of this estimate, the broad task given to MacArthur by the UN Security Council in its resolution of 27 June seemed overly ambitious. The resolution had called on member states to help the Republic of Korea "to repel the armed attack and to restore international peace and security in the area." In response to this call, the president first

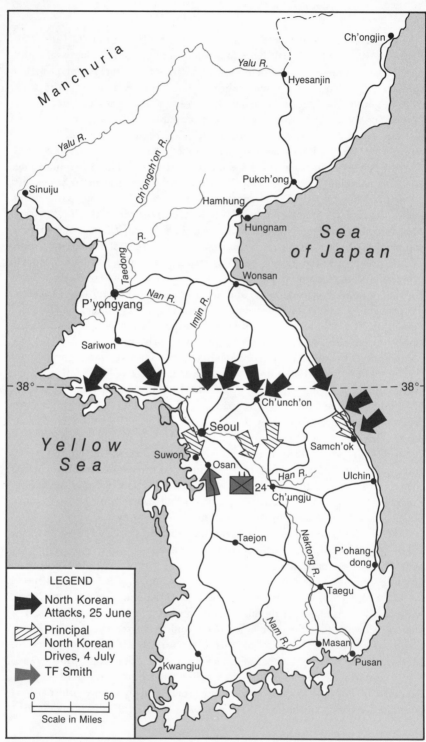

Map 9.1. The North Korean Invasion

authorized an increase in American air and naval activity against North Korea in support of the South Korean Army and later gave MacArthur authority to employ his ground forces to restore the prewar status quo.[3] In the early days of the war, the goal of restoring the boundary along the 38th parallel gave MacArthur all the direction he needed while confining the war to the Korean peninsula. Such an objective, universally appealing as an appropriate penalty for an act of international outlawry by the North Korean Government, avoided direct confrontation with the Chinese Communists and the Soviet Union. It was, perhaps, even more than MacArthur could accomplish on the battlefield.

MacArthur's ground forces were in poor condition to fight a conventional war in Korea. Of the ten Army divisions and eleven separate regiments on active duty when the war broke out, four infantry divisions—the 7th, the 24th, the 25th, and the 1st Cavalry—were assigned to the Eighth Army in Japan on occupation duty and were available immediately to MacArthur. The 5th Regimental Combat Team was in Hawaii, and the 29th Infantry regiment was in Okinawa. In addition, one infantry division, two infantry regiments, and a constabulary force roughly equal to a division were in Europe; two infantry regiments were in the Caribbean. The remainder constituted the general reserve, concentrated in the United States. Although the army maintained its authorized ten-division structure, it did so at the expense of combat readiness by eliminating units that were part of the mobilization base.[4] In 1949 and early 1950, the goal was minimum reduction of combat units and maximum elimination of "fat." Even though the percentage of combat forces in the Army increased, the statistic was deceiving, for it indicated a dangerous reduction in the support units—the "fat"—so essential for sustained combat. The only bright spot was the maintenance of the machinery for selective service. Otherwise, the Army was a hollow shell.

Simple numbers of divisions are misleading in other ways as well. All divisions except the one in Europe were under strength in each of their three regiments. Of the four divisions in Japan, three were below their authorized peacetime strength of 12,500, a figure which was itself only 66 percent of the wartime strength of 18,900. The 24th had 10,700 men, the 1st Cavalry had 11,300, and the 7th had 10,600. Only the 25th exceeded its peacetime manning with 13,000. Available manpower had been consolidated so that each regiment, except the 24th Infantry regiment of the 25th Division, had only two instead of the normal three battalions; none of the regiments had its authorized tank companies. Division medium-tank battalions were armed with M24 light tanks. Furthermore, artillery units were operating at reduced strength and with only two-thirds of their units.[5] To grasp the problem more concretely, consider the 24th Infantry Division.

As late as the spring of 1949, the primary mission of the 24th was to occupy the island of Kyushu, Japan. Its secondary mission was to train.

Clearly, the organization of the division reflected its mission. In the 19th Infantry regiment, only the 1st Battalion and the Headquarters Company and Company E of the 2d Battalion were operative. The 34th Infantry regiment had 1st and 3d battalions, but no Company I in the 3d, leaving that battalion with only three companies. The 21st Infantry regiment had only a 1st Battalion and the Headquarters Companies of the other two battalions. Even the battalions that were fully organized were under strength.[6]

In mid-1949, an abrupt change occurred simultaneously with the assignment of Lt. Gen. Walton H. Walker to command of the Eighth Army. First, training for combat readiness became the primary mission, and occupation duties reverted to secondary importance.[7] Consistent with this change in emphasis, in September, MacArthur's headquarters directed a new relationship between American military units and the Japanese people. His intent was to ease the rigors of the occupation. While vestiges of the occupation remained in the form of a curfew, "off-limits" restrictions, and other minor constraints, the effect on military units was to shift their concentration from military police duties to training.[8]

With the new mission came a rapid increase in strength of the 24th Division. Enlisted strength almost tripled, and officer strength doubled to a peak of 11,824 men in November. While the division could not hold that strength over the following months, training in the battalions at least proceeded with some hope of success. In July 1949, a new training program began, having as its first goal basic training of the new and partially trained fillers. Upon completion of basic training in mid-September, squad, platoon, and company training followed. Company-level tactical training was to be completed prior to the end of the year. In the first half of 1950, battalion training began and culminated in battalion testing. Regimental combat team and division training were to follow in the second half of the year.[9] Ambitious as Walker's training program was, the Army ran into insurmountable obstacles. It also ran out of time when the North Koreans attacked in June 1950. Perhaps most damaging, this was an army that really did not expect to go to war.[10] As had been the case in the Philippine Islands and China before World War II, American forces stationed in Japan after the war resembled a colonial army; they were concerned with administrative duties, not poised and ready for commitment to battle.

On the eve of the Korean War, the 21st Infantry regiment and the 52d Field Artillery Battalion—the units from which Brad Smith's task force had come— were in most ways typical of the units occupying Japan. The men of the 21st performed their duties in Camp Wood, a small post nestled in the middle of Kumamoto, a city of about 100,000 people on the southernmost island of Kyushu. Near Fukuoka, also on the island of Kyushu, batteries of the 52d Field Artillery Battalion occupied Camp Hakata.

The Gimlets liked life in Kumamoto. They enjoyed a healthy climate of leadership, first under Col. John A. Dabney and then, just before going to Korea, under the aggressive and paternal Col. Richard W. Stephens, whom the officers and soldiers affectionately called "Big Six." Stephens was a strong commander who enjoyed the respect of his men, probably because he tempered stern discipline with common sense and good spirits. He trained his regiment as best he could and took special pleasure in the keen competition provided by his regimental athletic teams. As noted, the 1st Battalion was commanded by Lieutenant Colonel Smith. Lt. Col. Carl C. Jensen commanded the 3d Battalion, rounding out a first-class team of senior leaders who imparted through their company commanders and senior noncommissioned officers an esprit that developed into an especially strong cohesiveness, a quality that distinguished the Gimlets from some other regiments when the fighting began in Korea.[11]

Among the junior leaders, officers of the grade first lieutenant and above were rich in combat service. Most of the NCOs were also World War II veterans. The other ranks were a mixed bag, mostly young soldiers who had been lured into the Army by the generous GI Bill. Their motivations had much to do with postservice education and low-interest loans and little to do with being prepared for battle. There were some "hard cases" as well among the lower ranks, as one would expect to find in a peacetime army. Many of these men moved frequently into and out of the stockade. Adventurous almost to a fault, they were often a valuable resource once the fighting began.[12]

Late in 1946, the wives and children of officers and NCOs began to arrive in Japan, and life in the "colonial army" took on traditional form. The social routine that developed was similar in every way to patterns in the Philippines and China before World War II. Virtually overnight, the Occupation Army became a nine-to-four organization. Officers and NCOs led comfortable lives in adequate, though not lavish, quarters, served by Japanese. Maj. Floyd Martin, the 1st Battalion executive officer, was offered three servants—the standard allotment for his rank—but wanted only two. Such a reaction was rare, and Martin had to argue long and hard before he won his case for a reduced staff. Rounds of dinner parties and Saturday nights at the officers' and NCO clubs brightened the men's lives. And once a month the officers and their wives dressed formally for a "Regimental Hail and Farewell."[13] The outcome was predictable: strong bonds of friendship and shared experiences united the officers and NCOs.[14]

For young soldiers of the other ranks, life in Japan was an adventure. Not only were they learning to live in the Army, but a new and strange culture beckoned just outside the camp gates.[15] While the officers and NCOs visited Kumamoto whenever they could escape the prying eyes of the military police, many young privates lived with Japanese women just outside the camp and thoroughly enjoyed life in that charming land. Their only natural enemy was venereal disease, and in most units this was dealt with privately by a discreet battalion surgeon and his staff of understanding medics. Not all, however, enjoyed such salutory neglect. In the 34th Infantry regiment, the regimental commander decided to stamp out V.D. once and for all. To an increasing degree, men of the 34th found themselves restricted to their post, treated more as prisoners than as soldiers. As a result, morale plummeted in the 34th, the regiment's performance deteriorated, and the regimental commander eventually lost his job.[16] Not surprisingly, when the 34th went into action in Korea, its performance was far worse than that of the 21st and the 19th Infantry regiments.

Heavy drinking was a problem in all units and all ranks. Boredom, loneliness, and old habits learned in the war took their toll. To combat the "soldiers' disease," sports became a focal point of regimental life. Good athletes were recruited—even "Shanghaied"—into the regiment to build football, basketball, baseball, track, and boxing teams. "Big Six" Stephens was a great sports lover, and the rest of the Gimlets shared his enthusiasm and supported their teams fully. Every Saturday during football season, the whole regiment turned out for the games. In 1949, the Gimlet football team won the division championship, and the regiment looked forward to another big season in 1950. Athletes were given a favored status and wide publicity, particularly members of championship teams. While they trained as all other soldiers, much of their time was spent in practice and on "special duty."[17] Nevertheless, on balance, a successful sports program probably reinforced a good climate of leadership, such as existed in the 21st.

Training for the troops was about as good as could be expected under conditions in Japan. For example, in 1948 and much of 1949, the strength of the 1st Battalion, 21st Infantry, was so low that meaningful training was virtually impossible. Company B was the only company that had enough people to permit daily training. Companies A and C had few people but joined Company B for training whenever possible. Company D was kept at full strength, but it was the military police company with full-time occupation duties. Company D rarely if ever trained with the battalion. Training, therefore, was confined to individual and some squad-level tactical exercises.[18]

In the spring of 1949, the 3d Battalion was a battalion in name only. There was no battalion staff, and the companies were manned by small cadres that served as caretakers. Kenwood Ross, formerly the 24th Division ordnance officer, recalled that in his periodic inspections he was often met at the first company of a battalion by the supply officer or motor officer, depending on the nature of the inspection. At the next company, the same officer would again meet him, and they would go through the same routine. Ross knew one officer who served as motor officer for three companies.[19] Ross complained that between 1945 and 1947, "we saw nothing but an exodus of the WWII veteran and his replacement, if at all, by a youthful, inexperienced boy. Small wonder that here were the makings of (three) weak divisions—the 24th, the 1st Cav, the 25th—which three years later would be ill prepared for what followed.''[20]

Soon after General Walker assumed command of Eighth Army in 1949, combat units received fillers, and the two battalions of the 21st Infantry swelled nearly to full strength.[21] Walker intended that Eighth Army no longer be an easygoing colonial army. He had successfully commanded one of General George Patton's corps in Europe and was an experienced and aggressive combat commander who knew how to train an army for war. His goal was to develop combined arms teams of infantry, armored, and artillery units working closely together at the company and battalion levels. Despite Walker's good intentions, such was not to be. Foremost among obstacles to effective combined-arms training was lack of training areas where units could shoot and maneuver. Japan was simply too populous to set aside precious land for such purposes. This prevented Eighth Army from holding regimental, divisional, or army exercises. Smaller areas, such as Mori on Kyushu, permitted limited maneuver of infantry battalions and artillery live fire but not simultaneously. In turn, lack of training space led to organizational changes. Because it was impossible for infantry regiments stationed in postage-stamp garrisons like Camp Wood to train with their organic tank companies, the tanks were eliminated from the tables of organization. Because the Army could not exercise larger units, other than by command-post exercises, Eighth Army's two corps headquarters, the Army's tactical control headquarters, were deactivated in April 1950. They were sorely missed in Korea and had to be reactivated in the summer in order to control combat operations. The absence of a third battalion in each regiment and its slice of supporting artillery had an equally important but as yet unforeseen result: the regiments of the 24th Division were never able to employ a strong reserve once they were committed to battle in Korea.[22]

At the battalion level, the consequences of lack of training were grave. The 21st Infantry had never maneuvered with live artillery and had no experience with tanks. Tactical training was confined to squad, platoon, and some company exercises in the small training areas beyond the limits of the city of Kumamoto. Even there, Japanese farmers began to encroach on the training reservation. In the 52d Artillery, the firing batteries were severely limited in live-fire exercises. The battalion could schedule only one trip a year to the Mori training area where it enjoyed sufficient space to shoot its 105-mm howitzers.[23]

Nevertheless, those things that could be practiced in garrison were done well. At Camp Wood, Colonel Stephens formed the Gimlets for physical training immediately after reveille each day. At 0730, the battalion fell out to follow the daily training schedule. Companies and platoons went to classes on a wide variety of subjects: communications, demolitions, mines and booby traps, field fortifications, flame weapons, weapons marksmanship, crew drill on crew-served weapons, and the inevitable close-order drill to reinforce discipline and prepare for Saturday morning parades. Practical exercises and training followed the classes. Recoilless rifles and 60-mm, 81-mm, and 4.2-inch mortar firing suffered from lack of ranges in the same ways as did artillery, so training concentrated on developing skills by crew drill and dry-firing exercises. In the 52d Artillery, the training was thorough but limited to communications, survey techniques, and the "cannoneer's hop" in which all members of the gun crew practiced each other's jobs under the watchful eye of the NCO in charge.[24]

Good as training could be in the hands of combat-experienced officers and NCOs, more often it fell short for a variety of reasons. No matter how skilled soldiers might be as individuals, they could not compensate for unit weakness. General Walker prescribed larger unit-training exercises, and most battalions in Eighth Army had progressed to the Army Training Test by the time the war broke out. Unfortunately and not surprisingly, many failed, chiefly because they could not adequately prepare. Both battalions of the 21st Infantry passed, but those of the trouble-ridden 34th Infantry failed.[26] Even in the 21st Infantry, a strong regiment, the inability to practice as battalions was crucially important in the transition to combat virtually overnight. There had been too few opportunities to iron out familiar working relationships, coordinations, standard operating procedures, resupply techniques, fire support, ammunition handling, and the myriad other arrangements that are so important in combat. Many otherwise-well-trained soldiers paid a bloody price for their regiments' lost opportunities.

Without exaggerating, it could be said that Eighth Army units were bordering on being unready for war. Even from the standpoint of materiel, the picture was not much better. All divisions in Eighth Army had old, worn equipment dating from World War II. Each lacked .30-caliber machine guns, spare machine-gun barrels, machine-gun tripods, mortar components, 57-mm recoilless rifles, all of their 90-mm antitank guns, and many radios. When Task Force Smith assembled for its move to Korea, other units of the 21st anteed up weapons and equipment to fill the 1st Battalion. When Company K arrived in Korea a week later, it carried two 81-mm mortar baseplates and two tubes but no bipods or sights. That company had no recoilless rifles either. The jeep taken to Korea by the Weapons Platoon of Company K was privately owned by one of the privates in the platoon.[27] Only thirteen high-explosive, antitank (HEAT) artillery rounds were to be found in the division, and they were given to the 52d Artillery for use with TF Smith.[28]

In the end, then, problems encountered during the first battle in Korea came down to training areas, shortages, and the distractions of colonial life in Japan. Because, as knowledgeable and skillful as were the officers and NCOs, few of them or their soldiers seriously believed that war was likely. The best of the leaders—Walker, Stephens, and Smith—knew that war was possible and fought against the obstacles. Others went through the motions and achieved a fatal sameness in training for lack of interest. In the end, none of these units, not even the Gimlets, was initially able to stop the enemy.

Moving south on a broad front, the North Koreans pressed the main attack to Seoul and to the Han River *(see Map 9.1)*. By 30 June, they were ready to cross. To slow them, the South Koreans blew up bridges and laid antitank minefields on all likely routes leading south from the river. Soon after daylight on the thirtieth, North Korean artillery pounded South Korean positions two miles east of Seoul and, under this cover, crossed an infantry company. Nevertheless, for three days, their advance slowed markedly until they could build a tank force on the south side of the river. The delay occurred partly because the South Koreans were beginning to recuperate. After the first few days of the war, particularly after the North Koreans lost their advantage in the air, the South Koreans pulled themselves together and began inflicting heavy casualties on the invaders.

On 4 July, the main body of North Koreans once again broke loose and rolled into Suwon in the west while another 20,000 captured Yoju and Wonju in the center. On the east coast, a ground column of some 10,000 men linked up with the amphibious force at Samch'ok. Their objective was Pusan, the only port left that could accommodate the entry of modern military forces in numbers large enough to affect the outcome of the war. The race for this decisive objective between North Korean forces, which were a mere 200 miles to its north, and American forces in Japan depended on MacArthur's ability to marshal and move enough combat troops to delay the North Koreans while the Joint Chiefs rushed reinforcements from the United States, sixteen sailing days away.

Initially, MacArthur's greatest advantage lay with his air and naval units. Aircraft from the Far East Air Force and the Navy soon controlled the sky and provided close air support to Korean army units, delaying, though not stopping, the enemy. By 3 July, Australian air units had joined a growing UN air force. Carrier-launched naval aircraft struck targets in North Korea on 4–5 July. Surface forces quickly assembled in Korean waters and secured the sea routes between Japan and Korea. From the very first, naval units functioned on a full wartime footing against air, surface, and undersea threats. On 1 July, the president ordered a blockade of the North Korean coast south of the 41st parallel on the east coast and 39° 30' on the west, well south of Manchuria and the Soviet Union. Thereafter, naval patrols prevented the infiltration of troops and supplies from the north and blocked transfer of supplies from China and the USSR to North Korea through its northern ports. But to stop the enemy short of Pusan, MacArthur needed more infantry on the westernmost enemy axis of advance.

It was for this purpose that MacArthur alerted the 24th Division to start moving to Korea. Maj. Gen. William F. Dean, commanding general of the 24th, received orders to send an infantry-artillery task force to Korea immediately. It was to be followed as quickly as possible by the rest of the division. Dean selected the 21st Infantry to provide the infantry and the 52d Artillery to send the guns because, being on Kyushu, they were closest to Korea. At 2245 on 30 June, Colonel Stephens, the regimental commander, received orders to send an infantry battalion to Itazuke Air Base for airlift to Pusan, Korea. Stephens telephoned Smith at his quarters and ordered him to prepare his battalion for movement. The 1st Battalion was to be reinforced by the 75-mm Recoilless Rifle Platoon (two guns) of Company M and two mortar platoons from the Mortar Company, as well as a battery of artillery from the 52d.[29] Moreover, the battalion received officers, NCOs, and other specialists from the 3d Battalion and other regimental and divisional units to fill under-strength units where needed. Lt. Carl Bernard and Lt. Ollie Conners, members of the 3d Battalion, assisted Lt. Col. Smith with the outloading at the airfield. Both were "abducted" by Smith when the task force actually took off for Korea. After fighting the first battle with Task Force Smith at Osan, Bernard returned to 3d Battalion, but Conners stayed with the 1st.[30] Such intermixing was not uncommon, and the unfamiliarity of some officers and NCOs with their men was initially to have a harmful effect on the way the task force performed.

By 0920 on 1 July, the battalion had arrived at Itazuke Air Base and was awaiting air lift. The wait turned out to be longer than expected, for heavy weather closed in at dawn. The first three aircraft that attempted the flight turned back when they found the airport at Pusan closed by low clouds and heavy rain.[31] The weather was to lighten sufficiently later in the morning to permit part of the battalion to fly to Pusan, but the storm over East Asia plagued combat operations for several days. As the sky cleared briefly, Air Force C-54 transports began slipping into Pusan, the first at 1100. Smith arrived at the head of Companies B and C, two of the recoilless rifles, two of the 4.2-inch mortars, half of his Headquarters Company, and half of the Communications Platoon. The task force quickly formed a truck convoy to the Pusan railway station. There they immediately boarded trains and headed north to Taejon, arriving the next morning. The remainder of the 1st Battalion stayed at Itazuke in Japan under the command of Capt. John Alkire, Company D commander. Later on 1 July, the rear half of the battalion moved to Fukuoka where it boarded a ship and sailed for Pusan.[32]

Before leaving Itazuke, Smith first learned what he was to do in Korea. General Dean told Smith to head for Taejon and stop the North Koreans as far north of Pusan as possible. Dean regretted that he had no more information than that, but Brig. Gen. John H. Church, commander of MacArthur's Advance Command and Liaison Group in Korea (ADCOM), would provide detailed intelligence and instructions when the two met in Taejon. On the morning of 2 July, General Church pointed to his map and told Smith that there was a "little action" north of Suwon and that the Americans were "to support the ROKs [soldiers of the Republic of Korea] and give them moral support." According to Church, "All we need is some men up there who won't run when they see tanks."[33] Church's confidence was shared by the Gimlets. Once the North Koreans realized that Americans had arrived, they would soon lose their zest for fighting. In a couple of weeks, they would all be back in Kumamoto.

Smith decided to rest his men while he moved forward with a small command group to reconnoiter the ground. As he proceeded north of Taejon, he issued at least three combat orders on as many terrain features that might serve as possible defensive sites. Thus it was that he found himself finally on top of the scrubby hill, about three miles north of Osan, looking for a way to give moral and other support to South Korean troops, allies he had neither seen nor talked to. From his vantage point, about 300 feet above the valley floor, Smith saw a road and railroad heading off to the northwest (see map 9.2). The hill on which he stood extended to his left and right, forming a low ridge perpendicular to the road. About a mile and a quarter to his front, the railroad parted from the road and swung around the east end of the ridge before rejoining the road less than a mile to the south. Observation and fields of fire over the principal high-speed avenues of approach were excellent, though concealment was poor. Smith could see almost all the way to Suwon, eight miles to the north. This, he decided, would be his initial defensive position.[34]

Returning to Taejon, Smith reported favorably on the Osan position to General Church. He was then instructed to start his men north by train to P'yongt'aek and Ansong, both south of Osan. There a company at each town dug in to await further orders. Brig. Gen. George B. Barth, acting assistant division commander, told Smith that General Church wanted him to move that night to the hill north of Osan. On 4 July, Smith reunited his two rifle companies and linked up with Battery A and the Headquarters and Service Battery of the 52d Field Artillery Battalion in P'yongt'aek before moving on to Osan. Smith and the artillery battalion commander, Lt. Col. Miller O. Perry, along with General Barth, went forward for a final reconnaissance of the Osan position and to select firing positions for the six 105-mm howitzers of Battery A. En route, the small reconnaissance party prevented skittish South Korean demolition teams from blowing up bridges that would have cut the road in and out of Osan.[35] Preventing premature blowing of the bridges was just the first of a series of uncoordinated problems encountered by the 21st Infantry. They could not make direct contact with responsible ROK Army headquarters. Subsequently, South Korean truck drivers abandoned their vehicles; railroad engineers backed their trains away from imagined dangers; and no one seemed capable of controlling refugees and keeping military routes cleared.

All the while, Korean soldiers identified as friendly could be seen moving within hailing distance but under no apparent control. On the other hand, South Korean troops—as well as Americans—were strafed by U.S. Air Force and Australian jets. In the early days, Korea was a poor example of coalition and joint coordination.

Just after midnight, Task Force Smith followed its commander north through steady rain to engage a still-unseen enemy. Working its way slowly through southbound mobs of retreating ROK soldiers and fleeing civilians, the truck convoy arrived at the ridge about 0300 on the fifth. Company B began to dig in on the left, including within its sector the main road, and Company C deployed to the right, positioning a platoon to the rear, in effect refusing the right flank (see Map 9.2). Each company received a 75-mm recoilless rifle, and the two 4.2-inch mortars were in general support about 400 yards behind Company B in the center of the battalion. In all, the front covered by the two companies was just under a mile in width. The artillery battery went into position west of the road about 2,000 yards behind the infantry. Perry placed one of his howitzers in an antitank role north of the battery and covered the road as it cut through Smith's ridge line. By first light on the fifth, all units were in place but not completely dug in. The artillerymen registered their guns, and the infantrymen cleaned and test fired their weapons. Seeking shelter from the constant rain, the Americans ate their morning C-rations and waited for the enemy.

There was hardly time. About 0700, Smith spotted a column of eight tanks on the road, which he correctly assumed were enemy. Calling for artillery fire, the task force commander took the tanks under fire about 2,000 yards to his front (see Map 9.2). The tanks, however, moved aggressively through the artillery, undamaged and probably unaware that they were fast approaching an American position. On they came, straight up the road, unimpeded by gunfire and safe from the unseen perils of antitank mines—for Task Force Smith had none in Korea. As the tanks neared 700 yards from the waiting task force, infantrymen manning the 75-mm recoilless rifles fired their weapons. Disregarding direct hits by the 75s, the tanks crept up the road to the crest of the ridge until the lead tanks came under the concentrated but ineffective fire of 2.36-inch rocket launchers. Once they had crested the ridge and started down the reverse slope, enemy tanks started taking hits from the 105-mm howitzer firing HEAT rounds from its antitank position in the rear. Although the 2.36-inch bazookas had not hurt the tanks, the artillery was another matter.[36] Apparently damaged, the two lead tanks pulled off the road and stopped. The crews of the two tanks jumped out, one surrendering and the other firing automatic weapons, inflicting the first American fatality of the war. The following tanks passed through the task-force position, firing as they drove by but not stopping to trade blows. Other tanks moving in smaller groups trailed the first six through the position and on south toward the 52d

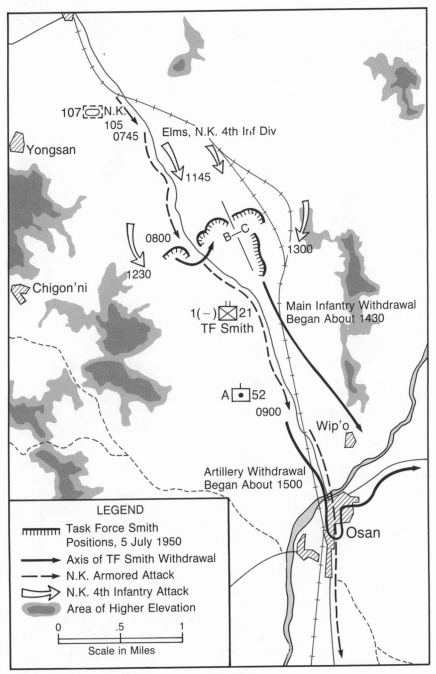

107 [⊖] N.K.
105
0745

Yongsan

Elms, N.K. 4th Inf Div

1145

0800

B — C

1300

Chigon'ni

1230

1(−) [⊠] 21
TF Smith

Main Infantry Withdrawal
Began About 1430

A [▣] 52
0900

Wip'o

Artillery Withdrawal
Began About 1500

Osan

LEGEND

⫼⫼⫼ Task Force Smith
Positions, 5 July 1950

→ Axis of TF Smith Withdrawal

--→ N.K. Armored Attack

⇨ N.K. 4th Infantry Attack

Area of Higher Elevation

0   .5   1

Scale in Miles

Map 9.2. Task Force Smith at Osan, 5 July 1950

Artillery positions. Once again, the North Korean tankers sought only to suppress the fire of the American howitzers in their effort to strike south to Osan and beyond. Unable to stop the tanks with high-explosive rounds, their only remaining ammunition, the artillerymen employed 2.36-inch bazookas. Here they were able to stop two more of the tanks by hitting their tracks.

By the time the armored rush was finished, some thirty-three tanks had tried to pass to the south. All but four had succeeded. About twenty of Smith's infantrymen were killed or wounded in the tank fight. Colonel Perry, a fearless and respected officer, was wounded in the leg but refused to leave the field or give up command of the artillery. Perry's heroic leadership extended to his officers and noncommissioned officers, who continued to serve the pieces after some of their men fled in momentary panic.[37] Inspired by the example of their officers and NCOs, the young artillerymen took heart and rejoined those who had stayed with the guns. But not much was left. The tanks had destroyed Perry's antitank howitzer, the remaining rounds of HEAT exploded, and its crew fell wounded. All the parked vehicles behind the infantry position were in flames or disabled. But worst of all, communication wire lines between the artillery and the infantry had been broken by the tanks. Radios had gone dead early in the action, so now Smith could no longer call for artillery fire. All the gunners could do was fire interdictory rounds at likely target locations. Damaged but not defeated, with enemy tanks somewhere in its rear, Task Force Smith awaited the next blow from North Korean infantry.

For about an hour, between 0900 and 1000, the front was quiet. Working energetically in the steady rain, the men improved their holes and prepared for the fight they knew was coming. No longer did anyone on that ridge expect the North Koreans to lose nerve at the sight of Americans. Major Martin, the executive officer, moved the ammunition to a central area within the battalion defensive position. Martin was anxious to protect his few reserves because he had no idea how or where he could find any more.[38] From his observation post, Smith gazed intently into the misty rain searching for telltale movement that would signal the advance of hostile infantry. Experienced as the battalion commander was, he was not prepared for what happened next. Emerging from the distant haze near Suwon, he saw three tanks leading a long convoy of trucks and a seemingly endless column of marching infantry. For an hour, the unbroken column marched toward the Americans until, Smith estimated finally, it stretched for about six miles. Here, indeed, was the main enemy column.

Smith and his increasingly apprehensive men held their fire until the leading tanks reached a point about 1,000 yards from the ridge (see Map 9.2). At that moment, Smith fired all the mortars and direct-fire weapons he had at the advancing troops. The enemy took a terrible beating but managed to set up a base of fire with the three tanks, dismount and deploy infantry into covered positions beside the road, and begin to move toward the defending

Americans. Heavy direct fire from Task Force Smith prevented a frontal approach, and the enemy moved around the position as if to conduct a double envelopment. To the west of the road, an enemy force seized a dominating hill top overlooking Company B's left flank. Smith immediately pulled the flank platoon across the road to rejoin its parent company. Enemy soldiers soon appeared on the high ground to the right of Company C and delivered heavy machine-gun fire into that flank as well. Because communications back to the 52d Artillery were still out, there was no chance of defeating the enveloping forces with artillery fire. Small-arms ammunition was low. Ever more enemy artillery and mortar fire pounded the Americans in their holes. Enemy troops began to work their way toward the rear, and still that enormous column of uncommitted infantry stood waiting for orders along the road to the front. The time was 1430. With no way to communicate with headquarters, far to the south, and no reinforcements or supplies on the way, Smith decided that his small command had done all it could do. Task Force Smith had halted the enemy column, forced its deployment, and cost the enemy unexpected casualties and delay. Now the Americans were being encircled. It was time—perhaps past time—to abandon any thoughts of holding at all cost; it was time to withdraw.

Withdrawing under fire in daylight is a most difficult and dangerous maneuver, and this time it proved particularly tough. Task Force Smith had to break contact without the means to cover its withdrawal with concentrated artillery fires. But remaining in place was by far the least attractive alternative. Smith decided, therefore, to withdraw through successive positions. Company C was to be first off; Company B initially was to cover the rest of the battalion. The infantryman were to withdraw toward Osan following the high ground just west of the railroad. Smith sent Company C and the rest of his men off the ridge while he stayed with Company B. Enemy pressure was intense because Smith had waited so long to withdraw. The position was already virtually overrun, and there was no chance to make a fighting withdrawal. Some of the soldiers fell back, leaving their crew-served weapons behind; others left their rifles.[39] Once the men had abandoned their weapons, an orderly withdrawal was impossible, and the men of Company C broke up into small groups seeking safety. Not surprisingly, their dead and some wounded also were left behind. When Company B pulled off, Smith moved back toward the 52d Artillery where he picked up Perry and his artillerymen. Removing the gun sights and breechblocks, Perry's men moved back to their trucks in Osan. Discovering only minor damage to the vehicles, they formed a small convoy and carefully circled east and then south toward Ansong, avoiding enemy tanks along the main road[40] (see Map 9.2). As the convoy drove to the rear, trucks picked up scattered infantrymen who were making their way cross country. Fortunately, the North Koreans chose not to pursue aggressively.

Night fell, offering greater security to the fugitives. Next morning, 6 July, Task Force Smith drove to Ch'onan and rendezvoused with more survivors from Company C. Task Force Smith now numbered only 250 men, just over half its original strength. During the next few days, the list of survivors lengthened as others made their way to safety, some performing heroic feats in their efforts to avoid capture and return to their own lines. Dusty Rhodes, an infantryman with Company B, was wounded lightly early in the fight and had gone back to the aid station for treatment. There he saw North Korean soldiers threatening the wounded. He and a companion decided to forego treatment and continue to the rear, however painful their wounds.[41] The final count of missing was 148 soldiers and 5 officers. Task Force Smith's withdrawal finally ended back at Taejon where it reorganized, reequipped, and prepared to return to the fight.

As Task Force Smith had ridden the rails north to Taejon on 2 July, the 34th Infantry regiment, also of the 24th Division and under command of Col. Jay B. Lovless, arrived by ship at Pusan. It was still raining and cold. On 4 July, the 34th moved north by rail. Passing through Taejon, the 1st Battalion continued on to P'yongt'aek, and the 3d turned off at Ansong, some twelve miles to the east (see Map 9.3). Just as their comrades in the 21st had been, the men of the 34th Infantry were confident, even unconcerned, boasting that the North Koreans would soon run when they realized they were fighting Americans. They, too, expected a quick return to Japan.

General Dean had given the regiment the mission of holding a line from Asan Bay, a major barrier that narrowed the front west of P'yongt'aek, to Ansong. The regiment was to block roads leading south using the same general positions first occupied by the two companies of Task Force Smith. As the survivors of Task Force Smith made their way south to Ch'onan, the 1st and 3d Battalions of the 34th Infantry formed thin lines, widely separated, with no reserves to meet the tanks and infantry that had overrun Smith's command. By this time, the fate of Task Force Smith was known among the senior officers, and General Barth, acting as assistant division commander, told commanders of the 34th to hold as long as they could but "not to end up like Brad Smith" if threatened with isolation. The purpose now was to gain time by delaying in successive positions.[42] For some reason, officers did not transmit the significance of the action at Osan to their subordinates. The men of the 34th continued in the belief that the "police action" would end quickly. Normal guard stood watch the night of 5 July.[43]

At P'yongt'aek, the 1st Battalion was the first of the 34th Infantry to confront North Korean tanks. The battalion, under command of Lt. Col. Harold B. Ayers, took a stand just north of the town. Although positioned along a small river, the battalion's defensive line was, according to Barth, weak with easily enveloped flanks.[44] At first light on the sixth, enemy tanks

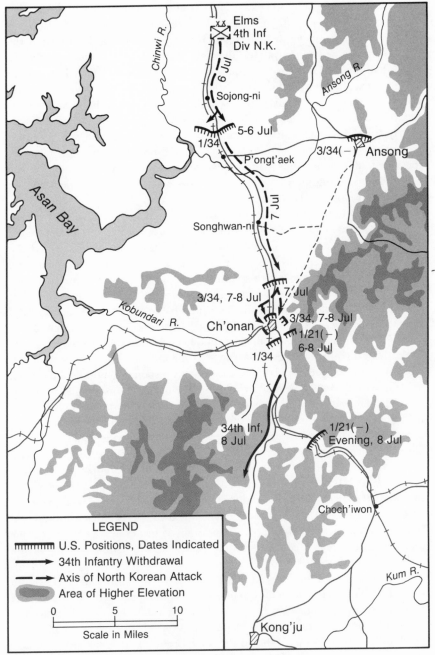

Chinwi R.

XX Elms
4th Inf
Div N.K.

6 Jul

Sojong-ni

5-6 Jul
1/34

P'ongt'aek

Ansong R.

3/34(−)   Ansong

Asan Bay

7 Jul

Songhwan-ni

Kobundari R.

3/34, 7-8 Jul

7 Jul

Ch'onan   3/34, 7-8 Jul

1/21(−)
6-8 Jul

1/34

34th Inf,
8 Jul

1/21(−)
Evening, 8 Jul

Choch'iwon

LEGEND

ꛛꛛꛛ U.S. Positions, Dates Indicated
→ 34th Infantry Withdrawal
⇢ Axis of North Korean Attack
▓ Area of Higher Elevation

0   5   10
Scale in Miles

Kum R.

Kong'ju

Map 9.3. Delaying Action, 34th Infantry, 5–8 July 1950

stopped at a blown railroad bridge in front of the American position. Unable to cross the intervening stream, the tanks—some thirteen could be counted—delivered supporting fire while North Korean infantry easily bypassed the bridge and fanned out to attack the defenders. Unlike Task Force Smith, which had inflicted numerous casualties on its enemy with spirited fire before falling back, the men of the 34th performed poorly. In Company A, it took fifteen minutes to build anything resembling an effective volume of fire. The regiment had had serious morale problems in Japan and was known to be poorly trained. Some of its officers were simply unfit for the task at hand. Colonel Lovless had commanded the regiment for only a short time following the relief of the previous commander and had to pay the price for the unfortunate timing of his assignment. Worse, Ayers had joined the 1st Battalion in Korea only days before.

Even though no effective fire slowed the enemy, the North Koreans halted after crossing the river to wait for their tanks to catch up. This gave the 1st Battalion a chance to break contact.[45] Satisfied that he had forced the enemy column to halt and deploy and without communications to regimental headquarters, Ayers ordered his companies to withdraw. By this time, the regimental S-3 had reached the command post of the 1st Battalion with orders from Lovless to hold as long as possible without endangering the battalion and then to withdraw to positions near Ch'onan. Ayers was to decide when to pull out. His decision already made, Ayers and his battalion were soon on the road back to Ch'onan in complete disarray.[46] In the meantime, the 3d Battalion at Ansong was also marching back to Ch'onan in response to regimental orders.

General Dean had wanted to hold the P'yongt'aek–Ansong line as long as he could. He was angry that his plans to delay farther north had failed. Dean nevertheless accepted the reality of enemy superiority and the failure of his own men and set about preparing a new scheme to slow the enemy advance. Ch'onan turned out to be the first place where elements of the 24th Division could concentrate in any strength. With the arrival of Companies C and D and Battalion Headquarters Company of the 1st Battalion, 21st Infantry, and the two battalions of the 34th Infantry, a new defensive position took shape (see Map 9.3). Even so, Dean was still smoldering at the precipitous withdrawal of the 34th Infantry and unwilling to sit and wait; so he ordered a battalion of the 34th forward to regain contact with the enemy and to fight a delaying action back to Ch'onan.[47]

Without hesitation, the 3d Battalion under Lt. Col. David H. Smith moved back north in search of the enemy, a task that proved to be surprisingly difficult. As the infantrymen marched along the road, they had to push their way through crowds of refugees fleeing south out of the area of danger. Just north of Ch'onan, troops of the 3d Battalion began to dig a defensive position on what appeared to be strong terrain with excellent fields of fire. But when Maj. John J. Dunn, the regimental S-3, arrived at the battalion defensive lines, he found troops withdrawing for no apparent reason and moving back south. Because he could not find the battalion commander and S-3 with the forward units, Dunn returned to the battalion command post to report the new development. Then, with considerable difficulty, Dunn headed the men back north to the position they had just vacated. As Dunn drove back to the position by jeep, he, the battalion S-3, and two company commanders were ambushed and badly wounded. The leading rifle company just to Dunn's rear formed a front toward the sound of gunfire and returned fire. But instead of advancing to rescue the officers wounded in the ambush, Dunn heard an officer order the line to fall back. Dunn, who was captured, recalled years afterward that the American force was superior by far to the ambush party and that the main body of the enemy did not arrive for another two hours. All in all, Dunn was disgusted with the showing of the 34th. So was General Dean. Earlier he had relieved the unfortunate Colonel Lovless and replaced him with Col. Robert R. Martin, a soldier of great experience, known to Dean for his aggressiveness and personal courage in World War II.

As its lead rifle company fell back, the remainder of the 3d Battalion, by now in considerable disorder, also turned south once again, heading for Ch'onan. Ordered to defend Ch'onan, the battalion commander, Lieutenant Colonel Smith, finally halted the 3d Battalion and took up a position along the northwest edge of the town (see Map 9.3). To its south, a newly arrived battery of artillery prepared to support the 34th. Just before midnight on the seventh, the battery fired its first fire mission against tanks and infantry east of Ch'onan. Martin personally led a small party of infantry into the town to contact the enemy. As he and his men engaged enemy tanks in the streets of Ch'onan, Martin grabbed a 2.36-inch bazooka and attacked the tanks. From a tiny hut, he personally confronted an enemy tank. The tank fired first, and Martin died on the spot. Thereafter, confusion swept the men of the 34th as the North Koreans built their strength. Under cover of an artillery white-phosphorus smoke screen, the survivors of the 3d Battalion evacuated Ch'onan, leaving their mortars, machine guns, and all but 175 of their comrades. Lieutenant Colonel Smith collapsed from exhaustion and returned to Japan. Neither the battalion nor its commander had withstood the rigors of combat. The regiment, too, left Ch'onan, to join the 21st Infantry in fighting a delaying action back to the Kum River. Dean had decided to make a stand along the river barrier.

Dean's intention was to withdraw to a division defensive position along the south side of the Kum River in order to hold the city of Taejon to the south. The 34th and the 21st were to withdraw simultaneously on parallel roads, delaying the enemy at successive strong points as they fell back (see Map 9.3). Upon reaching the Kum River, Dean hoped to consolidate these two regiments with the 19th Infantry in a force sufficiently strong to hold the line. In the withdrawal, the two regiments were to be supported by the first M24 light tanks to arrive in Korea, 105- and 155-mm artillery, and combat engineers. Because antitank mines were now available, the roads were to be blocked and bridges prepared for demolition. Just south of Ch'onan, the highway split, one branch running south to Kongju and the Kum River and the main road running southeast to Choch'iwon and then on to the Kum. Dean ordered the 34th Infantry to delay along the Kongju road and the 21st along the Choch'iwon road. Because the 34th was so badly hurt after the fight at Ch'onan, Dean relied on the newly arrived 21st, commanded by Colonel Stephens, for the main delay and to protect the supply line to the ROK I Corps to the northeast. To accomplish these tasks, Dean attached the 52d Artillery Battalion, a company of tanks from the 78th Tank Battalion, and a company of the 3d Engineer Battalion to the 21st.[48] Moving on to Choch'iwon with the 3d Battalion on 7 July, Stephens attempted to consolidate his regiment and the attached units in an effective series of delaying positions. For this, the regimental commander had to rely on the 3d Battalion and Companies A and D of the 1st Battalion.

Stephens reconnoitered north of Choch'iwon as soon as his train arrived in that town. Upon his return, he ordered Lieutenant Colonel Jensen's 3d Battalion to move into defensive positions on the northern outskirts of Choch'iwon. The next morning, Jensen advanced some six miles north of the town. Also on 8 July, after their return from Ch'onan, Stephens placed Companies A and D of the 1st Battalion on a ridge line covering the road, just east of Chonui, a short distance north of the 3d Battalion (see Map 9.4). During the late afternoon, General Dean sent Stephens a message confirming his oral orders to hold Choch'iwon until forced out by the enemy. A short time later, a second message arrived from Dean directing the 21st to hold Choch'iwon at all costs; the town would not be abandoned until the ROK Corps on the right had fallen back. Moreover, no help would be available to the 21st for at least four days.[49] Stephens immediately began detailed fire planning and registration of artillery and mortars. On 9 July, the engineers blew up a railroad bridge and a highway bridge north of Chonui to slow North Korean tanks. To assure better control of tactical air strikes, Stephens requested and received attachment of an air-ground support team. Within the regimental command post, the adjutant began organizing headquarters personnel into a tactical unit to defend the command post in case of a wide envelopment. Stephens then evacuated all civilians from the town of Choch'iwon in order to clear the area of potential refugees and also to remove all able-bodied men and women who might be North Korean guerrillas or spies.[50] Stephens intended to make a fight for Choch'iwon.

Action began about 1645 on the ninth in front of Companies A and D. Captain Alkire, who was still commanding the rear half of the 1st Battalion, spotted eleven tanks and several hundred infantry to his front (see Map 9.4). Alkire called for air strikes and artillery. The close air support was effective,

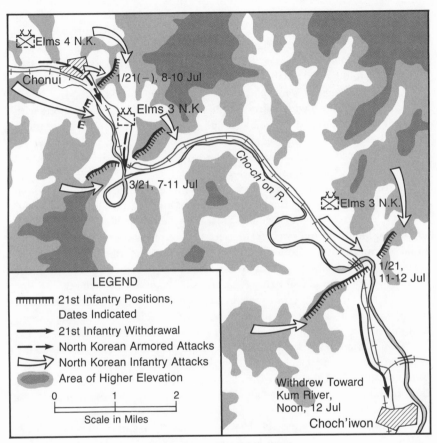

Map 9.4. Delaying Action, 21st Infantry, 8–12 July 1950

and five of the tanks were left burning. Subsequent air strikes along the road northwest of Chonui badly damaged a column of North Korean trucks and tanks. Sensing that the forward position was the place to be, Stephens moved forward to spend the night with Companies A and D.[51]

As dawn broke on the tenth, the valley and hills to the front were covered with a dense fog limiting observation of the North Korean approach. At 0600, the enemy moved out of close-in assembly areas with tanks and infantry against the forward edge of Companies A and D. About twenty tanks and 2,000 to 3,000 infantry moved against both the left and right flanks of the two companies. Four tanks pushed through the American lines and disappeared into the fog in the rear. Small-arms fire broke out on the left against Company A. At first, the enemy were held at bay by 4.2-inch mortar fire. But North Korean troops circled widely around the right flank and suddenly, along with the four tanks that had broken through, attacked the 4.2-inch mortars to silence them. Stephens had earlier lost telephone contact with the mortars, and now his radio communications were out as well. The mortarmen not killed abandoned their guns and ran for safety.

Artillery still delivered effective fire and turned back an attempted frontal attack. The attack against the left flank erupted anew about 1100 but was held in check by air strikes and artillery fire. Then, about 1130, friendly artillery fire began falling on the ridge. With wire torn out by the enemy tanks and no radio communication from the forward observers to the firing batteries, Stephens was cut off from the rear and unable to stop the fire. At about the same time, the men of Company A on the left began to run to the rear. Some formed a small perimeter, but most headed south. Stephens decided that with enemy tanks and infantry in his right rear and his left broken, it was time to pull out or lose everyone. At noon, he gave the order to fall back to the 3d Battalion. As small groups of infantrymen ran through the rice paddies to the rear, two American jet fighters strafed them, presuming the running figures were enemy. When the fugitives finally reached the lines of the 3d Battalion, they found their losses to be about 20 percent, the largest number from Company A.[52]

Immediately following the hasty withdrawal of Companies A and D, Colonel Stephens ordered the 3d Battalion to counterattack and retake the ridge. Lieutenant Colonel Jensen led the 3d Battalion forward and surprised the enemy, driving the North Koreans back nearly 2,000 yards. While in the forward position, Jensen looked for survivors from Companies A and D. He found ten. He also found six American soldiers with their hands tied, shot in the back of the head. About 2300, Stephens called Jensen and his battalion back to their original positions.[53] Upon arrival, Company K found enemy soldiers in their holes. It took another hour to clean them out and drive them off the hill. Companies A and D moved back to Choch'iwon where they rejoined the veterans of Task Force Smith. By 0730 on the eleventh, the 1st

Battalion was for the first time intact and manning a defensive line about two miles north of Choch'iwon.[54]

About the same time as Brad Smith was moving into his new position, the North Koreans hit the 3d Battalion *(see Map 9.4)*. In a carefully coordinated attack, the enemy first threw four tanks, about a thousand infantry, and heavy mortar fire at the battalion. Probably because some of their soldiers had occupied parts of the position the night before, enemy intelligence was especially good. The tanks once again drove straight through the infantry in search of the battalion rear. Infantry avoided the front in favor of bypassing the flanks in another double envelopment. As the attack progressed, enemy infantry strength increased to nearly 2,500. Enemy roadblocks prevented evacuation of the wounded and resupply of ammunition. Mortar fire fell steadily and was especially accurate, concentrating on the battalion and regimental CPs. The battalion's communication center exploded, as did the ammunition supply point. The 3d Battalion fought as long as it could, but before noon, it was surrounded, overrun, and ineffective. Then its men began to fight their way back to Choch'iwon in small groups.[55] In all, the battalion lost nearly 60 percent of its men, including Lieutenant Colonel Jensen, the battalion commander; the S-1; S-2; S-3; and the company commander of Company L. Of those few who escaped, 90 percent were without weapons, ammunition, canteens, helmets, and even shoes. In all, on 10–11 July, the 21st Infantry lost materiel and equipment of nearly two infantry battalions.

While the intensity of fighting in the sector of the 34th Infantry on the Kongju Road did not match that experienced by the 21st Infantry, the 1st Battalion of the 34th fought a series of delaying actions that paralleled the withdrawal of the 21st back to Choch'iwon. Enemy tactics were the same as those the 21st had faced, and the results uniformly favored the enemy, with one exception: in good weather, American units enjoyed the benefits of complete air superiority. The long lines of tanks, trucks, and infantry such as those dimly seen through the rain by Brad Smith in front of Osan were rich targets for fighter bombers of the Fifth Air Force and the Navy in clear skies. At Chonui and again at P'yongt'aek, UN pilots destroyed hundreds of massed vehicles along the P'yongt'aek-Chonui road. The effects of such serious losses were to accumulate as the days passed. Most importantly, UN control of the air forced the North Koreans to abandon daylight attacks in favor of night operations. Thereafter, enemy vehicles, weapons, and troop formations began to hide during the daylight and attack at night, a development that created a new set of problems for Eighth Army soldiers. Even with effective air support, the only hope for the men of the 24th Division was to retire behind the Kum River barrier. On 12 July, after a relatively brief delaying fight by the 1st Battalion, 21st Infantry, elements of the 21st and the 34th crossed the river.

Farther to the east, the newly arrived 25th Infantry Division was also drawing up to join in the fight. Moving from the vicinity of Osaka, Japan, the first of its regiments, the 27th's "Wolfhounds," moved to Andong northeast of Taegu in the east-central sector to back up ROK units fighting farther north. Within days, the 24th Infantry regiment and the 35th Infantry followed. General Dean, acting as overall commander until General Walker could establish his headquarters in Korea, ordered Maj. Gen. William B. Kean, commanding general of the 25th, to block the enemy drive coming from Ch'ungju *(see Map 9.5)*. This had the effect of drawing the 25th closer to the right (eastern) flank of the 24th Division as it stood behind the Kum River. It also permitted the 24th to move its 19th Infantry regiment into the defensive line behind the Kum River.[56] Such was the situation when Walker arrived in Korea on 13 July to take command of combat operations.

As Walker looked over the situation, the 24th Division defended his western (left) flank behind the Kum River *(see Map 9.5)*. The ROK 7th Division was no longer a factor. Across the river and slightly northeast were remnants of the ROK 1st, 2d, and Capital Divisions. East of this composite division were the ROK 6th Division, the ROK 8th Division, and, along the east coast, elements of the ROK 3d Division. Walker hoped that these scattered forces could hold a line across the peninsula by concentrating their resistance on the main roads that cut through the mountains toward Taegu, the port of P'ohang-dong, and the main port of Pusan. His hopes were severely jolted when the North Koreans easily crossed the Kum River around the flanks of the 24th Division.

When the 21st and 34th Infantry regiments found temporary refuge on the south side of the Kum River, they joined the third of the division's regiments, the 19th.[57] Dean ordered the battered 21st Infantry, a mere skeleton by this time, back to the Taejon airstrip. All that Stephens had left were 517 men in the 1st Battalion and 132 men in the 3d. He organized the survivors of the 3d Battalion into Companies K and M and attached them to the 1st Battalion. Another provisional group numbered 466 men. There was little they could do, so Dean put the Gimlets in reserve. At 0600 on 15 July, the 21st moved to a position at Orch'on about ten miles east of Taejon on the main Seoul-Pusan highway. There, it was to protect the rear of the 24th Division against a penetration of the ROK units to the east of Taejon. From its position high in the hills, the 21st was to sit out the Battle of the Kum River.

Pressed by the North Korean *4th Division,* the 3d Battalion, 34th Infantry, occupied low hills overlooking a blown highway bridge just north of the town of Kongju *(see Map 9.6)*. The 34th, almost as weak as the 21st, was in bad shape. After Colonel Martin had been killed, Lt. Col. Robert L. Wadlington, the executive officer, had taken command of the regiment. Soon after arriving at the Kum River, the S-2 and S-3 of the 34th regiment had to be evacuated

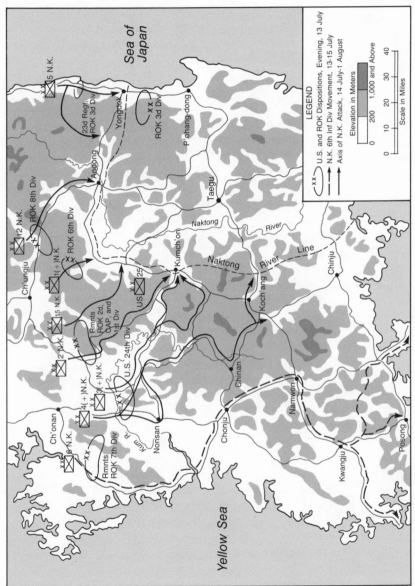

Map 9.5. The Front Moves South, 14 July–1 August 1950

LEGEND

xx U.S. and ROK Dispositions, Evening, 13 July

N.K. 6th Inf Div Movement, 13–15 July

Axis of N.K. Attack, 14 July–1 August

Elevation in Meters

0   200   1,000 and Above

0   10   20   30   40

Scale in Miles

Sea of Japan

Yellow Sea

5 N.K.

23d Regt, ROK 3d Div

Yongdok

ROK 3d Div

P'ohang-dong

ROK 8th Div

Andong

Taegu

12 N.K.

ROK 6th Div

Naktong   River

Ch'ungju

1(+) N.K.

US 25

Kumch'on

Naktong   River   Line

Chinju

15 N.K.

Rmnts ROK 2d, CAP, and 1st Div

Koch'ang

2 N.K.

U.S. 24th Div

Chinan

Ch'onan

4(+) N.K.

3(+) N.K.

Nonsan

Chonju

Namwon

6 N.K.

Rmnts ROK 7th Div

Kum   R.

Kwangju

Posong

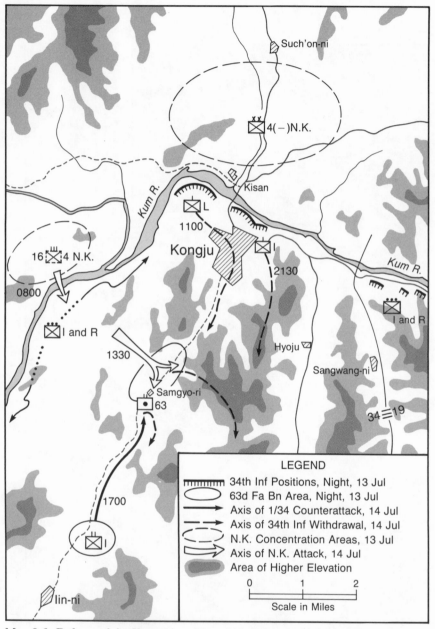

Map 9.6. Defense of the Kum River Line, 34th Infantry, 14 July 1950

for combat fatigue. Moreover, a composite force of forty men, comprising Company K, suffered from severe mental and physical fatigue and also had to be evacuated. Wadlington tried to cover all crossing sites over the Kum by placing the two companies of the 3d Battalion in front of the Kongju crossings and by stretching the Intelligence and Reconnaissance (I and R) Platoon several miles southwestward down the river. Wadlington's defense relied on the 1st Battalion, occupying a reserve area several miles south of Kongju, to provide depth to the position and to give him the ability to counterattack enemy bridgeheads. Good intentions and sound tactics were not enough to offset the lack of a third battalion. Once again, the under-strength American units were unable to handle the more numerous North Koreans. On 14 July, a regiment of the North Korean *4th Division* brushed aside patrols of I and R Platoon and moved immediately to attack the 63d Artillery Battalion's firing batteries south of Kongju. It then established a roadblock covering the road leading south from Kongju to the 1st Battalion position. Companies L and I of the 3d Battalion were no match for the North Korean assault forces crossing in the vicinity of Kongju. Company L gave up early in the day, and Company I held out until dusk. A counterattack by the 1st Battalion on the roadblock failed about 1700. With the withdrawal of Company I at 2130, the 34th Infantry sector of the Kum River line caved in.

On the right, the 19th Infantry stretched its line from where it tied into the 34th Infantry all the way to the ROK 2d Division on its east flank, covering some thirty miles of river front *(see Map 9.7)*. Col. Guy S. Meloy, Jr., concentrated his defense on the high ground overlooking the river above and below the village of Taep'yong-ni. Even though near full strength, Meloy could not hope to cover the entire front of thirty miles with his two battalions. With the collapse of the 34th Infantry on the left, the position was even more vulnerable, and Meloy sent Company G, reinforced with mortars, machine guns, tanks, and quad-.50s to that flank. But because the North Korean *3d Division* was probably concentrated to his front after following the 21st Infantry to the Kum, Meloy chose to concentrate his defense on the most likely crossing sites threatening the road leading south from Taep'yong-ni.

After initial probing efforts beginning on 14 July and lasting all day on the fifteenth, the North Koreans struck in full strength about 0300 on the sixteenth. Under cover of coordinated heavy indirect fire, enemy soldiers crossed on boats, rafts, and even by wading and swimming the 200 to 300 yards of water. They made successful crossings on the right in the gap between Companies C and E and on the left of Company B *(see Map 9.7)*. Once again, the North Koreans managed to use their favorite scheme of maneuver. Heavy fire and an infantry attack fixed the center of the 19th in position while enveloping forces skirted both flanks and headed for the American rear to attack mortars and artillery and to block the route of reinforcement and escape. Meloy and his men fought hard, but by 0630 the mortars and

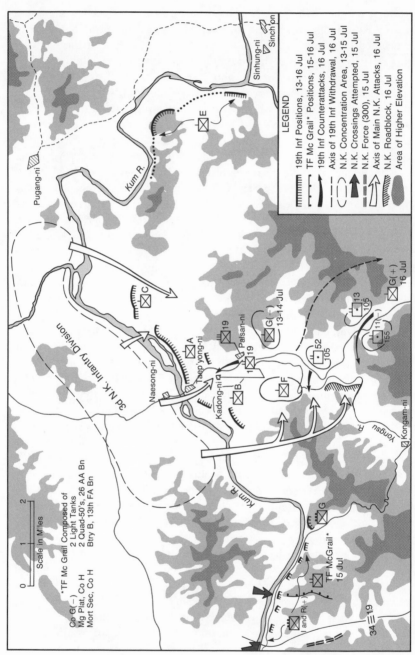

Map 9.7. Defense of the Kum River Line, 19th Infantry, 13–16 July 1950

LEGEND

19th Inf Positions, 13–16 Jul
TF Mc Grail* Positions, 15–16 Jul
19th Inf Counterattacks, 16 Jul
Axis of 19th Inf Withdrawal, 16 Jul
N.K. Concentration Area, 13–15 Jul
N.K. Crossings Attempted, 15 Jul
N.K. Force (300), 15 Jul
Axis of Main N.K. Attacks, 16 Jul
N.K. Roadblock, 16 Jul
Area of Higher Elevation

*TF Mc Grail Composed of
Co G(−)   2 Light Tanks
Mg Plat, Co H 2 Quad-50's, 26 AA Bn
Mort Sec, Co H Btry B, 13th FA Bn

Scale in Miles
0   1   2

3d N.K. Infantry Division

Kum R.
Kum R.
Yongsu R.

Sinch'on
Sinhung-ni
Pugang-ni
Naesong-ni
Taep'yong-ni
Kadong-ni
Paisan-ni
Kongam-ni

E
C
A
B
F
G
G
G(+) 16 Jul
G(−) 13–14 Jul

19
1 19

52 · 105
13 · 105
11 · 155

34 ≡ 19
TF McGrail*
15 Jul
I and R(+)

headquarters of the 1st Battalion in the center were under attack. A makeshift counterattacking force made up of headquarters officers, clerks, cooks, and mechanics, supported by a tank and a quad-.50 caliber antiaircraft artillery half-track, forced the enemy who had penetrated the center to withdraw back to the north side of the river. Still, the defense had been fatally penetrated on the left and right and could not hold much longer.

Enemy troops that crossed the river just west of Company B proved to be the main danger. As they worked their way south in the hills parallel to the main road, a small force turned east to attack Company F, the only regimental reserve, and fix it in position (see Map 9.7). The remainder of the North Koreans continued south where they encountered the guns of the 52d Artillery. Lieutenant Colonel Perry, still commanding the 52d though wounded fighting with Task Force Smith, took the enemy under direct fire with the guns of Battery B. Then, organizing a party of headquarters artillerymen and stray infantrymen, Perry led it against the attacking enemy soldiers and drove them further south. There, the enemy occupied a forty-foot bluff overlooking a sharp bend in the road constricted by the Yongsu River on the west and a steep slope on the east. From these positions dominating the narrow pass, the North Koreans blocked the movement of vehicles north and south and cut the only escape route for the 19th Infantry.

Learning of the roadblock, Colonel Meloy sent a message to Lt. Col. Thomas M. McGrail, commanding the 2d Battalion on the left flank where the 34th Infantry had been, to attack the roadblock with Companies G and H. Meloy then hurried to the site of the roadblock in order to coordinate and command its reduction. There, Meloy was wounded and taken out of action. After locating transportation to move his men, McGrail committed his battalion in two uncoordinated actions. The first, under his personal command, drove north up the road in a column of two tanks and four antiaircraft quad-.50 vehicles loaded with infantrymen. The small column took heavy casualties and fell short of breaking through by about 300 or 400 yards. The second thrust, by Company G, failed to close with the enemy before being ordered to withdraw south. The 19th never did break the enemy force at the roadblock, now stretching about a mile and a half between the relief forces to the south and the men of the 19th looking for a way out in the north. Only a small column of vehicles, led by a single tank carrying Meloy, finally broke through. Most men of the 19th Infantry moved into the hills searching for a safe route past the North Koreans to Taejon. All through the night of 16 July and throughout the seventeenth, stragglers worked their way back. In the end, the 19th Infantry suffered the same heavy losses that had exhausted the 21st and the 34th. Only Companies E and G were relatively intact. And another big fight loomed. Now the North Koreans were advancing on the important road junctions at Taejon. Moreover, the collapse on the Kum River line weakened the position of the ROK divisions to the east, and they, too, began to fall back to the south. There was not much space left to give away.

Although of little immediate consolation, reinforcements were on the way. The 5th Regimental Combat Team had sailed from Hawaii, and the 2d Infantry Division and the 1st Provisional Marine Brigade, from the continental United States. General Walker, therefore, took a hard look at the developing situation. After collecting all available data on the status of troops in Korea, those en route and scheduled to arrive in the next ten days, the organization of the Port of Pusan, and his ammunition and supply levels, he developed a concept of operations to delay the enemy. His idea was to use the 24th, 25th, and 1st Cavalry Divisions—the latter just released by Mac-Arthur—and the South Koreans to gain the maximum possible delay west and north of a general line following the Naktong River across to Yongdok on the east coast (see Map 9.5). If forced to fall back, he would defend Pusan with all available forces from behind the Naktong River line until such time as reinforcements arrived and Eighth Army could undertake a counteroffensive. If this concept were to succeed, Walker had to have time to put the 1st Cavalry Division in position. In order to complete shipping and deploying the 1st Cavalry Division, he needed a delay of two full days at Taejon. The task fell to the battered 24th Division.

Taejon was the most important communications center in southwestern Korea. Roads and a double-tracked railroad ran from Taejon through the mountains south to Taegu and south to Pusan. To hold Taejon, Dean placed the 24th Division between the city and the Kum River where its course twists through a broad valley to the east. Moving southeast down the valley, North Korean units forded the shallow river and easily attacked Taejon. There, the exhausted men of the 24th Division were heartened by the arrival of the first Sherman tanks (75-mm) in Korea and heavy-hitting 3.5-inch rocket launchers that had been airlifted from the United States. Nevertheless, the story turned out the same. On 19 and 20 July, they fought with spirit, but the defenders were no match for the encircling North Koreans. In the swirling confusion of battle northwest of the city, the 34th Infantry headquarters lost contact with its two battalions and did not know where its flanks were or what was happening out there.[58] A fiercely fought action in the center of the city held the enemy's anticipated frontal attack as other North Korean units passed to the rear in an attempt to cut off the Americans. Giving everything he had to inspire his men, General Dean fought bitterly to the end, leading 3.5-inch bazooka teams against advancing enemy tanks. Finally, he and his companions became separated as they tried to escape through roadblocks circling the city. General Dean, alone and injured, worked his way south for thirty-six days before he was finally captured. After the fight for Taejon, the 24th Division was badly hurt. Not only had it lost the commanding general, but it had lost 1,150 men of the 3,933 engaged there and virtually all the equipment the defenders had used. On 22 July, the 24th finally found relief when it was replaced by the 1st Cavalry Division. The 24th had given Walker the two days he needed.

The day before Taejon fell, President Truman had asked MacArthur for his personal appraisal of the situation in Korea. Replying later the same day, MacArthur asserted that the enemy had lost his chance for victory. The speedy commitment of the Eighth Army had forced the North Koreans to slow their advance by causing them to deploy, reform, and redeploy at successive delay positions. As a result, the enemy had resorted to costly frontal attacks to maintain momentum. Lengthening supply lines and increased consumption of ammunition and other supplies had begun to disrupt his logistical systems. There was still a hard campaign ahead; Americans must expect losses as well as successes, but, most important, the enemy no longer held the initiative. MacArthur concluded that the United Nations forces had a secure hold on southern Korea.[59]

The words were brave, but the price had been high. MacArthur's insight was correct, and the Eighth Army subsequently held Pusan, largely because of the time bought so dearly by the 24th Division. But success should not divert critical analysis of what happened in the delay. In all, Eighth Army and South Korean units delayed the North Koreans for over a month before falling behind the Naktong River line to defend the remainder of South Korea. For about two weeks, the 24th Division had carried the burden of American efforts. But performance of its units had not achieved as much as hoped for or as much as possible. A major part of the problem originated in lack of prewar preparation.

After World War II, the United States Army had demobilized to conform to the desires of the American people and government postwar policies. Overseas obligations to prevent the resurgence of fascism required occupation forces in Germany, Austria, Italy, Trieste, and Japan. But as demobilization proceeded, the overseas forces were thinly spread. Moreover, austere fiscal support during those years forced the Army to defer equipment modernization and extensive training in favor of meeting manpower costs. The army in Japan was a typical product of these policies. Military-police functions so necessary in an occupation were more important than combat readiness. In a few short years, the Eighth Army had changed from a proven combat formation into a colonial army.

Not surprisingly, the Eighth Army suffered accordingly. Its infantry regiments and artillery battalions were organized on a scale of two-thirds of their required units and, even at a reduced peacetime scale, were under strength. Divisions were short of equipment and parts and were unable to maintain themselves. Units conducted little training that was or could be effective. Nor was there any great interest in making it so. After all, the primary mission was to support the occupation, a far different matter from being ready for battle. Officers and soldiers alike succumbed to the life of a colonial army and lost the sharp edge they had honed in World War II.

Even the arrival of General Walker could not completely arrest deterioration. Walker altered the mission to make training the first priority; he rationalized the regimental organization, though still short one battalion combat team, to provide a basis for realistic training; and he filled the units to near their peacetime strength. Nevertheless, Walker was only partly successful. He never could fill the shortages of weapons and equipment; he could not create training areas for tank-infantry-artillery maneuvers; and he could never convince his officers and men that war was likely. In the year that Walker commanded the Eighth Army in Japan, he gained ground in the realm of training but not in overall combat readiness. He also ran out of time.

When war came, the Eighth Army was not ready to meet the demands of the battlefield. The army went to Korea lacking the most rudimentary support. There was no contact or coordination with the South Korean Army to ease the frictions of coalition warfare. There was no logistical structure from which to draw replenishment. There was no information about the enemy and none being generated beyond the painful experience of battle. There was no effective command-and-control network to guide Smith, Lovless, Stephens, and Meloy in their first engagements simply because radios failed and the distances between headquarters were too great. There was no effective air-ground coordination to exercise the only real advantage the Americans had.

Given these disadvantages, Task Force Smith did about as much as could be hoped for, and it performed reasonably well. Smith had put together a team quickly and on an ad hoc basis. He had integrated new officers and NCOs from other units into Companies B and C even before leaving Japan. He had chosen his ground wisely, delayed his enemy to the limit of his capacity, and then led most of the task force to safety in a dangerous withdrawal. He had worked smoothly with Perry, the artilleryman, until their communications broke down. Most of his officers and NCOs had performed with distinction, particularly in the withdrawal. His problems were serious but not of his making. He had no effective antitank defense because he had no tanks and no antitank mines and because the 2.36-inch rocket launchers and 75-mm recoilless rifles did not stop enemy tanks. He had no communications with higher headquarters, with his artillery, or even within his infantry much of the time. His radio batteries had gone dead, and enemy tanks cut the wire lines. He had no intelligence of the enemy, no means of resupply, and, because of the bad weather, no air support. Indeed, Smith had no help at all from any friendly forces; he could not even talk to the South Koreans.

Subsequently, the situation became even worse. Bad as things were for Task Force Smith, it fought well. Such was not the case in the 34th Infantry. Nowhere were the failures of the prewar Army more evident. In part because General Barth, Colonel Lovless, and Lieutenant Colonel Ayers were new to their responsibilities, command in the 34th broke down. Barth became involved in battalion-level operations to an extent that may have clouded the chain of command. Ayers was too quick to withdraw from P'yongt'aek, particularly without serious contact, and Lovless failed to support aggressively General Dean's concept of holding the line east of Asan Bay. Company commanders, junior officers, and noncommissioned officers mirrored the uncertainty of their commanders and in general performed badly. The regiment lost its bravest officers early and eventually lost the survivors to physical and mental collapse. In the end, all seemed more concerned with escape than with fighting. The contrast of its performance with that of the 21st ultimately resulted from the absence of aggressive leadership and unit cohesiveness.

Clearly, the North Koreans had much to do with the performance of units of the 24th Division. Weaknesses in American organization and preparation were aggravated by the contrasting excellence of the enemy. Most important, the North Koreans attacked with superior strength in tanks and infantry. Moreover, they attacked with a well-rehearsed, predictable, but remarkably effective scheme of maneuver. They fixed the American front with a tank charge, an infantry attack, or heavy shelling. As the Americans reacted to their front, North Korean infantry enveloped both flanks in search of the command post and indirect fire units in the rear. Once the mortars and artillery were defeated and communications disrupted, the enemy infantry formed roadblocks to prevent reinforcement and resupply while cutting the escape route. Once in the rear, their success was assured, for American units were ill prepared for the mental stress of being physically cut off. With only two battalions in each regiment, there was never an opportunity to deploy an adequate reserve. Occupying frontages designed to stop an enemy division, the thin battalions of the 24th really never had a chance. The soldiers lost their concentration and thought only of escape. Small-unit commanders found it impossible to fight their way out of these situations. Even much of Task Force Smith lost its cohesion during withdrawal as small knots of men hastily sought safety in the rear. The 34th Infantry never really made a fight, even behind the Kum River. The 19th Infantry fought well at the Kum River until it was cut off; then it suffered the same fate.

By the time Dean committed himself at Taejon, the 24th had worn itself out. The survivors were weakened, dispirited, and exhausted; they had to rest and reorganize. In time, they rebuilt the regiments of the 24th Division and fought with distinction. But to a man, they regretted the wasted years in Japan. There were no stronger advocates of a combat-ready peacetime army than the veterans of Task Force Smith and their comrades in the 24th Division.

10

The 1st Cavalry
and the Ia Drang Valley,
18 October–24 November 1965

GEORGE C. HERRING

The first battle of the Vietnam War in which the U.S. Army engaged large-scale North Vietnamese units took place in the rugged Central Highlands of South Vietnam in the fall of 1965 and matched the *32d, 33d,* and *66th North Vietnamese regiments* against the newly constituted U.S. 1st Cavalry Division (Airmobile). The battle was unusually bloody, each side inflicting heavy casualties in savage, often close-quarter fighting. At the time and since, both sides have claimed a great victory in that battle, and from the short term, the United States appears to make the better case. The 1st Cavalry thwarted a major North Vietnamese offensive in the highlands and inflicted losses as high as ten to one on the North Vietnamese regiments it faced. As with all such engagements, however, the more elusive long-term consequences may be more important. This engagement may have been a case in which generally effective tactics reinforced commitment to a dubious strategic concept. The perceived success of airmobile warfare in the Ia Drang and in particular the heavy losses inflicted on the enemy appear to have confirmed in the minds of U.S. Army leaders that their search-and-destroy approach was well calculated to achieve victory in the war.

The Battle of the Ia Drang Valley ushered in a new phase of the long and agonizing struggle for Vietnam. Since the late 1950s, North Vietnam and the United States had steadily increased their support for the contending factions in the civil war in South Vietnam. In 1965, each significantly escalated the way by committing its own forces directly to battle. The result was the first head-on clash between U.S. and North Vietnamese units, a classic blood bath between two very different types of armies. The People's Army of Vietnam (PAVN) reflected the preindustrial society from which it came. Lightly armed and equipped, it relied primarily on stealth and foot mobility. The 1st Cavalry Division (Airmobile) of the United States Army, on the other hand, represented the most advanced technology in the world and depended on mobility provided by the helicopter and the devastating firepower of modern weaponry.

By 1965, North Vietnam had created a formidable modern army, organized, trained, and equipped along Chinese lines. The PAVN numbered as many as 500,000 men and was backed by a ready reserve also of close to a half-million. Its divisions each possessed an authorized strength of 10,000 men, lightly armed and equipped for maximum mobility, although those fighting in South Vietnam were customarily under strength. Infantrymen generally carried Chinese-made pistols, 7.62-mm rifles, and three to five "potato-masher" grenades. Infantry divisions consisted of three infantry regiments when in the south, backed by weapons companies armed with 60-mm and 82-mm mortars, 57-mm and 75-mm recoilless rifles, and heavy machine guns. Training emphasized camouflage, the use of explosives, and small-unit tactics; field exercises were often conducted at night and under the most adverse conditions. The North Vietnamese made a virtue of the necessity of their light armament by constantly emphasizing that men, not weapons, constituted the decisive element in war. "People's war, not modern weapons and techniques, decides victory because war is the most acute form of struggle between man and man," party theoretician Truong Chinh proclaimed in 1965.[1]

The North Vietnamese Army attempted to compensate for its weakness in firepower by rigorous discipline, tactical superiority, and careful preparation. As much as 50 percent of the training time of the PAVN soldier was spent in political education, and political commissars accompanied every unit above the company level. In battle, the North Vietnamese attempted to use the terrain to best advantage, digging in even during rest periods and developing camouflage to a fine art. They avoided battle except under favorable conditions and attacked the enemy at weak points rather than strong ones. The North Vietnamese did not attempt to hold ground but rather sought to attack and withdraw before the enemy could react, hoping to inflict maximum casualties with rifles and automatic weapons in the opening moments of the fight. They were masters of the ambush. Actions of all sorts were planned and rehearsed with painstaking care. PAVN units might take as much as a month to prepare the battlefield, massing ammunition and supplies, digging intricate systems of underground trenches, and stocking food and ammunition at attack points, ambush sites, and along withdrawal routes. *PAVN or VC or both?*

Mobility and small-unit maneuver were the hallmarks of North Vietnamese tactics. To minimize the impact of enemy firepower, PAVN forces attempted to close with the enemy as quickly as possible and to maintain close contact, even to the point of "hugging" and hand-to-hand combat. They preferred to overwhelm enemy forces by massing strength at a single point, and they excelled at encircling maneuvers with fifty to seventy-five men. Survival on the battlefield often depended on the ability to disengage, and North Vietnamese tactical doctrine held that withdrawal was as important as the advance. At times, PAVN forces counterattacked to permit disengagement. If escape routes were blocked, they might attack a weak spot and slip away through the hole. Delaying forces were usually assigned the task of ambushing and harassing pursuers. Despite the lightness of its armament and a tendency to be repetitive and mechanistic in its tactical moves, the North Vietnamese Army was a formidable military force. Bernard Fall did not exaggerate when he described it in September 1965 as "one of the best infantry combat forces in the world, capable of incredible feats of endurance and raw courage even against vastly superior firepower and under the worst physical condition."[2]

The United States Army was also in a high state of battle readiness on the eve of its commitment to Vietnam. During the early 1960s, Secretary of Defense Robert McNamara had presided over a dramatic expansion and reorganization of the Army to meet the perceived threats of a direct Soviet attack on Western Europe, limited conventional wars along the lines of the Korean conflict, and so-called brush-fire wars in the Third World. McNamara increased the overall strength of the Army to nearly a million men, raised the number of combat-ready divisions from eleven to sixteen, expanded airlift capacity by 400 percent, and stockpiled huge quantites of equipment. The Army was reorganized to create a flexible, adaptable organization capable of meeting its varied missions. The ROAD (Reorganization Objectives Army Division) introduced in the 1960s included 15,000 men and was made up of three brigades plus headquarters and supporting units. A ROAD infantry division normally consisted of eight infantry and two armored battalions. The major virtue of the new scheme was its flexibility. Infantry, mechanized, armor, and airborne battalions were interchangeable and could be shifted about to form different types of divisions to meet different srategic and tactical needs.[3]

Changes in tactical doctrine accompanied the reorganization of the Kennedy era. Methods of conducting offensive operations did not vary drastically from those employed in World War II and Korea, but there were significant changes in concepts of defensive operations, and, in general, the defense assumed greater importance. This reflected a recognition that the United States and its allies would of necessity assume the defense of Europe and the fact that massed attacking forces would be especially vulnerable to nuclear attack. It was also a product of technology and reflected increased confidence among military planners in the power of the defense. Defensive doctrine during the 1960s enlarged the standard area to be defended from the 7,000 to 15,000 meters of World War II to 20,000 meters and emphasized mobility and rapid dispersal of forces as the keys to defensive operations. The major change, however, was the emphasis on destroying enemy forces rather than taking and holding territory as the object of defensive operations.[4]

Innovations in equipment drastically increased the mobility and firepower of the U.S. Army. The advent of armored personnel carriers and troop-carrying helicopters significantly altered the nature of infantry operations. Helmets, pistols, and mortars were similar to those used in Korea, and machine guns and artillery were improved versions of weapons long in use; but two new weapons vastly increased the firepower of the individual infantryman. The M79 grenade launcher permitted the use of grenades at ranges up to 350 meters with far greater accuracy than the old hand-thrown variety; they were particulary useful in ambushes and against machine-gun nests. Claymore mines, which weighed only 3.5 pounds, were easy to place, had a destructive area of up to 50 meters, and were also valuable in ambushes.[5]

Although the U.S. Army entered the Vietnam War among the best-equipped armies in history, the basic weapon of the foot soldier, the rifle, became a matter of considerable controversy. The standard-issue rifle as of 1965 was the M14. Designed for the open battlefields of Europe, it fired a 7.62-mm cartridge, was quite accurate at long ranges, and could be converted quickly to automatic firing. It was heavy and thus awkward to carry and fire, however, and as an automatic it had a horrendous kick and was difficult to aim, making it ill suited for combat in Vietnam where much of the fighting was at close range. In early firefights, the M14 was consistently outperformed by the Soviet-made AK47 used by some Viet Cong soldiers. By the time the U.S. committed significant combat forces to Vietnam, conversion to the new M16 rifle had begun. This rifle was much lighter and easier to carry and fire. It discharged volleys of small (.223-caliber), high-velocity, steel-jacketed bullets shaped so that on impact they spun over and over to inflict greater damage on victims. An experimental version, the AR14, had performed superbly in tests and in actual combat conditions in Vietnam and was adopted for standard issue. As a result of subsequent modifications added by Army ordnance, however, the M16 turned out to be unreliable, jamming at times and producing enough controversy to provoke a congressional investigation.[6]

A major innovation of the 1960s was the creation of an air-cavalry division. Helicopters had been effectively used in restricted roles in Korea, and as their technology improved, their potential began to seem almost limitless. They were widely employed during the advisory period in Vietnam and seemed increasingly to many tacticians to provide a solution to the fundamental problem of locating and engaging elusive guerrilla forces in difficult terrain. Over the vigorous opposition of some Army officers and the Air Force, McNamara took the lead in pressing for the creation of an entire division equipped with large numbers of its own helicopters.[7]

After intensive study and tests conducted by an experimental division over a period of several years, the secretary of defense activated the 1st Cavalry Division (Airmobile) in June 1965. The division's 16,000 men, artillery, and ground vehicles were to be flown into battle by some 400 huge Chinook and Iroquois helicopters. Six twin-engine Grumman OV1 Mohawks with infrared scanning devices were to be used for reconnaissance, while four giant "flying cranes" could lift an airplane, carry enough C-rations to feed a battalion for three days, or haul heavy artillery guns, their crews, and their ammunition. Although lightly armed and lacking staying power in battle, the division compensated with its fast-strike capability. Its helicopters could land as many as 10,000 troops in battle zones within hours. The division's greatest assets were its ability to cover all types of terrain, to maneuver over large areas, to react quickly to enemy attacks and reinforce embattled units, and to conduct raids behind enemy lines. "The air-mobile concept gives a commander a degree of surprise, freedom of action, and speed never before possible to ground combat," the division's commander, General Harry W. O. Kinnard, boasted.[8]

At the time of its activation, the First Team, as it proudly called itself, was among the elite forces in the Army. Many of its officers and key enlisted personnel had been hand picked, and it had assumed the black and gold horse head insignia of the prestigious and tradition-laden 1st Cavalry. Kinnard himself epitomized the style and elan of a unit that was to a considerable degree his brain child. A colorful and crusty Texan with a distinguished World War II combat record, he sometimes wore a black eye-patch emblazoned with the "Cav" insignia. The 1st Cavalry appears to have been designed explicitly for Vietnam, and it was no coincidence that it was the first division to go to war intact and to engage the enemy in battle.

Perhaps the major weakness of the U.S. Army on the eve of its involvement in Vietnam was its lack of intensive preparation for the type of war in which it would become engaged. All but ignored during the nuclear-war obsessions of the 1950s, counterinsurgency became a veritable fad in Kennedy's Washington, the result of a conviction widely shared by top administration officials that so-called wars of national liberation represented the new Communist strategy for world domination. Kennedy took the lead in promoting counterinsurgency, and the military services, sometimes grudgingly, followed. The president himself expanded the Special Forces and gave them a special elite status in the Army. The Green Berets in turn imparted some of their skills to more conventionally oriented units, especially after they began to acquire practical experience as advisers in Vietnam. By the mid-1960s, the Army had acquired a body of doctrine and a set of tactics for fighting guerrilla wars. Its adaptation was limited, however. Much of the leadership resisted what it regarded as little more than a passing fancy. Doctrine and tactics consisted for the most part of small-unit tactics for conventional war adapted for a different purpose. The Army never really grappled with the larger issues of strategy for counterinsurgency. "The elusive ideal of identifying the goals of military action within counterinsurgency was . . . overwhelmed by the more immediate task of developing tactical organizations, equipment, and doctrine." Whether these adaptations were successful against an enemy trained for the environment of Vietnam is still being debated; but the outlines of the larger failure are clear. As Harry Summers has written, "The sad truth is that in Vietnam our mind was never concentrated on how to win the war."[9]

The confrontation that brought the First Cavalry into battle with PAVN regiments in the Ia Drang took form in the spring and summer of 1965. Supported by steadily increasing aid from North Vietnam, Viet Cong insurgents had gradually expanded their grip on South Vietnam, by early 1965 controlling roughly half the territory and half the population. The possibility of a Viet Cong victory heightened a debate that had raged in Hanoi since the beginning of the war. Some leaders like Nguyen Chi Thanh, commander of Viet Cong forces, and Politburo member Le Duan wanted an unqualified commitment of North Vietnam's resources to attain a quick victory in the South. Others, like Vo Nguyen Giap, at least initially preferred a protracted guerrilla struggle in which the Viet Cong would bear the major burden and North Vietnam would play no more than a support role. The differences were apparently resolved by compromise sometime in the spring of 1965. Uncertain how the United States might respond and hopeful that South Vietnam would collapse of its own weight, the North Vietnamese moved cautiously, keeping the door for peace talks with the United States at least slightly ajar. Eager at the same time to capitalize on the favorable situation in the South, North Vietnam continued to infiltrate men and supplies and pressed the Viet Cong to intensify their military operations.[10] Even without a full-scale North Vietnamese commitment, the initial results seemed promising. Regiment-size main-force units mauled larger and better equipped Army of the Republic of Vietnam (ARVN) forces at Phuoc Binh and Dong Xoai in May 1965. During the summer, PAVN forces cut Highways 19 and 21, major routes from the highlands to the coast. Along with political chaos in Saigon, these military disasters portended a possible Viet Cong victory.

Apparently shocking some North Vietnamese leaders, the United States responded in July by drastically expanding the number of its troops in Vietnam and by committing its forces directly to battle, the closest equivalent to an American decision for war in Vietnam. Since taking office in November 1963, President Lyndon B. Johnson had sought to arrest the decay in South Vietnam with partial measures, but drastic expansion of the advisory effort and the bombing of North Vietnam had produced little demonstrable effect. In June 1965, General William C. Westmoreland, head of the Military

Assistance Command, Vietnam (MACV), warned the president that the United States must inject its own forces into the struggle. Westmoreland was convinced that North Vietnam was on the verge of moving to the third and decisive stage of guerrilla warfare and that it would soon launch a major offensive in the central highlands. Warning Washington that Hanoi seemed ready to commit whatever forces were required to "tip the balance" and that South Vietnam could not stand up "successfully to this kind of pressure without reinforcements," he urged Johnson to commit additional forces "as rapidly as possible during the critical weeks ahead."[11] Specifically, Westmoreland asked for an increase from the sixteen battalions deployed in Vietnam earlier in the year to forty-four. Westmoreland made clear his impatience with the "enclave" strategy then governing the use of U.S. forces. This strategic concept was the idea of Ambassador Maxwell Taylor to limit U.S. involvement by securing critical coastal areas. The ambassador believed this policy would reduce U.S. casualties, yet make clear American resolve. General Westmoreland, on the other hand, insisted that South Vietnam could not be stabilized until North Vietnamese and Viet Cong main-force units had been destroyed, and he asked for approval of an aggressive offensive strategy.

Johnson approved Westmoreland's recommendations but refused to commit the nation to the sort of war his military and civilian advisers urged. Alarmed by the drastic deterioration of the government of South Vietnam, he authorized Westmoreland in late June to commit U.S. forces to offensive operations against Viet Cong units. In late July, he approved the force level Westmoreland had requested. Recognizing that an additional 100,000 men might be required by early 1966, McNamara, supported by the Joint Chiefs of Staff, advocated a call-up of 235,000 reservists and National Guardsmen and an increase in regular forces of approximately 375,000 men, measures bearing a price tag as high as $8 billion. Johnson refused to go this far, however. He justified his decision on the grounds that even a partial mobilization for war might provoke a dangerous confrontation with the Soviet Union and China. In fact, he seems mainly to have feared that new taxes for that "bitch of a war," as he referred to Vietnam, would threaten what he called the "woman I really loved," the Great Society legislation then pending in Congress. He gambled that a slow, steady escalation of the bombing and the limited commitment of ground combat forces would be enough to coerce Hanoi into dropping its support for the Viet Cong and accepting a settlement on American terms.[12]

Armed with additional forces, Westmoreland set about developing a plan to save South Vietnam from disaster. During Phase I, projected to last until the end of 1965 and designed merely to "halt the losing trend," he proposed to use the bulk of his units to protect major military bases, air fields, and lines of communication; to defend that part of the countryside under government control; and, where possible, to conduct spoiling operations against Viet Cong base areas. To meet these needs, he strengthened Marine contingents in the I Corps along the northern coast, deployed the 2d Brigade, 1st Infantry Division, to the air base at Bien Hoa, and assigned the 1st Brigade, 101st Airborne Division, to Camranh Bay. The most important step, however, was the deployment of the 1st Cavalry to An Khe. Correctly anticipating that the major thrust of the enemy's offensive in the upcoming dry season would be in the central highlands, Westmoreland from the outset had pressed for deployment of a major offensive strike force there. The Joint Chiefs of Staff had at first opposed him, fearing that large-scale forces might be trapped in an American Dienbienphu and urging that U.S. units be assigned near the coast. Eventually, they compromised, positioning the Cav at An Khe where it could cover both the coast and the highlands.[13]

Despite a relatively high state of combat readiness, the transition from peace to limited war in Vietnam posed serious problems for the Army in general and the 1st Cavalry in particular. Major problems stemmed from shortages of key personnel. All mobilization plans had been based on the assumption that the reserves would be at least partially mobilized and enlistments extended, and when Johnson refused to take these steps, new methods had to be improvised. Among the units slated for deployment to Vietnam, large numbers of personnel were ineligible for overseas service. In the case of the 1st Cavalry, some 2,700 officers and men, many of them paratroopers (airborne troops of the 1st Brigade) and pilots, could not go. "I lost hundreds of pilots, crew chiefs, mechanics and so forth who were not eligible under a nonemergency situation for another Vietnam tour," General Kinnard noted in an interview many years later. Personnel had to be pirated from other units or hurriedly trained, causing serious problems with the Army's readiness down the line. The rapidity with which the 1st Cavalry was prepared for deployment also left little time for the sort of specialized training that was desirable if not absolutely essential. It did not get M16s until ten days before departure, permitting no more than hurried instruction in the care and use of the new rifle. The Cav had no experience in jungle warfare or the type of warfare then going on in Vietnam, and it absorbed nothing more than last-minute instruction in Viet Cong tactics before leaving the United States.[14]

These problems aside, the deployment of the division from Fort Benning to An Khe proceeded rapidly and relatively smoothly. By late August, advance units were hacking out of the jungle with machetes and entrenching tools bivouac space for 20,000 men and a 3,000-by-4,000-foot helipad, the largest in the world. The landing area could hold the division's 435 helicopters and was "paved" with an oil-based solution to keep down the high-ferrous-content topsoil. It was soon named the "Golf Course" because it had been neatly manicured to meet the precise specifications of the officer in charge. Six troop ships, four aircraft transports, and eleven cargo ships transported the men, planes, and supplies of the First Team to Qui Nhon. Despite major problems in unloading supplies caused by the inadequacy of the facilities at Qui Nhon, by 28 September, fewer than ninety days after it had been formally organized, the 1st Cavalry was in An Khe and had assumed responsibility for the security of its base. Within thirty days, it would go into battle.[15]

The military situation remained highly precarious at the time of the 1st Cavalry's arrival in South Vietnam. Throughout the early summer of 1965, the Viet Cong relentlessly chipped away at the South Vietnamese Army and government. Insurgent forces overran a government outpost at Bagia in Quang Ngai province, destroyed an ARVN battalion in Binh Duong province, and wiped out a Special Forces camp in Phuoc Long province. The Viet Cong responded to Johnson's escalation of the war by stepping up their own operations. Supported by North Vietnamese regulars, they besieged another Special Forces camp in the central plateau and overran the district town of Daksut in the highlands. Viet Cong terrorists kept up a war of nerves against U.S. bases in Danang, Bien Hoa, and even Saigon. Only at Chu Lai, near Danang, where a sweeping action by U.S. Marines in August produced heavy enemy casualties, did the United States and South Vietnam effectively resist the enemy onslaught.

In the meantime, North Vietnam completed preparations for a major offensive in the highlands to be carried out during the dry season of 1965–66. General Westmoreland has speculated, partly on the basis of information revealed in captured documents, that the North Vietnamese, by destroying U.S. and South Vietnamese forces in the highlands and on the coastal plain, hoped to cut South Vietnam in two and isolate Saigon, thus striking a knockout blow against the enemy.[16] The offensive represented a significant change in that a PAVN division was employed intact for the first time, apparently representing a major victory for Nguyen Chi Thanh and his followers in the ongoing strategic debate. The North Vietnamese certainly hoped to gain control of the highlands, which could then be used as a springboard for assaults against the northern coastal area and Saigon to the south. They may also have sought to throw U.S. forces off balance before the latter could prepare to launch offensive operations and to test the strength of their own units against those of the United States. American escalation appears to have caught North Vietnam off guard, however, creating a good bit of uncertainty as to how best to conduct the war, and it seems unlikely that even Thanh expected or aimed for a quick and decisive victory.

Whatever its strategic purpose, the Dong Xuan (Winter–Spring) campaign of 1965–66 called for an army corps to execute a series of operations in the area between the 17th parallel and a line running east to west from Pleiku. The first major operation, to be carried out by two North Vietnamese regiments, was called the Tay Nguyen (Western Plateau) campaign and aimed to strengthen the North Vietnamese-Viet Cong position around Pleiku and Kontum provinces by knocking out the Civilian Irregular Defense Group

(CIDG) camps that had been established by American Special Forces units among the Montagnard population to defend the highlands. North Vietnam's initial target was the CIDG camp at Plei Me. Located twenty-five miles south of Pleiku, the Plei Me camp guarded the southern approaches to Pleiku city and provided a checkpoint against enemy infiltration from Cambodia. The attack on Plei Me led directly to the battle of the Ia Drang.[17]

The North Vietnamese prepared for the Tay Nguyen campaign with the near-compulsive attention to detail that characterized most of their operations. Their "lure-and-ambush" plan, a familiar ploy, called for the *33d Regiment* to besiege the camp at Plei Me, forcing South Vietnam to send a relief column which would be ambushed by the *32d Regiment*. The two units would then combine to overrun Plei Me. The *32d* carefully reconnoitered the ambush site, stocking supplies of food and ammunition and conducting elaborate war games on primitive sand tables. After ten days of rigorous tactical exercises, the regiments moved to their respective positions. The *32d* spent more than a week preparing a four-kilometer area for the ambush. Meanwhile, the *33d* cut an elaborate system of trenches and firing pits around the unsuspecting Special Forces camp, working under cover of darkness, silently carrying the dirt away in hand baskets, and covering the trenches with brush to escape detection by the camp's Montagnard defenders.[18]

Shortly before midnight on 19 October, the *33d Regiment* opened the Battle of Plei Me with a withering barrage of mortar, small-arms, and recoilless-rifle fire. Although numerous signs had pointed toward a possible attack on Plei Me, "repetition" had "dulled belief," as General Kinnard later put it.[19] The camp's 350 Montagnard soldiers and nine American advisers were caught by surprise. They were also hopelessly outmanned. Had the purpose of the operation been simply to overrun the camp, the *33d* could easily have succeeded. North Vietnam's larger aims required the lure of a relief column, however, and while the *33d* kept the camp under unrelenting pressure, it delayed any breakthrough.

The United States and South Vietnam took advantage of the delay to bolster the defense of Plei Me. The ARVN II Corps commander, General Vinh Loc, immediately dispatched to Plei Me 250 South Vietnamese paratroopers and fourteen U.S. Green Beret advisers commanded by Maj. Charles Beckwith. In this case, as throughout the Ia Drang campaign, however, the United States relied on massive firepower to contain the enemy. In the first four days of the siege, U.S. planes flew more than 300 sorties, bombing, napalming, and strafing concentrations of enemy forces and using with special effectiveness newly developed cluster bombs, canisters that opened in mid-air and sprayed the ground with small but deadly explosive projectiles. The North Vietnamese sustained the siege in the face of this

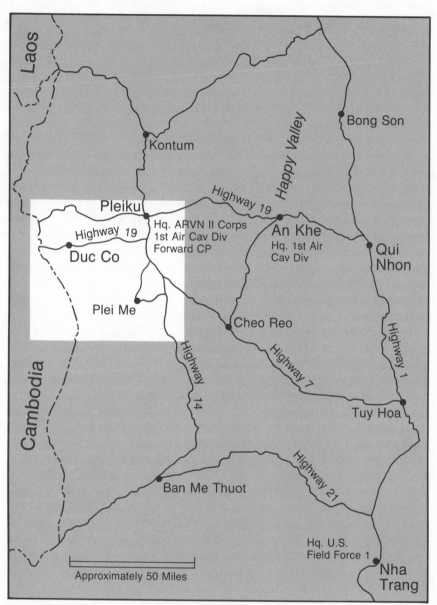

Map 10.1. Plei Me and the Ia Drang

pounding and even managed to shoot down two U.S. fighters and two helicopters; but they absorbed enormous losses.[20]

While the *33d Regiment* kept Plei Me under siege, the *32d* lay in wait for the anticipated relief force. The *32d* was made up of three battalions of infantry supported by mortar, machine-gun, and antiaircraft companies. It set the trap about five miles north of Plei Me along a narrow stretch of Provincial Route 21, the expected route of the relief column and an ideal ambush site surrounded by hills and covered by dense vegetation on both sides of the road. The *334th Battalion* positioned itself to cut off retreat or reinforcement from the rear. The *635th Battalion* prepared to attack the front, while mortar companies were to immobilize the tanks. A third battalion was held in reserve to deal with any additional forces that might be landed by helicopter or to support units that might be threatened. The North Vietnamese hoped to separate the relief force and cut it to pieces.[21]

The relief column was not dispatched to Plei Me until four days after the siege had begun. General Vinh Loc appears to have suspected the lure and ambush, and he claims to have deliberately delayed a response to permit time better to size up the enemy's intentions.[22] It seems clear, however, that the delay also resulted from uncertainty over whether or not the real enemy objective was a relief column or the city of Pleiku. A heated debate flared between American and South Vietnamese officers as to how best to deploy the limited forces at hand. Displaying the caution that characterized ARVN generals through much of the war, Vinh Loc tried to get the United States to send units of the 1st Cavalry into the possible ambush. Even after the United States agreed to use its own forces to defend Pleiku, Vinh Loc was reluctant to send anything more to Plei Me than a Ranger battalion and an armored cavalry squadron. Only under intense pressure from the Americans did he finally consent to send a relief column of 1,000 South Vietnamese troops led by tanks and armored personnel carriers.[23]

The delay paid handsome dividends. The larger relief force insisted on by the Americans proved adequate to withstand the North Vietnamese ambush. About 1800 on 23 October, the van of the ARVN column moved into the trap, meeting devastating fire that crippled a number of vehicles and caused heavy initial losses. Although badly shaken, the column did not give way. The tanks fanned out and maneuvered into something a journalist on the scene compared to "the old wild West wagon train circle." Their guns loaded with canisters of small shot blasted away at both sides of the road, mowing the "surrounding bush to stubble" and plastering "dozens of shredded enemy bodies" against shattered tree trunks.[24] The second part of the column withdrew in orderly fashion and hastily established a perimeter on a nearby hill. Makeshift ARVN defenses held out through the night against repeated enemy attacks. In the meantime, American aircraft and artillery, which had been called in the moment the battle had erupted, took a heavy toll of the

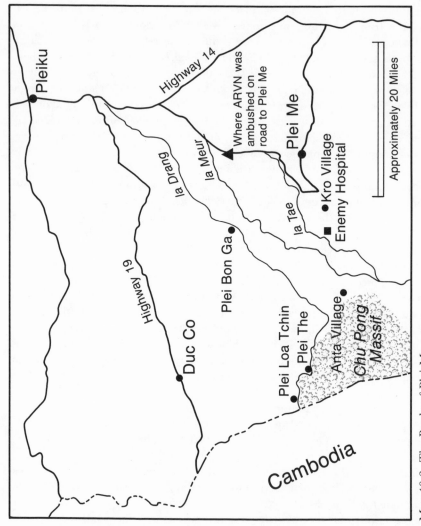

Map 10.2. The Battle of Plei Me

ambushers. Their trap failing, the North Vietnamese slipped away at daybreak. The battered ARVN forces had also endured as much as they could handle. The relief column took its time regrouping and would agree to move on to Plei Me only two days later and only after securing a firm commitment of air and fire support from units of the 1st Cavalry.[25]

By the time the column arrived at the embattled camp, the siege had been lifted. While awaiting the dispatch of ARVN relief forces, the *33d PAVN Regiment* had taken a beating from American aircraft. As of 25 October, U.S. planes had flown 422 missions in support of the camp—220 on 24 October alone, the heaviest single concentration of air support yet employed in the war. At times, the bombs fell so close to the camp that shrapnel flew about among its defenders. According to U.S. estimates, the North Vietnamese lost 850 killed and as many as 1,700 wounded.[26] Two battalion commanders were killed and another was seriously wounded, while some 300 weapons were captured and many more were destroyed. Their plan having failed, the *33d Regiment* broke the siege late in the evening of 25 October. Leaving behind a battalion to cover the retreat, the attacking forces began to withdraw to base camps near the Cambodian border.

The defense of Plei Me significantly improved the United States–South Vietnamese position in the Central Highlands. The camp itself was devastated from six days of steady bombardment, its narrow confines littered with debris and bodies, but it had endured a major challenge from vastly superior numbers of crack North Vietnamese troops. Had Plei Me fallen, Pleiku and Kontum would have been exposed, and Highway 19, a major east-west route, could possibly have been cut. The first phase of the enemy's dry-season offensive in the highlands had been frustrated, and the newly infiltrated North Vietnamese forces suffered heavy losses. The defense of Plei Me eased at least temporarily the threat to the highlands that had so disturbed Westmoreland in the summer of 1965.

With the base at Plei Me secure for the moment, Westmoreland decided to send the 1st Cavalry after the retreating North Vietnamese forces. He conceded later that the decision caused him some of the war's "most anxious moments."[27] The airmobile concept had not been tested in battle. The 1st Cavalry had only recently arrived in Vietnam, was still hacking out its base camp at An Khe, and had not had time to get acclimated. Under strength when it arrived, its ranks had been further thinned by a peculiar strain of malaria that resisted the usual treatment.[28] It would have to operate in unfamiliar and extremely inhospitable territory, and if contact with the enemy were made and it failed its first major test, the impact on the U.S. and South Vietnamese morale would be devastating.

Westmoreland accepted these risks. He had long been impatient with the defensive approach forced on him by necessity. He had insisted over the objections of the Joint Chiefs that the 1st Cavalry be brought to the highlands for just such a purpose, and the North Vietnamese retreat from Plei Me provided an opportunity to conduct offensive operations against sizable enemy units away from the security of their base areas. Thus, on 27 October, Westmoreland ordered the 1st Cavalry to begin search-and-destroy operations in the area west of Plei Me.

The mission assigned the Airmobile Division was formidable indeed. Its search area, the valley of the Ia (meaning "river" in Montagnard dialect) Drang, comprised about 2,500 square kilometers of desolate and unpopulated territory, long *terra incognita* to both the United States and the Saigon government. The only passable roads traversed the eastern and northern fringes. On the west the region was bounded by the Chu Phong massif, a rugged mountain extending out from the Cambodian border and rising 730 meters above sea level. Much of the valley was covered with thick jungle vegetation and trees as high as 100 feet. Even the "open" areas were covered with uncut shrubs and elephant grass as tall as a grown man. Flowing northeast to southwest, the Ia Drang, Ia Meur, and Ia Tac cut the area into hundreds of small compartments. Throughout the highlands and particularly in the Ia Drang, the climate combined with the topography to produce an aura that no one who fought there would forget. The "sudden, contrary mists offered sinister bafflement," Michael Herr has written, "where the daily heat and the nighttime cold kept you perpetually, increasingly on edge." The area was "spooky beyond belief."[29]

The U.S. Army relied on the helicopters of the 1st Cavalry to penetrate the Ia Drang. In fact, the region, almost impassable to "heavy" ground forces dependent on motorized transport, seemed ideal for the airmobile tactics of the 1st Cavalry. Helicopters—"slicks" (transports), "guns" (heavily armed gunships), and "hooks" (supply choppers)—were pivotal. Drastically modifying standard infantry tactics, reconnaissance helicopters discovered and fixed the enemy, then assault troops in a secure staging area boarded slicks. As they neared the battle zone, gunships, artillery, and often fixed-wing aircraft pounded the landing zone (LZ), raising their fires only as the troop-laden slicks swooped onto the LZ. If enemy contact was made, reinforcements would be brought in immediately and further artillery and tactical air support called in. Once secured, the LZ was used for various types of offensive (and sometimes defensive) operations.

The first phase of the Ia Drang campaign lasted from 28 October to 14 November and consisted of extensive air and ground searches by the 1st Brigade, punctuated with sporadic and violent clashes. The first major encounter took place on 1 November when scouts of the 1st Squadron, 9th Cavalry, stumbled onto an enemy regimental-aid station and field hospital hidden in a stream bed near Ia Tac. The scouts immediately called in reinforcements and after a short but heated engagement took the hospital, capturing large quantities of medical supplies and invaluable intelligence. In the early afternoon of the same day, a battalion-size North Vietnamese detachment counterattacked against three U.S. rifle platoons in the vicinity of the hospital. Reinforced by helicopter, the outmanned U.S. troops held off a series of furious enemy assaults over a six-hour period.[30]

Two days later, on 3 November, the 1st Squadron ambushed units of the *66th North Vietnamese Regiment* that were being staged forward. Using enemy maps captured at the field hospital, the cavalrymen set several traps at points where the infiltration and withdrawal routes of North Vietnamese forces intersected south of a Special Forces camp at Duc Co on the south bank of the Ia Drang. Within a short time, a North Vietnamese heavy-weapons company moved into the trap and was caught in such intense fire from claymore mines, M16 rifles, and M79 grenade launchers that it was unable to return fire. Suspecting that this company was but a small part of a larger force, the U.S. platoon leader, Capt. Charles B. Knowlen, immediately withdrew to base camp. Several hours later, the North Vietnamese attacked the base in force, the first of four assaults between midnight and 0400. The beleaguered U.S. squadron was eventually reinforced by helicopter, the first time this had been accomplished after dark, and by morning enemy attacks had diminished to sporadic sniper fire.[31]

The largest—and for the United States most costly—encounter of this phase of the campaign occurred on 6 November when two companies from the 1st Brigade ran into a well-placed ambush. While conducting patrols near the Ia Meur, Company B of the 2d Battalion, 8th Cavalry, encountered a platoon-size force of North Vietnamese and soon found itself engaged with an enemy who was well dug in and receiving reinforcements. Pinned down and nearly encircled, Company B was locked into savage fighting at such close range that artillery and air support could not be safely employed. Company C subsequently joined the fight by moving to attack the enemy's rear and also came under heavy fire. At nightfall, according to official U.S. sources, both sides disengaged. Each suffered heavy losses in this brief but extremely violent encounter. The official U.S. body count tallied 77 North Vietnamese killed in action and an estimated additional 121 dead. Twenty-six Americans were killed, another 53 wounded, and when Company B left the field, it was unfit for further combat.[32]

After another week of little more than sporadic combat, the two armies were drawn together almost by accident in a brief but violent clash that would comprise the centerpiece of the Ia Drang campaign. Having failed in their lure and ambush, the North Vietnamese improvised an alternate plan calling for the remnants of the *33d Regiment,* joined with the *32d* and the newly arrived *66th,* to launch a second attack on the Special Forces camp at Plei Me on 16 November, the first time a full PAVN division had been committed to a specific target in South Vietnam. In preparation for the attack, the three regiments began to assemble at staging areas between the Ia Drang and the Chu Phong massif.[33]

At precisely the same time, the United States Army Field Force (I,) without knowledge of North Vietnamese plans, shifted its search-and-destroy operations to the southwestern region of its operational zone, the very place where PAVN units were gathering. Searches in other areas had turned up nothing more than remnants of the retreating *33d Regiment*. The U.S. lacked fresh and reliable intelligence on the area, but the Chu Phong massif had been a Viet Minh stronghold in the war against France, and intelligence analysts surmised that it was now being used as a staging area for troops infiltrating into South Vietnam from the Ho Chi Minh Trail. Because Gen. Stanley "Swede" Larsen, Field Force (II) commander, believed that units of the *33d Regiment* and the hitherto invisible *32d Regiment* were regrouping east of Highway 21 and south of Plei Me, initial probes concentrated in that area— but without effect. Relieving the 1st Brigade, General Kinnard directed three battalions of the 3d Brigade to search the area around the Chu Phong massif.[34]

These decisions produced the Battle of Landing Zone X-ray, the most intense firefight of the Ia Drang campaign. General Kinnard later claimed to have used airmobility to lure the North Vietnamese into the kind of set-piece battle the French had never been able to obtain, but he appears to claim too much.[35] Although the Army had fairly reliable intelligence that the *33d* and *66th NVA Regiments* were in the Chu Phong area, it was in large part by chance that major PAVN forces happened to be in the immediate area chosen for the search. American units narrowly averted an ambush at X-ray and then several days later stepped into a disastrous ambush at a nearby landing zone, raising the question of who was luring whom. Throughout this phase of the campaign, moreover, the North Vietnamese retained the tactical initiative, beginning and breaking off contact when they chose. Their willingness to stand and fight in the face of devastating artillery fire and air strikes apparently reflected a calculated decision to absorb more punishment than necessary in order to learn "how the Americans fought."[36]

The battle for X-ray began almost inadvertently on 14 November. The commanding officer of the 1st Battalion, 7th Cavalry, Lt. Col. Harold Moore, chose the 100-by-200 meter spot at the base of the Chu Phong massif because it seemed the only one of several available clearings capable of handling eight to ten American helicopters. Ringed by scrub brush and tall trees and covered with thick elephant grass and huge ant hills, it turned out to be a less-than-ideal spot. Unknown to Moore, moreover, the North Vietnamese were only several miles away. The *66th Regiment* had already moved out from its mountain base for the second attack on Plei Me. When the 1st Cavalry began

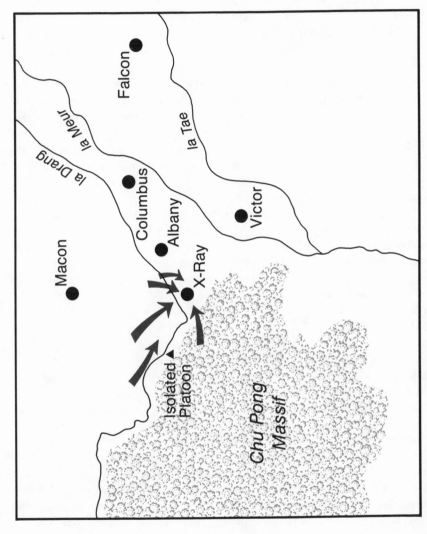

Map 10.3. X-Ray and Albany

landing nearby, the North Vietnamese were ordered to move toward X-ray for the attack.

Shortly after hitting X-ray, U.S. soldiers were engaged in some of the fiercest fighting of the war. A bit of luck combined with Moore's alertness spared the landing forces a potentially deadly ambush. Learning from a captured PAVN straggler that enemy forces were nearby, the colonel as a precautionary measure ordered a company to establish a position on a finger leading up the mountain where the North Vietnamese were suspected of being.[37] The company had moved only a short distance from the landing zone when it ran head on into two companies of North Vietnamese, initiating the battle before the attackers were ready. An American platoon was quickly cut off and surrounded by 250 North Vietnamese and subjected to fire so intense the men could not even dig foxholes. "We couldn't raise our heads more than a few inches without getting shot at," a survivor later recalled. Two efforts were made to rescue the trapped platoon, but the rescuers had to move uphill against heavy fire from entrenched enemy positions, and they were able to advance only a short distance from the landing zone. The platoon was cut off for more than twenty-four hours. Of its twenty-seven men, eight were killed and twelve wounded; it lost its platoon leader and sergeant in the early stages of the fight. It was saved only by artillery—which, in desperation, the sergeant who had assumed command had called in on his own position—and perhaps by the enemy's ignorance of the platoon's plight. Eventually, during the early afternoon of 16 November, the 2d Battalion, 5th Cavalry, under the comand of Lt. Col. Robert B. Tully, which had flown up to Landing Zone Victor and then marched overland, rescued the isolated platoon.[38]

While the remnants of the isolated platoon hung on, the landing zone itself became the scene of heavy fighting. By the time the four U.S. companies landed, they were engaged with an enemy force of 500 to 600 men. Fearful that his units might be separated and picked to pieces, Moore in the late afternoon pulled them back to the clearing to establish a perimeter. From the evening of 14 November to the morning of the sixteenth, the battalion defending X-ray, later reinforced by units from the 2d Battalion, 7th Cavalry, hurled back repeated assaults from elements of an attacking force of North Vietnamese totaling around three battalions. The enemy troops came off the mountain aggressively and well camouflaged. At times, they moved to the very edge of the defenders' foxholes, resulting in savage, close-quarter fighting, sometimes in hand-to-hand combat. One U.S. soldier was found dead, his hand clutching the throat of a dead enemy infantryman. On two occasions, Moore himself engaged with the attackers. Helicopters shuttled in and out of the landing zone under heavy fire bringing in men and supplies and taking out casualties. The noise and confusion were so great during the height of the battle that the Americans could communicate only by hand signal.

As at Plei Me, American firepower probably saved the embattled defenders of X-ray. From the onset of the battle, the Army and Air Force poured an incredible array of explosives on enemy positions in the area. Artillery from nearby Landing Zone Falcon fired more than 8,000 rounds— 4,000 of them on 14 November alone. During the first forty hours of the battle, Air Force fighter-bombers launched strikes every fifteen minutes. In their first use in "close" air support, B-52 bombers from Guam flew 96 sorties, dumping their massive loads up and down the Chu Phong massif, sometimes as close as 5,000 meters to friendly forces. Air Force and Army planes flew more than 350 sorties between 15 and 20 November.[39]

The battle of X-ray ended on 16 November. Unable to break the American perimeter and having absorbed enormous losses from American artillery and aircraft, the battered North Vietnamese withdrew from the area of the landing zone. Shortly afterward, the Americans vacated the turf they had defended so stubbornly. The Army recognized that the cost of a direct attack against the Chu Phong massif would be prohibitive. Because the enemy held the high ground, moreover, any forces remaining at X-ray would be vulnerable to artillery and mortar fire. Army spokesmen took great pains to explain to journalists that the withdrawal was not a retreat but rather the conclusion of a search-and-destroy mission. The Ia Drang Valley was itself of no strategic significance, they pointed out. "The idea was to kill as many communists as possible," a spokesman asserted.[40] Indeed, the losses suffered by both sides in the fight for the obscure clearing were enormous. U.S. estimates placed the North Vietnamese dead at more than 600, with an additional 1,215 supposedly killed or wounded. Although initially Army spokesmen described American casualties as "moderate," official reports indicated that the United States lost 79 killed and 121 wounded. Some companies were decimated.[41]

The blood bath continued the following day when the major part of a U.S. battalion walked into a disastrous ambush just north of the Ia Drang. At the end of the battle for X-ray, the 2d Battalion, 7th Cavalry, which had been sent as a reinforcement, was ordered to sweep six miles to the north to another landing zone named Albany where it would be evacuated by helicopter. In the meantime, the *8th Battalion* of the *66th PAVN Regiment* was proceeding in much the same direction to attack another nearby landing zone where Americans were located. North Vietnamese scouts discovered the American battalion, giving their unit about twenty minutes to put together an ambush. In a heavy canopy of jungle just short of Albany, the North Vietnamese hurriedly concealed themselves in trees, in ant hills, and behind bushes.[42]

The ambush (set up in an "L"-shape to catch both the lead units and the long column of 2d Battalion troops) had been skillfully devised, and the results were devastating. The snipers and machine gunners caught three of four American companies in a deadly trap. Some Americans who tried to flee the initial fire ran straight into the center of the ambush. The noise was deafening, and in the confusion GIs began firing on each other. A sergeant who was at the center of the column remembered that "suddenly everyone around me was getting hit and dying. I could hear the screams all around me, all over the place."[43] By the time the Americans realized that they were caught in an ambush, another participant later recalled, the North Vietnamese were "all around us, jumping out of trees and charging out of the bushes."[44] Shouting "Kill G.I. son of a bitch" in English, they rushed the panic-stricken Americans and engaged them in deadly hand-to-hand combat.

The battle at Albany continued through much of the day. Following the ambush, a wild, disorganized series of individual and small-unit fights broke out over a 1,000-meter space. All afternoon, an American participant remembered, there were "smoke, artillery, screaming, moaning, fear, bullets, blood, and little yellow men running around screeching with glee when they found one of us alive, or screaming and moaning with fear when they ran into a grenade or bullet."[45] Helicopters were unable to land reinforcements until early evening, and it would be several hours before the GIs could establish a crude perimeter and bring in artillery and air support. Although some Americans were probably napalmed, air support appears to have saved the companies from annihilation. All night long, the North Vietnamese maintained pressure on the perimeter and moved about the area killing the American wounded in cold blood. At daybreak, they quietly slipped away.[46]

Few events of the war can match Albany for sheer gore. The unfortunate U.S. units suffered at least 60 percent casualties. The official count tallied 151 GIs killed and 121 wounded of the roughly 450 in the unit. One company caught in the middle of the ambush suffered 93 percent casualties. By U.S. count, the North Vietnamese lost more than 400 men. The scene along the river resembled the "devil's butcher shop," one participant recalled, with "blood and mess" all over the place, dead snipers hanging from trees, and grotesque piles of as many as twenty tangled bodies. The ground was "sticky with blood," and a journalist who visited the battlefield reported that it was impossible to walk twenty paces without stepping on a corpse. There were stories of horrible North Vietnamese atrocities. A few Americans shot themselves to avoid capture, and significant numbers of GIs apparently were killed by friendly fire. Army spokesmen refused to admit an ambush. Those who had experienced Albany did not hesitate to use the word, however, and one participant could not refrain from mentioning that the units massacred along the Ia Drang had a direct line of descent from General Custer's 7th Cavalry, which had suffered a similar fate at the Little Big Horn.[47]

The fight at Albany marked the last major battle waged by U.S. forces in the Ia Drang campaign. The 1st Battalion, 5th Cavalry, engaged the enemy briefly on 18 November at Landing Zone Columbus. In the meantime, the battered 3d Brigade was ordered back to An Khe. It was replaced by the 2d

Brigade, which, along with an ARVN airborne brigade, conducted mopping-up operations from the Cambodian border to Chu Phong massif. Over the next few days, these units flushed out some scattered remnants of the *32d, 33d,* and *66th PAVN Regiments,* and the U.S. command concluded that the bulk of the enemy forces had withdrawn into sanctuaries across the border in Cambodia. By 24 November 1965, the battles of the Ia Drang were over.[48]

Glossing over or ignoring such things as the disaster at Albany, participants and official historians have claimed an unqualified and highly significant victory in this first major encounter with North Vietnamese regulars. According to official sources, the 1st Cavalry killed as many as 3,000 enemy soldiers and wounded more than 1,000, decimating the two North Vietnamese regiments it engaged.[49] The Cav's timely victory thwarted North Vietnam's end-the-war offensive in the highlands, reversing a tide that had been running against the United States and South Vietnam and staving off the South Vietnamese collapse that had seemed all but inevitable in the early summer. Army general and historian Dave Richard Palmer thus labels the Ia Drang "one of the war's rare decisive battles."[50] Implicit in these conclusions is the argument that General Westmoreland's search-and-destroy strategy was well chosen and could have worked if the Army had not been hemmed in with restrictions from Washington and subsequently undercut by declining public support.

This point of view contains a large element of truth. North Vietnamese sources make clear that the three regiments suffered staggering losses, and it would be some six months before they would return to battle.[51] Although the North Vietnamese probably had not expected the Winter-Spring campaign to produce victory, the successful defense of Plei Me and the bloody battles in the Ia Drang were still highly significant, easing the enemy threat to the highlands and forcing North Vietnam onto the defensive. As is usually the case, however, victory did not come without a price. The unavailability of documents makes it difficult to pinpoint at this stage the impact of the battle, but it seems to have had complex and ambiguous results, with long-term consequences that may have been quite costly.

Observing one of the most firmly established traditions of warfare, both sides claimed victory in the immediate aftermath of the battle. North Vietnamese spokesmen termed the Ia Drang a "valley of death" for Americans, gloated that more than 1,000 GIs had been killed in the week of X-ray and Albany alone, and chortled that some frightened American pilots had showered napalm on their own men. America's superiority in weapons and equipment had been proved meaningless, North Vietnam insisted. North Vietnamese soldiers had easily coped with the B–52s by deep shelter. Giap himself boasted that the vaunted 1st Cavalry had been put out of action and insisted that it was less formidable than ordinary American infantry units.

Liberation forces had proved they could neutralize American firepower by "catch-and-grasp" (hand-to-hand) combat, a PAVN spokesman claimed. The Americans could always be defeated in this way because they were not trained for that kind of fighting and did not like it. To mark the victory in the Ia Drang, the North Vietnamese government bestowed on the "soldiers and peasants" of the highlands two First-Class Military Merit awards.[52]

The United States had begun claiming victory before the battle had ended. On the day after fragmentary reports of the debacle at Albany began to appear in the press, Pentagon spokesmen, perhaps to deflect attention from the ambush, proclaimed that "this biggest battle of the war has been a resounding military success so far." They went on to identify the Ia Drang as a "major turning point" without explaining why, beyond saying that the United States had killed more than a thousand enemy soldiers while incurring only "moderate" losses itself.[53] General Westmoreland followed in several days with a statement labeling Ia Drang an "unprecedented victory . . . in terms of action, in the magnitude of the troops involved and in the degree of success of friendly forces."[54] A year later, President Johnson awarded the 1st Cavalry a unit citation for its exploits in the battle.

That part of the press that supported the war quickly picked up the refrain. In a column on 22 November, Joseph Alsop noted that the Ia Drang was exceptional among first battles of American wars. In contrast to Bull Run and Kasserine Pass, he pointed out, green American troops had taken on an enemy with seven-to-one numerical superiority and had won "remarkable victories on the enemy's chosen terrain."[55] The performance of the GIs was something "to marvel at," U.S. News agreed. Although inexperienced, they had proven themselves "tenacious, aggressive fighters," defeating the "best the Communists could throw at them." Indeed, given the problems they faced, they had performed far better than their fathers and brothers in the first battles of earlier wars.[56] The press singled out appropriate heroes of this first battle: Sp4c Nolan King, "a gangling sleepy-voiced Georgian in the best Sergeant York tradition," who had killed fourteen North Vietnamese, captured twenty-one, and seized seven weapons; and Pfc. Toby Braveboy of Coward, South Carolina, who had been separated from his unit for nearly a week and had survived for hours in the midst of the enemy by playing dead.[57]

On both sides, however, the bullish rhetoric appears to have masked deep concern with the implications of the bloodshed in the Ia Drang. Captured documents make clear that the fighting had a devastating effect on the North Vietnamese regiments involved. The extent to which spokesmen in Hanoi went out of their way to play down the importance of American firepower and to dismiss the fighting ability of the "tall but stupid" GIs suggested the depth of their concern.[58] Moreover, the failure of the dry-season offensive in the highlands appears to have rekindled the bitter internal debate over strategy. Thanh and his supporters claimed to have won great victories, arguing that if they had not taken on the United States they would have lost momentum and the Americans could have established secure forward bases from which to launch offensives of their own. Thanh continued to press for direct attacks against U.S. forces emphasizing close-quarter combat to neutralize American firepower. The heavy cost of the Ia Drang campaign appears, however, to have strengthened the hands of those like Giap who wanted to employ guerrilla tactics—to force the Americans to "eat rice with chopsticks"— instead of conventional war.[59] The debate would not be resolved for many months, but in the immediate aftermath of the Ia Drang, the North Vietnamese reverted to guerrilla warfare and tactical adjustments were made to enable PAVN units to cope with U.S. firepower more effectively.[60]

The Ia Drang also aroused concern in the United States. Journalists who had long since begun to question official statements almost as a matter of course cast a skeptical eye on the recent battles. Manifesting their lack of familiarity with less conventional forms of warfare, they wondered how the Army could claim a victory at X-ray when it had hurriedly vacated a position that had been defended at such cost, and they dismissed as hollow West-moreland's explanation that the withdrawal had been merely a tactical move. Firsthand reports of the debacle at Albany appeared on the same pages with the Army's claims of victory. The press quizzically compared official admission of "moderate" losses with reports of entire battalions being wiped out, wondered how the Army could refuse to call an ambush an ambush, and questioned how any one could speak of victory after seeing the piles of dead at the bloody landing zone. *New York Times* reporter Charles Mohr warned that the Army was feeding the American public a "steady stream of misinformation." Quoting cynical GIs who labeled body counts "WEG" (wild-eyed guesses), Mohr alleged, among other things, that the official estimates of enemy dead were grossly inflated.[61]

Even those who did not question the Army's explanation of events expressed concern with the battle's implications. Some unnamed military sources conceded that the United States was "involved in a dangerous game" and wondered in the aftermath of Ia Drang "who is the hunter and who the hunted."[62] Eager to claim victory but fearful that he might be misinterpreted, Westmoreland felt compelled to try to squelch any overoptimism that might develop from the headlines of success. A long war lay ahead, he warned, and "we must be prepared to accept this."[63] Indeed to many civilian commen-tators, Ia Drang was significant chiefly in that it heralded a new and more costly phase of the war. North Vietnam had "brutally served notice" on the United States that the war had changed, the *New York Times* observed. Instead of fighting and fading away, the enemy had refused to give ground and had "lavishly expended" lives in "determined attacks." This apparent change of approach, combined with reports of stepped-up infiltration, pointed to a "new, more dangerous" war, requiring large numbers of U.S. troops and perhaps leading to heavy casualties. Although the nation got only a vague and misleading impression of the extent of U.S. losses in the Ia Drang, much of the commentary in the press focused on the high rate of American losses.[64] Concern over the heavy losses was shared at the very top level of government. National Security Adviser McGeorge Bundy warned President Johnson on 27 November that the recent fighting indicated that "we may have to look forward to a pretty grim year."[65]

The impact of the battle on the 1st Cavalry itself is difficult to gauge. The individual brigades were self-contained and relatively isolated from each other, and those units not directly involved in the most intense fighting were probably not affected in any significant way. Among at least some of the troops at X-ray and Albany, however, the impact of this first encounter with the enemy appears to have been severe. Numerous participants have testified that in the immediate aftermath of the battle "morale was real low, the shock was real heavy."[66] Westmoreland wanted to keep the division in the western highlands to begin another campaign around Kontum, but the field force commander, General Stanley Larsen, insisted that time was needed for regrouping.[67] Indeed, what Michael Herr has termed the "animal terror" of the combat in the Ia Drang assumed an almost legendary quality. "No one who was around then can ever forget the horror of it," Herr would write, and those returning for new tours still "shuddered uncontrollably at what they remember: impromptu positions held to the last man and then overrun; Americans and North Vietnamese stiff in one another's death embrace, their eyes wide open, their teeth bared or sunk into enemy flesh."[68]

At the very least, U.S. soldiers emerged from these battles with a healthy respect for the enemy. After Plei Me, Major Beckwith told the press that the North Vietnamese were the "finest soldiers I have ever seen in the world except Americans," adding his wish that "we could recruit them." Another American who had survived the siege of Plei Me simply said, "Damn, give me 200 men that well disciplined and I'll capture this whole country."[69] In his after-action report on X-ray, Moore echoed these sentiments, describing the North Vietnamese infantryman as "well trained," "aggressive," a "deadly shot," and a determined fighter who battled to the death and could be particularly "fanatical" when wounded or cornered.[70]

Although the costly victory in the Ia Drang aroused considerable concern among Americans in Vietnam and in Washington, it appears not to have provoked any fundamental changes in policy or strategy. The extent to which Johnson was aware of what had occurred in the highlands remains unclear.[71] Whatever the case, he persisted in the course he had already staked out. After implementing a bombing pause and a noisy peace offensive to pacify an increasingly restless public, he approved Westmoreland's request for additional troops and the Joint Chiefs' proposals for expanded bombing in hopes that further escalation might find North Vietnam's breaking point.

The Army seems to have found in the Ia Drang confirmation for the approach it had already adopted. Westmoreland had been committed to an aggressive search-and-destroy strategy almost from the time American combat forces began arriving in Vietnam, and the favorable ratio of U.S. to enemy losses in the highlands apparently reinforced his belief that such an approach could destroy Viet Cong and North Vietnamese main forces and eventually break the enemy's will to fight.

Army officials also appear to have found in this first battle validation of existing equipment, doctrine, and tactics. After-action reports make clear that some problems developed with the M16, but MACV seems to have been pleased with its overall performance and urged that the entire army be equipped with it, leading to some problems later on.[72] Westmoreland claims to have been elated with the performance of the 1st Cavalry. Although it had gone into battle under strength and not yet acclimated to Vietnam, it had held up better in perhaps more difficult circumstances than its predecessors at the Kasserine Pass and the Pusan perimeter. Westmoreland attributed its "magnificent" performance against a skillful and determined enemy to the soundness of its training and tactics. The battles proved the value of airmobile operations, opening, in his later words, "a new chapter in the history of land warfare."[73] General Kinnard agreed. In Vietnam, he later said, the "name of the game" was "contact" and airmobility permitted the United States to "find those guys quickly and then . . . hold them long enough to do something about it."[74] In the aftermath of the Ia Drang, Army public relations officials boasted that the Cav's helicopters had shifted artillery batteries sixty-eight times and troop battalions forty-eight times in slightly more than a month, while simultaneously supplying isolated units and removing the dead and wounded. According to spokesmen, only four helicopters were shot down and 80 percent of the choppers were combat ready when the division retired from the Ia Drang. "We are freed from the tyranny of terrain," Kinnard exulted.[75]

Had the Army been more inclined toward self-criticism at this point, questions might have been raised about airmobile operations on the basis of the Ia Drang experience. The campaign had been enormously expensive, consuming some 550 tons of supplies a day, 50,000 gallons of aviation gasoline alone. The extensive flying time in a high-humidity climate took a heavy toll on the helicopters, and operations had to be carefully planned, sometimes restricted, and even canceled because aircraft were unavailable. At some points, fewer than 50 percent of the helicopters were actually in commission. The Cav was able to keep only one brigade in action at a time, and that brigade relied heavily on the Air Force for supply and tactical air support.[76]

In a more fundamental sense, questions might have been raised about the utility of airmobile tactics in this war and, in particular, about the relationship between tactics and strategy. Helicopters permitted the United States to locate an elusive enemy and at times to penetrate enemy strongholds, but they could not in all cases force the enemy to fight. In the Ia Drang, there was generally action when the North Vietnamese forced action. In addition, the United States inflicted the losses it did because the enemy stood and fought in the face of American firepower. Army officials wondered aloud why North Vietnam had apparently changed its tactics, but these officials seem not to have asked what would happen if it shifted back to a more passive approach. As Albany graphically demonstrated, moreover, on the ground and away from the security of safe landing zones, the 1st Cavalry was vulnerable. "Americans had almost as little foot mobility as their foe had helicopter mobility," Dave Richard Palmer has conceded.[77] In light of these factors, questions might have been raised about the ability of Westmoreland's search-and-destroy methods to bring the war to a successful conclusion.

These questions seem not to have been raised, however, and in the aftermath of the Ia Drang, the Army appears to have instituted only minor tactical changes to better exploit its weaponry. Lessons learned emphasized bringing in artillery and air support early and close, even at some risk to U.S. forces, to prevent the enemy from mingling where he could fight on his own terms. Techniques were to be developed to make air support more manageable and effective at night, and the use of napalm and white phosphorus against concentrations of North Vietnamese was encouraged because it seemed to have a particularly unsettling effect and make them vulnerable to rifle fire.[78] In its next battle, MASHER/WHITE WING, a division-level operation in Binh Dinh province, the 1st Cav would put into effect various of these changes but would also repeat certain of the mistakes of Ia Drang.

Although a significant victory, the Ia Drang may therefore also have been deceptive in its consequences. It did not produce significant changes in leadership, doctrine, or strategy. Rather, responsible officials seem to have interpreted it as indicating that the United States was on the right path. In fact, it set the tone for much of what lay ahead: more search-and-destroy missions, vast destruction, numerous "victories"—and ultimate frustration.

11

First Battles in Retrospect

JOHN SHY

A two-part idea has inspired this book: that first battles are peculiar, significantly unlike subsequent military operations of a war, and that this peculiarity is obscured by historical perspective, by our knowledge of what happened during and after the first battle. Each part of the idea requires close attention.

The peculiarity of first battles lies mainly in the lack of recent, relevant combat experience by the forces engaged. Sometimes, as in the 1942 North African campaign, only one side lacks this experience. But more often both sides will bring to the first battle preparations, expectations, and predictions largely untempered by direct knowledge—personal or organizational—of what actually happens in the violent shock of armed combat. Few would question the importance of this kind of experience to an armed force; yet it is precisely this kind of experience that the sporadic nature of war denies to an armed force in its first battle. Often only a few senior leaders will have had combat experience; sometimes no one will have had it. Weapons, doctrine, and organization inevitably will have changed since the last war, sometimes radically so, more often slightly but significantly. And invariably the precise circumstances of the new war are unique, however familiar the enemy or the terrain may be. Nothing comes through more strongly in the preceding case studies than the importance of these circumstances (which may be translated to mean "politics" in Clausewitz's broad sense of the word) to understanding the what and why of first battles. Political circumstances appear to have two major effects on first battles: limiting the military possibilities to certain resources and locations, and pushing strategy in certain directions at certain times. Of course, the enemy has a good deal to say about strategy, but an attentive reader will have been impressed by how often political circumstances

In addition to the editors, Thomas Collier, Robert Cummins, Roger Kaplan, Gerald Linderman, Jay Luvaas, Jonathan Marwil, and James Tobin have given valuable comments on this chapter.

at the beginning of a war, from the American Revolution to Vietnam, will affect the target and timing of strategy leading to the first battle. Subsequently, the military situation—the results of the first battle—plays a crucial role in strategy. But in the beginning, it is whatever causes the war—the politics of its outbreak, well beyond the control and responsibility of military commanders—that gives to the first battle much of its peculiar quality.

This peculiar quality of the first battle will usually vanish or be transformed once the battle is over. This vanishing trick is the second part of the idea that deserves special study. Once the results of the first battle are known, the events of the battle and what led up to it are seen in a new perspective; if the military outcome was decisive, the blunders of the defeated and the brilliance of the victor shape postbattle inquiry, while a stalemate—as in 1914—draws attention to the misguided optimism and mistaken predictions of both sides, perhaps to lost opportunities as well. In any case, the actual experience of the first battle—the perceptions, problems, calculations, decisions, and actions—is distorted by knowledge of the outcome. The normal human emotions of complacency and regret, euphoria and depression, are homely reminders of our natural tendency to read history backward, to look for the present in the past, neglecting all that for the moment does not seem relevant. But reading history backward destroys the integrity of the past. How many of us have tried in vain to explain to someone who was *not* present at an event that what happened cannot be understood solely in terms of the result, that the situation was complicated, that the actors were confused, that time was short? It is the same with first battles, only with far greater intensity and consequence. The results of the first battle so often structure the remainder of a war that observers simply cannot achieve the detachment and empathy needed to restore to the first battle its historical integrity. After two decades dust has not quite settled on the Ia Drang Valley, but at least now we can begin to add Vietnam to our list of cases in order to learn whatever first battles may have to teach us.

Both the peculiar quality of first battles and the difficulty caused by historical perspective in recapturing that quality are direct results of the roles ignorance and uncertainty play in first battles. All wars involve high levels of ignorance and uncertainty; if they did not, surprise, intelligence, and security would be far less important in warfare than they are. But it is at the very beginning of a war when lack of knowledge or of confidence may dominate the situation, before commanders can assess the results of their first realistic test of estimates, assumptions, guesses, predictions, hopes, and fears. It is this ignorance and uncertainty, lying at the heart of first-battle reality, that the authors of these case studies have tried to recapture as fully and accurately as possible. Each chapter has focused on the preconceptions and preparations, immediate problems, and the sequence of actions in the first battle. Each author has added his own assessment of the battle's impact. Here, in the final chapter, the task is to do what any attentive, interested reader ought to do: analyze, compare, and reflect on this peculiar kind of military experience. What follows is not in any sense meant to be definitive; rather, it is offered as a set of carefully considered thoughts, based squarely on the ten case studies, about the phenomenon of the first battle.

Of the ten first battles, the U.S. Army suffered five defeats (Long Island, Queenston, Bull Run, Kasserine, and Osan/Naktong) and won five victories. Four of those victories were very costly (San Juan, Cantigny, Buna, Ia Drang)—some might say too costly for the gains achieved. Only the two-day battle of the Rio Grande in 1846 was relatively cheap, although even there losses approached 10 percent of the force engaged. Won or lost, the first battle almost guarantees that inexperience will be paid for in blood. How far this costly inexperience would have been remediable by more and better training is an important and difficult question which will be discussed later. But here it can be said with some confidence that in only a few instances did inadequately prepared troops seem to fall apart *before* undergoing severe combat stress: most troops at Queenston in 1812 (certainly), some units at Kasserine in 1943 and from Osan to the Naktong in 1950 (probably), simply could not or would not fight effectively. But a close look at Long Island in 1776, Bull Run in 1861, Volunteer units in Cuba in 1898, National Guardsmen at Buna in 1942 and at Kasserine in 1943, and most occupation troops rushed to Korea in 1950 shows soldiers fighting perhaps better than might be expected, giving way only under heavy enemy pressure, and learning quickly under fire what they had not been taught before the first battle.

More glaring than poorly trained troops as a first-battle problem is the weakness of command-and-control. Virtually every case study emphasizes the lack of realistic large-scale operational exercises before the first battle, exercises that might have taught commanders and staffs the hard, practical side of their wartime business as even the most basic training introduces it to the soldier at the small-unit level. Virtually every case study indicates that the results of confusion, demoralization, and exhaustion at the command-and-staff level are at best bloody, at worst irremediable—a more crippling defect even than combat units falling apart, because units can often be relieved or replaced in time, headquarters almost never. Generals Putnam and Sullivan on Long Island simply did not know how to secure their vulnerable eastern flank. A common soldier would have been shot for a dereliction as serious as the Queenston mess in 1812, for which the president and the secretary of war must share responsibility with Generals Smyth and Van Rensselaer, when a simple, reasonable plan turned into an operational nightmare. Jack Bauer concludes that General Taylor's unsure touch in 1846 deprived his tactical victories of much strategic significance. At Bull Run, McDowell's defeat centered in the failure of divisions, especially division commanders, to do as they were told. At El Caney, General Lawton failed, at a high price in blood, to understand his mission, in part because General Shafter had failed to explain and emphasize it to him.

Cantigny is one of the only two first battles (Ia Drang is the other) conducted with professional skill at the command level. Yet even the American Expeditionary Forces and its showcase 1st Division, as well prepared an organization as the United States had ever sent to war, reveal command-and-control problems. Allan Millett tells us that the U.S. divisional structure was gigantic in part because GHQ AEF feared "that the U.S. Army could not provide enough division commanders and staffs to control a larger number of smaller divisions" (p. 160). But size exacerbated the technological problem of communications, which led the U.S. forces in France in 1918 to rely heavily on "elaborate planning and rigidly prescribed schemes of fire and maneuver" (p. 161). The rehearsals of the assault unit, the 28th Infantry, set up and conducted by the division operations officer, Lt. Col. George C. Marshall, are impressive evidence of professionalism at its best. Once committed to action, however, American units at Cantigny (and later in 1918) lacked flexibility; unexpected dangers were usually met with courage but at severe cost, while unexpected opportunities usually passed without being exploited. The critiques published during the summer by GHQ AEF emphasized that American operations were too rigid, stereotyped, and formalistic, depriving small-unit leaders of initiative. (German criticism of U.S. Army operations in Italy in 1943–44 would make similar points, contrasting American performance with the more flexible style of the French Expeditionary Corps.[1]) While there is room for debate on how to interpret the evidence, one conclusion strongly suggests itself, at least through the First World War: the professional response to the chronic American weakness in command-and-control was to plan more thoroughly, leaving as little to chance as possible. But thorough planning, with its natural deemphasis of unexpected situations (beyond the scope of contingency plans), led to rigidity and, often, heavy losses. In other words, the command-and-control weakness and its chosen professional remedy were but two aspects of a single larger problem: inadequate preparation of commanders and staffs for the real world of combat.

The Kasserine defeat is a classic study of how not to conduct a battle, with many up and down the chain of command to share blame with the II Corps commander, General Fredendall. How, for example, could Allied ground forces, allegedly on the offensive, have been so bereft of protection and support from the air as the 1st Armored Division and 34th Infantry Division were in Tunisia in February 1943? Had anyone but the ineffable George S. Patton succeeded Fredendall as corps commander, the likely American response to the command-and-control breakdown at Kasserine would have been more thorough planning, more caution, more rigidity; at the higher levels, that indeed may have been the response.

General Douglas MacArthur, both in the Buna campaign in 1942–43 and in South Korea in July 1950, kept his distance from the battle but also intervened in ways that complicated the command-and-control problem as much as they may have energized the combat units. Sending General Eichelberger out to "clean house" in the 32nd Division, bogged down in front of Buna, was almost certainly on balance the right move, as Jay Luvaas tells us, but it was made on the basis of bad intelligence. Eichelberger, a capable senior commander, might have done better with more discretion in executing his mission. "I want you to take Buna," was the order, to which MacArthur added "or not come back alive" (p. 211). Similarly, Roy Flint describes a lack of mutual understanding during July 1950 between MacArthur and General Walker, commanding the Eighth Army in South Korea, just as there was a similar difficulty between MacArthur and the Joint Chiefs of Staff. In general terms, MacArthur, again perhaps because of faulty intelligence, seemed not to share the less optimistic perceptions of both Walker and the Joint Chiefs. In particular, MacArthur's refusal (acting through his chief of staff, General Almond) to let Walker move Eighth Army headquarters, with its vital communications equipment, back to Pusan in late July suggests a lack of confidence in the subordinate commander. These are symptoms not only of MacArthur's personal style, which was—like Patton's—unique, but also of the chronic problem of command-and-control.

It is likely that this problem is more acute in *American* first battles because the size and structure of the prewar Army, and thus the prewar experience of senior commanders and staff officers, are—even today—dictated largely by peacetime needs, not by wartime probabilities. Headquarters in the U.S. Army habitually expend their time and energies on routine administration, seldom pushing, training, and testing themselves as they push, train, and test their troops. Perhaps it is natural for a hierarchy to act like a bureaucracy, comfortably keeping busy with the day-to-day tasks that all large organizations create for themselves. Of course, headquarters work hard, but the result too often seems to be that the troops, even when inadequately trained and armed, are readier for war than the men who lead them. The implied lesson is that senior commanders and their staffs might do well to free themselves from the routine busywork of peacetime military life and to plan and carry out frequent, more realistic training exercises for themselves, involving several command levels and arms, that will hone skills that otherwise must be bought with blood and, possibly, defeat.

Whether the command-and-control problem did not exist in the Ia Drang, obviated by good training and perhaps by the nature of airmobile operations in rugged terrain against a dispersed enemy, or whether more research and fuller documentation will uncover the old problem is at this time impossible to say. Based on the case study by George Herring in this volume, we can find little to question in battalion operations; but the evident surprise and heavy casualties at Landing Zone X-ray and Albany (14–18 November) indicate that further up the line, key people might have done better. Without laboring the point, all ten cases argue that realistic preparation and testing of senior commanders and their staffs for the complex, unnatural task of controlling large-scale combat can hardly be overemphasized, especially because such emphasis must overcome the combined resistance of peacetime routine, bureaucratized priorities, and professional traditions.

Related to the problem of command-and-control is the recurrent theme of "doctrine," how it shapes the first battle and is in turn affected by the experience of the first battle. At least one senior military historian has said that the word *doctrine* is too limiting for historical analysis and that a broader term such as *preconceptions,* which goes beyond explicit, official concepts for waging war, is more useful because it is more realistic. Certainly he has a point. Doctrine, of course, is supposed to be a clear set of guidelines for prewar preparations and wartime operations; but, in fact, doctrine is so often in flux or dispute that we must accept the condition as normal. When doctrine lacks clarity or credibility, soldiers at every level will fall back on other notions of warfare, whatever their source—prior experience, film images, even childish fantasies. Michael Herr, observing part of the Vietnam War, noted the powerful influence that Hollywood versions of war exerted even on professional soldiers.[2] The long, tedious debate during the Jefferson and Madison administrations, centered on William Duane's *American Military Library* and its critics, virtually guaranteed an absence of acceptable doctrine in 1812; that doctrinal vacuum was filled by a mixture of Napoleonic visions of quick victory and a growing sense of panic. While keeping the focus on doctrine and its role in first battles, we can also be ready to admit the importance in some cases of a wider circle of mental factors, unofficial, often vague, sometimes not wholly conscious. The shakier the doctrine, the more likely that this wider circle of factors will come into significant play. Doctrine, whether explicit or implicit, is never absent; defined simply, it is the general consensus among military leaders on how to wage war.

A number of our case studies emphasize the role of doctrine in the first battle, when ideas—memory and prediction—must fill the void of experience. According to Ira Gruber, George Washington accepted the standard European doctrine of the eighteenth century: long-service soldiers highly drilled in linear tactics, led by gentlemanly officers; set-piece, large-scale battles produced by skillful maneuvers designed to exploit terrain; wars limited as much by logistics and organization as by a prevailing consensus on the laws of war and an aristocratic code of honor. Whether Washington might have done better with a doctrine adapted to the conditions of North America, to decentralized democracy, and to revolutionary war must remain a question. But it is a fact that European doctrine guided him in 1776, while the battles of Brandywine, Germantown, and Monmouth, as well as Steuben's drilling of American troops at Valley Forge, indicate that Washington saw no reason to reject or even modify the doctrine after the defeat at Long Island in 1776. Finally, Gruber tells us that eighteenth-century doctrine, considered at the strategic level, was ambiguous, emphasizing operations best suited to limited war but drawing heavily on historical models that stessed decisive victories.

Similarly, Union commanders in the Civil War accepted and applied what they understood to be Napoleonic doctrine: an emphasis on offensive action; a deemphasis of caution and defensive tactics; a reliance on surprise and audacity to win a quick, decisive victory despite the fact that the introduction of a practical rifled infantry weapon since 1815 had changed the whole calculus of land warfare. Implicit also in Napoleonic doctrine was a hardened, battlewise combat force. When General McDowell took the offensive in 1861 with an audacious maneuver designed to surprise his Confederate enemy, he failed miserably. Of course, McDowell lacked the veteran army that Napoleon maneuvered at Rivoli and Austerlitz. The defeat at Bull Run produced one of the two classic responses to unsuccessfully applied doctrine: "The doctrine is sound, but next time apply it better." For two years and more, Union commanders sought quick, decisive victory through audacious, offensive maneuvers. Not until 1864 would the Union Army's commanders be prepared to dig in, avoid reckless infantry assaults, and maintain contact with the enemy when decisive victory did not come quickly.[3] The Vietnam War seems to reveal a similar pattern, with a costly victory in the Ia Drang battle reinforcing a big-unit, high-tech doctrine of search and destroy, itself the wisdom of World War II as distilled by Fort Benning.

The question reasonably arises: what alternative doctrines were demonstrably better in 1776, 1861, or 1965? Answer: no one can say with real confidence. Failure to answer this very difficult question satisfactorily, however, does not invalidate what some first-battle experiences teach us about the role of doctrine—that doctrine may entail a kind of commitment that closes minds to alternative possibilities, and that failure or difficulties in applying doctrine may do less to change the doctrine than to strengthen the commitment; stubbornness and moral courage are qualities more easily distinguished from one another on paper than on the battlefield.

In several other first battles, doctrine played a somewhat different role. Queenston, with other fiascos of the War of 1812, doubtless induced just enough grudging acceptance of military professionalism within postwar American society to moderate thereafter the extreme doctrine of a citizen soldiery. Neither of the brief encounters of 1846 and 1898 raised doctrinal questions, but both had significant—probably unfortunate—effects on postwar doctrine. After the Mexican War, field artillery commanders were expected to operate aggressively, pushing their guns up with the leading infantry units; faced with infantry rifles in the Civil War, this new part of artillery doctrine proved suicidal, although commanders were slow to learn the lesson. Ultimate victory at Santiago in 1898 seemed to confirm the viability of infantry-assault doctrine, which persisted in relying on direct-fire artillery support, although Graham Cosmas wonders "what would have happened at San Juan Hill if the Spaniards also had had Gatlings" (p. 147). The long-term effects of the Rio Grande are discernible as late as Cantigny in 1918.

Osan/Naktong, the first battle of the Korean War, is interesting as a kind of doctrinal fossil. One army organized and armed to refight World War II attacked another, similarly prepared army; the U.S. Army intervened, lost its first battle, won the second, lost the third against the Chinese, but finally fought its way to an attritional stalemate within the first year of the war, operating always within the doctrinal terms of 1943–45. The Korean War was not a revolutionary war and was only incidentally a guerrilla war; atomic weapons were not used; and U.S. (UN) forces enjoyed both air supremacy over the battle area and considerable sympathetic support throughout the world. During the early 1950s, Army service schools chanted the litany that Korea had demonstrated the soundness of Army doctrine. Again, this is not to suggest that doctrine was unsound, but only to point out how combat experience affected thinking.

Kasserine offers yet another version of how doctrine and the first battle can interact. The impressive success of German armor in Poland, France, and Russia had led to a new doctrinal concept in the U.S. Army, that of the "tank destroyer"—a mobile, high-velocity antitank gun, with protection for its crew from small-arms fire, employed in an aggressive (i.e., not static) manner. At Kasserine, neither equipment nor training for tank-destroyer operations was adequate, and the new doctrine failed as German armor sliced through American positions, severely undermining the credibility of the tank-destroyer concept within the Army. Although new, fully tracked tank destroyers firing long-barreled 90-mm guns were soon available and the defeated commander of the 1st Armored Division was sent back to run the Tank Destroyer Center at Camp Hood, Texas, the doctrine in its original form simply could not survive the Kasserine debacle. The new orthodoxy, according to Martin Blumenson, was that "tanks became the primary antitank weapons" (p. 263).

Jay Luvaas, in his account of the Buna battle, points to yet another form of interaction. The doctrine of jungle warfare, as set forth in FM 100–5 and FM 31–20, seems eminently clear and sensible, well suited to what would actually happen in New Guinea. But no one seems to have taken the doctrine very seriously. The choice of the unready 32d Division instead of the available

41st, trained and conditioned for mountain and jungle operations, is inexplicable in view of FM 31-20's emphasis on special preparation as critically important to these kinds of operations.

Cantigny may be the most interesting case of all because the role of doctrine in 1918 was so closely linked to the broader, political context of military operations. Schooled in an army whose traditions and experience emphasized offensive infantry action as the route to victory, General Pershing was determined not to let the AEF be subverted by the cautious, defensive doctrines of trench warfare employed by European forces on the Western Front. For that reason, Pershing fought to preserve the independence of AEF battalions and divisions from French or British operational control; his fight corresponded at the political level with President Wilson's insistence that the United States, by declaring war on the Central Powers in 1917, had not joined the Allies but was merely an ''Associated'' member of the alliance. The American political commitment to maintaining an independent role in waging war against Germany reinforced Pershing's doctrinal commitment to methods of tactical training and employment significantly in conflict with prevailing tactical doctrine in the French and British Armies. His first battle, at Cantigny, together with subsequent battles at Belleau Wood and Soissons, strongly suggests that GHQ AEF might have been too optimistic about the feasibility of open warfare and that some doctrinal revision might have been in order. But the political context would have made such revision very awkward, even if Pershing had felt moved to undertake it, and of course there is no evidence that he did. The point once again is not that doctrinal mistakes were made or that politics kept Pershing from making military adjustment, but rather that the role doctrine played in and after the first battle may be strongly shaped by factors that seem quite unrelated to doctrinal considerations as such.

Politics, like doctrine, is a category that eludes clear definition but in general directs attention to the motivational heart of war. For what do people fight? How hard will they fight? Much military writing ignores these questions or relegates them to the motivational responsibility of the military commander. But every first battle reminds us how compelling politics, in the broadest sense of motivation, are in the actual conduct of warfare. The political connection at Cantigny, not only to maintain at every level U.S. ''independence,'' but also to ''showcase'' at the earliest opportunity the combat capability of the U.S. Army, is an exceptionally clear example. But each of the other nine cases is similarly instructive.

The port of New York in 1776 may have been indefensible against concentrated British land and sea power. Yet Washington simply had to make the attempt. Congress, shortly before the British offensive began, declared the independence of the ''United States,'' in effect foreclosing any negotiated settlement short of what even many Americans considered a radical political goal. After more than a year of armed conflict, Congress had committed the American resistance movement to all-out war—this at a time when the British government had shown signs of wanting to reach some compromise on the points at issue between London and the colonies. Under those political circumstances, for Washington to abandon a leading American city and one of the greatest harbors in the world without a fight was simply unthinkable. From August to November, Washington, his army, and Congress paid a high price at Long Island and in subsequent battles around New York for the political choice made in early July. Forced to retreat through New Jersey in December, Washington had virtually no military means to prevent the political collapse whose danger had made him fight for New York in the first place; thousands of Americans, including a few revolutionary leaders, thinking that the noble experiment had failed, flocked to the British side. Nothing except two brilliant—and lucky—little counterstrokes at Trenton and Princeton arrested political collapse long enough to rebuild an army. No one can be blamed for letting politics shape strategy and operations in 1776; instead, it could have been no other way—unless perhaps Congress had decided against declaring independence.

The Battle of Queenston in 1812, considered politically, looks like the reciprocal of Long Island in 1776. Washington had been delighted by the Declaration of Independence because he expected it to unify and mobilize the American people to wage war; all doubts and confusion would be dispelled by the official adoption of a clear, if radical, political objective. In 1807, however, President Jefferson had rejected war when a British frigate attacked an American ship just off the Virginia coast, killing and wounding American sailors and humiliating the United States. Jefferson, his successor Madison, and the Democratic-Republican Party for the next five years tried a variety of legal and economic measures to avoid war without sacrificing vital American interests. In 1812, they finally failed, but the five-year effort had seriously eroded and splintered the national will to wage war, which had been fairly strong in the immediate aftermath of the 1807 incident. The organization and conduct of the Niagara campaign of 1812 reflects the political disarray in which the war was undertaken. As Theodore Crackel points out, even the importance of the Niagara front was a result of the political alienation of New England after 1807, which had made it impossible to mount an offensive against the proper objective—the St. Lawrence valley and the key city of Montreal, on which all of Upper Canada (modern Ontario) depended. Even with better trained troops and more competent, cooperative commanders, American military operations on the Niagara front would have been constrained within the iron limits set by earlier political decisions.

Bull Run in 1861 as described by Glenn Robertson is a similar case with interesting variations. Military mobilization by the Federal government had set off a second wave of secessions in the upper South. Having paid a high political price for choosing to prepare for war, Lincoln was politically pressed to justify that choice. The three-month term of the first 75,000 volunteers set a deadline for action; to argue, militarily, that the Union Army was not yet ready for war and, especially, that it lacked the power and skill needed for offensive operations, was virtually irrelevant. Something impressive had to be done quickly. Franklin D. Roosevelt was responding to a not-dissimilar situation in 1942 when he told the Joint Chiefs of Staff that, somewhere, by the end of the year, American troops must be fighting the German Army. Exactly where the battle took place and with what specific objective were secondary considerations. Washington, Jefferson, Lincoln, and Roosevelt faced wars in which American morale and unity were crucial but fragile elements of their strategic problems. Only Jefferson chose to test the fragility of the national mood; Washington, Lincoln, and Roosevelt instead did what popular attitudes wanted them to do, and Long Island, Bull Run, and Kasserine—three horrendous military defeats—were the consequences of their decisions. But the consequences of the opposite course—for the administration, for the party in power, and for the nation—were even worse as a direct consequence of Jefferson's choice. Obviously, there are no easy answers, although among military historians, exemplified by Matthew Forney Steele, whose *American Campaigns* instructed several generations of professional soldiers, there is a long tradition of deploring and denouncing "political interference" in strategy and operations, as if war and politics could be kept in separate, sealed compartments. Such views are worse than idle; they are positively harmful because they are so out of touch with the realities of historical experience, particularly in the opening stage of any war. Political leaders may, of course (like soldiers), make mistakes, but their wartime decisions are inescapable; and even a decision not to "interfere" is, ultimately, political in its effects.

The Korean and Vietnam Wars have become notorious for the degree to which politics affected strategy. In each, however, the American military commander may also be seen to some degree as having imposed his view of strategy on the broader political situation. In 1965, the introduction of large U.S. combat forces in South Vietnam was intended primarily to support aerial operations against North Vietnam. By midsummer, General Westmoreland appeared to have convinced his political superiors, Secretary McNamara and President Johnson, that those forces could not simply secure and defend the enclaves from which air attacks were being launched but that U.S. ground forces must strike out offensively to seize the strategic initiative in South Vietnam. Whatever doubts they may have had about this shift in strategy (and it appears that both Ambassador Maxwell Taylor and the U.S. Marine Corps shared those doubts), the administration deferred to the commander in the field, whose expertise and responsibility elicited respect even from political leaders as tough as McNamara and Johnson. In Korea, MacArthur was preparing a counterstroke even before it was clear that UN forces could halt the southward drive of the North Korean Army; this apparent confusion of strategic priorities troubled those in Washington who bore political responsibility for the consequences of what would happen in Korea. Yet they deferred to MacArthur, who had been Army chief of staff when Truman was a county judge and his Joint Chiefs very junior officers. In the event, the brilliant Inchon counteroffensive seems to have justified their deference; but within a few months, their early reluctance to interfere would contribute to a major, damaging crisis. The spectacular firing of MacArthur, after having failed for nine months to give and enforce clear orders to the field commander, leaves the Truman administration with some important share of responsibility for the irreparable decline of public confidence in the direction of the Korean War.

Buna offers some support to those who might argue that no one—not Harry Truman, not Omar Bradley—could effectively impose political direction on MacArthur. Ordered by Roosevelt and Marshall to conduct the defense of Australia in 1942, MacArthur chose to interpret his mission broadly by defending Australia as far north of New Guinea as possible. Clearly his own goal was to liberate the Philippines. The strategic concept of economizing Allied forces in the southwest Pacific while massing for a main effort through the Central Pacific was vitiated by the Buna campaign, the first in an escalating chain of very expensive offensive operations in the Southwest Pacific. The logistical cost of supporting *two* soldiers under MacArthur would have paid for *five* under Eisenhower. Even the choice of an unready division to take Buna, with all the unhappy results of that choice, when a much better prepared U.S. division was available, may have been dictated by MacArthur's determination to sustain the offensive after the battle for Buna. It is reasonable to suppose that no one in the White House, including the president and General Marshall, could face the political dangers that cracking down on MacArthur in 1942–43 might have entailed.

It is less a matter in any of these cases of deciding who was right and who wrong than it is of simply recognizing the pervasive effect of political factors on the first battle. Beyond this simple recognition, we should note how complex and various the interplay of political and military factors often is; rather than regarding political intrusion as abnormal or deplorable, professional soldiers might better prepare for the inevitable, and discard the idea that "purely military" is a useful category.

Politics dominated both the Mexican and the Spanish-American Wars. The Polk administration engineered the Mexican War and waged it in a way that would, among other things, minimize its political value to the victorious American field commanders. While military considerations after the Rio Grande battles argued in favor of shifting the strategic center of the war,

Polk's desire to limit General Taylor's prestige also played a role in sending a force under General Scott to Vera Cruz. Unlike Polk, the McKinley administration surely did not engineer the war with Spain, nor did any such partisan political concerns deflect military operations. War came primarily because of growing public outrage with what appeared to be extremely brutal counterinsurgency operations against Cuban rebels, not far from U.S. territory, and a chain of broken promises by the Spanish government to ameliorate the situation in Cuba. Domestic politics pushed McKinley into the war, and then domestic politics—acting through the National Guard—pushed the War Department, against its own better judgment, into creating a volunteer Army. Only a few Volunteer regiments served in General Shafter's V Corps at San Juan, but their inadequate training and armament created some fairly serious problems in the conduct of the battle, Rough Rider heroics to the contrary notwithstanding. In a word, politics are inescapable.

A fourth recurrent feature of these first battles, along with command-and-control problems, the role of doctrine, and the pervasiveness of political factors, concerns what may be called "preparedness." How ready was the Army to fight, relative to its enemy? Of course, both doctrine and command-and-control may be regarded as aspects of preparedness, but the critical importance—and prominence—of each has justified their separate treatment. Here we can deal with the more mundane side of preparedness, or readiness: planning; force levels; training status; arms and equipment; and shortages, replacements, and supply. All of this should be judged not in terms of some ideal standard of preparedness but against the realistic standard of enemy preparedness.

Preparedness has never been reckoned the strong suit of U.S. military capacity. More or less invariably, the outbreak of war has meant frantic improvisation, not least in raising, arming, training, and deploying ground forces adequate to the conflict. Each of our case studies more or less illustrates the point. Earlier wars were fought by volunteer soldiers usually innocent of prewar military experience or training. After the Civil War, the Regular Army, the National Guard, and—eventually—laws prescribing compulsory and reserve service became central features of readiness for the first battle. Yet this gradual shift from pure improvisation to a measure of organized preparedness does not explain very much about what happens in the first battle. Because combat is a two-sided activity, our attention is quickly drawn to the other side and to the question of how well prepared the enemy was to fight.

British forces (with German allies) in 1776, Japanese in 1942, German in 1943, and Vietnamese in 1965 are the outstanding cases of a veteran enemy defeating or severely punishing its U.S. Army opponent. At the Rio Grande, on San Juan Hill, at Cantigny, and in South Korea, the Army faced an enemy force modern for its day but with serious weaknesses. The Mexican Army in 1846 was afflicted by the troubles of Mexican society itself: an officer corps with little professionalism and a soldiery drawn from the lowest economic and educational levels. The Spanish garrison of Cuba was a veteran fighting force, but it was dispersed and aware that its chances for victory were slim. The German reserve formations facing the U.S. 1st Division in 1918 were composed of older men, something less than the best of the German Army, and the survivors of more than three years of grueling warfare. The North Korean Army in 1950, armed and trained by the Soviet Union, had only the cutting edge of modernity—automatic weapons in the hands of a numerous infantry who knew how to use them, mortars and light artillery to support the infantry, and Soviet T-34 tanks that could not be stopped by available U.S. antitank weapons in the opening battles of July. But the UN counteroffensive of September revealed serious weaknesses in the North Korean Army—in logistics, mobility, and command-and-control—weaknesses that had been present from the outset. Enemy forces at Queenston in 1812 and at Bull Run in 1861 were not much better prepared than the U.S. Army they faced.

Relative numbers in each first battle, often seen as a crude indicator of strength, deserve attention. Only at Long Island and Osan/Naktong, where the Americans were greatly outnumbered, and at San Juan and Buna, where Americans greatly outnumbered their enemies, were relative numbers crucial. In each case, the more numerous side won the battle. In the other six first battles, there was either rough equivalence of deployed numbers or at least not enough disparity in numbers to be a major factor in the result. Some Canadian historians emphasize that "thousands" of Americans at Queenston were defeated by a few hundred men, but this enlarges the battle area unrealisticaly to include all those U.S. troops east of the Niagara River.

Numerical strength might be seen not as a static part of the prebattle balance sheet but as a dynamic indicator of accessibility and isolation of the battle area. For whatever reasons, U.S. numerical superiority at Queenston in 1812 simply could not be brought to bear. Even a much larger U.S. strategic reserve could not have stopped the North Koreans in July 1950 because of the remoteness of the battle area and the limits on global mobility. Less Confederate mobility almost certainly would have meant a victory for numerically superior Federal troops at Bull Run in 1861, whatever gross deficiencies afflicted the Union Army. The isolation of the Spanish and Japanese garrisons in 1898 and 1943 meant victory for numerically stronger U.S. forces, despite heavy casualties.

Numbers count in the first battle, as does the readiness of the enemy to fight, but only up to a point; at that point, attention swings back to the U.S. side. Almost by definition, the first battle is fought by green troops. Although there is an enormous range of qualitative difference between the raw levies that fought at Queenston or Bull Run and the professional forces that attacked at the Rio Grande, Cantigny, or the Ia Drang, in these five (as well as the other five) first battles the U.S. Army betrayed its greenness. Even the most intensive training will be less-than-adequate preparation for actual combat. Veterans of combat agree that certain vital lessons can be learned only under fire. In general, it seems that nothing but experience teaches soldiers and armies how to hold the delicate balance between courage and caution; too much audacity jeopardizes the survival on which victory must rest, but excessive caution usually means that fleeting chances to win are missed. The best-prepared U.S. Army forces (the 1st Division in 1918 and the 1st Cavalry Division in 1965) seemed too reckless of their own losses, brave and aggressive but seriously hurt by their first battles; they were blooded by them, literally. Something similar may have happened to the 2d Division under General Lawton at El Caney, where the objective got lost in the sheer fury of the battle, and at Buna, where senior officers seemed unwilling to assess realistically either the problems of the battle area or the limitations of U.S. forces.

Troops less well prepared—at Long Island, Rio Grande, Kasserine, and Osan/Naktong—or those hardly prepared at all—Queenston and Bull Run— tend to err in the other direction, becoming discouraged by early losses and difficulties, although the accounts in this volume indicate that we must not be too pessimistic about the fighting capacity of inadequately trained troops, provided they get minimally competent leadership. Queenston, of course, is the extreme case of all-round lack of preparedness, but failures of planning and leadership were so gross there that it is not clear how much blame should be placed on the soldiers themselves. What happened at Kasserine approaches the Queenston extreme; why it happened remains less than clear. There were failure and breakdown at so many points in Tunisia that it is not easy to build a satisfactory explanation, and perhaps II Corps was meeting an opponent as capable as any in modern military history. But American combat units fought at Kasserine, with confusion doing more than fear or panic to undercut the effectiveness of resistance. The 24th Division in 1950 faced a comparable situation; unready in almost every sense for combat, its performance was mixed: some units did badly, others much better, with leadership a key factor in a vital but essentially hopeless fight. Other cases of what might seem to be troop-unit breakdown in the first battle—at Long Island, Bull Run, some Volunteer regiments in Cuba, and the 32d Division at Buna—appear less clear-cut upon closer examination. Obviously, everything possible should be done to prepare troops for combat, but the level of training and discipline is only one factor among many in determining the outcome of the first battle.

For none of these battles, surprisingly, is it possible to argue that the outcome hinged on some lapse in planning or on some critical missing item of supply. The "for-want-of-a-nail" school of military history has always been popular, and there are surely important cases in which faulty planning (Schlieffen Plan and its modifications to 1914) or logistical failure (Rommel in

JOHN SHY

western North Africa in 1942) was crucial. But in not one of these ten first battles can it be reasonably concluded that a specific failure in planning or logistics probably decided the outcome. Even planning for Queenston was adequate; execution was atrocious. Enemy armor might have been slowed—if not stopped—by better, almost-available antitank weapons in 1943 and 1950; but the fact is that they were not yet available. New York and Massachusetts Volunteers, armed with old Springfields, simply could not cope in 1898 with the Mauser-armed Spanish infantry, but their failure did not alter the result of the battle. The Federal plan for Bull Run, as Glenn Robertson points out, was not bad. Similarly, Washington and his subordinates had not forgotten about the Jamaica Road into the left flank of the American position at Long Island; they simply did not take effective measures to secure it. This list might go on, but the point is that planning and logistical failures seem less prominent than one might have expected.

Other recurrent features of the first battle are worth noting; one is defense versus offense. The experience of first battles appears to support the offensive tradition and doctrine of the U.S. Army. When the Army took the offensive, it won the first battle five times out of seven (Rio Grande, San Juan, Cantigny, Buna, and Ia Drang); only twice was it defeated (Queenston and Bull Run). All three defensive battles were lost (Long Island, Kasserine, and Osan/ Naktong). But once again, closer examination forces us to refine the picture. Looking at both sides in each battle, we see that although defenders won only two out of ten battles (Canadian militia and British regulars in 1812 and Confederates in 1861), several other cases indicate that the strength of the defensive is not to be underestimated. Taylor's little army on the Rio Grande was advancing, but it fought mainly on the defensive. The enemy defenders at San Juan, Cantigny, and Buna exacted a heavy toll on their attackers, and in a different strategic environment each might have caused the American attacks to fail altogether. Despite their tactical victories, enemy forces at Kasserine and in South Korea could not achieve strategic decisions. And battalions of the 1st Cavalry Division, while deployed aggressively, fought defensively, winning the Ia Drang battle by decimating their North Vietnamese attackers. In the ancient argument between offense and defense, the first-battle experience of the U.S. Army offers no simple resolution. We must carefully distinguish the level of action (strategic, operational, or small-unit) and then consider the facts of each case.

In the Falklands War, British Rear Adm. John Woodward committed his landing force despite the absence of most of those elements believed to be vital to successful amphibious operations. Typically, military historians, like sports commentators, are obsessed by the key play or break—the moment, event, or personality that seems to make the difference between victory and defeat. For all who try consciously to learn from experience, the role of chance is fascinating. With the decline of belief in Providential determinism, certainly since Machiavelli, Western thinkers have made a place for *fortuna*—the unexpected, the uncontrollable—in their explanations of why things happen as they do. There is of course a modern countertradition, best expressed in secular deterministic philosophies like Marxism, which regards chance primarily as a refuge for the lazy-minded. To the idea that an event or a personality was "just one of those things," the modern determinist answers that "it was no accident" and invites us to deepen our analysis. For the student of warfare, these are not idle, academic quarrels but important choices to be made from the armory of analytical weapons. Much military history and thought argues, following Machiavelli, that the heroic leader can impose his will on a chance-filled battlefield; Admiral Woodward, well aware that he could not "play the percentages," sent his landing force in with maximum speed and determination. But if the Argentine missiles had hit a British carrier instead of a destroyer or a container ship, what then? Even Machiavelli conceded that not all heroes are victors.

Others may read differently the record of these ten first battles, but my own sense is that they have a sobering effect on the popular fascination with chance. In each case, there are people and events that may be assigned to the category of "chance," but, arguably, not one makes a vital difference. At Long Island, the British had learned not to repeat the mistake of Bunker Hill, and the Americans did not seem to grasp what was needed to protect an open flank against a large force. Ira Gruber suggests that the untimely illness of General Greene, leaving the less competent Putnam and Sullivan to command on Long Island, may explain the American failure to cover the left flank; but Greene's subsequent role in the American defeats at Fort Washington and Fort Lee indicates that even he was as yet too inexperienced to salvage victory at Long Island. At Queenston, General Brock was a fine leader who rallied Canadian defenses, but American incompetence surely would have snatched defeat from a far less able enemy commander. The effect of James Wilkinson in splitting the American command into factions is more difficult to assess; its specific effect at Queenston was, according to Theodore Crackel, at most problematical. Lieutenant Sims' bizarre performance, in losing most of the oars for the Niagara River crossing, may be a purer instance of chance in battle, although he also reflects the high degree of confusion and low level of professionalism on the American side. Chances on both sides at the Rio Grande seem virtually to cancel one another (as the determinist argues that they will almost always). Bull Run, seen in the context of the entire Civil War, suggests that not chance, but great new difficulties in conducting a tactical offensive, doomed whichever side tried to attack in 1861. The Spanish navy taking refuge in Santiago harbor was the chance that gave ground operations their pattern and that also decided their ultimate outcome in 1898; but otherwise chance played no discernible crucial role.

U.S. operations at Cantigny seem eminently designed to eliminate chance, and they largely succeeded. Tensions between the German commanders, Rommel and von Arnim, probably saved the U.S. II Corps from something even worse than befell it at Kasserine; but tensions between the British General Anderson and his non-British subordinates, and the lack of combat aptitude among key U.S. commanders, were chance events that contributed heavily to the German opportunities. Again, chance seems to neutralize chance. Losing the field artillery to Japanese air attacks near Buna was certainly bad luck for U.S. and Australian troops, but the base locations and operational ranges of Japanese and Allied air forces, relative to surface operations, can hardly be called an accident. Colonel Smith and General Dean behaved heroically in leading a shaky American defense against the overwhelming North Korean advance, but surely in every U.S. division we can expect to find at least a few Deans and Smiths among its senior commanders. Pure chance produced the ferocious meeting engagements in the Ia Drang at Landing Zones X-ray and Albany, but numerous airmobile probes by elements of the 1st Cavalry Division had been trying to create just such encounters, and apparently the North Vietnamese had decided to test U.S. forces in battle, so little is left to call accidental in the Ia Drang battle, except perhaps the specific times and places of combat. Lesson: the more we know about a battle, the smaller the role we assign to chance.

Trying to assess the long-term effects of first battles, we note that in three cases—those American victories in which a well-prepared army had performed fairly well (1846, 1918, 1965)—the first battle had a "hardening" effect, creating a postbattle confidence that approached complacency, making the Army less flexible during subsequent operations. Long Island, Queenston, and Bull Run were defeats to which there were so many contributory factors that effective lesson learning appears to have been lost in the "noise" of postbattle recriminations and shake-ups. Even Buna, a costly victory, does not seem to have taught any important lessons to guide subsequent Army operations in the Pacific, although the painful experience of the campaign certainly had confirmed prewar Army doctrine for mountain and jungle warfare. The Army learned major lessons from the Spanish-American War, but they were not taught by the first battle at San Juan; rather, they came from a more general postwar sense of inefficiency and mismanagement. Only Kasserine and Osan/Naktong, both shocking defeats, seem to have had the kind of healthy instructive effect that one might reasonably expect from every first-battle experience. Why? The answer may lie in the fact that these two defeats were, indeed, shocking. In 1943 and 1950, the Army thought it would do better than it actually did. Unlike the defeats at Long Island, Queenston, and Bull Run, where expectations were either much lower or unrealistically higher, the expectations in Tunisia and Korea seem realistic, and yet they were brutally shattered by the first battle. Perhaps those are the psychological preconditions for effective learning: no easy way to explain away disaster and anxious determination to rectify the problem. In any case, the Army quickly learned from its defeats at Kasserine and Osan/ Naktong.

Recurrent features of our ten first battles have provided one set of subjects for discussion; a second set is provided by important changes since 1776, trends that have transformed warfare since the battle of Long Island. There is a natural tendency to assume that only the most recent military experience is relevant because so much has been altered by these deep, long-term changes. But whether we can learn more from Kasserine and Ia Drang than from Queenston or Bull Run should not be an assumption but a question for serious consideration. Behind the assumption lies the certain knowledge that military technology in particular is today radically unlike that available to Washington or even Pershing. It is this modern absorption with technology and with rapid technological change that makes us doubt the relevance of the more remote past.

Until the Mexican War, armies could maneuver freely within sight of one another. Artillery could fire effectively well over a mile, but lack of mobility and limited impact kept artillery to a secondary role except against fortified positions. The chief weapon was the smoothbore musket, inaccurate but deadly within a hundred yards. Massing infantry musket fire was the central concern of tactics, with drill and discipline the preferred means to this tactical end. The Revolutionary and Napoleonic Wars brought a new flexibility in the training and employment of troops in battle, but no tactical innovation could transcend the restrictions imposed by the smoothbore musket. Troops, supplies, and (for the most part) information moved over bad roads at a walking pace; water, where available, was the preferred mode of transportation—cheaper, faster, usually safer.

Changes began to appear in the Mexican War. The commander-in-chief and his field commanders jumped time and space with the new electric telegraph. Polk and his service secretaries could coordinate the movements of American forces on the East and West Coasts with those operating in southern Texas. General Taylor moved his army into disputed territory almost as soon as Washington sent orders to do so. During the battle, aggressive handling of new, light, mobile artillery by U.S. commanders stopped Mexican attacks before they could begin; the visible battle area was becoming a more dangerous place for maneuvering infantry.

At Bull Run, not field artillery but the new infantry rifle, deadly as far as a man could see to aim its spinning projectile, transformed the visible battle area into a killing ground. Firearms had driven cavalry to the fringes of the battle area long before Bull Run, but in 1861 riflemen drove artillery off the ridge lines and stopped infantry attacks with horrendous losses. At first, it seemed that telegraphic communications and new steam transportation could do nothing to overcome the remarkably strengthened defense; but in time the more populous and mechanized North deployed vast armies, fed by rail and coordinated by telegraph, that would overwhelm Confederate forces, with Union steamships strangling the Southern economy and slicing along its vital river valleys. New technology, by making battles indecisive and very bloody, protracted the war, but technology also made it possible, eventually, for a determined Federal government to win.

In Cuba, smokeless powder and breechloading, magazine-fed rifles reiterated the tactical lesson of Bull Run, but neither the timing nor the conditions of the San Juan battle were quite right to teach the big new lesson: that rifled artillery, firing high-explosive shells, directed by observers wired to the gun crews who used on-carriage recoil systems to keep their weapons aimed accurately, was becoming king of the battlefield. Before 1914, few had grasped that the net effect of massive, long-range, accurate, destructive artillery fire would be to make organized defenses (already strengthened by highly accurate, rapid-fire infantry weapons) almost impenetrable. By 1918, when the 1st Division moved out of its trenches into the attack at Cantigny, a "battle" no longer was an event that might decide a campaign or a war in one or two days of spectacular combat; it had become a brutal effort, endlessly repeated, to weaken enemy morale and resources without paying too high a price. Looking at the plan prepared for the Cantigny battle by Lieutenant Colonel Marshall's G-3 section, with its neatly drawn unit boundaries and phase lines and its very limited terrain objectives, and contrasting it with the operation carried out by a force of comparable size under General Howe against Washington in 1776 and with that attempted by General McDowell with a slightly larger force in 1861, we can see graphically what had happened to warfare by the early twentieth century.

None of this would change after 1918; that is, Buna, Osan/Naktong, and Ia Drang remind us how tough organized, high-technology defenses can be, while Kasserine also reminds us—as do certain aspects of the other three modern battles—that the extremes of defensive, attritional warfare reached on the Western Front in 1914–18 were never typical of warfare elsewhere, even during the First World War, wherever forces did not fill the space available for maneuver. German armor drove around and cut off dispersed American defenses at Kasserine in 1943, just as North Korean divisions found the open flanks and moved around UN forces in 1950. Unlike the hard-pressed Japanese at Buna in 1942, the hard-pressed battalions of the 1st Cavalry Division in 1965 could bring massive artillery and air support to bear on the attacking enemy and could usually leave the battle area itself to avoid defeat or unacceptable losses. The great technological changes since 1918 (excluding nuclear weapons)—air power and armored mobility—have changed the calculus by which modern defensive firepower plays its role, but they have by no means destroyed that role. Buna, Kasserine, Osan/Naktong, and Ia Drang all indicate that the critical change is in the degree to which one side or the other can isolate the battle area, preventing movement of forces and fire support into and out of the battle area during the limited time in which modern defenses struggle to stop the attacker. Given anything like an even break, the tactical defense will win.

But before concluding on the basis of American experience that it is changing technology that has driven land warfare from brief, decisive battles of the classic age to the protracted attritional campaigns of modern times, we should recall the exceptions to the trend and try to account for them. Washington, badly beaten in the battles around New York in 1776, fought on because he was fighting a revolutionary war, viable as long as popular support for it did not collapse. Whether or not better British leadership in 1776 would have changed this result is a question wide open to debate. Not debatable is the importance of politics in the Revolutionary War and of Washington's own decision to wage a more cautious, attritional war after 1776; neither factor was much affected by technology. And then there are the modern cases, outside American experience—France in 1940 and the Middle East in 1967 quickly come to mind—in which the latest technology, plus some major breakdown on the losing side, leads to a truly lightning war. Technology, if nuclear weapons are excluded from consideration, surely has pushed us toward longer, bloodier, less conclusive land warfare, but the trend refers to probabilities, not to the confident prediction of actual results in a specific case.

John Keegan, in the concluding chapter of his remarkable book *The Face of Battle,* has asked whether the modern battlefield is "habitable" and thus whether battle itself, in any meaningful sense, will be possible in the future.[4] The most modern means of finding and hitting targets are so effective, as we have glimpsed them in the Yom Kippur War of 1973 and again when Exocet missiles sank the British destroyer *Sheffield* and the container ship *Atlantic Conveyor* in 1982, and the compression of time by modern electronic and propulsion systems so great, that the human capacity to respond, endure, and simply survive in such an environment may indeed be far too limited. But two points must be made: one is that battles, at least first battles, remain likely, however incapable human beings may be of waging them effectively. The other point is that from Long Island to Ia Drang, battle has already undergone radical transformations in less than two centuries. In our own set of ten cases, one major threshold was being crossed at Bull Run in 1861, and land warfare had crossed another by 1918. If we were to broaden our survey and extend it backward in time, we would see yet another threshold, crossed long before 1776, when massed infantry, drilled and disciplined to fire short-range, bayonet-tipped muskets to maximum effect and to endure horrific losses while doing so, transformed the wild melee of traditional battle into a highly organized, routinized, controlled activity. When Washington rejected the more informal, individualistic American style of warfare in favor of European professionalism, he simply was choosing what all informed observers regarded as the demonstrably superior system. At Long Island and Queenston, Bull Run and Cantigny, Kasserine and the Ia Drang, if one looks closely and thoughtfully, there is the spectacle of men trying to do more than they can do, of flesh and blood and brain unable to meet the test of British and German fusiliers in closed ranks moving in on half-trained farm boys, of brave Union gun crews blown away by rifle fire as they tried to unlimber their batteries, of soldiers trained for open-field tactics hugging their holes while German artillery rained death on them, of Iowa National Guardsmen wondering what was happening as dozens of unidentified armored vehicles rumbled around their hilltop position in a blinding sandstorm, of confident and well-armed but immobilzied troopers flat on their faces and praying for air strikes as fire comes at them from every point of the encircling Vietnamese jungle. Courage and professional capacity, which rightly receive so much attention, are not the only issues here; we also confront the spectacle of battle, especially the first battle, overwhelming people, blocking even the best efforts of individuals and organization to cope and act effectively.

In one sense, there is nothing new in this; soldiers cut off and overrun at Long Island in 1776 would not need instruction from the survivors of LZ Albany in confusion and sudden death. But in another sense, the effect of technology in making battles more frequent and lethal, and in protracting the periods of intense combat, invites us to reconsider traditional concepts of battle itself. Unless the battlefield becomes so automated that the human fighter is in no more danger than anyone else—science-fiction wars fought by robotic weaponry controlled by real men (and women) from deep, deep bunkers—then we will need to pay very close attention to that complex, vital, unpredictable, and delicate system at the heart of the battlefield—the human being. The human element must function, and be able to function, in battle; before the first battle, this imperative raises a question unanswerable before the event. In terms of the human capacity to respond, how much has technological change really altered the face of battle?

The chief human response to changing military technology has been organizational and pedagogical: increasing specialization in the new technology, more and more schooling to teach specialists the new tasks. Washington's staff was a handful of loyal, literate young men whose education was liberal, not professional; General Howe's staff was surprisingly similar. As late as the Mexican War, artillery units were trained and often used as infantry. Since then, the key task of military leadership has become the management of a complex organization of technical specialists, and the standard professional path to leadership has come to mean spending much of a military career in school, as teacher or student. Engineering—fortification and siegecraft—was among the first set of military tasks to demand specialized schooling and organization, with the procurement and distribution of supplies second. Jefferson established West Point in 1802 mainly to provide the engineering specialists needed to make the citizen-army concept workable. Keeping written records, housing and moving troops, caring for bodies and souls, and enforcing rules had even by 1776 produced small corps of adjutants, quartermasters, surgeons, chaplains, and judge advocates. Newer specialties would center on the tools of war as each became more important, plentiful, expensive, and complicated. The narrow specification of tasks and the schools designed to teach those tasks have become features of the military profession so common that it is difficult to imagine an army without them. At least it is difficult to take seriously an army, like Washington's, composed of soldiers virtually unspecialized, led by officers largely unschooled. But this is almost certainly a mistake, a failure of modern imagination, a blind spot in our own heavily schooled, highly specialized mental equipment. The very process of military modernization, with its ever-narrowing division of tasks and roles and its emphasis on rational procedures and measurable results, has made it more difficult than it was in 1776 or 1861 to deal effectively with the marvelously resilient, poorly understood human machine at the center of the system. The vital question about military change during the last two centuries is how much, or how little, this human element has changed in response to changes both in technology and in the broader environment within which battle takes place. The question is acute when we apply it to first battles, where we must depend so heavily on memories, myths, and guesses about how people will behave.

The simplest aspect of the question concerns how soldiers were recruited for their first battles. Voluntary and compulsory service appear to be the only recruiting alternatives. In fact, men who volunteered, like Washington's soldiers at Long Island or the Union troops at Bull Run, were to some extent compelled to do so by community pressure or economic need. At the same time, compulsory service—strictly applicable to only three of our ten cases: Cantigny, Buna, and Kasserine—seems to work only when there has been a voluntary acceptance of compulsion. The local draft board, invented in 1917, worked wonderfully well to produce manpower for four wars until, during the Vietnam War, it became the object of suspicion and dislike—less the expression of a community's sense of patriotism and justice, as it had been in 1917, 1941, and even 1951; more the bureaucratic symbol of a dubious war. Without popular support, compulsory service is not likely to be effective.

The trend since 1776 has clearly been in the direction of more dependence on compulsory service, though not simply because modern men are less willing than their ancestors to serve voluntarily. The modern draft, with its system of specified exemptions, has been as much the instrument for managing the total national labor force as it has been a way of forcing men into the Army. In 1917, volunteers were actually turned back so that manpower intake could be carefully controlled; the lesson of 1861, when facilities were swamped by an outpouring of volunteers, contributing to the disorganization and demoralization that weakened the Army's effort at Bull Run, was well learned by 1917.

A critical element in this trend away from reliance on the spontaneous volunteer is the legal requirement for *personal* service. During the eighteenth and nineteenth centuries, the law, when it occasionally "drafted" men for war, expected only an able-bodied person, not a specific person. The hiring of substitutes was commonplace in the Revolutionary and Civil Wars. Although it did not affect the battles at either Long Island or Bull Run nor any other first battle before 1900, the older popular attitude toward military service that made substitution acceptable surely had some effect on motivation. By making compulsory service less honorable, substitution seems to have raised the incentive for men to volunteer; conversely, not to volunteer was seen as more or less dishonorable.

All this was changed fundamentally by the two world wars; total war put the total manpower at the nation's service, with economic roles being morally equated—at least in theory—to active military service. Some of the soldiers who fought at Buna and Kasserine had volunteered before Pearl Harbor to serve in the 32d or 34th Divisions (both National Guard), but by 1942, no soldier in those units could claim that his service was not, in the strictest sense of the word, compulsory. The soldiers who fought at Osan/Naktong had volunteered, but surely not for anything so strenuous as stopping the whole North Korean Army, and the U.S. Army would rely during the Korean War on the most difficult kind of compulsion—"selective service," which selected some men for battle while selecting others to stay at home. To make selection more equitable, combat soldiers served only nine months in Korea before being sent home. A similar system, with one year as the term, was used in the Vietnam War; but for the first time since the Civil War there was massive draft resistance and evasion, and the whole system was on the verge of collapse when it was abandoned, in 1975, for a return to voluntary service. The men of the 1st Cavalry Division in 1965, however, were volunteers—professional soldiers who were psychologically ready for combat, conscious that they were members of an elite fighting force.

Military commentators and historians, from Washington through Emory Upton down to Robert McNamara, have preferred the long-service professional soldier to the citizen-soldier who voluntarily takes up arms in an emergency. But most of those who have emphasized professionalism have also favored a general legal obligation to serve militarily. In other words, advocates combine the professional levels of training of the voluntary system with the large, controllable pool of manpower provided by compulsion. In historical fact, the two systems are not readily combined; the voluntary system may produce limited numbers of professionally capable soldiers (or larger numbers of ill-trained volunteers), while the compulsory system is much more likely to solve the problem of numbers than the problem of adequate training. Lack of public support or acceptance will undermine either system, especially compulsion. Whether the most recent shift, from compulsory to voluntary service, is a new trend or merely a blip on an older trend toward military obligation as part of citizenship, remains open to debate. My own sense, looking backward, is that it must be a blip; the demands of modern warfare and Great Nationhood cannot be (some argue should not be) met by those relatively few who, for whatever reason, are attracted to military service.

Motivation remains the key to both systems, and Secretary McNamara's insistence that military service is nothing more than another kind of labor, to be hired at whatever price the labor market would charge for it, is only a recent example of how the policy debate on manpower has been characterized for two centuries by naive, superficial thinking. What brings a man (or woman) to the Army, and what—beyond adequate training and leadership—makes better or worse soldiers, remains a mystery. Very few soldiers can perform satisfactorily in their first battle, but given a chance most seem to adapt quickly to the challenges of combat. Between Long Island and Ia Drang there is less clear evidence of change than there is between all ten first battles and our present sense that, unlike any previous experience, soldiers in the next first battle will never get the chance to adapt once the first shots have been fired.

Increasing specialization has of course changed the Army a great deal since 1776; more soldiers, with primary tasks only remotely related to armed combat, have raised alarmingly the size of Army "tail" relative to Army "tooth." But if we look at individuals rather than at the organization, it is less clear that the modern soldier must learn and know more than his earlier counterpart in order to survive and function effectively. Specialization means, among other things, that more is done today for the typical soldier by other soldiers. A soldier at Queenston or San Juan needed to do much more himself. Nor should we underestimate the burden that the complexities of earlier weapons and tactics placed on the individual. We may like to think and say that never has the combat soldier faced such a severe challenge as he does today, but we may actually mean that cooks, clerks, and electronic repairmen are still somehow expected to retain the wide range of soldierly skills of an earlier, simpler organization. Is this a realistic perception of past and present? Probably not.

Turning from the soldier in the ranks to the directing elements of Army organization, to the NCOs and the officers below general rank, we see the same long-term trend toward more schooling and specialization. But there is far less change in recruitment and motivation. Washington believed that gentlemen made the best officers; West Point came under repeated attack for denying access to those who lacked a middle-class education and some political connections; current Army policy makes college-level education a prerequisite for commission. In one form or another, the belief persists that being an officer needs some kind of social prerequisite. With social criteria thus narrowing the pool of potential officers, the NCO has been all the more important in the U.S. Army. But NCOs historically have come from that small group of soldiers who elect to stay in the Army. The prospect of being a commissioned officer always seems to attract a sufficient number of young Americans, but very few are drawn to the life and status of a sergeant; consequently, the chronic shortage of good NCOs may have always been the weakest link in the Army chain, in part of course because of the inevitable inadequacies of the most junior officers. Rereading each chapter in an attempt to see where and how junior leadership played its role, one is dismayed by our neglect of the NCO. Social scientists dealing with the military profession are as guilty of this neglect as the military historians. But where did those precious sergeants come from? How does a democratic society that has never been sympathetic to the occupation of soldier produce enough of these sergeants? Many think they know the answers, but it is time for more historical study than the questions have yet received.

From Long Island to the present, unhappy observers of the Army have noted that good human material in the ranks has failed to realize its potential because of inadequate leadership at the junior and middle levels, from squad to battalion. Good leadership, when it appears at those levels in our first battles, stands out. We may reasonably ask whether more schools, or new systems of incentive that do not address directly the question of what produces, after ten years of service, an effective sergeant or captain, can substantially improve a problem that is not new but recurrent since 1776.

In this section on changes since Washington lost his first battle, the emphasis has been as much on human continuities as on the transforming effects of technology. Perhaps this is a historian's natural bias, seeing always the relevance of even the remote past; at least it challenges the widespread current belief that things were never as tough as they are now and that the simpler people of the past have nothing truly important to teach us. On the other hand, the popular expression about reinventing the wheel betrays an irrepressible doubt that everything important has changed. So if we simply read these accounts of first battles, knowing that some things change and some do not, trying our best to sort out which is which, we have done what the past expects of us.

Notes

CHAPTER 1. AMERICA'S FIRST BATTLE:
LONG ISLAND, 27 AUGUST 1776

1. For the persistence and nature of warfare in colonial America, see Douglas Edward Leach, *Arms for Empire: A Military History of the British Colonies in North America 1607-1763*, The Macmillan Wars of the United States (New York: Macmillan, 1973), and John E. Ferling, *A Wilderness of Miseries: War and Warriors in Early America*, Contributions in Military History, no. 22 (Westport, Conn.: Greenwood Press, 1980).

2. For an example of a campaign against Indians, see Douglas Edward Leach, *Flintlock and Tomahawk: New England in King Phillip's War* (New York: Macmillan, 1958); of an engagement in the French and Indian War, C. P. Stacey, *Quebec, 1759: The Siege and the Battle* (New York: St. Martin's Press, 1959); and of the opening engagements of the revolution, Christopher Ward, *The War of the Revolution*, ed. John Richard Alden, 2 vols. (New York: Macmillan, 1952), 1:32-51, 73-98, 181-201; 2:665-78.

3. The fifteen British officers are listed in Henry P. Johnston, *The Campaign of 1776 around New York and Brooklyn*, ed. Leonard W. Levy, Era of the American Revolution (New York: DaCapo Press, 1971), 1:134-36. Biographical sketches of William Howe, Henry Clinton, Robert Pigot, Hugh Percy, James Grant, Charles Cornwallis, and John Vaughn may be found in Leslie Stephen and Sidney Lee, eds., *Dictionary of National Biography*, 22 vols. (London: Oxford University Press, 1949-1950); of Alexander Leslie, James Agnew, Francis Smith, James Robertson, Edward Mathew, and Sir William Erskine in John Grant Wilson and John Fiske, eds., *Appletons' Cyclopedia of American Biography*, 6 vols. (New York: D. Appleton, 1887-1889); of Samuel Cleveland in Francis Duncan, *History of the Royal Regiment of Artillery*, 2 vols., 3d ed. (London: John Murray, 1879), 1:124, 127, 188-89, 207, 301, 308-09, and in *Gentleman's Magazine*, Sep 1794, p. 864; and of Valentine Jones in *Gentleman's Magazine*, Nov 1779, p. 566. The service of these officers while with particular regiments may be traced through Great Britain, War Office, *A List of the General and Field-Officers as They Rank in the Army* . . . (London: J. Millan, 1755-), published annually after 1755, and through Charles H. Stewart, comp., *The Service of British Regiments in Canada and North America* . . . , rev. ed. (Ottawa: Department of National Defense Library, 1964).

4. The twenty-one American generals are listed in Johnston, *Campaign of 1776*, 1:126-31. Biographical sketches of George Washington, Rufus Putnam, Israel Putnam, James Clinton, John Morin Scott, William Heath, Thomas Mifflin, George Clinton, Joseph Spencer, Samuel Holden Parsons, John Sullivan, William Alexander Lord Stirling, Alexander McDougall, Nathanael Greene, John Nixon, Oliver Wolcott,

Nathaniel Woodhull, and Henry Knox are in Allen Johnson and Dumas Malone, eds., *Dictionary of American Biography,* 20 vols. (New York: Charles Scribner's Sons, 1928-36); of John Fellows and James Wadsworth in *Appletons';* of Nathaniel Heard in Larry R. Gerlach, *Prologue to Independence: New Jersey in the Coming of the American Revolution* (New Brunswick, N.J.: Rutgers, 1976), pp. 332, 372.

5. Ira D. Gruber, "George III Chooses a Commander in Chief," in Peter J. Albert and Ronald Hoffman, eds., *Arms and Independence: The Military Character of the American Revolution* (Charlottesville: University Press of Virginia, 1983), and comparison of biographical sketches in n. 3 above.

6. Ira D. Gruber, *The Howe Brothers and the American Revolution* (Chapel Hill: University of North Carolina Press, 1974), pp. 56-59; William B. Willcox, *Portrait of a General: Sir Henry Clinton in the War of Independence* (New York: Knopf, 1964), pp. 9-39; Franklin and Mary Wickwire, *Cornwallis, the American Adventure* (Boston: Houghton Mifflin, 1970), pp. 8, 17-29, 45-46; Sir Lewis Namier and John Brooke, *The House of Commons, 1754-1790,* 3 vols., The History of Parliament (New York: Oxford University Press, 1964), 3:269-70; and *Dictionary of National Biography* (for Percy).

7. James Thomas Flexner, *George Washington in the American Revolution (1774-1783),* 4 vols., George Washington (Boston: Little, Brown, 1965-72), 2:104-08.

8. For authoritative sketches of Washington, Greene, and Sullivan, see George Athan Billias, ed., *George Washington's Generals* (New York: William Morrow, 1964), pp. 3-21, 109-62; of Putnam, *Dictionary of American Biography.*

9. Charles Evans, *American Bibliography . . . ,* 12 vols. (Chicago: Blakely Press, 1903-34), 2:95-5:301; Charles Knowles Bolton, *The Private Soldier under Washington* (Port Washington, N.Y.: Kennikat Press, 1964), p. 109.

10. North Callahan, *Henry Knox: General Washington's General* (New York: Rinehart, 1958), p. 35.

11. Callahan, *Knox,* pp. 29-30, 35-36; Theodore Thayer, *Nathanael Greene: Strategist of the American Revolution* (New York: Twayne, 1960), pp. 20-21, 24, 47-48; Richard K. Showman, ed., *The Papers of General Nathanael Greene,* 3 vols. to date (Chapel Hill: University of North Carolina Press, 1976-   ), 2:28, 235; John C. Fitzpatrick, ed., *The Writings of George Washington . . . , 1745-1799,* 39 vols. (Washington, D.C.: Government Printing Office, 1931-44), 1:385, 2:150, 3:27-28.

12. Ira D. Gruber, "British Strategy: The Theory and Practice of Eighteenth-Century Warfare," in Don Higginbotham, ed., *Reconsiderations on the Revolutionary War,* Contributions in Military History, no. 14 (Westport, Conn.: Greenwood Press, 1978), pp. 14-22, quoting p. 21.

13. Guy Frégault, *Canada: The War of the Conquest* (Toronto: Oxford University Press, 1969), provides the basis for this interpretation.

14. My interpretation is based on the evidence—but not the arguments—of Reginald Savory, *His Britannic Majesty's Army in Germany during the Seven Years War* (Oxford: Clarendon Press, 1966).

15. Ms notebook, Hugh, Lord Percy, F/3/22, Alnwick Castle, Northumberland, England; Ms jnl, Henry Clinton, sub: Seven Years' War in Germany; Ms notebook, Henry Clinton, 1768-76, Clinton Papers, John Rylands Library, Manchester, England.

16. Robert S. Quimby, *The Background of Napoleonic Warfare: The Theory of Military Tactics in Eighteenth-Century France* (New York: Columbia University Press, 1957), pp. 6, 26-174.

17. Ms notebooks, Hugh, Lord Percy, F/3/5, F/3/22, Alnwick Castle; Ms letterbook, Henry Clinton, box titled "Memoranda," Clinton Papers, William L.

Clements Library, Ann Arbor, Michigan; Ms reflections, Henry Clinton, box marked "Arnold, Gibraltar, Intelligence . . . Tactics," Clinton Papers, Clements Library; Ms return, William Howe, 7 Apr 1774, sub: review of *4th Regiment of Foot*, War Office Papers, Class 27, vol. 30, Public Record Office, Kew, Surrey, England (hereafter cited as W.O. 27/30).

18. Stacey, *Quebec, 1759*, pp. 138-55; Ward, *The War of the Revolution*, 1:87-94.

19. Johnston, *Campaign of 1776*, 1:104-38; Charles H. Lesser, ed., *The Sinews of Independence: Monthly Strength Reports of the Continental Army* (Chicago: University of Chicago Press, 1976), pp. 26-28.

20. Gruber, *Howe Brothers*, and Willcox, *Portrait of a General*, provide numerous illustrations of the effects of divided authority and personal influence on British planning.

21. R. Arthur Bowler, "Logistics and Operations in the American Revolution," in Higginbotham, ed., *Reconsiderations on the Revolutionary War*, pp. 54-71; R. Arthur Bowler, *Logistics and the Failure of the British Army in America, 1775-1783* (Princeton: Princeton University Press, 1975).

22. E.g., Charles P. Whittemore, *A General of the Revolution: John Sullivan of New Hampshire* (New York: Columbia University Press, 1961), pp. 31, 51, 149-52; Showman, *Papers of Greene*, 1:216-17, 285-86; 2:18, 98-99, 109-11, 121-25, 220-21, 252-53.

23. Bowler, "Logistics and Operations," p. 56.

24. James A. Huston, *The Sinews of War: Army Logistics 1775-1953*, Stetson Conn, ed., Army Historical Series (Washington, D.C.: Government Printing Office, 1966), p. 16. This paragraph is drawn from Bowler and Huston.

25. Johnston, *Campaign of 1776*, 1:68-90, 122-25; Gruber, *Howe Brothers*, pp. 100-04; Huston, *The Sinews of War*, pp. 18-30.

26. Sylvia R. Frey, *The British Soldier in America: A Social History of Military Life in the Revolutionary Period* (Austin: University of Texas Press, 1981).

27. James W. Hayes, "The Social and Professional Background of the Officers of the British Army, 1714-1763," M.A. thesis, University of London, 1956; Ira D. Gruber, "For King and Country: The Limits of Loyalty of British Officers in the War for American Independence," in Edgar Denton, ed., *Limits of Loyalty* (Waterloo, Ont.: Wilfrid Laurier University Press, 1980), pp. 25-40.

28. Johnston, *Campaign of 1776*, 1:104-25.

29. Don Higginbotham, "The American Militia: A Traditional Institution with Revolutionary Responsibilities," in Higginbotham, ed., *Reconsiderations on the Revolutionary War*, pp. 83-103; Bolton, *Private Soldier*, pp. 13-34; Charles Royster, *A Revolutionary People at War: The Continental Army and American Character, 1775-1783* (Chapel Hill: University of North Carolina Press, 1979), pp. 3-43; James Kirby Martin and Mark Edward Lender, *A Respectable Army: The Military Origins of the Republic, 1763-1789* (Arlington Heights, Ill.: Harlan Davidson, 1982), pp. 6-48.

30. Martin and Lender, *A Respectable Army*, pp. 40-48; Bolton, *Private Soldier*, pp. 26-31.

31. John R. Sellers, "The Common Soldier in the American Revolution," in Stanley J. Underdal, ed., *Military History of the American Revolution*, The Proceedings of the 6th Military History Symposium United States Air Force Academy, 10-11 Oct 1974 (Washington, D.C.: Government Printing Office, 1976), p. 152.

32. Ibid. and quoting Edward C. Papenfuse and Gregory A. Stiverson, "General Smallwood's Recruits: The Peacetime Career of the Revolutionary War Private," *William and Mary Quarterly* 30 (1973): 132.

33. Flexner, *Washington*, 2:23-97; Gruber, *Howe Brothers*, pp. 20-35, 80-85.

34. Ms ltr, Howe to Lord George Germain, 25 Apr 1776, Colonial Office Papers, class 5, vol. 93, Public Record Office. Gruber, "British Strategy," pp. 22–24.

35. Gruber, *Howe Brothers,* pp. 4–83.

36. Quoted in Johnston, *Campaign of 1776,* 1:58–59.

37. Ibid., 1:48–92; Ltrs, Washington to President of Congress, 14, 30 Jul 1776, Fitzpatrick, *Writings of Washington,* 5:274, 354.

38. Ms ltr, Howe to Lord George Germain, 7 Jul 1776, C.O. 5/93.

39. Gruber, *Howe Brothers,* pp. 91–106.

40. Ms ltr, Howe to Germain, 6 Aug 1776, C.O. 5/93.

41. Johnston, *Campaign of 1776,* 1:64–91, 95, 101, 104–06, 131–32.

42. Ibid., 1:84.

43. Ibid., 1:64–84, 101–03; Douglas W. Marshall and Howard H. Peckham, *Campaigns of the American Revolution* (Ann Arbor: University of Michigan Press, 1976), pp. 22–23, provides a detailed contemporary drawing of the American works at Brooklyn on 27 Aug 1776.

44. Ltr, Francis, Lord Rawdon to Francis, Earl of Huntingdon, 3 Sep 1776, *Report on the Manuscripts of the Late Reginald Rawdon Hastings . . . ,* 4 vols., Great Britain, Historical Manuscripts Commission Reports (London: His Majesty's Stationery Office, 1928–47), 3:181–82; Ms ltr, William Hotham to Sir Charles Thompson, 1 Sep 1776, Hotham Deposit, DD HO/4/17, Brynmore Jones Library, Hull University, Hull, Humberside, England.

45. Gruber, *Howe Brothers,* pp. 109–10; Johnston, *Campaign of 1776,* 1:137–43.

46. Johnston, *Campaign of 1776,* 1:143–58.

47. Ibid., 1:159.

48. Henry Clinton, *The American Rebellion: Sir Henry Clinton's Narrative of His Campaigns, 1775–1782,* William B. Willcox, ed., Yale Historical Publications: Manuscripts and Edited Texts, 21 (New Haven: Yale University Press, 1954), pp. 41–42.

49. Ibid., p. 42.

50. Ibid.; Whittemore, *Sullivan,* pp. 33–40; Douglas Southall Freeman, *George Washington; A Biography,* 7 vols. (New York: Charles Scribner's Sons, 1948–57), 4:157–62.

51. Ms ltr, Howe to Germain, 3 Sep 1776, C.O. 5/93; Clinton, *The American Rebellion,* pp. 42–44; Whittemore, *Sullivan,* pp. 36–40; Alan Valentine, *Lord Stirling* (New York: Oxford University Press, 1969), pp. 179–87; Johnston, *Campaign of 1776,* 1:161–92.

52. Howard H. Peckham, ed., *The Toll of Independence: Engagements and Battle Casualties of the American Revolution,* Clements Library Bicentennial Studies (Chicago: University of Chicago Press, 1974), p. 22, is the source for American losses; Gruber, *Howe Brothers,* p. 112, for British.

53. Quoting ltr, Sir James Murray to Mrs. Smyth, 31 Aug 1776, Eric Robson, ed., *Letters from America 1773 to 1780* (New York: Barnes & Noble, [1953]), p. 33; Jnl, Henry Duncan, 26 [–27 Aug 1776], John Knox Laughton, ed., *The Naval Miscellany I,* Publications of the Navy Records Society, vol. 20 (London: The Navy Records Society, 1902), p. 123; Ltr, Carl Leopold Baurmeister to Baron de Iunckheim, 2 Sep 1776, Bernhard A. Uhlendorf, ed., *Revolution in America; Confidential Letters and Journals 1776–1784 of Adjutant General Major Baurmeister of the Hessian Forces* (New Brunswick, N.J.: Rutgers University Press, 1957), p. 37.

54. Ltr, Samuel H. Parsons to John Adams, 29 Aug 1776, and Daniel Brodhead to ———, 5 Sep 1776, Johnston, *Campaign of 1776,* 2:34, 64; Jnl, Ambrose Serle, 27 Aug 1776, Edward H. Tatum, Jr., ed., *The American Journal of Ambrose Serle Secretary to Lord Howe 1776–1778* (San Marino: The Huntington Library, 1940), p. 79.

55. Quoting ms ltr, Howe to Lord George Germain, C.O. 5/93; Ltr, Baurmeister to Iunckheim, 2 Sep 1776, Uhlendorf, ed., *Revolution in America,* p. 36.

56. Ltr, Percy to the Duke of Northumberland, 1 Sep 1776, Charles Knowles Bolton, ed., *Letters of Hugh Earl Percy from Boston and New York 1774-1776* (Boston: Goodspeed, 1902), p. 68; Jnl, Archibald Robertson, 27 [Aug 1776], Harry Miller Lydenberg, ed., *Archibald Robertson, Lieutenant General Royal Engineers, His Diaries and Sketches in America 1762-1780* (New York: New York Public Library, 1930), p. 93.

57. Jnl, Henry Duncan, 26 [-27 Aug 1776], Laughton, *The Naval Miscellany I,* p. 123.

58. Quoting Clinton, *The American Rebellion,* p. 43, and Jnl, Robertson, 27 [Aug 1776], Lydenberg, *Archibald Robertson,* p. 93.

59. Ltr, Murray to Mrs. Smyth, 31 Aug 1776, Robson, *Letters from America,* p. 33.

60. Ms Ltr, Howe to Lord George Germain, 3 Sep 1776, C.O. 5/93; Ltr, Murray to Mrs. Smyth, 31 Aug 1776, Robson, *Letters from America,* p. 34.

61. Quoting Jnl, Ambrose Serle, 27 Aug 1776, Tatum, *American Journal of Serle,* p. 79; Ltr, John Haslet to Caesar Rodney, 31 Aug 1776, Johnston, *Campaign of 1776,* 2:52.

62. Ltr, Howe to Lord George Germain, 3 Sep 1776, C.O. 5/93; Clinton, *The American Rebellion,* pp. 43-44.

63. Jnl, Robertson, 27 [Aug 1776], Lydenberg, *Archibald Robertson,* p. 94; Jnl, Mackenzie, 26 Oct 1776, *Diary of Frederick Mackenzie . . . During the Years 1775-1781 in Massachusetts Rhode Island and New York,* 2 vols. (Cambridge: Harvard University Press, 1930), 1:89.

64. Ltr, Percy to a Gentleman in London, 4 Sep 1776, Bolton, *Letters of Percy,* p. 71.

65. Ltr, Baurmeister to Iunckheim, 2 Sep 1776, Uhlendorf, *Revolution in America,* pp. 37-38. Quoting Ltr, Francis, Lord Rawdon to Francis, Earl of Huntingdon, 3 Sep 1776, *Report on the Manuscripts of Hastings,* 3:181-82; and Ltr, Sir James Murray to Mrs. Smyth, 31 Aug 1776, Robson, *Letters from America,* p. 33.

66. Jnl, Ambrose Serle, 27 Aug 1776, Tatum, *American Journal of Serle,* p. 78.

67. Ms ltr, Henry Clinton to Charles Mellish, 25 Sep 1776, Mellish Manuscripts, Manuscripts Department, University of Nottingham, Nottingham, England.

68. Ltr, Jasper Ewing to Judge Yates, 30 Aug 1776, Johnston, *Campaign of 1776,* 2:50; quoting Ltr, Sir James Murray to Mrs. Smyth, 31 Aug 1776, Robson, *Letters from America,* pp. 33-34; Ms Narrative, Andrew Snape Hamond, 25-27 Aug 1776, William Bell Clark and William James Morgan, eds., *Naval Documents of the American Revolution,* 8 vols. to date (Washington, D.C.: Government Printing Office, 1964-   ), 6:353; Ms ltr, William Howe to Lord George Germain, 3 Sep 1776, C.O. 5/93.

69. Ltr, Charles Stuart to Lord Bute, 3 Sep 1776, E. Stuart-Wortley, ed., *A Prime Minister and His Son* (London: John Murray, 1925), p. 84. Robson, *Letters from America,* p. 33, n. 2, confuses the two incidents.

70. Ltr, Brodhead to ———, 5 Sep 1776; Jnl, Samuel Miles, n.d.; and Ltr, George Washington to the Massachusetts Assembly, 19 Sep 1776, Johnston, *Campaign of 1776,* 2:64-65, 61-63, 32.

71. Whittemore, *Sullivan,* pp. 36-38; Ltr, Baurmeister to Iunckheim, 2 Sep 1776, Uhlendorf, *Revolution in America,* pp. 37, 39.

72. Ltrs, Samuel H. Parsons to John Adams, 29 Aug 1776, John Ewing to Judge Yeates, 14 Sep 1776; and quoting John Haslet to Caesar Rodney, 31 Aug 1776, Johnston, *Campaign of 1776,* 2:33-34, 51, 52.

73. Ltr, Samuel H. Parsons to John Adams, 29 Aug 1776, ibid., 2:33-34; and Jnl, Jabez Fitch, 27 Aug 1776, W. H. W. Sabine, ed., *The New-York Diary of Lieutenant Jabez Fitch . . .* (New York: By the author, 1954), p. 30.

74. Ltr, George Washington to the Massachusetts Assembly, 19 Sep 1776, Johnston, *Campaign of 1776*, 2:32; Jnl, Ambrose Serle, 27 Aug 1776, Tatum, *American Journal of Serle*, pp. 78-79; Valentine, *Lord Stirling*, pp. 188-89, which provides a long extract from Stirling's letter to Washington describing the battle.

75. Ltrs, Samuel H. Parsons to John Adams, 8 Oct 1776 (quoted), and John Morin Scott to John Jay, 6 Sep 1776, Johnston, *Campaign of 1776*, 2:35, 37.

76. Ltr, John Haslet to Caesar Rodney, 31 Aug 1776 (quoted), ibid.; Memo, "Reasons of Council of War for Evacuating Long Island," [29 Aug 1776], Fitzpatrick, *Writings of Washington*, 5:508-09.

77. Ltr, Parsons to John Adams, 29 Aug 1776, Johnston, *Campaign of 1776*, 2:34.

78. Ltrs, Parsons to John Adams, 29 Aug 1776, and Silliman to his wife, 29 Aug 1776, ibid.; Jnl, Henry Duncan, 29 [Aug 1776], Clark and Morgan, *Naval Documents*, 6:372.

79. Freeman, *Washington*, 4:165-70, 179.

80. GO, 31 Aug 1776, Ltr, George Washington to the Massachusetts Assembly, 19 Sep 1776, and Ltr, John Morin Scott to John Jay, 6 Sep 1776, Johnston, *Campaign of 1776*, 2:31, 33, 37-38; Memo, "Reasons of Council of War for Evacuating Long Island," [29 Aug 1776], Fitzpatrick, *Writings of Washington*, 5:508-09.

81. Ward, *The War of the Revolution*, 1:233-36.

82. Quoting Ltr, Sir James Murray to Mrs. Smyth, 31 Aug 1776, Robson, *Letters from America*, p. 35; and Jnl, Henry Duncan, 30 [Aug 1776], Clark and Morgan, *Naval Documents*, 6:372.

83. Quoting Ms jnl, Sir George Collier, 30 Aug 1776, Collier Manuscripts, 35 Ms/0085, National Maritime Museum, Greenwich, England. Ms ltr, Richard Lord Howe to William Hotham, 28 Aug [1776], Hotham Deposit.

84. Quoting Jnl, Ambrose Serle, 30 Aug 1776, Tatum, *American Journal of Serle*, pp. 82-83; and Ms Ltr, William Leslie to his father, 2 Sep 1776, Leven and Melville Muniments, sec. IX, no. 513, Scottish Record Office, Edinburgh, Scotland.

85. Gruber, *Howe Brothers*, pp. 112-20.

86. Ibid., pp. 113-303; Gruber, "British Strategy," pp. 24-31.

87. Royster, *A Revolutionary People at War*, p. 148, quoting John Adams to Abigail Adams, 2 Sep 1777. I have explored the divergence between Washington and Congress in Ira D. Gruber, "The Anglo-American Military Tradition and the War for American Independence," in Kenneth J. Hagan and William R. Roberts, eds., *Against All Enemies: Interpretations of American Military History from Colonial Times to the Present* (Westport, Conn.: Greenwood, 1986), pp. 21-47.

88. Bolton, *Private Soldier*, pp. 48-72; Martin and Lender, *A Respectable Army*, pp. 66-78, 94-115. Royster, *A Revolutionary People at War*, analyzes the ideological and psychological challenges that a standing army presented to republicans; and Robert A. Gross, *The Minutemen and Their World* (New York: Hill and Wang, 1976), the mounting opposition to military service in one community.

CHAPTER 2: THE BATTLE OF QUEENSTON
HEIGHTS, 13 OCTOBER 1812

1. On the reorganization of the Army under Jefferson, see Theodore J. Crackel, "Mr. Jefferson's Army: Political Reform of the Military Establishment, 1801-1809," Ph.D. dissertation, Rutgers University, 1985.

2. In addition to the infantry, the Army consisted of four regiments of artillery, two of dragoons, and one of riflemen. Of this, all but two artillery regiments had been added in 1808. The rifle regiment could trace its origins to the American experience in

the Revolutionary War but had traveled a circuitous route. Regiments of riflemen had, in the years since, been popularized in Britain and France but had disappeared from the United States. They were rediscovered by Americans who had observed the success of riflemen in Europe.

3. James A. Huston, *The Sinews of War: Army Logistics, 1775-1952* (Washington, D.C.: Government Printing Office, 1966), pp. 102ff.

4. H. C. B. Rogers, *The British Army of the Eighteenth Century* (London: George Allen & Unwin, 1977), p. 68.

5. Sir John Moore, quoted in Peter Young, *The British Army 1642-1970* (London: William Kember, 1967), p. 112.

6. David Dundas, *Principles of Military Movements* (1788), pp. 12-13.

7. The Militia Act of 1792 had prescribed Steuben's system of discipline, originally adopted in 1779, for all the enrolled militia, a provision that was not repealed until 1820 when the militia was brought into line with the system of discipline and field exercise observed by the regular army. John F. Callan, *Military Laws of the United States* (Philadelphia: George W. Childs, 1863), p. 99.

8. Richard H. Kohn points out that Hamilton and other Federalist leaders knew that the New Army they were building "must be capable tactically and strategically of waging the new warfare then sweeping Europe" but seems to have found no real evidence to suggest that any serious doctrinal reforms were considered. *Eagle and Sword: The Federalists and the Creation of the Military Establishment in America, 1783-1802* (New York: Free Press, 1975), pp. 244ff.

9. Even that debate seems to have been precipitated by the new danger of war with England after the *Chesapeake* affair.

10. Maximillian Godefroy, *Military Reflections, on Four Modes of Defense, for the United States* (Baltimore: Joseph Robinson, 1807), p. 42. Duane suggests in the preface to *American Military Library* that his work was prompted by the British attack on the *Chesapeake* (22 June, 1807), but in his careful critique of Godefroy's book he noted that he began directing his efforts to such work "the moment" he first "perused" that book (*Aurora*, 2 Nov 1807). Duane's first number appeared in late November or early December: Ltr, William Duane to Thomas Jefferson [Dec 1807], "Letters of William Duane," *Proceedings of the Massachusetts Historical Society* (May and Jun 1906): 304-05.

11. [William Duane], "On National Defense," *Aurora*, 30, 31 Oct, 2, 3, 4, 5 Nov 1807. This series seems to begin with No. 2, dated 30 Oct; and [William Duane] "On A National Militia," *Aurora*, 10, 11, 12, 14 Nov 1807.

12. *Aurora*, 30, 31 Oct 1807.

13. *Aurora*, 14 Nov 1807.

14. William Duane, *The American Military Library*, 2 vols. (Philadelphia: William Duane, 1809). Ltr, William Duane to Thomas Jefferson [Dec 1807], "Letters of William Duane," *Proceedings of the Massachusetts Historical Society* (May and Jun 1906): 304-05.

15. William Duane, *A Military Dictionary* (Philadelphia: William Duane, 1810).

16. Issac Maltby in *The Elements of War* argued that Duane's work was "valuable for officers on active service, but too voluminous for militia officers" (Boston: T. B. Wait and Co., 1813), p. xv. The comprehensive nature of the work was, of course, the original object. Duane had written Jefferson at the beginning of the project that he intended to "collect all that is to be had in the best books . . . which may lead judicious men to inquire and think, and inform those who are uniformed." Ltr, William Duane to Henry Dearborn, 16 Mar 1808, Microfilm Publication M221, Letters Received by the Secretary of War, National Archives; Ltr, William Duane to William Eustis, 7

May 1809, M221, NA; Ltr, William Duane to Thomas Jefferson [Dec 1807], "Letters of William Duane."

17. Ltr, Willian Henry Harrison to Charles Scott, 10 Mar 1810, reprinted in *National Intelligencer,* 21 Sep 1810.

18. Ltr, William Henry Harrison to Charles Scott, Apr 1810, reprinted in *National Intelligencer,* 1 Oct 1810.

19. (Daniel Parker) Memo (post 1814), Daniel Parker Papers, Historical Society of Pennsylvania. See also Roger L. Nichols, *General Henry Atkinson, A Western Military Career* (Norman: University of Oklahoma Press, 1965), pp. 24–25.

20. On the Wayne affair, see Kohn, *Eagle and Sword,* pp. 178–82.

21. Winfield Scott, *Memoirs of Lieut.-General Scott* (New York: Sheldon & Company, 1864), pp. 36–37.

22. Ltr, Wade Hampton to William Eustis, 10 Jun 1811, William Eustis Papers, Library of Congress.

23. Ltr, William Eustis to Wade Hampton, 16 Jul 1811, William Eustis Papers, Library of Congress. Eustis' reference to "party" refers not to political party but to factions within the Army.

24. Duane reported in September 1811 that "I shall soon put to press four *handbooks* on the discipline of the four arms—infantry—Light troops—Artillery—Cavalry." Ltr, William Duane to [H. A. S. Dearborn] [Sep 1811], Dearborn Papers, Boston Public Library.

25. [William Duane], "A Bird's Eye Sketch of the Military Concerns of the United States, Respectfully Addressed to the Consideration of Congress," 21 Apr 1812, Morris Swett Library, U.S. Army Field Artillery School, Fort Sill, Okla.

26. *National Intelligencer,* 2 May 1812; Alexander Smyth, *Regulations for the . . . Infantry of the United States* (Philadelphia: Fry and Kanmerer, 1812), p. xiv.

27. Ltr, William Duane to Thomas Jefferson, 17 Jul 1812, Jefferson Papers, Library of Congress. The changes to Smyth were, of course, to bring it in line with the newly prescribed organizational structure.

28. *Annals of Congress,* 12th Cong., 1st Sess., 30 Jun 1812, p. 1566.

29. Ibid., 1 Jul 1812, p. 1571.

30. Scott, *Memoirs,* 1:52–53.

31. Ltr, J. W. Livingston to Alexander Smyth, 4 Nov 1812, in E. Cruikshank, ed., *Documentary History of the Campaign upon the Niagara Frontier in 1812,* 4 vols. (Welland, Ont.: Lundy's Lane Historical Society, n.d.), 4:80 (hereafter cited as Cruikshank).

32. William King, "Report on the State of [the] 14th Regiment of Infantry," 5 Oct 1812, in Cruikshank, 4:241–42.

33. Ibid. On medical matters, see Mary C. Gillett, *The Army Medical Department, 1775-1818* (Washington, D.C.: Government Printing Office, 1981).

34. Charles H. Stewart, *The Service of British Regiments in Canada and North America, A Resume* (Ottawa: Department of National Defence Library, 1962).

35. Returns indicate that American troops opposite Queenston on 12 October numbered 3,170: 350 regulars under Lt Col Chrystie, 550 regulars under Lt Col Fenwick, 558 militia under Brig Gen Miller, and 1,682 militia under Brig Gen Wadsworth. "Return of the Troops, Lewiston," 12 Oct 1812, in Solomon Van Rensselaer, *A Narrative of the Affair of Queenston: In the War of 1812* (Boston: Leavitt, Lord & Co., 1836), app., p. 19.

36. Ltr, Stephen Van Rensselaer to William Eustis, 14 Oct 1812, in Cruikshank, 4:80.

37. Ltr, Stephen Van Rensselaer to Henry Dearborn, 8 Oct 1812, in Solomon Van Rensselaer, *A Narrative,* app., p. 8.

38. Ltr, Stephen Van Rensselaer to William Eustis, 14 Oct 1812, in Cruikshank, 4:80.

39. Ltr, Stephen Van Rensselaer to Henry Dearborn, 8 Oct 1812, in Solomon Van Rensselaer, *A Narrative,* app., p. 11. There is no evidence that any tactical plan was agreed upon for the action across the river. One can only assume that the forces would have formed up and marched forward until they made contact with the enemy, at which time they would have deployed.

40. Lt Col Thompson Mead, 17th Regiment of Detached Militia, 18 Nov 1812, in Cruikshank, 4:92-93.

41. From a letter of unknown authorship, dated 17 Oct 1812, [Philadelphia] *Aurora,* 29 Oct 1812, in Cruikshank, 4:125. Contemporary sources place little weight on the "constitutional" aspects of this refusal to cross into Canada—that the militia was not required to engage in operations outside the United States—though later historians often emphasized it.

42. Ltr, John Chrystie to Thomas H. Cushing, 22 Feb 1813, in Cruikshank, 4:98.

43. Ibid.

44. Ltr, Stephen Van Rensselaer to William Eustis, 14 Oct 1812, in Cruikshank, 4:82.

45. Lt Col Thompson Mead's report, 17th Regiment of Detached Militia, 18 Nov 1812, in Cruikshank, 4:92-93.

46. Ltr, Henry Dearborn to Alexander Smyth, 21 Oct 1812, in Cruikshank, 4:152.

47. Ltr, William Duane to Thomas Jefferson, 14 Feb 1813, "Letters of William Duane," p. 360.

48. Ltr, Thomas Jefferson to William Duane, 4 Apr 1813, Jefferson Papers, Library of Congress.

49. *Annals of Congress,* 12th Cong., 2d Sess., 12 Jan 1813, pp. 43, 710.

50. Duane believed that only with the ability to train a sizable and effective force on short notice could a large standing army be dispensed with. His *Hand Book* and the forces that could be rapidly trained with it in time of danger promised to provide an alternative to a larger regular establishment.

51. William Duane, *Hand Book for Infantry,* 5th ed. (Philadelphia: William Duane, [1814]), p. 10.

52. Ibid., p. 97.

53. Ibid., p. 10.

54. William Duane, "Notes on the Progress of the New System of Discipline," in *The System of Infantry Discipline,* appended to the 5th edition of the *Hand Book.*

55. Duane, *Hand Book,* p. 87.

56. Ibid., p. 16.

57. *Annals of Congress,* 12th Cong., 2d Sess., 16, 17 Feb, 1, 2 Mar 1813, pp. 114, 117, 1075-76, 1364. In this way, Congress maintained its insistence on a hand in governance of the force and in the formulation of doctrine.

58. It was no coincidence that, just one day before, the author was again commissioned and brought into the office of the inspector general. There, in the midst of other tasks, he continued to work on similar handbooks for riflemen and for cavalry.

59. [William Duane], "Memorandum Concerning the Elementary Discipline," [May 1814], Daniel Parker Papers, Historical Society of Pennsylvania (hereafter Duane, "Memorandum").

60. Ibid.

61. Duane, "Notes."

62. William [Southland] Hamilton, "[Report] Respecting a System of Discipline for the Infantry," 27 Mar 1814, Daniel Parker Papers, Historical Society of Pennsylvania.

63. Charles Francis Adams, ed., *Memoirs of John Quincy Adams Comprising Portions of His Diary from 1795 to 1848,* 12 vols. (Philadelphia: J. B. Lippincott & Co., 1875), 5:112. That charge apparently had some currency because Duane at least once offered to forego his profits if that would be helpful. (Duane, "Memorandum.")

64. At the same time, three rifle regiments were added, bringing that total to four. The artillery, which had been increased from one regiment of twenty companies to three such regiments in 1812, was consolidated in May 1814 into a single artillery corps of twelve battalions of four companies each. Though the number of companies was reduced by one-fifth, the total number of men authorized was actually increased by increasing company size.

65. The Hampton faction made significant gains in 1814 at Wilkinson's expense—and at the expense of all those allied with him. The reorganization of the Army at the war's end saw the dismissal of a bitter Wilkinson and nearly all his supporters and the complete domination by those who had adhered to the Hampton faction.

66. Ltr, Winfield Scott to William H. Winder, 16 May 1814, quoted in Charles Winslow Elliott, *Winfield Scott, the Soldier and the Man* (New York: Macmillan, 1937), p. 148.

67. Scott, *Memoirs,* 1:119-21.

68. Ltr, Jacob Brown to James Monroe, 28 Nov 1814, Jacob Brown Papers, Library of Congress.

69. Ltrs, William Duane to Daniel Parker, 26 Oct, 2 Nov 1814, Daniel Parker Papers, Historical Society of Philadelphia.

70. *Annals of Congress,* 13th Cong., 3d Sess., 10, 23 Nov 1814, pp. 550-51, 638.

71. Ltr, William Duane to Daniel Parker, 25 Nov 1814, Daniel Parker Papers, Historical Society of Pennsylvania.

72. Ltr, Jacob Brown to James Monroe, 28 Nov 1814, Jacob Brown Papers, Library of Congress.

73. Duane sent a copy of his letter to the secretary of war; its receipt and a note as to its subject are recorded in the Register of Letters Received (Microfilm M22, National Archives), but the letter itself was not located.

CHAPTER 3: THE BATTLES ON THE RIO GRANDE:
PALO ALTO AND RESACA DE LA PALMA, 8-9 MAY 1846

1. The political background of the war can be traced from several perspectives in: K. Jack Bauer, *The Mexican War 1846-1848* (New York: Macmillan, 1974), pp. 16-29; James Morton Callahan, *American Foreign Policy in Mexican Relations* (New York: Macmillan, 1932), pp. 151-57; Norman B. Graebner, "The Mexican War: A Study in Causation," *Pacific Historical Review,* 49 (Aug 1980): 405-26; Clayton Charles Kohl, *Claims as a Cause of the Mexican War* (New York: New York University Press, 1914); Frederick Merk, *Manifest Destiny and Mission in American History* (New York: Alfred A. Knopf, 1963), pp. 24-88; David Pletcher, *The Diplomacy of Annexation* (Columbia: University of Missouri Press, 1973), pp. 66-271 passim; Glenn W. Price, *Origins of the War with Mexico* (Austin: University of Texas Press, 1960); George Lockhart Rives, *The United States and Mexico, 1821-1848,* 2 vols. (New York: Chas. Scribner's Sons,

1913), 2:53-80, 119-22; Charles Sellers, *James K. Polk, Continentalist* (Princeton: Princeton University Press, 1966), pp. 259-65; Justin H. Smith, *The War with Mexico*, 2 vols. (New York: Macmillan, 1919), 1:74-101, 425-39.

2. Army of Occupation, Orders No. 1, 6 Aug 1846, Army of Occupation General Orders (hereafter AOGO), Records of the Office of the Adjutant General (RG94), National Archives (NA).

3. Ltrs, Taylor to Adj Gen, 25 Jul, 15 Aug 1846, U.S. Congress, House, *Mexican War Correspondence* (hereafter *Mexican War Correspondence*), 30th Cong., 1st sess., H. Ex. Doc. 60, 1848, pp. 97, 99-100; Adj Gen Roger Jones to Taylor, 13 Sep 1845, Adjutant General, Letters Sent (AGLS), RG 94, NA, 21:946.

4. Accounts of the life at Corpus Christi can be found in: Emma Jerome Blackwood, ed., *To Mexico with Scott* (Cambridge: Harvard University Press, 1917), pp. 17-21; Croffut, *Fifty Years in Camp and Field*, pp. 193-207; William S. Henry, *Campaign Sketches of the War with Mexico* (New York: Harper & Bros., 1847), pp. 14-52; Nathan S. Jarvis, "An Army Surgeon's Notes of Frontier Service," *Journal of the Military Service Institute of the United States*, 40 (1907): 435-40; George Gordon Meade, *Life and Letters of George Gordon Meade*, 2 vols. (New York: Chas. Scribner's Sons, 1913), 1:25-35; Richard F. Pourade, ed., *The Sign of the Eagle* (San Diego: Copley Press, 1970), pp. 5-6; George Winston Smith and Charles Judah, eds., *Chronicles of the Gringos* (Albuquerque: University of New Mexico Press, 1968), pp. 25-26.

5. Ltr, Marcy to Taylor, 13 Jan 1846, *Mexican War Correspondence*, p. 90.

6. See Proclamation, Gen de brig Francisco Mejía, 18 Mar 1846; Ltr, Jenés Cardenes to Taylor, 23 Mar 1846; Brig Gen W. J. Worth, Min of Interv with Gen de brig Rómulo Díaz de la Vega, 28 Mar 1846, all in ibid., pp. 125-38.

7. Smith, *The War with Mexico*, 1:99, 439.

8. Ltr, Lt Robert Hazlett to ———, 22 Apr 1846, Robert Hazlett Papers, U.S. Military Academy Library.

9. The original complement of six guns per battery dropped to four in 1842 when the companies were reduced to 64 men. It rose to six again after the Act of 13 May 1846 increased the size of the light artillery companies to 100 men. The light artillery companies were designated either horse batteries, in which all men rode horses (only Captain Samuel Ringgold's C/3 Arty was so mounted), or mounted batteries, in which the men normally marched on foot but rode limbers and caissons for rapid movement on the battlefield. William E. Birkheimer, *Historical Sketch of the Organization, Administration, Material and Tactics of the Artillery, United States Army* (New York: Greenwood Press, 1968), pp. 54, 57-58, 62, 364.

10. Ibid., pp. 59-60, 321-22; Albert G. Brackett, *History of the United States Cavalry, from the Formation of the Federal Government to the 1st of June, 1863* (New York: Greenwood Press, 1968), pp. 35, 159-60; Stanley L. Falk, "Artillery for a Land Service: Development of a System," *Military Affairs*, 28 (Fall 1964): 103; William Addleman Ganoe, *The History of the United States Army* (Ashton, Md.: Eric Lundberg, 1964), pp. 143, 145-46, 168; James A. Huston, *The Sinews of War: Army Logistics 1775-1953* (Washington, D.C.: Office of the Chief of Military History, 1966), pp. 129-30; Harold L. Peterson, *Notes on Ordnance of the Civil War, 1861-1865* (Washington, D.C.: The American Ordnance Association, 1959), n.p.; H. L. Scott, *Military Dictionary* (New York: Greenwood Press, 1968), pp. 29, 45, 426, 477, 565, 577; Smith, *The War with Mexico*, 1:450; Russell F. Weigley, *History of the United States Army* (New York: Macmillan, 1967), p. 171; Cadmus Marcellus Wilcox, *History of the Mexican War* (Washington, D.C.: Church News Publishing Co., 1892), p. 246. See also Grady McWhiney and Perry D. Jamieson, *Attack and Die* (University: University of Alabama Press, 1982), pp. 27-40.

11. W. A. Croffut, ed., *Fifty Years in Camp and Field* (New York: G. P. Putnam's Sons, 1909), p. 215; Isaac Ingalls Stevens, *Campaigns of the Rio Grande and of Mexico* (New York: D. Appleton & Co., 1851), p. 12.

12. Smith, *The War with Mexico,* 1:157.

13. Ltr, Taylor to Adj Gen, 25 Mar 1846, *Mexican War Correspondence,* pp. 129–32; Blackwood, *To Mexico with Scott,* pp. 23–30; Ulysses S. Grant, *Personal Memoirs of U. S. Grant* (Cleveland: World Publishing Co., 1952), p. 31; Henry, *Campaign Sketches,* pp. 59–60; Wilcox, *History of the Mexican War,* p. 35.

14. Fort Texas was subsequently named Fort Brown, from which Brownsville, Texas, draws its name.

15. Ltr, Taylor to Mejía, 28 Mar 1846, *Mexican War Correspondence,* p. 393.

16. Ltrs, Marcy to Taylor, 13 Jan 1846, *Mexican War Correspondence,* p. 393; Gen de div José María Tornel y Mendivil to Gen de div Manuel Arista, 4 Apr 1846, Justin H. Smith Papers, Latin American Collection, University of Texas, 11:224–25; Manifesto, Paredes, 23 Apr 1846, *Niles National Register,* 70 (30 May 1846): 199; Ltr, Gen de div Pedro de Ampudia to Taylor, 17 Apr 1846, *Mexican War Correspondence,* pp. 138–40.

17. Ltrs, Taylor to Adj Gen, 30 May 1846, *Mexican War Correspondence,* pp. 302–03; Arista to Ampudia, 30 Apr 1846, Mejía to Arista, 4 May 1846, Papers Captured with Gen Arista's Baggage, New York Historical Society; Arista, Advise [*sic*] to American Soldiers, 20 Apr 1846, Army of Occupation, Letters Received (AOLR), RG 94, NA, Box 2.

18. Rpt of Board, 23 Apr 1846, AOLR, RG 94, NA, Box 2; Army of Occupation, Orders No. 50, 23 Apr 1846, AOGO, 1; Henry, *Campaign Sketches,* pp. 77–78; Meade, *Life and Letters,* 1:67–68.

19. Ltrs, Taylor to Adj Gen, 15 Apr 1846; Ampudia to Taylor, Taylor to Ampudia, 12 Apr 1846, *Mexican War Correspondence,* pp. 138–40.

20. Ltrs, Arista to Taylor, 24 Apr 1846, U.S. Congress, House, *Correspondence between the Secretary of War and Generals Scott and Taylor and between General Scott and Mr. Trist,* 30th Cong., 1st sess., H. Ex. Doc. 56, 1848, p. 395; Taylor to Ampudia, 22 Apr 1846, *Mexican War Correspondence,* pp. 145–47; Albert C. Ramsey, trans., *The Other Side* (New York: John Wiley, 1850), pp. 39–40; Smith, *The War with Mexico,* 1:149.

21. Army of Occupation, Orders No. 46, 15 Apr 1846, AOGO, 1.

22. Munroe, Memo of interrogation, 23 Apr 1846, AOLR, Box 2; Ramsey, *The Other Side,* p. 42; José María Roa Bárcena, *Recuerdos de la Invasión Norteamericana, 1846-48,* 3 vols. (Mexico: Editorial Porrua, 1947), 1:62; Smith, *The War with Mexico,* 1:149; Blackwood, *To Mexico with Scott,* p. 39.

23. Ltrs, Capt W. J. Hardee to Taylor, 26 Apr 1846; Thornton to Capt W. W. S. Bliss, 27 Apr 1846, *Mexican War Correspondence,* pp. 290–92; Torrejón to Taylor, 25 Apr 1846, AOLR, Box 2; Torrejón to Arista, 26 Apr 1846, Papers Captured with Arista's Baggage; Taylor to Crittenden, 15 Sep 1846, Mrs. Chapman Coleman, ed., *The Life of John J. Crittenden,* 2 vols. (Philadelphia: J. B. Lippincott & Co., 1871), 1:251.

24. Ltrs, Jones to Taylor, 20 Apr 1846, Taylor to Adj Gen, 26 Apr 1846, *Mexican War Correspondence,* pp. 96–97, 288.

25. Ltrs, Walker to Taylor, 2 May 1846, Capt G. A. McCall to Bliss, 30 Apr 1846, AOLR, Box 2; Emilio del Castillo Negrete, *Invasión de los Norteamericanos en México,* 2 vols. (Mexico: Imprenta del Editor, 1890), 1:167; John S. Jenkins, *History of the War Between the United States and Mexico* (Auburn, N.Y.: Derby & Miller, 1851), pp. 98–99.

26. Jenkins, *History of the War,* p. 99; Army of Occupation, Orders No. 53, 29 Apr 1846, AOGO, 1.

27. Smith, *The War with Mexico,* 1:162–63; Roa Bárcena, *Recuerdos,* 1:63.
28. Ltr, Taylor to Adj Gen, 3 May 1846, *Mexican War Correspondence,* pp. 289–90; Army of Occupation, Orders No. 55, 1 May 1846, AOGO, 1; Smith, *The War with Mexico,* 1:163.
29. Ltrs, Ampudia to Mejía, 2 May 1846, Arista to Mejía and Ampudia, 3 May 1846, Papers Captured with Arista's Baggage; Roa Bárcena, *Recuerdos,* 1:63.
30. Jenkins, *History of the War,* pp. 103–04; *Niles National Register,* 70 (20 June 1846): 254; Charles Spurlin, "Ranger Walker in the Mexican War," *Military History of Texas and The Southwest,* 9 (1971): 264.
31. The siege of Fort Texas is described in: Ltrs, Hawkins to Bliss, 10 May 1846, with enclosures, U.S. Cong., Senate, *Message from the President . . . Relative to the Operations and Recent Engagements on the Mexican Frontier,* 29th Cong., 1st sess., Sen. Doc. 388, 1846 (hereafter *Recent Engagements*), pp. 31–36; Taylor to Adj Gen, 5 May 1846, Brown to Bliss, 4 May 1846, *Mexican War Correspondence,* pp. 292–94; Ramsey, *The Other Side,* p. 44; Smith, *The War with Mexico,* 1:176, 464.
32. Ltr, Taylor to Adj Gen, 7 May 1846, and Army of Occupation, Orders No. 58, 7 May 1846, *Mexican War Correspondence,* pp. 294–95, 487.
33. Holman Hamilton, *Zachary Taylor,* 2 vols. (Indianapolis: Bobbs-Merrill Co., 1941–51), 1:177; Smith, *The War with Mexico,* 1:163–64.
34. Ltr, Taylor to Adj Gen, 16 May 1846, *Recent Engagements,* p. 3.
35. Ibid., p. 5.
36. Arista had brought only 650 rounds of artillery ammunition to the battlefield.
37. The description of the Battle of Palo Alto is drawn from: Ltrs, Taylor to Adj Gen, 16 May 1846, with enclosures, *Recent Engagements,* pp. 2–30; Arista to Min Guerra y Marina, 8 May 1846, Nathan Covington Brooks, *A Complete History of the Mexican War* (Chicago: Rio Grande Press, 1965), pp. 135–36; Pedro de Ampudia, *El Chidadano General Pedro de Ampudia ante el Tribunal Respectable de la Opinión Publica* (San Luis Potosí: Imprenta del Gobierno, 1846), pp. 17–23; Brooks, *Complete History,* pp. 125–33; Henry B. Dawson, *Battles of the United States by Sea and Land,* 2 vols. (New York: Johnson, Fry & Co., 1858), 2:447–50; Lester R. Dillon, Jr., *American Artillery in the Mexican War 1846-1847* (Austin: Presidial Press, 1975), p. 25; Rhoda van Bibber Tanner Doubleday, ed., *Journals of the Late Brevet Major Philip Norbourne Barbour* (New York: G. P. Putnam's Sons, 1936), pp. 54–55; Grant, *Memoirs,* pp. 43–45; Henry, *Campaign Sketches,* pp. 90–94; Louis C. Duncan, "A Medical History of General Zachary Taylor's Army of Occupation in Texas and Mexico, 1845-1847," *Military Surgeon,* 38 (1921): 86–88; Jenkins, *History of the War,* pp. 108–12; *Niles National Register,* 70 (27 Jun 1846): 265; Oficial de Infantria, *Campaña Contra los Americanos del Norte* (Mexico: Ignacio Cumplido, 1848), pp. 8–14; Ramsey, *Other Side,* pp. 45–50; Roswell Sabine Ripley, *The War with Mexico,* 2 vols. (New York: Harper & Bros., 1849), 1:116–24; John Sedgwick, *Correspondence of John Sedgwick, Major General,* 2 vols. (n.p., 1903), 1:15–16; Smith, *The War with Mexico,* 1:164–69, 465–66; Smith and Judah, *Chronicles of the Gringos,* pp. 65–67; Wilcox, *History of the Mexican War,* pp. 51–58.
38. Ltr, Arista to Gen. de brig Morlet, 8 May 1846, Papers Captured with Arista's Baggage.
39. Ltrs, Conner to Sec of Navy George Bancroft, 3 May 1846, *Niles National Register,* 70 (13 Jun 1846): 198; Munroe to Conner, 8 May 1846, David Conner Papers, New York Public Library; Munroe to Bliss, 9 May 1846, AOLR, Box 2; K. Jack Bauer, *Surfboats and Horse Marines* (Annapolis: U.S. Naval Institute, 1969), pp. 15–17.
40. Stevens, *Campaigns of the Rio Grande and of Mexico,* p. 20; Sedgwick, *Correspondence,* 1:16, assigns the council to the night of the ninth.

41. Ltr, Capt G. A. McCall to Capt B. D. Alden, 5 June 1846, Alden Papers, U.S. Military Academy.

42. Ibid.

43. Henry, *Campaign Sketches,* p. 97.

44. Samuel G. French, *Two Wars* (Nashville, Tenn.: The Confederate Veteran, 1901), p. 51.

45. May claimed to have personally captured la Vega, but in reality the Mexican was taken by a bugler, Private Winchell. Smith, *The War with Mexico,* 1:467; Samuel E. Chamberlain, *My Confession* (New York: Harper & Bros., 1956), pp. 108-09.

46. Smith, *The War with Mexico,* 1:174-75.

47. The chief sources for the description of the Battle of Resaca de la Palma are: Ltrs, Taylor to Adj Gen, 17 May 1846, with enclosures, *Recent Engagements,* pp. 6-26; McIntosh to Bliss, 2 Dec 1846, *Mexican War Correspondence,* pp. 1102-04; Childs to Belknap, 12 May 1846, Adj Gen, Letters Received 1846, RG 94, NA, C-454; McCall to Capt B. R. Alden, 5 Jun 1846, Alden Family Papers, U.S. Military Academy Library; Ampudia, *El Cuidadano . . . Ante el Tribunal,* pp. 18-23; Blackwood, *To Mexico with Scott,* pp. 50-51; Abner Doubleday, *From Mexican War to Rebellion,* Doubleday Papers, New York Public Library, pp. 125-33; Doubleday, *Journals of Barbour,* pp. 58-59; Grant, *Memoirs,* pp. 45-46; Henry, *Campaign Sketches,* pp. 94-100; Oficial de Infantria, *Campaña contra los Americanos del Norte,* pp. 15-20; Ramsey, *The Other Side,* pp. 50-55; Ripley, *The War with Mexico,* 1:125-31; Wilcox, *History of the Mexican War,* pp. 58-65; *Niles National Register,* 70 (20, 27 Jun 1846): 251-53, 265; Brackett, *History of the Cavalry,* pp. 56-59; Brooks, *Complete History,* pp. 137-47; Dawson, *Battles of the U.S.,* 2:451-53; Duncan, "Medical History," pp. 88-89; Jenkins, *History of the War,* pp. 112-17; Roa Bárcena, *Recuerdos,* 1:84-85; Theophilus F. Rodenbough, *From Everglades to Cañon with the Second Dragoons* (New York: D. Van Nostrand, 1875), pp. 514-15; Smith, *The War with Mexico,* 1:169-76, 466-67; Smith and Judah, *Chronicles of the Gringos,* pp. 67-71.

48. Ltr, Childs to Belknap, 12 May 1846, loc. cit.

49. Ltrs, Taylor to Adj Gen, 18 May 1846, Adj Gen, Letters Received 1846, T-161; 21 May, 3, 10 Jun 1846, *Mexican War Correspondence,* pp. 300, 305-06, 547-48; Brig Gen P. F. Smith to Bliss, 22 May 1846, AOLR, Box 3; Erna Risch, *Quartermaster Support of the Army* (Washington, D.C.: Quartermaster Historian's Office, 1962), pp. 267-68; Smith, *The War with Mexico,* 1:178.

50. 9 *U.S. Stat.:* 10-11; *Cong. Globe,* 29th Cong., 1st sess., pp. 782-83, 792-804; U.S. Cong., Sen., *Report of the Secretary of War Showing the Number of Troops in the Service of the United States Since the Commencement of the War,* 30th Cong., 1st sess., S. Ex. Doc. 36, 1848, pp. 28-29, 36-37; Ltr, Jones to Marcy, 25 Aug 1845, AGLS, 21:826. The law also authorized recruiting the companies of regulars up to full 100-man strength. Jones to Taylor, 12 May 1846, ibid., 22:627.

51. 9 *U.S. Stat.:* 17. The 26 Jun 1846 Act also authorized the organization of the volunteers into brigades and divisions.

52. Ltr, Marcy to Scott, 25 May 1846, U.S. Cong., Sen., *Message of the President of the United States . . . Relative to the Calling of Volunteers or Militia Into the Service of the United States Without Legal Authority,* 29th Cong., 1st sess., S. Doc. 378, 1846, pp. 7-9; Milo Milton Quaife, ed., *The Diary of James K. Polk during His Presidency 1845 to 1849,* 4 vols. (Chicago: A. C. McClurg & Co., 1910), 1:397, 407-08; 421; Winfield Scott, *Memoirs of Lieut.-General Soctt, LL.D.,* 2 vols. (New York: Books for Libraries Press, 1970), 2:384-85. Scott recognized, as Polk did not, that sufficient troops for a campaign on the Rio Grande and their logistic support would not be available before September. Polk, on the other hand, sensed the political requirement for action to maintain

support for the war. Ltrs, Scott to Taylor, 18 May 1846, *Message Relative to the Calling for Volunteers*, pp. 10-12.

53. Ltrs, Jones to Kearny, 14 May, 13 Jun 1846; Capt W. G. Greeman to Taylor, 20 Jun 1846, all in AGLS, 22:640, 850, 890; Scott to Taylor, 12 Jun 1846, *Mexican War Correspondence*, pp. 323-27; Quaife, *Diary of Polk*, 1:438-39; Sellers, *Polk*, pp. 422, 426-27; Pletcher, *The Diplomacy of Annexation*, pp. 461-62.

CHAPTER 4. FIRST BULL RUN, 19 JULY 1861

1. *War of the Rebellion: A Compilation of the Official Records of the Union and Confederate Armies*, Series 3 (Washington, D.C.: Government Printing Office, 1880-1901), 1:22 (hereafter cited as *O.R.A.;* no series will be indicated unless other than Series 1); Marvin A. Kreidberg and Merton G. Henry, *History of Military Mobilization in the United States Army, 1775-1945* (Washington, D.C.: Department of the Army, 1955), p. 88; Emory Upton, *The Military Policy of the United States* (Washington, D.C.: Government Printing Office, 1904), p. 225. For a graphic display of troop deployment in 1860, see Francis Paul Prucha, "Distribution of Regular Army Troops before the Civil War," *Military Affairs* 16 (Winter 1952): 169-73.

2. Mark Mayo Boatner III, *The Civil War Dictionary* (New York: David McKay Company, 1959), p. 728; Ezra J. Warner, *Generals in Blue: Lives of the Union Commanders* (Baton Rouge: Louisiana State University Press, 1964), pp. 429-30; Kreidberg and Henry, *Military Mobilization*, p. 85. For full-length biographies of Scott, see Arthur D. Howden Smith, *Old Fuss and Feathers* (New York: The Greystone Press, 1937), and Charles Winslow Elliott, *Winfield Scott: The Soldier and the Man* (New York: Macmillan, 1937), especially the latter.

3. Kreidberg and Henry, *Military Mobilization*, pp. 85-88; Warner, *Generals in Blue*, pp. 208-09, 573-74; Ezra J. Warner, *Generals in Gray: Lives of the Confederate Commanders* (Baton Rouge: Louisiana State University Press, 1959), p. 312; A. Howard Meneely, *The War Department, 1861: A Study in Mobilization and Administration* (New York: Columbia University Press, 1928), pp. 25-27, 108-09.

4. Kreidberg and Henry, *Military Mobilization*, pp. 88-89; Russell F. Weigley, *History of the United States Army* (New York: Macmillan, 1967), pp. 240-41; E. J. Stackpole, "Generalship in the Civil War," in *Military Analysis of the Civil War: An Anthology by the Editors of Military Affairs* (Millwood, N.Y.: KTO Press, 1977), p. 96.

5. Kreidberg and Henry, *Military Mobilization*, pp. 30, 90-91; Fred Albert Shannon, *The Organization and Administration of the Union Army, 1861-1865* (1928; reprinted, Gloucester, Mass.: Peter Smith, 1965), 1:27-29; Meneely, *War Department*, pp. 24, 104. For an account of the service of one of the best prewar militia units, see William Miller Owen, *In Camp and Battle with the Washington Artillery of New Orleans* (Boston: Ticknor and Company, 1885).

6. Kreidberg and Henry, *Military Mobilization*, p. 89. The official accounts of Twiggs' surrender of U.S. troops in Texas can be found in *O.R.A.*, 1:503-78. See also Caroline Baldwin Darrow, "Recollections of the Twiggs Surrender," in Robert Underwood Johnson and Clarence Clough Buel, eds., *Battles and Leaders of the Civil War* (New York: The Century Co., 1884-87), 1:33-39.

7. *O.R.A.*, Series 3, 1:69, 145-46, 303; Kreidberg and Henry, *Military Mobilization*, pp. 92-93; Weigley, *United States Army*, pp. 198, 200. Although they did not secede, Kentucky and Maryland furnished no troops under Lincoln's call of 15 April 1861. Officially, Virginia furnished none, but the western section of the state provided 900 men without state government sanction.

8. *O.R.A.*, 51, pt. 1: 339, 369-70; *O.R.A.*, Series 3, 1:138, 2:237; Elliott, *Winfield Scott*, pp. 718-19, 721-23; Kreidberg and Henry, *Military Mobilization*, pp. 90-91, 97, 116, 116n; Theodore Ropp, "Anacondas Anyone?" in *Military Analysis of the Civil War*, pp. 89-94; Weigley, *United States Army*, pp. 199-200; Meneely, *War Department*, pp. 169-70, 175-76, 180, 195-96. For a bitter opponent of Scott's policy, see Upton, *Military Policy*, pp. 235-36.

9. *O.R.A.*, Series 3, 5:690-93; *O.R.A.*, Series 4, 1:126-31; E. Merton Coulter, *The Confederate States of America, 1861-1865* (Baton Rouge: Louisiana State University Press, 1950), pp. 308-09; Albert Burton Moore, *Conscription and Conflict in the Confederacy* (New York: Macmillan, 1924), pp. 1-5; Kreidberg and Henry, *Military Mobilization*, pp. 134-35. For the Confederate Regular Army, see Richard P. Weinert, "The Confederate Regular Army," in *Military Analysis of the Civil War*, pp. 16-26.

10. The numbers cited in the text are from Maurice Matloff, ed., *American Military History*, rev. ed. (Washington, D.C.: Government Printing Office, 1973), p. 188. See also Upton, *Military Policy*, pp. 236-38; Warner, *Generals in Gray*, pp. xxiii-xxv, 62-63; Weigley, *United States Army*, p. 229; Kreidberg and Henry, *Military Mobilization*, pp. 115-16; William Addleman Ganoe, *The History of the United States Army*, rev. ed. (Ashton, Md.: Eric Lundberg, 1964), pp. 250, 252-53; Oliver Lyman Spaulding, *The United States Army in War and Peace* (New York: G. P. Putnam's Sons, 1937), pp. 243-44; Ellsworth Eliot, Jr., *West Point in the Confederacy* (New York: G. A. Baker & Co., 1941), p. 10. Although the figures for officers differ somewhat from source to source, there is general agreement that only twenty-six enlisted personnel of the U.S. Army joined the Confederate forces.

11. Weigley, *United States Army*, p. 226; Francis A. Lord, *They Fought for the Union* (Harrisburg, Pa.: The Stackpole Company, 1960), pp. 60, 193-95; Kreidberg and Henry, *Military Mobilization*, pp. 11-118; Coulter, *Confederate States*, p. 329; H. C. B. Rogers, *The Confederates and Federals at War* (New York: Hippocrene Books, 1975), pp. 29-30.

12. Lord, *They Fought*, pp. 160-62; Rogers, *Confederates and Federals*, pp. 32-33; Berkeley R. Lewis, *Small Arms and Ammunition in the United States Service, 1776-1865* (Washington, D.C.: Smithsonian Institution Press, 1956), pp. 49-50; Harold L. Peterson, *Notes on Ordnance of the American Civil War, 1861-1865* (Washington, D.C.: The American Ordnance Association, 1959), unpaginated; R. M. Johnston, *Bull Run: Its Strategy and Tactics* (Boston: Houghton Mifflin, 1913), p. 8

13. Grady McWhiney and Perry D. Jamieson, *Attack and Die: Civil War Military Tactics and the Southern Heritage* (University: University of Alabama Press, 1982), pp. 62-64; L. Van Loan Naisawald, *Grape and Canister: The Story of the Field Artillery of the Army of the Potomac, 1861-1865* (New York: Oxford University Press, 1960), pp. 37-38; Warren Ripley, *Artillery and Ammunition of the Civil War* (New York: Van Nostrand Reinhold Company, 1970), pp. 17-28, 45-46, 109-10, 366-67, 370; Peterson, *Ordnance*, unpaginated.

14. McWhiney and Jamieson, *Attack and Die*, pp. 27-47; Weigley, *United States Army*, p. 235.

15. McWhiney and Jamieson, *Attack and Die*, pp. 48, 67-68; Weigley, *United States Army*, pp. 235-36, 239; John K. Mahon, "Civil War Infantry Assault Tactics," in *Military Analysis of the Civil War*, pp. 263-65.

16. McWhiney and Jamieson, *Attack and Die*, pp. 49-53, 61-62, 65; Lord, *They Fought*, pp. 41-43. See also Nathaniel Cheairs Hughes, Jr., *General William J. Hardee: Old Reliable* (Baton Rouge: Louisiana State University Press, 1965), pp. 41-50, and Thomas V. Moseley, "Evolution of the American Civil War Infantry Tactics" (unpublished Ph.D. dissertation, University of North Carolina, 1967), pp. 262-69.

17. Shannon, *Organization*, 1:162, 172; Lord, *They Fought*, pp. 39-40; Newton Martin Curtis, *From Bull Run to Chancellorsville* (New York: G. P. Putnam's Sons, 1906), p. 26; William T. Sherman, *Memoirs of General William T. Sherman* (New York: D. Appleton and Company, 1875), 1:192; H. Seymour Hall, "A Volunteer at the First Bull Run," *War Talks in Kansas: A Series of Papers Read before the Kansas Commandery of the Military Order of the Loyal Legion of the United States* (Kansas City, Mo.: Press of the Franklin Hudson Publishing Company, 1906), pp. 148, 151.

18. Kreidberg and Henry, *Military Mobilization*, p. 119-20; Lord, *They Fought*, pp. 20-30; Shannon, *Organization*, 1:152, 173; Thomas S. Allen, "The Second Wisconsin at the First Battle of Bull Run," in *War Papers Read before the Commandery of the State of Wisconsin. Military Order of the Loyal Legion of the United States* (Milwaukee, Wis.: Burdick, Armitage & Allen, 1891), 1:375; Augustus Woodbury, *A Narrative of the Campaign of the First Rhode Island Regiment. In the Spring and Summer of 1861* (Providence, R.I.: Sidney S. Rider, 1862), p. 35 (hereafter Woodbury, *First Rhode Island*).

19. Russell F. Weigley, *The American Way of War: A History of United States Military Strategy and Policy* (New York: Macmillan, 1973), p. 92; Matthew Forney Steele, *American Campaigns* (Washington, D.C.: Byron S. Adams, 1909), 1:130; Johnston, *Bull Run*, pp. 13-16; Benjamin Franklin Cooling, *Symbol, Sword, and Shield* (Hamden, Conn.: Archon Books, 1975), pp. 40-48.

20. William C. Davis, *Battle at Bull Run* (Garden City, N.Y.: Doubleday & Company, 1977), pp. 5-13, 42; James B. Fry, *McDowell and Tyler in the Campaign of Bull Run, 1861* (New York: D. Van Nostrand, 1884), pp. 7-10; U.S. Congress, *Report of the Joint Committee on the Conduct of the War*, pt. 2 (Washington, D.C.: Government Printing Office, 1863), p. 37; Warren W. Hassler, Jr., *Commanders of the Army of the Potomac* (Baton Rouge: Louisiana State University Press, 1962), pp. 3-6; Meneely, *War Department*, p. 138; Cooling, *Symbol*, p. 48; George W. Cullum, *Biographical Register of the Officers and Graduates of the U.S. Military Academy, at West Point, N.Y., from Its Establishment, March 16, 1802, to the Army Reorganization of 1866-67* (New York: D. Van Nostrand, 1868), p. 559; Warner, *Generals in Blue*, pp. 297-98, 309. Mansfield remained in command of the troops north of the Potomac in Washington.

21. Joseph E. Johnston, *Narrative of Military Operations* (New York: D. Appleton and Company, 1874), pp. 13-14; Gilbert E. Govan and James W. Livingood, *A Different Valor: The Story of General Joseph E. Johnston, C.S.A.* (Indianapolis: The Bobbs-Merrill Company, 1956), pp. 11-34; Alfred Roman, *The Military Operations of General Beauregard in the War between the States, 1861 to 1865* (New York: Harper & Brothers, 1884), 1:66-67; T. Harry Williams, *P. G. T. Beauregard: Napoleon in Gray* (Baton Rouge: Louisiana State University Press, 1955), pp. 1-67; Cullum, *Biographical Register*, 1:343-44, 548-49; Davis, *Bull Run*, pp. 20, 31-34, 49-51.

22. Steele, *American Campaigns*, 1:131-32. For a visual display of the opposing troop dispositions, see Vincent J. Esposito, ed., *The West Point Atlas of the Civil War* (New York: Frederick A. Praeger, 1962), map 18.

23. *O.R.A.*, 2:472, 847; Johnston, *Narrative*, pp. 17-25; Johnston, *Bull Run*, pp. 32-51; Davis, *Bull Run*, pp. 28-31; Steele, *American Campaigns*, 1:132-33. Cocke's suggestion was made as early as 15 May 1861.

24. *O.R.A.*, 2:719-21; *Report of the Joint Committee*, pt. 2: 35-37, 62; Meneely, *War Department*, pp. 182-85; Johnston, *Bull Run*, pp. 53-54, 60-61, 70; Davis, *Bull Run*, pp. 72-75; Steele, *American Campaigns*, 1:131, 133; Sherman, *Memoirs*, 1:179; Weigley, *American Way of War*, pp. 93-95, 135. According to the foremost strategic theorist of the day, Antoine Henri, Baron de Jomini, the goal of strategy should be to direct the mass of one's forces against the decisive point. Richmond, seat of the Confederate government, was seen as the decisive point in the summer of 1861, and this view

continued to prevail in the federal command structure long after First Bull Run. For opposing views on the importance of Jominian ideas in the Civil War, see T. Harry Williams, "The Military Leadership of North and South," in David Donald, ed., *Why the North Won the Civil War* (Baton Rouge: Louisiana State University Press, 1960), and McWhiney and Jamieson, *Attack and Die,* pp. 147-154.

25. *O.R.A.,* 2:156-66, 692-94, 701-03; *Report of the Joint Committee,* pt. 2: 36, 55-56, 62; Johnston, *Bull Run,* pp. 67-75, 80-81; Davis, *Bull Run,* pp. 45-48, 73-75, 77-80, 86-89. In fairness to Patterson, it must be stated that part of his dithering was due to contradictory messages sent him by Scott. The Pennsylvanian's own account of events can be found in Robert Patterson, *A Narrative of the Campaign in the Valley of the Shenandoah, in 1861* (Philadelphia: Sherman & Co., 1865).

26. *O.R.A.,* 2:324; *Report of the Joint Committee,* pt. 2: 37-38; Fry, *McDowell and Tyler,* pp. 9-11; Davis, *Bull Run,* pp. 76-78; Steele, *American Campaigns,* 1:133-34, 148.

27. Cullum, *Biographical Register,* 1:190, 401, 595; 2:30; Warner, *Generals in Blue,* pp. 204, 402-03, 422-23, 441-42, 514; Fry, *McDowell and Tyler,* p. 12; *O.R.A.,* 2:309, 314; Johnston, *Bull Run,* pp. 91-92, 97; Davis, *Bull Run,* pp. 39, 40. For the status of individual units, see Frederick H. Dyer, *A Compendium of the War of the Rebellion* (1908; reprint, New York: Thomas Yoseloff, 1959), 3: passim. At the time of First Bull Run, Tyler was a brigadier general of Connecticut volunteers only. He did not become a brigadier of U.S. volunteers until March 1862.

28. Warner, *Generals in Blue,* pp. 57, 243-44, 377-78; Cullum, *Biographical Register,* 1:232; 2:191; *O.R.A,* 2:309, 315, 390, 392, 393; Johnston, *Bull Run,* pp. 92-93, 97; Davis, *Bull Run,* p. 59; Dyer, *Compendium,* 3: passim; Dangerfield Parker, "The Regular Infantry in the First Bull Run Campaign," *The United Service,* 13 (1885): 521, 523; Allan R. Millett, *Semper Fidelis: The History of the United States Marine Corps* (New York: Macmillan Publishing Co., 1980), p. 94. Hunter is credited with only 2,485 men in *O.R.A.,* 2:309, but since one of his brigades, Porter's, marched with 3,700 on 21 July (*O.R.A.,* 2:383), the division total must have been far greater than that. See the statement of James B. Fry in Johnson and Buel, *Battles and Leaders,* 1:194.

29. Cullum, *Biographical Register,* 1:295-96; 2:72, 184-85, 369; Warner, *Generals in Blue,* pp. 159, 227-28, 237, 558; Davis, *Bull Run,* pp. 39-40; Johnston, *Bull Run,* 93-94, 97; Dyer, *Compendium,* 3: passim; *O.R.A.,* 2:309, 315. Of Heintzelman's twelve regiments, two would not be present at First Bull Run, one because it had been left behind at Fairfax Court House and the other because its term of enlistment had expired that very day.

30. *O.R.A.,* 2:309, 315; Davis, *Bull Run,* p. 76; Dyer, *Compendium,* 3: passim; Johnston, *Bull Run,* p. 96.

31. Cullum, *Biographical Register,* 1:266-67, 351; Warner, *Generals in Blue,* pp. 37, 113-14; Davis, *Bull Run,* pp. 44-45, 76; *O.R.A.,* 2:309-15; Dyer, *Compendium,* 3: passim; Johnston, *Bull Run,* pp. 95-96.

32. Cullum, *Biographical Register,* 1:400, 529, 602; 2:70-71, 167, 225; Warner, *Generals in Gray,* pp. 28-29, 56-57, 79, 83-85, 163, 192; Davis, *Bull Run,* pp. 15-16, 54-59, 110; Johnston, *Bull Run,* pp. 103-06, 109.

33. *O.R.A.,* 2:441; Johnston, *Bull Run,* pp. 38-42, 127-30; Davis, *Bull Run,* pp. 59-63; Oliver Otis Howard, *Autobiography of Oliver Otis Howard* (New York: The Baker & Taylor Company, 1908), 1:147. Apparently acting on his own responsibility, Cocke eventually entrenched one of his regiments. *O.R.A.,* 51, pt. 1: 26-27.

34. *O.R.A.,* 2:447-48; Roman, *Military Operations,* 1:92; Johnston, *Bull Run,* pp. 127-30; Davis, *Bull Run,* pp. 64, 110; Esposito, *West Point Atlas,* map 21; E. P. Alexander, *Military Memoirs of a Confederate* (1907; reprint, Bloomington: Indiana University Press, 1962), pp. 13-16.

35. *O.R.A.*, 2:324; *O.R.A.*, 51, pt. 2: 688; Allen, "Second Wisconsin," pp. 379-82; Parker, "Regular Infantry," p. 523; Sherman, *Memoirs*, 1:181; *Report of the Joint Committee*, pt. 2:39; Edward K. Eckert and Nicholas J. Amato, eds., *Ten Years in the Saddle: The Memoirs of William Woods Averell* (San Rafael, Calif.: Presidio Press, 1978), p. 292 (hereafter Eckert and Amato, *Averell Memoirs*); Johnston, *Bull Run*, pp. 114-20; Davis, *Bull Run*, pp. 91-99.

36. *O.R.A.*, 2:307, 312, 328-29; *Report of the Joint Committee*, pt. 2: 46-47; J. G. Barnard, *The C.S.A. and the Battle of Bull Run* (New York: D. Van Nostrand, 1862), p. 47 (hereafter Barnard, *Battle of Bull Run*); Johnston, *Bull Run*, pp. 121-26; Davis, *Bull Run*, pp. 99-102. Misunderstanding the purpose of McDowell's reconnaissance, Chief Engineer J. G. Barnard joined Tyler at Centreville instead of accompanying the army commander when invited to do so.

37. *O.R.A.*, 2:473, 478-79, 980-81; Johnston, *Narrative*, p. 33; Roman, *Military Operations*, 1:90-91; Johnston, *Bull Run*, pp. 87-89, 130; Davis, *Bull Run*, pp. 103-10.

38. *O.R.A.*, 2:307, 311-14, 329-30, 441-45, 461-65; *Report of the Joint Committee*, pt. 2: 39; Fry, *McDowell and Tyler*, pp. 21-36; Howard, *Autobiography*, 1:150-51; Barnard, *Battle of Bull Run*, p. 49; Eckert and Amato, *Averell Memoirs*, p. 292; James B. Fry, "McDowell's Advance to Bull Run," in Johnson and Buel, *Battles and Leaders*, 1:179; James Longstreet, *From Manassas to Appomattox* (1896; reprint, Bloomington: Indiana University Press, 1960), pp. 38-41; Johnston, *Bull Run*, pp. 130-37; Davis, *Bull Run*, pp. 112-31.

39. *O.R.A.*, 2:308, 317-18, 324, 326, 330-31, 336-44; *Report of the Joint Committee*, pt. 2: 29; Johnston, *Bull Run*, pp. 137-48; Davis, *Bull Run*, pp. 151-58. The two most knowledgeable authorities on the campaign differ strongly in their evaluation of McDowell's plan. R. M. Johnston found it fatally flawed, while William C. Davis considered it to be quite sophisticated for an officer with McDowell's limited amount of field experience. McDowell's probable estimate of the situation is cast in a modern format by Thomas O. Blakeney in "The Commander's Estimate and General McDowell," *Military Review* 33 (December 1953): 9-17.

40. *O.R.A.*, 2:473; Johnston, *Narrative*, pp. 33-37; Fry, "McDowell's Advance," p. 182; Johnston, *Bull Run*, pp. 150-51, 154-57; Davis, *Bull Run*, pp. 132-34, 148-51. Patterson's lengthy but unconvincing defense of his actions is in *Report of the Joint Committee*, pt. 2: 78-142, and also in his equally lengthy *Narrative*. Both his campaign and his apologia are analyzed in Thomas L. Livermore, "Patterson's Shenandoah Campaign," in Theodore F. Dwight, ed., *Papers of the Military Historical Society of Massachusetts* (Boston: Houghton, Mifflin and Company, 1895), 1:3-58.

41. Cullum, *Biographical Register*, 1:539; 2:127, 132-33, 150; Warner, *Generals in Gray*, pp. 23-24, 82, 151, 279-80; Clement A. Evans, ed., *Confederate Military History* (Atlanta, Ga.: Confederate Publishing Company, 1899), 6:394-95; *O.R.A.*, 2:470; Johnston, *Narrative*, pp. 27, 33; Davis, *Bull Run*, pp. 18, 83-84, 133; Johnston, *Bull Run*, pp. 107-10.

42. *O.R.A.*, 2:473; Johnston, *Narrative*, pp. 36-38; James I. Robertson, Jr., *The Stonewall Brigade* (Baton Rouge: Louisiana State University Press, 1963), pp. 33-37; Johnston, *Bull Run*, pp. 109, 151-54; Davis, *Bull Run*, pp. 134-41; Angus James Johnston II, *Virginia Railroads in the Civil War* (Chapel Hill, N.C.: University of North Carolina Press, 1961), pp. 28-30.

43. *O.R.A.*, 2:473-74, 479-80, 486; Johnston, *Narrative*, pp. 38-41; Johnston, *Bull Run*, pp. 157-63; Davis, *Bull Run*, pp. 143-48; Douglas Southall Freeman, *Lee's Lieutenants: A Study in Command* (New York: Charles Scribner's Sons, 1942), 1:50-51, 726-27.

44. *O.R.A.*, 2:348–49, 357–58, 368, 558–59; *Report of the Joint Committee*, pt. 2: 30, 41–44, 150, 160–61, 200–04, 212; Alexander, *Military Memoirs*, pp. 30–31; Willey Howell, "The First Battle of Bull Run," *Journal of the United States Infantry Association* 6 (July, 1909): 32; Johnston, *Bull Run*, pp. 164–68, 174–77, 183; Davis, *Bull Run*, pp. 159–66; Longstreet, *From Manassas to Appomattox*, pp. 54–55. Longstreet was one of Tyler's few defenders.

45. *O.R.A.*, 2:331, 382–84, 395–96, 559–61, 563; Woodbury, *First Rhode Island*, pp. 87–96; Parker, "Regular Infantry," pp. 525–26; Alexander, *Military Memoirs*, p. 33; Fry, "McDowell's Advance," p. 184; Eckert and Amato, *Averell Memoirs*, pp. 296–97; Johnston, *Bull Run*, pp. 181–89, 195–97; Davis, *Bull Run*, pp. 166–68, 171–75. Heintzelman's division was to have crossed at a ford nearer the Stone Bridge but could not find the road to it. Therefore, it followed Hunter to Sudley Springs.

46. *O.R.A.*, 2:481; Johnston, *Narrative*, pp. 38, 41–42, 45; Roman, *Military Operations*, 1:99, G. T. Beauregard, "The First Battle of Bull Run," in Johnson and Buel, *Battles and Leaders*, 1:205; J. E. Johnston, "Responsibilities of the First Bull Run," in Johnson and Buel, *Battles and Leaders*, 1:246; Johnston, *Bull Run*, pp. 168–70; Freeman, *Lee's Lieutenants*, 1:55–60. Bartow's two regiments were united with Bee's two under the latter's command.

47. *O.R.A.*, 2:349, 369, 384–85, 402, 559; Johnston, *Narrative*, pp. 45–46; Woodbury, *First Rhode Island*, pp. 98–100; Johnston, *Bull Run*, pp. 191–201; Davis, *Bull Run*, pp. 175–88.

48. *O.R.A.*, 2:353, 369, 384–85, 396, 418; *Report of the Joint Committee*, pt. 2:214; Woodbury, *First Rhode Island*, pp. 100–02; Fry, "McDowell's Advance," p. 187; Hassler, *Commanders*, p. 21; Steele, *American Campaigns*, 1:146; Johnston, *Bull Run*, pp. 210–12, 214; Davis, *Bull Run*, pp. 187–88, 192–93.

49. *O.R.A.*, 2:481; Owen, *Washington Artillery*, pp. 36–37; Robertson, *Stonewall Brigade*, pp. 37–39; William M. Robins, "The Soubriquet 'Stonewall.' How It Was Acquired," *Southern Historical Society Papers*, 19:164–67; Freeman, *Lee's Lieutenants*, 1:733–34; Johnston, *Bull Run*, pp. 201–03, 206–07; Davis, *Bull Run*, pp. 195–98.

50. *O.R.A.*, 2:474–75, 491–92; Johnston, *Narrative*, pp. 48–49; Roman, *Military Operations*, 1:102–04; Beauregard, "The First Battle of Bull Run," pp. 210–11; Johnston, "Responsibilities," p. 248; Freeman, *Lee's Lieutenants*, 1:65–66; Johnston, *Bull Run*, pp. 203–05; Davis, *Bull Run*, pp. 208–09, 212–14; Davis, *Bull Run*, pp. 189–92, 198–200.

51. *O.R.A.*, 2:347, 394, 406; *Report of the Joint Committee*, pt. 2: 143–44, 168–69, 243; Johnston, *Narrative*, pp. 49–50; Naisawald, *Grape and Canister*, pp. 10–13; Johnston, *Bull Run*, pp. 208–09, 212–14; Davis, *Bull Run*, pp. 200–05.

52. McWhiney and Jamieson, *Attack and Die*, p. 38; *O.R.A.*, 2:347, 394, 481, 483, 494; *Report of the Joint Committee*, pt. 2: 144–47, 169–77, 216, 218–21; Naisawald, *Grape and Canister*, pp. 13–15; Ralph W. Donnelly, "Federal Batteries on the Henry House Hill, Bull Run, 1861," in *Military Analysis of the Civil War*, pp. 310–14; Arthur C. Cummings, "Thirty-third Virginia at First Manassas," *Southern Historical Society Papers*, 34:367–70; Robertson, *Stonewall Brigade*, pp. 40–41; Johnston, *Bull Run*, pp. 215–16; Davis, *Bull Run*, pp. 205–12. The two guns Griffin removed from Henry House Hill were subsequently lost during the Federal retreat.

53. *O.R.A.*, 2:332, 349–50, 353–54, 358–60, 369–70, 403, 406, 409; Fry, *McDowell and Tyler*, pp. 56–61; Sherman, *Memoirs*, 1:186–87; *Report of the Joint Committee*, pt. 2: 149; E. D. Keyes, *Fifty Years' Observation of Men and Events, Civil and Military* (New York: Charles Scribner's Sons, 1885), pp. 433–34; Robertson, *Stonewall Brigade*, pp. 41–43; Steele, *American Campaigns*, 1:146–47; Johnston, *Bull Run*, pp. 216–23; Davis, *Bull Run*, pp. 214–19, 233–34.

54. *O.R.A.*, 2:418, 476, 495-96, 519, 522-23, 530-31; Howard, *Autobiography*, 1:158-60; Johnston, *Narrative*, pp. 51-52; Roman, *Military Operations*, 1:107; Johnston, *Bull Run*, pp. 223-24, 226-29; Davis, *Bull Run*, pp. 139-40, 219-27. The brigade Smith led into battle was actually Elzey's. When his own brigade was delayed in reaching Piedmont, Smith accompanied Elzey's regiments and assumed command of them by virtue of his superior rank. After Smith was wounded, Elzey regained command of his old unit.

55. *O.R.A.*, 2:334, 403, 409, 418, 496-97, 556-57; Howard, *Autobiography*, 1:160-61; Johnston, *Narrative*, p. 52; Allen, "Second Wisconsin," p. 391; Hall, "A Volunteer," pp. 156-57; Johnston, *Bull Run*, pp. 229-30; Davis, *Bull Run*, pp. 227-33. The position of the units comprising the final Confederate line is carefully delineated in Freeman, *Lee's Lieutenants*, 1:728-32.

56. *O.R.A.*, 2:350, 354, 385, 390, 483, 497, 519, 524-25, 532-33, 535-36, 543-44; Parker, "Regular Infantry," p. 529; Howard, *Autobiography*, 1:161-62; Keyes, *Fifty Years*, p. 434; Longstreet, *From Manassas to Appomattox*, pp. 51-52; Johnston, *Narrative*, pp. 53-56; Freeman, *Lee's Lieutenants*, 1:74-75; Johnston, *Bull Run*, pp. 231-49; Davis, *Bull Run*, pp. 234-42.

57. G. F. R. Henderson, *Stonewall Jackson and the American Civil War* (1898; reprint, New York: David McKay Company, 1968), pp. 117-18; Bruce Catton, *The Coming Fury* (Garden City, N.Y.: Doubleday & Company, 1961), pp. 464-65; Allan Nevins, *The War for the Union: The Improvised War, 1861-1862* (New York: Charles Scribner's Sons, 1959), pp. 220-21; Johnston, *Narrative*, pp. 60-65; Johnston, "Responsibilities," pp. 252-53; Roman, *Military Operations*, 1:116-17; Alexander, *Military Memoirs*, pp. 49-50; Barnard, *Battle of Bull Run*, pp. 101-02; Cooling, *Symbol*, pp. 57-61; Freeman, *Lee's Lieutenants*, 1:77-78; Johnston, *Bull Run*, pp. 249-52; Davis, *Bull Run*, pp. 244-45.

58. *O.R.A.*, 2:568, 570, 571; *O.R.A.*, 51, pt. 1: 17-19; Owen, *Washington Artillery*, pp. 43-45; Johnston, *Bull Run*, pp. 253-66; Davis, *Bull Run*, pp. 198, 245-46, 253.

59. Williams, *Napoleon in Gray*, pp. 91-92; Freeman, *Lee's Lieutenants*, 1:81-96; Steele, *American Campaigns*, 1:145; Johnston, *Bull Run*, pp. 173-75; Davis, *Bull Run*, pp. 246-49.

60. Johnston, *Bull Run*, pp. 269-70, 273; Davis, *Bull Run*, pp. 252-55; Steele, *American Campaigns*, 1:144-45; Howell, "First Battle of Bull Run," p. 29; Elliott, *Winfield Scott*, p. 730; Sherman, *Memoirs*, 1:181; *Report of the Joint Committee*, pt. 2: 31, 48, 62, 77, 151, 160, 205, 207; Barnard, *Battle of Bull Run*, p. 93; Livermore, "Patterson's Shenandoah Campaign," pp. 50-51; William Swinton, *The Twelve Decisive Battles of the War: A History of the Eastern and Western Campaigns* (New York: Dick & Fitzgerald, 1867), p. 44.

61. Johnston, *Bull Run*, pp. 270-72; Davis, *Bull Run*, pp. 253-54; Steele, *American Campaigns*, 1:146.

62. Johnston, *Bull Run*, pp. 226-67, 272; Davis, *Bull Run*, pp. 246, 249-50, 253-55; *O.R.A.*, 2:324; Hassler, *Commanders*, p. 23; *Report of the Joint Committee*, pt. 2: 245-46; Johnston, *Narrative*, pp. 56-57; Beauregard, "First Battle," p. 218; Williams, *Napoleon in Gray*, p. 81; Shannon, *Organization*, 1:166-67, 181-82; Steele, *American Campaigns*, 1:147.

63. *O.R.A.*, 2:345-48, 361-68, 372-73, 377-82, 390-94, 407, 416-17, 436-37; Johnston, *Bull Run*, pp. 257-58; Millett, *Semper Fidelis*, pp. 94-95; Naisawald, *Grape and Canister*, pp. 24-25; Stephen Z. Starr, *The Union Cavalry in the Civil War* (Baton Rouge: Louisiana State University Press, 1979), 1:64; John C. White, "A Review of the Services of the Regular Army During the Civil War," *Journal of the Military Service Institution of the United States*, 45:376-77; 46:467-72; 48:82, 401. The performance of

Sykes' battalion is especially remarkable because it was composed of companies from three different regiments and one of the companies was newly recruited. Dyer, *Compendium*, 3:1710-11; Theo F. Rodenbough and William L. Haskins, eds., *The Army of the United States* (1896; reprint, New York: Argonaut Press, 1966), pp. 422, 443-44, 520.

64. *O.R.A.*, 2:753, 766, 769; *O.R.A.*, 51, pt. 1: 443; Howard, *Autobiography*, 1:169; Eckert and Amato, *Averell Memoirs*, pp. 305-06; Shannon, *Organization*, 1:183; Kreidberg and Henry, *Military Mobilization*, pp. 93, 135. Scott preferred Henry W. Halleck to McClellan, but Lincoln believed that the public would respond more favorably to a man who had produced victories, small though they were. Elliott, *Winfield Scott*, p. 733.

65. McWhiney and Jamieson, *Attack and Die*, pp. 81-111. See also Mahon, "Civil War Infantry Assault Tactics," pp. 253-65, and Edward Hagerman, "From Jomini to Dennis Hart Mahan: The Evolution of Trench Warfare and the American Civil War," in John T. Hubbell, ed., *Battles Lost and Won: Essays from Civil War History* (Westport, Conn.: Greenwood Press, 1975), pp. 31-54.

66. Rogers, *Confederates and Federals*, pp. 32-34; Naisawald, *Grape and Canister*, pp. 35-37; *O.R.A.*, 2:420, 422, 548.

67. Michael Howard, *War in European History* (New York: Oxford University Press, 1976), pp. 97-98; Edwin A. Pratt, *The Rise of Rail-Power in War and Conquest, 1833-1914* (Philadelphia: J. B. Lippincott Company, 1916), pp. 1-50; Rogers, *Confederates and Federals*, pp. 90-107; Johnston, *Virginia Railroads*, pp. v-vi. See also Robert C. Black III, *The Railroads of the Confederacy* (Chapel Hill: University of North Carolina Press, 1952); George Edgar Turner, *Victory Rode the Rails* (Indianapolis, Ind.: Bobbs-Merrill Company, 1952); and Thomas Weber, *The Northern Railroads in the Civil War, 1861-1865* (1952; reprint, Westport, Conn.: Greenwood Press, 1970). According to Rogers, *Confederates and Federals*, p. 90, "Never before or since the American Civil War have the opposing armies depended so much on railways for movement and supply."

68. Shannon, *Organization*, 1:177-78, 181, 184, 190; Kreidberg and Henry, *Military Mobilization*, pp. 119-23; Curtis, *From Bull Run to Chancellorsville*, p. 76; *O.R.A.*, 30, pt. 3: 226; *Report of the Joint Committee*, pt. 2: 142-43; Sherman, *Memoirs*, 1:192; Robertson, *Stonewall Brigade*, p. 46.

69. *O.R.A.*, 5:67, 567; *O.R.A.*, 25, pt. 2: 614-15, 651, 728-30; *O.R.A.*, 51, pt. 1: 434-35, 913-14, 960-61; Hassler, *Commanders*, p. 31; Lord, *They Fought*, pp. 56-59, 66; Rogers, *Confederates and Federals*, pp. 30-31, 70-71; Johnston, *Narrative*, p. 73; Freeman, *Lee's Lieutenants*, 1:670-71; Naisawald, *Grape and Canister*, pp. 274, 329-30; Jennings C. Wise, *The Long Arm of Lee* (1915; reprint, New York: Oxford University Press, 1959), pp. 413-14; William E. Birkhimer, *Historical Sketch of the Organization, Administration, Materiel and Tactics of the Artillery, United States Army* (Washington, D.C.: James J. Chapman, 1884), pp. 79-86; Meneely, *War Department*, pp. 193-94.

70. Howard, *Autobiography*, 1:168; Shannon, *Organization*, 1:186-87; Stanley L. Swart, "The Military Examination Board in the Civil War: A Case Study," in Hubbell, *Battles Lost and Won*, pp. 241-59; Kreidberg and Henry, *Military Mobilization*, pp. 118-19; Upton, *Military Policy*, p. 261; Meneely, *War Department*, pp. 194-95, 315-16; Elliott, *Winfield Scott*, pp. 733-46.

71. Freeman, *Lee's Lieutenants*, 1:97-98; Davis, *Bull Run*, pp. 257-61. One officer, Capt. Frank Crawford Armstrong, led a company of the 2d U.S. Dragoons at Bull Run but joined the Confederacy the following month and eventually became a brigadier general in the Confederate Army. Warner, *Generals in Gray*, pp. 12-13; *O.R.A.*, 2:393.

CHAPTER 5. SAN JUAN HILL
AND EL CANEY, 1–2 JULY 1898

1. For a summary of armed services reform in this period, see James L. Abrahamson, *American Arms for a New Century: The Making of a Great Military Power* (New York: The Free Press, 1981). Army developments are covered in: Graham A. Cosmas, *An Army for Empire: The United States Army in the Spanish-American War, 1898–1899* (Columbia: University of Missouri Press, 1971), ch. 1–2. For the Army schools, see Timothy K. Nenninger, *The Leavenworth Schools and the Old Army: Education, Professionalism, and the Officer Corps of the United States Army, 1881–1918* (Westport, Conn.: Greenwood Press, 1978).

2. Cosmas, *Army for Empire*, ch. 3–5.

3. The best overall account of the war with Spain is David F. Trask, *The War with Spain in 1898* (New York: Macmillan, 1981); for planning and development of strategy, see ch. 4–7. For early naval plans, see Ronald Spector, *Professors of War: The Naval War College and the Development of the Naval Profession* (Newport, R.I.: Naval War College Press, 1977), pp. 89–95. Cosmas, *Army for Empire*, ch. 4 and pp. 177–81, relates strategy to Army mobilization. Older but still indispensable is French Ensor Chadwick, *The Relations of the United States to Spain: The Spanish-American War*, 2 vols. (New York, 1911), especially, for Santiago, vol. 2.

4. Fifth Corps order of battle can be found, among other places, in Society of Santiago de Cuba, *The Santiago Campaign* (Richmond, Va.: Williams Printing Co., 1927), app. 1 (hereafter *Santiago Campaign*). For details of its organization, see *Annual Report of the Major General Commanding the Army to the Secretary of War, 1898* (Washington, D.C.: Government Printing Office, 1898), pp. 148–49, 321, 365, 367, 393–95 (hereafter MGCAR 98). Lt Col William H. Carter, *From Yorktown to Santiago with the Sixth U.S. Cavalry* (Baltimore: The Lord Baltimore Press, 1900), pp. 285–87 (hereafter Carter, *Sixth Cavalry*). Ralph C. Deibert, *A History of the Third United States Cavalry* (n.p., 1933), p. 34.

5. Cosmas, *Army for Empire*, pp. 201–02; see ch. 5 for a general discussion of Army supply problems.

6. *U.S. Army Infantry Drill Regulations*, special ed. (New York: D. Appleton & Co., 1898), passim. John K. Mahon and Romana Danysh, *Infantry, Part I: Regular Army*, Army Lineage Series, 2 vols. (Washington, D.C.: Office of the Chief of Military History, 1972), 1:33–34, 38. Vardell E. Nesmith, Jr., "The Quiet Paradigm Change: The Evolution of the Field Artillery Doctrine of the United States Army, 1861–1905" (Ph.D. dissertation, Duke University, 1977), pp. 2–3, 256–62. *Santiago Campaign*, p. 183.

7. Cosmas, *Army for Empire*, p. 194. *Santiago Campaign*, pp. 58–59. Carter, *Sixth Cavalry*, pp. 272–77, describes prewar training.

8. For the formation of the wartime officer corps, see Cosmas, *Army for Empire*, pp. 148–51. Information on V Corps officers is drawn from Francis B. Heitman, *Historical Register and Dictionary of the United States Army*, 2 vols. (Washington, D.C., 1903). For participant comments, see *Santiago Campaign*, p. 286, and MGCAR 98, p. 577.

9. Shafter is sketched in Cosmas, *Army for Empire*, pp. 193–94. For his frontier activities, see Robert M. Utley, *Frontier Regulars: The United States Army and the Indian, 1866–1891* (Bloomington: Indiana University Press, 1977), pp. 350–55.

10. Breckinridge's comment is in MGCAR 98, p. 591. Cosmas, *Army for Empire*, pp. 171–72, discusses problems of wartime corps and division staff formation. Shafter's staff are listed in Chadwick, *Spanish-American War*, 2:20–21.

11. The embarkation is recounted in Cosmas, *Army for Empire*, pp. 195-96, and Trask, *War with Spain*, pp. 178-86. Much of the inefficiency stemmed from the absence at Tampa of anything like a separate base command. Statistics are from Chadwick, *Spanish-American War*, 2:19-20.

12. Cosmas, *Army for Empire*, p. 197. Trask, *War with Spain*, pp. 186-90, 194-96.

13. For summaries of Spanish dispositions and the conditions at Santiago, see Trask, *War with Spain*, pp. 196-203; Cosmas, *Army for Empire*, p. 209; Chadwick, *Spanish-American War*, 2:26-29, 49-47; and Herbert H. Sargent, *The Campaign of Santiago de Cuba*, 3 vols. (Chicago: A. C. McClurg & Co., 1907), 2:8-13, 45-53 (hereafter Sargent, *Santiago Campaign*). Severo Gomez Nunez, *La Guerra Hispano-americana: Santiago de Cuba* (Madrid: Imprenta del Cuerpo de Artilleria, 1901), ch. 2 and pp. 57-58, 98-100 (hereafter Nunez, *Guerra: Santiago*), gives a view from the Spanish side. Octavio A. Delgado, "The Spanish Army in Cuba, 1868-1898: An Institutional Study" (Ph.D. dissertation, Columbia University, 1980), 1: ch. 4 and 6, discusses the sources and character of Spanish troops. For an American view of Spanish arms and fortifications, see MGCAR 98, pp. 597, 599-600.

14. Shafter describes his plan in MGCAR 98, pp. 149-50. For the Army-Navy controversy and varying evaluations of its merits, see: Cosmas, *Army for Empire*, pp. 207-09; Trask, *War with Spain*, pp. 204-08; Chadwick, *Spanish-American War*, 2:24-25, 58; and Sargent, *Santiago Campaign*, 2:24-44. See also *Santiago Campaign*, pp. 341-42.

15. Cosmas, *Army for Empire*, pp. 206-09, 212-13. Chadwick, *Spanish-American War*, 2:29-40, 48-67. MGCAR 98, pp. 150-52, 593. Nunez, *Guerra: Santiago*, pp. 64-81, 117-18.

16. MGCAR 98, pp. 151-52. Cosmas, *Army for Empire*, pp. 209-12. Ltrs, Shafter to Major General J. Wheeler, 26, 27 Jun 1898, William R. Shafter Papers, Stanford University, Stanford, Calif.

17. Chadwick, *Spanish-American War*, 2:49-50, 65-66, sums up living conditions during the first days on shore. For an individual view, see Matthew F. Steele ltrs to Mrs. Steele, 27, 28 Jun 1898, Matthew F. Steele Papers, U.S. Army Military History Institute (USAMHI), Carlisle Barracks, Pa. *Santiago Campaign*, p. 69, contains comment on wool uniforms. For health conditions, see ltr, Shafter to Alger, 27 Jun 1898, in U.S. Army Adjutant General's Office, *Correspondence Relating to the War with Spain and Conditions Growing out of the Same, . . . between the Adjutant General of the Army and Military Commanders in the United States, Cuba, Porto Rico, China, and the Philippine Islands, from April 15, 1898, to July 30, 1902*, 2 vols. (Washington, D.C., 1902), 1:60 (hereafter *Correspondence*).

18. Cosmas, *Army for Empire*, p. 213. MGCAR 98, pp. 152-53. *Correspondence*, 1:60, 64. For examples of information reaching Shafter, see ltrs, Wheeler to Shafter, 26, 27, 28 Jun 1898, Shafter Papers.

19. Sargent, *Santiago Campaign*, 2:91-92. Ltr, Matthew F. Steele to Mrs. Steele, 28 Jun 1898, Steele Papers. *Correspondence*, 1:66-67. MGCAR 98, p. 389. *Santiago Campaign*, pp. 297-98.

20. MGCAR 98, pp. 152, 319. For Shafter's early interest in El Caney, see Chadwick, *Spanish-American War*, 2:61, 67-68. *Santiago Campaign*, pp. 16-17. Wheeler also thought El Caney an easy target; see ltrs to Shafter, 28, 29 Jun 1898, Shafter Papers.

21. Shafter's telegram is in *Correspondence*, 1:68; see also p. 60. His adjutant general recalls his reluctance to storm the city in *Santiago Campaign*, p. 9; see also pp. 15-16. William R. Shafter, "The Capture of Santiago de Cuba," *The Century Magazine* (Feb 1899): 621-22.

22. MGCAR 98, pp. 152, 411, 594. *Santiago Campaign*, pp. 17, 115. Major Philip Reade, Inspector General, 1st Division, Report (hereafter cited as Reade Report), in U.S. Congress, Senate, *Report of the Commission Appointed by the President to Investigate the Conduct of the War Department in the War with Spain*, 8 vols. (Senate Doc. no. 221, 56th Cong., 1st Sess., 1900), 1:351-52. Chadwick, *Spanish-American War*, 2:76-77.

23. General Vara del Rey also commanded one of the two brigades into which the Santiago garrison was organized, controlling troops at a number of positions north of Santiago. MGCAR 98, pp. 319-20. Sargent, *Santiago Campaign*, 2:101-02. Nunez, *Guerra: Santiago*, pp. 115-17, 120-21. *Santiago Campaign*, pp. 116, 277-78, contains participant views of El Caney, its defenses, and the terrain around it.

24. Quotation is from MGCAR 98, p. 594; see also pp. 367, 412.

25. Quotations are from MGCAR 98, pp. 360-61, 322; see also pp. 153, 317-18, 320-23, 362, 366-67, 378-79, 381. *Santiago Campaign*, pp. 327-28.

26. For comment on Lawton's failure to disengage, see Trask, *War with Spain*, pp. 236-38; and Chadwick, *Spanish-American War*, 2:83-84. MGCAR 98, pp. 171, 454-55. Vara del Rey's report is recounted in Nunez, *Guerra: Santiago*, pp. 143-44.

27. MGCAR 98, pp. 357-59, 855-56. For the Navy view, see Chadwick, *Spanish-American War*, 2:98-100.

28. Sargent, *Santiago Campaign*, 2:93-95, 98-101, 108-110, summarizes the terrain and Spanish dispositions. See also Nunez, *Guerra: Santiago*, pp. 137-40, 143.

29. MGCAR 98, pp. 154-55, 161, 388-90, 453. McClernand describes his role in *Santiago Campaign*, p. 18. Sargent, *Santiago Campaign*, 2:111-12. Copies of many of the messages sent back and forth are in the Shafter Papers.

30. Sargent, *Santiago Campaign*, 2:110-11. Shafter's and Kent's versions are in MGCAR 98, pp. 153, 164. McClernand's story is in *Santiago Campaign*, pp. 19-21.

31. For one of many recollections of a lack of briefing, see *Santiago Campaign*, pp. 78-79. The quotation is from Reade Report, p. 352. Sumner recalled being instructed initially to "move to the San Juan Creek and hold it." MGCAR 98, p. 371.

32. Reade Report, pp. 353-55. MGCAR 98, pp. 370, 372, 439, 441. *Santiago Campaign*, pp. 22-23. Matthew F. Steele to Mrs. Steele, 3 Jul 1898, Steele Papers.

33. Grimes' report is in MGCAR 98, p. 409. Nunez, *Guerra: Santiago*, pp. 140-42. Matthew F. Steele to Mrs. Steele, 3 Jul 1898, Steele Papers. Msgs, Miley to Shafter, 1 Jul 1898; Shafter to McClernand and Grimes, 1 Jul 1898; McClernand to Shafter, 1 Jul 1898; Shafter Papers. Capt Charles D. Parkhurst, "The Artillery at Santiago," article in Shafter Papers.

34. The 1st Cavalry Brigade filed few after-action reports. The most detailed account is in Carter, *Sixth Cavalry*, pp. 289-93. See also MGCAR 98, p. 369. Msg, Miley to Shafter and McClernand, 1 Jul 1898, 1000, Shafter Papers.

35. The 2d Cavalry Brigade is better covered by reports; see MGCAR 98, pp. 154, 326-27, 336, 342-43, 371. Memoirs of this brigade are also numerous. Just two examples are: Bigelow, *Reminiscences of the Santiago Campaign*, and Theodore Roosevelt, *The Rough Riders* (New York, 1899).

36. Chief Signal Officer, *Report . . . to the Secretary of War for the Fiscal Year Ending June 30, 1898* (Washington, D.C.: Government Printing Office, 1898), pp. 19, 88-91, 93. MGCAR 98, p. 390. Typical troop reaction to the balloon and the fire it drew can be found in Matthew F. Steele to Mrs. Steele, 3 Jul 1898, Steele Papers. Msg, Derby to Shafter, 1 Jul 1898, 0930, Shafter Papers.

37. Carter, *Sixth Cavalry*, pp. 289-93. MGCAR 98, pp. 335-36, 369. *Santiago Campaign*, pp. 226-29.

38. The first quotation is from L. W. V. Kennon, "Company E, 6th U.S. Infantry at Fort San Juan," manuscript in Crook-Kennon Papers, USAMHI. The

second is from Reade Report, p. 357; see also pp. 355, 361. John E. Woodward Diary, 1 Jul 1898, in Spanish-American War Collection, USAMHI. Matthew F. Steele to Mrs. Steele, 7 Jul 1898, Steele Papers. Straggling is mentioned in msg, McClernand to Shafter, 1 Jul 1898, Shafter Papers. MGCAR 98, pp. 164, 278-81, 292, 298-99, 421-22, 425, 440-41, 596; this document prints unit after-action reports down to the company level, many of which, written within days of the battle, contain vivid detail.

39. Msgs, Shafter to McClernand, 1 Jul 1898; McClernand to Miley, 1 Jul 1898; and McClernand to Shafter, 1 Jul 1898, 1135; all in Shafter Papers.

40. MGCAR 98, pp. 153-54, 164-65, 305. Reade Report, pp. 352-53. *Santiago Campaign,* pp. 413-18.

41. For detailed reports, see MGCAR 98, pp. 279-81, 285-91, 295, 298-300, 303-04, 363-66, 433. Kennon, "Company E," gives a more dramatized narrative.

42. MGCAR 98, pp. 164-65. Reade Report, pp. 354-56, 364. Matthew F. Steele to Mrs. Steele, 10 Jul 1898, Steele Papers.

43. MGCAR 98, pp. 154, 165, 421-24, 430-31, 439-42, 445-46.

44. The Spanish view is in Nunez, *Guerra: Santiago,* pp. 143-44. MGCAR 98, pp. 155, 411, 413, 419. *Santiago Campaign,* pp. 188-89.

45. Parker's report is in MGCAR 98, pp. 457-59; see also pp. 395, 422 for the infantry's view. John H. Parker, *History of the Gatling Gun Detachment, Fifth Army Corps, at Santiago* (Kansas City, Mo., 1898), describes the entire Gatling gun experiment.

46. Nunez, *Guerra: Santiago,* pp. 142, 144-47.

47. McClernand's version is in *Santiago Campaign,* pp. 23-25. Sumner's account is in MGCAR 98, p. 371.

48. Ltr, Matthew F. Steele to Mrs. Steele, 10 Jul 1898, Steele Papers.

49. Chadwick, *Spanish-American War,* 2:91-93. MGCAR 98, pp. 154, 326-27, 336, 340-41, 343, 369. Carter, *Sixth Cavalry,* pp. 293-98. Deibert, *Third Cavalry,* pp. 34-35. Matthew F. Steele to Mrs. Steele, 3 Jul 1898, Steele Papers. Msgs, Wheeler to McClernand, 1 Jul 1898, 1300, 1320, and 1330; and Sumner to Shafter, n.d., Shafter Papers.

50. MGCAR 98, pp. 298, 303-04, 306, 440, 449. *Santiago Campaign,* p. 418.

51. MGCAR 98, p. 422.

52. Ibid., pp. 166, 280-82, 286, 288-90, 300-01, 304, 315, 365, 424, 431-32, 450. Kennon, "Company E." *Santiago Campaign,* pp. 27, 418.

53. MGCAR 98, pp. 165-66, 391-95, 397-98, 441. Reade Report, p. 355.

54. Nunez, *Guerra: Santiago,* pp. 144-48. MGCAR 98, pp. 154-55, 166, 173, 291-92, 304, 326, 329, 335-36, 400-01, 411, 413, 422-24, 446, 459. Reade Report, pp. 355, 363-64. Spanish solid shot are described in Matthew F. Steele to Mrs. Steele, 3, 6 Jul 1898, Steele Papers. Msgs, Miley to Shafter and McClernand, 1 Jul 1898, 1405 and 1620; Kent to McClernand, 1 Jul 1898, 1445 and 1635; Wheeler to Shafter, 1 Jul 1898, 1650, 1745, 2020; Shafter Papers.

55. MGCAR 98, pp. 320-21, 381, 384-88, 412, 594. *Santiago Campaign,* pp. 270-74.

56. The quotation is from *Santiago Campaign,* p. 276; see also p. 358. MGCAR 98, pp. 318, 386-88, recounts actions and claims of the 12th and 25th Infantry.

57. Sargent, *Santiago Campaign,* 2:105-06, reproduces Shafter's message. For Lawton's explanation, see msg, Lawton to Shafter, 1 Jul 1898, 1645, Shafter Papers.

58. MGCAR 98, pp. 171-72, 361-63, 367, 385, 455. Nunez, *Guerra: Santiago,* pp. 130-32. *Santiago Campaign,* p. 328. Lawton at first doubted that he had done the garrison much damage; see his msg to Shafter, 1 Jul 1898, 1645, Shafter Papers.

59. MGCAR 98, pp. 155, 171-72, 321. McClernand's version of the giving of the order to Lawton and a cavalry officer's criticism of Lawton's neglect to reconnoiter

are in *Santiago Campaign,* pp. 29–30. Msg, Lawton to Adj Gen V Corps, 1 Jul 1898, 2230, Shafter Papers.

60. The quotation is from MGCAR 98, p. 401; for other reports of 2 Jul action, see pp. 155–56, 167–68, 286–87, 326, 359, 395, 398, 410–11, 413, 415, 420. *Santiago Campaign,* pp. 32–33, 190–92. Carter, *Sixth Cavalry,* p. 298. Nunez, *Guerra: Santiago,* pp. 152–53, 211–13. Matthew F. Steele to Mrs. Steele, 5, 6, 10 Jul 1898, Steele Papers. Woodward Diary, 2, 6, 7 Jul 1898.

61. Sargent, *Santiago Campaign,* 3, appendices R and V give detailed breakdowns of both United States and Spanish casualties. Shafter's figures are in MGCAR 98, p. 157; for examples of officer and enlisted loss rates, see pp. 292, 343, 368. In the entire campaign, 14 percent of 869 officers were killed or wounded and 9 percent of 17,349 enlisted men; in individual regiments and brigades, the officer loss rate was even higher. See for example Carter, *Sixth Cavalry,* p. 300. Nunez, *Guerra: Santiago,* pp. 132–33, 148–51, gives a partial breakdown of Spanish losses, apparently excluding the men captured at El Caney.

62. Trask, *War with Spain,* pp. 245–54; and Cosmas, *Army for Empire,* pp. 215–17, describe the reappraisals following the battles; the Roosevelt quotation can be found in the latter volume, p. 215. For contemporary views, see: MGCAR 98, pp. 158, 577–78; Reade Report, p. 356; Matthew F. Steele to Mrs. Steele, 5, 12 Jul 1898; and Woodward Diary, 3, 6 Jul 1898; the second quotation is from Woodward Diary, 16 Jul 1898. Shafter's hesitations can be followed in *Correspondence,* 1:70–75. McClernand gives a version of the 2 Jul council of war in *Santiago Campaign,* pp. 30–32. Nunez, *Guerra: Santiago,* p. 215, claims the Americans were intimidated by the heavy resistance the Spaniards had put up.

63. A convenient summary of the criticisms of Shafter can be found in Trask, *War with Spain,* p. 246. Sargent, *Santiago Campaign,* 2:134–66, is a balanced but highly critical, near-contemporary view of Shafter's conduct, as well as of Spanish tactics.

64. Chadwick, *Spanish-American War,* 2:24–25. Shafter himself attributed success to "the intrepid gallantry of the company officers and men, and the benefits derived from the careful training and instruction given in the company in recent years in rifle practice and other battle exercises." MGCAR 98, p. 157.

65. Cosmas, *Army for Empire,* pp. 199–201, 217–22, 230–44. Trask, *War with Spain,* ch. 15–18.

66. For the ordnance evaluation, see Cosmas, *Army for Empire,* p. 244; see also ch. 8–9 for the war scandals and their effects. For the artillery question, see MGCAR 98, pp. 411–12, 577–78; Nesmith, "Quiet Paradigm Change," pp. 269–71, 339; and Parkhurst, "Artillery at Santiago." Parker's views on the machine gun are in MGCAR 98, pp. 9–460, and his *History of the Gatling Gun Detachment.*

67. Cosmas, *Army for Empire,* ch. 9. Root's achievements are summed up in his *Five Years of the War Department* (Washington, D.C.: Government Printing Office, 1904). Army developments to 1914 are conveniently summarized in Russell F. Weigley, *History of the United States Army* (New York: Macmillan, 1967), ch. 14.

68. Trask, *War with Spain,* is the best current summary of the combat and diplomacy that ended the conflict. For the Santiago siege see also Cosmas, *Army for Empire,* pp. 217–30; and Nunez, *Guerra: Santiago,* pp. 213–19, 224–25.

CHAPTER 6. CANTIGNY, 28–31 MAY 1918

1. Richard D. Challener, *Admirals, Generals, and American Foreign Policy, 1898-1914* (Princeton, N.J.: Princeton University Press, 1973). See also James W. Pohl, "The

General Staff and American Military Policy: The Formative Period, 1898–1917"
(unpublished Ph.D. dissertation, University of Texas–Austin, 1967).

2. For descriptions of the prewar Army and land-force policy, see especially
Russell F. Weigley, *History of the United States Army* (New York: Macmillan, 1967), pp.
313–54; James L. Abrahamson, *American Arms for a New Century: The Making of a Great
Military Power* (New York: Free Press, 1981); John P. Finnegan, *Against the Specter of the
Dragon: The Campaign for American Military Preparedness, 1914–1917* (Westport, Conn.:
Greenwood Press, 1974); Marvin A. Kreidberg and Merton G. Henry, *History of
Military Mobilization in the United States Army, 1775–1945* (Washington, D.C.: Depart-
ment of the Army, 1955), pp. 175–240; and Maj Gen William Harding Carter, *The
American Army* (Indianapolis, Ind.: Bobbs-Merrill, 1915).

3. "Report of the Secretary of War" and "Report of the Chief of Staff," *War
Department Annual Reports, 1915,* 3 vols. (Washington, D.C.: Government Printing
Office, 1916), 1:7–40, 139–68. For technical details on field artillery of the World War
I period, see Capt Leslie E. Babcock, *Elements of Field Artillery* (Princeton, N.J.:
Princeton University Press, 1925). See also ms, Janice E. McKenney, 1982, sub:
"Artillery," U.S. Army Center of Military History.

4. "Report of the Chief of Ordnance," *War Department Annual Reports, 1915,*
1:703.

5. The quote is from Notebook 20, entry: 15 May 1913, Robert L. Bullard
Papers, Manuscript Division, Library of Congress (MD/LC). The description of
Army War College teachings is taken from the lectures and class exercises, Class of
1912 (Sep 1911–May 1912), archives of the Army War College, U.S. Army Military
History Institute (USAMHI), Carlisle Barracks, Pa. On the School of the Line and the
Staff College, see Timothy K. Nenninger, *The Leavenworth Schools and the Old Army:
Education, Professionalism, and the Officer Corps of the United States Army, 1881–1918*
(Westport, Conn.: Greenwood Press, 1978).

6. The analysis of doctrine comes from "Combat," a section of Office of the Chief
of Staff, War Department, *Field Service Regulations 1914* (Washington, D.C.: Government Printing Office, 1914), as well as Col John F. Morrison, *Training Infantry* (Fort
Leavenworth, Kans.: U.S. Cavalry Association, 1914) and Capt Oliver L. Spaulding,
Jr., *Notes on Field Artillery* (Leavenworth, Kans.: U.S. Cavalry Association, 1908).

7. On the nature of prewar maneuvers, I have based my description on: Brig Gen
Tasker H. Bliss, *Report of the Commander of Maneuvers and Chief Umpire, Connecticut
Maneuver Campaign, August 10–20, 1912* (n.p., 1912), USAMHI; Ltr, Brig Gen Tasker
H. Bliss to Brig Gen J. J. Pershing, 2 Jun 1913, Tasker H. Bliss Papers, MD/LC; Ltr,
Maj Gen F. Funston to Gen L. Wood, 23, 31 Mar 1914, Leonard Wood Papers, MD/
LC; Ltr, Maj Gen J. F. Bell to Brig Gen William H. Carter, "Report of the Second
Division," *War Department Annual Reports, 1913,* 4 vols. (Washington, D.C.: Govern-
ment Printing Office, 1914), 3:113–20; Ltr, Wood to Maj Gen H. L. Scott, 26 Mar
1915, Hugh L. Scott Papers, MD/LC; Lt Gen Hunter Liggett, *Commanding an
American Army* (Boston: Houghton Mifflin, 1925), pp. 1–3; Col Robert L. Bullard,
"Impressions of Service with the 2d Division in Texas," *Infantry Journal* 11 (Nov–Dec
1914): 353–59, and 12 (Jul–Aug 1915): 32–37; Ltr, Bliss to Scott, 24, 26 Jul 1916,
Scott Papers; Memo, Brig Gen James Parker, "Report of the Instruction of National
Guard Troops," 24 Jan 1917, Clarence Edwards Papers, Massachusetts Historical
Society, Boston; and Militia Bureau, War Department, *Report on Mobilization of the
Organized Militia and National Guard of the United States, 1916* (Washington, D.C.:
Government Printing Office, 1916).

8. Ordnance analysis is based on Office of the Assistant Secretary of War and
Director of Munitions, *America's Munitions, 1917–1918* (Washington, D.C.: Govern-

ment Printing Office, 1919). See also David A. Armstrong, *Bullets and Bureaucrats: The Machine Gun and the United States Army, 1861-1916* (Westport, Conn.: Greenwood Press, 1982).

9. Memo for the Commandant, Army War College, "Study of the Results of the Army Educational System as Evidenced by the Records Made by Officers in the World War," 22 Oct 1923, copy in "Book File," Pershing Papers; Memo, Adj Gen's Office, War Department, "Percentage of Officers of the Several Staff Corps and Departments and of the Several Arms of the Line Who Are Graduates of the Military Academy," 14 Jun 1913, Wood Papers. In addition to Nenninger and Abrahamson, cited above, see also Allan R. Millett, *The General: Robert L. Bullard and Officership in the United States Army, 1881-1925* (Westport, Conn.: Greenwood Press, 1975).

10. Entry, Diarybook 8, 16 Jun 1917, Bullard Papers.

11. The General Staff, His Majesty's Army, *German Army Handbook, April 1918* (1918; reprint, London: Arms and Armour Press, 1977).

12. Timothy K. Lupfer, *The Dynamics of Doctrine: The Changes in German Tactical Doctrine During the First World War,* Leavenworth Papers No. 4 (Fort Leavenworth, Kans.: Combat Studies Institute, USAC&GSC, 1981).

13. Memo, Bliss to the secretary of war, "A Study of Deficiencies to Be Supplied in Case the United States Should Ever Have to Organize a Military Force of 500,000 Men for Service at Home or Abroad," 19 May 1915, Tasker H. Bliss Papers, MD/LC; Memo, Brig Gen M. M. Macomb to the chief of staff, "Organization and Cost of a National Volunteer Force," 21 Jun 1915, File 9053, Army War College Correspondence Files, Records of the War Department General Staff, RG 165, NA; Corresp of the Office of the Chief of Staff, WDGS Report 12460, 28 Feb 1916, RG 165; U.S. Congress, Senate, "Government Manufacture of Arms, Munitions, and Equipment," Sen. Doc. 664, 64th Cong., 2d Sess. (1917); Ltr, Adj Gen W. M. Wright to Maj Gen H. L. Scott, 24 Mar 1917, Scott Papers; Ltr, Brig Gen J. McA. Palmer to Maj Gen R. C. Davis, 7 Aug 1925, John L. Hines Papers, MD/LC.

The best scholarly accounts of the American war effort are Edward M. Coffman, *The War to End All Wars: The Military Experience in World War I* (New York: Oxford University Press, 1968), and David M. Kennedy, *Over Here: The First World War and American Society* (New York: Oxford University Press, 1980). See also Historical Section, Army War College, *The Genesis of the American First Army* (Washington, D.C.: Government Printing Office, 1938); Daniel R. Beaver, *Newton D. Baker and the American War Effort, 1917-1919* (Lincoln: University of Nebraska Press, 1966), and Edward M. Coffman, *The Hilt of the Sword: The Career of Peyton C. March* (Madison: University of Wisconsin Press, 1966).

14. In addition to Donald Smythe, *Pershing* (Bloomington: Indiana University Press, 1986), see Frank Vandiver, *Black Jack: The Life and Times of John J. Pershing,* 2 vols. (College Station: Texas A&M University Press, 1977); Edward M. Coffman, "John J. Pershing: General of the Armies," in B. F. Cooling III, ed., *Essays in Some Dimensions of Military History* 4 (Carlisle Barracks, Pa.: U.S. Army Military History Research Collection, 1976): 48-61; and Frederick Palmer, *John J. Pershing* (Harrisburg, Pa.: Military Service Publishing, 1948). John J. Pershing, *My Experiences in the World War,* 2 vols. (New York: Frederick J. Stokes, 1931) remains an important source on the AEF.

15. Office of the Chief of Staff, GHQ AEF, "A Strategical Study on the Employment of the A.E.F. against the Imperial German Government," 25 Sep 1917, File 681, GHQ AEF Secret General Correspondence, Records of the American Expeditionary Forces, RG 120, NA.

The principal printed source of AEF documents on plans and policies is vol. 1 of Historical Division, Department of the Army, *United States Army in the World War, 1917–1919,* 17 vols. (Washington, D.C.: Government Printing Office, 1948) (hereafter *USA/WW*), which may be supplemented by a personal analysis by Maj Gen James G. Harbord (AEF chief of staff during 1917), *The American Army in France 1917–1919* (Boston: Little, Brown, 1936).

16. GHQ AEF, "Final Report of G-3," 2 Jul 1919, *USA/WW,* 14:1–60, summarizes plans and operations; Historical Section, Army War College, *Order of Battle of the United States Land Forces in the World War: American Expeditionary Forces: Divisions* (Washington, D.C.: Government Printing Office, 1931), describes divisional organization. The travails of the 1st Division are described in unit memoranda and reports scattered throughout the twenty-nine volumes of *World War Records, First Division, A.E.F., Regular* (Washington, D.C.: Society of the First Division, 1928–30) (hereafter cited as *WWR/1st Div* by vol., unpaginated). The collection is basically organized by unit. See also The Society of the First Division, *History of the First Divison during the World War, 1917–1919* (Philadelphia: Winston, 1922).

17. Memo, HQ, 1st Division, 5 Aug 1917, *WWR/1st Div,* 20; Maj Frank Parker, "The Infantry Division," 30 Mar 1917, Frank Parker Papers, Southern Historical Collection, University of North Carolina–Chapel Hill; the final company organization may be found in the records of the 28th Infantry, war diaries, Oct–Dec 1917, vol. 17, *WWR/1st Div.*

18. Army General Staff College, AEF, 3d Course, "Division on the Offensive" (19 Dec 1917) and "Division in the Attack" (22 Dec 1917), General Staff College File, GHQ AEF Historical Files, RG 120; HQ 1st Division, "Provisional Manual for Infantry Signal Detachments," 23 Aug 1918, *WWR/1st Div,* 20; CG, 1st Artillery Brig to CO, Field Artillery School, 7 Jul 1918, *WWR/1st Div,* 20; G-3 memo, 1st Div, 13 Apr 1918, *WWR/1st Div,* 19. For French doctrine, see Lt Col Paul Azan, French Army, *The War of Positions* (Cambridge, Mass.: Harvard University Press, 1917). On the development of World War I artillery doctrine, see Lt Col Alexander T. Jennette, "Mass Fire in WWI," *Field Artillery Journal* 43 (May–Jun 1975): 40–45.

19. The 1st Division's training memoranda and schedules for 1917 are reprinted in *WWR/1st Div,* vol. 19, with the fundamental guidance in GHQ AEF, "Program for Training the 1st Division, A.E.F.," 12 Oct 1917, interpreted in Memo, Maj Gen R. L. Bullard, "Requirements of our G.H.Q. in France," 15 Dec 1917, *WWR/1st Div,* vol. 20. The account of the division G-3 is important on the division's training: George C. Marshall, *Memoirs of My Services in the World War, 1917–1918,* edited by Brig Gen James L. Collins, Jr. (Boston: Houghton Mifflin, 1976).

20. Practically all the senior officers of the 1st Division in May 1918 left substantial accounts of their service with the division, including frank evaluations of their peers. Marshall's memoir has already been cited. See Diarybook 9 (1918), Bullard Papers; Robert L. Bullard, *Personalities and Reminiscences of the War* (Garden City, N.Y.: Doubleday, Page, 1925); George B. Duncan, "Reminiscences of the World War," n.d., copy in the possession of Edward M. Coffman, University of Wisconsin–Madison; Beaumont B. Buck, *Memories of War and Peace* (San Antonio, Tex.: Naylor, 1935); Hines correspondence files (1918) and "Remarks to the General Staff College," 1919, and "Battle Command of a Regiment," 19 Jun 1923, Hines Papers; Ltrs, F. Parker to Mrs. F. Parker, Jan–Jun 1918, Parker Papers; and Campbell King, "My Tour in France," n.d., Campbell King Papers, Duke University Library. Bullard characterized Ely in *Fighting Generals* (Ann Arbor, Mich.: Edwards, 1944), pp. 43–45; see also Allan R. Millett, "Hanson E. Ely," *Dictionary of*

American Biography: Supplement Six, 1956-1960 (New York: Scribner's, 1980), pp. 190-92, based on Ely family records and letters.

Pershing's views of the division's leadership may be found scattered throughout his diary notes for Oct 1917-Mar 1918, Pershing Papers. Other important observations come from diary entries, Jan-Mar 1918, P. L. Stackpole (aide to Maj Gen H. Liggett), Stackpole Papers, George C. Marshall Library, Lexington, Va.; Robert Alexander, *Memories of the World War* (New York: Macmillan, 1931); Henry T. Allen diary, entries, Jan 1918, Henry T. Allen Papers, MD/LC. Another keen observer of regular senior officers was citizen-colonel-newspaperman Robert R. McCormick, who published his memoirs, *The Army of 1918* (New York: Harcourt, Brace and Howe, 1928). French opinion is summarized in Lee Kennett, "The A.E.F. through French Eyes," *Military Review* 52 (Nov 1972): 3-11.

21. In addition to the organizational and personal accounts cited above, the following sources provide detailed evaluations of the 1st Division's training from a variety of perspectives: Brig Gen A. W. Brewster, IG, to AG AEF, report on inspection of the 1st Division, 19 Sep 1917, Corresp File 745, Office of the Inspector General, AEF, RG 120; IG, AEF to Commander in Chief, AEF, "Tactical Inspection of the First Division, November 26-28, 1917," Ibid.; Col G. Van H. Moseley, G-5, AEF, to Commander in Chief AEF, "Report of Inspection, February 15-17, 1918," 19 Feb 1918, Moseley Letterbooks, 1917-19, George Van Horn Moseley Papers, MC/LC; Memo, Col F. Conner, G-3, AEF, sub: prospective availability of divisions and other troops, 17 Feb 1918, *USA/WW*, 2:208-10; entries, "Military Notebooks," 26 Jan-14 Mar 1918, Bullard Papers; CG 1st Division to Commander in Chief AEF, "Miscarriage of Two Raids Organized for the 1st Division . . . ," 7 Mar 1918, *WWR/1st Div*, 20; Shipley Thomas (a regimental staff officer in the 1st Division), *The History of the A.E.F.* (New York: Doran, 1920), pp. 55-56; Theodore Roosevelt, Jr. (battalion commander, 26th Infantry), *Average Americans* (New York: G. P. Putnam's Sons, 1919); Maj Gen Joseph D. Patch, USA (Ret.), *A Soldier's War: The First Infantry Division, A.E.F.* (Corpus Christi, Tex.: Joseph Dorst Patch, 1966); and 1st Lt H. H. Caswell, "History of the 3rd Machine Gun Battalion of the 1st Division, A.E.F.," unpublished mss., 1919 with addenda, 1971, provided the author by H. H. Caswell, Ann Arbor, Mich.

Contemporary French assessments of the division are found in File 17 N 109-2, archives of the French Military Mission to the American Expeditionary Forces, Service Historique de l'Armée de Terre, Vincennes, France: "Rapport du Captaine Seligmann, Officier de Liaison près la 1 Division Americaine," 13 Jan 1918; Lt Col Sezille des Essarts, "Rapport sur l'Occupation d'un Secteur Par la 1 D.I.U.S.," 9 Mar 1918; "Rapport du Lieutenant Colonel Sezille des Essarts, Officier de Liaison pres la 1 D.I.U.S.," 13 Mar 1918.

22. Cable, Commander in Chief, A.E.F. to Chief of Staff, USA, 29 Mar 1918, "AEF Confidential Cables Sent," Harbord Papers; Pershing, *My Experiences in the World War*, 2:353-66; GHQ AEF, Second Section, supplement to "Summary of Intelligence No. 78," 28 Mar 1918, GHQ AEF, *Summary of Intelligence, 1918*, copy in Ohio State University Library.

23. On the movement into the Cantigny sector, see Thomas, *The History of the A.E.F.*, pp. 70-71; Capt Ben H. Chastaine, *History of the 18th U.S. Infantry* (New York: Hymans Publishing, 1920), pp. 45-58; "Regimental Chaplain," *The Story of the Sixteenth Infantry in France* (Frankfurt: Martin Flock, 1919), pp. 22-29; "Regimental Adjutant," *The Twenty-Sixth Infantry in France* (Frankfurt: n.p., 1919), pp. 17-22; *Brief History of the Fifth Field Artillery, 1st Division, American Expeditionary Forces, 1917-1918* (Nancy and Strasbourg: Berger-Levrault, 1918), pp. 11-15; *History of the Sixth Field*

Artillery, 1798-1932 (Harrisburg, Pa.: HQ, 6th Field Artillery, 1933), pp. 188-95; *History of the Seventh Field Artillery (Field Division, A.E.F.) World War, 1917-1919* (New York: Little and Ives, 1929), pp. 36-64; Maj Thomas F. Farrell et al., *A History of the 1st U.S. Engineers, 1st U.S. Division* (Coblenz: n.p., 1919), pp. 19-22; Patch, *A Soldier's War*, pp. 83-109; war letters of 1st Lt Elden Sprague Betts (26 Apr-6 Jun 1918) in "An Argonne Cross," unpublished ms., Parker Papers; Jeremiah M. Evarts (Capt, 18th Infantry), *Cantigny* (New York: Scribner's, 1938); and Roosevelt, *Average Americans,* pp. 120-61.

24. On Bullard's health, see Bullard ms autobiography, pp. 135-36, Bullard Papers; Pershing-Harbord letters, 10-29 Apr 1918, "Pershing-Harbord Correspondence," Harbord Papers; diary entries, 16, 17 Apr 1918, Pershing Diaries, Pershing Papers; and Ltr, Maj R. H. Lewis to Col F. Conner, 22 Apr 1918, *WWR/1st Div,* vol. 20.

On the relief investigation, see Ltr, Col M. Craig, C/S, I Corps, to C/S, GHQ AEF, 17 Apr 1918; Ltr, Brig Gen J. G. Harbord to Maj Gen R. L. Bullard, 19 Apr 1918; Ltr, Lt Col B. Winship, Assistant Inspector General, I Corps, to C/S, I Corps, "Investigation of Evacuation of Ansauville Sector by 1st Division," Jul 1918; JAG, AEF to C/S, AEF, "Conditions Attending Departure of the First Division from Sector Early in April," 21 Apr 1918, all copies in Summerall Papers.

On the Seicheprey affair, see Pershing, *My Experiences in the World War,* 2:9, 16; entries, 23, 24 Apr 1917, Stackpole Diary, Stackpole Papers; and Col J. H. Parker to Col J. McA. Palmer, 22 Apr 1922, "Chapter Notes, Vol. XVII," John McAuley Palmer Papers, MD/LC.

On Pershing's speech and state of mind, see diary entry, 16 Apr 1918, Pershing diaries, Pershing Papers; entry, 16 Apr 1918, in Charles G. Dawes, *A Journal of the Great War,* 2 vols. (Boston: Houghton Mifflin, 1921), 1:92-93; and Duncan, "Reminiscences of the World War," p. 82.

On training, see C. King, "Tour in France," p. 3; Maj P. H. Clark, liaison officer with GQG French Army, to Gen J. J. Pershing, 10 Apr 1918, John J. Pershing Collection, RG 200, NA; "Digest: Reports on Training, 1st Division," May 1918, *WWR/1st Div,* vol. 19; and Frederick Palmer, "Notes of Observation with the First Division," Apr 1918, Pershing Papers.

25. For maps and terrain photographs, see the American Battle Monuments Commission, *Terrain Photographs: American World War Battlefields in Europe, 1st Division, Cantigny and Montdidier-Noyon Defensive* (19 Apr-13 Jul 1919), set in the Army Military History Institute, and the more accessible American Battle Monuments Commission, *American Armies and Battlefields in Europe* (Washington, D.C.: Government Printing Office, 1938), pp. 414-16, and the maps published by the commission for each combat division. The author visited the battlefield in Sep 1975.

26. The division's service in Picardy is described in the unit and personal accounts cited above, but see the documents in the "Cantigny" section of *USA/WW,* 4:259-348; Marshall, *Memoirs,* pp. 75-118; Duncan, "Reminiscences of the World War," pp. 83-85; and entry, 25 Apr 1918, "War Notes," 1, Moseley Papers.

27. The German side of the Battle of Cantigny is well documented except for the *271st RIR.* The surviving messages, war diaries, orders, and after-action reports of the *26th Reserve Division* appear in several postwar collections: volume 1 in the four volumes of German documents that are part of *WWR/1st Div* and volume 4 of *USA/WW* as well as the historical files of the 1st Division in RG 120. The most complete collection is Maj P. B. Harm, ed. and trans., *Cantigny Operation,* compiled for the Historical Section, Army War College, 1928, which I used in the U.S. Army Military History Institute Library. See also War Department General Staff, *Histories of Two Hundred and*

Fifty-One Divisions of the German Army Which Participated in the War (1914-1918) (Washington, D.C.: Government Printing Office, 1920).

28. 1st Division Field Orders 15 (10 May 1918) and 18 (20 May 1918), *WWR/1st Div*, vol. 4; Gen C. A. Vandenberg to Maj Gen R. L. Bullard, 12 May 1918, *WWR/1st Div*, vol. 25; French X Corps Order 201-32.7, 15 May 1918, *USA/WW*, 4:272-75.

29. Entry, 27 May 1918, Pershing diaries, and Ltr, Gen J. J. Pershing to Maj Gen R. L. Bullard, 28 May 1918, Pershing Papers; Memo 1355, G-3, 1st Division, "Cantigny Operation," *WWR/1st Div*, vol. 13; Cable 1223-S, Commander in Chief, AEF to AG USA, 1 Jun 1918, *USA/WW*, 2:434.

30. The full attack order for the 28th Infantry is Regimental Field Order 3, 26 May 1918, in vol. 10, *WWR/1st Div*, which incorporated Division FO 18 and its subsequent appendices, already cited.

31. HQ 1st FA Brig., 1st Division, "Report on Operation Against Cantigny," *WWR/1st Div*, vol. 14; HQ 1st FA Brig., "Firing Order for Cantigny Operation," 27 May 1918, *WWR/1st Div*, vol. 11; French X Corps Artillery memoranda, 18-26 May 1918, *USA/WW*, 4:276-91, 294; Marshall, *Memoirs*, pp. 90-92; statement of Maj Gen C. P. Summerall, Comd Gen, 4th Corps, American Expeditionary Forces, typescript, 28 Apr 1919, Summerall Papers.

32. The fullest account of the planning is Capt Paul B. Parker, "The Battle of Cantigny," in Class of 1923, Infantry School, *Monographs of the World War* (Fort Benning, Ga.: The Infantry School, n.d.), pp. 336-47. See also Buck, *Memories of War and Peace*, pp. 171-82, and Lt Col Hanson E. Ely, "The Attack on Cantigny," *National Service* 7 (Apr 1920): 201-08. Company organization is described in HQ 1st Division, Instructions 29, 13 May 1918, G-3 AEF Correspondence File, RG 120, and G-3 AEF memo, "Divisional Organization," 18 May 1918, *USA/WW*, 2:406-12.

33. Intelligence Section, HQ 1st Division, Intelligence Summary for 26-27 May 1918, *WWR/1st Div*, vol. 4; Capt Edward S. Johnson, "The Day before Cantigny," 1929, Infantry School monograph, Infantry School library (ISL); Fort Benning, Ga. (Johnson was the commander of one of the companies the raiders struck; he interviewed sixteen other witnesses of the action in the 28th Infantry sector.) The missing lieutenant's grave was later found behind German lines.

34. Entry, 27 May 1918, Pershing diaries, Pershing Papers; Marshall, *Memoirs*, pp. 94-95; Bullard manuscript autobiography, pp. 130-38, Bullard Papers.

35. Field messages and operations reports, 28th Infantry, 28 May 1918, 28th Infantry Historical File, 1st Division Organizational Records, RG 120, and as partially reprinted in *USA/WW*, 4:298-302. The most detailed chronology of the operation is HQ 1st Artillery Brigade, "Journal of Cantigny Operations, May 28-30, 1918," *WWR/1st Div*, vol. 11. This report includes the messages from Col Holbrook at the 28th Infantry PC to Summerall. Other artillery documents are in *WWR/1st Div*, vol. 11. The phone messages between CO 28th Infantry and CG 2d Inf. Brig. may also be found in vol. 15 of *WWR/1st Div*.

36. Parker, "The Battle of Cantigny"; HQ 1st Division, intelligence summary, 28 May 1918, *USA/WW*, 4:303. The German side of the battle is reported in HQ 26th Reserve Corps to Commanding General, *18th Army*, Operations Section Report No. 2137, 3 Jun 1918, which includes after-action reports from the *82d Reserve Division* and *25th Reserve Division* commanders from regimental to company level, in Harm, *Cantigny Operation*.

37. Parker, "Battle of Cantigny." Among the best descriptions of the conduct of the attack and the establishment of the regimental defense position come from the machine-gun officers with the 28th Infantry: reports, CO, Company C, 2d Machine Gun Bn., to CO, 28th Infantry, 2 Jun 1918, and CO, Company D, 2d Machine Gun

Bn., to CO, 28th Infantry, 2 Jun 1918, *WWR/1st Div,* vol. 15, and Capt Welcome P. Waltz, "Operations of Company C, 3rd Machine Gun Battalion at Cantigny," 1929, Infantry School monograph, ISL. In addition to 28th Infantry documents, the 3d Battalion's experience is analyzed in Maj Stuart G. Wilder, "Operations of Company M, 16th Infantry in the Cantigny Operations, May 28–June 6, 1918," 1930, Infantry School monograph, ISL. Wilder's company was the first into the 3d Battalion's zone when the 28th Infantry was relieved; he made a careful study of the terrain and positions of the troops, living and dead.

38. Telephone msgs, between 28th Inf., 2d Brig., and HQ 1st Div, 28 May 1918, *WWR/1st Div,* vol. 15; Gen J. J. Pershing to Maj Gen R. L. Bullard, 28 May 1918, Pershing Papers; reports of commanding officers, *271st RIR* and *272d RIR,* 1, 2 Jun 1918, in Harm, *Cantigny Operation.* Also useful are 1st Lt Claude L. Bowen, Jr., "Battle of Cantigny," 1939, and Capt C. F. Butler, "Battle of Cantigny," 1925, Infantry School monographs, ISL, both of which contain interviews with officers who participated in the action.

39. Telephone messages between 28th Inf., 2d Brig., and 1st Div, *WWR/1st Div,* vol. 15; HQ, 28th Infantry, "Reports on Cantigny and Consolidation of Position," 2 Jun 1918, 28th Infantry Historical File, 1st Division Organizational Records, RG 120, which includes battalion messages to Ely and the reports of his three battalion commanders, written on 2 or 3 Jun 1918.

The role of the 18th Infantry is described in Chastaine, *History of the 18th U.S. Infantry,* pp. 45–58, and Brig Gen B. Buck to Col F. Parker, 1 Jun 1918, Parker Papers.

40. HQ 18th Army, "Estimate of the Situation," 1 Jun 1918, in Harm, *Cantigny Operation.*

41. Telephone messages and reports between 28th Inf., 2d Brig., and 1st Div, 29 May 1918, *WWR/1st Div,* vol. 15; operations reports, CG 1st Div to G-3, GHQ AEF, 29, 30 May 1918, *WWR/1st Div,* vol. 12; Lt Col W. S. Grant to Col F. Conner, 30 May 1918, *WWR/1st Div,* vol. 12.

42. 1st Div, operations report, 30 May 1918, "Reports on Cantigny and Consolidation of Position," 2 Jun 1918, 1st Div Records, AEF, RG120.

43. Casualty figures predictably vary and are incomplete. I have used those in CG 1st Div to CG, French X Corps, 2 Jun 1918, but Ely gives 45 officers and 817 men in CO 28th Inf. C/S, AEF, 7 Jun 1918, 28th Infantry Historical File, 1st Division Organizational Records, RG 120; but his report probably does not cover some of his attachments, the 18th Infantry, and 1st Battalion, 26th Infantry. The French attachments had one casualty before withdrawing from Cantigny. German losses are in the war diaries, *82d Reserve Division* and *25th Reserve Division,* 31 May, 1 Jun 1918, in Harm, *Cantigny Operation* and *WWR/1st Div: German Documents,* vol. 1.

44. Memo No. 8, HQ 1st Division, 2 Jun 1918, copy in Parker Papers; Maj Gen A. W. Brewster to Gen J. J. Pershing, 15 Jul 1918, Bullard 201 File, Defense Personnel Records Center, St. Louis, Mo.; Cable, Pershing to AGWAR, 1 Jun 1918, "AEF Confidential Cables Sent," Harbord Papers; entries, 11, 30 Jun 1918, Pershing diaries, Pershing Papers; Maj P. H. Clark to Gen J. J. Pershing, 28 May, 3 Jul 1918, Pershing Collection, NA; Maj R. H. Lewis to Col F. Conner, 29 May 1918, *WWR/1st Div,* vol. 12; T. Bentley Mott, *Twenty Years as Military Attache* (New York: Oxford University Press, 1937), p. 307.

45. G-5, GHQ and 1st Army, AEF, "Notes on Recent Operations—No. 1," Aug 1918; "Combat Instructions," 5 Sep 1918; "Notes on Recent Operations—No. 3," 12 Oct 1918; "Notes on Recent Operations—No. 4," 22 Nov 1918; "Combat Instructions," 12 Oct 1918; and "Memorandum for Corps and Division Command-

ers, Subject: Reduction of Hostile Machine Gun Nests," 16 Oct 1918; all of the above in G-5, "Historical File," GHQ AEF and 1st Army, RG 120. For a German assessment, see HQ, Reserve Corps, Meuse Group East, "Lessons to be Drawn from Fighting on the West Bank of the Meuse," 3 Sep 1918, copy in Hines Papers.

46. CG, Army Artillery, and Chief of Artillery, AEF, "Artillery Operations, First Army, A.E.F.," *Field Artillery Journal* 12 (May-Jun 1922): 192-223; Maj Gen W. S. McNair, "Explanation and Execution of Plans for Artillery for St. Mihiel Operation and Argonne-Meuse Operations to November 11, 1918," 23 Dec 1918, 1st Army lectures, copy in Edwards Papers.

47. GHQ AEF, "Report of Superior Board on Organization and Tactics," 19 Apr 1919, G-3, "Historical Files," GHQ AEF, RG 120; Chief of Artillery to AG AEF, "Final Report," 1919, *USA/WW*, 15:177-208; "Study of the Armament and Types of Artillery Material to be Assigned to a Field Army," *Field Artillery Journal* 9 (Jul-Aug 1919): 289-347; Director, Army Center of Artillery Studies, AEF, to Chief of Field Artillery, USA, 12 Jul 1919, *USA/WW*, 15:342-46; G-5, GHQ AEF, final reports, Infantry Specialists School and Army Machine Gun School, *USA/WW*, 15:346-55; "Report of the G-5, GHQ, American Expeditionary Forces," Cmdr in Chief, AEF, "Historical Files," RG 120.

48. Bernard L. Boylan, "Army Reorganization 1920: The Legislative Story," *Mid-America* 49 (Apr 1967): 115-28; U.S. Congress, 66th Cong., 1st Sess., House of Representatives, Committee on Military Affairs, Hearings: "Army Reorganization" (3 Sep-13 Nov 1919), 2 vols. (Washington, D.C.: Government Printing Office, 1919); U.S. Congress, 66th Cong., 1st and 2d Sess., Senate, Committee on Military Affairs, Hearings: "Reorganization of the Army" (7 Aug-17 Dec 1919), 2 vols. (Washington, D.C.: Government Printing Office, 1920).

49. War Department Information Section, "General Pershing's Letter on Organization of the Army of the United States," 15 Jul 1921, copy, "Chapter Notes XVI," Palmer Papers; "Excerpts from Annual Reports of the Chief of Staff," *A Report of the Secretary of War to the President 1922* (Washington, D.C.: Government Printing Office, 1922), pp. 111-21; *Annual Report of the Secretary of War, 1923* (Washington, D.C.: Government Printing Office, 1923), pp. 1-30.

50. Maj E. F. Harding, ed. and comp., The Infantry School, *Infantry in Battle* (Washington, D.C.: The Infantry Journal, 1934), p. 77. See Chief of Staff, U.S. Army, *Field Service Regulations 1923* (Washington, D.C.: Government Printing Office, 1924).

51. Lt Col Oliver L. Spaulding, "The Tactics of the War with Germany," *Infantry Journal* 17 (Sep 1920): 228-40.

CHAPTER 7. BUNA, 19 NOVEMBER 1942-2 JANUARY 1943: A "LEAVENWORTH NIGHTMARE"

1. *New York Times*, 16 Nov 1942, 17 Nov 1942.

2. U.S. War Department, *FM 100-5: Field Service Regulations: Operations* (Washington, D.C.: Government Printing Office, 1941), p. ii.

3. U.S. War Department, *Field Service Regulations*, 1923, p. 11.

4. U.S. War Department, *Field Service Regulations*, 1941, p. 5.

5. Ibid., pp. 6-7; *Field Service Regulations*, 1923, p. 13. Mounted cavalry was abolished in the U.S. Army early in 1942. Maj Gen John K. Herr and Edward S. Wallace, *The Story of the U.S. Cavalry, 1775-1942* (Boston: Little, Brown and Company, 1953), p. 252.

6. Office of the Chief of Staff, *FM 100–5, Tentative Field Service Regulations,* 1939, pp. 203–31.

7. U.S. War Department, *Field Service Regulations,* 1941, pp. 182–240.

8. U.S. War Department, *FM 31–20. Basic Field Manual: Jungle Warfare* (Washington, D.C.: Government Printing Office, 1941), p. 40.

9. U.S. War Department, Office of the Chief of Staff, *A Manual for Commanders of Large Units (Provisional), vol. 1, Operations* (Washington, D.C.: Government Printing Office, 1930), pp. 39–51 (hereafter *A Manual for Commanders*).

10. Dudley McCarthy, *South-West Pacific Area—First Year. Kokoda to Wau* (Canberra: Australian War Memorial, 1959), p. 462 (hereafter McCarthy, *Kokoda to Wau*).

11. Samuel Milner, *Victory in Papua* (United States Army in World War II, The War in the Pacific) (Washington, D.C.: Office of the Chief of Military History, 1957), p. 193.

12. U.S. War Department, *Infantry Field Manual: Organization and Tactics of Infantry, The Rifle Battalion* (Washington, D.C.: Government Printing Office, 1940), pp. 18, 34.

13. U.S. War Department, *FM 7–5. Infantry Field Manual. Organization and Tactics of Infantry: The Rifle Battalion* (Washington, D.C.: Government Printing Office, 1942), pp. 11, 313–15 (hereafter *FM 7–5: The Rifle Battalion*).

14. U.S. War Department, *FM 7–15. Infantry Field Manual. Heavy Weapons Company, Rifle Regiment* (Washington, D.C.: Government Printing Office, 1942), pp. 2–3, 44, 100–01, 148–49. There is a curious discrepancy between this manual and *FM 7–5: The Rifle Battalion* with respect to the ranges of the weapons of the heavy weapons company. The latter gives the effective range of the heavy machine gun as 3,500 yards (p. 13) and a maximum of 2,000 yards for the 81-mm mortar (p. 14).

15. *FM 7–5: The Rifle Battalion,* p. 19.

16. Ibid., p. 20.

17. Ibid., p. 46.

18. Ibid., p. 48.

19. Ibid., p. 50.

20. Ibid., p. 7.

21. Larry I. Bland, ed., *The Papers of George Catlett Marshall. vol. 1. "The Soldierly Spirit." December 1880–June 1939* (Baltimore: Johns Hopkins University Press, 1971), p. 533.

22. U.S. Infantry School (Fort Benning, Ga.), *Infantry in Battle,* 2d ed. (Washington, D.C.: The Infantry Journal, Incorporated, 1939), p. vii.

23. Harold Whittle Blakeley, *The 32d Infantry Division World War II* (Madison, Wis.: The Thirty-Second Infantry Division History Commission, n.d.), p. 9.

24. Elbridge Colby, *The National Guard of the United States: A Half Century of Progress* (Manhattan: Kansas State University in conjunction with *Military Affairs,* 1977), ch. 10, p. 9.

25. "An Official Army Commentary" as quoted in Blakeley, *32d Division,* p. 9.

26. William F. McCartney, *The Jungleers: A History of the 41st Infantry Division* (Washington, D.C.: Infantry Journal Press, 1948), p. 5.

27. Blakeley, *32d Division,* p. 24.

28. Bell I. Wiley, "The Preparation of Units for Overseas Movement," in R. R. Palmer, Bell I. Wiley, and William R. Keazst, *The Procurement and Training of Ground Combat Troops,* United States Army in World War II: The Army Ground Forces (Washington, D.C.: Office of the Chief of Military History, 1948), pp. 572–73.

29. After the maneuvers the previous spring, Lt Gen Lesley McNair, Chief of Staff of GHQ, had rated the 41st as "the top ranking National Guard division and one of the three top divisions of the whole army." McCartney, *The Jungleers,* p. 6.

30. Transcript of Interv of Maj Gen Edwin F. Harding, Office of the Chief of Military History (OCMH) Collection, Military History Institute (MHI), Carlisle Barracks, Pa.

31. Robert L. Eichelberger, *Our Jungle Road to Tokyo* (New York: Viking Press, 1950), p. 11.

32. Transcript of Interv of Lt Gen Robert L. Eichelberger by Samuel Milner, 21 Nov 1948, World War II Papers, OCMH Collection, MHI.

33. Transcript of Interv with Maj Gen Edwin F. Harding, 10 Dec 1947, OCMH Collection, MHI.

34. Eichelberger, *Jungle Road*, p. 12. See also Milner, *Victory in Papua*, pp. 132-33.

35. Transcript of Interv of Maj Gen Edwin F. Harding, 10 Dec 1947, OCMH Collection, MHI. Maj Gen Horace H. Fuller commanded the 41st Infantry Division. Eichelberger, Harding, and Fuller all graduated from the U.S. Military Academy in 1909.

36. Transcript of Interv of Lt Gen Eichelberger, 20 Nov 1947, OCMH Collection, MHI.

37. McCarthy, *Kokoda to Wau*, pp. 159-87 passim.

38. GHQ, SWPA, Communique No. 151, 10 Sep 1942, as quoted in Supreme Commander for the Allied Powers, *Reports of General MacArthur: The Campaigns of MacArthur in the Pacific* (Washington, D.C.: Department of the Army, 1966), 1:70 (hereafter *Reports of General MacArthur*).

39. McCarthy, *Kokoda to Wau*, p. 235.

40. Ibid., pp. 234-40; John Hetherington, *Blamey: The Biography of Field-Marshal Sir Thomas Blamey* (Melbourne: F. W. Cheshire, 1954), pp. 158-70.

41. *Reports of General MacArthur*, 1:75.

42. Blakeley, *32d Division*, p. 33.

43. Ibid., pp. 36, 40; Milner, *Victory in Papua*, pp. 92-94; George C. Kenney, *General Kenney Reports: A Personal History of the Pacific War* (New York: Duell, Sloan and Pearce, 1949), pp. 99-106.

44. Quoted in McCarthy, *Kokoda to Wau*, p. 312.

45. The fighting along the Kokoda Trail is described in detail in Ibid., pp. 254-335. It is a story largely unknown to Americans.

46. *Field Service Regulations*, 1941, sec. 9, "Jungle Operations," p. 235.

47. Quoted in McCarthy, *Kokoda to Wau*, p. 312.

48. Interv of Harding by Milner, 10 Dec 1942, OCMH Collection, MHI.

49. Lido Mayo, *Bloody Buna* (Garden City, N.Y.: Doubleday and Company, 1947), p. 75.

50. 126th Infantry Report of Action, New Guinea Campaign, 12 Sep 1942-31 Jan 1943; 128th Infantry Regiment History, 15 Oct 1940-28 Feb 1943; 32d Division After Action Reports, Papuan Campaign. All official records of the 32d Division cited are in the Federal Record Center, Suitland, Md.

51. Milner, *Victory in Papua*, p. 169.

52. In 1942, no ocean-going vessels could proceed along the north coast of New Guinea beyond Milne Bay. Richard M. Leighton and Robert W. Coakley, *Global Logistics and Strategy*, The United States Army in World War II: The War Department (Washington, D.C.: Office of the Chief of Military History, 1955), vol. 1, 1940-43, p. 409.

53. Col Maxwell Emerson, "A Quartermaster Comments on the Buna Campaign," *The Quartermaster Review* (May-Jun 1951), 32:96-100. Emerson contends that it was a mistake not to include the entire 107th Quartermaster Battalion when the two regimental combat teams were ordered to New Guinea. The forty quartermaster

troops at Port Moresby were overworked and undermanned loading and unloading ships at night and operating the ration and ammunition dumps in the daylight. This situation was not rectified until the end of December. "Supply is easily fifty percent of jungle warfare," Emerson concludes. Leighton and Coakley note that even at the end of 1942, "the ratio of service support . . . was shockingly low." *Global Logistics,* 1:413. The illustrative problems mentioned in the above paragraph are mentioned in the 32d Division, G-2, G-3 Journal, 18–22 Oct, serial nos. 76, 133, 143, 244, 282.

54. McCarthy, *Kokoda to Wau,* p. 352; Milner, *Victory in Papua,* pp. 118–19.

55. Interv, Gen Eichelberger, 20 Nov 1947, OCMH Collection, MHI. At Buna, the 32d Division came under control of New Guinea Force, Gen Herring, an Australian, commanding; Herring opened an advanced headquarters at Popondetta on 28 Nov. Herring in turn was responsible to Gen Blamey, another Australian, who commanded Allied Land Forces, SWPA, and had been sent to New Guinea on 23 Sep to take personal command; Blamey's headquarters remained at Port Moresby. He, of course, reported to MacArthur, Supreme Commander, Southwest Pacific Area. Although GHQ remained at Brisbane throughout the campaign, MacArthur made a brief visit to New Guinea on 2–4 Oct, and on 6 Nov MacArthur and several members of the GHQ staff established an advanced headquarters at Port Moresby, where he remained until the fall of Buna, when he returned to the mainland on 9 Jan 1943. Throughout this phase of the campaign, the general impression in the United States, carefully cultivated by pictures and communiques coming out of GHQ (see the headlines quoted at the beginning of this chapter), was that MacArthur himself directed operations at Buna. As a matter of fact, he was never there. See Jay Luvaas, ed., *Dear Miss Em: General Eichelberger's War in the Pacific 1942–1943* (Westport, Conn.: Greenwood Press, 1973), pp. 54, 64–66.

56. Milner, *Victory in Papua,* pp. 137–39.

57. McCarthy, *Kokoda to Wau,* pp. 144, 531; Milner, *Victory in Papua,* p. 144.

58. Milner, *Victory in Papua,* p. 146.

59. Ibid., p. 100; Allied Forces, Southwest Pacific Area, "History of the Buna Campaign: December 1, 1942–January 25, 1943," pp. 42–44; Headquarters United States Army, Japan, "18th Army Operations," in Donald S. Detwiler and Charles B. Burdick, eds., *War in Asia and the Pacific 1937–1949,* 15 vols. (New York: Garland Publishing, 1980), vol. 7, monograph No. 37, pp. 6–33 (hereafter cited as "18th Army Operations"). There is a marginal note in Eichelberger's personal copy of *Victory in Papua* to the effect that MacArthur assured him, probably in mid-November, that there were about 1,500 enemy in the Buna beachhead. Copy in author's possession.

60. George H. Johnston, *The Toughest Fighting in the World* (New York: Sloan and Pearce, 1943), pp. 192, 208–09.

61. "And Sutherland in a talk with me near the Triangle called them 'hasty field intrenchments!!!' " Marginal note in Eichelberger's personal copy of *Victory in Papua,* p. 141. Copy in author's possession.

62. A detailed description of the Japanese defenses is found in Milner, *Victory in Papua,* pp. 140–43. See also War Department, Military Intelligence Division, *Papuan Campaign: The Buna-Sanananda Operation 16 November 1942–23 January 1943,* American Forces in Action Series (Washington, D.C.: War Department, 1944), pp. 14–16 (hereafter *Papuan Campaign*).

63. There were several attempts, some of them partially successful, to reinforce the garrison at Gona, but Allied airpower made it hazardous to disembark troops on the open beach. "18th Army Operations," pp. 32, 37–39.

64. A detailed account of the fighting for Gona is given in McCarthy, *Kokoda to Wau,* pp. 418–48.

65. "18th Army Operations," p. 31.

66. McCarthy, *Kokoda to Wau*, p. 394.

67. Eichelberger, *Jungle Road*, p. 27.

68. *Papuan Campaign*, pp. 9-11.

69. Blakeley, *32d Division*, p. 55.

70. Milner, *Victory in Papua*, pp. 128-30.

71. Ibid., pp. 168-70.

72. Ibid., p. 128.

73. Ibid.

74. Ibid., p. 140-41.

75. Ibid., p. 176.

76. Msg, Gen Harding to GOC, NGF, no. 936; Msg, Gen MacNider to CG, 32d Division, no. 146; Msg, Maj H. A. Smith to CG, 32d Division, no. 947; Msg, Gen Harding to NGF, no. 957, in 32d Division, G-2, G-3 Journal, 19 Nov 1942.

77. These were from the 1st Australian Mountain Battery, commanded by Maj O'Hare. The guns were 3.7-inch howitzers, "very accurate and fast weapons capable of getting off 12 rounds per gun per minute." The guns had been landed at Pongani airfield on 12 Nov and moved to its battery position by barge on the sixteenth. McCarthy, *Kokoda to Wau*, pp. 356-57. A sketch map of artillery dispositions in the Buna Area is found in Allied Forces, Southwest Pacific Area, "History of the Buna Campaign," p. 76A.

78. D. Clayton James, *The Years of MacArthur*, II, 1941-1945 (Boston: Houghton Mifflin, 1975), p. 241; *New York Times*, 20 Nov 1942.

79. In the initial strike, several bombs fell on Miller's position, causing six casualties; in the second attempt, eighteen additional Americans became casualties. One of the difficulties apparently was in letting ground troops know when the bombing was over, which was to have been done by having Very flares fired from the three planes of the last flight and by voice, for which ground sets were to have been tuned to a prearranged frequency. Msg, G-3 to Gen Whitehead, no. 1052, 32d Division, G-2, G-3 Journal, 21 Nov 1942. This remained something of a problem throughout the battle. Gen Eichelberger cited an incident when Gen Blamey was visiting the front, when American troops were strafed by American bombers and fired back "with everything they had." "Those planes think they are firing on the Japs at Sanananda three miles away. Our men got fed up and fired back," Eichelberger explained, Eichelberger, *Jungle Road*, p. 40.

80. Msg, G-3 to Gen MacNider, no. 1032, 32d Division G-2, G-3 Journal, 21 Nov 1942.

81. Msg, White Smith to Harding, Series 1107, 32d Division G-2, G-3 Journal, 21 Nov 1942.

82. Msg, Gen Harding to NGF, no. 1099, 32d Division G-2, G-3 Journal, 21 Nov 1942.

83. Blakeley, *32d Division*, p. 68.

84. Msg, G-3 to Smith, 126th, no. 1254, 32d Division G-2, G-3 Journal, 23 Nov 1942; transcript of Interv of Harding by Milner, 10 Dec 1947, OCMH Collection, MHI; Milner, *Victory in Papua*, pp. 179-80; McCarthy, *Kokoda to Wau*, pp. 361-63.

85. Milner, *Victory in Papua*, p. 184.

86. Msg, Gen Harding to White Smith, no. 1330, 32d Division G-2, G-3 Journal, 24 Nov 1942.

87. Msg, White Smith to G-3, no. 1339, 32d Division G-2, G-3 Journal, 24 Nov 1942.

88. Milner, *Victory in Papua*, pp. 184-88.

89. Quoted in ibid., pp. 191–92.

90. See McCarthy, *Kokoda to Wau,* p. 274.

91. Killed in action, 82; wounded in action, 325; missing in action, 85. Milner, *Victory in Papua,* p. 195n.

92. James, *The Years of MacArthur,* 2:243. For a sympathetic and well-balanced account of Harding's difficulties, see Leslie Anders, *Gentle Knight: The Life and Times of Major General Edwin Forrest Harding* (Kent, Ohio: The Kent State University Press, 1985), pp. 246–60.

93. Luvaas, *Dear Miss Em,* p. 32. Italics mine.

94. Ltr, Gen Sir E. F. Herring to Eichelberger, 27 Jan 1943, Robert L. Eichelberger Papers, William R. Perkins Library, Duke University, Durham, N.C.

95. The operations of the 3d Battalion of the 126th Infantry, which fought continuously for twenty-two days to hold the roadblock, are not treated here because the battalion was under Australian control. Obviously, the experiences of these men were similar to what American troops were enduring on other fronts. By 9 Jan 1943, this battalion, or rather what was left of it since bullets and illness had reduced the strength from 1,300 when it crossed the Girua to 158, was relieved by the 163d Infantry regiment of the 41st Division. These men were much better prepared than any of the regiments in the 32d Division. "For four months we were able to supervise their work and insisted upon a lot of scouting and patrolling, individual and squad combat, firing with ball ammunition, etc." Ltr, Eichelberger to MacArthur, 12 Jan 1943, copy in author's possession. See also McCartney, *The Jungleers,* pp. 27–29.

96. Eichelberger to Gen R. K. Sutherland, 20 Dec 1942, copy in author's possession.

97. Ltr, Eichelberger to Sutherland, 13 Dec 1942, copy in author's possession.

98. Ltr, Eichelberger to Sutherland, 16 Dec 1942, copy in author's possession.

99. Ltr, Eichelberger to Sutherland, 9 Jan 1943, copy in author's possession.

100. Ltr, Eichelberger to Sutherland, 3 Jan 1943, copy in author's possession.

101. *A Manual for Commanders,* 1:2.

102. MacNider had been wounded on 23 Nov, Waldron was wounded supervising an attack by Urbana Force on 5 Dec, and his successor, Brig Gen Clovis Byers, was shot eleven days later during an attack on the coconut grove, after which Eichelberger assumed personal command of all U.S. forces at the front.

103. Ltr, Eichelberger to Sutherland, 22 Dec 1942, copy in author's possession.

104. Blakeley, *32d Division,* pp. 89–91.

105. See Gen Clovis E. Byers, "Combat Leadership," *Marine Corps Gazette* 46 (Nov 1962): 27–29.

106. Eichelberger, *Jungle Road,* pp. 27–28.

107. Milner, *Victory in Papua,* p. 240.

108. Ibid., p. 241.

109. Quoted in ibid., p. 243.

110. Transcript of Interv of Maj Gen A. W. Waldron by Lt Hechler, 11 Mar 1944, OCMH Collection, MHI.

111. Luvaas, *Dear Miss Em,* p. 40.

112. Milner, *Victory in Papua,* p. 245.

113. G-3 Daily Periodic Reports, Buna Campaign, 4 Dec 1942–23 Jan 1943.

114. Allied Forces, SWPA, "History of the Buna Campaign," p. 54.

115. Ltr, Eichelberger to Sutherland, 24 Dec 1942, copy in author's possession.

116. Ltr, MacArthur to Eichelberger, 25 Dec 1942, copy in author's possession.

117. "You have probably eight or nine times the strength of the enemy. Use it in unison." Ltr, MacArthur to Eichelberger, 25 Dec 1942, copy in author's possession.

118. Ltr, Eichelberger to Sutherland, 7 Jan 1943, copy in author's possession.
119. Ltr, Eichelberger to Sutherland, 31 Dec 1942, copy in author's possession.
120. Luvaas, *Dear Miss Em,* pp. 37-38.
121. Ltr, Eichelberger to MacArthur, 25 Dec 1942, copy in author's possession.
122. Interv of Waldron by K. Hechler, 11 Mar 1944, OCMH Collection, MHI; *Papuan Campaign,* p. 42.
123. Johnston, *The Toughest Fighting in the World,* p. 218.
124. Quoted in ibid.
125. Ltr, Eichelberger to Sutherland, 14 Dec 1942, copy in author's possession.
126. Ltr, Eichelberger to Sutherland, 16 Dec 1942, copy in author's possession.
127. Milner, *Victory in Papua,* pp. 284-88.
128. Ltr, Eichelberger to Sutherland, 20 Dec 1942, copy in author's possession.
129. Milner, *Victory in Papua,* pp. 288-93.
130. Ltr, Eichelberger to MacArthur, 25 Dec 1942, copy in author's possession.
131. Milner, *Victory in Papua,* pp. 292-303; Blakeley, *32d Division,* pp. 104-07. In the fighting for the Government Gardens, the first two medals of honor earned in the 32d Division were awarded.
132. Quoted in McCarthy, *Kokoda to Wau,* p. 450.
133. Ibid., pp. 451-52.
134. Eichelberger, *Jungle Road,* pp. 44-45.
135. *Papuan Campaign,* p. 48; McCarthy, *Kokoda to Wau,* pp. 455-62. Australian casualties on 18 Dec were 11 officers and 160 men.
136. Ltr, Eichelberger to Sutherland, 27 Dec 1942, copy marked "Not sent." McCarthy, *Kokoda to Wau,* pp. 474-75.
137. Ltr, Eichelberger to Sutherland, 2 Jan 1943, copy in author's possession.
138. Luvaas, *Dear Miss Em,* p. 50.
139. Milner, *Victory in Papua,* pp. 370-72. About 60,000 Army and Marine Corps ground troops were deployed on Guadalcanal at one time or another during the six months of fighting, of whom 1,600 were killed in action and 4,245 were wounded. John Miller, Jr., *Guadalcanal: The First Offensive,* United States Army in World War II: The War in the Pacific (Washington, D.C.: Historical Division, 1949), p. 350.
140. Allied Forces, "History of the Buna Campaign," pp. 54, 64.
141. U.S. Army, Headquarters Army Ground Forces, "Report of Military Observer in Southwest Pacific Theater of Operations, Col. H. F. Handy, September 26 to December 23, 1942," p. 17, copy in MHI (hereafter "Handy Report").
142. Maj Gen O. W. Griswold to Lt Gen Leslie McNair, 29 Aug 1943, circulated by Headquarters, Army Ground Forces, as "Observer's Report . . . received in a personal letter," copy in MHI.
143. U.S. Army Headquarters, Army Ground Forces, Observer's Report of Col Herbert B. Laux, 20 Feb 1943, copy in MHI, p. 4 (hereafter "Laux Report").
144. Allied Forces, "History of the Buna Campaign," pp. 54-55.
145. U.S. Army Headquarters, Army Ground Forces, "Report of Colonel Harry Knight, Cavalry, covering observations in the Southwest Pacific Theatre, during the period October 16 to December 30, 1942," p. 12, copy in MHI (hereafter "Knight Report").
146. "Handy Report," pp. 15-16; "Knight Report," p. 6.
147. Allied Forces, "History of the Buna Campaign," p. 69.
148. Ibid., pp. 61-62.
149. Ibid., p. 70.
150. "Handy Report," p. 1; Allied Forces, "History of the Buna Campaign," p. 76. At Adelaide, where apparently the artillery training was the best, Harding had

been anxious to have artillery fire over his infantry, but there was some question whether firing over the troops was legal. Interv of Gen Harding with Samuel Milner, 10 Dec 1947, OCMH Collection, MHI.

151. "Knight Report," p. 15.

152. Ltr, Eichelberger to Gen Fuller, 14 Dec 1942, in Luvaas, *Dear Miss Em,* pp. 44-45.

153. Ltr, Eichelberger to Sutherland, 31 Dec 1942, copy in author's possession.

154. "Laux Report," p. 3.

155. U.S. Infantry School, *Infantry in Battle,* p. 1.

156. Leighton and Coakley, *Global Logistics,* 1:411.

157. Ltr, Eichelberger to Sutherland, 15 Jan 1943, copy in author's possession.

158. Alfred D. Chandler et al., eds., *The Papers of Dwight David Eisenhower: The War Years* (Baltimore: Johns Hopkins University Press, 1970), 2:904-05.

159. Ibid., p. 828.

160. Ltr, Eichelberger to Sutherland, 9 Jan 1943, copy in author's possession.

161. History of the 126th Infantry Regiment (during the period beginning 1 Feb 1943 and ending 30 Jun 1945), 32d Division.

162. Ltr, Col Rex E. Chandler to Lt Gen Leslie J. McNair, 11 May 1943, Rex E. Chandler Papers, World War II Miscellaneous Collection, Archives, U.S. Army Military History Institute.

163. Blakeley, *32d Division,* pp. 131-32.

164. Ibid., p. 147.

CHAPTER 8. KASSERINE PASS, 30 JANUARY-22 FEBRUARY 1943

1. Mark Skinner Watson, "The Deterioration of the Army between Wars," in *Chief of Staff: Prewar Plans and Preparations,* reprinted in *20th Century War: The American Experience* (Leavenworth, Kans.: Combat Studies Institute, Command and General Staff College, 1982), p. 197.

2. Ibid., pp. 195-99.

3. Walter Millis, *Arms and Men: A Study of American Military History,* reprinted in *20th Century War,* pp. 178-80; Watson, "Deterioration," pp. 196-97; Jean R. Moenk, *A History of Large-Scale Maneuvers in the United States, 1935-1964* (Fort Monroe, Va.: Historical Branch, Office of the Deputy Chief of Staff for Military Operations and Reserve Forces, U.S. Continental Army Command, Dec 1969), p. 2.

4. Watson, "Deterioration," p. 202; Russell F. Weigley, *History of the United States Army* (New York: Macmillan, 1967), pp. 415-17.

5. Watson, "Deterioration," pp. 195-99; Christopher R. Gabel, "The U.S. Army GHQ Maneuvers of 1941" (Ph.D. dissertation, Ohio State University, 1981), p. 9 (hereafter Gabel, "Maneuvers"); Moenk, *A History,* p. 3; Forrest C. Pogue, *Marshall: Ordeal and Hope* (New York: Viking Press, 1966), pp. 6-7, 11, 16-17, 31.

6. A basic source for the material following on the Army between the wars is Weigley, *History,* pp. 395-420.

7. See Millis, *Arms and Men,* pp. 179-80.

8. Weigley, *History,* p. 403; see Watson, "Deterioration," p. 200.

9. Millis, *Arms and Men,* p. 178.

10. T. Harry Williams, *The History of American Wars from 1745 to 1918,* excerpted in *20th Century War,* pp. 151, 155.

11. George Hofmann, "The Demise of the U.S. Tank Corps and Medium Tank Development Program," *Military Affairs* (Feb 1973), reprinted in *20th Century War,* pp. 184, 186, 188; see Millis, *Arms and Men,* p. 177.

12. Hofmann, "Demise," p. 190; Martin Blumenson, *The Patton Papers, 1885-1940* (Boston: Houghton Mifflin, 1972), pp. 959-60.

13. See Ernest N. Harmon, *Combat Commander* (New York, 1970); Millis, *Arms and Men,* p. 177; Maj Gen Robert W. Grow, unpublished manuscript, author's copy.

14. Hofmann, "Demise," pp. 190, 185-86; Gabel, "Maneuvers," pp. 32-52.

15. Weigley, *History,* p. 414; I. B. Holley, *An Enduring Challenge: The Problem of Air Force Doctrine,* Harmon Memorial Lectures in Military History (Colorado Springs, Colo.: USAF Academy, 1974).

16. George F. Howe, *The Battle History of the 1st Armored Division* (Washington, D.C.: Combat Forces Press, 1945), pp. 4ff.

17. Weigley, *History,* p. 419.

18. Basic sources for training and maneuvers are Moenk, *A History,* preface and pp. 1-26; and Martin Blumenson, *Mark Clark* (New York: Congdon and Weed, 1984), pp. 48-60.

19. See Blumenson, *The Patton Papers, 1885-1940,* pp. 787-88.

20. Weigley, *History,* p. 402.

21. Gabel, "Maneuvers," p. 3.

22. Moenk, *A History,* pp. 25-26.

23. See Forrest C. Pogue, *Education of a General* (New York: Viking Press, 1963), p. 247ff.

24. Command and General Staff College, *Annual Reports,* 1920, p. 13; 1929-30, p. 9; 1935-36, p. 10.

25. Weigley, *History,* pp. 409, 411, 418-19; Blumenson, *The Patton Papers, 1885-1940,* pp. 729-31, 841-42, 844, 853-54, 868, 960; Gabel, "Demise," pp. 14-15.

26. Gabel, "Demise," pp. 33-34.

27. Ibid., pp. 9-10; Weigley, *History,* p. 419.

28. Millis, *Arms and Men,* p. 180.

29. Martin Blumenson, *Kasserine Pass* (Boston: Houghton Mifflin, 1967), p. 9.

30. Basic sources for this section are Weigley, *History,* pp. 461ff; Moenk, *A History,* pp. 25ff; Gabel, "Demise," passim; Kent Roberts Greenfield, Robert R. Palmer, and Bell I. Wiley, *The Organization of Ground Combat Troops, The Army Ground Force,* U.S. Army in World War II (Washington, D.C.: Government Printing Office, 1948), passim (hereafter Greenfield, *Organization*).

31. Gabel, "Demise," pp. 21, 197-200; Blumenson, *The Patton Papers, 1885-1940,* p. 945.

32. Blumenson, *Mark Clark,* p. 45-46.

33. Moenk, *A History,* p. 33; Blumenson, *The Patton Papers, 1885-1940,* pp. 943-46, 948-49.

34. Lt Col Emory A. Dunham, *Tank Destroyer History,* Study No. 29 (Washington, D.C.: Historical Section, Army Ground Forces, 1946), p. 28.

35. Blumenson, *The Patton Papers, 1885-1940,* pp. 953-54.

36. Howe, *Battle History,* pp. 4ff.

37. Moenk, *A History,* pp. 61-62.

38. Martin Blumenson, *The Patton Papers, 1940-1945* (Boston: Houghton Mifflin, 1974), pp. 29ff; Blumenson, *Mark Clark,* p. 53.

39. Moenk, *A History,* pp. 64-67.

40. Blumenson, *The Patton Papers, 1940-1945,* pp. 41ff; Gabel, "Demise," pp. 94, 309.

41. Gabel, "Demise," pp. 307ff, 342, 344, 346, 348, 356; Howe, *Battle History,* pp. 10-11; Greenfield, *Organization,* p. 323.

42. Howe, *Battle History,* pp. 11ff.

43. Ibid., p. 9.

44. Basic sources for this section are Dunham, *Tank Destroyer History,* passim; Greenfield, *Organization,* pp. 83-84, 428-29; Gabel, "Demise," pp. 300ff.

45. Watson, "Deterioration," p. 202.

46. Moenk, *A History,* pp. 41-42; Weigley, *History,* pp. 420, 427.

47. Blumenson, *Mark Clark,* pp. 50-51; Blumenson, *The Patton Papers, 1885-1940,* p. 954.

48. See Watson, "Deterioration," p. 202.

49. Greenfield, *Organization,* pp. 43-45; Moenk, *A History,* pp. 34, 38, 41, 44-45; Gabel, "Demise," p. 17.

50. Moenk, *A History,* pp. 68-70; Gabel, "Demise," passim.

51. Gabel, "Demise," p. 202.

52. Ibid., p. 257.

53. Ibid., pp. 57-71, 313-14, 325ff.

54. Greenfield, *Organization,* p. 46.

55. Weigley, *History,* p. 435.

56. Greenfield, *Organization,* pp. 54-55.

57. Ibid.

58. Moenk, *A History,* p. 15; Blumenson, *The Patton Papers, 1940-1945,* pp. 58-76.

59. Blumenson, *Mark Clark,* pp. 48-50.

60. Moenk, *A History,* p. 74, 78.

61. Blumenson, *Mark Clark,* p. 64.

62. Greenfield, *Organization,* pp. 418-19.

63. The following is taken from Ann Larson, "Volunteer Citizen Soldiers of Southwest Iowa, 1930-1945" (National Endowment for the Humanities project, 1981), copy in author's possession.

64. Moenk, *A History,* p. 43.

65. See Louis Morton, "Germany First: The Basic Concept of Allied Strategy in World War II," in Kent R. Greenfield, ed., *Command Decisions,* reprinted in *20th Century Warfare,* pp. 229-32, 236; Maurice Matloff and Edwin M. Snell, *Strategic Planning for Coalition Warfare, 1941-42,* U.S. Army in World War II (Washington, D.C.: Government Printing Office, 1953).

66. See Blumenson, *Kasserine Pass,* pp. 56-68.

67. The following is taken from Howe, *Battle History,* passim; George Howe, *Northwest Africa: Seizing the Initiative in the West,* U.S. Army in World War II (Washington, D.C.: Government Printing Office, 1957), passim; and Blumenson, *Kasserine Pass,* passim.

68. Blumenson, *Kasserine Pass,* p. 190.

69. See ibid., pp. 231-37, for an account of a particular mine-laying expedition characterized by nervousness, fear, lack of control, the absence of information, and an unwillingness to perform normal missions in time of danger.

70. Ibid., p. 296.

71. Gabel, "Demise," p. 327.

72. The following is from Greenfield, *Organization,* pp. 300-02, 317, 326-27.

73. Ibid., pp. 329, 427-28, 430; Dunham, *Tank Destroyer History,* pp. 30-31; Gabel, "Demise," pp. 331-34.

74. Greenfield, *Organization,* pp. 428-30.

75. Ibid., p. 420.

76. Moenk, *A History,* pp. 86, 89.

77. Greenfield, *Organization,* p. 412; Gabel, "Demise," pp. 327-28; Martin Blumenson, *Breakout and Pursuit,* U.S. Army in World War II (Washington, D.C.: Government Printing Office, 1963), pp. 207-08.

78. Greenfield, *Organization,* p. 412.

79. Ibid., p. 433.

80. Ibid., p. 221.

81. Ibid.

82. Ibid., p. 316.

83. Blumenson, *Kasserine Pass,* p. 303.

CHAPTER 9. TASK FORCE SMITH AND THE 24TH
DIVISION: DELAY AND WITHDRAWAL, 5-19 JULY 1950

1. The author is indebted to the excellent historical research conducted by the Army historians of the Office of the Chief of Military History. In particular, I relied on Roy K. Appleman's *South to the Naktong, North to the Yala (June-November 1950),* United States Army in the Korean War (Washington, D.C.: Office of the Chief of Military History, 1961). Except where noted otherwise, this narrative is based on Appleman's work. In addition, the photographs in U.S. Department of the Army, *Korea—1950* (Washington, D.C.: Office of the Chief of Military History, 1952) are a superb primary record of military operations in the Korean War. They offer a treasure of detail concerning uniforms and equipment, terrain, road conditions, weather, tactics, weapons employment, and the health and morale of American troops. The reader will also want to read Edwin P. Hoyt's *The Pusan Perimeter* (New York: Stein and Day, 1984), which covers the events of this chapter as well as the rest of the Eighth Army on into the defense of Pusan.

2. Testimony of Gen J. Lawton Collins in U.S. Congress, Senate, Committee on Foreign Relations, *Military Situation in the Far East, Hearings to Conduct an Inquiry into the Military Situation in the Far East and the Facts Surrounding the Relief of General of the Army Douglas MacArthur from his Assignment in that Area,* 82d Cong., 1st sess., 1951, pt. 2, p. 1188 (hereafter *Military Situation in the Far East*).

3. U.S. Department of State, *Bulletin* 23 (10 Jul 1950): 57980; Gen Omar N. Bradley's testimony, *Military Situation in the Far East,* pt. 2, p. 954; statement by the president of the United States, 27 Jun 1950, ibid., pt. 5, p. 3369; Secretary of State Dean Acheson's testimony, ibid., pt. 3, pp. 1729, 1782.

4. U.S. Department of the Army, *Semiannual Report of the Secretary of the Army, 1 July to 31 December 1949* (Washington, D.C.: Government Printing Office, 1950), p. 136.

5. Appleman, *South to the Naktong,* p. 49; Matthew B. Ridgway, *The Korean War* (Garden City, N.Y.: Doubleday and Co., 1967), p. 34; J. Lawton Collins, *War in Peacetime: The History and Lessons of Korea* (Boston: Houghton Mifflin Co., 1969), p. 66.

6. *History of the 24th Division,* 1949, vol. 1, RG 407, i, National Archives, Washington, D.C.

7. Ibid.

8. Ibid., G1 Report, pp. 2-3.

9. Ibid., pp. vii-viii.

10. Ltr, Col (ret.) Floyd R. Martin to author, 29 Apr 1983; Ltr, Kenwood Ross to author, 7 Dec 1982; Interv, Henry L. (Dusty) Rhodes, 15 Apr 1983. The interview with Dusty Rhodes, a veteran of Company B, 21st Infantry regiment and Task Force Smith, took place at a reunion of a number of veterans of the 21st Infantry on 15–17 Apr 1983. The author appreciates the help he received from these soldiers, particularly their recollections about life in Japan before the regiment moved to Korea.

11. Ltr, Floyd R. Martin to author; Interv, Dusty Rhodes; Ltr, Carl Bernard to author, 6 Dec 1982.

12. Ltr, Kenwood Ross to author; Interv, Dusty Rhodes and Edwin A. Eversole.

13. Interv, Floyd R. Martin; Ltr, Floyd R. Martin to author.

14. Ltr, Carl Bernard to author.

15. Ibid.

16. Interv, Floyd R. Martin.

17. Interv, Dusty Rhodes and Carl Bernard.

18. Ltr, Floyd R. Martin to author.

19. Ltr, Kenwood Ross to author.

20. Ibid.

21. Ltr, Floyd R. Martin to author.

22. Ltr, [an anonymous officer in the 24th Division] to Office of the Chief of Military History, 5 Aug 1950, DA file OPS 091 Korea, National Archives.

23. Interv, Edwin A. Eversole.

24. Ibid.

25. Interv, Carl Bernard, Edwin A. Eversole, and Floyd Martin; Ltrs, Carl Bernard and Floyd Martin to author.

26. Interv, Floyd R. Martin; Ltr, Floyd R. Martin to author.

27. Interv, Elmer J. Grinok.

28. Interv, Edwin A. Eversole.

29. 21st Infantry Regiment War Diary, 30 Jun 1950, RG 407, National Archives (hereafter cited as 21 Inf WD and a date). Maj Gen William F. Dean, *General Dean's Story*, as told to William L. Worden (New York: Viking Press, 1954), p. 17.

30. Ltr, Carl Bernard to author.

31. 21 Inf WD, 1 Jul 1950.

32. 21 Inf WD, 2 Jul 1950.

33. Appleman, *South to the Naktong*, p. 61. Ltr, Brig Gen C. B. Smith (USA, Ret) to Lt Col John Speedy, 9 Jul 1984.

34. Interv, Edwin A. Eversole; Ltr, Smith to Speedy. Eversole claims that Smith told the reconnaissance party that "we are going to stay here until the last man." Smith denies this "categorically" in his letter to Speedy.

35. Brig Gen George B. Barth, "The First Days in Korea," *United States Army Combat Forces Journal* 2 (Mar 1952): 22; Ltr, Smith to Speedy.

36. Ltrs, Carl Bernard and Floyd Martin.

37. Interv, Edwin A. Eversole.

38. 21 Inf WD, 5 Jul 1950; Interv, Floyd Martin.

39. Barth, "The First Days in Korea," p. 23; Ltr, Floyd R. Martin.

40. 21 Inf WD, 5 Jul 1950; Ltr, Smith to Speedy.

41. Interv, Dusty Rhodes.

42. Barth, "The First Days in Korea," p. 22; Dean, *General Dean's Story*, p. 21. In addition to Appleman's *South to the Naktong*, see also Russell A. Gugeler, *Combat Actions in Korea* (Washington, D.C.: Office of the Chief of Military History, 1970). Ch 1, "Withdrawal Action," covers the first engagement of the 1st Battalion, 34th Infantry, in detail.

43. Gugeler, *Combat Actions,* pp. 6-7.

44. Barth, "The First Days in Korea," p. 22.

45. Ibid., p. 24.

46. Gugeler, *Combat Actions,* pp. 10-11.

47. Dean, *General Dean's Story,* pp. 23-24.

48. Ibid., p. 26; 21 Inf WD, 8 Jul 1950.

49. Ibid.

50. Ibid., 9 Jul 1950.

51. Ibid.

52. Ibid., 10 Jul 1950.

53. Ibid.

54. Ibid., 11 Jul 1950.

55. Ibid.

56. [Capt Allan A. David, ed.], *Battleground Korea: The Story of the 25th Infantry Division* (Arlington, Va.: 25th Infantry Division Association, 1951).

57. The story of the fight at the Kum River is from Appleman, *South to the Naktong.*

58. Dean, *General Dean's Story,* pp. 30-31.

59. James F. Schnabel, *Policy and Direction: The First Year,* United States Army in the Korean War (Washington, D.C.: Office of the Chief of Military History, 1972), p. 112.

CHAPTER 10. THE 1ST CAVALRY AND THE IA DRANG VALLEY, 8 OCTOBER-24 NOVEMBER 1965

1. Quoted in Bernard Fall, "The New Communist Army," in Bernard Fall, ed., *Vietnam Witness* (New York: Praeger, 1966), 253.

2. This section is based on ibid., pp. 225-54; Harvey H. Smith et al., *Area Handbook for North Vietnam* (Washington, D.C.: 1967), pp. 397-400, 403-05, 409-11; Maj Robert Doughty, *The Evolution of US Army Tactical Doctrine* (Fort Leavenworth, Kans.: Combat Studies Institute, 1979), pp. 32-35 (hereafter Doughty, *Tactical Doctrine*); John H. Hay, Jr., *Tactical and Materiel Innovations* (Washington, D.C.: 1974),pp. 3-6; and 1st Cavalry Division (Airmobile), "Combat Operations After Action Report, Pleiku Campaign, 23 October-26 November 1965" (unpublished ms, Center of Military History, Washington, D.C.), pp. 13-14 (hereafter 1st Cavalry Division, "After Action Report").

3. Russell H. Weigley, *A History of the U.S. Army* (New York: Macmillan, 1967), pp. 540-42. In South Vietnam, no "normal" infantry divisions were deployed. Most featured nine infantry battalions, and only the 4th Infantry Division contained an armored battalion.

4. Doughty, *Tactical Doctrine,* pp. 22-25.

5. Hay, *Tactical and Materiel Innovations,* pp. 51-53.

6. Weigley, *U.S. Army,* p. 546; James Fallows, *National Defense* (New York: Vintage Books, 1982), pp. 76-95.

7. John J. Tolson, *Airmobility, 1961-1971* (Washington, D.C.: Department of the Army, 1973), pp. 3-61; *Time,* 25 Jun 1965, pp. 31-32; *New York Times,* 19 Oct, 20 Nov 1965.

8. Valuable detail on the history of the 1st Cavalry can be found in ibid., and in J. D. Coleman, ed., *1st Air Cavalry Division—Memoirs of the First Team—Vietnam August 1965-December 1969* (Tokyo: 1970); Edward Hymoff, *The 1st Air Cavalry Division* (New York: 1967), and in Harry W. O. Kinnard oral history interv, The Army Aviation

Papers, U.S. Army Military History Institute, Carlisle Barracks, Pa. The Kinnard quote is from Hymoff, *1st Cavalry,* p. 8.

9. Doughty, *Tactical Doctrine,* pp. 26-28; Weigley, *U.S. Army,* pp. 542-45; Harry G. Summers, Jr., "The Bitter Triumph of Ia Drang," *American Heritage* 35 (Feb/Mar 1984): 58.

10. North Vietnamese strategy is capably summarized in Wallace Thies, *When Governments Collide* (Berkeley: University of California Press, 1980), pp. 328-29, and Patrick J. McGarvey, *Visions of Victory* (Stanford, Calif.: Hoover Institution Press, 1969), pp. 7-9.

11. *The Senator Gravel Edition—The Pentagon Papers,* 4 vols. (Boston: Beacon Press, 1971), 3:470-85, 4:290-99 (hereafter *Pentagon Papers [Gravel]*); William C. Westmoreland, *Soldier Reports,* Dell ed. (New York: Dell Publishing Co., 1980), pp. 180, 184.

12. The best analysis of Johnson's decisions for war is Larry Berman, *Planning a Tragedy* (New York: Norton, 1982). See especially pp. 79-128.

13. *Pentagon Papers (Gravel),* 4:296-97. See also Msg, Westmoreland to CINCPAC, 13 Jun 1965, in ibid., 4:606-08.

14. Richard Hermes, "Department of the Army: The Buildup, 1965-1967" (unpublished ms, Center of Military History), ch. 4, pp. 9-39, ch. 5, pp. 36-42, and ch. 6, pp. 8-52 (hereafter Hermes, "The Buildup"); "First Strike at River Drang," interv by Alexander S. Cochran, Jr., with Maj Gen Harry W. O. Kinnard, *Military History* (Oct 1984): 45. For personal accounts of the deployment of the 1st Cavalry to Vietnam, see Lt Col Kenneth D. Mertel, "The Year of the Horse" (unpublished ms, Center of Military History), chs. I and II, and Robert Mason, *Chickenhawk* (New York: Penguin Books, 1984), pp. 51-69.

15. Hermes, "The Buildup," ch. 5, pp. 36-42; *New York Times,* 19 Oct, 20 Nov 1965; *Time,* 24 Sep 1965, pp. 33-34, 22 Oct 1965, p. 28; and Hymoff, *1st Cavalry,* p. 12.

16. Westmoreland, *Soldier Reports,* p. 203.

17. Maj William P. Boyle and Maj Robert Samambria, "The Lure and the Ambush" (unpublished ms, Center of Military History), pp. 1-3.

18. Ibid., pp. 4-5; *Time,* 5 Nov 1965, p. 31a; *New York Times,* 28 Oct 1965.

19. Lt Gen Harry W. Kinnard, "A Victory in the Ia Drang: The Triumph of a Concept," *Army* 17 (Sep 1967): 73.

20. *New York Times,* 28 Oct 1965.

21. Boyle and Samambria, "Lure and Ambush," pp. 6-8.

22. Maj-Gen Vinh Loc, *Why Pleime?* (Pleiku: Center of Military History, 1966), pp. 55-63.

23. Kinnard, "A Victory in the Ia Drang," p. 73; 1st Cavalry Division, "After Action Report," p. 124; George MacGarrigle, draft chapters on the Ia Drang campaign, Center of Military History, ch 5, pp. 39-55 (hereafter MacGarrigle).

24. *New York Times,* 28 Oct 1965.

25. MacGarrigle, ch 5, pp. 39-55.

26. The body count has been one of the most controversial issues of a controversial war. At this stage, the Army seems to have tabulated the counts as conscientiously as possible, and there are no indications of the heavy padding that became standard operating procedure later on. The counts were compiled hurriedly and under the most difficult circumstances, however, and there is evidence to suggest that at least in certain cases they may have been inaccurate. Mertel, "Year of the Horse," ch 6, pp. 6, 20, admits that in actions in which his unit participated, the North Vietnamese dragged away all of their dead and the body count was based on interrogation. In his study of

the Ia Drang, MacGarrigle points out that in one engagement the casualties for a particular enemy unit equaled 100 percent of the soldiers engaged in battle. In the *New York Times*, 26 Nov 1965, Charles Mohr reported that the pressures for high body counts were great and quoted cynical GIs who referred to the estimates as WEGs, "wild-eyed guesses."

27. Westmoreland, *Soldier Reports*, p. 203.

28. On the malaria problem, see ibid., pp. 348-349, and Maj Gen Spurgeon Neel, *Medical Support of the U.S. Army in Vietnam, 1965-1970* (Washington, D.C.: Center of Military History, 1973), 38. The 1st Cavalry reported a total of more than 1,000 cases of malaria from October to December 1965. See Field Forces Vietnam, "Command Report for the Quarter Ending 31 December 1965," 14 Jan 1966, Center of Military History.

29. Michael Herr, *Dispatches* (New York: Knopf, 1978), pp. 93-95.

30. Kinnard, "A Victory in the Ia Drang," pp. 78-79.

31. Ibid., pp. 80-83; Mertel, "Year of the Horse," ch 6, pp. 6-20.

32. Kinnard, "A Victory in the Ia Drang," pp. 83-84; *New York Times*, 8 Nov 1965.

33. Kinnard, "A Victory in the Ia Drang," p. 84.

34. Ibid.

35. Ibid., p. 85.

36. Documents captured during the Cedar Falls operation of early 1967 provided presumably reliable information indicating that the North Vietnamese willingness to accept heavy losses in the Ia Drang resulted from a calculated decision. See *Time*, 25 Aug 1967, p. 22.

37. Col Harold Moore, "After Action Report, Ia Drang Valley Operation, 1st Battalion, 7th Cavalry, 14-16 November 1965" (unpublished ms, Center of Military History), p. 3. For the X-ray battle, see also Hymoff, *1st Air Cavalry*, pp. 29-31, and Peter Arnett's firsthand reports in *Louisville Courier-Journal*, 16 Nov 1965, and *Lexington* (Ky.) *Herald*, 17 Nov 1965.

38. *New York Times*, 8 Nov 1965.

39. Moore, "After Action Report," pp. 10-12. See also John A. Cash, "Fight at Ia Drang," in John Albright et al.: *Seven Firefights in Vietnam* (Washington, D.C.: Center of Military History, 1970), pp. 3-40.

40. *New York Times*, 17 Nov 1965.

41. Moore, "After Action Report," p. 13.

42. 1st Cavalry Division, "After Action Report," p. 94; Kinnard, "A Victory in the Ia Drang," p. 88.

43. *Washington Post*, 19 Nov 1965.

44. *New York Times*, 19 Nov 1965.

45. Jack P. Smith, "Death in the Ia Drang Valley," *Saturday Evening Post* 240 (28 Jan 1967): 83.

46. Official accounts of the Ia Drang either ignore or convey a misleading picture of the disaster at Albany. Cash, "Fight at Ia Drang," and Dave Richard Palmer, *Summons of the Trumpet* (San Rafael, Calif.: Presidio Press, 1978) (a capable military history by an officer who served in Vietnam), do not even mention the fight at Albany. Gen Kinnard claims that the United States "won the day." Although many details remain murky, the outlines of the action and the profound emotions it evoked can be gleaned from Smith, "Death in the Ia Drang Valley"; *Washington Post*, 19, 20 Nov 1965; and 1st Cavalry Division, "After Action Report," pp. 93-94.

47. Ibid. See Cochran interv.

48. Kinnard, "A Victory in the Ia Drang," pp. 89-90.

NOTES TO PAGES 321–324

49. The official count was 1,519 enemy killed by actual body count, an estimated additional 2,042 killed and 1,178 wounded and 1,023 weapons captured.

50. Palmer, *Summons of the Trumpet,* p. 93.

51. The North Vietnamese division would not return to action until May 1966. The heavy losses are also confirmed in the captured documents printed in Vinh Loc, *Why Pleime?,* p. 161.

52. North Vietnamese claims of victory are reported in *Washington Post,* 21 Nov 1965. Giap's comments are in McGarvey, *Visions of Victory,* pp. 44, 214, and in Vo Nguyen Giap, *The Military Art of Peoples War* (New York: Monthly Review Press, 1970), p. 271. The unidentified North Vietnamese colonel is interviewed by a British correspondent in the *New York Times,* 8 Dec 1965. North Vietnamese claims appear to have expanded since the end of the war. A recent study produced by the High-Level Military Institute contends that the American "Air Cavalry Division was defeated in its first engagement" and claims that the North Vietnamese killed 1,700 GIs, shot down 59 planes, destroyed five 105s, and captured 73 weapons in the campaign. See the translation and synopsis of *The Anti-U.S. Resistance War for National Salvation, 1954–1975* in Joint Publications Research Service #80968, 3 Jun 1982. Official U.S. figures indicate that 300 Americans were killed and 524 wounded.

53. *Washington Post,* 20 Nov 1965.

54. Ibid., 21 Nov 1965.

55. Ibid.

56. "Fighting Gets Tougher—So Does American GI," *U.S. News and World Report,* 13 Dec 1965, pp. 39–41.

57. *Time,* 3 Dec 1965, pp. 33–34.

58. McGarvey, *Visions of Victory,* p. 14.

59. Thomas Hughes to Dean Rusk, 21 Apr 1967, "Hanoi's Attitudes as Reflected in Recently Captured 1966 Documents," Lyndon B. Johnson Papers (Lyndon B. Johnson Library, Austin, Tex.), National Security File: Country File, Vietnam, Box 157.

60. Thies, *When Governments Collide,* pp. 329–30, and McGarvey, *Visions of Victory,* pp. 7–9. For the enemy tactical adjustments, see *Time,* 25 Aug 1967, p. 22, and Vinh Loc, *Why Pleime?,* pp. 136–38.

61. *Washington Post,* 19–21 Nov 1965, and *New York Times,* 19–21 Nov 1965. Mohr's comments are in *New York Times,* 26 Nov 1965.

62. *New York Times,* 21 Nov 1965.

63. *New York Times,* 27 Nov 1965.

64. Standard operating procedure required only that specific casualty figures be given out on a weekly basis and for all of Vietnam, not for a particular day or battle. For the latter, casualties were described only as light, moderate, or heavy. Even here, the Army may have fudged a bit, admitting only to "moderate" casualties for the week of X-ray and Albany. For the comment on casualties, see *New York Times,* 21 Nov 1965.

65. Bundy to Johnson, 27 Nov 1965, McGeorge Bundy File, National Security File, Johnson Papers.

66. Al Santoli, *Everything We Had* (New York: Random House, 1981), p. 42. See also the comments of a GI in "Fighting Gets Tougher," p. 40.

67. MacGarrigle, ch 6, p. 43.

68. Herr, *Dispatches,* p. 94.

69. *Time,* 5 Nov 1965, pp. 31–35; *New York Times,* 28 Oct 1965.

70. Moore, "After Action Report," pp. 17–18.

71. White House files for this period have not been processed, and it is therefore impossible to determine what the president knew about the fighting in the Ia Drang and what impact it may have had on him.

72. For the performance of the M-16, see 1st Cavalry Division, "After Action Report," p. 126; Moore, "After Action Report," p. 17, and Kinnard to Deputy Chief of Staff, 10 Jan 1966, "Quarterly Command Report," Center of Military History.

73. Westmoreland, *Soldier Reports*, pp. 202–04; William C. Westmoreland, *Report on the War in Vietnam* (Washington, D.C.: Government Printing Office, 1968), pp. 98–99, 110.

74. Kinnard oral history interv, Army Aviation Papers.

75. *Newsweek*, 13 Dec 1965, p. 28; in his 1967 Army article describing the Ia Drang operations, Kinnard cited such statistics as 5,048 tons of cargo airlifted by helicopters and planes from Pleiku to the combat area, movement by air of 67 artillery batteries and evacuation of some 2,700 refugees—all with only 59 aircraft hit and 4 lost ("A Victory in the Ia Drang," p. 90).

76. 1st Cavalry Division, "After Action Report," pp. 125–30.

77. Palmer, *Summons of the Trumpet*, p. 97. S. L. A. Marshall comments similarly on a later campaign conducted by the 1st Cav in *Vietnam: Three Battles* (New York: Dial Press, 1971), pp. 167–68.

78. Moore, "After Action Report," pp. 17–18. See also 1st Cavalry Division, "After Action Report," p. 127; Kinnard to Deputy Chief of Staff, 10 Jan 1966, "Quarterly Command Report," Center of Military History; "Tactical Tips," attached to Command Report for Quarter Ending 30 Dec 1965, Center of Military History.

CHAPTER 11. FIRST BATTLES IN RETROSPECT

1. Chester G. Starr, *From Salerno to the Alps* (Washington, D.C.: Infantry Journal Press, 1948), p. 198.

2. Michael Herr, *Dispatches* (New York: Knopf, 1977), pp. 46, 70, 187ff, 290ff.

3. Two recent books are original attempts to deal with the problem sketched here. Grady McWhiney and Perry D. Jamieson, *Attack and Die* (University: University of Alabama Press, 1982), emphasizes the effect of rifled weapons on operations. Michael C. C. Adams, *Our Masters the Rebels* (Cambridge, Mass.: Harvard University Press, 1978), stresses a crippling lack of confidence in the Union command, especially in the East.

4. John Keegan, *The Face of Battle* (London: Jonathan Cape Ltd., 1976), pp. 325–36.

About the Editors
and Contributors

CHARLES E. HELLER (lieutenant colonel, USAR) is Chief of Mobilization Requirements, Operations and Training Division of the Mobilization, Operations and Training Directorate at the Army Reserve Personnel Center (ARPERCEN), St. Louis, Missouri. He has been Army Reserve Advisor and faculty member at the Combat Studies Institute, U.S. Army Command and General Staff College, Fort Leavenworth, Kansas, as well as director of the Summer Session at the University of Massachusetts at Amherst. He has served as an Individual Mobilization Augmentee at the Army's Center of Military History and in a variety of other Army Reserve assignments and has also served on active duty with the 8th Infantry Division in Germany. His publications include *Leavenworth Paper* No. 10, "Chemical Warfare in World War I: The American Experience, 1917–1918," and articles on topics ranging from the American Civil War to World War II.

WILLIAM A. STOFFT (brigadier general, USA) is the Chief of Military History for the U.S. Army. He was previously the Assistant Deputy Commandant at the Command and General Staff College, Fort Leavenworth, Kansas, where he also taught military history and strategy and was director of the Combat Studies Institute. He has also been an assistant professor of history and social sciences at West Point. He has held command and staff positions in Europe and the United States with the 2d and 3d Armored Divisions, completed two tours in Vietnam, and commanded a battalion at Fort Knox, Kentucky. In Washington, D.C., he served in the Office of the Chief of Staff, working on officer education.

K. JACK BAUER, professor of history at Rensselaer Polytechnic Institute, is a specialist in American military and naval history. He has served on the staff of the National Archives and in the historical sections of both the United States Marine Corps and the United States Navy and as John F. Morrison Visiting Professor of Military History at the United States Army Command and General Staff College (1977/78); he has lectured at the Naval War College and in the ROTC Workshop in Military History at West Point. His books include *Surfboats and Horse Marines* (1969), *The Mexican War, 1846–1848* (1974), *Soldiering* (1977), *The New American State Papers: Naval Affairs* (1981), *United States Navy and Marine Corps Bases* (coeditor, 1985), and *Zachary Taylor* (1985).

MARTIN BLUMENSON (lieutenant colonel, USAR, retired) served as historical officer with the Third and Seventh Army Headquarters in Europe during World War II, commanded the Third Historical Detachment in Korea, was chief historian of Joint Task Force Seven for the Pacific atomic weapons tests in 1956, and for ten years was a senior historian in the Office of the Chief of Military History. He has taught at the United States Merchant Marine Academy, Hofstra College, Acadia University, the Army War College, Bucknell University, George Washington University, and the National War College. He has held the Ernest J. King Chair at the Naval War College, the Mark W. Clark Visiting Professorship at The Citadel, and the Harold K. Johnson Chair at the Military History Institute. Blumenson's more than a dozen books include a full study of the first American engagement of World War II in Europe, *Kasserine Pass* (1967), *The Patton Papers, 1885–1940* (1972), *The Patton Papers, 1940–1945* (1974), *Mark Clark* (1984), and *Patton: The Man behind the Legend, 1885–1945* (1985).

GRAHAM A. COSMAS has taught American history at the University of Texas at Austin and the University of Guam. In 1973 he joined the staff of the History and Museums Division, United States Marine Corps, and since 1979 has been with the United States Army Center of Military History. In 1984/85 he served as the Harold K. Johnson Professor of Military History at the Military History Institute, Carlisle Barracks, Pennsylvania. Cosmas is the author of *An Army for Empire: The U.S. Army in the Spanish-American War, 1889–1899* (1971) and coauthor of a monograph on the United States Marines in the Dominican Republic from 1916 to 1924 and of a book on medical support of the European Theater of Operations in World War II; he has also drafted a volume on Marine operations in Vietnam in 1970/71. Cosmas's principal research interest is the United States Army from 1880 to 1917.

THEODORE J. CRACKEL (lieutenant colonel, USA, retired) is a Senior Consultant with the General Electric Company in Washington, D.C. He has taught political and military history and strategy formulation at West Point, the Command and General Staff College, and the Army War College. He has also been a Senior Fellow with the Heritage Foundation.

ROY K. FLINT (brigadier general, USA) is Dean of the Academic Board and former professor and head of the Department of History at the United States Military Academy, West Point. He has graduated from the United States Army Command and General Staff College, the British Staff College, the Armed Forces Staff College, and the Air War College. He has written numerous articles on subjects ranging from the American Revolution to the United States Army in Vietnam. He currently lectures at the Army, Navy, and Air Force War Colleges on strategy and the Korean War and is writing a history of the Korean War.

IRA D. GRUBER, a professor of history and chairman of the Department of History at Rice University, has studied the American Revolution, especially from the British side, for twenty-five years. He has been a fellow at the Institute of Early American History and Culture and has taught at Duke University, the College of William and Mary, and Occidental College. His publications include *The Howe Brothers and the American Revolution* (1972) and a series of articles about British strategy and the British army officer during the Revolutionary era. In 1979/80 he was John F. Morrison Professor at the United States Army Command and General Staff College and in 1984/85 was visiting professor of military history at the United States Military Academy.

GEORGE C. HERRING has taught at Ohio University and is on the faculty of the University of Kentucky. His publications include *Aid to Russia, 1941-1946: Strategy, Diplomacy, the Origins of the Cold War* (1973), *The Diaries of Edward R. Stettinius, Jr., 1943-1946* (1975), and *America's Longest War: The United States and Vietnam, 1950-1975* (1979). Herring has also served as editor of *Diplomatic History*.

JAY LUVAAS, a former member of the Department of History at Allegheny College, is now professor of military history at the United States Army War College. He has served as Visiting Professor of Military History at the United States Military Academy at West Point, Harold Keith Johnson Visiting Professor of Military History at the United States Army Military History Institute, and professor of military history at the United States Army War College. His publications include *The Military Legacy of the Civil War: The European Inheritance* (1959) and *The Education of an Army: British Military Thought, 1815-1940* (1964). He edited and translated *Frederick the Great on the Art of War* (1966) and edited *The Civil War: A Soldier's View* (1958) and *Dear Miss Em: General Eichelberger's War in the Pacific* (1972).

ALLAN R. MILLETT (colonel, USMC Reserve), a professor of history and director of the Program in International Security and Military Affairs at the Mershon Center, Ohio State University, is a specialist in the history of American military policy and institutions. He is the author of *The Politics of Intervention: The Military Occupation of Cuba, 1906-1909* (1968), *The General: Robert L. Bullard and Officership in the United States Army, 1881-1925* (1975), and *Semper Fidelis: The History of the United States Marine Corps* (1980) and coauthor of *For the Common Defense: A Military History of the United States of America* (1984).

W. GLENN ROBERTSON, a member of the Combat Studies Institute of the United States Army Command and General Staff College at Fort Leavenworth, Kansas, has spent most of his career studying the Civil War. His Ph.D. dissertation was on the Bermuda Hundred Campaign of 1864. He has taught at institutions ranging from the Hampton Institute to the University of New Mexico. His writings encompass military topics from the early national period to the Korean War. His most recent work is *Counterattack on the Naktong* (1986, in the Leavenworth Paper Series).

JOHN SHY, professor of history at the University of Michigan, has also taught at Princeton. He has been Fulbright Professor at London University, Harmsworth Professor at Oxford, and a visiting professor at the United States Army War College. His publications include *Guerrillas in the 1960s* (with Peter Paret, 1961), *Toward Lexington* (1965), *A People Numerous and Armed* (1976), and chapters on Jomini and revolutionary warfare in the 1986 edition of *Makers of Modern Strategy*.

Index

Eustis, William, 38
Evans, Col. Nathan G., 92–93, 97–100, 103
Ewell, Brig. Gen. Richard S., 82–83, 92–94, 103

Falklands War, 342–43
Fall, Bernard, 302
Ferdinand, Prince of Brunswick, 6
Feuquieres, Marquis de, 5
Field Artillery School, 184
Field Service Regulations, 152–53, 184; 1941 version of, 187, 190, 197, 207
First Armored Division, 233–34, 238, 240–41, 246–47, 252, 258, 261, 263, 330, 334, 340–41, 346
First Cavalry Division (Airmobile), 300–301, 303–8, 311–14, 316, 321, 324, 326, 341–42, 346, 349, 401
First Expeditionary Division, 157–66, 168–70, 178–79
First U.S. Army, 182, 229, 237
Flint, Roy, 331
Foch, Gen. Ferdinand, 163–64
Fort Benning, Ga., 190, 223, 233, 307, 333
Fort Dix, N.J., 235
Fort George, N.Y., 43, 45, 47, 53
Fort Knox, Ky., 233
Fort Leavenworth, Kans., 152, 155, 213–14, 224, 230, 238
Fort Lee, N.J., 343
Fort Monroe, Va., 89
Forts, 33
Fort San Juan, Cuba, 130
Fort Sill, Okla., 230
Fort Sumter, S.C., 82–84, 88
Fort Texas, 63–66, 73, 77
Fort Washington, N.Y., 343
Franco-Austrian War of 1859, 106
Franklin, William B., 92, 99, 101
Fredendall, Maj. Gen. Lloyd R., 241–54, 257–58, 260–62, 330
Frederick the Great, 35
Freeman, Douglas Southall, 108
French and Indian Wars, 2, 5–6
French forces: in World War I, 155–67, 169–72, 175, 178–79, 184; in World War II, 241–47, 250, 260, 330, 335
French Revolution, 36
Friendly Fire, 320
Fuller, J. F. C., 231
Funston, Maj. Gen. Frederick, 153

Gaines, Brig. Gen. Edmund P., 59
Garcia, Gen. Calixto, 113, 120–23, 130, 143–44
Gas, 167, 184
Gatling battery, 116, 138–40, 147, 334

Geerds, Lt. Col. Henry A., 198
German forces: in World War I, 149–52, 155–56, 163, 165–79, 330, 335, 340, 344, 346; in World War II, 226, 231–33, 240, 246–52, 254–60, 262, 265, 334, 339
Giap, Vo Nguyen. *See* Vo Nguyen Giap
GI Bill, 271
Gimlets, 266, 271–75, 277, 290
Godefroy, Maximillian, 37
Goe, Capt. J. B., 140
Grant, Gen. James, 23, 27–28
Great Britain, 149, 152, 157
Great Depression, 226
Green Berets. *See* Special Forces
Greene, Nathaniel, 3–4, 18, 343
Grenade launchers, 303, 315
Grenades, 207, 210
Grenadier regiments, 59
Griffin, Capt. Charles, 100–101, 105
Grimes, Capt. George S., 131–32, 135, 138
Griswold, Maj. Gen. O. W., 221–22
Grose, Col. John E., 211–12, 218
Ground-air coordination, 228, 235, 237–38, 264
Gruber, Ira, 332–33, 343
Guadalcanal, 194, 199, 221
Guam, 148
Guerrillas, 119, 125
Guerrilla warfare, 119, 125, 141, 303–6, 323, 334

Haig, Gen. Sir Douglas, 163
Hale, Col. J. Tracy, 209, 211, 224
Hampton, Gen. Wade, 38–39, 53, 362
Hand Book for Infantry (Duane), 40, 49, 51–52, 54, 60
Handy, Col. H. F., 221
Harcourt, Maj. Henry G., 207
Hardee, Maj. William J., 86
Harding, Maj. Gen. Edwin F., 192, 198, 203–6, 208–11, 221, 224
Harney, Brig. Gen. William S., 82
Harper's Ferry, 87–89
Harrison, William Henry, 38, 52–53
Hart, B. H. Liddell, 231
Hartle, Maj. Gen. Russell P., 239
Harvey, Edward, 4
Haslet, John, 28
Hawkins, Capt. Edgar S., 66
Hawkins, Brig. Gen. Hamilton S., 135, 137, 139–40
Heintzelman, Col. Samuel P., 92–95, 97, 99, 101, 104
Helicopters, 301, 303–4, 307, 311, 314–20, 325–26
Herr, Michael, 314, 324, 333
Herring, Lt. Gen. Sir Edmond, 195, 208, 210–11, 221